# Delius and his Music

# Delius and his Music

Martin Lee-Browne
& Paul Guinery

with a Foreword by Sir Mark Elder

THE BOYDELL PRESS

First published 2014
The Boydell Press, Woodbridge

ISBN 978 1 84383 959 0

The Boydell Press is an imprint of Boydell & Brewer Ltd
PO Box 9, Woodbridge, Suffolk IP12 3DF, UK
and of Boydell & Brewer Inc.
668 Mt Hope Avenue, Rochester, NY 14620-2731, USA
website: www.boydellandbrewer.com

A catalogue record for this book is available from the British Library

Designed and typeset in Warnock Pro
by David Roberts, Pershore, Worcestershire

# Contents

# Illustrations

*Text Illustrations*

The authors and publishers are grateful to all the institutions and individuals listed for permission to reproduce the materials in which they hold copyright. Every effort has been made to trace the copyright holders; apologies are offered for any omission, and the publishers will be pleased to add any necessary acknowledgement in subsequent editions.

The quality of a good number of the pictures we have used is not as good as we would have liked, for the simple reason that they are well over 100 years old. Paul Brooks, of Design & Print, Oxford, has, however, worked wonders on them, and hopefully they contribute a period feel to the book!

All of the music examples in this book were prepared by Paul Guinery, with the assistance of Andrew Jones, from the full scores in the Collected Edition, now in the public domain.

# Sources and Abbreviations

These are the main sources we have consulted, with the abbreviations used for them in the footnotes and list of further reading. There have, of course, been many more, details of which are given where appropriate in the footnotes. A selection of the numerous other books, articles and theses about Delius which the authors consider particularly relevant to this book are listed before the Index.

| | |
|---|---|
| *AJ* | Alan Jefferson, *Delius*, Master Musicians (London: J. M. Dent & Sons, 1972) |
| *AMC* | Sir Thomas Beecham, *A Mingled Chime: Leaves from an Autobiography* (London: Hutchinson & Co., 1944) |
| *CE* | *Frederick Delius: Complete Works*, ed. Sir Thomas Beecham, prepared for publication by Robert Threlfall (London: Boosey & Hawkes, Schirmer, Stainer & Bell, Thames Publishing, Universal Edition, in conjunction with The Delius Trust, 1990). This is also known as the 'Collected Edition'. |
| *Companion* | *A Delius Companion*, ed. Christopher Redwood (John Calder, 1980) |
| *DSJ* | *The Delius Society Journal*, no. 43 onwards (1974–) |
| DTA | The Delius Trust Archive |
| *FD&PW* | *Frederick Delius and Peter Warlock: A Friendship Revealed*, ed. Barry Smith (Oxford: Clarendon Press, 2000) |
| *Fenby 1* | Eric Fenby, *Delius as I Knew Him* (London: Faber & Faber, 1936; rev. edn 1981) |
| *Fenby 2* | Eric Fenby, *Delius*, The Great Composers (London: Faber & Faber, 1971) |
| *Gardiner* | Stephen Lloyd, *H. Balfour Gardiner* (Cambridge: Cambridge University Press, 1984) |
| *Gillespie* | Don C. Gillespie, *The Search for Thomas F. Ward, Teacher of Frederick Delius* (Gainesville: University Press of Florida, 1996) |
| *Grieg & Delius* | Lionel Carley, *Grieg and Delius: A Chronicle of their Friendship in Letters* (New York: Marion Boyars, 1993) |
| *Hudson* | Derek Hudson, *Norman O'Neill: A Life of Music* (London: Quality Press, 1945) |
| *Letters* | *Delius: A Life in Letters*, ed. Lionel Carley, vol. 1: *1862–1908* (London: Scolar Press 1983); vol. 2, *1909–1934* (London: Scolar Press 1988). The letters are numbered consecutively through both volumes, and are simply referred to as (e.g.) 'Letter 185'. The volumes are referred to as *Letters 1* and *Letters 2*. |

| | |
|---|---|
| *Lloyd* | *Fenby on Delius*, ed. Stephen Lloyd (London: Thames Publishing, 1996) |
| *Lowe* | Rachel Lowe, *Frederick Delius, 1862–1934: A Catalogue of the Museum Archive of The Delius Trust, London* (London: The Delius Trust, 1974) |
| *Lucas* | John Lucas, *Thomas Beecham: An Obsession with Music* (Woodbridge: The Boydell Press, 2008) |
| *M&C* | Robert Montgomery and Robert Threlfall, *Music and Copyright: The Case of Delius and his Publishers* (Aldershot: Ashgate 2007) |
| *MA&L* | *Frederick Delius: Music, Art and Literature*, ed. Lionel Carley (Aldershot: Ashgate, 1998) |
| *MMB* | Clare Delius, *Frederick Delius: Memories of my Brother* (London: Ivor Nicholson & Watson, 1935) |
| *Palmer* | Christopher Palmer, *Delius: Portrait of a Cosmopolitan* (London: Duckworth, 1976) |
| *Paris Years* | Lionel Carley, *Delius: The Paris Years* (Rickmansworth: Triad Press 1975) |
| *Pictures* | *Delius: A Life in Pictures*, ed. Lionel Carley and Robert Threlfall (Oxford: Oxford University Press, 1977) |
| *PW* | Peter Warlock, *Frederick Delius* (London: Bodley Head, 1952). This is a revised version of *Frederick Delius* by Warlock's *alter ego* Philip Heseltine (London: Bodley Head, 1923), and includes an introduction and 'Additions, Annotations and Comments' by Hubert Foss. |
| *PW Letters* | *The Collected Letters of Peter Warlock*, ed. Barry Smith, 4 vols (Woodbridge: The Boydell Press, 2005) |
| *RT Catalogue* | Robert Threlfall, *A Catalogue of the Compositions of Frederick Delius: Sources & References* (London: The Delius Trust, 1977) |
| *RT Supplement* | Robert Threlfall, *Frederick Delius: A Supplementary Catalogue* (London: The Delius Trust, 1986) |
| *TB* | Sir Thomas Beecham, Bart., *Frederick Delius* (London: Hutchinson & Co., 1959) |
| *Young* | Percy M. Young, *A History of British Music* (London: Ernest Benn, 1967) |
| *WS&SS* | Lyndon Jenkins, *While Spring and Summer Sang: Thomas Beecham and the Music of Frederick Delius* (Aldershot: Ashgate, 2005) |

# Foreword

### Sir Mark Elder, CBE

C AN there be more to say about Delius, so often regarded in the past as an
eccentric, odd-ball rebel with limited craft – the 'bad boy' of English(?)
music? Yes, I believe that *Delius and his Music*, building on the substantial
amount of existing knowledge about the composer's life and music, does just
that. Each work is analysed and placed in the context of his life in an entirely
new and very approachable way, showing that Delius was a conscious artist, a
true original and innovator who knew just what he wanted and how to achieve
it technically.

Following the pioneering biographies by Philip Heseltine and Sir Thomas
Beecham, together with Eric Fenby's first-hand account of the years he spent as
the composer's amanuensis, came Lionel Carley's impeccably researched and
highly revealing account of Delius's life, told through his correspondence. The
monumental task of editing and publishing Delius's complete works, begun
by Beecham in the 1950s, has been brilliantly completed by Robert Threlfall,
so that we now have an authoritative Collected Edition. The *Delius Society
Journal* has also published – and continues to publish – many valuable articles
covering a wide range of topics. Delians are well served. However, *Delius and
his Music*, this latest addition to the bookshelves, offers, I think, something
significantly different.

It is a compete survey of Delius's music. In the case of the mature
compositions, Paul Guinery has provided extensive and refreshingly reader-
friendly musical analyses and comments which shed much light on just
how Delius approached and solved questions of structure and form. Little
technical knowledge is assumed, and the emphasis is very much on verbal
description. But for those to whom reading a score is not difficult, there are
detailed references to the Collected Edition, and many of the music examples
usefully show Delius's very full orchestrations in newly prepared, short-score
reductions.

Martin Lee-Browne has provided a sufficiently detailed biography to place
the various works in the context of Delius's life. He fills in the background
of the literary and artistic movements of which Delius was so keenly aware –
particularly during the crucial years when he lived in Paris in the 1890s. There
are abundant references to Delius's many acquaintances – for he made friends
easily. The image we have of the recluse in his final decade – an austere,
dogmatic and difficult character, tortured by chronic illness – is worlds away
from the fun-loving, gregarious and charming young man that he was in his
prime – and that comes through strongly in this new account. There is also
generous space given to contemporary critical opinion, mainly in newspaper

reviews, showing how Delius's works were received at the time – a fascinating insight.

Confirmed Delians – and hopefully some doubters – will, I am sure, be encouraged to go beyond the well-known pieces, and explore more of the extended output of a unique composer. I hope that this entertaining and comprehensive guide will open up for them a completely new musical world through scores which, at first hearing, might have seemed impenetrable.

For my own part, ever since I was a student, I have found myself drawn into the very special poetic landscapes of Delius. His music has a very strong bond between man and nature, and his most significant works are certainly among the greatest music this country has produced. I am convinced that this book goes a long way towards making that evident. *The Song of the High Hills*, for instance, may have been inspired by Delius's experiences in Scandinavia, but anybody who has been on the top of the Yorkshire Dales will find this music movingly atmospheric. Delius's scores repay repeated listening, understanding and thought, and I hope very much that this important new study will make many more friends for this great man.

# Preface

*'For me, music is very simple; it is the expression of a poetic*
*and emotional nature.'*                    (Frederick Delius)

*'... I believe myself in no doctrine whatever – and in nothing*
*but in Nature and in the great forces of Nature ...'*
                                            (Frederick Delius)

*'In the long run, words about music are less important than the*
*music.'*                    (attributed to Dmitry Shostakovich)

### Delius's Life and Times

I N *Musical Opinion* for June 1962, Deryck Cooke wrote, 'It is significant that
there has been no thorough and comprehensive study of [Delius's] music.'
Now, just over fifty years later, this is the first one.

A number of books have been written about Frederick Delius's life, and there
are probably very few, if any, new facts of significance still to be discovered
about it. On the other hand, relatively little has been written about his music
in detail. Arthur Hutchings's *Delius* (1946) covers the highest proportion of
the works, with a modest number of musical examples, in a little over half
his book; Eric Fenby's *Delius as I Knew him* (1936) and *Delius* (1971) do the
same on a more restricted basis; Alan Jefferson's *Delius* (1972) has twenty-one
pages on 'Delius's craft', again with a few examples; and, finally, there is Philip
Heseltine (writing under his pseudonym Peter Warlock) in his *Frederick Delius*
(1923, revised with additions, annotations and comments by Hubert Foss).
All of them attempt to describe the music – more often than not extremely
vividly – but not, however, to analyse how it is 'put together' and develops.

This book is therefore intended to make good that omission. It is, first and
foremost, about the music – and is addressed both to 'average' or 'ordinary'
listeners (if they will forgive the *soubriquets*) who are attracted to its sounds
and style on a first or early hearing and can follow a score (or at least read music
a little), and particularly to A-level and university students and researchers.
The analyses and descriptions of the works are, however, interspersed with
biography, critical reviews of their early performances, and (to a lesser extent),
references to the contemporary English musical scene and a number of Delius's
closest friends. The plentiful number of those reviews interestingly show that
critical opinion of Delius's music is much the same today as it was in 1891 (the
year in which he had his first public performances) – totally divided, but on
balance probably more 'against' than 'for'.

Every one of Delius's published works is covered. The approach we have
adopted is to relate what is known about their inspiration, origins and gestation

(if anything is known, that is – Delius very rarely spoke or wrote about what he had in mind); then to analyse them; and finally to show how their early performances were received by critics and friends. Although many of those performances did not take place until well after the work was completed, it would seem preferable to have all the reviews for each work immediately after the analysis, rather than in strictly chronological order later in the same chapter or a following one. For example, *Appalachia* was first performed in 1904 (Chapter 4, 1902–5), but as the first English performance was not until 1907, reviews of it should perhaps logically be covered in Chapter 5 (1906–10); they are, nevertheless, in Chapter 4. We hope that that does not make the biographical train of dates too difficult to follow. Exceptionally, however, in the case of the works included in the 1889 all-Delius concert at the St James's Hall, because that was the first occasion on which Delius's music was noticed by the English critics, the first reviews of the complete programme are all grouped together in the paragraphs dealing with that concert in Chapter 3. Lengthy discussions of individual works are presented as headed subsections, while the titles of works that are discussed more briefly appear in the text in boldface at the first mention.

Appendix 1, in two parts, contains a complete list of all Delius's works, with their dates, catalogue references, and, in the case of those involving the orchestra, details of their first performance and their orchestration. The prime sources for that are Robert Threlfall's encyclopaedic *A Catalogue of the Compositions of Frederick Delius: Sources and References* (London: The Delius Trust, 1977), its sequel *Frederick Delius: A Supplementary Catalogue* (London: The Delius Trust, 1986), and the monumental *Frederick Delius: Complete Works* (the 'Collected Edition'), also prepared by Threlfall for publication for The Delius Trust. It is almost impossible adequately to express the tremendous debt of gratitude we both owe him, for without those volumes it would have been impossible to produce this book. Equally profuse thanks are due to Dr. Lionel Carley, Archivist of The Delius Trust, for allowing me freely to make use of his magnificent two-volume *Delius: A Life in Letters*. It is an indispensable companion, not only to this book, but, indeed, for anyone interested in Delius's life. Dr. Carley has also read, and wisely commented on, our drafts – a labour of love! There are many different manuscript versions of most of Delius's works, and it is beyond the scope of this book to examine them. For those readers who are interested, however, detailed and interesting descriptions are to be found in Robert Threlfall's *Catalogue* and *Supplement* to it.

I have taken much material on the biographical side from the books by Sir Thomas Beecham, Clare Delius, Philip Heseltine, Alan Jefferson, and Robert Threlfall and Robert Montgomery, as well as occasionally from other Delian scholars. I sincerely hope that I have not plagiarised any of them, but if I have done so it was unintentional; there are, of course, only a limited number of ways of expressing specific ideas and relating facts, and I apologise if there are any references for which credit is not given in the footnotes.

Sir Thomas Beecham's biography *Frederick Delius* – though not always completely accurate as to facts – is another marvellous read, with many vivid pages and paragraphs of comment about Delius, his wife Jelka and the music, all written in Beecham's inimitable style – elegant, sensitive and often very amusing. Such passages could have graced a good number of pages in this book, but to my disappointment Lady Beecham declined my request for permission to quote them. I have therefore been obliged to make paraphrases and include footnote references instead. However, I have included those quotations which I feel are most important, in particular in the last paragraph of the book.

When selecting concert and recital reviews to quote from I have largely limited myself to those in *The Times*, *The Musical Times* and *Musical Opinion*, and the reason for that is entirely practical. *The Times* is the only national paper of the period in question that is indexed and available online (or, until recently, on microfiche at the British Newspaper Library at Colindale in North London), while *The Musical Times* and *Musical Opinion* are readily available on the shelves, or can be quickly produced, in music libraries. Other contemporary newspapers, such at *The Era* and *The Saturday Review*, which usually contained more thoughtful reviews than was ever possible in daily papers, could for all practical purposes only be seen in bound volumes at the British Newspaper Library. Unfortunately, the Library closed in 2013, though the majority of its vast stock is now available to order into any Reading Room of the British Library at St Pancras.

As completion of the draft of this book drew near, it became tempting to include reviews of some post-1934 performances up to the present day – particularly those by Sir Thomas Beecham which are listed Maurice Parker's two-volume *Calendar* (see below, List of Further Reading), and those by other conductors who espoused the Delian cause. But apart from making this book too unwieldy, it would also have been impossible to carry out the necessary research given the closure of the Colindale library. It is fair to say, however, that few reviews over the past thirty years added much to our understanding of Delius's music over and above what was written by critics during his lifetime – in particular the perspicacious ones such as Samuel Langford and Ernest Newman. Indeed, a good many about the 250 or so concerts which included Delius's music as part of the celebrations of his 150th anniversary in 2012 were, surprisingly, as far off the mark and pejorative as some of those that greeted the early performances of, say, *Paris* and *Sea Drift*. I believe, however, that the reviews I have used provide a good conspectus of mainly well-balanced praise and criticism.

All but the very latest issues of *The Delius Society Journal* are also available through the website of The Delius Trust and The Delius Society (http:\\www.delius.org.uk), where there is also a detailed timeline of Delius's life.

We would have liked to include the texts of the works for voices and orchestra but, sadly, considerations of space precluded that. However, almost certainly anyone wishing to follow the analyses in detail will do so with a CD and its accompanying booklet. There is a complete Delian discography, immaculately compiled by Stephen Lloyd, available on the website of The Delius Trust and The Delius Society. Given that it is expected to be updated on a regular basis, we have decided not to include one in this book, as it would necessarily have to be selective, and in due course become out of date.

Idiosyncrasies of grammar and spelling in quotations from letters – Delius's in particular – and reviews have been retained, and occasionally confirmed by '[*sic*]'. Paul Guinery and I may not always have been very logical in anglicising the titles of the works (other than the songs) with French, Norwegian or German titles, but we have used the ones which seem most appropriate or commonly adopted. In the hope of encouraging both general readers and researchers to explore other aspects of both English music generally and Delius in particular, I have deliberately included a large number of footnotes

In addition to our appreciation of the help – indeed, inspiration – we have received from Robert Threlfall and Lionel Carley, we owe the greatest of thanks to Stephen Lloyd and Lewis Foreman for much wise advice and information; to the late Lyndon Jenkins for his encouragement; to Norman Jones and local librarians for translations of reviews in German newspapers and periodicals; to Barry John Ould, the secretary of The Percy Grainger Society; Rupert Ridgewell of the British Library; and the staff at the British Newspaper Library, the Victoria Music Library, the Staffordshire Library and the Leeds Central Library. We are also most grateful to the following for permission to reproduce paintings or photographs, and to quote from writings, in which they own the copyright: The Delius Trust and The Delius Society, Professor John Bergsagel, Lionel Carley, Jeff Driggers, Familenverbindung Delius of Bielefeld, Roger Fenby, Elisabeth Ferry, The Gerhardi/Steinweg Collection of Lüdenscheid, The Grainger Museum at the University of Melbourne, Sir John Eliot Gardiner, the family of Alan Jefferson, Lyndon Jenkins, Katherine Jessel, Michael Kennedy, The Schou Foundation of Palsgaard, St Leo Abbey Archive, The Bantock Estate, The Harrison Sisters Trust, *The Musical Times* and *Musical Opinion*.

We are very lucky to have had the advice, patient help and skills of Megan Milan, Rohais Haughton, and Rosie Pearce of Boydell & Brewer in converting our manuscript into a finished book, and our especial thanks go to our copy-editor Marianne Fisher, who made most helpful comments and suggestions for making the book more readable, and to David Roberts who not only designed and typeset it so beautifully, but in the course of doing so, corrected a host of our infelicities andslips in the most erudite and kindly way possible. No authors courld possibly have wanted a greater attention to detail, or more perspicacious comments. Lastly, but most certainly not least, we are extremely grateful to The Delius Trust and The Delius Society for their generous grants towards the cost of this book.

*Martin Lee-Browne*

## *The Musical Analyses*

A TTEMPTING to describe music through words can be a frustrating business, particularly so in the case of Delius, whose sound-world, unique and instantly recognisable, remains strangely elusive. We know a piece of Delius when we meet one, but how difficult it is to define or explain what makes it what it is.

In the course of many years spent introducing music broadcasts for the BBC, for which I must have written hundreds of scripts, I was sometimes surprised to be told by listeners who were clearly passionately keen and knowledgeable that they 'did not understand music'. This, I came to realise, was their way of apologising for a lack of technical knowledge. In my view, this was an unnecessary admission, since, in one sense, there is nothing really to understand. After all, to savour a culinary dish, it is not obligatory to know the exact list of its ingredients or how it was cooked: it is the taste, together with the texture, which directly stimulate the palate, and you either like the flavour or you do not. Similarly, when looking at a great painting, there is no need to analyse how much blue was added to green to produce that particular shade of yellow, or exactly how the brush strokes were applied by the artist. On the other hand, the question, 'yes, but exactly *how* was it done?', is not invalid: there is inevitably a layman's fascination for the tricks of the trade, even if providing a lucid explanation of them is far from straightforward. But therein lies the challenge.

Not so long ago, I was chatting to a stranger at a social function when the conversation turned to music and, in particular, to Delius. 'Oh, it's all so depressing', he claimed. 'What, *all* of it?' I queried. He then admitted that he only really knew two works, both of which, incidentally, I have always considered rather uplifting. Though his evaluation is not untypical, that is definitely not the Delius I know and love, and there is obviously some work still to be done in clearing a path through the woods and putting paid to such generalisations and downright misconceptions. It is a belief in the value of that exercise which has spurred me on to attempt a commentary in words on the music of a composer who, in my opinion, was a towering figure and a genius at his craft.

However, I do acknowledge that there are at least two major barriers which have to be crossed if Delius is to be freed from the stigma of being hard to grasp. Firstly, there is the undeniable complexity of his harmonic style, with its constantly shifting chromaticism, and its intense and restless feeling of never settling for too long in any particular key-centre. That can be off-putting, though, ultimately, it is also a question of taste. The second problem is that some works of Delius can give the impression of wandering aimlessly, as if there is no firm hand on the tiller – and this is where this book will, I hope, be of assistance. Delius's music is rarely expressed through traditional outlets such as sonata form, but, on the contrary, creates its own architectural forms and structures which sometimes, on first hearing, can seem confusing or puzzling.

The idiosyncrasies of the building itself may need to be defined and described, but with a floor-plan and a map of the terrain it should eventually be possible to get a sense of orientation.

To put it another way: it is far more profitable to approach Delius's scores by accepting them on their own terms and going with the flow than by trying to impose a preconceived framework on them. The more I study Delius, the more I find the accusation that he had no idea of overall form to be misguided and invalid. I have come to realise that there is indeed an experienced director behind the scenes watching over the development of the plot, a conscious artist at work shaping and moulding the proportions and content of scores which, at first hearing, may yet come across as capricious or amorphous.

However, having said all this, I am in no doubt that Delius himself would have thrown up his hands in horror at each and every one of my analytical attempts to pin his music down in words. I am sure he would have insisted that the music speak for itself, without a word of explanation on his part; during his lifetime he certainly expected performers to react to it intuitively. I cannot imagine him, for example, ever being interviewed by one of today's music presenters and agreeing to 'talk us through' one of his pieces. To a great extent, I sympathise with him.

The descriptions of some of the early, minor works, occurring mostly in the opening chapters of this book, were undertaken by my co-author (for which I am grateful, as it eased my burden considerably), but I alone take responsibility for all the remaining analytical commentaries. These, as well as the inevitable judgments and evaluations, express my own, subjective opinions. For example, I personally would place the three string concertos among Delius's finest works; equally, I would unquestionably rate as masterpieces works which some may find either too austere for their taste – such as *An Arabesque, North Country Sketches* and *Fennimore and Gerda* – or may even, in the case of the wonderfully imaginative *Requiem*, consider distasteful. On the other hand, admirers of *Irmelin, The Magic Fountain* and *Poem of Life and Love* will find that I have been severe in my evaluations of those particular works. But Delius's output was so large and his range – *pace* his detractors – so broad, that there is plenty of room for diverse opinions and I hope, at least, that I have not been unfair or unreasonably negative.

I have deliberately tried to avoid using too many technical terms, although when discussing harmony, for example, this is unavoidable. I have also tried to eschew the type of scholarly analysis that, whilst irreproachably accurate, is simply unreadable and reduces everything to a series of mathematical formulae. My own approach may veer too much towards the descriptive for some tastes, but I must admit to being influenced by the way in which Eric Fenby, for one, spoke and wrote so vividly and inspirationally about Delius; certain phrases of his have stuck in my mind: 'bleak figurations with icy fingerings from the harps', and 'bravura passages with meadowland dallyings in oboe arabesque [leading] to rapture in the strings'. Too flowery for some, perhaps, but to me, much more evocative, and far more useful, than just invoking pedal points, Neapolitan sixths or Phrygian cadences.

Those who read music, and who have access to scores, will, I hope, find it helpful to follow the copious references in my descriptions to bar numbers, or rehearsal figures or letters. It should be noted that a reference such as 'Fig. 6+3' or 'Fig. 6-3' means the third full bar after, or before, Figure 6, *counting bar 1 as Figure 6 itself*.

Since Delius often wrote for very large forces, it would be impractical to reproduce orchestral scores in full. So, among the 250 musical examples included, many are my own reductions onto just two or three staves, with instrumentation indicated; and I have certainly not always attempted to show every detail of the original, but merely what was necessary to illustrate the point I wanted to make. Here I must pay tribute to my copyist Andrew Jones and say how very grateful I am for all the hours of work he has put in to transform my hand-written manuscript arrangements into such expert and professional settings.

Delius wrote six operas, four of which are substantial works, and a detailed musical commentary on these would require a separate volume in itself. I have therefore restricted myself to a more general overview, concentrating on the highlights of each score, including their significance in Delius's development as a composer for the stage. Similarly, I have made no attempt to deal with all the songs individually; since they number more than sixty, I have simply made a representative selection and discussed these in Chapter 9. Otherwise, there is some mention, ranging from just a paragraph, to several pages with musical examples, of each and every work that Delius wrote.

Delians are supremely lucky in having a complete edition of the scores, numbering over thirty volumes, which have been edited by Robert Threlfall with devotion and impeccable scholarship. The two parts of Appendix 1 give the titles of works as they appear in his indispensable *Catalogue* and *Supplementary Catalogue*, to which there are also cross-references, as well as to the relevant volumes in the Collected Edition.

I would, indeed, like to thank Robert Threlfall for reading through one of my first analytical efforts and indicating that I might not be wasting my time; also my dear friends Joy and Roger Brison, who provided such sympathetic support and encouragement; Dr. Lionel Carley, whose literary experience and wise comments were invaluable and which I did not hesitate to act upon (especially concerning my over-indulgent use of the exclamation mark); finally, it need hardly be said, I must thank Philip, who has had to put up with an occasionally fractious writer – and has coped.

I can only hope that readers will find the musical commentaries helpful as maps and aids to navigation for some of the more complicated journeys through Delius's music. But in the end, it is always the music itself, and not words about it, that counts for the most, and to which we must return. Although I have come to be infinitely more aware of what is going on behind the scenes in Delius's music than I was when I started this project, the theatrical illusion has not been spoilt for me. For I think that Beecham got it absolutely right when he pinpointed the supreme value of Delius and his inimitable artistry as being sheer beauty of sound. That may be an unfashionable concept nowadays, but it will do for me.

*Paul Guinery*

CHAPTER 1 ✼ 1862–1888

# Youth

The English Musical Scene – Bradford –
Norway – Florida – Leipzig – first works –
*Six Part Songs – Florida Suite – Hiawatha*

W HEN Delius was born, in 1862, music-making was flourishing in England – in cathedrals, churches, town halls, village halls and private houses. On the other hand, it was 167 years since the death of the last English composer of real note, Henry Purcell (1659–95), and the most highly regarded composers in the second half of the nineteenth century were probably Sir George Smart (1776–1869);[1] Sir Alexander Macfarren (1813–87), who wrote a vast amount of music, including nine symphonies and twenty-four operas;[2] Sir William Sterndale Bennett (1816–75), whose best music was for the piano; and Sir John Stainer (1840–1901), most of whose work was religious and included the well-known oratorio *The Crucifixion*.[3] By today's standards, however, their music was at best only competent and mildly interesting. Their better works can be enjoyable on an occasional hearing, but there is no question of their having the stature of their Continental counterparts: in Germany, Brahms, Bruckner, Wagner and Liszt; in France, Fauré, Bizet, Saint-Saëns and Franck; and, in Russia, Rimsky-Korsakov, Tchaikovsky, Musorgsky, Balakirev and Borodin – a good number of whom were well advanced in their careers, and writing some of their finest works.

The well-known gibe referring to England as being *Das Land ohne Musik* (*The Land without Music*) probably dates from the mid-1880s.[4] At that time, however, the astonishing English Musical Renaissance is generally considered

[1] 'The inspiration of the provincial festivals', although 'as a composer ... he was negligible; More than that, he was a menace': *Young*, p. 442.

[2] 'Never was more earnest composer, more prolific writer; never did man strive more zealously for the art of his country; yet Heaven had endowed him only with talent and not genius': lecture to The Worshipful Company of Musicians in 1904; printed as F. J. Sawyer, 'English Opera after Purcell', in *English Music [1604–1904], being the Lectures Given at the Music Loan Exhibition of the Worshipful Company of Musicians* (London: Walter Scott, 1906), pp. 264–92, at p. 283.

[3] They were all knighted for their academic and administrative qualities rather than for their composing.

[4] It has been attributed to a number of German musicians and critics, including the conductor Hans von Bülow (which seems a little unlikely, given that he conducted in this country in 1873, 1878 and 1888) and the critic Eduard Hanslick. It was also the title of a book by Oskar Schmitz published in Germany in 1914.

to have started – with the première of the thirty-two-year-old Hubert Parry's 'dramatic cantata' *Scenes from Shelley's 'Prometheus Unbound'* at the 1880 Gloucester Three Choirs Festival; when Hans Richter[5] conducted the first performance of Elgar's *Variations on an Original Theme ('Enigma')* in London's St James's Hall on 19 June 1899, it could be said with true certainty that English music was at long last alive and well again. The style was still very Germanic – but from the mid-1880s, three young composers, two English and one French, began writing music that was completely different from anything that had ever been heard before. Little of it owed anything to the old forms: it was full of new harmonies, new choral and orchestral sounds, using a wider range of metre (although always with an underlying musical pulse), and it mirrored the rise of the Impressionist school of painting. They were Ralph Vaughan Williams,[6] Frederick Delius and Claude Debussy.[7]

Over the ten or so years either side of the 'Enigma' Variations, the musical world in mainland Europe was rocked, very largely in France and Germany, by a complete change in all that music had 'been about' since 1750. The traditional sonata form, counterpoint, key structures and 'abstract' music were quite quickly abandoned. Now audiences heard Hugo Wolf's *Italian Serenade* and Rimsky-Korsakov's *Capriccio Espagnol* (both 1887), Satie's *Gymnopédies* (1888), Schoenberg's *Verklärte Nacht* (1899), Scriabin's *Le Poème de l'extase* (1908), Janáček's *On an Overgrown Path* (1908–11), Strauss's *Elektra* (1909) and Stravinsky's *Petrushka* (1911). It was indeed a time of musical evolution and revolution.

The music of Vaughan Williams and Delius – throughout their composing lives – was, however, worlds apart from any of those, for it was heavily influenced in the former's case by folksong, and in the latter's by Nature. Compare Vaughan Williams's three *Norfolk Rhapsodies* (1905–6) or *On Wenlock Edge* (1909), Delius's *In a Summer Garden* (1908) or *The Song of the High Hills* (1911–12), or, indeed, Debussy's String Quartet (1893) and *Trois nocturnes* (1899) with any of those nine works just mentioned: although equally 'modern', they inhabit utterly different worlds. Delius would spend his life composing music that bore no relationship to anything, good or bad, that had been written before by anyone. Like Elgar (born five years before him), he formed his own style, astonishingly, without having had a traditional musical education. Both Elgar's and Delius's early pieces were hardly more than trifles (and, curiously, not very dissimilar in style), but from 1889 they trod completely different paths. Ten years later, having written *Paris*, Delius emerged, at the

---

[5] Hans Richter (1843–1916): celebrated Austrian conductor who became a great friend of Wagner, and in 1876 conducted the first performance of *Der Ring des Nibelungen* at Bayreuth; thereafter he worked extensively in England.

[6] Ralph Vaughan Williams, OM (1872–1958).

[7] (Achille-) Claude Debussy (1862–1918).

age of forty-seven, as a new and unique musical voice of the early twentieth century.[8]

In the middle of the previous century, commercial and industrial England was prosperous and successful (despite the appalling way so many, though certainly not all, employers treated their workers – the very people who ultimately made their businesses thrive). Perhaps surprisingly, an offshoot of that prosperity and success was the enormous amount of music-making mentioned above. One of the country's most important activities was the wool trade. It had flourished, in particular, in the Cotswolds, where the sheep were bred, and in the North of England, where the wool was turned into textiles – although decline set in at the beginning of the Industrial Revolution. No doubt seeing the opportunities for shipping high-quality cloth back to Germany, many German businessmen emigrated to Bradford in Yorkshire – which, with Leeds, had, over the course of the century, risen to become one of the wool capitals of the world. Their impact was such that even today part of Bradford is still known as Little Germany.

Probably in the late 1840s, three brothers living in Bielefeld in north-western Germany, Ernst Oswald Friedrich, Julius Friedrich Wilhelm and Emil Theodor Delius, came in turn to England. Ernst set up as a middleman in Manchester, to be joined first by Julius and then by Emil; they called their business Delius & Company: Stuff and Yarn Merchants, and, as the business flourished, in 1873 Ernst and Julius set up a branch at 5 Burnett Street in Bradford, later moving it to 61 East Parade.[9]

Julius became a naturalised Englishman in 1851,[10] and in 1856 he married a Bielefeld girl, Elise Pauline Krönig. They lived in Bradford for the rest of their lives, and had fourteen children: the fourth, born on 29 January 1862, was baptised Fritz Theodor Albert.[11] The Deliuses' family home was in Claremont, a quiet residential street not far from the centre of the city.[12] Julius was an excellent employer and a considerable public philanthropist – but in the family home he was a martinet. The household was run on strict Teutonic lines, and, like most Victorian fathers, he expected everyone to accept what he said – which they did until, as we shall see, at the age of twenty-one, Fritz refused. Nevertheless, although he did not play or sing himself, Julius was very fond

---

[8] There is a good overview of Delius's life and music in Michael Trend's *The Music Makers: The English Musical Renaissance from Elgar to Britten* (Wiedenfeld & Nicholson, 1985), pp. 33–46.

[9] For more information on the Delius family's connection with Bradford, see www.bradlibs.com/localstudies/delius [accessed 19 March 2014].

[10] *The Musical Times* 120 (1979), p. 990.

[11] He changed his name to Frederick in 1902.

[12] Delius was in fact born at 6 Claremont, one of a row of three semi-detached houses. It was rented by the family until 1863, when they moved across the street into no. 3; some ten years later they expanded into no. 1, making their address 1–3 Claremont: see Philip Jones, 'The Delius Birthplace – A Solution', *DSJ* 67 (1980), 5–9.

of music and often gave musical evenings in the house: visitors included the violinist Joachim and the cellist Piatti, and Fritz was taken to hear the Hallé Orchestra,[13] whose regular visits from Manchester to Bradford had started as the result of some lobbying by Julius. He was a happy boy, bilingual, 'a born rider',[14] and good at cricket[15] – but, infinitely more importantly as it was to turn out, he also proved to be really musical. When he was quite young, Fritz began to learn both the piano and the violin – the latter, when he was only six or seven, with William Bauerkeller of the Hallé, then, in about 1872, with George Haddock, the founder of the Leeds College of Music.[16] Many years later, he told Philip Heseltine[17] that:

> My first great musical impression was hearing the posthumous Valse of Chopin [in E minor] which a friend of my father's played for me when I was ten years old. It made a most extraordinary impression on me. Until then I had only heard Haydn, Mozart and Beethoven, and it was as if an entirely new world had been opened up to me. I remember that after hearing it twice I could play the whole piece through from memory ...[18]

Although, he admitted later, 'not, of course, very correctly'.[19] Other important experiences were a performance of 'The Ride of the Valkyries' by the Hallé (under Hallé himself),[20] and being taken to *Lohengrin* at Covent Garden.[21] These were undoubtedly the start of the great love of Wagner's music that Delius retained for the whole of his life. After three years at a local preparatory school, in 1874 he was sent to Bradford Grammar School.[22] He only spent four years there – maybe he did not do well – and in 1878 his parents sent him to The London International College at Isleworth in

---

[13] Founded by Sir Charles Hallé in 1858, it is Britain's second-longest-established professional orchestra. Hallé (1819–95) was an Anglo–German pianist and conductor, and his wife was one of the leading lady solo violinists of the time.

[14] *MMB*, pp. 26 and 40. (It should be noted that Clare Delius is not now regarded as a very reliable biographer of her brother.)

[15] Cricket was first played at Bradford Grammar School in the 1870s.

[16] Lionel Carley, 'Delius and the Violin: The Student and his Teachers', *DSJ* 146 (2009).

[17] Philip Arnold Heseltine (1894–1930): he was introduced to Delius in 1911, and wrote the first biography of Delius in English (*PW*) in 1923, when Delius was still alive (see below, Chapter 6).

[18] *PW*, p. 32.

[19] *TB*, p. 18.

[20] Delius, 'Memories of Childhood' (manuscript in The Grainger Museum at The University of Melbourne, reproduced in *Letters 1*, appendix 1).

[21] *AJ*, p. 9.

[22] Where one of his fellow pupils was John Coates (1865–1941), who became one of the finest English tenors.

Middlesex.[23] 'The only subjects that interested him were geography, which stirred the *Reiselust* [desire to travel] in him, French and German.'[24]

It was, however, the other things he did during the three years he spent there that really mattered. He continued his violin lessons – now with Carl Deichmann, who had been much involved in Wagner's visit to England in May 1877 – and he also played in an amateur orchestra in Chiswick.

Isleworth was only some fourteen miles from the centre of London, and soon Fritz was frequently going to concerts and the opera. There was much to be heard and seen – and the annals of The Philharmonic Society[25] give a good picture of concert life in England at its 'upper level' at this time. Brahms was perhaps 'the' composer of the period – an 1876 concert of the Society began with the *German Requiem* and finished with some of his *Hungarian Dances* (via Beethoven's Symphony no. 2, Mendelssohn's *Ruy Blas* overture and Joachim playing a Spohr violin concerto!). In 1879 Joachim gave Brahms's Violin Concerto and Symphony no. 2 for the first time in England. Richter's 1880/1 concert series for the 'Phil.' included Beethoven's Symphony no. 9 (the 'Choral') and Liszt's *Mephisto Waltz*, as well as Wagner's *Siegfried Idyll* and the *Prelude and Liebestod* from *Tristan und Isolde*. During that season there were also (mainly new) pieces by Harold Thomas, J. F. Barnett, Alberto Randegger, Charles E. Stephens, George Henschel, Julius Benedict, Arthur Sullivan, Hubert Parry and the two Macfarren brothers – a wide conspectus of orchestral music, good and not-so-good. At the London opera houses in 1880, Fritz's last year at Isleworth, *The Flying Dutchman* and *Carmen* had their first English performances; the initial run of *HMS Pinafore* finished after 571 consecutive performances at the Opera Comique, off the Strand; and at His Majesty's Theatre one could have seen Boito's *Mefistofele*, Gounod's *Faust*, Verdi's *Aida* and Bellini's *La Sonnambula*.

After leaving Isleworth at Christmas 1879, when he was eighteen, Fritz joined the family firm. Julius sensibly believed that he should learn the business from the bottom, and he was therefore sent to work with its agent, a Mr Baxter, in the Gloucestershire town of Stroud. The Baxters invited Fritz to live with them, rather than in an hotel, and he was thus able to spend his allowance from the firm on train trips to London for more music.[26] He then became an apprentice manager at a textile mill in Chemnitz in Saxony (known as 'Das Sächsische [the Saxon] Manchester'); he may or may not have done well

---

[23] It was founded in 1866, by the industrialist and statesman Richard Cobden and others, as an attempt to provide a progressive style of education with much international content. It had 'sister colleges' in Paris and Bonn.

[24] *PW*, p. 33.

[25] See, for example, Cyril Ehrlich, *First Philharmonic: A History of The Royal Philharmonic Society* (Oxford: Clarendon Press, 1995). The Society became 'Royal' in 1912.

[26] Stroud station, on the Cheltenham & Great Western Union Railway line between Gloucester and London, was opened in 1845.

there, but he had some lessons with Hans Sitt, the city's musical director and a celebrated violin teacher.[27] The great musical centres of Berlin, Dresden and Leipzig were easily accessible from Chemnitz – Fritz saw *Die Meistersinger von Nürnberg* in Berlin, and it seems very probable that he went to concerts and operas in the other cities. Next, he was dispatched to Norrköping in Sweden. The city was the centre of Sweden's wool trade, and, with little to occupy his free time there, Fritz worked hard and profitably at his job. Having finished his business tasks, he then took the opportunity of enjoying something of what other parts of Sweden had to offer. Stockholm was an extremely civilised city, and the contrast between it and industrial Bradford quite unbelievable. He went on to investigate Norway, where the beauty of the mountains, fjords and the countryside completely overwhelmed him. Seeing them was without doubt the first 'defining moment' of his life, and the influence of those high, lonely places on him was almost beyond description.[28]

That stimulating experience could not, of course, last. In the autumn of 1881, Julius learned that Fritz was no longer paying proper attention to the needs of the business, and – his success at Norrköping notwithstanding – he was summarily ordered home. The next attempt to keep Fritz on the straight and narrow path was sending him to Saint-Étienne in deepest France, a commercial town about 60 km south-west of Lyon. As well as wool, its main industries in the late nineteenth century were coal mining and bicycle making, and it was famed for ribbon and *passementerie*. Business cannot, however, have occupied many of his waking hours, for early in 1882 he found time to play truant for a few weeks in the culturally vibrant Monte Carlo – staking his all at the gaming tables, where he managed to make enough to cover the cost of lodgings, food, more violin lessons, going to concerts, and to opera in the recently opened Salle Garnier. He was, though, being followed by another employee of Delius & Co., who reported his gallivanting to Julius – and, needless to say, back he was summoned to Bradford yet again. Halfway there, however, on his way across Paris, he called in on Julius's brother Theodor – who had left the family firm and was living the life of a sophisticated bachelor in the rue Cambon, not far from the Opéra.[29] Fritz probably asked him for some advice. Exactly what ideas he went away with a few days later is unknown, but his uncle must have given him considerable moral support, and it is probable that he suggested that Fritz should find a different occupation, albeit still in commerce and not (at this stage) as a musician.

Unfortunately for Julius, everywhere he sent Fritz (save for Norrköping), good music was available either on the doorstep or within a reasonable distance, and all his efforts to encourage Fritz to follow in his footsteps had only succeeded in turning him against a career with Delius & Co. Instead, he

---

[27] Carley, 'Delius and the Violin'; see also Philip Jones, 'A Reluctant Apprentice: Delius in Chemnitz', *DSJ* 118 (1996), 17–28.

[28] *TB*, p. 21.

[29] *MMB*, p. 99.

became increasingly determined on a musical one. Their relationship had by now reached a very low ebb, and Julius made three final attempts at persuasion. On the strength of Fritz's original success in Norrköping he was sent back to Scandinavia. Not surprisingly, though, this second trip was a success only from Fritz's point of view: the high hills, the mountains and the other scenic marvels of what had already become his beloved Norway were even more exhilarating than before, and walking in them, in solitude and wonder, was a life-changing experience. Furthermore, he had by now learned enough Norwegian to enable him to start reading the works of Bjørnstjerne Bjørnson[30] and Henrik Ibsen,[31] the country's foremost writers – indeed, he would also become widely read in French and German. Holding the purse-strings, though, naturally enabled Julius soon to oblige his son to return to Bradford once more – and he then used what turned out to be his last-but-one card, by arranging for him to go and work in the office of his uncle Ernst's wool business in Manchester; that idea, of course proved to be a signal failure. So too was Julius's final attempt at getting Fritz to become a dedicated and successful representative of the firm. In 1883, he was sent to Paris – but, yet again, his time there brought little or no benefit to the business. Julius therefore had simply no alternative but to accept that Fritz was not destined to become a wool merchant, and could not be forced. Julius was convinced that it would be impossible for him to make a respectable living from music, and that a different business career was the only alternative – so, to reduce the parental opposition to his becoming a musician, Fritz did his best to keep his father thinking that he would be reasonably content with that.

As Fritz reached the age of twenty-one that year, he can now be referred to as Delius.

Delius had a Bradfordian friend of much the same age, Charles Douglas, who was likewise thoroughly disenchanted at the prospect of joining his own father's dyeing business, and wanted to live an outdoor life in some foreign country. One or other of them saw in a local paper an advertisement for the sale of land in Florida 'suitable for growing oranges, lemons, pineapples and all kinds of tropical fruits', and they decided that this was the answer to all their problems. To Delius's undoubted joy and relief, Julius agreed to take an option on an orange plantation, Solana Grove,[32] on the St Johns River, about thirty miles south of Jacksonville in Florida, and to provide some funds for the venture. On 2 March 1884, the two young men therefore sailed from Liverpool

---

[30] Bjørnstjerne Bjørnson (1832–1910): one of Norway's greatest poets, as well as a celebrated and powerful playwright. In 1910, he was awarded the Nobel Prize for Literature. He was also a great patriot, and became heavily involved in politics. Delius would meet him in 1891.

[31] Henrik Ibsen (1828–1906): with Bjørnson, he was Norway's most celebrated playwright, and also a hugely significant poet. He and Delius first met in the autumn of 1897.

[32] Most writers have called it 'Solano', but Delius always used 'Solana'.

to New York, and then down to Georgia, completing the journey to Jacksonville by train. Delius's sense of happiness and independence when he arrived at the property must have been simply overwhelming.

Solana Grove was around 140 acres, with a well-built wooden bungalow with two living rooms, two bedrooms and an outside kitchen; it fronted onto the huge, slow-flowing river, and all around was forest, with exotic and often huge trees, and vast swamps. The sounds, the silences, scents and the majesty of the river were utterly different from those of the Norwegian landscape Delius remembered so well – only the magical dawns and evenings being common to both:

> Florida! Ah! Florida! I loved Florida – the people, the country – and the silence! ... I wanted to get away as far as possible from parental opposition to my becoming a musician ... [At Solana Grove] I used to get up early and be spellbound watching the silent break of dawn over the river; Nature awakening – it was wonderful! At night the sunsets were all aglow – spectacular. Then the coloured folk on neighbouring plantations would start singing instinctively in parts as I smoked a cigar on my verandah.[33]

The intense beauty of the place and its surroundings, the warm and humid climate, the enjoyment that he got from talking to the black plantation workers, and the simplicity of life on the edge of the river were not in the least conducive to the business of cultivating the plantation, but they were to provide the stimulus for Delius's first two sizeable compositions, *Florida* and *Hiawatha*. Whatever inclination he had to work, however, was frustrated by two things: firstly, he struck up a strong friendship (which flourished for many years) with Jutta Bell, the Norwegian wife of a neighbour, and a distant relative of Edvard Grieg.[34] She was apparently a good musician, and to judge from the help she later gave Delius over the libretti of two of his early operas, she very probably encouraged him to pursue a musical career.[35] Secondly, Charles was not turning out to be the industrious companion that Delius had hoped – and Delius was certainly not going to do two men's work!

At this point, what was undoubtedly the second 'defining moment' in Delius's life occurred. Charles succumbed to malaria, and Delius went to Jacksonville to find a doctor. When he arrived, the doctor was out, so Delius decided to wait for him. He went into Merryday & Paine's nearby music shop,

[33] Eric Fenby, 'On Delius in Florida', in *Programme for the 24th Annual Delius Festival, Jacksonville, Fla., 1984*, quoted in *Gillespie*, p. 9; see also Letter 69 and the note on p. 114 of *Letters 1*.

[34] Jutta Bell (Jutta Mordt Bell, or Jutta Bell-Ranske) (1857?–1934): she and Delius met up again some ten years later, in Paris, and they worked together for a while on the libretti of *The Magic Fountain* (1894–5) and *Koanga* (1895–7).

[35] See Mark A. Stoneman, 'Delius in Florida: The Delius Festival of Jacksonville', in *MA&L*, pp. 36–56, at p. 38; *Lloyd*, p. 65. On Grieg, see below, n. 62.

sat down at a piano and began to improvise. After a while, another visitor to the shop heard him and introduced himself as Thomas F. Ward; he was an organist in his thirties from New York, who had come to the area for his health. Each immediately recognised the other as a 'kindred spirit' – and, talking non-stop about music, Delius so completely forgot about Charles that it became too late to return to Solana Grove that night. When he did so the following day, he found that one of his neighbours had decided that Charles needed more care and attention than Delius was likely to provide, and had taken him off to his own home. Delius returned to Jacksonville, bought a piano, met Ward again and invited him to stay for a while.[36] Ward accepted readily, they settled down together, and he turned out to be an extremely sound musician. So, for probably the next six months[37] – while the native caretaker and foreman, Albert Anderson, looked after the plantation as best he could – Ward taught Delius strict counterpoint and fugue,[38] as well as some orchestration, and (being an organist) almost certainly introduced him to a large amount of Baroque and Classical music.[39] In the event, neither counterpoint nor fugue would have any place in Delius's music – but his orchestration was to become one of the hallmarks of his unique style.

There is confusion among the biographers as to the exact order of the next events – largely because whatever letters Delius may have written or received while he was in America have not been traced – but in essence this is what happened between the summer of 1884 and early 1885. Possibly urged on by Ward, Delius wrote to his father at least once, and possibly twice, explaining that he was now seriously studying music with a friend; that he had come to the conclusion that orange growing was simply not for him; and asking permission to leave America, to study at the great Conservatorium at Leipzig (the oldest in Germany, founded by Mendelssohn). Julius refused, and sent a Mr Tattersfield out to Solana Grove, perhaps primarily 'to report on the situation, and read the riot act which [Julius] was unable to pronounce in person',[40] perhaps to exercise the option on the plantation – but most probably both, as Julius became the property's sole owner.[41] When he learned, either from Mr Tattersfield or in

[36] *TB*, pp. 27–8. In *PW*, p. 40, however, there is no mention of Charles Douglas at all.

[37] One biographer says it was six months (*PW*, p. 40), but Gillespie believes that it could have been longer (*Gillespie*, p. 54). *Gillespie*, pp. 48–58, covers the whole of the period of the Delius/Ward friendship.

[38] There is a manuscript 'Early counterpoint exercise written by Delius for Thomas Ward on the plantation in Florida', in Delius's hand, in The Grainger Museum at the University of Melbourne (Catalogue no. MD C2/DELI – 10): see *Grainger's Collection of Music by Other Composers*, ed. Phil Clifford (Melbourne: University of Melbourne Press, 1983), p. 227.

[39] *PW*, p. 42.

[40] *MMB*, p. 75.

[41] At some stage, Julius Delius transferred the plantation to Fritz, who, in 1912, sold it to his conductor friend Hans Haym (see below, Chapter 3). Haym's son Rudolf

a letter from Fritz himself, that Fritz now appeared to have no intention of making a go of orange growing, he must have been dumbfounded, as the only possible motive for his purchase of the plantation outright was to lock his son into a business life. Then, probably in September 1884, Ward left Solana Grove and returned to being an organist in Jacksonville – and Delius noted that 'We corresponded, but I never saw him again.'[42]

The future for Delius, now on his own, looked very uncertain – but there was yet another surprise. 'At this point, Providence stepped in, in the form of his elder brother [Ernst] who arrived suddenly from Australia'[43] – 'complete with a keg of whisky!'[44] – and agreed to take over the estate. He, too, had flatly refused to join Delius & Co., and taken up sheep farming; the venture had not, though, worked out as he had hoped, and he was now looking for something new to do. Delius's sister Clare felt that Fritz had been extremely keen to leave the Grove, but that:

> Some member of the family must, in all decency, be left to look after papa's property. Ernst wanted something to do, and here was the very job for him … For a few days he worked hard enough for two men, and then suddenly decided, the keg of whisky having been exhausted, that he had had enough of plantation life. His boat was still tied to the bank. He got into it and vanished down the St. John's [*sic*] river, nobody knows for certain where. He was heard of in Sumatra some years later and apparently finally made his way back to New Zealand, from which country the news of his death reached the family.[45]

Delius may or may not have stayed on long enough to satisfy himself that Ernest would be able to cope – but in the summer of 1885 he left Solana Grove for Jacksonville, where he set himself up as a music teacher. The town was a fast-growing place, still being rebuilt after the Civil War, and he found enough work to enable him to pay his way for a while. He then saw an advertisement in a local newspaper for someone to teach music to the two daughters of a Professor John Frederick Rueckert, who lived at Danville in Virginia, some 500 miles to the north. Danville was a flourishing and civilised town with several

---

later unsuccessfully tried to farm it (see St Pancras Library, *Catalogue for Delius & America Exhibition*, 1972, pp. 1 and 5; see also *Letters 2*, p. 82). Rudolf Haym may have sold it to Fritz's foreman, Albert Anderson. Claire Delius wrongly thought that the building completely disintegrated through neglect (*MMB*, pp. 83–4), but in 1961 it was dismantled and reconstructed on the campus of The University of Jacksonville: see, *inter alia*, Roger Buckley, 'A Visit to Solana Grove', *DSJ* 77 (1982), 15–19; Richard Suddath, 'A Favour for a Friend: An Account of the Restoration of the Delius House', ed. Thomas H. Gunn, *DSJ* 96 (1988), 3–7.

[42] *Fenby 2*, p. 22.

[43] *PW*, p. 43. All the other biographers say that he came from New Zealand.

[44] *MMB*, p. 79.

[45] Ibid., pp. 79–80.

newspapers, a debating society, a number of schools and two music societies.[46] Rueckert had been a student at the Leipzig Conservatorium,[47] and his business was selling organs and pianos. He told Delius that he would do his utmost to get him other pupils, so Delius accepted the job, and arrived to discover that Rueckert was as good as his word – he found himself advertised in the papers as 'the celebrated and well-known Professor Delius ... [who] was willing to give lessons to a selected number of musical aspirants.'[48] It seems highly likely that the arrival of a supposedly famous, clearly talented, and handsome young man created a lot of interest among the elegant young ladies of the town. He was soon teaching not only the Rueckert daughters but also those of smart and wealthy tobacco merchants being educated at Roanoke Female College – almost certainly in their grand houses on 'Millionaires' Row' – and earning a good living for himself. He also got to know an influential member of the community, Robert S. Phifer, who was 'looked upon as the leading musician in Danville – [and who] really established the classical movement' there.[49]

At that time, the Leipzig Conservatorium was undoubtedly the most prestigious of all the music colleges in Europe, and Rueckert must have talked to Delius about it. Delius became determined to go there and, as the result of his pouring out his woes about the impossibility of spending his life with Delius & Co., the very sympathetic Phifer took it upon himself to write to Julius, urging him to allow his son to embark on a musical career. Julius did not reply to that letter, but he later wrote to Phifer asking if he had any news of his son – and was astonished to learn that he was supporting himself perfectly adequately with his music teaching. Delius stayed in Danville for the school year, and then, for no apparent reason, left for New York – no doubt leaving behind him a large number of heartbroken young ladies. Although Sir Thomas Beecham[50] later suggested that his mother disagreed,[51] Delius realised that his musical abilities would enable him to 'hold his own' in back in Europe. Julius, not having heard from him since he left Solana Grove, must have become very worried about what he was up to, and a private detective was sent, presumably

---

[46] For fuller descriptions, see William Randel, 'Delius in America', in *Companion*, pp. 147–66, at p. 158; Mary Cahill, *Delius in Danville* (Danville: Virginia Historical Society, 1986).

[47] Now the Hochschule für Musik und Theater.

[48] *MMB*, p. 84.

[49] Ibid., p. 87. On p. 85 there is a reference to one of Delius's female pupils, who called him 'one of my early sweethearts'.

[50] [Sir] Thomas Beecham, 2nd Baronet, CH (1879–1961): English conductor and impresario. From the early twentieth century until his death, he had an immense influence on the musical life of Britain, and was the first English conductor to have an international career. As will be seen in Chapter 5, and thereafter *passim*, he did more in his lifetime than anyone else to champion and perform Delius's music.

[51] Sir Thomas Beecham, *Frederick Delius* (London: Hutchinson & Co., 1959), p. 33. This book is probably the best biography of Delius.

to Jacksonville, to find him. In due course, the sleuth ran him to earth, possibly in New York – where, it has been suggested,[52] albeit without any actual evidence, Delius was for a while the organist of a church in Manhattan. The detective then delivered a message from Julius that must have caused Delius utter astonishment: he could, after all, go to the Leipzig Conservatorium for eighteen months, and at Julius's expense too. There was, however, a sting in the tail, because when he had finished the course he would have to return to America and continue to earn his living (albeit a musical one) there. That did not deter Delius in the least, and, having possibly spent a few days on Long Island, he left New York for Liverpool on the RMS *Aurania*.[53]

### FIRST WORKS

O F Delius's first compositions, all that survive from his two-and-a-quarter years in America are three songs (see Chapter 9) and two piano pieces. A piano was one of the absolute necessities of Delius's life, and to discover that he could buy one in Jacksonville must have been a great excitement. Having it delivered to Solana Grove proved to be another of the major turning points in his life. From his very young days, Delius had developed a technique (albeit one not necessarily based on textbooks) that made him at least competent and possibly quite good, and he became a confident improviser. Some of his writing for the keyboard is significant, in particular the piano parts of the later songs and the sonatas for violin and cello.

The polka *Zum Carnival* (1885?: *RT* IX/1; *CE* vol. 33) is believed to have been written in 1885, but it was not published until 1892 – in Jacksonville. This is strange, since by that time Delius was living in Paris. Almost certainly while he was in Jacksonville he made the acquaintance of the publisher, A. B. Campbell, and, probably as a friendly gesture, promised him his first composition. A 'jiggety' little piece, 2/4 in C major, with accents on the second beat of the bar, it is not difficult to play – and, as a naïve and jolly pot-boiler, it would have been commercially just what a publisher wanted for amateur pianists. The manuscript is missing, but that of the second piece, *Pensées Mélodieuses* (1885: *RT* IX/2; *CE* vol. 33), survives. It is clearly dated 10 June 1885, though it was never published in Delius's lifetime.[54] It is a pleasant enough little piece, but without question a 'first effort', and the dotted rhythm of its main idea, which is repeated in about two-thirds of its ninety-six bars, becomes somewhat monotonous. Unlike most of Delius's other piano music, it has specific pedalling instructions.

---

[52] *AJ*, p. 18; *MMB*, p. 89; *TB*, p. 31.

[53] The crossing time from New York to Liverpool was between six and seven days: see information available through www.gjenvick.com [accessed 3 April 2014].

[54] Its two pages are reproduced as plates 16 and 17 in *RT Catalogue*, and it is printed in *CE* vol. 33.

D ELIUS'S time in America was the watershed of his life. Many years later, in his *Delius as I Knew Him*, Eric Fenby[55] wrote:

> The three months he had spent entirely alone at his orange-grove in Florida before going to Leipzig had been a revelation to him. 'I was demoralised when I left Bradford for Florida,' he told me; 'you can have no idea of the state of my mind in those days. In Florida, through sitting and gazing at Nature, I gradually learnt the way in which I should eventually find myself, but it was not until years after I had settled at Grez that I really found myself. Nobody could help me. Contemplation, like composition, cannot be taught.

By August 1886, only eight weeks after arriving back in England, Delius was in lodgings in Leipzig, first at 8 Marschnerstrasse and then at 5 Harkortstrasse, and he started at the Conservatorium at the end of the month. He quickly became friendly with several Norwegian fellow students, including Christian Sinding[56] and the violinists Arve Arvesen,[57] Johan Halvorsen[58] and Halfdan Jebe.[59] Although then young and innocent, Jebe became an extraordinary character: a 'violinist, composer, world-traveller and libertine, whose personality seems to have fascinated all with whom he came into contact'[60] – Delius in particular, for he later wrote: 'Jebe is the only man I have ever loved in all my life.'[61] Another of Sinding's friends then currently in Leipzig was Edvard Grieg[62] – and Sinding's introduction of him to Delius was the third of the four

---

[55] Eric Fenby (1906–77): a young man who became Delius's amenuensis in 1928, and subsequently wrote a famous book about their work together, *Delius as I Knew Him* (*Fenby 1*), and an introduction to Delius and his music (*Fenby 2*): see below, Chapters 8 and 10, *passim*.

[56] Christian Sinding (1856–1941): Norwegian composer who arrived at Leipzig in the same term as Delius. They became close friends, and there are over sixty letters from Sinding to Delius in the DTA. His piano piece, *The Rustle of Spring*, became very popular with good amateurs.

[57] Arve Arvesen (1869–1951): after leaving Leipzig he went to Paris, where he and Delius continued to see much of each other – although their paths did not cross subsequently. He taught the violin, became the director of music in various Scandinavian cities and finally the principal of the Conservatorium at Bergen.

[58] Johan Halvorsen (1864–1935) spent the same two years at Leipzig as Delius. He then taught and performed in Aberdeen, and subsequently in various European cities.

[59] Halfdan Jebe (1868–1937): a lifelong friend, to whom Delius dedicated *An Arabesque* in 1911: see *Letters 2*, pp. 380–1.

[60] John Bergsagel, 'Delius and Danish Literature', in *MA&L*, pp. 290–310. See also Don Gillespie, 'Halfdan Jebe in Atlanta', *DSJ* 149 (2011), 34–40.

[61] Letter 377, and see *Letters 2*, pp. 380–1.

[62] Edvard Hagerup Grieg (1843–1907) became Norway's probably most celebrated musician, as a composer – drawing much of his inspiration from Norwegian folk melodies – a conductor and a brilliant pianist, particularly in his own music. He married Nina Hagerup, a singer (1845–1935), in 1867.

'defining moments' of Delius's life (after his first visit to Norway and meeting Ward). Although Grieg was the elder by nineteen years, they got on exceedingly well – so much so that Grieg soon became Delius's musical 'guru', and perhaps one of the relatively few people whom Delius ever asked for an opinion of his work. They remained the closest of friends until Grieg's death in 1907.

In Leipzig, there was, of course, a vast amount of music going on, and celebrated composers, conductors and instrumentalists often came to give concerts and recitals – Brahms and Tchaikovsky conducted their own works, Mahler and Arthur Nikisch were in the pit at the Opera House (the latter doing *Tristan und Isolde*), while Busoni[63] and the celebrated Brodsky Quartet[64] gave chamber music recitals. Delius's violin teacher from his Chemnitz days, Hans Sitt – now the professor of violin at the Conservatorium – was the viola player in the Quartet. Delius resumed lessons with him, although probably only for two terms. He was taught composition (and possibly the piano) by the professor of composition, Carl Reinecke,[65] and by Salomon Jadasson[66] – both elderly and completely set in their ways, and whose teaching 'proved useless'.[67] Many of the attitudes and much of the teaching at the Conservatorium were very old-fashioned – Sinding and Grieg used to deride it as 'Die Doppelfugeanstalten' ('The Double Fugue Institution') – and how much knowledge and inspiration Delius actually gained from being there can only be a matter for speculation.[68] There are, as one might expect, notebooks containing contrapuntal exercises, but he seems to have had little time for the teaching staff – indeed many years later he said of Thomas Ward: 'I didn't know what a good teacher he was until I went to the Conservatoire. The professors there had no insight whatever compared with his. His instruction was intuitive;

---

[63] Ferruccio (Benvenuto) Busoni (1866–1924) was an Italian composer, arranger and pianist, who later conducted the second performance of *Paris*.

[64] Adolph Brodsky (1851–1929): celebrated Russian violinist and teacher, in the 1880s a professor at Leipzig. His string quartet became one of the finest in Europe, and in 1895 he became the principal of The Royal Manchester College of Music (later The Royal Northern College of Music). He played Elgar's Violin Concerto with the composer conducting, and the Brodsky Quartet were the dedicatees of Elgar's String Quartet.

[65] Carl (Heinrich Carset) Reinecke (1824–1910): one of the most influential musicians of his time, he taught, among others, Grieg, Sinding, Jánaček, Albéniz, Svendsen, Max Bruch and the conductor Felix Weingartner.

[66] Salomon Jadassohn (1831–1902): German composer and a typically academic teacher, whose *A Practical Course in Ear Training* became very popular. On account of his Jewish origins, however, he was not well liked at the Conservatorium, and, in *PW* at p. 45, Heseltine described him as 'neither a beautiful player or a cultured musician'.

[67] Fenby, quoted in *Lloyd*, p. 55.

[68] There is an excellent description of student life in Leipzig by a contemporary of Delius there, Percy Pitt (who became a well-known conductor of opera in London – see Chapter 5, n. 39), quoted in *Letters 1*, pp. 6–7.

just what I needed.'[69] Although his formal lessons must have helped to some degree, in all probability he learned far more from listening to music and talking to other diploma students. As he said in a letter to Grieg, 'I have never lived through such a congenial time. It has been a cornerstone in my life. I hope there will be three more to come.'[70]

In the summer of 1887, he went alone on a walking holiday to Norway – which greatly deepened his love of the country. He kept a remarkably full diary of his travels every day between 15 July and 18 August, and for a further few days until 1 September.[71] Besides these he also had a 'Red Notebook' (as it is known) inscribed 'March 26th/86/Danville Va'. The scenery, his journeys, and his encounters with people are described in the latter in vivid detail,[72] and it is clear that he was even more bowled over by Norway than on his first two visits. Indeed, after he had left Leipzig, he wrote to Grieg:

> Do you know what I have in mind, 'please don't faint': to live in Norway. That is 8 months of the year & 4 months in Leipzig or Paris. When I come to Norway I will look out for a nice place where I can live and work in peace. Perhaps you can help me to find something like this.[73]

Many years later, in 1921–2, he and Jelka did indeed build a very modest single-storey house, which they called Høifagerli, at Lesjaskog, a tiny village on the west coast of Norway, between Bergen and Trondheim – although they never lived there, and in fact only went there twice.[74]

Back in Leipzig, on Christmas Eve 1887 the Griegs invited Sinding, Halvorsen and Delius to what turned out to be an unforgettable evening:

> After the meal we were, without exception, all plastered, but the programme had to be adhered to and it offered music, music and still more music! What a Christmas Eve! … Mr Delius played a piano piece which he called 'Norwegische Schlittenfahrt' with great talent.[75]

The manuscript of *Norwegische Schlittenfahrt* (*Norwegian Sleigh Ride*) (*RT* IX/3) is now lost – but in 1889–90 Delius included an orchestrated version of it, titled just *Winter Nacht* (*Winter Night*), in the *Drei symphonische Dichtungen* (see below, Chapter 2).

---

[69] *Lloyd*, p. 126.

[70] Letter 6.

[71] There is a transcription of the diary in *Letters 1*, appendix 3.

[72] It also contains the very first sketches for *The Song of the High Hills*. It is held at The Grainger Museum in Melbourne, Australia, and Professor Roger Buckley, a former chairman of The Delius Society, is currently transcribing and annotating it. The other diaries are in the DTA.

[73] Letter 12.

[74] There are some photographs of Delius and his great friend Balfour Gardiner sitting on the veranda there, both wearing suits and ties!

[75] *Grieg & Delius*, p. 34.

It seems, however, that he enjoyed himself far too much in Leipzig to get round to writing more than a few pieces of music – for all that survives from his five terms at Leipzig are the *Six Part Songs*, the orchestral suite *Florida*, and the preliminary sketches for *Hiawatha*.

## SIX PART SONGS

(1885?–91: *RT* IV/1; *CE* supp. vol. 17)

*Durch den Wald* (von Schreck?); *An den Sonnenschein*
(Robert Reinick); *Ave Maria* (unknown); *Sonnenscheinlied*
(Bjørnstjerne Bjørnson); *Frühlingsanbruch* (Carl Anderson);
*Her ute skal gildet staa* (Henrik Ibsen)

A MEMBER of the Delius family is recorded as one of founders, in 1846 or 1856 (the authorities differ), of the Bradford Liedertafel, one of many groups, originally of German origin, which sang male voice partsongs, partly for their own pleasure but also giving regular concerts in the town.[76] Julius may well have been a later member. The group very probably rehearsed in each others' houses, and, if so, possibly the Delius house, 1–3 Claremont – so that the young Fritz almost, as it were, had partsongs in his blood. The songs were not sophisticated compositions, but strophic settings[77] of a wide variety of poets and sometimes folktales, more often than not four-square, jolly, and not difficult to sing. The notebooks Delius kept when he was in Leipzig include a considerable number of sketches for such songs.

This collection is for SATB[78] choir, with German texts (translated for the Collected Edition[79] by Lionel Carley), and although they are, not surprisingly, very straightforward, they are well put together for a twenty-three-year old, and (except perhaps for the last one) have a discreet charm. The first in the set was *Lorelei* (H. Heine), listed as *RT* IV/1[1], but the style of handwriting and notation is different from anything else written by Delius, and it is not now thought to have been his.[80]

*Durch den Wald* ('Durch den Wald wie schimmert es sonnig im Grün' – 'Through the woods a glimmering of sunlight in green') is the first music in which Delius used his very characteristic lilting 6/8 time signature. *An den Sonnenschein* ('Oh! Sonnenschein' – 'Oh! Shining, shining golden sun') is entirely in block harmony, with no real deviation from the home key of G. The words of *Ave Maria* are untraced – they are not the same as those of the

---

[76] *Young*, note to p. 535; *DSJ* 58 (1977), 5; *DSJ* 67 (1980), 7.

[77] I.e. having the same melody for all its verses, and sometimes a refrain repeated at the end of each verse.

[78] Soprano, alto, tenor and bass.

[79] For details of the *Collected Edition*, see above, List of Sources and Abbreviations, *supra CE*.

[80] *RT Supplement*, p. 48.

Schubert/Walter Scott song. This is the first of only two pieces by Delius which might be called 'church' or 'religious' music (the other is the wedding music in Scene IV of *A Village Romeo and Juliet*), and they are both almost entirely predictable, very like an anthem or hymn tune by, say, Stainer. *Ave Maria* is not unlike the Schubert setting – quiet, slow and stately. *Sonnenscheinlied* ('Es war so ein heller Sonnentag' – 'It was such a bright and sunny day') is also in 6/8, and there is a nice hint of originality in the slowing-up at 'träumen' at the end of the third line, 'Da lag ich zu sinnen und träumen' ('I lay thinking and dreaming'). *Frühlingsanbruch* ('Was dämmert im Ost in dem purpurnen Höhn?' – 'There's a glow in the East in the purple hills') is a welcome to Spring. Probably written in 1887 (in mauve ink!), it is another completely straightforward piece, the third of the set in 6/8. The Collected Edition includes *Her ute skal gildet staa* ('Yes, here we shall feast as the sun goes down') – not one of the original six songs and a not very appealing one at that, which jogs along, yet again in 6/8. However, the number of bars in each phrase varies, which prevents it from being completely four-square – and there is a most un-Delian three-bar quasi-fugal entry of the parts about half-way through.

Songs numbers 3 and 5 were first performed on 11 January 1974 in St John's Smith Square, London, by The Linden Singers under Ian Humphris:

> Two early songs of Delius were practically throwbacks to Mendelssohn, but the rest afforded an excellent view of early-twentieth-century English choral music with its pleasant washy slidings.
>
> *The Times* 12 January 1974

Song number 7 was included in a concert by the Derwent Singers in Nottingham on 25 June 1977. When the others were first sung is not known.

## FLORIDA
## (TROPISCHER SZENEN FÜR ORCHESTER)
### (1887: *RT* VI/1; *CE* vol. 20)

T HIS was Delius's first significant, full-scale work. It dates from 1886–7
and is dedicated to 'the People of Florida'. It is a set of vivid reminiscences
of Delius's time at Solana Grove, possibly begun in America, but certainly
completed when he was in Leipzig; early in 1888 it was given a private
run-through in a restaurant (probably Bonorand's) in the Rosental Park, with
Grieg in the small audience. The conductor was Hans Sitt, and his sixty or so
players were members of a Leipzig military band whose fee was a barrel of
beer.[81] After that, the work lay dormant for nearly half a century until Beecham
revived the greater part of it in 1937. Despite the warm advocacy of his classic
1956 recording, it has never quite become the repertoire work Beecham hoped
it would. It has an untroubled youthfulness and charm about it that are most
appealing; with its refreshing lack of complexity it is no denigration at all to
say that the score is superior 'light music'. Naturally the sound-world of the
twenty-five-year-old composer is mostly untypical of his later style – there is
plenty of Grieg and Sinding in it and, indeed, Smetana: but then most young
composers are inevitably derivative. What is really most remarkable about it
is its orchestration, which is self-assured and very effective. The run-through
that Delius heard must have been rather rough round the edges, but at least he
knew how to fix most of the faults and he did rewrite part of it, claiming later
that he learnt more in half-an-hour listening to *Florida* than from all of his
studies at Leipzig.

The four movements represent a time-span from the rising of the sun to
nightfall. *Daybreak* falls into two equal but highly contrasting parts, and opens
imaginatively with shimmering (*tremolandi*) muted violins above A minor
chords that unfold on descending clarinets, horns and bassoons. A plangent
oboe solo weaves a line of repeated melodic sequences falling step-wise by
semitones (Fig. 1+3):

Ex. 1.1

A string texture reminiscent of the 'Forest Murmurs' in Wagner's *Siegfried*, with
pentatonic wisps of melody from the woodwind and horns (Fig. 1+15), leads to
a more definite 'tune', again on 1st oboe:

---

[81] Frederick Delius, 'Recollections of Grieg', in *Letters 1*, p. 395.

Ex. 1.2

Ex. 1.2 turns out to be a resourceful development of the earlier melody, but this time firmly in A major. The texture fills out and the violins explore a broader idea of their own in C sharp minor (Fig. 3+7); again fairly episodic (how Delius loved his sequences, even at this age!), this builds to some *tutti* climaxes (Figs 4+14 and 5+2), the orchestral textures full but never bloated. The music begins to steer itself towards D major at the same time as it falls away and pulls up at a double bar, concluding the first part of this movement. (The two small cuts in this opening section, as marked in volume 20 of the Collected Edition, are presumably Beecham's editorial suggestions rather than Delius's; they only amount to some nineteen bars in all, but Beecham observes them in his 1956 recording and they justifiably eliminate some musical padding.)

The second part of the movement has become familiar in its own right as *La Calinda*, an African ritual dance which was imported to the southern states of the USA via the West Indies. Delius was clearly fond of this section, as he subsequently incorporated it into the second act of his opera *Koanga*; it has now become popular as a stand-alone piece for the concert hall. It has a tripartite, A–B–A structure driven by a *moto perpetuo* pulse of quaver–crotchet–quaver; its copious themes are memorable and well contrasted. They include the main oboe tune:

Ex. 1.3

and a more widely stepping tune, heard first on the upper woodwind:

Ex. 1.4

This is passed to the strings (Fig. 8+3); a further idea is established in the form of a scale-inflected tune with a pseudo-oriental 'twist' to its intervals (flutes and 1st clarinet, then strings) (Fig. 8+11). An extensive middle, the B section, shifts to the dominant of A major (where Beecham suggested another cut), and is built around sweeping flourishes on strings and woodwind with some robust writing for the brass (Fig. 11+17 *et seq.*). Delius manages a most effective transition back to a shortened repeat of the opening A section, taking the kettle off the boil at just the right moment (Fig. 13+7) and then allowing the music to wind down to *andante* eleven bars from the end, where it dies out completely – as if the dancers are exhausted.

The brass are *tacet* for the second movement, *By the River*, which suggests the full heat of the day with a languorous 12/8 *andantino* that flows along in a rich E flat tonality. The fortunate strings now have the best tune of the whole suite:

Ex. 1.5

This is a sinuous, strangely poignant idea and has a second melody appended to it at Fig. 1+1. The flute and piccolo arabesques (Fig. 2+1) that decorate its repeat are most effective. There is a central section in the mediant (G major) that also aims at the heart-strings with a beautiful viola melody (Fig. 3-1). This is first presented with an accompaniment of divided cello and double-bass chords, whilst the harp scatters three-part chords above – a wonderful effect. We return to E flat, via a transposition of the counter-melody, for the third section (Fig. 5+1), which is more or less a mirror image of the first with just a few nips and tucks – all refreshingly straightforward. As with the other three movements of the suite, the ending is hushed and all the better for it. This movement is a gem and it is not surprising that it was extracted as an encore by Beecham, as one of his 'lollipops'.

*Sunset*, the third movement, expands the orchestration somewhat by calling for separate players for the bass clarinet and cor anglais, not used elsewhere in the suite – an early indication of Delius's characteristic profligacy. As in *Daybreak*, the outer sections frame a central dance. An introductory *moderato* of twenty-two bars with an E minor-ish feel introduces a somewhat bland four-bar theme on the cellos doubled by the 1st clarinet to a pulsing flute accompaniment. This leads (Fig. 1+1) to the slightly faster main body of this section in a D major key-centre and with a developed version of the cello/clarinet idea which is soon taken up by the violins in canon with woodwind:

Ex. 1.6

This is not an especially distinguished theme, and it does come in for a lot of repetition over the next forty-five bars. Delius also repeats it in the final *molto tranquillo* section of this movement by which time, frankly, it has outlived its limited appeal. But if the bread of the sandwich is disappointingly bland, the 'filler' is much more tasty: a spirited (and later very loud) *danza*, marked in the revised score 'Auprès de la Plantation' ('By the Plantation'):

Ex. 1.7

Delius may possibly be quoting a genuine traditional tune, or at least giving his own imitation of one. In his *pizzicato* lower strings, off-beat tambourine and harp, Delius suggests that banjos are strumming and the perky little tune has a nice 'blues' twist, with an unexpected G sharp in the fourth bar of the melody. The dance also has a *più animato* subsection (Fig. 5+1) with a more aggressive feel, enhanced by some *tutti* outbursts and subsequently driven even harder (Fig. 7+1). The banjo texture makes a curtailed appearance (Fig. 9+5) before the opening material is repeated *molto tranquillo*. Some ears may hear the two-bar oboe phrase (Fig. 10) as being not unlike the baritone solo 'Oh honey, I am going down the river in the morning', from near the end of *Appalachia* (Letter Dd+9) – an interesting anticipation.

The first dozen or so bars of *At Night*, the last movement, bring us full circle, as Delius directly quotes the oboe passage from near the opening of *Daybreak* (cf. first movement at Figs 1+3 to 1+15) before the music relaxes into a flowing three-in-a-bar, prefaced by a chorale for the four horns. The harmonies are especially Grieg-like; indeed, this movement as a whole has a Nordic feel. The theme, lyrical but not outstandingly memorable, is taken up by the violins and violas in D major (Fig. 1+1); a counter-melody in E major (Fig. 2+1) adds additional warmth to some glowing orchestration. Then, at Fig. 4+1, Delius quotes the viola melody from *By the River*, embellishing it this time with an arching counter-subject in the violins and a fuller texture. Although it is lovely to hear it again, its return may seem somewhat redundant. The E major idea comes back quietly (Fig. 4+13) on the 1st violins followed by the horn chorale (Fig. 6+1), this time with harp and cello arpeggios. This overall mood of tranquil recollection is consolidated by a beautifully imaginative touch: at the beginning of the *più tranquillo* coda (Fig. 7+1) Delius sketches an outline of the tune using just the first nine notes of it (but in a different rhythm) on the 1st clarinet, with muted violas doubled high up on the cellos. It is a wonderful touch of imagination and lingers in the ear as the music dies away to nothing.

Taken overall, *Florida* is not a consistent masterpiece: the level of thematic inspiration is uneven and Delius relies too often on repetition and sequence. Considering, however, that this score came so early in his career it is remarkable, and Beecham was quite justified in rescuing it from oblivion.

In the right conductor's hands it can enchant and beguile the ear with that sheer beauty of sound that was to become such a hallmark of Delius's mature style.

Hoping that he could get an English first performance, at the end of 1888 Delius sent copies of the score and parts of *Florida* to August Manns,[82] who directed the Crystal Palace Concerts. Most disappointingly, however, after a five months' delay he returned them, saying that he did not have enough rehearsal time in which to prepare it as well as the music for 'the general daily Entertainments'. A further fifty-eight years were to pass before *Florida* had its second performance (albeit inexplicably omitting the second movement), on 1 April 1937 by The London Philharmonic Orchestra under Beecham. *The Times* was not impressed:

> The Royal Philharmonic Society completed its 125th season last night with a 'Coronation Concert' at Queen's Hall ... [Arnold Bax's 'Overture to a Picaresque Comedy'] was followed by a suite 'Florida,' which Frederic Delius wrote 50 years ago in Leipzig, and which was oddly labelled 'First performance.' Nevertheless, Mr Edwin Evans was able to quote Clare Delius's account of the real first performance in Leipzig when Grieg heard it and prophesied the composer's successful future from it. Grieg was a man of prescience. Listening to 'Florida' today one doubts whether Sir Thomas Beecham would think it worth playing if it bore any other name than that of Delius. But it was pleasant enough, though it seemed to take up more time than it deserved.
>
> 2 April, 1937

but *The Musical Times* liked it rather better:

> 'Florida,' a suite in four movements, dates from Delius's Leipzig days, and dates almost odorously, if with a certain fragrance. Its melody, harmony and sentiment are roses and lavender; but Grieg had good reason to say, when he heard a private performance, that Delius would go far as a composer. Though the orchestration is too luscious for its themes, it is made and coloured by a hand that knows its palette, and the music has a flow and inventiveness that bespeak a real creative power. As a document the suite was worth the devoted attentions that Sir Thomas Beecham gave to it.
>
> April 1937

---

[82] (Sir) August (Friederich) Manns (1825–1907): The 'father' of popular concerts in London, he worked as the Director of Music at The Crystal Palace for forty-six years. This was an enormous and revolutionary cast-iron and glass building erected in London's Hyde Park for the Great Exhibition of 1851 – after which it was moved to Sydenham in south London, where its main use was for the popularisation of music. The Saturday Concerts there ran for almost fifty years, until 1901.

## HIAWATHA
(1888: *RT* VI/2; *CE* supp. vol. 6)

THIS is Delius's second orchestral work, finished in January 1888. Musical associations with Longfellow's *Hiawatha* inevitably bring to mind Samuel Coleridge-Taylor, whose trilogy of cantatas based on the epic poem were completed between 1898 and 1900, and remained phenomenally popular for about half a century. So it may come as a surprise to learn that Delius had already been there a decade earlier with what he referred to (in a letter to Grieg) as 'my symphonic poem "Hiawatha"', and on the title page of the manuscript full-score as 'Ein Tongedicht', the two terms being fairly new ones for a descriptive orchestral work as favoured by Liszt and Richard Strauss respectively. Delius originally gave indications of the programme of the work in the score but later vigorously scratched them all out, with the exception of two stanzas from Longfellow's poem inscribed in the final pages which refer to Hiawatha's departure; he probably meant to excise these as well, but simply overlooked them. Incidentally, there is no question of Coleridge-Taylor being influenced by Delius's score, since it was never heard in public in either his or the composer's lifetime. Indeed, until 2009, *Hiawatha* was an unperformable score in the sense that several pages of the original orchestral manuscript were missing, removed by Delius himself for reasons that are still not clear. However, Robert Threlfall, of The Delius Trust, has been able to give the score a belated start in life by ingeniously 'closing the gaps', as he put it, and without the need to compose any fresh material. The new full score was published in 2008. While no one would claim it as a neglected masterpiece, it is still well worth hearing as an example of the young composer making steady progress in learning his craft. In its new performing version, at just over seventeen minutes, the work in no way outstays its welcome, and whilst the main themes are not as distinctively memorable as in *Florida*, they are appealing and effectively contrasted – even combined at one point.

The construction is straightforward: a brief introduction of a pastoral nature leads to the presentation of the two principal themes, plausibly depicting Hiawatha and his beloved Minnehaha. The central section, imbued with rhythms of the dance, doubtless evokes Hiawatha's celebrated wedding feast. The final section, with a significant oboe solo, implies a tender portrait of the happy couple, and leads into a succinct recapitulation of the main themes and thence to a coda whose unexpected mood of desolation (timpani strokes and string *tremolandi*) suggests the death of the heroine. Hiawatha's theme returns (this is where Delius left in the references to Hiawatha's departure), and the work dies away in a resplendent orchestral sunset complete with soft horn calls, shimmering strings and harp arpeggios.

If it marks no particular advance on *Florida* (and only one year separates them), then at least *Hiawatha* consolidates Delius's uncanny flair for orchestration: the vivid instrumental colours that glow so memorably in

*Florida* are just as vibrant in this score, and are further proof that Delius's limited musical studies were not holding him back but, on the contrary, were empowering him to strike out on his own, thanks to two gifts that cannot be taught at conservatoires, namely imagination and audacity.

The 'completed' work was first played (following its recording) at the English Music Festival in Dorchester-on-Thames on 23 May 2009 by the BBC Concert Orchestra, conducted by David Lloyd-Jones. Although of considerable interest to Delians, there was no press coverage other than in *The Times*, which deigned only to give it the briefest of mentions:

> The ... concert was full of novelties. Here was the first public performance of Delius's tone-poem of 1888, a lightly exotic, congenial score, realised with passion and authority.
>
> 25 June 2009

but a review of the recording was a little more interesting:

> It makes for a luminous musical image of the poem, less robust than Coleridge-Taylor's Cantata, but imbued with rippling sounds of nature, graced with passionate themes and orchestrated with lustre.
>
> *The Daily Telegraph*, 11 August 2009

DELIUS left Leipzig at Easter 1888, having achieved what can only be described, at best, as two mediocre reports on some twenty-one months' work. His diploma was worded rather more encouragingly, and included the comment that his 'moral demeanour had been exemplary' – a statement that, had they ever seen it, might have surprised perhaps quite a number of those ladies in Paris among whom he would live and enjoy himself from May that year until the summer of 1897. Transcriptions of the reports and the diploma are included below, in Appendix 2). Academically, he had not been successful – indeed, the authorities thought that he had done so little work that it took a year to get them to hand over the diploma – but he had heard a great deal of music, and, very significantly, he and Grieg had become the best of friends.[83]

The Delius family could trace its origins back to at least 1554. For around the first 200 years very few of them were concerned with commerce or finance, but they almost exclusively served the learned professions, the civil service or the army. Gradually, however, they became increasingly involved in trade and industry. Given that family history, how could Julius not have had a deep and instinctive wish to see Delius join him in Delius & Co.? He found it impossible to accept that his son could make a living as a musician as effectively as he himself had in the sphere of business (albeit perhaps not such a rich one), but in the long run, of course, the son was proved right.

---

[83] Their friendship is fully described in *Grieg & Delius*.

By now, however, there was no way in which Delius, as he had previously promised Julius, was going to return either to America or to any form of business, and having Grieg as a very good friend proved to be his trump card. Back in February 1888, very probably at Delius's request, Grieg had written him a letter which was unusually formal and obviously intended for Julius's eyes – although whether he actually saw it is unclear:

> I was pleasantly surprised, indeed stimulated, by your manuscripts and detect in them signs of a most distinguished compositional talent in the grand style, which aspires to the highest goal. Whether you will reach this goal only depends upon what turn your affairs take. If you will permit me, in the interests of your future, to offer you a piece of advice, (it is as an older artist that I take the liberty of doing this) it would be this, that you devote yourself now, while you are still young, fully to the pursuit of your art, rather than accept a formal position, and that you follow both your own true nature and the inner voice of your ideals and your inclinations.[84]

It so happened that Grieg was coming to London for a concert in May, and Delius therefore invited him and his wife Nina out to dinner – and as he said, somewhat laconically, later:

> My parents were in London at the time, and we all had dinner together at the Hotel Metropole and Grieg persuaded my father to let me continue with my musical studies.[85]

Julius, no doubt familiar with some of Grieg's piano music and songs, was deeply impressed that his son should be on such friendly terms with the internationally famous composer and pianist, and by the end of the dinner, in a complete *volte face*, Julius had agreed that there should be no further thoughts of Delius returning to Florida or retaining any connection with Delius & Co. Furthermore, he not only accepted his son's wish to go to live in France, at least for a while, but even promised to continue paying his allowance of £104 a year. Delius was simply astonished, and two days later he was off.

The story of his early life is a classic illustration of the father–son relationship in which the father thinks that his particular occupation in life is one of the best – for it has made him successful – and his paternal instinct makes him want to see his achievement carried on, preferably by his eldest son, then his eldest grandson, and down through succeeding generations. In this case, however, it was never destined to happen, but Julius must nevertheless take considerable credit for having, in the end, allowed the young man to do what he wanted with his life.

---

[84] Letter 3.

[85] *Grieg & Delius*, p. 47.

# The Young Composer in Paris

Parisian life – *Zanoni* – *Rhapsodische Variationen* –
*Paa Vidderne* (melodrama) – *Three Pieces* for string
orchestra – String Quartet (1888) – *Romance* for violin
and piano – *Idylle de printemps* – *Suite d'orchestre* no. 1 –
*Sakuntala* – *Suite de trois morceaux caractéristiques* – *Drei
symphonische Dichtungen* – Two piano pieces – *Légendes
(Sagen)* – *Marche française* – *À l'amore* – *Petite Suite
d'orchestre* no. 2 – *Suite* for violin and orchestra – *Irmelin* –
*On the Mountains* – *Maud* – Violin Sonata in B major –
*Légende* for violin and piano – String Quartet (1892–3)

I N the late 1880s and the 1890s, Second-Empire Paris was an astonishing
city, full of contrasts – stunning architecture and appalling slums, great
luxury and desperate poverty, an amazing mix of people – and in full artistic,
intellectual and musical flow:

> The city was abuzz with a thousand scandals, with literary and poetic
> gatherings of the arguably avant-garde, with eventful dissident
> exhibitions, *soirées* liberally sprinkled with cursed, damned or anti-
> establishment artists, and sophisticated society dinners given by well-
> known and admired academe painters. The Exposition Universelle of
> 1889, which Delius attended ... particularly demonstrated the vitality of
> the *vie parisienne* and all its spheres of activity in the period of peace
> and insouciance after the Franco–Prussian War of 1870 ... [For the
> artists in particular, the city was] full of images of the muffled noise of
> the luxurious salon of an Academy jury member; the hammering of the
> rain on the meagre and sordid slum of a cubby-hole studio at the end
> of a narrow courtyard, unpaved and unlit, belonging to a poor *débutant*
> artist; in certain *quartiers*, multi-coloured and international blocks of
> artists' flats, near hearty cafés or ill-famed cabarets; brasseries, with
> their celebrated drinking bouts – and [in many cases] refined decor,
> thanks to the continuous municipal policy of embellishment, of health
> improvements and renovation of the *quartiers*.[1]

In Thomas Beecham's words:

> Prosperity and elegance abounded, and the very air seemed to vibrate
> with life and excitement. The world of music was dominated by Massenet,

---

[1] Elisabeth Ferry, 'The 1880s: The Ambience and Artistic Life of Paris', *DSJ* 143 (2008),
22–31, at p. 22. See also articles on Paris in *DSS*143 (2008).

Gounod, Franck and Fauré, with Debussy just appearing on the horizon; that of letters by Anatole France, Emile Zola, Paul Verlaine and Guy de Maupassant. Led by Manet, Monet, Renoir and Degas, painting was entering upon the noonday of Impressionism, and around those great personalities were grouped small circles of lesser effulgence and it was to these, rather than to the haunts of musicians, that Frederick was drawn from the first.[2]

Delius arrived in Paris on 6 May 1888, and was welcomed into his uncle Theodor's apartment in the rue Cambon. A month or so later, he wrote to Grieg:

> I have now settled down a bit & must confess that I feel very happy here. There is something in the atmosphere that is quite different from Germany or England. The hustle & bustle here is extraordinary, one is bound to think that every street-urchin enjoys life … I am meeting a lot of artists, musicians and writers. But I can't do much work.[3]

The next eleven years or so were 'arguably the most fascinating … of his life – a time when he was on intimate terms with many of the artistic and literary giants of the age.'[4] By 1890, he found himself in the circle of the Franco-Norwegian musician William Molard (1862–1937) and his wife Ida, a Swedish sculptress, who had a studio in the rue Vercingétorix, in the very centre of Montparnasse. It was a popular meeting-place for artists, musicians and writers:

> Life within the gateway of No. 6 rue Vercingetorix was quite unlike that on the outside. Indeed, life at the Molards' was often bizarre. With a mixture of brilliant and tragic figures, of true originals and commonplace spongers all coming together in the salon, 'Les Molard' soon became something of an institution among Scandinavians travelling to Paris, and to many other curious souls as well. Theirs was a place you just had to visit and to drink in the atmosphere, rather like the Boulevard Saint-Michel, Notre Dame or the Opera.[5]

There Delius got to know the Swedish playwright August Strindberg, the artists Paul Gauguin[6] and Georges-Daniel de Monfreid,[7] and the French composers

[2] *TB*, p. 51.

[3] Letter 7.

[4] *Paris Years*, p. 13.

[5] Thomas Millroth, *Molards Salong* (1993), quoted in David Eccott, 'Florent Schmitt', in *MA&L*, pp. 113–53, at pp. 118–19.

[6] Eugène Henri Paul Gauguin (1848–1903): he became one of the leading post–Impressionist artists. Originally a successful stockbroker, he turned to painting, gradually abandoning imitative art for expressiveness through colour. From 1891 he mainly lived and worked in the South Seas.

[7] Georges–Daniel de Monfreid (1856–1929): a great friend of Gauguin, who painted, sculpted, and collected art.

Florent Schmitt[8] and Maurice Ravel.[9] He was introduced, possibly by Theodor, to Gabriel Fauré[10] and André Messager.[11] As well as making friends in the Parisian artistic community, however, Delius also immersed himself in the low side of life in the city – described by the American writer Henry James, who lived there in 1876, as 'the biggest temple ever built to material joys' – and its strong attraction for him did not wane until the early 1900s, when he married and finally 'settled down'. Sometimes dressed in old and shabby clothes, he would go to circuses and music halls, frequent disreputable cafés, enjoy mistresses and prostitutes – and even, like many other people at the time, make visits to view the corpses in the Morgue. Then there was yet another side to his life: Theodor was the epitome of the man-about-town, knowing everyone and perfectly at home at the decorous soirées and dinner parties of the Parisian 'smart set'. He introduced Delius to them with great success: his nephew's striking good looks helped (as they had in Danville) to turn many ladies' heads, and it seems very likely that he forged a fair number of romantic relationships.

In August, he took a break at Saint-Malo in Brittany – probably necessitated more by his non-musical activities than because he was exhausted with composing – and stayed there until October, spending much time exploring the coastline.[12] Nevertheless, away from the distractions and pleasures of Paris, he in fact did a great deal of work: he wrote seven songs; partly completed a set of orchestral variations, the *Rhapsodische Variationen*; finished a melodrama, *Paa Vidderne*; and tried (and failed) to write an opera, **Zanoni** (1888: *RT* I/1). Although he was to do so later, it seems unlikely that at that stage in his life Delius had become involved in occultism, and it is therefore somewhat curious that the opera was to have been based on an 1842 romantic novel by Edward Bulwer-Lytton,[13] the plot of which is about the occult aspirations of

---

[8] Florent Schmitt (1870–1958): he wrote interesting and unusual music in all forms except opera. German Romanticism and oriental exoticism both appealed to him, and he was a brilliant orchestrator, but he is now largely forgotten. He made piano reductions of four of Delius's operas.

[9] (Joseph-)Maurice Ravel (1875–1937): he and Debussy became the two most celebrated French composers. His music is highly sophisticated and stylish; he was a brilliant orchestrator, an important innovator in pianistic style who extended the bounds of harmony, and on occasion a successful experimenter with musical form.

[10] Gabriel Urbain Fauré (1845–1924): one of the foremost French composers, organists and teachers of his generation. Delius's Letter 92 records that at a soirée in March 1899, Fauré 'and a few of the best young French musicians played my opera' – although which one is not known.

[11] André Charles Prosper Messager (1853–1929): a very versatile French musician of high standing – composer (of ballets and twenty-three light operas, some of which became extremely popular), conductor, pianist, critic and opera administrator.

[12] Delius's brief diary entries for this holiday are in *Letters 1*, appendix 5.

[13] Edward Bulwer–Lytton, 1st Baron Lytton, PC (1803–73): English politician, poet, playwright and best-selling novelist. It was he who coined the famous phrase 'It was a dark and stormy night.'

Rosicrucians in the late eighteenth century. He first turned it into a play, but then, because (perhaps not surprisingly) 'as an opera it doesn't go well,'[14] he began writing incidental music to it. He got as far as producing a draft piano score,[15] but thereafter did nothing more to it – very probably because by that time his mind was simply overflowing with other new ideas.

Next came Delius's first essay in variation form, the **Rhapsodische Variationen für grosses Orchester** (1888: *RT* VI/3; *CE* supp. vol. 4). Judging from his comments about the teaching at Leipzig, it may well have been Thomas Ward, rather than the professors there, who introduced him to the possibilities inherent in the idea of successive statements of an idea or theme, each altering in shape, mood, metre and rhythm, complexity and (in the case of orchestral music) sound. Dated Saint-Malo, September 1888, the manuscript runs to thirty-two pages. Delius got as far as the end of the sixth variation, but the seventh peters out after twelve bars. It is not known how many more he envisaged, but presumably he had in mind some sort of finale. The work was first published as part of the Collected Edition in 1997, but has never been performed.

The key throughout is E major, and the theme, *moderato* – given out twice by the horns, then twice by the trumpets, and then once again by the horns – is simple in the extreme:

Ex. 2.1

Only two of the variations are really of interest: Variation 4 is a charming *eleganza* waltz for the strings, accompanied by woodwind and horns, and Variation 6, *lento con gravità e molto espressione*, for strings alone, flows nicely. The others must be described as simply student work.

Delian scholars and biographers[16] have not drawn sufficient attention to the extent of the emotional support and musical advice that Grieg gave him. Delius's letters during this year are full of expressions of unbounded gratitude for Grieg's friendship, and of appreciation for constructive suggestions about his work:

> Hearty thanks for your kind letter which gave me much pleasure. I definitely believe that mankind has instinct. My instinct has seldom led me astray, my reason often. When I first met you it was no longer instinct for I had already been acquainted with you so long through your music. I believe nothing reveals a human being so openly as music. A poet can

---

[14] Letter 10.

[15] It is in the DTA.

[16] With the singular exception of Lionel Carley in his *Grieg & Delius*.

(probably) dissemble but a composer must show himself or nothing at all. You have absolutely no idea how I look forward to next summer, when we will talk of all this.[17]

That admiration, and their conversations and correspondence, led, directly or indirectly, to Delius's melodrama, *Paa Vidderne*.

## PAA VIDDERNE[18]
### (1888: *RT* III/1; *CE* vol. 14)

T HE melodrama – a text or poem set for voice and orchestra or piano, with an actor or singer declaiming or reciting, not singing, the words – was originally an eighteenth-century invention, adopted by (among many others) Beethoven, Weber, Schubert and Berlioz for both the opera house and the concert hall. The subject matter of the text was usually of a dramatic or violent nature, and needed a strong voice to put it across.[19] The genre became quite popular in the early twentieth century – *Enoch Arden* by Richard Strauss (1864–1949), *Erwartung* by Arnold Schoenberg (1874–1951) and *Façade* by William Walton (1902–83) are perhaps the best known, and both Granville Bantock[20] and Arnold Bax[21] wrote them.

Spurred by his walking holiday in Norway at the beginning of 1887, Delius started writing a melodrama soon after he arrived in Paris the following spring – the first of two works both somewhat confusingly entitled *Paa Vidderne*.[22] After some revision, it was finally finished in October, and dedicated to Grieg. It is a setting for reciter and orchestra of a poem of the same name in eleven sections by Ibsen (in a German translation), dealing with the challenge of achieving individuality as a person – a tale of a young man testing himself in the mountains. Delius originally had a tenor voice in mind, but he eventually decided on a reciter, and there is a note on the score instructing the conductor to give careful attention to the balance between voice and orchestra. Much of the language used is colloquial, giving it an immediacy that in fact serves

---

[17] Letter 12.

[18] Pronounced 'Paw *vih*-dehr-nuh'.

[19] A closely related idea was *Sprechstimme* – a notated combination of speaking and singing, spectacularly used by Schoenberg in his gigantic *Gurrelieder*.

[20] [Sir] Granville Bantock (1868–1946): composer, conductor and musical administrator. He wrote two melodramas: *The Blessed Damozel* (to words by Dante Gabriel Rossetti) and *Thorvenda's Dream* (to his own words). He and Delius met in 1907, and they became extremely good friends.

[21] [Sir] Arnold Edward Trevor Bax (1883–1953): composer, especially of symphonies and symphonic poems. His melodrama for speaker and piano was, curiously, also a setting of *The Blessed Damozel*.

[22] The second, for orchestra, is covered later in this chapter under the title *On the Mountains*.

to intensify the seriousness of the idea, the gradually mounting passion and the surge of the story. The protagonist says goodbye to his mother and, armed with a rifle, sets off into the mountains ('Vidda'); he finds a girl standing in the summer moonlight and, up on the hill, they make love 'as the soft winds whispered by'. In his sleep, he dreams of his wedding to the girl, and of his longing for her:

> How sad – how hard – to part from the one you love.
> But to be immersed in the cool waters of longing makes
>     a man clean and whole.
> So here I stand, my soul re-born.
> My blood runs cool and clear.
> And now I trample underfoot this life of mine, half-lived,
> this past of sinning and remorse! ...
> I stand refreshed, so near to God
> and to my real self!

Next day, he comes upon a curious stranger:

> There is sorrow in his laughter;
> his lips speak but say no word ...
> His eye is cold: I fear its depths –
> depths I can scarcely dream of –
> depths of a blue black lake
> born of the glacier's ice ...
> between us there grew a strange bond,
> which I could not break.[23]

He is, as it were, Delius's *doppelgänger*, or double, calling him to give up his home life in the valley for a higher fulfilment in the mountains, mirroring the reality of Delius having turned his back on a commercial life to become a creative artist. In the autumn, the young man thinks of going back, but by the time he actually tries to, he is stopped by the winter snow. At Christmas, the stranger reappears, and together they watch his mother's house consumed by fire, 'with your cat and the Christmas pudding!'; then 'A cloud passed over the moon and the hunter was gone.' Finally, in the summer, the young man (it is tempting to call him 'Delius') lies on the hill and hears wedding bells ringing in the valley – for his love, who is marrying another man; he sees people riding to church, then the girl leading the procession on horseback, with everyone dressed-up, then even the church itself. He is able, however, to look at it all dispassionately, and his grief is transfigured: the stranger returns and says: 'My friend, from what I have just heard, my journey was unnecessary; I am not needed here.' The last two lines of the poem sum it up beautifully: '... up here

---

[23] The extracts from the poem quoted here are taken from Lionel Carley's translation, which can be found in the sleeve notes for the recording on Classico CLASSCD 364.

in the mountains I have freedom and God. / Men lose their way in the valley!'[24] These are sentiments that were to become the very essence of *Over the Hills and Far Away*, the partsong *On Craig Ddu*, the beginning of Part 2 of *A Mass of Life*, and especially *The Song of the High Hills*.

The music is very powerful and straightforward (the beginning bears a striking resemblance to that of another energy-laden work written ten years later, Strauss's *Ein Heldenleben*), and the instantly recognisable 'Delian triplet' pervades much of the work, in many variations:

Ex. 2.2

Grieg understood the techniques needed for a successful melodrama, as he himself had written one, *Bergliot*, to a poem by Bjørnson some seven years earlier:

> I should like to say a few words about [your] melodrama, I have read it and re-read it and in it have found splendid music indeed. A pity that the general run of performance would fall short of your intentions. You see, you have composed with an unbelievable lack of consideration for the declaimer, and I am convinced that this lack of consideration will exact a cruel revenge if ever you should put the piece to the test.[25]

to which Delius replied:

> Thank you for your kind letter & candid criticism. It pleased me perhaps a little more than you think for it has shown me that you are the person I always thought you to be. How good it does one to discover that about someone whom one esteems – & loves.[26]

He was obviously concerned lest Grieg might think him guilty of plagiarism, for in the same letter he said: 'I must tell you that I had not seen a single work in this genre before I composed "Paa Vidderne".' Perhaps, however, Grieg had mentioned *Bergliot* in passing at some time or other, and the idea had stuck in Delius's mind until he came across Ibsen's poem.

*Paa Vidderne* remained unperformed until 1981, when it was marvellously recorded for Norwegian television. The text was spoken by the leading Norwegian actor Svein Sturla Hungnes, in its original language rather than the German translation that Delius used, and the Oslo Philharmonic Orchestra was conducted by Charles Farncombe; the recording was broadcast by on 17 May. The work's first concert performance was given in London on 7 February

---

[24] Ibid.

[25] Letter 14.

[26] Letter 15.

1984 by Leslie Head and the Kensington Symphony Orchestra at St John's Smith Square. Allan Hendrick was the speaker, using the Carley translation;[27] later that year, on 15 July, Hungnes did it again in Norwegian at the Cheltenham Festival, with the Hallé Orchestra under Sir Charles Groves. Sadly, no reviews of either of those two concerts can be traced.

P ROBABLY in late 1888, Delius wrote to Grieg from Saint-Malo saying, 'I have also written 3 pieces for string orchestra'. These are listed in the *Catalogue* as **Three Pieces for string orchestra** (1888: *RT* VI/4), but they do not appear to have survived, either in an identifiable draft or otherwise.

In October 1888, Delius returned to Paris, but he soon moved out of his uncle's house to a small, two-roomed cottage called the Chalet des Lilas à la Chaumière, in the village of Ville d'Avray, out towards Versailles. This was only thirty-five minutes by train away from the city – no distance at all, of course, for the musician anxious to go to concerts or the opera, or, despite his protestations, the young-man-about-town seeking diversions from hard work:

> it stands quite alone on the bank of a small lake in a wood. So I am at work again. Close by there is a small restaurant where I eat. It is really lovely here, not a soul & all around woods and hills. You would think a 100 miles from Paris'[28]

His first composition there was probably a **String Quartet** (1888: *RT* VIII/1), for in December 1888 Delius wrote to Grieg saying, 'I have a string quartet ready and have sent it to Sinding to give to Brodsky.' Sinding replied that it looked 'damn good', and that 'You are indeed a real devil for work', but also commented that 'some stoppings are impossible to execute'.[29] However, only the third and fourth movements, and an eleven-bar fragment of the second movement, survive (in the Delius Trust Archive). The fragment was used by Delius many years later in the *scherzo* of the 1916 String Quartet (see below, Chapter 7).

The lure of Parisian life still proved irresistible, and Delius was soon back in the comfort of Theodor's apartment, not only for Christmas and the 1889 New Year but a few weeks longer as well. (One wonders if Theodor, very much the 'suave dandy', knew that his nephew was probably gallivanting around the less salubrious parts of the city, and if so, what he thought.) But at least Delius continued working while he was there, for he wrote to Grieg, 'Perhaps I am crazy, but I am writing incidental music for Emperor & Galilean.'[30] *Emperor and Galilean* was a huge play in ten acts by Ibsen, on the truly un-Delian subject of a Roman emperor, Julian the Apostate. Why, after failing to make anything of

---

[27] In this performance, the reciter did not use a microphone, so the work was heard as Delius envisaged it in 1888.

[28] Letter 13.

[29] Letter 15 and n. 1.

[30] Letter 18.

*Zanoni*, Delius should have chosen yet another work on an extremely obscure subject is another mystery, and there is no indication of how he got to know of it; however, Sinding, doubtless well aware of Delius's tendency not to finish something before a new idea seized him, advised against undertaking such a huge task. None of Delius's sketches appear to have survived.

In February 1889 Delius went home to Bradford – probably to recover from a chest infection, and perhaps he wanted to tell his father face to face how well he was getting on in France. The visit also gave him another opportunity to meet Grieg. On the 28th, Delius heard him conduct his Piano Concerto, with Sir Charles Hallé as the soloist, in Manchester, and then again in London on 14 March.

In April, Delius returned to Ville d'Avray, and by early June he had probably written the **Romance for violin and piano (*op. posth.*)** (1889: *RT* VII/2; *CE* vol. 31a). This was his first attempt at a work for violin and piano. It is dated 1889, and is dedicated to 'his friend Fred' – the conductor Alfred Hertz (1872–1942),[31] who ten years later, in 1899, would give the first-ever all-Delius concert, at the St James's Hall in London.[32] It did not appear in print for nearly a century, finally coming out in 1986 – hence the *op. posth.* designation. It is a lyrical, genial work with an opening *andante tranquillo* in D flat, modulating half-way through to F, followed by a contrasting dance-like *vivo* section in C that builds to a climax and then recalls the opening section in theme and mood. Even at this early stage, Delius shows that he had a fine ear for harmonic nuance – there is a good example in the fourth bar of the opening piano solo where the music takes a sudden and unexpected turn into C flat. Once the violin has entered it never has a bar's rest, a characteristic that extends to the *Légende* and the Violin Sonata in B major, which also work the player hard. The writing for the piano is unimaginative, consisting of a stream of chromatically inflected chords linked with passing notes, not truly idiomatic for the instrument.

By the end of June 1889 Delius was longing to go off to Norway again – for the fourth time. As he wrote to Grieg:

> How I long once again to wipe all the dust and dirt from my feet, & to set foot on this fresh, fragrant moorland! How splendid if we can live for a while in this [*sic*] hut & enjoy something of the uncivilised life.

He travelled by train and boat, meeting his Leipzig friend, the violinist Arve Arvesen, and walking with Grieg and Sinding in the Jotunheim mountains.

---

[31] The dedication must have been added after the piece was written, as Hertz was then only nineteen, and it seems unlikely that he and Delius had yet met. He began his career in Germany, holding posts in, among other places, Frankfurt, Halle and Elberfeld, and he subsequently went to America, directing the Metropolitan Opera in New York and then the San Francisco Symphony Orchestra, both for a good many years. He became an advocate for Delius's music in Germany, and a good friendship grew up between them.

[32] See below, Chapter 3.

Back at Theodor's yet again in September, Fritz decided to move from Ville d'Avray, which he had found very damp, further out of the city to Croissy-sur-Seine, on the opposite side of the river from Saint-Germain; there he rented a wing of an old, Louis-XIII house, 8 Boulevard de la Mairie, with a pleasant garden that was 'an oasis of tranquillity'.[33]

It was probably soon after moving in there that Delius wrote the **Idylle de printemps (Morceau symphonique pour orchestre)** (1889: *RT* VI/5; *CE* vol. 21c). As is so often the case with Delius, there is no mention of this work in letters to his friends, either before or after it was written, but he must surely have been inspired by the sounds of spring in the peaceful garden of his new home. It is a very atmospheric little work, lasting about eleven minutes, and – although the central climax is quite Wagnerian – the piece stands as Delius's second attempt at a 'sound world' that he would make very much his own: an impression or tone poem inspired by Nature or the seasons. It was undoubtedly the seed from which the miraculous *In a Summer Garden* was created nineteen years later, and subsequently *On Hearing the First Cuckoo in Spring, Summer Night on the River, A Song before Sunrise* and *A Song of Summer*. The work remained unpublished until it appeared in the Collected Edition in 1991. Its first public performance was given by Ronald Corp and the New London Orchestra in St John's Smith Square, London, on 2 November 1995, and on 14 October 2010 the Hallé Orchestra under Sir Mark Elder played it in Manchester's Bridgewater Hall:

> A surprise … was the Delius piece … a pleasant surprise at that and after a hundred and twenty years a Hallé première too. Delius's *Idylle de Printemps* is an orphan piece that no one else seemed to want to hear … this symphonic fragment, played splendidly by the Hallé and headily perfumed with sweet pastoral ardour, could easily serve as an interlude to a Delius opera.
>
> www.musicweb-international.com, 20 October 2010

> Frederick Delius's rarely-heard *Idylle de Printemps* could have benefited from an editor's blue pen, and it leaned shamelessly on Wagner and Grieg. But in this performance it had an attractive, naive charm.
>
> *The Daily Telegraph*, 15 October 2010

*Idylle de Printemps* was very quickly followed by the **Suite d'orchestre no. 1** (1889: *RT* VI/6; *CE* supp. vol. 2), the manuscript of which is signed and dated May 1889. Formerly, there was much confusion on the parts of Heseltine and Fenby – the future great advocates of Delius's music – about the contents of this piece, because none of them knew of the existence of a letter from Delius to Grieg in June 1889 listing all five movements: *Marche – Berceuse – Scherzo – Duo – Tema con variazione.*[34] The only known performance was on 13 May

---

[33] *Paris Years*, p. 24.

[34] *Grieg & Delius*, p. 84, and *RT Supplement*, p. 73.

1978, given by Dr David Tall and the Beauchamp Sinfonietta at the Stratford-upon-Avon College of Further Education. *The Delius Society Journal's* review of the concert said: 'Less strongly characterised than other compositions of the earliest period ... this short work nonetheless made a pleasing impression.'[35]

The *Marche* is a gentle, wistful piece, with attractive writing for the woodwind, and is actually quite unsuited to a parade ground! It was rewritten in 1890 as the *Marche caprice* (and as such became part of the *Suite de trois morceaux caractéristiques*). Delius uses the smallest forces he ever employed – though the orchestra for the 'Seven Danish Songs' is the same – with distinction and a feeling for contrast. The *Berceuse* is scored for just single wind, one horn and strings without double basses; the *Scherzo* for piccolo, double wind, four horns and strings; the *Duo* for double woodwind and strings; and the *Tema con variazione* has the same orchestra as the *Marche*.

Delius had not yet written anything that, in its entirety, would be unquestionably recognisable as 'mature Delius'. Nevertheless, there are a good number of short passages or even individual bars which were a foretaste of things to come – particularly the way he uses solo woodwind instruments with flair and sensibility – and much of his early orchestral music has a definite style of its own. Then, for no apparent reason, the next work proved to be significantly different from anything he had written before.

---

[35] Robert Threlfall, 'World Première of 1890 *Petite Suite d'orchestre*', *DSJ* 60 (1978), 23–4, at p. 24.

## SAKUNTALA[36]
### (1889: *RT* III/2; *CE* vol. 15b)[37]

ELIUS'S *Sakuntala* – his tenth work using the orchestra, and the first
for voice and orchestra – is a setting of a poem by the Danish painter
and poet Holger Drachmann.[38] The style of the music is far removed from
the composer's earlier scene painting, marches and romances, and it marks a
huge advance in his musical progress. It also holds a special, if small, place in
musical history. A number of composers orchestrated some of their own songs
which originally had a piano accompaniment, but this was the first published
song specifically written for voice and orchestra by anyone since 1800. Richard
Strauss had written an orchestral song, *Der Spielmann und sein Kind*, in 1878,
at the age of fourteen, but it remains unpublished and it is extremely unlikely
that Delius would have heard it; Strauss did not write his next orchestral songs
until 1896–7. Mahler's first song cycle of 1894–5, was originally published with
a piano accompaniment, and only subsequently in an orchestrated version.
Consequently, in 1889 Delius was ahead of them both.

Drachmann's poem is based on a story, part myth and part history, as told by
the Sanskrit playwright Kālidāsa. Sakuntala, a Brahmin girl, becomes pregnant
by a king, Dusyant, none of whose several wives have borne him children.
Tricked by them, he abandons her, but shortly before she is to give birth, she
returns to his court. Unfortunately, she had lost her wedding ring while bathing
in a river; so, when she arrives, Dusyant does not recognise her, and she is
forced to leave. The ring is, however, found by a fisherman inside one of his
catches; he convinces Dusyant of her true identity, and the couple live happily
ever after.

Drachmann saw Kālidāsa's play in Munich, and not only found in it many
vivid similarities between the story and his own failed first marriage, but was
so smitten by the actress playing Sakuntala that he wrote the poem then and
there, whilst he was still sitting in the theatre. It does not tell the story, but it
reflects Drachmann's sad and hopeless longing for the actress: all four of the
eleven-line verses end 'Sakuntala / Sakuntala!', and the penultimate line of
the second is 'Behold, how I trembling gaze and sigh'. The music is by far the
most beautiful, emotional and sophisticated that Delius had written to date – it

---

[36] Pronounced 'Sha-*koon*-ta-la'.

[37] Boosey & Hawkes also publish a vocal score with a piano accompaniment (reduced
by Robert Threlfall).

[38] Holger Henrick Herhol Drachmann (1846–1909): he qualified at the Royal Danish
Academy of Fine Arts, and won immediate fame for his pictures of the sea and
beautiful sailing ships in storms, but from about 1872 he turned to writing poetry
and became the national Danish poet *par excellence*. He was a 'typical bohemian
with a turbulent private life – the women in which often caused great scandal':
Michael Green, 'The Influential Danish Poets', *DSJ* 142 (2007), 55–60, at p. 58.

almost anticipates the anguish of the solo part in *Sea Drift*. The 12/8 rhythm is continually varied and fluid, but never descends into a jog-trot:

Ex. 2.3

The key changes, meanwhile, from G to E flat, to G sharp, B major, and back again, are very subtly managed, and both the vocal line and the orchestration are full of imagination. They always complement each other, and neither has supremacy. For an early work, it is a remarkable achievement.

*Sakuntala* is only known to have been performed three times. The first took place ninety-eight years after the piece was completed – on 19 June 1987 at York University's Summer Music Festival, by the University Chamber Orchestra under Peter Seymour, with Ian Partridge as the soloist. In a damning criticism, however, *The Yorkshire Post* thought that:

> the work's most striking feature, considering the intensity and luxuriance of Drachmann's poem on which it is based, is the restricted emotional compass of the music, its lack of melodic character and general want of passion … the orchestration was pianistic to a fault.

The second performance was given by Ian Barratt and the North Oxfordshire Scratch Orchestra, conducted by Raymond Head, on 6 November 1987. Finally, there was a BBC studio broadcast on 13 June 1994 (when Delius was the 'Composer of the Week')[39] with Neil Mackie as the singer and Vernon Handley conducting the BBC Symphony Orchestra.[40] The piece well deserves revival.

---

[39] The next occasion was in April 2012 (Delius's 150th anniversary year).

[40] 'News Round-Up', *DSJ* 114 (1994), 24–6, at p. 24.

TOWARDS the end of 1889, Delius began the second of the series of small works that, even though they were no more than trifles, were undoubtedly helping him to improve his orchestration skills. This was the **Suite de trois morceaux caractéristiques** (1889–90: *RT* VI/6(a)), comprising *La Quadroone (une rhapsodie floridienne)* (*CE* vol. 21c), *Scherzo* (*CE* vol. 21c), and *Marche caprice* (*CE* vol. 21a). The cor anglais, so often the singer of sad tunes, has one as the main theme of *La Quadroone*,[41] a nicely flowing *allegretto grazioso*. In fact it is the only theme – less striking than most of those in both of the other two *Suites* – and the whole movement is based on it. The orchestration, however, is most interesting – the wind parts are full of contrasts between individual instruments and different combinations of instruments; there are deft touches on the harp and percussion; and, demonstrating great restraint, the trombones only play for seventeen bars out of the total of 142, and in only five of them are they marked above *mezzoforte*. The *Scherzo* is delightful – no Beethovenian or Brucknerian 'muscle' for Delius! – and could almost be a successor to Berlioz's *Queen Mab* and Mendelssohn's *Midsummer Night's Dream*. It dances along in 6/8, with an infinitely more attractive main theme than *La Quadroone*. That theme again provides the main material, but in the middle there is an intriguing sixteen-bar sequence for the wind choir and then the strings, that puts the accent on the last quaver of the bar:

Ex. 2.4

Much stopping and unstopping of horns (and chords for all four of them), two-note chords for the timpani and much staccato string writing all show the advances Delius was making in his craft. As for the *Marche caprice*, that started life as the un-marchable-to *Marche* in the 1889 *Petite Suite d'orchestre*, and Delius revised it substantially in 1890.

After the *Suite*, Delius made a start on what were to become the first and third of the **Drei symphonische Dichtungen** (1889–90: *RT* VI/7). Although not heard until 1946, these three pieces have since found modest places in the orchestral repertoire. They are charming pastoral invocations, painted in a rather more Wagnerian style than the *Idylle de printemps*. The first piece, *Summer Evening* (*Sommer Abend*, *CE* vol. 21a), makes much use of the 'Delian triplet':

---

[41] The title is interesting. 'Quadroon' means a person who is a quarter black, and was often used as a term of abuse in the eighteenth and nineteenth centuries. Quadroon balls were common in Florida and Mississippi, among other southern American states, and were intended to encourage mixed-race women to form liaisons with rich white men. This music is not in the least dance-like, and the subtitle might have been intended to indicate that the piece was a memory of a slave girl who worked for Delius at Solana Grove and became involved in the quadroon system.

Ex. 2.5

This is absent from only six bars out of the whole seventy-four, albeit with a little variation in the use of different orchestral colours, but it does not in fact outstay its welcome. The third piece, *Spring Morning* (*Frühlings Morgen*, *CE* vol. 21b), is less distinctive, and is obviously indebted to Grieg, with its constant repetitions of a pentatonic main theme (i.e. one using just five notes within an octave):

Ex. 2.6

The middle piece of the three is *Winter Night (Sleigh Ride)* (*Winter Nacht* [*Schlittenfahrt*], *CE* vol. 21b). This began life as the piano piece *Norwegischer Schlittenfahrt*,[42] which Delius played to the Griegs and Sinding at Christmas 1887, and then orchestrated in 1888 or 1890. It is in simple A–B–A–B form: A is an *Allegretto con moto* in 2/4 with a jaunty piccolo tune, and the sleigh bells jingle through every bar; B is an *Andante molto tranquillo* in 3/4 (a stop to look at the snowy landscape, or for a warming *akvavit*?) with a very brief climax, and on its second appearance B is only twelve bars long, as the sleigh disappears into the foggy distance, *molto rit.* and *pp*.

Fifteen years after Delius's death, Beecham mentioned to The Delius Trust the possibility of a fourth movement, *Autumn*, being published, but there is no evidence that it was, nor have any sketches or score come to light. A piece of that name, apparently by Delius and arranged by Beecham, was included in the programme of the Queen's Hall Promenade Concert on 17 September 1931[43] – but there is no reference to it in the letters that Delius and his wife wrote to the conductor, Henry Wood, having heard the concert on the radio, warmly thanking him for his performances.[44] All three pieces were given their first performances by Richard Austin[45] and the Royal Philharmonic Orchestra

---

[42] See above, Chapter 1.

[43] Available through www.bbc.co.uk/proms/archive [accessed 18 March 2014].

[44] It could possibly have been *Autumn (The Wind Soughs in the Trees)* from *North Country Sketches* – but if so why did Beecham have to arrange it?

[45] Richard Denis Oliver Austin (1903–89): the son of Frederic Austin (see below, Chapter 4, {n. 000}). In 1934, he succeeded Sir Dan Godfrey (1868–1939) as music director of the (as it was then) Bournemouth Municipal Orchestra. Godfrey had held the post for forty-one years, and was a tireless champion of British music (including some of Delius's).

in the Central Hall, Westminster, on 8 November 1946, as part of that year's Delius Festival, although they were not actually published until 1951. In the context of the huge amount of Delius's music played at the festival, it is not surprising that they went unnoticed by the critics.

By now well settled at Croissy – he was to stay there until the spring of 1892 – Delius next sketched a couple of piano pieces, a theme and variations for piano and orchestra, two more short works for orchestra, and wrote his fourth orchestral suite. He also set nineteen songs.

The more one listens to early Delius, the more it seems clear that he must have learned a great deal more from his concert-going and his friends in Leipzig than he did from his teachers there. How else would he have heard the sound of a cor anglais and thought of using one in *La Quadroone*? In later years, however, he acquired a copy of Berlioz's famous *Grande Traité d'instrumentation et d'orchestration modernes*, published in 1843/4,[46] from which he would have learned much about the capabilities and qualities of the various instruments (i.e. their compass, 'pitch transposing', tone colour and so on) – though he had not a high opinion of the author, and 'described Berlioz as a vulgarian.'[47]

In the late 1880s Delius also wrote another two piano pieces: **Valse and Rêverie** (1889–90: *RT* IX/5; *CE* vol. 33). Neither of these got past the sketch stage – although the *Valse* is complete, the last five bars of *Rêverie* were left in almost indecipherable manuscript. In the former, these 'arpeggiated' figures are repeated in all but the last five bars:

Ex. 2.7

The piece is infinitely more chromatic and richer in texture than anything Delius had written before. *Rêverie* is even more interesting. Again very chromatic, and with occasional bars of twos in the right hand against threes (and even fives) in the left, it could almost be by Fauré (whose early *barcarolles, nocturnes* and *impromptus* would have been played in many recitals in Paris at around this time), and it certainly looks like Fauré on the page:

---

[46] Its most celebrated successors, Rimsky-Korsakov's *Principles of Orchestration* and Cecil Forsyth's *Orchestration* were not published until 1913 and 1914 respectively, the latter by Macmillan & Co.

[47] *Fenby 1*, p. 195.

Ex. 2.8

There is no tempo marking, but the gentle speed at which it should be played is obvious.

Both pieces give the feel of 'formless exploration' – as if Delius was playing with ideas and notes simply to see where they led him – but in them there are many tiny phrases which anticipate future works. He later incorporated the sketches into a projected *Rhapsody* – in fact a theme and variations – for piano and orchestra (*RT* VII/4(a) (*RT Supplement*); *CE* supp. vol. 4), on which he was probably working around 1900–3; only some 200 bars are extant, and the fragment has never been performed publicly. A somewhat revised version of the *Valse* was included as the second of the *Five Piano Pieces* published in 1925 (see below, Chapter 8).

As has already been seen, Delius was an inveterate traveller – he once said to Grieg 'I have got a devilish wanderlust again'[48] – and at the end of May 1890 he returned to Leipzig with the Norwegian composer Johan Selmer,[49] whom he had met a few months earlier, and possibly William Molard as well, to see Wagner's *Der Ring des Nibelungen*. During the three weeks they spent there, he met Sinding again and managed to get a (presumably scratch) orchestra together, paying them fifty marks for a two-and-a-half hour run-through of some of his works – although we do not know which ones. Unfortunately, however, the occasion brought his budding friendship with Selmer to a virtual halt, because at the beginning of the rehearsal Selmer marched in and insisted that Delius let him rehearse a piece of his own (a 'Finnish March') – which took twenty-five minutes of the allotted time. Selmer offered a very abject apology,[50] but the relationship never really recovered.

It was probably in 1890 that Delius met the Norwegian artist Edvard Munch (1863– 1944) at Molard's studio; they became firm friends, and Munch sketched his portrait twice. It seems that Munch quite liked music, and (although he then knew nothing of Delius's) they may have considered working together, as

---

[48] Letter 27.

[49] Johan Peter Selmer (1844–1910): heavily influenced by Berlioz, Lizst and Wagner, his main works are for large orchestra (often being programme music), some with soloists and/or chorus; he also wrote a substantial amount of piano music. He greatly interested in social and philosophical matters.

[50] Letter 29.

in a letter of 24 June 1899 Munch said to Delius, 'If only we could work out that plan, with engravings and music – and I. P. Jakobsen [*sic*]?'[51] That was an exciting suggestion, but exactly what the project was, sadly nobody knows. Their correspondence lasted until 1929, by which time Delius had become very ill.

During this period, Delius left a considerable amount of what he was writing unfinished – probably because he had so many ideas in his head – and (as can be seen from the list of works in Appendix 1) in 1889–1900 he began or completed twenty-one separate scores. Trying to work out the order in which they were finished or left on one side is an almost impossible task; the ordering here simply matches that in Robert Threlfall's *Catalogue*.

Among the uncompleted works is **Légendes – Sagen** (1890: *RT* VII/2; *CE* supp. vol. 4). The inspiration, in view of its alternative title, might well have been that visit to Leipzig and the Norse mythology on which Wagner based *Der Ring des Niebelungen*. However, what the *Légendes* were about is a complete mystery – as is the bilingual title: *légendes* is the French for 'tales', and *sagen* the German. The work is another theme and variations; there are only fifty-two pages of manuscript extant, with the virtuoso piano part complete (or at least playable), whereas the orchestral accompaniment is merely sketched-out.

Within weeks of returning to Paris, Delius was off again – this time to Jersey, Normandy and Brittany – getting home again in mid-October. How hard he worked while he was away nobody knows, but he undoubtedly returned to his desk well refreshed. Two more orchestral trifles, **Marche française** (1890: *RT* VI/6(b)) and **À l'amore** (1890?: *RT* VI/8), may very well have been inspired, or written, during his holiday, but he again failed to finish them. Only the first seventeen and forty-nine pages respectively survive. Both were to have been orchestral works, and the fragment of the latter is the beginning of a movement; interestingly, it is on the same paper and in the same style of writing used for *Légendes*. They have been neither performed nor published. Robert Threlfall thought that *À l'amore* is a mistake for *À l'aurore* (*To the Dawn*), which makes more sense.[52]

The next work was the **Petite Suite d'orchestre no. 2** (1890: *RT* VI/9; *CE* supp. vol. 2), which Beecham thought pleasant and very well scored, but lacking Delius's (even then) characteristic style.[53] The three movements are labelled *Allegretto ma non troppo – Con moto – Allegretto*, and the only known performance was given on 2(?) May 1999 in Vienna, by the Camerata Internazionale under Richard Owen. This 'was also a triumph, and presented the work with appropriate sweetness without sugar-coating as is often the case in weaker performances of Delius'.[54]

[51] Jens Peter Jacobsen (1847–85): Danish author (see below, Chapter 3).

[52] *RT Supplement*, p. 78.

[53] *TB*, p. 60.

[54] This and other past concerts and reviews are available through www.cameratany. org [accessed 18 March 2014)

## SUITE FOR VIOLIN AND ORCHESTRA
### (1890–1: *RT* VII/1; *CE* vol. 28)
### *Pastorale – Intermezzo – Elégie – Finale*

B Y the end of his studies at Leipzig, Delius had become a proficient violinist. It is therefore no surprise that he should have thought of composing something substantial for the instrument, and this happy suite was the result. The solo part is quite virtuosic, and it might well have been written with either Arvesen or Jebe in mind.[55] In the *Pastorale* (marked *Andante quasi allegretto*), the Delian triplet is much in evidence, and the soloist has a sweet line over a gentle accompaniment; the jolly *Intermezzo* is marked *Allegro molto vivace*, and scurries along, one-in-bar; rhapsodic phrases in the solo part characterise the *Elégie*, marked *Andante cantabile* and with a passionate central climax; and the *Finale* (*Allegro moderato*) could almost have come out of the Mendelssohn Violin Concerto – it has a lovely flow and freedom.

Like *Florida*, this suite had to wait nearly a hundred years for its first performance – finally given on BBC Radio 3 on 28 February 1984 by Ralph Holmes and the BBC Scottish Symphony Orchestra, conducted by Vernon Handley. A month later, Holmes played it again in London, and then in Cheltenham, on both occasions with the Young Musicians Symphony Orchestra under James Blair. After the London performance, it received one of the best criticisms of the première of any of Delius's early works:

> A marked and fingered copy of the solo part of Delius's Suite for Violin and Orchestra tantalizingly survives, but with no record of any performance. So the Young Musicians Symphony Orchestra, conducted by James Blair, did their characteristic bit and engagingly presented its first public performance on Saturday night.
>
> Ralph Holmes was the soloist; and few violinists could have brought out as affectingly and unselfconsciously as he the warm but tough pastoralism which pervades its four movements. Delius, in this robust early work, knew just how to strengthen what is often little more than salon sentiment by nudging and fracturing rhythm and harmony in just the right places. And Mr Holmes, too, whether in the hurdy-gurdy Intermezzo or the elegiac Adagio, reinforced his expansive playing with a sharp-edged, sinewy energy. The brass principals of the orchestra, who had partnered Mr Holmes so admirably in the Delius, enjoyed themselves no end in Malcolm Arnold's Four Cornish Dances.
>
> *The Times*, 26 March 1984

---

[55] See above, Chapter 1. Delius kept up with Arvesen until about 1907: see Letter 222.

D ELIUS badly wanted to write operas – indeed, a few years later he wrote 'I want to tread in Wagner's footsteps, and even give something more in the right direction.'[56] So far, however, he had found it impossible to find a suitable libretto – witness his abandonment of plans to set *Zanoni* and *Emperor and Galilean*. So, in, or perhaps somewhat before, 1890 (and possibly urged on by Nina Grieg) he decided to write his own.[57]

## IRMELIN

### (1890–2: *RT* I/2; *CE* vol. 1)

T HE action is set in medieval times and fuses two stories: the legend of Princess Irmelin who, much to her father's displeasure, rejects a series of suitors; and the fairy-tale of the princess who falls in love with a swineherd, which Hans Christian Andersen also used, though in a different version. In Delius's plot, Act 1 focuses on the listless, melancholy Irmelin, sexually frustrated, and dreaming of an ideal lover, 'young, fair and strong'. Various claimants for her hand have come calling, but she has rejected them all. Her loving but stern father, the king, has now fixed a limit of six months to all this prevarication and insists she choose one of three knights who are, respectively, old, young, and warlike. Irmelin will have none of them. The second act introduces Nils, a prince who is also searching for the partner of his dreams. He has followed the 'Silver Stream', a symbol of his quest, but has missed the way and ended up consorting with a band of outlaw robbers led by Rolf. Nils has not disclosed his true identity and is working for them as a swineherd, seduced by the debauchery of the outlaws' camp with its bevy of loose women. But at the end of the act, he determines to tear himself away and is allowed to leave. He manages to find the Silver Stream again and re-embarks on his search for pure love. The final act sees him arriving at the king's court just as Irmelin is about to be forcibly betrothed to the warlike knight. While knight and king are off hunting, Nils and Irmelin become passionately attracted to each other, and agree to meet later that night in the grounds of the palace. There and then, as dawn breaks, they declare their undying love. 'And thou wilt follow

---

[56] Letter to Jutta Bell, 29 May 1894. That year he saw *Tannhaüser*, and *Parsifal* twice, and told her that in Munich he intended to see *Der Ring*, *Tristan und Isolde* and *Die Meistersinger* three times each!

[57] In 1892, when he had virtually completed *Irmelin*, Delius went to stay with the English writer Richard Le Gallienne (1866–1947) and his wife at what is now 33 Church Road, Hanwell, Middlesex, to discussed a possible collaboration over a plot for an opera about the Greek youth Endymion, who was kissed every night by the moon goddess Selene. During his visit they went to see the first performance of *Lady Windermere's Fan* by Oscar Wilde, to whom Delius was introduced. Le Galliene was a wide-ranging writer whose work included contributions to the celebrated literary periodical *The Yellow Book*, a translation of Wagner's *Tristan und Isolde*, war poems and *The Romance of Perfume*.

me where'er I lead thee?' asks Nils, and Irmelin replies: 'Ay! E'en to the end of the world.' Nils bids farewell to the Silver Stream ('I need thee no longer') and, as the score puts it, the couple simply 'wander hand in hand joyfully through the wood, wondering at and discovering new beauties everywhere [until they] disappear from sight'.

Although he had a real feeling for literature and was extremely well read, on the evidence of this libretto, Delius himself was no writer. What little action there is, is expressed in banal and clichéd language. These rhyming couplets of Irmelin and Nils in Act 3 are typical:

> Am I dreaming? Am I dreaming?
> Are these moonbeams o'er me streaming?
> Is this face and is this kiss
> but a dream, so soon to miss?
> Are these arms which clasp so tight
> soon to vanish with the night? ...
> Oh, let me nevermore awake.
> But dream and kiss for love's own sake!

This is one of the most ecstatic moments in the score, but it is scuppered by the amateurish bathos of the text. The construction of the opera is at best eccentric, at worst careless: Irmelin and Nils do not meet until almost two-thirds of the way through, whilst the scenes at the robbers' camp are most unconvincing. Neither is there any dramatic conflict: Irmelin's father, who might have provided some, is really only capable of stern bluster; Rolf, the robber baron, makes no serious attempt to prevent Nils leaving his entourage – and so on. The lack of action is one reason why Delius may have defensively called *Irmelin* a 'lyric drama' rather than an opera.

All this may be put down to inexperience, and Delius would not have been the first young composer to write a bad or immature first opera. Having said that, there are certainly worthwhile pages in *Irmelin*, remarkable for a young man whose published vocal output at this point consisted only of some fifteen songs. With no substantial orchestral works to his credit, Delius nevertheless produced nearly 400 pages of manuscript – two hours of music in all, scored for large forces. The strength of *Irmelin* is its sheer beauty of sound. The whole score glows with an inner warmth and radiance. There is a bloom on it which makes one think of the vivid palettes of pre-Raphaelite painters such as Holman Hunt and Rossetti. Essentially, it is in the orchestra that the heart of the score lies. Through-composed in the Wagnerian manner (there are few 'set-piece' arias or concerted numbers), the orchestra weaves a potent web of sound that is 'gorgeous' in the true sense of the word, and which even surpasses the sumptuousness of much of *Florida*.

Unlike Wagner, however, Delius does not employ a sophisticated network of *leitmotifs*. There are really only two principal themes that recur consistently. The first opens the work and is associated with the princess; it has two sections, the first a sequence of arching woodwind solos above a G sharp minor harmony:

Ex. 2.9

Thirty-two bars later it gains a memorable appendage:

Ex. 2.10

Delius often varies the harmonisation of Ex. 2.10, nowhere more strikingly than in the prelude to Act 3:

Ex. 2.11

Nils has his own theme, which is also strongly associated with the Silver Stream:

Ex. 2.12

There are other, minor themes (i.e. at bar 393 *et seq.* in Act 3, and subsequently at bar 588, an arabesque figuration on woodwind which stands for the growing erotic attraction of the hero and heroine), but nothing as pervasive as Exs 2.9 and 2.10.

Each act has an extended instrumental introduction (and Act 3 even has an additional prelude before the second scene), and these offer some splendid opportunities for the orchestra. The world of Wagner's *Tristan und Isolde* is never far away; for example in the very opening scene, a dialogue between Irmelin and her maid recalls that of Isolde and Brangäne. The majority of the music for Irmelin and Nils is in the form of monologues or soliloquies, unavoidably since they do not actually meet until Act 3. Their first love duet occurs towards the end of Act 3 Scene 1, where Delius imaginatively suggests their initial awkwardness (another parallel with the lovers in *Tristan*) by thinning the texture down to sparse arpeggios on harp and cellos with very simple woodwind counter-melodies. He does a fine job of building up the increasing attraction of Irmelin and Nils, but allows their voices to mingle for just three bars or so before being interrupted by the return of the huntsmen. Consequently the essence of their love duet is in the following scene, extremely passionate and containing the finest pages in the score. Having said that, the vocal lines are not especially memorable in themselves and one feels that they have been fitted to the orchestral texture rather than the other way round. But that is often Delius's way when composing for voices and orchestra, and there is ample evidence of it in his later scores. The fact that the voices of Irmelin and Nils are united, more or less of necessity, only in this final duet does at least serve to lead the opera forward and give it an effective focus. But the passage beginning at bar 990 – 'The dawn is breaking, / rosy hues tint the sky' – really cries out for some memorable vocal lines which Delius, at the critical moment, fails to supply. A similar charge could be levelled at the two solo scenes for Nils in Act 2.

Elsewhere the musical characterisation is thin. The scenes at court in Act 1 are pretty feeble stuff; the music for the king, for example, sounds perfunctorily virile in its marching, dotted rhythms. Given the parental opposition in Delius's own life, one might have expected his inspiration to rise to something more sinister. The music for the hunt uses every cliché in the book and there are some embarrassing passages for an off-stage chorus of country folk, tra-la-la-ing away in the distance where mercifully their doggerel text may not be too audible – an error which Delius regrettably compounds towards the end of Act 2 Scene 3. The equivalent 'court' of the outlaws in Act 2 contains some of the weakest music in the score, and Rolf and his followers never come to life: 'despite his carousels at the *crémerie* [Delius] seemed unable to write convincingly for the brigands or for rough people of any sort.'[58] Perhaps a really effective drinking song or some properly seductive music for the female camp followers would have done the trick – how unfortunate that Delius would not see *Parsifal*, with its Flower Maidens, for another ten years, for he might there have learned something.

[58] *AJ*, p. 28.

*Irmelin* is like the proverbial curate's egg, good only in parts, but perhaps one should not be too hard on this apprentice work. It is one of enormous promise, containing some beautiful music and, if nothing else, served Delius as a necessary musical exercise in how to write for the stage. He did not, however, seem to have been concerned about getting it performed, and it was not in fact heard until 4 May 1953, when Beecham staged the first of five performances in The New Theatre at Oxford. Audiences were poor and, according to one report, 'undergraduates ... became increasingly unruly and noisesome as the evening went on.'[59] Beecham never forgave the university city for its indifference to a unique event. He thought *Irmelin* the best first opera he knew – despite a number of weak passages – and considered it both attractive and strong.[60]

Of course, Beecham was thinking about the music rather than the libretto, and others were not so enthusiastic about the opera in its entirety:

> If a test of success in the theatre is the suspension of time and probability, the casting of a spell and the appeasement of the spirit, then *Irmelin* is a successful opera. But it is not what most people mean by a successful opera: there is no conflict, no passion and little development of character or situation ... It should perhaps be called an idyll for the theatre ... The music, which here and there betrays an unexpected wisp of Wagner in its constitution, is even at this early stage in his career characteristic Delius in melody, harmony, and, above all, in a sluggish rhythm, but it is fresher and less cloying than in his later work ... He constructed his own libretto without verbiage or episodical distraction, and the opera is only too long by the separation into two scenes of the last act, which could have been put together and so have saved an *entr'acte* and some pointless dancing ... It need hardly be said that the protagonist was Sir Thomas Beecham at the head of his orchestra: he knows as no one else where Delius kept his magic. We have come to expect this, but what is astonishing is that he can by taking [the] train to Oxford, shake out of his suitcase an unknown and exquisite opera all of a piece and without apparent effort.
>
> *The Times*, 5 May 1953

> ... [the music is] true Delius, immature but prophetic ... [The composer] lacked at that time the most rudimentary knowledge of stage technique ... there is practically no action. Some of the naïvetés are staggering.
>
> Ernest Newman in *The Sunday Times*, 10 May 1953

> ... one of the main sources of dramatic weakness is the feeling ... that the characters appear unable to control their own destinies.
>
> *Redwood*, p. 236

---

[59] D. R. Scorgie, '*Irmelin* at Oxford', *DSJ* 65 (1979), 23.
[60] *TB*, p. 58.

I N March 1891, Delius made brief visits to Bradford – perhaps out of a sense of filial duty – and London, and at the end of June he set off yet again for Norway. There he travelled around, seeing friends (including the Griegs and the Bjørnsons) and enjoying the mountains. He stayed until the autumn, for what must always be one of the most exciting times in a composer's life – the first public performance, with the preceding rehearsals, of any of his works. It was his latest composition, *On the Mountains*, given by the Music Society at Christiania (now Oslo) on 10 October 1891, conducted by Iver Holter, a friend of both Grieg and Delius.

### ON THE MOUNTAINS
### (PAA VIDDERNE – AUF DEM HOCHGEBIRG – SUR LES CIMES)
(1890–2: *RT* VI/10; *CE* vol. 22)

I BSEN'S poem *Paa Vidderne* clearly held something for Delius, as only two years after setting it as a melodrama he started this purely orchestral piece, using the same title. The full heading to the manuscript score reads:

> Paa Vidderne (*Auf dem Hochgebirg*)
> Symphonische Dichtung nach dem Gedicht von Henrik Ibsen
> *Sur les cimes*: Poème symphonique d'après une poésie de H. I.
> *On the Mountains*: Symphonic poem after H.I's Paa Vidderne

In England it is usually called *On the Mountains*, to avoid confusion with the earlier work.

There is no obvious reuse of the material of the melodrama, and for all practical purposes they are completely different works. *On the Mountains* is far more forceful than anything Delius had written before, and its quiet episodes have little charm or sense of wonder; furthermore Delius continued to be obsessed by triplets, for there are, yet again, hardly two consecutive bars in the whole piece in which they do not appear. Only the barest outline of the poem can be read into the music – the cellos' upwards-striding figure in the very first bars (which then appears in a number of different guises throughout the work) is presumably the lad starting off up the mountains, and the love scene obviously begins at letter H in the full score. There is no music clearly depicting the stranger, but the triumphant last pages must surely be expressing the phrase 'Now I am steel' from the last verse of Ibsen's poem, and its final two lines: '... up here in the mountains I have freedom and God.'

Among the reviews of the concert were the following:

> The programme concluded with an interesting composer-début: 'Paa Vidderne', a concert overture for large orchestra by Fritz Delius. The young composer – he is only 28 years old – whose portrait [one of Munch's sketches mentioned above] we today present to our readers, is

an Englishman by birth; but in temperament and upbringing, with long stays in America, France, Germany and Norway, he is a cosmopolitan.[61] Through his admiration for our art and Nature, he has an affection for our country, and he knows it and its cultural life as few foreigners do. 'Paa Vidderne', inspired by Ibsen's poem, is the first work of his in a larger form to be publicly performed. It is a fine, captivating composition, rich in fantasy and colour, which, both in its musical content and its in part excellent form, stands far above what one might expect of a 'prentice' work: it will repay a degree of concentration but is, as it stands, art that is good, mature and noble. The composition made a good impression, and the conductor was called forward.

*Verdens Gang* (Oslo), 12 October 1891 (transl. Carley)

The final item was 'Paa Vidderne' by Fritz Delius, which the composer calls 'Concert Overture',[62] a name associated with a form that gives the impression of something well regulated and clear. However, 'Paa Vidderne' is more rhapsodic than that. We are once again confronted with one of the many 'programmatical musicians', who try to make an audience understand a work of the imagination without explaining what it is about … Modernism is also evident in the composition: some parts succeed, but others are merely experiments. Dr. Delius may have some talent – the work leaves one with that impression; however, on the basis of hearing a composition without form, it is difficult to tell how that talent may develop.

*Kunst og Literatur*, 13 October 1891
(transl. Norwegian National Library)

Although Delius must have known that this was the first time that any of his music had been played in public, until the mid-1960s it was generally believed that it was in 1897, when *Over the Hills and Far Away* was given at Elberfeld. However, an article in *The Musical Times*[63] reported the finding of a copy of the programme for the concert – which must have therefore been the greatest occasion in Delius's life so far.

Delius must have been absolutely thrilled when the work was done again – with some revisions, and apparently some financial help from Theodor[64] – on

---

[61] This could well be the first time that Delius was referred to as a 'cosmopolitan' – a word nowadays often used, quite correctly, to describe him, as in Christopher Palmer's *Delius: Portrait of a Cosmopolitan* (London: Duckworth, 1976).

[62] Delius used this title in letters, and the programme called it a 'Concertoverture for stort orkester', but that does not appear on the manuscript score.

[63] Rachel Lowe, 'Delius's First Performance', *The Musical Times* 106 (1965), pp. 190–2 (Rachel Lowe was at that time Archivist of The Delius Trust); see also *Companion*, p. 178.

[64] *MMB*, p. 115.

25 February 1894, at an interesting concert in Monte Carlo.[65] The English composer and singer Isidore De Lara (see below) claimed in his memoirs[66] that he was responsible for the decision to programme the work – and the organisers were evidently under the impression that they were giving the first performance:

> The seventh international concert of the season was also dedicated to English works. [It was a] rich programme, which featured the overture to *La Bohémienne* [*The Bohemian Girl*] by Balfe; *Benedictus* by Mackenzie; an orchestral suite (first performance) by M. Oakeley;[67] an overture *di Ballo* by Arthur Sullivan; *Fire Dance* for harp (Mlle Thérenet) by Parish Alvars;[68] *Saint David*, a march by Godfrey;[69] and finally a symphonic poem *On the Mountains* (first performance) by Delius, which was especially noted by the true musicians and which M. Teck's orchestra played marvellously.
>
> *Le Figaro*, 2 March 1894

> A series of so-called International Concerts is being given this winter on Sundays by M. Arthur Steck's band. On February 25 the programme was selected from works of British composers – at any rate, they were announced as 'œuvres anglaises' – and included the names of ... [as above] and one Delius, whoever he may be ... It seems a pity that the authorities did not call to their councils someone with a competent knowledge of the resources of the English school, and thus save themselves from such inadequate expressions of what the foremost British musicians have been doing for the last fifty years.
>
> *The Musical Times*, 1 April 1894

The first English performance was not given until 8 November 1946 – as part of Beecham's second great Delius Festival[70] – when *The Musical Times* gave it a good review:

> This is an early work that dates from 1892, and remains unpublished after a single performance abroad. As was only to be expected, it adds little

---

[65] Presumably given by the Monte Carlo Philharmonic Orchestra, which was founded in 1856.

[66] Isidore De Lara, *Many Tales of Many Cities* (London: Hutchinson, 1928).

[67] Possibly [Sir] Herbert Stanley Oakeley (1830–1903).

[68] Elias Parish Alvars (1808–49) was a celebrated English harpist who wrote over eighty works for solo harp, many of extreme difficulty.

[69] Probably a member of the celebrated family of bandmasters who lived between 1790 and 1935. It is unlikely, however, to have been Sir Dan Godfrey (1868–1939), conductor of the Bournemouth Municipal Orchestra for forty-one years and a tireless champion of British music, since he does not seem to have written anything himself.

[70] See below, Chapter 10.

to what we already know of Delius's but it reveals a remarkably assured hand for a man of thirty and has an exuberance and forthrightness that are welcome in themselves, though far removed from Delius's later style, of which the work contains only occasional faint adumbration. Magnificently played by the RPO [Royal Philharmonic Orchestra], 'On the Mountains' made a favourable impression and is well worth occasional revival.

December 1946

*The Times* (which never seemed to be very keen on Delius's music), however, was unenthusiastic:

The verdict … on 'On the Mountains' was that as a young man's essay in the late romantic manner it was a striking enough work for its time, but that, though not obviously derivative, it can be spared [*sic*] as not very characteristic in the light of his subsequent production.

9 November 1946

B EFORE he left for Norway, Delius may well have begun his only song cycle (as distinct from sets of songs), *Maud* (1891: *RT* III/3; *CE* vol. 16). The poems ('Birds in the high hall-garden', 'I was walking a mile', 'Go not happy day', 'Rivulet crossing my ground', and 'Come into the garden, Maud') were by Alfred, Lord Tennyson[71] (1809–92), who became the Poet Laureate in 1850 and was a Fellow of The Royal Society. He is regarded by many as the chief representative of Victorian poetry, and perhaps the most musical English poet of his time. The twenty-eight widely differing poems making up his *Maud* cycle – which he described as a 'monodrama' – were written in 1855, and Delius was in fact the first English composer to set any of them.[72] For tenor and a modest orchestra, they were (like *Sakuntala*) orchestrated from the outset, and, so far as is known, have only been performed in public once, and never recorded.

Delius was seriously handicapped by the jogging rhythms of the poems, and there are pages and pages of accompaniment which consist of little besides frankly tedious muted *tremolandi* in the strings, supporting the soloist and the wind lines. The very low *tessitura* and range of the voice part are other good reasons for the neglect of this work – but they are surprising faults, as by now Delius had quite considerable experience of writing for the voice. Nevertheless, the Delius scholar Christopher Redwood said that 'Anyone who studies this

---

[71] A technically incorrect form of address: after Alfred Tennyson had been created the 1st Baron Tennyson, he should have called himself just Lord Tennyson, but no doubt did not wish to lose the christian name with which he had acquired his fame.

[72] 'Go not, happy day' was set by Franz Liszt in 1879 and by Massenet in 1880; possibly Saint-Saëns used one of the poems too. A total of twenty-two English composers from Parry to Michael Head (1900–76) set a few of them – but the only other cycle, using thirteen poems in all, was composed in 1898 by Sir Arthur Somervell (1863–1937).

score will be in no doubt whatever that Delius had achieved a formidable mastery of compositional technique by this stage in his career'[73] – and Beecham thought that the cycle deserved a place among Delius's better songs.[74]

Delius had spent two years in Croissy, but when he returned from Norway in November 1891 – partly, no doubt, to be closer to the new social milieu into which he had been bought, but almost certainly because he was also missing the bright lights and sensual pleasures of Paris itself – he moved into a new apartment within easy walking distance of the centre of the city, at 33 rue Ducouëdic,[75] in Montparnasse. Possibly Theodor gave him some help with the rent. Lionel Carley writes that Delius 'persuaded the *propriétaire* to knock two little rooms into one, and this made a pleasant two-windowed apartment containing a grand piano, a red carpet and a square table. Next to it was a tiny bedroom and an equally tiny kitchen.'[76] Nina Grieg – perhaps somewhat naïvely – was concerned about how he was spending his time:

> I cannot really understand, at least as far as I know you, how you can live in Paris and not in the country. Do you not long for trees and fields, for quiet paths, where no-one walks?[77]

It was towards the end of 1892 that Delius made the acquaintance of the English composer and singer Isidore de Lara[78] – an unusual character who lived in France, socialising with the good and the great of Paris and Monte Carlo, and a tireless chaser of the ladies. De Lara introduced Delius to the smart salons of the Parisian aristocracy – which at that time were deeply immersed in the esoteric mysteries of occultism:

> Occultism was very much a craze of the period. Curtains were being drawn, candles lit and hands laid on tables, across the length and breadth of Paris. The courses of the stars were studied, bumps were felt, heads and hands analysed, cards consulted, to the general excitement of a large section of society.[79]

Delius had some involvement in all this, about which Beecham wrote amusingly.[80]

---

[73] Christopher Redwood, 'Delius's Five Songs from Tennyson's *Maud*', *DSJ* 127 (2000), 16–20, at p. 16.

[74] In an early draft of *TB*.

[75] *Paris Years*, p. 29. It seems that the street is now called rue du Couëdic or Couédic.

[76] Ibid.

[77] Ibid.

[78] Isidore de Lara (1858–1935): his operas became very popular, particularly in Monaco (where he lived for some ten years); he also wrote songs, and during the Great War became a minor musical philanthropist.

[79] *Paris Years*, pp. 33–4.

[80] *TB*, p. 61; see also Letter 45.

Notwithstanding his earlier plans to make an opera out of *Zanoni*, how or why Delius originally became interested in the occult is not known, but it certainly occupied much of his time during the next few years. In the autumn of 1893, at least 'allied' to work, he met and then co-operated with the celebrated occultist Dr Gérard Encausse (1865–1917, who called himself Papus) on an extraordinary booklet, *Anatomie et physiologie de l'orchestre*, which explored the mystic properties and characteristics of the orchestra.[81]

Around this time, Delius's output tailed off quite considerably, and between 1891 and 1893 he produced very little – or, at least, very little that has survived:[82] as he once said, he 'ruthlessly destroyed' a considerable amount of his work. Beecham thought that he had temporarily exhausted himself in the three previous years, and needed to consider exactly where he was going in life,[83] but it is clear that he was still very much enjoying both Parisian high and low life, and spending much time with his artistic and literary friends. He did not, however, entirely give up, and the first work he seems to have written at rue du Couëdic was the Violin Sonata in B Major.

[81] *TB*, p. 34. See Paul Mathews, 'Delius and the Joining of French and German Orchestration' (2003), available online at http://issuu.com/paulmathews/docs/mathews_delius_2003 [accessed 3 April 2014]

[82] See below, Appendix 1.

[83] *TB*, p. 34.

## VIOLIN SONATA IN B MAJOR (*OP. POSTH.*)

(1892: *RT* VIII/2; *CE* vol. 31a)

*Allegro con brio – Andante molto tranquillo –*
*Allegro con moto*

T HE Violin Sonata in B major is the first of four for violin and piano, but since it was never published during Delius's lifetime (the score was not even engraved until 1977) it has been designated an *op. posth*. We know that Delius was at a private performance given in Paris in 1893 at the lodgings of the pianist Harold Bauer, who on that occasion accompanied the violinist Achille Rivarde.[84] The percipient Grieg had praised the sonata as a work full of talent, singling out the slow movement, and Delius did try to get this substantial, half-hour work into print, but Max Abraham, head of the publishing-house C. F. Peters, rejected it. His reasons for doing so are interesting:

> ... the form is too free, the key is changed too frequently and the first and last movements are so difficult to play that reasonably large sales for the work are unthinkable.[85]

Was this judgement justified? The answer is yes, to some extent, but only if one looks at the piece – as Abraham had to – from a commercial point of view. B major is not a particularly straightforward key, and F sharp major – which Delius uses for the second movement (*Andante molto tranquillo*) – is even less so. There is also much truth in the criticism that – at least for a potential amateur market – the writing is strenuous and tricky, with much of it placed in the instrument's high register, which can cause problems of intonation. The violin part weaves itself restlessly around the stave with hardly the most obvious of intervals between the notes. It is also quite true that the music does not settle for very long in one key but modulates freely and frequently.

But these unclichéd characteristics are also the sonata's great strengths: '[It] has an immediacy about it that is hard to resist – the sheer *joie de vivre* of the outer movements is infectious.'[86] That is exactly where the sonata scores: in its youthful, virile vigour and its outpouring of seemingly spontaneous emotion. Delius is not at all interested in following textbook sonata form. For example, the opening movement is almost monothematic: the second subject, with its dotted note-values, is related rhythmically to the first and it appears in the subdominant key of E major rather than the expected dominant, F sharp; likewise the development section begins in A flat (which must have disturbed Abraham). But to be pedantic about all this is to destroy the work's

---

[84] (Serge) Achille Rivarde (1865–1940): he became a professor at The Royal College of Music in 1899, where his pupils included Margaret Harrison, the sister of May and Beatrice for whom Delius would write his Double Concerto.

[85] Letter 43.

[86] Tasmin Little, liner note to Conifer CD 75606–51315–2.

considerable vitality and *élan*. It is a young man's music, that of a free soul, and anyone who experiences the sonata in performance must quite rightly give up trying to work out what it is 'doing' structurally and just savour the exhilarating moments. The middle movement that so appealed to Grieg is highly expressive; apart from fifteen bars of piano solo at the start, the violin rests for only four bars out of a total of 157 (a similar situation occurs in the finale, *Allegro con moto*, which also happens to be the weakest of the three movements in terms of melodic invention). One could criticise Delius's piano writing in the slow movement for being unduly chordal – a similar objection holds good for the outer sections of the Cello Sonata – but it is perfectly playable and there are some *bravura* passages in the finale. In short, the Sonata in B major is a world away from the three 'numbered' ones, but on its own terms it is a very good play and a very good listen. It has a counterpart in Richard Strauss's early Violin Sonata in E flat, op. 18, written four years before Delius's, and which the latter may have known: neither is typical of the mature composer, but both are irresistibly winning.

T HE Violin Sonata was quickly followed by the ***Légende* for violin and piano** (1892: *RT* VII/3; *CE* vol. 31a). Although written in 1892, it was not published until 1916 (by Forsyth Bros of Manchester), by which time, of course, it was hardly representative of Delius's style. It is tempting to think that maybe the *Légende* held a special place in his heart and that he yearned to see it in print. The truth, however, is that by 1916 the composer was in London, temporarily exiled from Grez on account of the War, and needing to earn money from even a modest success in the field of salon music, which is really what this charming but slight piece is. A letter from Beecham[87] confirms that he had bought the *Légende* outright for £150 from the composer (as well as three other works, including *North Country Sketches*), but that after publication the generous conductor intended to hand the copyright back to Delius.

The *Légende* cannot, however, have earned much – it is certainly no *Chanson de matin*. But it is appealing and mellifluous enough and quite unabashed by its influences – Dvořák and Grieg. The latter could have written the opening violin theme in E flat, though perhaps not the semitonal, rocking idea which permeates the contrasting B section that follows after an unconvincing modulation to E major. The opening A section then returns more forcefully with a chugging quaver accompaniment and some rather laboured padding in the form of harmonic sequences. The B section also reappears in an imaginative treatment; then the A section comes back again, and soon develops to reach a climax (with a high A flat for the violinist). The coda, marked *vivo*, reveals Delius's lack of experience with the genre of popular music, as he gives the violin twenty-eight bars of muted semiquaver figuration, high up on the E string. These are tricky to bow and pitch, and would have put the piece out of the reach of the average non-professional. But in all fairness,

---

[87] Letter 408.

Delius had not originally written the work specifically for the amateur market, though one wonders whether an editor at Forsyth might not have had a quiet word with him. This penchant for awkwardly chromatic, semiquaver string figurations caused problems later on in Delius's concertos, as we shall see.

There is no record of a performance of this version, but the later, orchestrated one was first performed at the 1899 St James's Hall concert (see below, Chapter 3) after which one critic laconically wrote: 'This was followed by a Légende for violin and orchestra somewhat vague in form, but picturesque and well laid out for the instrument.'

Finally, Delius also worked in this period on another **String Quartet** (1892–3: *RT* VIII/4). There is some confusion about just how many early quartets he wrote, and Beecham, and again Heseltine and Fenby all say different things.[88] Although included in Robert Threlfall's *Catalogue*, only a few fragments of this 1892–3 work survive, as do some of another quartet of the same period.[89]

I N the last three of the four years covered by this chapter, Delius had written several serious and quite substantial works – *Sakuntala, Irmelin, On the Mountains,* and *Maud* – as well as some attractive violin music. Whilst none of them can be described as mature Delius, he had broken away from salon music – as the individual movements of *Florida* and *Hiawatha* might perhaps be described – and they represent a considerable advance both in his practical techniques and his maturity as a composer. It would be only another nine years before he arrived at the peak of his achievements.

---

[88] *RT Catalogue*, p. 175.
[89] *RT Supplement*, p. 101.

# Coming to Maturity

*Over the Hills and Far Away – The Magic Fountain –
Légende for violin and orchestra – Badinage – Koanga –
American Rhapsody – Romance for cello and piano – Jelka
Rosen – Grez-sur-Loing – Folkeraadet – 'Seven Danish
Songs' – Piano Concerto (two versions) – Mitternachtslied
Zarathustras – La Ronde se déroule – St James's Hall
concert – Paris – A Village Romeo and Juliet – Lebenstanz –
Margot la Rouge*

D URING these next eight years, Delius wrote four operas, a piano concerto, six orchestral works and fifteen songs – and by the end of the period he had become a mature composer, with his own utterly distinctive style. However, his great problem – admittedly one that almost all aspiring composers face at the start of their careers – was actually getting anything played or published. There had been the *ad hoc* performance of *Florida* at Leipzig in 1888, and the two professional ones of *On the Mountains* in Norway in 1891 and Monte Carlo in 1894 – but that was that, and, notwithstanding the encouragement of a few friends, it would not be until 1897 that another note of Delius's was heard in public. The principal reason for the lack of performances can only have been that the mainly salon-type, 'easy-listening', music that Delius was still writing in the early 1890s simply stood little chance of acceptance by the major conductors, publishing houses and concert promoters, when by this time audiences in German concert halls and opera houses had already heard works such as *Parsifal* (1882), Debussy's *L'Enfant prodigue* and Bruckner's Symphony no. 7 (1884), and Strauss's *Tod und Verklärung* (1890 – the same year that Delius began his *Suite* for violin and orchestra). Nevertheless he persevered.

The musical public's taste in songs, on the other hand, had not advanced anything like as much as that for orchestral music, and so publishers were more willing to take them. In fact, Delius had done reasonably well. Augener Limited of London had issued *Fünf Lieder (aus dem Norwegischen)* in 1890 and then *Three Songs, the Words by Shelley* and *Sieben Lieder (aus dem Norwegischen)* in 1892. In 1896, 'Le Ciel est par-dessus le toit' (one of the *Deux Mélodies* with words by Paul Verlaine) appeared in a French magazine; then, in the same year, L. Grus Fils of Paris produced a book of *Cinq Chansons, musique de Fritz Delius* (the 1888 'O schneller mein Ross', two of the *Sieben Lieder*, one of the Shelley songs, and the second of the *Deux Mélodies*).

Away from his desk, Delius was torn between the 'high solitudes' of Norway with a few good friends, and the lively café life of Montparnasse with many. In the summer of 1893, he spent much of a three months' holiday in Norway with

Sinding, and on his return to Paris in September he began to frequent a small but celebrated *crémerie* run by Madame Charlotte Caron at 13 rue de la Grande Chaumière. This had become a busy meeting place for many artists, musicians and writers. As Delius described it:

> artists received unlimited credit. Paintings were sometimes accepted in lieu of payment, and at one period six or seven magnificent Gauguins were to be seen on the walls. It was a little place of the utmost simplicity, where hardly ten people could sit down at a time and where one's meal generally cost one a franc, or a franc-fifty including coffee.[1]

## OVER THE HILLS AND FAR AWAY
## (FANTASIA – FANTASIE OUVERTÜRE)
### (1893–7: *RT* VI/II; *CE* vol. 23a)

A PART from writing two songs and finishing the String Quartet he had begun the previous year (see Chapter 2), the sole composing event in 1893 seems to have been the start of the *Over the Hills and Far Away*. Delius must, of course, have 'doodled', and almost certainly begun a number of things, but nothing else has come to light or is mentioned in correspondence. He loved the company of his friends and acquaintances in the Parisian artistic world – although curiously he had relatively little to do with the musicians – and he continued also to move in 'high society' and the world of cafes and prostitutes.[2] None of those three milieux could, however, have been more different from what is likely to have been the inspiration of this orchestral work.

Delius was very much a cosmopolitan, and did not in fact write a single complete work in England. Much of his music was inspired by the scenery, sounds and even silences, of America, Norway (in particular the Jotunheim mountains) and France, and the writings of their authors and poets. He wrote very little that unquestionably sounds 'English', but this work could well be a picture of the Yorkshire Moors that he knew and had roamed over in his boyhood.[3] The reasons why it took probably four years to finish are not

---

[1] Frederick Delius, 'Recollections of Strindberg', *The Sackbut* 1/8 (December 1920), pp. 353–4.

[2] Philip Heseltine was seemingly ignorant of the life that Delius led in Paris between 1888 and 1897, and probably after that (or he was perhaps being loyal to his mentor): in *PW*, p. 48, he writes that 'Unlike the majority of young artists, Delius did not come to Paris to develop and indulge an abnormal taste for absinth, venery or sartorial eccentricities. He led a very quiet life ...'. See also Letter 96, from an unknown admirer: 'I love you with all my heart ...'.

[3] Although it has, however, been suggested that Norway might have been the stimulus for it: see *Palmer*, p. 41; Lionel Carley, 'Introduction', in *MA&L*, pp. 1–12, at p. 3; Barrie Iliffe, '*Eventyr* and the Fairy Tales in Delius', in *MA&L*, pp. 273–89, at p. 275.

hard to guess – they can all be deduced from the ups and downs of Delius's multifaceted life. The title is that of a seventeenth-century English song which was included in, among other things, John Gay's *The Beggar's Opera* (1728) – but how Delius came to use it is a mystery.

Fenby aptly summed up the charming naïvety of the 'fantasy overture' by identifying its 'youthful vigour and boyish tunefulness'. A hushed introduction with a rising, fanfare-like string motif answered by horn calls sketches an atmosphere of wide-open spaces and leads into a sensuous melody on lower strings. A more virile, fully scored passage gallops briefly across, then ends with an uncharacteristically decisive cadence, as if Delius is stamping his foot or shaking his fist at us. A group of secondary themes follows: an undulating one, predominantly for strings, then a very touching woodwind idea which is considerably varied, even though no formal development section follows. The opening material is recalled, and the original sequence of musical ideas followed through, before this refreshingly uncomplicated work culminates unexpectedly (and again untypically for Delius) in a loud 'bang', complete with cymbal crash. Beecham was fond of *Over the Hills* and one can quite see why: it does not outstay its welcome, and presents its attractive melodies with skill and effective instrumentation.

Back in 1890, at the age of twenty-nine, Hans Haym (1860–1921) had been appointed the director of the Concertgesellschaft (Concert Society) at Elberfeld – a prosperous industrial town on the banks of the River Wupper, to the north-east of Cologne, which had a flourishing orchestra and choir.[4] Haym was born in Halle, some 40 km from Leipzig (which, because of the standing of its Conservatorium, was probably then regarded as the greatest musical town in Europe); at university he studied philosophy and classical philology, and he did not embark on a musical career until he was in his mid-twenties. It was therefore to his considerable credit that it was only some five years later that he secured the relatively prestigious Elberfeld post. Although he became quite well known as a pianist, and rather less well known as a composer, he was primarily an excellent conductor, and performed appreciably more new music than most of his German contemporaries:

> This earnest, likeable young man soon established a happy and lasting relationship with the town and his performers. He continued [his predecessor's] policy of blending the old with the new, and although for the most part he had to defer to the conservative tastes around him he was as generous as he could be in introducing the works of younger composers.[5]

Haym came into Delius's life through a young painter, Ida Gerhardi, whom

---

[4] Jelka described it as 'a dismal town, full of black smoke, modern industry, machines and ugly people.' Renamed Wuppertal in 1930, it also boasted a magnificent suspended railway.

[5] Lionel Carley, 'Hans Haym: Delius's Prophet and Pioneer', in *Companion*, p. 189.

Delius met in 1896.[6] She had taken to helping Delius to promote his music, and, as she happened to know Haym, she wrote to him in September 1897 asking if he would perform one of Delius's orchestral pieces.[7] The outcome was far beyond anything that she or Delius could have anticipated. Not only did Haym conduct the first performances of *Over the Hills and Far Away* on 13 November that year, and then *Paris* in 1901, but he followed them with the Piano Concerto and *Appalachia* (both 1904), as well as giving the German premières of *Mitternachtslied Zarathustras* in 1903 and, in 1909, a complete performance of *A Mass of Life*. As a result, he not only became one of the firmest of Delius's friends,[8] but also, despite a great deal of opposition from the committee of the Elberfeld Concert Society, his most powerful advocate and supporter in Germany – in exactly the same way as, a decade later, Beecham and, to a lesser extent, Henry Wood,[9] were to in Britain. Haym stayed at Elberfeld until 1920, the year before his death, and in addition to those first performances he gave a number of subsequent ones of Delius's major works.

The critics were either openly hostile towards *Over the Hills and Far Away*, or very guarded in their views. On 16 November 1897, the *General Anzeiger für Elberfeld-Barmen* reported that 'We may safely overlook a quite new, but fairly uninteresting apprentice work by one Mr. Fritz Delius', while the *Täglicher Anzeiger für Berg und Mark* commented:

> In contrast to the Brahms, the performance of the first item on the programme, the new Fantasy-Overture by Fritz Delius 'Over the Hills and Far Away', which the orchestra played from manuscript, did not fulfil our expectations. Even though the opening did arouse our interest and keen anticipation (the work is certainly rich in original ideas, attractive melodies and much skilful orchestration), nevertheless, logical connections and, above all, a clear progression of thoughts, were lacking. In addition, the orchestral colours were often too garish and were too thickly applied. Not infrequently the sound came across as too

---

[6] Ida Gerhardi (1862–1927): by the early 1900s she would become an established portrait painter with a strong reputation, and she showed at large exhibitions in Paris and Berlin. She painted Delius three times, and also gave him help in finding a tenant for Solano Grove (see below). For an excellent discussion of her, see Annegret Rittmann, '"Our Prophetic Little Lady Friend": The Artist Ida Gehardi', in *MA&L*, pp. 168–83.

[7] Letter 74, n. 2.

[8] There are over fifty letters and postcards from Haym to Delius: for some, see the Index of Correspondents on p. 432 of *Letters 1*.

[9] [Sir] Henry (Joseph) Wood, CH (1869–1944): a celebrated English conductor who was a very powerful force for music in England (and particularly English music) for most of his long career. In 1895, he and Robert Newman, the manager of the Queen's Hall in London, founded the Promenade Concerts there (which he conducted until 1944), and he directed and conducted at many of the major music festivals around the country.

overbearing. Without doubt, the young composer is very talented and in time will certainly achieve greater things.

16 November 1897

Another review was marvellously pompous:

The second subscription concert in the Casino on Saturday began with a novelty which has not yet appeared in print: the Fantasy-Overture 'Over the Hills and Far Away' by Fritz Delius. According to our information, the composer has so far not produced anything on a bigger scale. What we know of him is that he comes from Westphalia,[10] is at present completing his musical studies with Hofkapellmeister Stavenhagen in Weimar and is engaged in composing an opera, though when that will eventually be completed, cannot be foretold even by the Muses who were present at Delius's cradle. Among those same Muses opinions differ; after hearing the Fantasy-Overture on Saturday, there can be no doubt of course that Mr. Delius has deprived us of our sharpest critical barbs. By describing his music as a 'Fantasy', he has allowed himself considerable liberties in providing any connections for his ideas and harmonic structure. As the composition developed we were reminded, amongst other things, of the influence of Grieg's musical language. After the first few bars, a programme is indicated, and indeed, to all intents and purposes, this is what Delius offers us: programme music – a kind of Impressionistic creation, a rising main theme which functions as a glimpse into the Eternity of 'Over the Hills and Far Away'. It is not quite clear to us whether Mr. Delius, by unleashing an uproar of musical sounds, intends to depict the wide horizon obscured by raging storms. In any case, we are of the opinion that the changes of tempo which serve to bridge the sections, are somewhat confusing. The ending of the work, with its cheerful mood, reinforces our distinct impression that Mr. Delius is not asking us the momentous question posed by Goethe's Wanderer: 'What is the meaning of all this pain? What is the meaning of the stormy blast?' As an orchestrator he has a well-expressed individuality and, technically, he produced admirable results; however, we feel that a potentially imposing artistic personality has not yet appeared and therefore we are inclined to doubt whether the somewhat perfunctory and polite applause which greeted the performance was a true indication of the work's worth. Or was Mr. Delius's brief 'Fantasy Overture' regarded simply as a well-intentioned introductory overture to the Concert and that its value (or not) as a composition hardly mattered, since all our thoughts were directed towards the appearance of the famous singer Carl Scheidemantel?

*Elberfelder Zeitung*, 15 November 1897

---

[10] The region of northern Germany between the rivers Ruhr and Weser, including the cities of Bielefeld, Dortmund, and Minden.

Delius must have been disappointed by reactions like that, but he never lost heart.

1894 was infinitely more stimulating for Delius than 1893 – although no more productive – because not only did *On the Mountains* have its second performance, in Monte Carlo on 25 February, but around then he almost certainly met the painter Paul Gauguin, who had moved into the upstairs of the building in the rue Vercingétorix where the Molards had their studio. There, Gauguin started giving parties attended by a variety of those in the Parisian artistic world. Edvard Munch arrived in Paris in 1889, about a year after Delius; he began attending those getherings, and they probably got to know each other in 1890. Then in the late summer of 1894, August Strindberg (1849–1912)[11] arrived, and they formed an interesting little group – two painters, a writer and a composer. Delius also got to know two other composers (both pupils at the Paris Conservatoire) who were to play a modest part in his life: Florent Schmitt and Maurice Ravel. Schmitt, whom he had first met (very probably at the Molards) in 1892 or 1893, began preparing a vocal score of *Irmelin*; that was soon to be followed by *The Magic Fountain*, then *Koanga*, and finally *A Village Romeo and Juliet*.[12] Meanwhile Ravel, almost certainly introduced to Delius in the latter year, would in due course produce a vocal score of *Margot la Rouge*.[13] Apart from a couple of songs, Delius did not in fact finish anything this year, but in the summer he made a start on *The Magic Fountain*, with his friend from Florida days, Jutta Bell, giving him help with the libretto. In the late summer he visited Bayreuth and Munich.

*The Magic Fountain* was finished by midsummer in 1895, but otherwise it was a quite dreadful twelve months for Delius. First, he learned that he had contracted syphilis – although whether as the result of an early affair in America, his enjoyment of the Parisian 'low life', or dalliances with one of his more appropriate 'lady-friends' is not known;[14] then news reached him that Delius & Co. was in financial difficulties, with the result that Julius (also concerned that his son was apparently making little or no progress with his

---

[11] Who, by coincidence, had lived at Grez-sur-Loing for a year or so in the mid 1880s, probably when Delius was in Virginia.

[12] The scores of *Irmelin* and *The Magic Fountain* are in the archive of Boosey & Hawkes Ltd; that of 'the Original prelude to Act III of *Koanga*' is reproduced in Boosey & Hawkes' 1974 vocal score; and that of *A Village Romeo and Juliet* (partly in Schmitt's hand, and partly in FD's) is in the DTA.

[13] His score of *Margot la Rouge* is in the DTA.

[14] Anthony Payne's article on Delius in volume 5 of *The New Grove Dictionary of Music and Musicians* says that he probably caught it during his Florida days – but others have doubted whether he did in fact have it at all, and suggested that he died of other causes: see *DSJ* 79, 80, 82 and 84 (1983–4). The current authors do not intend to join in the controversy.

composing) cut his allowance in half; finally, Delius had a serious quarrel with Theodor, who refused to help fund a performance of *The Magic Fountain*.[15] Almost nothing else is known of how Delius spent the rest of the year – but he must have been pleased to have completed the new opera.

## THE MAGIC FOUNTAIN
### (1894–5: *RT* I/3; *CE* vol. 2)

I N 1896 Delius admitted to 'a vague idea' of writing a trilogy dealing respectively with (American) Indians, gypsies, and Negroes and quadroons.[16] This project was only partly carried out: his next opera, *Koanga*, would indeed focus on the latter group, but the gypsy theme only emerged tangentially in the plot of *A Village Romeo and Juliet*; American Indians, however, figure prominently in the story of *The Magic Fountain*, and what is remarkable is that Delius should have pioneered this. Although the American-born composers Arthur Nevin and Charles Wakefield Cadman would later explore Indian folklore in their operas *Poia* (1907) and *The Land of the Misty Water* (1912), Delius pre-empted them by several years.

The action of *The Magic Fountain* takes place in the sixteenth century. On board his ship, a Spanish nobleman, Solano,[17] and his crew are becalmed off the coast of Florida. Solano is a philosophic dreamer who is on a quest to find the Fountain of Eternal Youth; he believes that drinking its waters will guarantee him immortality. A catastrophic storm wrecks the vessel, but Solano survives and is washed up on a beach where he is discovered by Watawa. Born a princess, she is the last of her tribe, all of whom have been slaughtered by white invaders. Natives from a local village, led by Chief Wapanacki, bear the unconscious Solano away. In the second act, the Spaniard tries to find out more about the legendary fountain, and Wapanacki tells him that its secrets can only be revealed by the seer and guru Talum Hadjo, who lives a hermit's life in distant swamplands. Watawa and Wapanacki plot together: she seeks a murderous revenge for her tribe, but he refuses to kill an unarmed guest and wants to bide his time, hoping to get his hands on the stranger's gold. Watawa knows of Solano's quest for the Magic Fountain and, what is more, she also knows that without the necessary spiritual preparations made over the course of many years, drinking the waters of the fountain will result in instant death. Consequently, she is only too eager to act as Solano's guide. After the Indians leave on a war expedition, she and Solano set off together.

---

[15] It is not known where – although there was a possibility of it being given in Prague, which came to nothing.

[16] See above, Chapter 2, n. 41.

[17] The original manuscript has 'Solana' throughout, but in the second 'a' was scratched out and 'o' substituted.

A transformation scene brings them through dense forests to Talum Hadjo's hut. Watawa tells the hermit about Solano and seeks advice: should she avenge her ancestors? The guru deters her from outright murder, but confirms that the waters of the fountain will do her work for her and that she must let 'her heart decide'. The scene is transformed again to the Everglades, and as Solano and Watawa journey on, it is clear that he is becoming obsessed with her. The final act opens on the shores of a lake. Watawa is in anguish: she now realises that she, too, is attracted to her companion and confesses as much. The couple fall into each other's arms and kiss passionately. As they do so, spirit voices are heard, and the Magic Fountain is revealed with its attendant God of Wisdom. Solano at first refuses to believe in the deathly properties of the water, but Watawa is insistent and to prove it, and perhaps to save her lover, she drinks first and dies. Solano then chooses to follow her example, so that he can join her in 'the sweet magnolia grove' of death.

It is not hard to conjecture how Delius came up with this romantic and fanciful plot. While the legend of the Fountain of Eternal Youth goes way back to Herodotus and other authors of classical antiquity, it became especially popular in the sixteenth century. The first governor of Puerto Rico, Juan Ponce de León, is supposed to have been searching for such a fountain when he crossed the Atlantic in 1513, and the story thereafter became strongly associated with Florida, where Delius probably heard it recounted. It works best on a purely symbolic level, with its theme of love triumphing over illusory desires for immortality (a premonition of one of Delius's later *idées fixes*), but in doing so it cries out for richly poetic language and this the composer simply could not provide. His clunky text is written, like *Irmelin*, in doggerel verse: 'What can it be, this strange, vague anguish, / floating, quiv'ring in the air? / Labour'd breathing cramps my thinking, / stifled sobs seem ev'rywhere' – preposterous lines when given to a character like Watawa. Moreover, the mechanism of the plot is at times obscure and confusing, and in an amateurish way characters insist on telling each other what they already know, just so that we, the audience, can eavesdrop. Watawa's transformation from a monster of bloodthirsty revenge who is consumed by hatred at the end of Act 2, into the loving creature of Act 3, is hardly credible, even though the *volte-face* is measured by an interval and some attempt to show her subsequent self-reproach and doubts. But at least there is some development in Watwa, whereas Solano is a cardboard character whose lack of self-awareness is unappealing. On page 11 of the score he admits he does not 'grasp the meaning [of] a fountain ready for those prepared', and on page 268 he is still in denial of what he calls 'those Indian legends'. The subsidiary characters of Wapanacki and Talum Hadjo are likewise bland and uninteresting. Although Delius told Jutta Bell in 1896 that he did not 'believe in realism in opera', there has to be a measure of credibility in plot and character or the audience's sympathies will never be engaged.

On the other hand, the orchestral 'voice' of the opera, which, as in *Irmelin*, is where the real musical interest lies, is consistently sumptuous and imaginative. The transformation sequences of Act 2 Scene 2, and of Act 3, give splendid opportunities for instrumental colour, which Delius seizes with alacrity, giving full play to his ample brass and horn sections and exploiting the richly sensuous sounds of the cor anglais, bass clarinet and sarrusophone (or double bassoon). Delius recycles material from the *Florida Suite*, notably the opening theme of the first movement, which he quotes in the introduction to Act 1 (bar 16 *et seq.*), and excerpts from the third movement, which serve for the tribal war dances in Act 2 and for some of the transformation music at the end of Act 2 (bar 692 *et seq.*). On her initial appearance, Watawa has a little motif heard on the 1st clarinet (Act 1, bars 557–9), but this is not distinctive and later Delius hardly refers to it at all. Unlike in *Irmelin*, there are no consistently used *leitmotifs* standing for ideas or characters. Generally the vocal lines are also less memorable than in the earlier work, and melodic distinctiveness is thin on the ground – the composer does not seem to be setting out to write take-home tunes. Instead, there is a great deal of lyrical, but ultimately bland, pentatonic music. Likewise the few set-pieces are disappointing: one might have expected a really distinctive *arioso* from Solano on board ship in Act 1, or from Talum Hadjo in Act 2, but this never really happens. There are also moments when the action, such as it is, stalls – notably in Act 2 in the scenes between Watawa and Wapanacki.

Some of the most effective writing occurs in Act 1 where Delius suggests the becalmed vessel and its languorous, weary crew with great imagination. The *lento molto* introduction opens with sixteen bars of quiet chords, one per bar, and with subtly changing harmonies. Delius pulls off the same trick again at the end of the introduction, and it is a magical effect:

Ex. 3.1

The sailors' choruses are also striking, often moving only step-wise and in unison over a monotonous, dragging *ostinato* accompaniment. There is a very effective chorus in 4-part canon ('The sails hang rotting on the masts, heigh ho! / The chains lie rusting in the sea, heigh ho!'), most unusual for Delius but which works well:

Ex. 3.2

The storm scene whips up a tremendous amount of weather and is violent enough, though Delius is actually only adopting the usual musical clichés for a tempest: chromatic chords slithering up and down in contrary motion, underscored by diminished sevenths. On the whole, though, this act is well constructed and without *longueurs*. But in Act 2, opportunities are missed to make something really striking of the Indian locale: the braves and squaws occasionally hum a little in a less than meaningful way, and the war chant section beginning at letter O is no better. Delius was clearly not interested in introducing any authentic folk tunes or melodies at this point. Act 2 ends rather strikingly with a musical question mark: a soft E flat minor chord on strings but with the seventh of the scale (D flat) obtruding in the 2nd bassoon.

The finest pages of *The Magic Fountain* are really in the third act, and one just has to ignore the incongruities of the story and its banal text, and concentrate instead on the sheer beauty of sound. Delius enjoys painting the scenery in extravagant and sensuous textures – the orchestra includes two harps – and the orchestral introduction is very fine in its misty evocation of the moonlit tropical Everglades, with their luxuriant forests and colourful flowers. The love duet of Watawa and Solano reaches heights of passion but, unlike with Irmelin and Nils, Delius is reluctant to combine their voices in a true duet. Unfortunately, the composer's taste falters in subsequent pages, which depict the lovers kissing and then incongruously falling asleep as the 'vapoury forms of beautiful women' rise from the lake in a ballet sequence accompanying the appearance of the fountain. This should have been a climactic moment in the opera, and Delius lets us down. He meanders around repeating A flat minor arpeggios before beginning a regrettably vacuous passage in B flat with the spirit voices simply repeating *la–la–la* (a propensity of Delius's that can be hard to take). Worse is to come, with a key change to D flat and a sequence ('Play, fountains, play') which belongs more to a third-rate musical comedy. The composer exonerates himself with Solano's ecstatic address to the fountain, doused in a refreshingly limpid dash of C major (bar 469 *et seq.*), but the final scene in which the lovers meet their deaths fails to move us as it should, and ends with the orchestra swooning perfunctorily in D flat.

The verdict on *The Magic Fountain* has to be that it is a failure and, along with *Margot la Rouge*, the weakest of Delius's stage works. It is certainly no advance on *Irmelin* – quite the contrary. For this difficult and symbolic material Delius should have found himself a proper poet with a gift for elevated language. The opportunities for characterisation and local colour offered by the unusual material are left unexploited. Ultimately Delius is more interested in the scenery than in his cast, and for a successful opera that simply will not do.

*The Magic Fountain* was the last but one of Delius's six operas to be given its première – on 30 July 1977, in a concert performance at the Golders Green Hippodrome in North London, conducted by Norman Del Mar. The concert was subsequently broadcast by the BBC on 20 November, and then released on records.[18] Twenty years later, starting on 22 June 1997, there were eight performances in English at the Kiel Opera House, in an interesting production conducted by Walter E. Gugerbauer. One critic certainly did not enjoy himself:

> Musically, the long orchestral passages are distinctly reminiscent of Grieg's Peer Gynt, without reaching those standards. The arias and duets on the other hand seem entirely random in their melody production. The anyhow underemployed chorus was more to be heard than seen.
>
> *Schleswig-Holsteinische Landeszeitung*, 26 June 1997

while another tried his hand at analytical gobbledegook:

> Structurally, Delius often works with extensive formations made up of simple canonic elements combined. This [pattern] is interwoven with an elaborate, restlessly ranging yet uncontentious harmony, finely structured by a meticulously finished orchestral language rich in pedal tones and mixtures, never solid but always fluid. Max von Schillings[19] complained about 'Delius's paintbox where [the] colours intermingle' – a wicked

---

[18] For an article looking back on the broadcast, see Gordon Lovegreen, 'THAT Opera in Retrospect', *DSJ* 62 (1979), 7–10.

[19] Max (von) Schillings (1868–1993 – he abandoned the 'von'): a German conductor. He worked first at Bayreuth, then (at this time) in Munich, Stuttgart, and finally at the Berlin State Opera from 1919 to 1925. He and Delius probably first met around 1900. He was the dedicatee of *Sea Drift*, writing to Delius: 'Accept these brief thanks for sending "Seadrift", the dedication of which is a great and genuine joy to me.'

misrepresentation of a more sensitive musicality devoid of all robustness and never betraying the secret of its profound melody for cheap effect.

*Frankfurter Rundschau*, 24 June, 1997[20]

The opera was eventually given its first British production in February and March 1999 – by Scottish Opera under Richard Armstrong,[21] at the Edinburgh Festival Theatre and The Theatre Royal in Glasgow. The critical reception was generally favourable, with the music again being much more highly rated than the libretto.[22]

Almost nothing is known ever to have been written about *The Magic Fountain*, although Alfred Hertz did say to Delius in an 1898 letter: 'the music is so original, & the conception of the whole so poetic that, really, my boldest expectations were exceeded.'

A FTER finishing *The Magic Fountain* in the middle of 1895, Delius then reworked the 1892 *Légende* as the **Légende for violin and orchestra** (1895: *RT* VII/3; *CE* vol. 28). Unlike the earlier *Romance* for violin and piano, Delius thought enough of his original version of this piece to orchestrate it. The differences between the two are considered in *RT Catalogue* and *RT Supplement*. This version received its first performance four years later, on 30 May 1899 in St James's Hall, London, as part of the all-Delius concert which he organised and paid for himself.[23] It was, however, only mentioned in passing in a few of the reviews, almost all of which were about Delius's music in general.

Happily, 1896 was a huge improvement on the previous year. By February, Delius was sketching his next opera, *Koanga*; in early June he went to Norway, starting work on *Koanga* properly, and then walking in the Jotunheim mountains; by the middle of September he was back in Paris, having visited Denmark and Germany on the way. Interestingly, he also went back to Bradford yet again, this time for Christmas. Moreover, in the January occurred the event which, though not quite the last 'defining moment' of his life, would prove to be without question the greatest: he met a young German painter called Jelka Rosen.

Jelka's family, mainly lawyers and diplomats, came from Schleswig-Holstein, and her mother was one of the daughters of the composer Ignaz Moscheles (1794–1870). Jelka (actually christened Helena Sophie Emilie) was born in August 1862 in Belgrade, and when the family moved to Detmold she became

---

[20] This and the previous quotation are taken from the article 'The Première Staged Production of *The Magic Fountain*', *DSJ* 122 (1997), 50–60.

[21] (Sir) Richard Armstrong, CBE (1943–).

[22] Some reviews can be found in *DSJ* 125 (1999).

[23] There is a suggestion in one of Delius's letters that it was in fact first played in London in January 1897 (see *RT Catalogue*, p. 163), but there is no further record of that.

friends with another girl already mentioned above, Ida Gerhardi. They were both pupils at one of the most highly respected private art academies in Paris: the Académie Colarossi, opposite Madame Caron's *crémerie* in the rue de la Grande Chaumière. The Académie had been established in the nineteenth century as an alternative to the very conservative École des Beaux-Arts (the teaching arm of France's foremost artistic institution, the Académie des Beaux-Arts), and, unlike the École, had a liberal reputation, principally because it accepted female students and allowed them to draw from the nude male model. Jelka lived and worked in a *pension* in the avenue du Maine, a street along which many of the regulars at the *crémerie*, including Delius, often walked on their way there, so she may well have seen him from her window.[24] They actually met at a dinner party, when they discovered that they shared a strong interest in Nietzsche's writings; soon they were close friends, and possibly in love.[25] She had taken to going to paint in the little village of Grez-sur-Loing, near the Forest of Fontainebleau, at a house in the main street[26] with a garden going down to the river, belonging to the Marquis de Cazeaux; by the spring she was quite often enjoying Delius's company there, and in due course they married.

Until the early 1870s, the Académie des Beaux-Arts was France's foremost artistic institution, and it had very strict views and rules as to what kind of paintings and drawings it would accept for exhibitions – the 'approved' subjects were almost exclusively portraits, or historical or religious themes. In 1874, however, a group of young painters, mainly in their mid-thirties – Monet, Pissarro, Sisley, Renoir, Manet, Degas, Berthe Morisot and others – banded together under the title of the *Société anonyme coopérative des artistes, peintres, sculpteurs, graveurs, etc.* and held an exhibition that earned them the name of Impressionists. They completely changed the nature of painting, taking overall views of their subjects rather than exploring their details, and painting landscapes, townscapes, the insides of cafés and theatres, and informal portraits of the middle classes. They matched their new ideas with new techniques: the use of blurred outlines, imprecision, and either seemingly crude and random brushstrokes and splodges of colour, or what became known as *pointillism* – painting with tiny individual dots or strokes (*pointes*) which blend together so as to reveal a picture when viewed from a few feet away. As the writer Horst Keller puts it, the Impressionists viewed the world around them

in a kind of 'innocence of vision' … bathed in light, whether in the streets of the capital, or in the social scene, sometimes at a race

---

[24] *MMB*, pp. 104–5.

[25] In Letter 59 he said to her 'I believe you are after all about the best woman I ever met.' See also *TB*, p. 79; *MMB*, p. 105.

[26] Now 94 rue Wilson – the street was named after the Great War in honour of the American president Woodrow Wilson.

meeting ... or just the gentle idleness of a pleasant summer's day in the meadows.[27]

They also frequently worked *en plein air*, direct from their subjects – a method which simply did not allow them the precision and detail that their predecessors had sought.

Delius must have seen many of the Impressionists' drawings and paintings in the galleries and studios around Montparnasse, at artistic gatherings and in private houses. Jelka used both of their basic techniques, and the two can be compared in her 'broad brushstroke' 1912 portrait of Delius and the *pointilliste* painting *The Garden at Grez*.[28] One might say that, from a musical point of view, Delius had also been attracted to these two methods. Perhaps unsurprisingly, after his marriage to Jelka they almost came to define his mature style. Jelka was, however, much more than a traditional Impressionist – some of her work is quite powerful. Although The Delius Trust has reproductions of some twenty of her paintings,[29] the whereabouts of the majority is unknown.

Although he probably did not realise it for some years, Delius had found in Jelka a very special person indeed, and her importance to him cannot be overstated. Without her inestimable and wonderful loyalty – as strong in his old age and infirmity as when he was young and well – he would surely never have achieved all that he did. Philip Heseltine wrote:

> it was amongst the painters and literary men rather than the musicians that Delius found kindred spirits and true friends, chiefest and best of whom was Jelka Rosen, who became his wife, and, with her unfailing sympathy and devotion, allied to materially practical as well as great artistic abilities, has ever proved an ideal companion and helpmate to him.[30]

while Hubert Foss was most sympathetic:

> Important as was the formative and developing influence of the Parisian years, Delius' greatest gain from them was his wife, Jelka Rosen, both spiritually and materially. Heseltine's tribute to her ... is as prophetic as it is true. Throwing up her career as a painter, she devoted her entire life to Frederick ... No separate memoir of such a woman, however richly deserved, could ever be written, for she immersed herself utterly in her husband's music, in the making and the management of it, in providing

---

[27] Horst Keller, *The Art of the Impressionists* (Oxford: Phaidon Press, 1980), p. 35. Good examples of the two styles are Alfred Sisley's *The River Bank at Saint-Mammès* (1884) and Georges Seurat's *The Bridge at Courbevoie* (1886–7).

[28] Unfortunately, questions of space make it impossible to reproduce these paintings here, but they can be found in *Pictures*, plates 6 and 8.

[29] Three of them are on the covers of *DSJ* 137 (2005), 138 (2005), and 140 (2006); a fourth appears in *DSJ* 142 (2007), 3.

[30] *PW*, p. 48.

the bodily and spiritual needs of the remote thinker, and in continual literary assistance in his operas and vocal works.[31]

and Fenby said:

> One thing was ever uppermost in my mind [when I was helping Delius] at Grez, and that was that only there, and with such constant care as his wife lavished on him, could he go on living. Her name deserves a very prominent place on the scroll of those who have given themselves unstintingly for others.[32]

There is, too, an affectionate portrait of her in Beecham's *Frederick Delius*,[33] and over the years there have been numerous other properly generous tributes.[34]

THOUGH the exact date is unknown, it was probably around this time that Delius wrote the insubstantial but attractive little piano piece **Badinage (Danse lente)** (mid-1890s?: *RT* IX/4; *CE* vol. 33). *Badinage* is not in fact a very appropriate title, as the word means 'humorous or playful jest' – which (although the tempo direction is *giocoso*) this piece is not. Just *Danse lente* would have been more appropriate, as the music flows along in 4/4 with a nice lilt, almost like a French cabaret song. The key signature is D flat, and after two pages it moves via a single bar of D major into E flat for the middle section (hardly a modulation of which the professors of harmony at the Leipzig Conservatorium would have approved!), the tune of which is rather too like the first and last sections to give the piece any real variety.

---

[31] Hubert Foss, 'Additions, Annotations and Comments', in *PW*, p. 148.

[32] *Fenby 1*, p. 30.

[33] *TB*, p. 79.

[34] For a good memoir of Jelka, see Heinrich Simon, 'Jelka Delius', *The Monthly Musical Record* 65 (December 1935), 219–20; reprinted in *Companion*, pp. 131–4.

## KOANGA

(1895–7: *RT* I/4; *CE* vol. 3)

THIS is Delius's third opera. He began sketching it in 1895,[35] but it was not until 1896 that he started work on the actual score. The plot is taken from an 1880 novel by George Washington Cable (1844–1925) entitled *Les Grandissimes*, after a French-American Creole family in Louisiana. One episode of the book involves the slave Mioko-Koanga, a prince of the Jaloff tribe in Africa who is also known as Bras-Coupé – Delius's original working title. At an early stage Delius asked Jutta Bell to help him fashion a libretto, but when she declined he turned instead to an English author and poet 'of much merit', Charles Keary.[36] Keary – with whom Delius was later to fall out – produced a first draft which the composer set, but it was considerably revised (and translated) for the first performance in Germany. Those changes were so radical that in places they altered the whole sense of the plot. The situation was further complicated in 1933 when Jelka translated the German libretto back into English, with unhappy results – although that version was published as a vocal score in 1935. In 1974, Douglas Craig and Andrew Page completely revised the libretto to make a modern, performable version which tidied up many incongruities; the preface to the published vocal score sets out in detail the convoluted history of all these revisions and changes. The music, however, remained unaltered and was published as a full score in 1980, with the 1974 revisions as the now official libretto.

*Koanga* is set in eighteenth-century Louisiana on a plantation bordering the Mississippi. It is framed by a prologue and epilogue set in a later era, in which a group of planters' daughters persuade an old slave called Uncle Joe to tell them a familiar tale of 'grief and love'. This turns out to be the story of Koanga and Palmyra. The latter, a quadroon with blood of the Dahomey race in her, is maid to Clotilda, wife of the plantation owner, Don José Martínez. The estate overseer, Simon Pérez, rouses the slaves at dawn and brutally urges them to get to work. He is besotted by Palmyra and wants to marry her, but she will have nothing to do with him. As the plantation owner arrives, a new slave is dragged in: Koanga, an African prince and a priest of the Voodoo cult. Koanga mourns for his lost homeland and proudly swears that he will never submit to his owners. Martínez threatens him but is restrained by Pérez, who realises that force is useless. Martínez now has a better idea: let Palmyra be used as bait for the stubborn slave. Koanga is instantly attracted to her and agrees that if she is given to him in marriage, he will co-operate and renounce his Voodoo faith. Pérez is appalled – as is Clotilda, who seems to have a strong desire to protect the girl. This is explained at the beginning of the second act, when Clotilda secretly admits to Pérez that Palmyra is actually the illegitimate child of her

---

[35] *RT Catalogue*, p. 28.

[36] Charles (Francis) Keary (1848–1917): see Letter 62, n. 1, and Letter 67.

own father and that she has brought her up from birth; Palmyra's marriage to a slave would therefore be an outrage. Pérez vows to stop the union, but as his reward he wants Palmyra for himself. Later, he tells the girl who she really is, ordering her to forget Koanga and marry him instead. Once again she rejects him. Koanga now appears in his finery ready for the wedding ceremony, which includes the Creole dance *La Calinda*. Before the priest can officiate, Palmyra is abducted by Pérez and his men. Koanga is enraged and strikes Martínez down, swearing revenge in the form of a curse bringing terrible afflictions to the estate. He escapes into the forest, rededicating himself to the protection of his gods.

The final act takes place in a swamp at nightfall. Koanga has attracted followers, and they enact an extended ceremony of Voodoo rituals. But he then has a vision of Palmyra back on the estate, mortally sick, and rushes off to be with her. The scene changes to the plantation, where the slaves and the land they work have all been afflicted by Koanga's curse. Palmyra appears, and Pérez once again exerts his claims and tries to embrace her. At that moment, Koanga appears and kills Pérez with his spear. But he in turn is brutally attacked by Martínez's men, and as he lies dying he turns back to his old religion in repentance. Palmyra is deeply moved by his faith and, dedicating herself accordingly to Voodoo, chooses death by stabbing herself. A substantial orchestral interlude leads to the epilogue, where Uncle Joe has just finished the story for his young listeners.

It is worth recounting the plot in some detail if only to underline the fact that, in comparison with Delius's previous operas, *Koanga* is positively action-packed. Acts 1 and 2, in particular, are full of development in terms of story and character, and are tautly constructed in a hard-driven sequence of events. Dramatic tension, so notably lacking in *Irmelin* and *The Magic Fountain*, is no problem here. Only in the opening scene of Act 3 does the momentum flag: the Voodoo ceremonies are somewhat prolonged, and set to rather disappointingly dull music. Elsewhere, however, the overall feeling is of energy and vigour. Indeed, *Koanga* feels like a proper opera, something Delius himself was aware of when he told Jutta Bell that 'it is more of an opera than the last one – with quartets, trios, quintets and chorus.' There are also powerful solo moments, notably for Koanga, who has a superb, if taxing, baritone part: his opening *arioso* 'O Voodoo Manian' begins *forte* on a middle C, and in its opening bars ranges up to G above the stave. He has equally potent solos during the aborted wedding in Act 2; in the great scene that ends that same act when he realises he has been betrayed; in the Voodoo scene at the start of Act 3; and in his terrible curse as he lies dying. Ex. 3.3 (from Act 1) is typical of the vocal demands that Delius makes.

Koanga is the only character with a distinctive *leitmotif*, and Delius works it into the orchestral texture with many variations; it is usually to be heard somewhere, whenever Koanga's name is mentioned (Ex. 3.4).

Palmyra has relatively few solo opportunities: there is nothing much for her in Act 1, and originally there was nothing in Act 2 either – that is until

Ex. 3.3

Moderato

Koanga

O Voo-doo Ma-nian, my fa-thers from your graves a-venge me, a-

-venge me on my vile be-tray-ers, You hosts a-rise a-gain

and let the trai-tors' blood in ri-vers flow!___ Let___ them be

burned o-ver a thou-sand fires!

Ex. 3.4

Delius bowed to pressure from a rebellious soprano and added an aria for the Elberfeld première. That aria is 'The hour is near', which he stuck rather abruptly into the middle of the wedding chorus (Figs. 10–11 in the vocal score). Elsewhere, Palmyra's finest moments are in her duets with Pérez, which are in one sense the only love duets (albeit one-sided) in the score. It is a real oddity that there is no extended love duet for Palmyra and Koanga, as there is for Irmelin and Nils, and for Watawa and Solano, but then the plot hardly allows for this. Koanga's death scene is a monologue, and only after he has perished does Palmyra launch into a solo which lasts a mere forty bars before her suicide. Delius, though, intended the orchestra to transform this into a *Liebestod*, and sharp-eared listeners will note more than a hint of the famous opening bars of Wagner's *Tristan* in the orchestra:

Ex. 3.5

Quite why Delius quotes Irmelin's theme on the cor anglais a few bars later is something of a mystery. Once Palmyra falls silent, her song is taken up in a great outpouring of purely orchestral sound which is ravishingly beautiful – Beecham was quite right to make a separate extract of this final scene. At Fig. 41+1 the music settles down into D flat with an arching melody on the cellos that includes the hallmark Delian triplet, before quoting a chorus first heard in Act 1 (to the words 'O Lawd, I'm goin' away'), perfectly scored on muted strings with exquisite harmonies and dying down to a *pianissimo* G flat chord. There, surely, the opera should have ended, not with the framing scene that complements the opening. Both are unnecessary, and the epilogue seems an artistic misjudgement which actually spoils the close of the opera – the intrusion of jolly G major is surely regrettable.

The way that Delius uses the chorus of Negro slaves in the first two acts of *Koanga* is remarkable for its time and worthy of detailed examination. As in *Appalachia*, Delius does not appear to be quoting authentic slave songs but, rather, writing convincing pastiches – although it is important to remember that the words, as they now appear in the published editions of vocal and full scores, are not what Delius originally set: they are adaptations by Douglas Craig and Andrew Page from other folk material, although they serve their purpose very well indeed. The chorus 'Oh Lawd, I'm goin' away' is heard twice to great effect early in Act 1: forcefully at first, then more tenderly in counterpoint to the solo line of Pérez – it is the tune that Delius partly quotes in the third movement of *Florida*. The chorus-writing is also most effective when the slaves are heard off-stage in the fields, and Delius uses a striking technique of superimposing their songs upon the on-stage action: 'John, say you got to reap what you sow' is heard twice during the dialogue between Pérez and Martínez (Fig. 12+1 *et seq.*), and 'D'lilah was a woman fair' is interjected twice, firstly during an on-stage quartet (just after Fig. 25+1) and then again during a quintet (Fig. 31+1). These are inventive and theatrically effective strokes, and the only problem is that of verbal congestion for the audience: since each character is given a separate text to sing, the result, allied to the additional choral text, is a veritable Tower of Babel. Moreover, some vital motivation for the plot (for example, Koanga renouncing his Voodoo gods in favour of Palmyra) is completely lost. Delius unexpectedly opens Act 2 with an unaccompanied chorus behind the scenes ('Now once in a way') and twice interpolates the haunting 'He will meet her when the sun goes down', anticipating *Appalachia*. There is another notable chorus during the wedding scene, 'How clearly calls the voice of our homeland', which acts like a commentary on Koanga's heartfelt solo (Fig. 12+1). In contrast, the choruses in Act 3 are limited to the opening Voodoo ceremonies and are neither folk-like nor, indeed, particularly memorable.

The famous dance *La Calinda* is borrowed from *Florida*, and Delius ingeniously weaves choral parts into it without having to alter the original instrumental version. It is not in fact the only borrowing: the orchestral introduction to Act 3 recycles the Act 2 prelude of *The Magic Fountain* almost note-for-note, occasionally adding extra bars and altering the harmony (e.g. Figs 1+9 to 1+12.) The orchestration includes banjos, sparingly but effectively used in choral and dance numbers, and the instrumental textures are generally much less opaque than in Delius's previous operas, letting the voices cut through far more naturally. The orchestra also has a vivid voice of its own, nowhere more so than in Act 2, just before Koanga reminds Palmyra of his homesickness and shame, but also of his commitment to her. The orchestra is eloquent as Koanga gazes around him:

Ex. 3.6

*Koanga* marks a considerable advance in Delius's operatic development and shows a much greater sense of the theatre than either *Irmelin* or *The Magic Fountain*. The dramatic impact is telling, and seems to owe something to the new *verismo* movement: Delius may have heard *Pagliacci* and *Cavalleria rusticana* in Paris, if not Puccini's *Manon Lescaut* (though Fenby said that he in fact loathed Puccini). The composer certainly deserved a better libretto and even though the clumsiness and illogicality of the original text have mostly been improved in the new version, there are still rough edges. But clearly Delius was not just writing to a formula – if he had been, the work might originally have met with more success. In *Koanga* Delius honed his skills and it left him poised to write an operatic masterpiece – indeed, that is just what he would do two years later.

The opera was probably finished in 1897, either during Delius's second visit to America (discussed below) or after his return to Paris – and excerpts from it were included in the 1899 concert at the St James's Hall. None of the reviews, however, did more than briefly mention them. The first production of the complete opera at the Elberfeld opera house in March 1904 was said to be the most spectacular musical event of the year, with Fritz Cassirer conducting, and the leading American baritone Clarence Whitehill as Koanga.[37]

---

[37] Cassirer apparently first found the score back–stage in the opera house – and Jelka designed the costumes: I. A. Copley, 'A Delius Miniature and Some Memories', *Music & Letters* 43 (1962), 4–6, at p. 4.

Cassirer (1871–1926) was Delius's second great advocate in Germany. Born into a well-off Jewish family that ran a fine art business with galleries in Berlin, he studied in Munich and then, back in Berlin, with the composer Hans Pfitzner. After three appointments in small German opera houses, he became the music director and conductor at the Stadttheater in Elberfeld, where he was introduced to Delius's music by Haym and the conductor Julius Buths – another strong supporter. Like Haym and Delius, Cassirer and Delius became extremely good friends: 'We have come to such an understanding of each other', Cassirer wrote to Delius,[38] before they holidayed together in 1904.[39] In addition to the première of *Koanga*, he would also give the first performances of *A Village Romeo and Juliet* and help Delius with the libretto for *A Mass of Life*.[40]

*Koanga* was not performed in England until September 1935, when Beecham conducted it three times at Covent Garden, and then on another seven occasions in various cities in the North of England. In Germany and in England, the notices were generally favourable; the music was considered to be better than the libretto, although some of the more serious reviews commented on the lack of drama and characterisation.[41] Beecham thought that the work was charming and original, but that *Irmelin* and *The Magic Fountain* were superior, in that both their plots were driven by supernatural elements that controlled the destinies of the protagonists (i.e. the Silver Stream and the Fountain of Eternal Youth). The later *A Village Romeo and Juliet* and *Fennimore and Gerda* share the same idea – the principal characters being completely influenced by an ominous power.[42]

A LTHOUGH there is no direct evidence, Delius's next work was probably his ***American Rhapsody: Appalachia*** (1896: *RT* VI/12; *CE* vol. 22) – not to be confused with the later *Appalachia* for chorus and orchestra (see Chapter 4), although the latter was a substantial reworking of this relatively short piece. It seems likely that Delius first became aware of American music while he was in his early teens and living with his family in Bradford. An American university choir toured in England and other countries between 1873 and 1878, and gave several concerts in Bradford – singing both standard partsongs and gospel music – and Delius could well have been taken to hear them. In her biography, Clare Delius tells how a local businessman:

---

[38] Letter 167.

[39] Beecham, however, took a slightly different view of their relationship, saying that Cassirer had an over-enthusiastic view of the worth of Delius's early works, and was too much of a Delius-worshipper: *TB*, p. 132.

[40] There are some interesting letters from Cassirer to Delius in *Letters 1*.

[41] A number of reviews can be seen in *DSJ* 113 (1994).

[42] *TB*, p. 130.

and his brothers, together with some of their friends got up a Christy Minstrel performance at Fred's instigation. The performance was given in [the businessman's] stables. The thing was done in style ... I remember at one of these performances how, as Fred was leading the chorus in 'Shine, shine moon',[43] the last of the candles which, placed in saucers, constituted the footlights, went out, leaving the performers to conclude their pointed invocation to the moon, in pitch darkness.[44]

It would seem logical for *American Rhapsody* to have been inspired by Delius's second visit to America, but that cannot be the case, as he did not go back there until the following year. It is also curious that he wrote it when his music had already veered away from his early, lighter style, with the relatively sophisticated *Paa Vidderne* and *Over the Hills and Far Away*. After the quiet start, the music that would in due course become the 'Old Slave Song' of *Appalachia* appears three times in close succession in the middle (although quite differently presented), while the traditional *Yankee Doodle* makes several appearances, and is combined with the minstrel show song *Dixie* in the main climax.

Like many of Delius's early works this had to wait many years for its first performance – by the London Philharmonic Orchestra under Edward Downes at a Royal Philharmonic Society concert in the Royal Festival Hall, London, on 10 December 1986 – but it seems to have attracted insufficient interest to warrant a review anywhere.

*American Rhapsody* was in all likelihood followed by the **Romance for cello and piano** (1896: *RT* VIII/5; *CE* vol. 31c). 'Dédiée à Monsieur Joseph Hollman' (1852–1927), a celebrated Belgian cellist,[45] this piece is only 105 bars long, and is in three sections: the first *lento tranquillo*, the second *molto tranquillo* in E (with seven bars *a tempo vivo* in the middle), and the third marked 'Tempo 1', back in B. Much use is made of the Delian triplet. Although there seems to be no record, Hollman presumably played it somewhere not long after Delius wrote it; however, the first confirmed performances were given by Julian Lloyd Webber at the Helsinki Festival on 22 June 1976, and then in London two days later. For once, *The Times* review was most favourable:

Hitherto, cellists have had four works by Delius at their disposal, although a fifth, early work was known about. That is the Romance (1896), which has just been published. It received its first British performance,

---

[43] This was one of a set of plantation songs with words and music by, somewhat improbably, Sir Alfred Scott-Gatty, KCVO, KStJ, FRSA (1847–1918). He was not only the Garter Principal King at Arms but also a prolific writer of children's and popular songs which (according to his obituary in *The Musical Times*) had an enormous vogue.

[44] *MMB*, p. 45.

[45] Of whom there is a brilliant drawing in the British Museum's collection. He had a cello piece and two songs performed in the Proms between 1897 and 1914.

two days after its premiere at the Helsinki Festival, by Julian Lloyd Webber and Yitkin Seow last night ... The new work proved to be a modest recital piece, after the manner of the Caprice and Elegy, carefully constructed, working its way through the bass, tenor and treble clefs to a central climax, and then down again. Although a comparatively early work, one could not fail to admire Delius's sure handling of the tenor register of the instrument, so notable a feature of the lovely Concerto and, to a lesser extent, of the weaker Double Concerto. And, although some of the piano writing did incline towards characteristically block chordal support, given the feeling for the ebb and flow of the music which those two performers earlier revealed in the Cello Sonata, the instruments go hand-in-glove to produce finely woven, gently nostalgic phrases.

26 June 1976

The first half of 1897 saw one of the most intriguing episodes in Delius's life – his return, with Halfdan Jebe, to Solana Grove, via Jacksonville in January, and via Danville on their way home in late May. The journey is virtually undocumented, and there is no clear evidence as to why they actually went. The most straightforward and plausible reason put forward is that Delius wanted to see for himself what had happened at the plantation during the eleven years since he left it under the management of his old Negro foreman, Albert Anderson. Delius was probably worried that it might be in a very bad way, in all likelihood producing very little income, and in the event it would still be another two years before he managed to find a tenant. Jelka was desperately worried that he would never come back to her – with good justification, as he only wrote to her once, probably in April, when he simply told her that he had been:

> basking in the sunshine and enjoying this lovely place ... [I am] sorry that I cannot bring back some of the flowers or a piece of the moonlight nights or something of the magnolia blossoms and orange blossoms. The sunsets here are something remarkable and always different varying between the most delicate colour on some nights to the most lurid and ferocious hues on others.[46]

He made no mention of the property at all. It has, however, been suggested that another (or even the sole) reason for the trip was that he wanted to find his Negro mistress. She is believed to have been a local, seventeen-year-old black girl, possibly called Chloe Baker, by whom, so he later told Percy Grainger,[47] he had fathered a child. The search, however, was fruitless.[48] Lastly, some say he might possibly also have been trying to extricate himself from the clutches of a

---

[46] Letter 69.

[47] Percy (Aldridge) Grainger (1882–1961): see below, Chapter 5, n. 31 *et seq.*

[48] Letter from Grainger to Richard Muller, 5 October 1941; see also articles by Tasmin Little in *DSJ* 91 (1986) and 122 (1997), and by William Randel in *DSJ* 96 (1988).

Parisian mistress, the Princesse de Cystria; if so, that failed, as she managed to get on the same ship to New York (and possibly even followed Delius and Jebe to Florida), and indeed she and Delius later continued their relationship.[49]

Early in 1897, the Marquis of Cazeaux decided to sell his house in Grez. Having fallen in love with the place the moment she first saw it, Jelka was quite unable to accept the prospect of never painting there again. She therefore managed to persuade her mother to find about half the 35,000 francs needed, and in May they bought it jointly.[50] Jelka invited Ida Gerhardi to join her, and the two young women set up house together.[51] It was here that Delius first met Ida: in the early days of their friendship she did a great deal to help promote his music, and she painted Delius three times. Indeed, there was possibly an intimate friendship between them[52] – but, as Delius's visits to the property became more frequent, it was Jelka who captured his real affections, and at some stage he displaced Ida by moving in permanently.[53] The house was then to remain Delius's and Jelka's home until their deaths. Nevertheless, he still kept his apartment in Montparnasse – and, despite his and Jelka's now deep affection for each other, he continued (at least spasmodically) to enjoy the coarser pleasures of the city. In 1898 (two years after they first met) Florent Schmitt had finished a letter to him 'Amusez-vous et surtout flirtez bien avec les charmantes miss(es) and ladys'[54] – while Alfred Hertz remembered an occasion in the early 1900s when Delius had taken him to see 'six whores' in Paris before inviting him home to dinner with Jelka.[55] Many years later Percy Grainger would write not only that 'Fred set out to enjoy life, did so, and did not regret paying the price it cost',[56] but that he 'practiced immorality with puritanical stubbornness'.[57]

1897 was reasonably productive for Delius – no doubt because, in spite of his absences, he was now thoroughly established at Grez and felt much more secure and settled. In this year he finished *Koanga* and wrote the three other works (*Folkeraadet*, the 'Seven Danish Songs' and the Piano Concerto), though the order in which they were produced is uncertain.

---

[49] It did, however, eventually come to an end in 1902: see Letter 137.

[50] There is a lovely description of the property in *MMB*, pp. 136–9.

[51] This was in fact a condition of the purchase, stipulated by Jelka's mother: see Eric Fenby 'Jelka Delius', *DSJ* 79 (1983), 7–12, at p. 10.

[52] *Letters 1*, p. 93. On the other hand, curiously, all Delius's letters to her began 'Dear Fräulein Gerhardi' – hardly endearing.

[53] Beecham wrote an amusing description of these events in *TB*, pp. 90 *et seq.*

[54] David Eccott, 'Florent Schmitt', in *MA&L*, pp. 113–53, at p. 127.

[55] *Letters 1*, p. 94.

[56] Letter to Eric Fenby, 6 December 1936.

[57] The expression was used in John Bridcutt's documentary film for the BBC, 'Delius: Composer, Lover, Enigma' (first broadcast 25 May 2012).

## FOLKERAADET

(1897: *RT* I/5; *CE* vol. 7)

WHILE living in Paris, Delius had met the Norwegian playwright and writer Gunnar Heiberg (1857–1929), who visited Delius in Grez in July 1897. Norway and Sweden had been united as a single kingdom since 1814, but the Norwegians' strong patriotism created resentment on the part of the Swedish, and a Norwegian demand to alter the constitution led to the establishment of political parties in 1884. Heiberg had just finished a five-act play called *Folkeraadet* (*Parliament*) – which Delius was able to read in the original Norwegian – a satire on 'the professional politician who mouths patriotic sentiments from the platform, and encourages others to sacrifice their lives in wars in which he is usually careful not to participate'.[58] Delius readily accepted Heiberg's request that he write some incidental music to it, and the work was finished in time for the first run of the play only three months later.

The music consists of a prelude to Act 1, interludes before Acts 2, 3 and 5, and two extremely brief 'Melodramas' (of nine and ten bars respectively) to be played during the second and fifth acts. The prelude and the first two interludes, respectively marked 'Con moto', 'Con spirito' and 'Allegro energico' are mainly jaunty and quite brassy, while the last is a 'Marcia, lento solenne', with a forceful ending 'Allegro moderato con umore'. Like the *American Rhapsody*, however, the work does not show any appreciable advance in Delius's compositional skills.

The most notable thing about it was its première on 18 October, at the Christiania Theatre in Oslo, conducted by Per Winge: it caused an uproar. In an attempt to emphasise the satire of the play, Delius had incorporated the theme of the Norwegian National Anthem, 'Ja, vi elsker', into the third and fourth interludes – in the latter, turning it into a funeral march in a minor key. Although he had not deliberately 'sent it up', a substantial part of the audience took great exception to what he had done, and there was serious booing, hissing, jeering and whistling to counteract the applause from Delius's and Heiberg's supporters. The demonstrations were repeated at every performance, but nevertheless the play continued to attract large audiences, enjoying a *succès de scandale*; the music got good and bad reviews, reflecting the differing reactions of the audience. The climax of the protests came on 1 November, when a twenty-five-year-old painter fired a revolver, albeit loaded only with blanks, at Winge three times before he was forcibly removed by the police (who were by now attending every performance). In the event, Delius withdrew the music twice during the run, the second occasion on 4 November at the request of the orchestra, who did not appreciate their efforts being sabotaged, and for the remainder of the run of the play the orchestra pit was empty. Delius does

---

[58] *MMB*, p. 117.

not seem to have been particularly upset at the failure, and it certainly did not affect his continued love for Norway and its people.[59]

The last two movements were included in the St James's Hall concert, but *Folkeraadet* was not performed complete until 12 January 1974, when it was recorded by the BBC Concert Orchestra under Ashley Lawrence for subsequent broadcasting.

## 'SEVEN DANISH SONGS'
### (1897: *RT* III/4; *CE* vols 15a and 15b)

*Silken Shoes (Seidenschuhe, or Silkesco over gylden Laest)
(J. P. Jacobsen); Irmelin [Rose] (J. P. Jacobsen); Summer
Nights (On the Seashore) (Holger Drachmann); In the
Seraglio Garden (Im Garten des Serails) (J. P. Jacobsen); Wine
Roses (J. P. Jacobsen); Through long, long Years (Red Roses)
(J. P. Jacobsen); Let Springtime come then (Den Lenz lass
Kommen) (J. P. Jacobsen)*

THAT Delius is nowadays properly regarded as a true cosmopolitan is clearly evidenced by the choice of texts for his sixty-nine songs, which were selected from Norwegian, Danish, German, French and English poets. Arguably the Danish influence is the greatest, for he wrote fifteen songs to Danish poems by Hans Christian Andersen (1805–75), Holger Drachmann (1846–1908), Jens Peter Jacobsen (1847–85) and Ludwig Holstein (1864–1943).[60] But this particular group of songs, which follows *Maud* as Delius's second set with an orchestral accompaniment, uses texts by just two poets: Jacobsen and Drachmann.

Jacobsen was an interesting character. Originally a botanist of some standing, he translated Charles Darwin's *The Origin of the Species* and *The Descent of Man* into Danish, and became one of the foremost Darwinians in Denmark. As an author he produced only two novels (*Niels Lyhne* would provide the story for Delius's *Fennimore and Gerda*), some short stories, and a single book of often dreamy, melancholic and wistful poems (one of which Delius used for the 'mysterious, troubled landscape'[61] of *An Arabesque* in 1911); despite this, he was one of Denmark's most influential writers, and began the 'naturalist' movement there. The naturalists believed that imaginative literature should be based on scientific knowledge, describing believable everyday realities and people as they really are (as distinct from, for example, Romanticism or Surrealism, in which subjects may receive highly symbolic, idealistic, or even supernatural treatment). Holger Drachmann, on the other hand, was a successful painter of

---

[59] See Lionel Carley, 'Folkeraadet: Performance and History' in *MA&L*, pp. 211–59.

[60] See generally John Bergsagel, 'Delius and Danish Literature' in *MA&L*, pp. 290–310; Michael Green, 'The Influential Danish Poets', *DSJ* 142 (2007), 55–60.

[61] Christopher Palmer, sleeve note to Unicorn-Kanchana DKP(CD)9063.

ships and the sea, and when he turned to writing they were a constant influence on his work. Like Jacobsen, he came under the influence of the Danish critic and writer Georg Brandes (1842–1927), but unlike him Drachmann was a prolific writer, producing many novels and plays, and much poetry.[62]

These songs have both orchestral and piano accompaniments, and it is probable that the latter came first. In the autograph score dated 1897 the accompaniments are all orchestral, but it seems that the piano ones date from 1894 onwards. Although Delius probably conceived them as a set, they did not appear as such: numbers 1, 2 and 4 were published by Harmonic Verlag in 1906, numbers 3, 5 and 6 by Stainer & Bell in 1973, and number 7 by Tischer & Jagenberg in 1915. Although all Delius's 'Danish' songs 'were first composed in their original language' [i.e. Danish],[63] they were not in fact so published until 1998.[64] Of the present seven, five were originally published with both German and English words, and two with English ones alone. Delius made all the English translations, six of the seven German ones were by Jelka, and that of *Wine Roses* was by Jacobsen's own translator.

This is a beautiful set of songs by any standards, with vocal lines that are a joy to sing, and it is strange that (even given the general failure of concert promoters to programme almost any Delius) they have only been rarely performed. An analysis of them will be found in Chapter 9.

The first hearing of numbers 6, 7, 2, 3 and 5 (in that order) was in Delius's concert at the St James's Hall on 30 May 1899, and this might well have been the spur for Delius to orchestrate them. They were sung by the French soprano Christianne Andray, with Alfred Hertz conducting. Numbers 1 and 4 received their premières at a concert of the Societé National de Musique in Paris on 16 March 1901, with Christianne Andray again, and Vincent D'Indy conducting. Debussy was there, and wrote a scathing few words in the Parisian literary and artistic magazine *La Revue blanche*: 'very sweet songs, very pale, music to lull convalescent ladies to sleep in the rich quarters'.[65]

---

[62] There are many references to Jacobsen and Drachmann (as well as those other Danish poets) in the 'Delius and Denmark' section of *DSJ* 142 (2007).

[63] Letter 533.

[64] As *CE*, supp. vol. 5.

[65] Claude Debussy, 'A la Société Nationale', *La Revue blanche* 24 (April 1901), 550–1, at p. 551.

## PIANO CONCERTO
### (1897–1907: *RT* VII/4; *CE* supp. vol. 3 [1904 version]; *CE* vol. 29a [1907 version])

F INALLY, 1897 saw the genesis of what was to become the Piano Concerto. This now exists for performance in two separate forms: as a three-movement version dating from 1904 and in a later revision into one continuous movement, dating from 1907. Tracing the relationship between these two versions involves a tortuous journey, which begins in 1897 when Delius completed a one-movement *Fantasy* for piano and orchestra. It was never performed in public, although the composer did play it through privately with Busoni on two pianos. Then, in the autumn of 1904, a seemingly different work for piano and orchestra (more imposingly called a concerto) was scheduled for performance in Germany at the Stadthalle, Elberfeld, with Julius Buths as the soloist and the Elberfelder Konzertgesellschaft, conducted by Hans Haym. In fact this was not a different work but an evolution of the old one. The 1897 *Fantasy* had consisted of three longish sections linked together, the third being a shorter repeat of the first whilst the second provided contrasting music in a much slower tempo. By 1904 Delius's concept of the work had radically changed, though it is not known why, and he had decided to recast the bulk of the material in three separate movements. Maybe other musicians (Buths, perhaps?) had advocated this restructuring in order to give the work a better chance of succeeding as a conventional concerto rather than a fantasy, a term implying something more lightweight. Whatever the reason, it involved Delius writing a completely new third movement. The original middle section of the *Fantasy* was able to form the basis of a self-contained slow movement, whilst the outer sections were conflated into the opening *Allegro*.

In this three-movement form the retitled concerto had several successful performances, but it was soon destined to undergo yet further transformation, back in the direction from which it had come. For Delius now decided to discard the newly written third movement altogether, and return to a revision of his original material and its structure as a one-movement work in three sections. But even that is not quite the end of this complicated story. Delius consulted the virtuoso Theodor Szántó[66] and asked for advice about the effectiveness of the solo part. It was possibly the worst thing he could have done. Szántó was not content just to retouch the piano part here and there: he radically rewrote it so that hardly a bar remained unaltered or unadorned with the most conventional virtuoso flim-flam. The effect is something like the musical equivalent of a medieval church being insensitively Victorianised. Regrettably Delius himself sanctioned this vulgar refurbishment (though it has to be said that he put his foot down about yet further adornments which

---

[66] Theodor Szántó (1877–1934): an Hungarian pianist and composer, he settled in Paris in 1905 and was introduced to Delius in 1906.

the pianist tried to add in later years). In this travestied form the concerto was performed by Szántó at a Promenade Concert in Queen's Hall[67] on 22 October 1907, with Henry Wood conducting,[68] and it remained popular in England for many years: Benno Moiseiwitsch was a notable exponent, recording it in 1946 (with the Philharmonia Orchestra under Constant Lambert), and reviving it at the 1955 Proms with Malcolm Sargent conducting.

Taking the 1904 three-movement version first, it is one of the few examples of Delius following the textbook rules of traditional sonata form (another is the early Violin Sonata in B major). The opening 'Allegro ma non troppo' introduces a first-subject group in the home key, C minor, consisting of several distinct ideas: a hymn-like one from the strings (bars 1–10) answered by a downward flourish from the piano; a soaring string melody on the 1st and 2nd violins (bars 11–16) backed by forceful piano chords; a lyrical *molto espressivo* motif sung by the piano above left-hand arpeggios (bars 16–24) interrupted by anguished chromatic scales from the strings (bars 25–7); and a further piano melody shaped by harmonic sequences (bars 28–30) leading to some octave passage-work that gives the required virtuoso feel to this opening. These are all strong concepts and they occur succinctly in the space of just over thirty bars. The briefest of links (bars 33–5) from piano and woodwind then leads to the second subject (in E flat, the relative major) introduced by the four horns and answered by the strings, an idea which is soon taken up solo by the piano. Delius muses on this attractive theme for a while, but then takes us straight on to the development section (bars 70–127) which displays considerable variety of texture (the soloist sometimes heroic, sometimes poetic) as it playfully investigates a selection of the copious material already heard. The recapitulation is begun by the piano (bar 128) announcing the opening theme chordally and *fortissimo* before Delius takes us over the exposition material once more, with the second subject now in the tonic major as the textbooks say it should be. The piano provides a brief but forceful coda.

The second movement, 'Largo', is a fine inspiration, mostly restrained and poetic and cast, like the slow movement of Grieg's concerto which clearly inspired it,[69] in the rich key of D flat. The main theme also owes much to the Norwegian composer – though Delius's piano writing tends to be essentially chordal in texture, a stylistic trait that also characterises his later piano parts in the songs and string sonatas. Not that he is incapable of writing Chopinesque passage-work when he wants to – an example being the semiquavers which ripple above the strings' announcement of the theme from bar 15 onwards. This

---

[67] Queen's Hall, in Langham Place off Upper Regent Street, was London's principal concert hall from 1893 until 1941, when it was destroyed in an air-raid.

[68] The concerto was subsequently performed again at the Proms 21 times up until 2012.

[69] Grieg had given Delius a copy of his own Piano Concerto in 1897, the year in which they first met.

movement is more or less monothematic, although there is a subsidiary idea which is introduced lyrically by the strings in bar 42 and taken up extensively by the piano (bar 45 onwards). The main theme returns very quietly in the piano and lower strings (bar 61) and this highly effective – and affective – movement then dreams its way to a hushed close.

The opening of the finale, 'Maestoso con moto moderato', is certainly a bold conception, not only for its 5/4 time signature but also for its scoring: three bassoons and cello, with the piano filling in the chordal harmonies. The main theme fits its prescribed metre awkwardly and the extra beat seems just that, adding an unnatural limp as the music treads its heavy-footed – and unmemorable – way. There is a second theme (4/4) in E flat (bars 38–47) introduced by the strings and subsequently heard in the piano, but again it is not especially distinctive. There is a brief development section (bar 61 *et seq.*) before the recapitulation, where we find the concerto's only cadenza, a poetic affair beginning at bar 154 (Delius recycled portions of it some years later for the Violin Concerto – see Chapter 7); a forceful coda at bar 195 ends this unsatisfactory movement, a somewhat unworthy companion to the rest of the work.

Delius was undoubtedly right to revert, in 1907, to the structure of the 1897 *Fantasy* and discard the finale altogether in favour of a tripartite structure based on just the first two movements. The exposition and development sections of the 1904 first movement now lead without a break into the slow movement, which is then linked to the original first movement recapitulation but with the cadenza omitted. This was not just a scissors and paste job: in restructuring, Delius also refashioned some of the material to make the joins fit. But what was far and away more drastic – in fact an utterly disastrous miscalculation – was to have allowed Szántó to rewrite and expand the original piano part so fundamentally that hardly one bar was left intact. The revision is vulgar and overblown. Compare the examples below in which Delius's delicate semiquaver passage-work in the second movement of 1904 (bars 15–18) (Ex. 3.7) is unnecessarily inflated by Szántó in its 1907 version (Ex. 3.8):

Ex. 3.7

Ex. 3.8

*dolce e leggiero*

**pp** *sempre una corda*

*legato*
Ped          ✻ Ped                    ✻

Elsewhere there are countless instances of strenuous but otiose double-octave reworkings along with torrential chromatic runs and arpeggios (Exx. 3.9, 3.10). The passage between Figs. 11+1 and 13+1 in the 1907 version is another particularly gruesome example. If only Delius had contented himself with reorchestrating passages from the 1904 score where he felt the soloist needed a lighter accompanying texture. But the damage has been done and the Piano Concerto in its 1907 manifestation is not much loved, even by avid Delians; the general verdict is that it is inflated and bombastic. What would now be the best compromise (though involving yet another version!) would be to discard the weak third movement of 1904 and recast the first and second movements according to the structure of 1907, retaining the original orchestration and piano part without the Szántó accretions – in other words back to where the fantasy-concerto sprang from in 1897.[70]

After Szántó's 1907 first performance of 'his' version, views on the work were mixed:

Like several modern concertos, the work is written in three continuous movements, all of which are based on one theme with various modifications. Mr Delius has got a good theme, which leads itself very well to elaborate treatment; his subsidiary themes, too, are good, the second subject of the first movement being particularly beautiful, and both this and the theme of the *largo* (a modification of the main subject) are worked up into imposing climaxes, in which there are moments of inspiration. But in spite of all this, the concerto as a whole is not quite

---

[70] For a much fuller discussion of the differences between the two versions, see Robert Threlfall, 'The Early Versions of Delius's Piano Concerto', in *Companion*, pp. 239–48.

Ex. 3.9

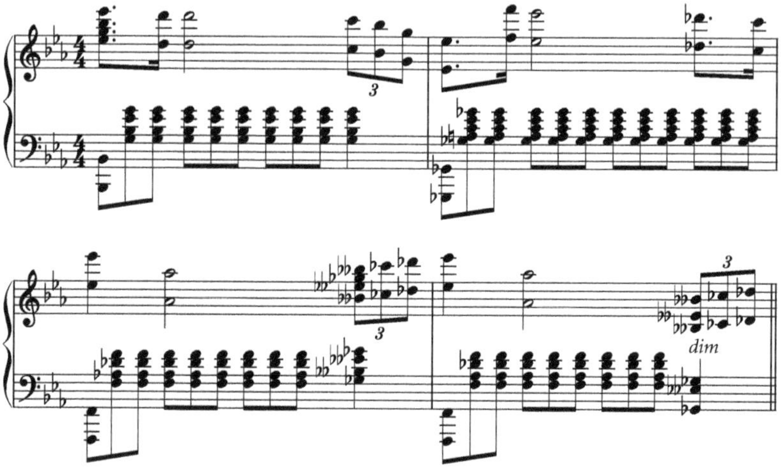


Ex. 3.10

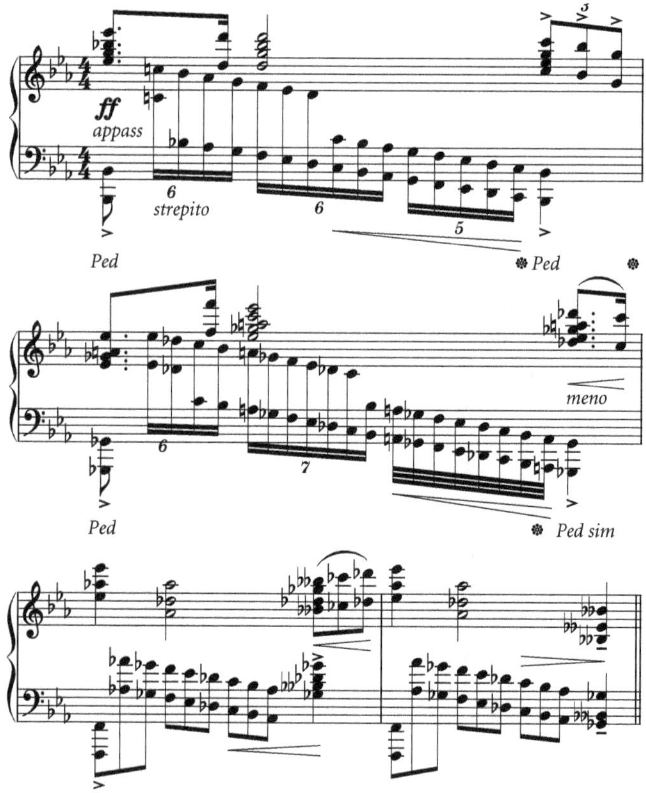

successful. In the first place, a feeling of monotony is engendered by the fact that almost every tune in the concerto is written *maestoso*, or, if not actually *maestoso*, it is *largo* or *moderato in tempo* and in treatment is heavy, and sometimes even pompous. The orchestration, too, is frequently heavy, and the piano part is often accompanying the orchestra with series of chords and arpeggios, something in the manner of the opening of Tchaikovsky's B♭ minor concerto – a trick which gives too much solidity when it is too often repeated; and finally there is a good deal of decoration for the piano which is purely formal and not very interesting; successions of scales, for instance, and long runs up and down the instrument, in thirds. M. Szántó played his part with great energy, but he had a tendency to bang, and frequently hurried the time too much and got ahead of the band.

*The Times*, 23 October 1907

On a first hearing the work conveys the impression that intimate acquaintance would be required fully to appreciate the significance of the music, albeit the style is sufficiently direct to at once stir the imagination of the listener and excite his admiration. The chief characteristics of the concerto are virility and strenuousness. Passionate passages deepen into poignancy, but a tranquil spirit ultimately prevails, and in the last movement the glorified treatment of the principal theme of the work seems to suggest triumph over adverse influences. The solo part was most brilliantly played by Mr. Theodor Szántó, a newcomer of whom we should hear more. The concerto received an enthusiastic reception.

*The Musical Times*, November 1907

while Delius received the following letter:

33 Oakley Street
Chelsea SW

Dear old Frederico,

I dare not talk to you to-night before that heterogeneous mob, & I could not write about your work. Frankly I did not think the interest sustained to the end, *because* the end was so badly played. But up to 2-3rds – till after the Largo – the poignancy of the emotion was so strong that had you gone on I must have collapsed. I think I never was so moved by modern music as by that, in spite of horns 'cracking' etc. And for that reason, old hand as I am, I could not write. My notice conveys nothing, I fear, though it may show one or two that I felt the sincerity of the composition. Also I felt not a little bitter at all the youths being there & regarding themselves as your equal – But for the genuine emotion, for the sheer loveliness of that Largo, I thank you sincerely & from the bottom of a heart that I thought was growing stoney & cynical & hard as nails.

At 1.15 tomorrow

Yrs gratefully & cordially

Robin H. Legge[71]

The work was played again only eight days later, on 29 October, in Berlin with August Schmidt-Lindner as the soloist; Max Schillings conducted, and after the performance he wrote to Delius:

> Thus your piano concerto appears to have been found too serious. The reception in the evening was very warm; Schmid Lindner [*sic*] played his part excellently and with affection, I think we did justice to the work, but what I have read about it so far is sheer nonsense; someone discovered that you have now gone over to the unrestrained impressionistic manner of the new French school & moreover your work is 10 years old & belongs to a "long-outmoded" movement in its melody & austere form. Priceless!
>
> I greatly enjoyed your work. Certainly the instrumentation is rather heavy; but of course it is not really a concerto *for* piano but *with* piano. I am not quite sure about the ending (from the Maestoso on); it seems to me as if it is rather too terse? Or am I wrong? I am rather ashamed that you had so colossal a success with the concerto in London, & it is a bad sign for Berlin. But there too it will probably change![72]

It is notable that, by the middle of 1915, Beecham had conducted the concerto (in the 1904 version, with four different soloists, including Percy Grainger) no fewer than eight times; on 8 February 1915 the soloist was Benno Moiseiwitsch, and one critic thought it 'One of the most obviously beautiful of this composer's works';[73] in December 1916, William Murdoch played it in Liverpool: 'a noble work that deserved more frequent hearing … he appeared in the uniform of the Grenadier Guards, of whose band he is at present a member.'[74]

As mentioned at the beginning of Chapter 2, in his early days in Paris, Delius had made a good friend of the painter Georges-Daniel de Monfreid, who was now acting as an informal agent for Paul Gauguin. During the spring or summer of 1898, Delius made up his quarrel with his uncle Theodor over the funding of a performance of *The Magic Fountain* – which was lucky, as Theodor then unexpectedly died, leaving Delius a legacy of 25,000 francs. In the November Delius learned from de Monfreid that Gauguin's striking, and now famous, painting *Nevermore* – a naked woman reclining on a bed, her head resting on a yellow cushion – was for sale. On 11 November Delius took him a cheque for 500 francs, and de Monfreid wrote to Gauguin saying that

---

[71] Letter 230. Robin (Humphrey) Legge (1862–1933): at that time a staff critic on *The Daily Telegraph*, of which he later became music editor.

[72] Letter 234.

[73] *The Musical Times* 60, March 1915.

[74] *Liverpool Echo*, 8 December 1916.

Delius had bought it 'because it is a *beautiful painting*. An opinion which I fully share'.[75] It originally hung in Delius's music room, but he sold it in 1920, when somewhat financially embarrassed, and after Jelka had painted a copy of it for them to keep.[76] Within the next six months, however, there was to be a far bigger call on the legacy.

## MITTERNACHTSLIED ZARATHUSTRAS
### (1898: *RT* II/1; *CE* vol. 10)

I N 1889, Delius had spent over two months of the summer in Norway, partly at the home of his friend, Arve Arvesen. This visit sparked off Delius's deep and lifelong interest in the works of the German philosopher and writer Friedrich Nietzsche,[77] with whom he immediately and passionately identified:

> When, one wet day, a few years later, [Delius] was looking for something to read in the library of a Norwegian friend with whom he was staying during a walking tour, and had taken down a book, *Thus Spake Zarathustra*[78] – a book, for all and none – by one Friedrich Nietzsche, he was ripe for it. That book, he told me, never left his hands until he had devoured it from cover to cover. It was the very book he had been seeking all along, and finding that book he declared to be one of the most important events of his life. Nor did he rest content until he had read every work of Nietzsche that he could lay his hands on; and the poison entered into his soul.[79]

In her *Memories of Frederick Delius*,[80] Jelka wrote:

> At that time [early in 1896] I was full of enthusiasm for Nietzsche's Zarathustra which I was reading, and I was greatly surprised when this young Englishman said he knew and loved Zarathustra

and about six months later she asked him:

> I wonder whether you are composing Nietzsche? I am longing for that. I have discovered several other poems of his, and send you a little one: the others are all longer. Would you like copies? I hope you may feel inspired by this one! The big ones are very fine: Dionyssos – Dithyramben.[81]

---

[75] *Letters 1*, p. 140.

[76] *Letters 1*, p. 141.

[77] Friedrich (Wilhelm) Nietzsche (1844–1900); see below, Chapter 4.

[78] *Also sprach Zarathustra: ein Buch für Alle und Keinen* (*Thus Spake Zarathustra: A Book for All and None*), written between 1883 and 1885.

[79] *Fenby 1*, p. 171.

[80] Jelka Delius, 'Memories of Frederick Delius', in *Letters 1*, appendix 7.

[81] Letter 65. The text of the poem is included in it.

He replied: 'The verses you sent me are beautiful many thanks – I shall compose them.'[82] In the event, he did not, but within some eighteen months he had completed his next major work – the choral and orchestral *Mitternachtslied Zarathustras*. After Delius's death, Jelka wrote about an evening probably in the second half of 1897, not long after he had moved into her house:

> Fred was still working in his empty room downstairs, when he called me and Ida to hear a song he had written to words of Nietzsche. It was the 'Mitternachtslied' from Zarathustra: 'O Mensch! gib Acht!' etc. and formed the nucleus of the great 'Mass of Life'. It was quite wonderful. We sat on cushions on the floor, and Fred at the piano with a flickering candle played to us that solemn and intense song '... Doch alle Lust will Ewigkeit ...'; the greatest yearning of humanity was expressed so beautifully, and I was overcome with the wonder of it all, that in my house this had been created, that Fred was so gifted and had all his life before him to create such beautiful things. I resolved to give him all help and assistance in my power.[83]

That song (now published as *Noch ein Mal* in *CE* Volume 18b) was quite soon expanded into the present work.

Delius selected the text himself from parts 2, 3 and 4 of the seventy-ninth chapter of *Also sprach Zarathustra*, and the work was dedicated to his cousin Arthur Krönig. It was first performed at the concert in the St James's Hall the following May, but notwithstanding its relative success, there seemed no possibility of another performance in England – so Delius turned to the Continent. In 1900, he tried, but failed, to interest the great conductor Artur Nikisch – in a letter to Ida he said, 'I cannot quite understand why such a good musician should be scared by Zarathustra.'[84] However, Delius had another idea. When Hans Haym had given the first performance of *Over the Hills and Far Away* in 1897, Buths was in the audience. As Jelka later wrote:

> [He] came over for this concert, and altho' he was rather forbidding and critical, one could notice that he was very interested. A year or so later, Fred sent him the score of his 'Midnight Song from Zarathustra.' Buths went to great pains studying it, and to this end copied out the whole orchestral score. In the end he wrote to Fred that he could not in all conscience perform it.[85]

So, although Delius told Jelka on 25 October 1900 that:

> I went to Düsseldorf this afternoon & had a chat with Buths, who is a very nice man. He promised to look at my things later in the season but

[82] *Ibid.*, n. 10.

[83] Jelka Delius, 'Memories of Frederick'.

[84] Letter 110.

[85] Jelka Delius, 'Memories of Frederick'.

his programmes were already settled for this season. I took Zarathustra with me & will send it to him later on …'[86]

There is no evidence that, despite Buths's apparent 'feel' for the music, a performance resulted. Delius's next hope was Siegfried Ochs (1858–1929), the conductor of the Berliner Philharmonische Chor, and a month later, when Delius was in Berlin, he wrote to Jelka and Ida: 'I shall go to Ochs tomorrow morning with Zarathustra – But really hope for nothing here.'[87] He was proved right, as he found that Ochs was away.

At last, however, *Mitternachtslied* did have its second performance, under Haym in Elberfeld on 15 November 1902, with Delius (not surprisingly) in the audience. Max Schillings, who was also there, thought the work 'very interesting and *Stimmungsvoll* [atmospheric]', but in the event he was unable to do it himself – and he recommended it to Hermann Suter,[88] who conducted it at the Tonkünstlerfest in Basel on 12 June 1903, again with Delius present.[89] Haym was very keen to know how it had gone, and Delius must also have written to Grieg telling him about that performance, for Grieg wrote:

> Congratulations on Basel! Do send me the piece when it comes out. What a pity it is from 'Zarathustra'. I have to think of Strauss, and I have no stomach for Strauss![90]

To which Delius replied:

> I don't need to tell you my *Mitternachtslied* has absolutely no relationship with the Strauss Zarathustra, which I consider a complete failure.[91]

*Mitternachtslied Zarathustras* was never published, but six years later, in 1904, Delius incorporated it in its entirety – with a few vocal changes, but the original orchestration – into the final movement of *A Mass of Life*.

In the autumn of 1898, Delius set Nietzsche again, in the four *Songs to Poems by Friedrich Nietzsche* (see below, Chapter 9). He sent them to Krönig, who replied: 'We will study your songs with great pleasure. I consider Nietzsche quite unsuitable for musical treatment. He is not sombre enough.'[92]

---

[86] Letter 112.

[87] Letter 114.

[88] Hermann Suter (1870–1926): eminent Swiss conductor, who was also a composer. He worked in Zurich from 1892 until 1902, when he moved to Basel, where he was the director of the Conservatorium for three years at the end of his life. *A Dictionary of Modern Music and Musicians*, ed. A. E. Hull (London: J. M. Dent, 1924) describes him as 'Without doubt the most eminent Swiss conductor. His oratorio performances have justly become famous.'

[89] In the programmes for both concerts, it was referred to by Delius's original titles, *Das Trunkene Lied* or *Das Nachtlied Zarathustras*.

[90] *Grieg & Delius*, Letter 78.

[91] Ibid., Letter 80

[92] Letter 83.

## LA RONDE SE DÉROULE
## (THE DANCE GOES ON)
### (1899: *RT* VI/13; *CE* vol. 24a)

THIS piece followed *Mitternachtslied Zarathustras*. As we have seen, Delius had first been to Norway in 1881, working for Delius & Co. – and, having completed the firm's business in Sweden, on his way back to England he travelled via Norway, and was completely bowled over by it. He quickly realised that he had a 'secret affinity' with the mountains and fjords, and they became a constant source of inspiration to him for the next thirty years. He was introduced to Scandinavian literature, and not only became extremely well read in it, but in due course also came to know a large number of Scandinavian writers. It was in fact another ten years before he first went to Denmark, and then only for a short while – but, most significantly, one evening he had dinner in Copenhagen with the Danish lyric poet Helge Rode,[93] who became his 'oldest and most constant friend'.[94] In 1898, Rode wrote a play, *Dansen Gaar*, and Delius originally considered writing some incidental music to it – but in the event it never materialised, and instead the play became the inspiration for this orchestral piece, written the following year. The imagery in the work, with its Nietzschean overtones, clearly appealed to Delius, and he quoted some lines from it at the head of the autograph score:

> The Dance of Life. My picture shall be called the dance of life! There will be two people who are dancing in flowing clothes on a clear night through an avenue of black cypresses and red rose bushes. The earth's glorious blood will gleam and blaze in the roses, Claire [the poet's love]. He holds her tightly against himself. He is deeply serious and happy. There will be something festal about it. He will hold her to himself so firmly that she is half sunk into him. She will be frightened – frightened – and yet something will awaken inside her. Strength is streaming into her from him. And before them is the abyss.

The piece was played only a few months later, at the St James's Hall concert in May, with the ink barely dry on the copyists' parts. It is not known to have been performed since, and was never published. However, Delius revised and extended it in 1900–1 to become *Lebenstanz* (*Life's Dance*) (see below).

---

[93] Helge Rode (1870–1937): one of the Danish poets who helped to revive lyric poetry in the 1890s, he might have been introduced to Delius by Edvard Munch, whose picture *The Dance of Life* was painted in 1900. Rode was also a playwright and a journalist.

[94] John Bergsagel, 'Frederick Delius and Danish Literature', at http://thompsonian. info/edansklitt.htm [accessed 18 March 2014].

D ELIUS had been getting more and more exasperated by his failure to interest any English publishers other than Augener in his music, which had produced a few songs, and he started seriously thinking about promoting an orchestral and choral concert himself. At the end of 1898, he therefore went to London to start organising it, and although he had made little progress by the end of the year, the situation then improved dramatically. He was introduced (possibly by Jutta Bell) to a concert agent, R. Norman-Concorde, who had a grandiose plan for a 'London Permanent Opera'; both saw it as an opportunity for putting on one or more of Delius's three as yet unperformed operas – primarily *Koanga*. Delius, however, soon realised that the scheme would not work, and enlisted Norman-Concorde's help in mounting a concert instead. It entailed a huge amount of work, and although there were disappointments along the way it eventually took place on 30 May 1899, at the St James's Hall.[95] Alfred Hertz came over from Breslau and conducted an *ad hoc* orchestra of ninety-four,[96] a small professional choir, an enormous amateur chorus and eight soloists. The publicity was very good, and consequently there was 'a fairly large and by no means unappreciative audience which listened from half-past eight until nearly midnight'.[97] That audience included a gratifying number of critics – and the concert was 'unquestionably the main talking point of the day in musical circles'.[98]

The programme was:

1. *Over the Hills and Far Away*
2. *Légende* for violin and orchestra (John Dunn)
3. *Folkeraadet* (third and fourth movements)
4. *Five Danish Songs* (Christianne Andray)
5. *La Ronde se déroule*
6. *Mitternachtslied Zarathustras* (Douglas Powell)
   Interval

---

[95] Opened in 1858, it had façades to both Regent Street and Piccadilly, and was built by the music-publishing firms Chappell & Co. and Cramer & Co., specifically to attract to central London the large audiences who went to the concerts at Crystal Palace.

[96] See *PW*, p. 56, and the lavish concert programme. It was led by Delius's Norwegian friend Halfdan Jebe, and included some of London's top-class players – among them the clarinettist Charles Draper, the horn players Adolf Borsdorf and A. E. Brain and the double bassist Claude Hobday, all now legendary figures who were founder members of the London Symphony Orchestra in 1904.

[97] *PW*, p. 57.

[98] *Letters 1*, p. 142.

7. Excerpts from *Koanga*:

Prelude to Act III, Quintet and Finale of Act I

Act II complete (Ella Russell, Tily Koenen, G. A. Vanderbeek, William Llewellyn and Andrew Black)[99]

All were first performances except for the first and third items.

As was to become the norm, the reviews were divided, and both in view of the importance of the concert in Delius's career, and to get a broad picture of how the music struck the critics, an unusually large number of them is quoted here. The *Sunday Sun* declared that:

It is not easy to associate optimism with a composer who takes for a subject for musical illustration such a work as 'Also sprach Zarathustra' by Friedrich Nietzsche. M. Delius' music is bizarre and cacophonous to a degree almost unapproached. There is nothing beautiful in ugliness, though M. Delius evidently is not of my way of thinking. The ugliness of some of his music is really masterly. Oh! if he could be persuaded to look on the brighter side of things, to give us music that would cheer us, not that which blights us as a March wind blights young shoots. If M. Delius may be claimed as one of the rising English school of composers it is his manifest duty 'to cheer up'. It is so much more easy to be a pessimist than an optimist. His gifts are undeniable. Would that some god would give him the gift to see himself as I see him. I want to be cheered by music not depressed. Life itself gives one one's share of the blues. Heaven help us if our young composers are going to assist!

4 June 1899

Others wrote in the same vein:

but in St James's Hall I must own that banjos seemed incongruous to me after long quotations, or reminiscences, from *Tristan*.

*The Saturday Review*, 3 June 1899

although the following week the same paper (but presumably another critic) took a different view:

Every bar of Mr Delius's music shows high musicianship, an astonishing mastery of notes, and a degree of vital energy quite as astonishing.

*The Saturday Review*, 10 June 1899

Most of the critics (who had probably gone rather unwillingly) were, however, full of praise:

we recognise in Mr Delius a composer of strong originality. His music is sure to be warmly discussed ... we own to having been deeply impressed,

[99] Interestingly, Russell and Black both reduced their fees (normally forty guineas) by one-half and two-thirds respectively, and the other singers did not charge at all. (See Letter 97).

and we gladly welcome the advent of a composer who has something to say, and is not afraid of saying it.

*The Morning Post*, 31 May 1899

It is long since we have heard so striking a work [as *La Ronde se déroule*]. The music palpitates with excitement and sends the blood tingling through one's veins. It is splendidly graphic and intensely engrossing ... Here again [in *Mitternachtslied*] Mr. Delius shows himself deeply impressive and original. He does not shrink from employing the strangest and most perilous harmonic progressions ... We have said enough to show that in Mr. Delius we recognize a musician of very great and noble talent. His music is essentially of today, or, rather, of tomorrow, which is all in its favour. That it may speedily make its way is our most earnest wish.

*The Morning Post*, 3 June 1899

Mr. Delius has fully justified his appeal to the musical public, that he has shown himself to be possessed of genuine, we might also add commanding, talent, and that his further acquaintance is eminently desirable.

*The Morning Advertiser*, 21 May 1899

Certainly, it may be hoped that enterprising concert managers may no longer allow his unquestionable talents to languish unrecognised ... He is a musician not only of promise but of achievement.

*The Westminster Gazette*, 31 May 1899

Much has been written concerning the music of Mr Fritz Delius, who gave an orchestral concert at the end of May. Of one thing the composer may be sure: his compositions aroused considerable interest, and we shall be glad to hear these and others again.

*Musical Opinion*, July 1899

In a two-page article in *The Musical Standard* on 3 June 1899, E. A. Baughan wrote:

Personally, I admit that some of Mr. Delius' music sounded discordant to my ears, harsh, uninviting, and ugly. But I could hear that he made it so with a definite purpose in view, and I can quite imagine that I might get to like those discords if I knew them better. That is what happened with Wagner's music.

The most sympathetic and complete review was in *The Musical Times*:

Until May 30 last the name of Mr. Fritz Delius was scarcely known in England, but from the talent displayed in his compositions at his concert on that date at St. James's Hall it is probable that in the near future we shall make intimate acquaintance with some of his compositions. In spite of their frequent wildness, lack of reticence, and occasionally apparent want of knowledge of the best means to secure the desired effects, they possess a boldness of conception and virile strength that command and hold attention. ... The programme, consisting entirely of his own compositions, was in itself indicative of ambitious aims and extensive musical knowledge. It opened with a Fantasia for orchestra entitled 'Over the hills and far away,' which, by reason of the expressiveness of its themes and the deft use of the instruments, created a favourable impression. This was followed by a Legende for violin and orchestra, somewhat vague in form, but picturesque and well laid out for the solo instrument, played by Mr. John Dunn.

Two remarkable movements from an orchestral suite, formed from incidental music to a drama entitled 'Folkeraadet,' excited much attention. The first movement given (the third number of the suite) was an *Allegro energico* in C, specially notable for the brilliancy of its orchestration and extraordinary treatment of the Norwegian National air. The second performed (the fourth number of the suite) illustrates a change of popular sentiment, from grief for the dead to derision on the discovery of a deception, a strange incident which is set forth with great dramatic power and sense of humour. A symphonic poem based upon a morbid story and entitled 'The Dance goes on,' also showed decided gifts of musical expression. Criticism must be reserved on a setting for baritone solo, male chorus, and orchestra of an incoherent poem, called 'Also Sprach Zarathustra,' by Friedrich Nietzsche, as some of the band parts were apparently wrong, and more than once cacophony rather than music reigned supreme. The vocalist was Mr. Douglas Powell. But although opinions may differ on the musical value of this last-named composition, and also of a long excerpt from an opera, entitled 'Koanga' ... there can be no doubt concerning the expressive character of several miscellaneous songs, which were rendered by Mdlle. Christianne Andray, for those entitled 'Through long, long years' and 'On the seashore' are remarkable for poetical conception and perfect sympathy with the text.

June, 1899

Four years later, the critic and writer John F. Runciman (1851–91) summed up the reports of the concert:

The truth was that we didn't know what the devil to make of this music; and most of us were frank enough to say so. That there was intention, real mastery of notes; that every sound proceeding from the orchestra was meant by the composer; that there was no bungling, not from beginning to end an unanticipated effect – all this every competent critic knew. But the strains sounded unpleasant in our ears. ... [However] Delius has already done enough to justify me in calling him the biggest composer we have produced for many a long day.[100]

---

[100] *PW*, pp. 61–2.

And many years later Percy Young wrote:

> The reaction to this concert was that which has since become typical of the English towards 'modern music'. The (reasonably large) audience was polite; the critics, having nothing to work on, were generally perplexed by the alternating languors and asperities of a harmonic idiom that seemed to stem from no legitimate antecedents, and by the generally exotic flavour. They stood firm on the sole assumption that the composer had something to say, but were not sure that they understood his method of saying it. *The Yorkshire Post*, however, displayed an exceptional warmth: '[The] hearty force and intense life [of the music] are, however, such that it is with a feeling of patriotic pride that we are able to say that Mr. Delius was born and brought up in Yorkshire.'[101]

Delius told Jutta Bell on 4 June that 'The concert turned out far better than I had expected & may be called an artistic success',[102] and two days earlier Norman-Concorde had written to him:

> You have had a magnificent success far greater than could have been hoped for ... I was extremely sorry that you had to go – it was a business mistake as you wd have been the lion of the season ... and wd also have made many musical and moneyed friends who wd probably have subscribed something in the future – However I am glad for your happiness & your arts sake that you went. London was telling on you.[103]

In a classic show of disinterest, on reading a report in the *Yorkshire Times* Julius is said to have commented simply, 'I see that Fritz has given a concert.'[104]

Unfortunately, the cost was far more than the 85 guineas (around £8,000 today) that Norman-Concorde had originally quoted (including two shillings a day for sandwich-men carrying advertisements around the streets).[105] The orchestra had to be enlarged, extra rehearsals were needed, the impressive programme book had musical illustrations as well as the *Koanga* words, and a great deal was spent on advertising. In the event, the bill that Norman-Concorde sent him was around £450 (something in the region of £45,000– £50,000 today). Norman-Concorde had not, however, managed to secure any backers, so, after they had exchanged a good many very 'uncomfortable' letters, Delius had no alternative but to pay up from his own pocket.

---

[101] *Young*, p. 536. There are some interesting comments on the concert in Arthur Hutchings, *Delius* (London: Macmillan & Co., 1948), pp. 27–32.

[102] Letter 100.

[103] Letter 100, n. 1.

[104] *MMB*, p. 131.

[105] Letter 90.

Sadly, however, and notwithstanding the generally good reviews, the concert failed to bring Delius to the lasting notice of the musical public as a whole, and he had to wait another eight years before he had anything else played in an English concert hall. In those days it was virtually impossible for a composer to get his larger works performed unless he were able to interest an impresario or a conductor; but 'between 1899 and 1907 there was no highly gifted compatriot with the insight, the money or the influence to do for Delius what Beecham did in the following decades.'[106] His music, quite simply, confounded most of those who had never heard it before.

In the late summer, Delius went to Germany to try to get some interest from publishers, but failed again. He also spent time in Paris, Norway and Denmark. The autumn then saw him begin his largest purely orchestral work to date – *Paris*.

---

[106] Hutchings, *Delius*, p. 32.

## PARIS
### (EIN NACHTSTÜCK – THE SONG OF A GREAT CITY)
(1899–1900: *RT* VI/14; *CE* vol. 23b)

G IVEN Delius's love for, and intimate knowledge of, the less public and
well-known parts of Paris, it is hardly surprising either that he wrote
a musical impression of the city, or that it should be subtitled 'Nachtstück'
('Nocturne'). It is impossible to say whether there is an 'autobiographical'
element in the work, or anything which could possibly be thought specifically
to describe Delius's experiences in the cafés, dance halls, brothels, ateliers and
streets of Montparnasse and elsewhere. Delius did, however, copy a poem by
an unknown author on the flyleaf verso of an early autograph score (although it
was subsequently crossed out in blue pencil):[107]

> Mysterious city!
> Asleep whilst the crowds hurry bye [*sic*]
> To their many pursuits and pleasures
> Awakening as the twilight ~~softly~~ deepens
> ~~Tinging all things with mystery~~
>
> City of pleasure,
> of strange sensations
> of brazen music and dancing
> of painted and beautiful women.
>
> Secret city,
> unveiling but to those
> who ever shunning day
> return home in the pale blue light
> of scarcely breaking dawn
> and fall asleep to the song of awakening streets
> and the rising dawn.

As Philip Heseltine perceptively said, 'For Delius, Paris is not so much the capital
city of France as a corner of his own soul, a chapter of his own memoirs.'[108]

In analysing *Paris*, it is best to divide the score into seven separate sections
of alternately slow and faster music. With this composer one should not be
surprised that there is no apparent attempt to use any textbook formula such
as sonata form. But it should become clear that there is definitely a firm grasp
of structure. Sections I, III, V and VII form 'pillars' of essentially slow music,
each of relatively substantial duration, whilst sections II, IV and VI constitute
the 'arches' between them. These arches are briefer, each comprising around
two minutes of quick-moving music. The quicker music is mostly in compound

---

[107] *RT Supplement*, p. 199.
[108] *PW*, p. 118.

time signatures, usually 6/8 (even the 4/4 march in section IV has a 12/8 feel to it), thereby giving a sense of rhythmic unity to these three hedonistic episodes. Furthermore, Delius ensures a satisfying feeling of coming full circle by making sections I and VII, which serve as introduction and coda respectively, mirror each other in mood and musical material. *Paris* may sound merely rhapsodic or even disorganised on first hearing; in fact it is anything but, and is constructed with care and craftsmanship.

The work uses a large orchestra: 3 flutes (3rd doubling piccolo), 3 oboes, cor anglais, 3 clarinets, bass clarinet, 3 bassoons, double bassoon, 6 horns, 3 trumpets, 3 tenor trombones, bass tuba, timpani, bass drum, percussion (cymbals, glockenspiel, castanets, triangle, tambourine), 2 harps and strings.

I. 'Adagio – Lento molto': Delius usually excelled at beginnings and endings, and the opening of *Paris* is no exception. He begins down in the depths with a pedal D natural on the double bassoon, timpani and double basses. The bass clarinet huskily intrudes in the second bar, sketching some melodic fragments:

Ex. 3.11

This is answered by divided cellos, like distant horn calls. The 1st oboe gives voice to a curiously folk-like tune, more pastoral than urban, and there are other little wisps of half-themes, all of them heavily veiled in the shadowy atmosphere. Philip Heseltine commented that 'the programme annotator would be delighted to discover seven or eight distinct themes in as many pages ... and dismayed to find that none of these are developed in the conventional manner.'[109] Nevertheless two important themes are reworked in later sections, the first a rhythmic fragment on the 1st and 2nd bassoons, subsequently picked up by the 1st oboe and 1st horn:

Ex. 3.12

The other idea is an arching, oriental-sounding melody on the bass clarinet, immediately echoed by the cor anglais:

Ex. 3.13

109 Ibid.

Delius selects these last two ideas for further treatment on various groups of instruments in a subsection beginning just after a double bar (Fig. 4+1): washed over by undulating triplet figurations on upper strings and harps, they are cunningly juxtaposed. Furthermore, at Fig. 5+1 a further quotation of the little folksong tune is added to the texture by the 1st oboe and 1st clarinet, with an entry in canon of Ex. 3.13 in the cellos and double basses. Delius's studies at Leipzig are here paying dividends. The dotted rhythm of Ex. 3.12 is also exploited to give an *ostinato* effect on flutes, clarinets and timpani. This all builds impetuously to a climax (Fig. 6+1) and then just as suddenly subsides – one of those swift musical deflations at which Delius was so adept. A 'Lento molto' passage (Fig. 7+1) then reintroduces Ex. 3.11 on bass clarinet, higher in the register than before and now over tremulous violas and cellos. This introductory section, as it dies away, dovetails into the first example of truly quick music in the score (Fig. 8+1)

II. 'Vivace': The influence of Richard Strauss has been detected here by several commentators, and there is indeed a similar feel and texture in passages from *Till Eulenspiegel* and *Ein Heldenleben*, where there are chromatic scurryings in woodwind and strings in a 6/8 metre. Strauss, though, would probably not have played with his triangle, glockenspiel and tambourine quite as much as Delius does. This fleeting section – under two minutes long – feels as if we have suddenly turned a corner into Montparnasse, with garish lights and stray noises-off from cabarets and *cafés-concerts* evoked by most of the brass (Fig. 9+3), aided later by violas and bass clarinet (Fig. 10+5). (These are reworkings, it seems, of unpublished sketches which Delius headed 'Scènes Parisiennes' and 'Episodes et Aventures'). There are no really substantial themes to grab onto in this excursion into the *demi-monde* – just little wisps of melody, although fragments of a slightly developed version of the folksong from the introduction are bandied around in woodwind and horns (Fig. 11+10). But something more definite is about to emerge as this section slackens in pace and dynamic, and we reach a double bar with changes of time and key signature.

III. 'Adagio con espressione – Con grazia – Molto adagio': This section can be subdivided into three parts. The first ushers in a glorious and subtly harmonised melody on the violas:

Ex. 3.14

Its outline is traceable from an oboe theme in *Hiawatha*:

Ex. 3.15

There, its harmonic accompaniment is somewhat prosaic; here it is utterly transformed, 'like opening a magic window to Innocence'.[110] The melody is passed on to woodwind and, notably, to the 1st trumpet (Fig. 13+11) as the music soars aloft in a premonition of 'high hills' to come, even though these were still twelve years in the future. This broad theme in C major is like a cool draught to sober us up, and its upward-leaping shape is reflected (in diminution) in a little motif introduced by the 1st and 2nd bassoons, 3rd and 4th horns, and by the cellos; it is further refined by upper strings:

Ex. 3.16

This will assume some importance later on. These are undoubtedly some of the most exhilarating pages in the whole of *Paris* – but the music suddenly comes down to earth (Fig. 14+6), as cellos and double basses are given a version of Ex. 3.14 under vigorous, but mundanely chugging, strings. (One can imagine the young Eric Fenby tut-tutting at this, just as he did over a similar passage in *Poem of Life and Love* before it was excised from the revision of *A Song of Summer*.)

The central subsection marked 'Con grazia' (Fig. 15+1), built around a suggestion of the leaping outlines of Ex. 3.16 in a variant in woodwind and strings, is only a brief recollection (lasting under twenty bars) of the festive mood of section II. Since there is no programme note, we are left guessing as to why we are back on the boulevards again for this snatch of *gaîetés*, which includes a reference (this time on the 1st violins) to the *chansons populaires* of Fig. 9+3. But soon the lights are abruptly dimmed for the concluding subsection.

This is a 'Molto adagio' (Fig. 16+9), a truly haunting passage with a melancholy, almost ghostly tinge. Divided 1st violins sigh expressively above poignant harmonies, although soon there is a sense of consolation from a gentle, rocking figure anticipated by the 1st oboe (Fig. 16+10) and 1st clarinet (Fig. 16+12), and then sketched in by solo violin above a variant of Ex. 3.16 on a solo cello (Fig. 17+1); after the briefest of interruptions by sounds of distant boulevards the violin is then doubled by the 1st flute (Fig. 17+7). But the most tender voicing of this idea comes *con espressione* again from a solo cello and the 1st horn:

Ex. 3.17

*mp con espressione*

The 1st violins simultaneously add a reference to the first two bars of Ex. 3.13 – a wonderful example of real composition of the material. The full significance of this heart-rending passage could have been known only to the composer – 'a corner of his soul' indeed.

IV. 'Allegretto grazioso – Tempo di marcia': The cello and horn theme (Ex. 3.17) is developed rhythmically in the first part of this section (Fig. 18+9), which recalls the equally boisterous 6/8 feel of section II. Flutes, trombones and violins take up Ex. 3.17; the rhythmic insistence of Ex. 3.12 also manages to emerge from the thick texture in the upper strings (Fig. 20+8). Delius lets the tempo relax a little but then whips it up again to lead seamlessly into a subsection in march tempo (Fig. 23+1). This is more dance-like than military, as its softer, more feminine key of G flat would suggest. It is based on a theme:

Ex. 3.18

This is in fact a development of Ex. 3.17 (it can be found foreshadowed by the 1st trumpet and violas at Fig. 21+2). Delius eventually builds up quite a head of steam before jamming the brakes on with some decisive punctuation: a pair of G flat chords in harps and strings (Fig. 25+1).

V. 'Meno mosso – Molto lento (Adagio molto)': There is now a sudden change of mood and texture (Fig. 25+2): tranquil music which, like section III, offers us a fascinating view of the shape of things to come in Delius's maturity. The music stays essentially in flat keys as a rising–falling motif emerges in the 2nd violins (Fig. 25+4), interspersed with Ex. 3.17 from the 1st horn decorated by a solo violin, echoed gently by the 1st trumpet (Fig. 26+2) and then by the 1st flute. The tempo pulls back even further to 'Molto lento' (Fig. 27+1) and then to 'Adagio molto' as a little arching melody, like the outline of Ex. 3.16, is heard on the 1st oboe:

Ex. 3.19

This is imitated by the 1st flute and cushioned by a similar figure on a solo violin: such figurations will soon become utterly characteristic of Delius's sound-world. This delicate and exquisitely textured music is another of the finest passages in the whole of *Paris*.

VI. 'Vivace (Allegretto) grazioso': Section V does not resolve harmonically but dies away *pppp* on a half-cadence and leads (Fig. 28+1) straight into the soul-mate of sections II and IV. The influence is once again Straussian, with thick textures and chromatic harmony – with perhaps a rather heavy hand in the percussion department (Delius clearly relishes his glockenspiel!). Ex. 3.18

swaggers forth prominently in the horns (Fig. 31+1) in counterpoint with Ex. 3.17 from piccolo, 1st flute and glockenspiel. By now there are other familiar melodic fragments swirling around in the mixture. The mood of *joie de vivre* climaxes *con tutta forza* around Fig. 32+1, then characteristically deflates in some half-dozen bars as a sinister passage begins (Fig. 33+1). Practically the full orchestra unites in a rare homophonic texture: it is as if dawn is breaking, a warning that it is time to draw a line under dissipation and stagger home to the garret. Lower woodwind and brass sound a gloomy A minor chord *ppp* and call a halt to proceedings.

VII. 'Molto tranquillo – Tempo primo': Delius here telescopes material from the opening introduction to form a much shorter coda. Ex. 3.12 returns (Fig. 34+1) on the 1st bassoon and 1st horn; then the pace levels out to the initial 'Adagio' of the whole work as a pedal note hovers (uncertainly this time) between D flat and D natural; the bass clarinet murmurs its opening theme again (Ex. 3.11), interspersed with mutterings of Ex. 3.12 from the woodwind and horns. The little rustic tune from the opening returns on the 1st oboe (Fig. 36+3); the piccolo has a distant flourish *pppp* (Delius rather impractically asked the player to *draussen spielen* [go outside to play it]). The shape of Ex. 3.19 is hinted at by the 1st flute (Fig. 36+9), and then by the 1st oboe and 1st clarinet. All this is a remembrance of things past, and just when we might be expecting a dying fall towards the final double bar, the music unexpectedly shakes its fist at the breaking dawn and increases in dynamic intensity to *fortissimo*, consolidated by a strong *tutti* G major chord, though with an E natural hinting ambiguously at the relative minor. But it's a gesture, nothing more, and the music fades swiftly away to a hushed close.

I N December 1900, Delius went to Berlin and tried, unsuccessfully, to see Arthur Nikisch (1855–1922), the celebrated conductor of both the Berlin Philharmonic and the Leipzig Gewandhaus orchestras – presumably taking the score of *Paris* with him. On the 14th he wrote to Jelka, 'As far as I can see I have absolutely no chance here – Strauss plays his own things – Weingartner plays his own things and Nikisch plays nothing new.'[111] He subsequently wrote to Nikisch (although he did not send a score), but seems not to have had a reply. Nikisch was the epitome of the martinet conductor of those days – but he had great charisma and, interestingly, he often used his eyes, rather than arm and hand motions. Nevertheless, fourteen years later Nikisch did give the first performances of *On Hearing the First Cuckoo in Spring* and *Summer Night on the River* in Leipzig.[112]

---

[111] Letter 115.

[112] And the next, perhaps equally surprisingly, was given by Wilhelm Mengelberg a year later in London.

1  2–3 Claremont, Bradford

2  St Johns River, Florida, *c.* 1888, by William Henry Jackson

3 Julius Delius

4 Elise Delius

5 Solana Grove in 1939

**6** Thomas Ward

**7** Edvard Grieg in 1889

**8** 8 boulevard de la Mairie, Croissy

9 Delius in 1888

10  Delius in 1899

11  Ida Gerhardi: self-portrait, 1920

**12** Jelka Delius *(third from left, standing)* and Ida Gerhardi *(right)* in the Académie Colarossi

**13** Theodor Delius

**14** The street in Grez, *c.* 1934, with Delius's house on the left

15  Jelka Delius by Ida Gerhardi

**16** River Loing at Grez

**17** Hans Haym

**18** Julius Buths

19 Fritz Cassirer

20 Henry Wood *c.* 1906

21 Walt Whitman in 1887

**22** Friedrich Nietzsche, *c.* 1880

**23** Frederic Austin in 1908

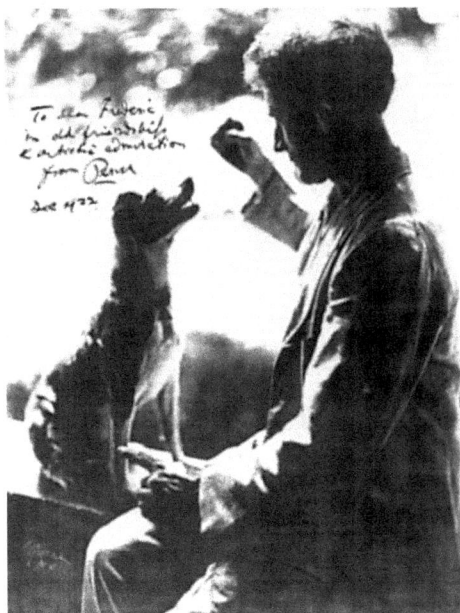

**24** Percy Grainger in 1922

25 Thomas Beecham in 1911

**26** Balfour Gardiner, *c.* 1905

**27** Norman O'Neill in 1903

**28** Philip Heseltine in 1915

29 Granville Bantock, c. 1908

30 Beatrice Harrison

31 Charles Kennedy Scott in 1925

32 Albert Coates

**33** Delius and Eric Fenby in 1920

**34** Delius and Jelka in the garden at Grez, *c.* 1919

1 2–3 Claremont, Bradford

2 St Johns River, Florida, *c.* 1888, by William Henry Jackson

3 Julius Delius

4 Elise Delius

5 Solana Grove in 1939

6 Thomas Ward

7 Edvard Grieg in 1889

8 8 boulevard de la Mairie, Croissy

**9** Delius in 1888

10 Delius in 1899

11 Ida Gerhardi: self-portrait, 1920

12  Jelka Delius *(third from left, standing)* and Ida Gerhardi *(right)* in the Académie Colarossi

13  Theodor Delius

14  The street in Grez, *c.* 1934, with Delius's house on the left

15  Jelka Delius by Ida Gerhardi

**16** River Loing at Grez

**17** Hans Haym

**18** Julius Buths

**19** Fritz Cassirer

**20** Henry Wood *c.* 1906

**21** Walt Whitman in 1887

**22** Friedrich Nietzsche, *c.* 1880

**23** Frederic Austin in 1908

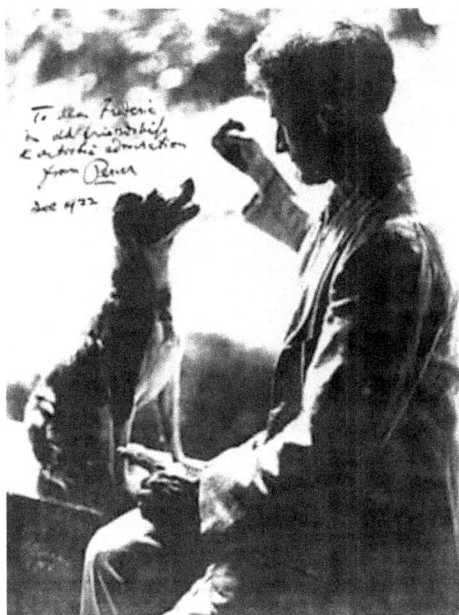

**24** Percy Grainger in 1922

25  Thomas Beecham in 1911

**26** Balfour Gardiner, *c.* 1905

**27** Norman O'Neill in 1903

**28** Philip Heseltine in 1915

**29** Granville Bantock, *c.* 1908

**30** Beatrice Harrison

**31** Charles Kennedy Scott in 1925

**32** Albert Coates

33  Delius and Eric Fenby in 1920

34  Delius and Jelka in the garden at Grez, *c.* 1919

Having introduced *Over the Hills and Far Away* for the first time four years earlier, Hans Haym had become very excited about Delius's music, and Ida Gerhardi therefore had little difficulty interesting him in *Paris*. On the other hand, notwithstanding that he was the dedicatee and in spite of their friendship, Delius had become somewhat unexcited about Haym, concerned that he was not really in sympathy with the music. Having been at a rehearsal for a planned performance in 1900 (admittedly with an orchestra of only forty), on 1 November Delius wrote to Jelka, 'Everything went wrong ... he was too slow and of absolutely no significance.'[113] But it was really too late to do anything about it. For Delius to 'stand down' one of the only two conductors who had to date shown a real interest in his music would undoubtedly have been embarrassing in terms of his and Jelka's friendship with Ida Gerhardi – and, of course, he badly wanted to have the work performed. He need not, however, have worried; although something delayed the programming (and the performance did not in fact take place for another thirteen months), Haym was able to reassure him on 6 December 1901 that:

> Paris will be done! Six extra musicians & the second harp will probably be put on your account, the Concert Gesellschaft will be responsible for the rest. The first rehearsal is on Wednesday aft. at the latest. Hope you will be able to be there! Best wishes!

Eight days later, on 14 December, the work had its première in the Stadthalle at Elberfeld, with Delius and Jelka in the audience.

Delius had supervised the last rehearsals and, as there is no evidence to the contrary, it must be assumed that he was at least satisfied – indeed, he must surely been thrilled at having achieved the first hearing of his music in Germany for four years. One wonders, though, how he reacted to this in an Elberfeld paper:

> The nocturne 'Paris' has an imposing opening, conjuring up unidentifiable sounds such as would be heard at night in Montmartre – a deep, droning, background noise that is followed by rising figurations played repeatedly by the double bassoon. If all these bizarre effects had been left out and only the elegiac, melodious, poetic parts (which are full of deep feeling) had been allowed to remain, we would have had, in fact, a tone poem, an unforgettable impression truly reflecting its subject-matter, of the kind we experience when standing at night in the deserted square in front of the Sacré Cœur. But the composer grabs us by the arm, shoves us into an omnibus and then hurries us on from one cabaret to the next. We flit across the Seine and are straightway amongst the throng *chez* Bullier.[114] However, he doesn't let us hear the gypsy melodies of the boulevard cafés,

---

[113] Letter 112, n. 2.

[114] Chez Bullier (or just 'Bullier') was a celebrated café and dance hall in Montmartre, created by François Bullier in the 1840s; it features in Puccini's *La Rondine*.

although we are aware of cymbals and tambourines, generally coming from two cabarets at the same time. At the close the audience reacted to the work with hissing and mild applause.

*Täglicher Anzeiger für Berg und Mark, Elberfeld*, 15 December 1901

or this, in a Düsseldorf one:

In this tone poem, the night-life of the great 'Babel of Sinfulness' on the Seine is portrayed by the composer with heavy truncheon blows and a musical hullabaloo. The lovable Jacques Offenbach, with his light touch, was much better at describing the frivolous, laughing, lusty young sounds of the metropolis at night

*Neueste Nachrichten*, 16 December 1901

Sad to say, but perhaps not unexpectedly, it has not proved possible to find a good, supportive review for that performance.

Early in 1902 Delius sent the score to Richard Strauss, who replied:

Charlottenburg, 2 March 1902

Dear Herr Delius,

I have read your score Paris with great interest! I am afraid I cannot decide to perform the work for the time being: the symphonic development seems to me to be too scant, and it seems moreover to be an imitation of Charpentier which has not quite succeeded – perhaps I cannot quite imagine the effect of the piece, and I beg you kindly to forgive me and in any case not to be discouraged if, with regret, I return your score to you unperformed.

Perhaps I shall have the pleasure of greeting you personally in Paris and of chatting to you at greater length.

With sincerest greetings
Yours
Richard Strauss.[115]

Ida Gerhardi, continuing her efforts to secure more performances of *Paris*, approached Ferruccio Busoni[116] – and she may not have quite known how to take this from him:

What are you doing with this miserable score? What are you doing, peddling it around like this? ... it is early enough if I have the score on 1 Sept but *not later and with faultless orchestral parts*. I am a novice at conducting, the work is difficult and unknown, so I must not take too many risks.[117]

---

[115] Letter 134.

[116] Ferruccio Busoni (1866–1924): an Italian all-round musician, particularly celebrated for his piano playing and his fiendishly difficult transcriptions for piano. He and Delius met at Leipzig in 1886, and around 1898 Delius introduced Gerhardi to him.

[117] Letter 142, n. 1.

After he had performed it in Berlin on 15 November 1902, the music fared no better at the hands of the critics. They wrote about 'an abstract blend of sound without any comprehensible logic, without any sort of power',[118] and of the 'unpleasantness of sound … this weak, feeble attempt [to portray Paris in music]'.[119] Beecham later wrote that the performance was one 'of such atrocious ineptitude' that Delius would never forget it.[120]

The next performance was given by Julius Buths (1851–1920). He was the son of an oboe player and fourteen years Delius's senior. He studied in Cologne, Berlin, Italy (as a holder of the Meyerbeer Travelling Scholarship), and in Paris. His first conducting post was in Breslau in 1879; four years later he moved to become the director of music at Elberfeld, where he brought the standard of music in the town up to a high standard. He translated Elgar's *The Apostles* and *The Dream of Gerontius* into German, and in 1902 he gave the first German performance of the latter at the famous Lower Rhine Festival; he became the director at Düsseldorf in 1890, and in 1902 the director of the newly established Conservatorium there. In due course, he would conduct the first performance of *Lebenstanz*.

*Paris* was done in Düsseldorf's Tonhalle, on 12 February 1903, after which, for a change, the report in the principal local newspaper must have gladdened Delius's heart:

> How powerfully this vision of nocturnal Paris works on the human sensibility, doubly so since it springs from the heart of an artist who has such a finely-tuned, sensuous temperament! … The way the Delius work is constructed is as cleverly contrived as it is effective; the whole score enriches the repertoire of programme music in such an interesting way. This piece was very warmly received thanks to an exemplary performance – lively and rhythmic …
> *Düsseldorfer General Anzeiger*, 14 February 1903

Haym conducted it again, at Elberfeld on 24 October 1904, in a programme which (amazingly, considering the Concert Society management's opposition to Delius's music in general) included *Lebenstanz*, as well as the first performance of the original version of the Piano Concerto, with Buths, in a change of role, as the soloist. Before the concert, Haym wrote a 'preview' of the work in the main Elberfeld paper, and after the concert their critic wrote:

> A lively discussion about Delius developed amongst the concert-goers, working up almost to the level of a quarrel; one person declared roundly to another in the heat of the argument that Delius understood simply nothing about the art of music. On the other hand, the Delius worshippers that I heard in the corridors expressed themselves differently: 'Enchanting,

---

[118] *Berliner Börsen Zeitung*, 16 November 1902.
[119] *Berliner Tageblatt*, 19 November 1902.
[120] *TB*, p. 125.

entrancing, isn't it? Delightful!' – and the very clever ones said: 'It is wonderful, but I will not give my opinion yet, I still do not understand it sufficiently.' Of course, in the matter of understanding, it will have been difficult for many – despite this, we do not wish to be ungallant and not venture an opinion, so I believe that his music is truly an advancement.

*Täglicher Anzeiger für Berg und Mark, Elberfeld*, 26 October 1904

The next performance of *Paris* was in December 1905, in Brussels (an unexpected location, perhaps), conducted by Sylvain Dupuis.[121] He reported the concert to Delius:

I am afraid that not all of [the audience] understood its finesse but everyone acknowledged that it had come from the pen of a composer of real talent. The main criticism was on the broad development of your impressions of night, and it was regretted that your intentions on this subject were not known. It would have been preferable to have, so it ran, an explanatory text. I congratulate you nevertheless, and am glad to have had the opportunity of performing your work under excellent conditions.[122]

The English première was given in Liverpool by Beecham and the New Symphony Orchestra on 11 January 1908. At the end of 1907, Beecham had written the first of his many letters to Delius, saying that he thought the orchestra would really enjoy playing the work, and asking how he could get hold of the performing material. He also invited Delius to meet him, to look at the draft programme for Beecham's next season of concerts.[123] Delius went to the London rehearsal on 9 January 1908, and reported to Jelka:

Just a word to say that all is going well – I was at the rehearsal this morning which went very well – Beecham takes good tempi & the orchestra likes the piece – I leave tomorrow for Liverpool ...[124]

On the day after the actual performance he told her:

Beecham played 'Paris' very well indeed – It was not quite a finished performance & he was perhaps a bit nervous but in London no doubt they will play it better – The success was mediocre. I don't think that anybody but a few musicians understood it.[125]

[121] Sylvain Dupuis (1856–1931): Belgian conductor and composer who mainly worked in Liège and its Conservatory, as well as at the Théâtre de La Monnaie in Brussels. It was Henry Wood who drew his attention to *Paris*.

[122] Letter 185.

[123] Letter 245.

[124] Letter 255.

[125] Letter 256, n. 1.

However, at least one critic enjoyed himself:

> [It] made a favourable impression. It is an exceedingly clever work, full of orchestral device and resource, and withal of melodic as well as constructive interest.
>
> *The Musical Times*, February 1908

but when Beecham repeated the work in London on 26 February, the following day *The Times* music critic wrote:

> Last night, at the Queen's Hall he gave the first of what should prove to be a very attractive series of five orchestral concerts, which are to be devoted partly to the compositions of the newer men, such as Bantock, Holbrooke, Delius, Fauré and d'Indy, and partly to the works of older composers which, for one reason or another, are seldom given a hearing ... Later on the band played ... a symphonic poem 'Paris: The Song of a Great City' by Frederick Delius which has done for the French capital what Elgar, in his *Cockaigne* Overture, and Mackenzie in his suite *London Day by Day*, have done for the English [one]. The work has melodious moments and is richly scored for a large orchestra. But the composer's free use of the 'extra' instruments for the sake of colour breaks up the surface into so many points of high light that the general effect is spotty and untidy, and one longs for a moment of repose. Everyone has his own impressions of Paris, and this symphonic poem undoubtedly represents the composer's; but it is a pity that for musical purposes he could not have felt a little more of the poetry and passion that breathe in every page of the score of the French opera that is a sort-of-apotheosis of the city – Charpentier's *Louise* ...[126]
>
> 27 February 1908

There were, curiously, two different views in *The Musical Standard* of 7 March. The first reads:

> The first performance [*sic*] was given of Mr. Frederick Delius' 'Paris: the Song of a Great City.' The work is of the Impressionistic School, and the programme annotators inform us that through it all 'there runs a lyrical element ... a thread of romance ... which add refinement and poetry to the dancing and the gaiety.' Frankly, I found no lyricism in the work; there certainly are dance rhythms, and of a reflection of French gaiety I could discover nothing. The work seemed to me morbid to the verge of dullness, and heavy and leaden in purport. Certainly at times there is a powerful fracas, but so far as I could see it is bizarre and incomplete. Of the charm, grace and finesse which one associates with the French there is nothing. According to Delius these things do not exist, and he has

---

[126] It is curious that Delius should have twice been compared to Charpentier! (See Richard Strauss's letter, above).

pictured Paris in very jaundiced, gloomy colours. I imagine the Parisians would keenly resent it ... But this chaotic piece of patchwork which he has given to the world as his 'Impressions of Paris' will in all probability find its way to the limbo of those tentative and uncertain productions which are not held in honour by musicians.

while the second described the piece as:

... a virile piece of work, which contains some very beautiful music.

*The Musical Times* was not as keen as it had been after the première:

Mr Frederick Delius's is an original work, but it cannot be said to conjure up a specifically Parisian atmosphere. It must therefore be judged as abstract music, and from this standpoint it is undoubtedly interesting and clever.

April 1908

And, after Beecham had done it a third time, 'by general request', on 14 April, again at Queen's Hall, the same periodical took a very similar view:

The power and beauty of much of this important work were again apparent, but it was not any easier than before to feel that the peculiar brooding of the music naturally associated itself with the psychological states induced by a night in Paris, unless indeed the mood of the music is meant to be that of a detached philosophical spectator.

*The Musical Times*, May 1908

Following the first American performance of *Paris* – by the Boston Symphony Orchestra under Max Fiedler on 29 November 1909 – *The Boston Globe* warned of moral impediment in its byline 'Wild Night of Orgy is Set to Music'. Simultaneously attracted to and repelled by the work, and in a very American style of writing, its critic found partial refuge with his puritan forefathers:

For every euphonious platitude of orthodox musical creed which Mr. Fiedler and the orchestra expounded in Mozart's 'E-Flat' major symphony yesterday afternoon, they added doubly distilled heresy in the cacophonous profanities of a new musical pagan, Hon. Frederick Delius.

Surely the latest rebel from the faith will cause the guardians of appreciable form and intelligible melody much grief. He is a bold and wanton offender. Because of a conductor abreast of the times, and an orchestra which can work up complex scores quickly, Boston is down to the minute in the ways of orchestra literature.

[The performance] could only give the general contour of the work, with its eagerly following train of quick-lived, sharply-varied episodes, kaleidoscopic swiftness and vividity of outline, surging chaos of myriad voices, high-sounding splendors of their beat and din, plangent dissonances, the lull of receding tumults and a passing melody overheard to fill it, the swift-pacing stride in the wake of the crowd, its feverish unrest, its fickleness, its caprices, its sordidness, its superb animalism, its picturesque abandon.

Save for a moment's pause within doors now and then to watch the ingratiating danseuse pirouette to piquant music or to hear a ballad prettily sung in some cafe, the work is gorged with the clamor of humanity and its complexity of warring moods. Once initiated into Parisian night-time mysteries, the pace runs on unflagging, until in gigantic dissonant chords – the first evidence of simultaneous polyphony – the revelers shudder, perhaps only yawn, at their orgy, and conclude to go home.

To those who hold that night was made for less mutinous infringement of the law, musical and otherwise, this new piece of impressionism will doubtless seem monstrous and deplorable. However, to others who occasionally fancy the sweetness of rebellion and the clangor and stress of life, it will be fascinating, absorbing and thrilling.

27 November 1909

The less morally disposed anonymous critic of the *Boston Journal* attempted to deal with the work in musical terms, but also succumbed to strong visual images of Parisian street life:

> There is a greater resemblance to Debussy than to Strauss … There is no turbulence, no frenetic climax. The kaleidoscopic picture has a subdued tone, varied now and then by shrill notes, as of some peddler crying his wares or some brazen urchin or grisette flaunting authority in the face; and there are even melodious suggestions of merry celebrations. The piece is modern in the most extreme sense of that term, but not yet clear enough in its expressiveness to create a mood and arouse the imagination. The audience applauded in a manner that plainly indicated a desire to hear the work again.

27 November 1909

while the *Boston Daily Advertiser* said:

> The work by Delius stunned us. We have been to Paris several times, but we never knew it was as bad as that.

27 November 1909[127]

Even by 1915, however, few seemed really to understand *Paris* – in its March issue that year, *The Musical Times* said: 'Although it is difficult to see where the Paris we know comes in, there can be no doubt as to the abstract beauty of the music.'

---

[127] This and the two preceding quotations are taken from Don Gillespie and Robert Beckhard, 'On Hearing the First Delius in America: Critical Reaction to Frederick Delius's Music in the United States, 1909–1920', in *MA&L*, pp. 57–98, at pp. 59–60. There are further reviews of early performances of *Paris* in *DSJ* 143 (2008).

T HAT was written after Beecham had done *Paris* for the seventh time, and not surprisingly, Robert Threlfall notes that the earliest extant autograph full score 'bears clear signs of use for performance'[128] – for the work was not published until 1909, so that all performances of it up till then would probably have been conducted from that score or a copyist's copy of it, with handwritten parts. Copyists were perhaps the greatest unsung heroes of the musical world until about the turn of the nineteenth century, for without them few performances of orchestral music, indeed of almost any music, could ever have taken place. Music was first printed in the late 1700s, but it would have been both expensive and difficult to obtain. The only alternative was to use copyists' manuscripts, which reproduced the composer's full scores, orchestral parts, vocal scores, songs and piano music in a clear hand, using a calligraphy pen, good quality paper and a ruler to produce the staves.[129] The work needed a sound knowledge of musical notation, musical theory, the conventions of different styles of music (in relation, for example, to ornamentation) and the planning of page turns. In their own way, the best copyists' productions were real works of art.

Until 1906, there were no printed full or vocal scores, or sets of orchestral parts, of any of Delius's music available.[130] Then, on 1 January that year and on Cassirer's recommendation, Delius was approached by the Berlin publishers Harmonie Verlag. Between then and June 1907, contracts were signed with them for *Appalachia, Sea Drift, A Village Romeo and Juliet, A Mass of Life* and the Piano Concerto. By the time *Paris* appeared in print, however, Delius had changed publishers – as he was to do quite regularly for the rest of his life – and was using the Leipzig firm of F. E. C. Leuckart.[131] Some of the music remained unpublished almost up to the end of his life, and after – for example *Cynara* (for baritone and orchestra) was written in 1907 but not printed and published until 1931, and the *Drei symphonische Dichtungen* of 1889–90 were only issued in 1951.

Returning now to 1899, towards the end of the year Delius began his fifth opera, *A Village Romeo and Juliet*.

---

[128] *RT Supplement*, p. 81.

[129] Letter 152, penultimate paragraph.

[130] But it is still quite common for orchestras today to play Delius using either lithographed copies of copyists' parts or pirated photocopies of printed parts with all the publisher's information deleted.

[131] *M&C*, pp. 24–5.

## A VILLAGE ROMEO AND JULIET
## (ROMEO UND JULIA AUF DEM DORFE)
(1897?–1901: *RT* I/6; *CE* vol. 4)

T HIS opera is based on a short story or novella by the Swiss writer Gottfried Keller called *Romeo und Julia auf dem Dorfe*, included in the first volume of his collection *Die Leute von Seldwyla* – a subject that Delius had first considered in 1897.[132] For the libretto, he originally turned to C. F. Keary, whose work on *Koanga* had seemed to satisfy Delius, but whose efforts on this occasion proved uninspiring. Meanwhile, Jelka felt that setting German words might help Delius come closer to the emotional heart of Keller's world, and so Gerhardi asked her brother Karl-August, a poet, if he would like to produce a draft of just the first Act. But his efforts were also far from what the exacting composer had in mind, and Delius reluctantly went back to Keary. What he produced was still not satisfactory, so in the end Delius decided to write his own text – originally in German, later producing an English translation which, according to Ida, 'fell from him like a ripe apple' – although in fact it now sounds extremely stilted.[133] At any rate, Delius finished it in 1899 and started on the music in the autumn or winter of that year; the libretto was later translated into German by Jelka for the Berlin première.

This 'lyric drama', as Delius called it, takes place in mid-nineteenth-century Switzerland. The action unfolds in a series of six scenes of which the second and third, and the fifth and sixth, play continuously. The Romeo and Juliet of the title are Sali and Vrenchen (or Vreli), son and daughter respectively of two neighbouring farmers, Manz and Marti. The two children have formed an affectionate bond, despite the fierce rivalry of their fathers whose fields are separated by an uncultivated 'wildland', the owner of which has died, leaving an illegitimate son who cannot legally inherit and who leads a homeless existence under the name of The Dark Fiddler. Each farmer suspects the other of surreptitiously encroaching on the wildland with his plough, and this leads to a bitter quarrel; as a result, the children are forbidden to play together.

Six years pass, by which time the farmers' dispute has led to a ruinous law-suit which has impoverished both families. Sali and Vreli are now in their mid-teens and their childhood affection has deepened into love. Sali, in a fit of temper, assaults Vreli's father, who never recovers his faculties; but even this disaster does not affect the feelings of the two young people, and they share dreams of being married. However, conformity to the world's notions of respectability proves elusive: ever the outsiders, even when trying to snatch

---

[132] Ida Gerhardi so stated in letters to her brother Karl-August: see *RT Supplement*, p. 25; see also Letter 71, n. 1.

[133] It did, even before the first performances in 1907. In a letter to Delius on 26 November, Cassirer (who was to conduct them) said 'The text was completely impossible': *TB*, p. 140.

a few hours' relief from their sorrows by visiting a fairground, Sali and Vreli eventually make their way to a lonely inn called The Paradise Garden. There they once again encounter The Dark Fiddler, who tries to persuade them to join him and his band of vagabond companions and go with them into the mountains. When the two lovers hesitate, they are mocked for their supposed conventionality. What they really yearn for, as Sali puts it, is 'to be happy one short moment and then to die: were that not eternal joy?' So they resolve to end their life together by drowning and, climbing aboard a barge, they deliberately sink it as they float away down the river.

This fanciful and somewhat whimsical tale, with two very ordinary young people as its hero and heroine, is far from the usual stuff of Grand Opera *c.* 1900. In fact, by the tenets of the day, it would have been classed as sordid: the protagonists are without exception working class or vagrants, and the common assault and suicide included in the plot hardly count as heroic deeds. Once again Delius was breaking new ground (as he had done in *Koanga*) by deliberately ignoring the conventions and clichés of the opera house of his day. So it is nothing short of miraculous that he manages to create an engrossing and highly moving piece of music-theatre that works far more effectively on stage than anything he had previously attempted. In *A Village Romeo and Juliet*, Delius aspires to a level of poetic symbolism rather than realism, always a difficult ambition to bring off in the opera house. But he achieves his aims with distinction, unlike the flawed attempts he had made in his previous operas. For the first time, the various ingredients of the plot and the score really do fit together, and musically Delius attains a level of inspiration that he is able to sustain. The opera is not only his operatic masterpiece, but it marks a watershed in his overall development as a composer: it is the first important score in which his authentic, undiluted voice is consistently heard.

As we have seen earlier, Delius had mostly shown himself inadequate to the task of depicting passionate relationships on stage with any sort of conviction: Nils and the Princess, Solano and Watawa, Koanga and Palmyra – none of these couples had been really been brought to life in his music. By contrast, *A Village Romeo and Juliet* represents a real breakthrough: at last Delius manages to ignite both human and musical sparks from the poignant story of Sali and Vreli.

The winds of change sweep through the score right from its exhilarating opening bars, a bracing violin melody reinforced by clarinet above rippling strings, with four horns binding the texture together in a warm C major:

Ex. 3.20

This feeling of warmth and sensuousness is not restricted to the orchestra: it also permeates the voice parts. Ex. 3.21 shows an example of this from early in Scene 2, where Sali's vocal line is finely shaped and gratifying to sing, its lyricism counterpointed in the orchestra by a characteristic triplet figure whose outline recurs in many other bars, lending an overall rhythmic unity to the score:

Ex. 3.21

The lovers' meeting in the wildland in Scene 3, where the red poppies are symbolically in full bloom, produces the sort of genuine duet writing that was so lacking in Delius's first three operas. The passage beginning at Fig. 41+1 is noteworthy ('Our childhood's happy days ... they seem so long ago!'), although the finest moments for Sali and Vreli are to be found a little later, in the fourth scene, whose pages are undoubtedly a highlight of the opera. First, there is a short but memorable monologue for Vreli as she sits alone in the dark, her father's house stripped of everything except a bedstead and a bench. Her lament is infinitely touching and has a modal quality, rare in Delius:

Ex. 3.22

After Sali's entrance, Delius builds the music with assurance, introducing a swaying 12/8 rhythm at Fig. 12+1 ('O Sali, I should have died, had you not come') that kindles a passionate intensity; note how independent the vocal lines are from the orchestral ones:

Ex. 3.23

The duet is constructed in sections that are sharply contrasted in both metre and key, in this case leading convincingly into some remarkable pages in which the lovers fall asleep and simultaneously dream of their wedding in the old church of Seldwyla. This sequence (beginning at Fig. 30+1) is a *tour de force*: Delius exploits the full potential of his massive orchestra, with tolling bells vividly and richly evoked on low woodwind, brass and strings, with both the harps and a tam-tam adding splashes of colour. Not even Rimsky-Korsakov in his reorchestration of *Boris Godunov* did it better. Given that Delius was an unbeliever, the religious music in this scene is surprisingly effective: the solemn march that begins at Fig. 31+1 avoids being too obviously churchy and builds magnificently towards Fig. 35+1, with reiterated triplet chords in woodwind and horns; then, after a brief chorus for voices and organ, the music dies away before rising again in intensity to reach a shattering climax at Fig. 39+1, followed

by a manic peal of bells brilliantly evoked in the orchestration. The evocation
of dawn breaking, as the vision fades at Fig. 42+1 and the scene returns to the
sleeping lovers, produces some of the most sensuous orchestral music Delius
ever wrote. Ex. 3.24 shows just a few bars of its rapturous lyricism:

Ex. 3.24

This scene, ending with the lovers' impulsive decision to go and enjoy the
fun of the fair (marked by an exhilarating transposition into the 'sharp' keys of
A and E after predominantly sensuous D flat and B flat), is arguably the finest
sustained sequence in all of Delius's stage works – he never puts a foot wrong
either in terms of technique or taste, and here his inspiration is at its peak.

The fifth scene, evoking the fairground, is another impressive feat of musical
imagination. Delius subverts the normal view of him as an unworldly, cerebral
poet of Nature, by demonstrating the earthy sense of fun and love of life that
marked his days as a man about town in the Paris of the 1890s:

Ex. 3.25

That waltz is exactly the sort of thing that would have been heard at a country fair, and its honest vulgarity is reflected in a deliberately clumsy arrangement for an on-stage brass band. There is an ebb and flow about this whole scene, with its interweaving of chorus and solo voices, which recalls a similar treatment by Gounod in the *kermesse* scene in *Faust*, an opera which Delius must surely have known.

Linking Scenes 5 and 6 is an orchestral interlude now known separately in the concert hall as *The Walk to the Paradise Garden*. Originally it was only forty-five bars long, but later another eighty-seven were added to give more time for changing the set; whether that was done for the première performances in Berlin in 1907 or the first London production in 1910 is not clear.[134] At all events, the passage draws on themes from various parts of the work and illustrates how ingenious Delius was in subtly varying his material. For example, the little motif heard on the 1st oboe and cor anglais at Fig. 51+5, which dominates the coda to the interlude, is derived from a woodwind figuration at Fig. 19+2 in Scene 1; whilst Ex. 3.21 (from Scene 2) mutates into Ex. 3.26:

Ex. 3.26

This figuration evolves most memorably (at Fig. 45+3) into Ex. 3.27 which Delius quarried from the horn solo later at Fig. 85+10, when Sali suggests that he and Vreli follow the vagabonds into the mountains:

Ex. 3.27

The ending of the opera, which could so easily have resulted in bathos, again shows how much Delius had matured as a man of the theatre. A sensitive production cannot fail to move both heart and mind as the distant voices of three bargemen drift across the scene from the river, suggesting to the young lovers the means of terminating their existence: 'Shall we also drift down the river? ... to be happy one short moment', sings Sali. Then comes an exquisite moment as the vocal line, soaring up to a G sharp, tugs at the heart-strings (Ex. 3.28).

The duet that follows ('See the moonbeams kiss the woods') is beautifully accompanied by tremulous strings (note also how Delius drew on the little downward phrase in the violas, incorporating a perfect fifth [Fig. 95+1], when

[134] See *Fenby 2*, p. 49; *Lowe*, p. 78; *RT Catalogue*, pp. 38–9; *RT Supplement*, p. 25.

Ex. 3.28

he subsequently came to write the interlude between Scenes 5 and 6 [Fig. 39+5]). The duet soars ecstatically in a poignant climax at Fig. 99+1 (as in many similar passages, the influence of *Tristan und Isolde*, a score much admired by Delius, comes through strongly). The sinking of the barge is vividly evoked by the orchestra in swaying, syncopated rhythms from lower woodwind and strings, whilst the two harps suggest the lapping of the waters, and the upper strings, divided, provide a shimmering halo of sound in a warm B major. A magical effect.

Amongst the other principal characters, the two warring farmers are not given particularly memorable music. The Dark Fiddler, though, has much more musical personality in his three appearances, even if the last of them (in Scene 6) involves him in a pointless recapitulation of the story of the quarrel. He is an interesting figure – an illegitimate outsider whose behaviour is enigmatic. Initially he is friendly towards Sali and Vreli; later, he comes across as menacing and unpleasant in mocking them as he does. He is also a tempter with something of the devil about him, and this wily deviousness is aptly reflected by the composer in an idiosyncratic theme:

Ex. 3.29

There is not the space here to pay more than passing tribute to Delius's masterly orchestration in *A Village Romeo and Juliet* which shows a huge advance on that of *Koanga* and, indeed, on anything else he had written up to then. Despite having a big orchestra in the pit, Delius knows that sometimes less is more, and he orchestrates with discrimination and restraint – especially where full brass is concerned – so that the textures never become congested and muddy, as had sometimes happened in his previous operas. It is, however, the orchestra that is usually the leading partner in the musical argument – a characteristic of all Delius's large vocal works – and to which he assigns the majority of the memorable phrases in the score; the vocal lines, by and large, are nowhere near as distinctive. For example, few composers would have been so perverse as to deny the singers a chance to take over at some point the lyrical Ex. 3.27 – indeed, many would have built an entire love duet out of such a marvellous idea. But not Delius.

*A Village Romeo and Juliet* is without doubt the most important full-scale work Delius had written up to 1901, and it marks a turning point for him. It is both the beginning of a new phase in his development and the onset of his maturity. Ironically, it also proved to be the last full-length opera that he wrote.

T HE opera was first performed, perhaps not unexpectedly, in Germany – although with a considerable amount of difficulty. The faithful Fritz Cassirer was the conductor at the Komische Oper in Berlin, but when he first mooted the idea the Intendant, Hans Gregor, had serious objections to the libretto. Eventually, however, after a discussion that lasted half the night, an *ad hoc* committee agreed that '1. The music was magnificent ...; 2. The text was completely impossible ...; and 3. A success could only be expected with an elaborate and rich production.'[135] Delius made a number of changes – possibly including providing an initial spoken prologue[136] – and the performance eventually took place on 21 February 1907:

> In its overall construction, Delius's music shows a most sensitive and cultivated mind at work, especially in terms of harmony and orchestration. As for any stronger sense of expressiveness, it does not possess remarkable powers of invention; on the whole the atmosphere of the individual scenes is well done, but dramatic verve, however, is lacking. The most effective moments are the impressive third tableau; the scene at the Fair; and the ending.
>
> *Neue Zeitschrift für Musik*, 7 March 1907

---

[135] Cassirer reported the problems very fully to Delius in Letter 203.

[136] Letter 203 – although it is not mentioned in either the *RT Catalogue* or the *RT Supplement*.

Delius, together with Debussy, is one of the most interesting members of the 'get rid of Wagner' movement. So it is in that sense that one must approach his opera which was christened at the last moment an 'idyll'. His music is not the sort of music we are used to: there are no melodies in the traditional sense of the word and everything is soaked in a tumultuous sea of sound. But a feeling of such great integrity pervades the entire work – it speaks so intensely to the heart – that one feels that here is someone standing alone but whose aims are really worth taking note of.

Delius's art reaches out quite deliberately into the realm of pathos; his music must be judged on its own terms; there are no signposts to familiar realms of melody or harmony; we find instead a totally personal style, an endless flow of shimmering, gleaming orchestral sound ... A recognisable melodic line can hardly ever be discerned. The tragedy of the young couple is portrayed with great skill and intensity, faintly reminiscent of the age-old love song of Tristan, but through different means. There is a scene in which the two youngsters dream of their marriage ... a vision in which Sali and Vrenchen are united. Here the music rises to its greatest heights of beauty. Chaste, yet at the same time radiant, it develops and builds to an unsentimental climax, and then gently dissolves again. Even sceptics could appreciate this new artistry in all its purity ... Delius invites the collaboration of his audience in giving free rein to their own fantasies in the flood of musical images, colours and sounds. Everything is enveloped in a warm mist and emerges as if from a distance. In an absolute sense, Delius's music is only so beautiful in so far as it is appropriate for what it is depicting on stage. But as an experiment in using fresh methods to draw expressiveness from the orchestra and to create novel scenic effects, it is to be heartily welcomed.[137]

Beecham conducted the first English performance at The Royal Opera House in London on 22 February 1910,[138] with Walter Hyde as Sali and Ruth Vincent at Vrenchen. Although the production was notable for the merry-go-round that Beecham hired from a travelling circus for the Fair scene, the music was not greeted with much excitement or praise. The outspoken Mr Baughan of *The Musical Standard* (which was generally by far the least stuffy of the English musical periodicals) did not bother to hide his disdain, in almost Beecham-like prose:

And now we have to speak of Delius's 'The Village Romeo and Juliet.' The opera was played for the first time at Covent Garden on Tuesday night, February 22. It is said to have won success in Germany. The libretto is none

---

[137] Fritz Jacobsohn, *Hans Gregors Komische Oper, 1905–1911* (Berlin: Oesterheld, 1911).

[138] As part of his astonishing three seasons there that year – 190 performances of thirty-four operas, of which he conducted seventy-four, and was the impresario for the rest.

too interesting, and the music seldom holds one's attention. There are six scenes, and the orchestral interludes are, for the most part, written in the familiar Delius manner: that is to say, we are expected to be impressed by a succession of harmonies, made non-eloquent by absence of rhythmic impulse – the life of music! – and melodic interest of phrase. It is a very easy thing, indeed, to string a lot of chords together: some musicians do not consider the act represents the art of composition. We expect a *composer* to put some work into what he calls upon us to consider. Apart from that aspect of the matter– and the excess of sequential and pedal passages – this chord business produces unutterable boredom. For it is so horribly monotonous, a little of it goes a long way, and it carries no meaning. We have already said it is not composition. In some portions of the opera Mr. Delius writes in a normal manner, but he seldom succeeds in giving us any thing striking or even interesting. The love duet, however, is appropriate, and in the Dream Scene, after the marriage service is over, there is some music that has a certain fascinating brilliancy; and the Roundabout Scene is decidedly attractive. On the whole, however, 'The Village Romeo and Juliet' is a singularly dull opera. The music shows taste, non-sensationalism, and is particularly well scored. But we would have willingly exchanged these qualities for blatant vulgarity if that vulgarity embodied some sort of human vitality. Edge-less music of the kind is not wanted, and its lack of substance and value should not be held up for us to admire. H. S. R., in The Daily Mail, thinks Delius 'is one of the great composers of the day; of that there is no doubt.' And he concludes his notice as follows: 'The great English opera has yet to be written, but we believe that Frederick Delius is the man to write it.' He also believes that were it not for the fact that 'The Village Romeo and Juliet' has so poor a libretto the opera would be the most important contribution to English opera that has been produced for many years. Well – the critic has every right to his own opinions. For our part, we could not discover that Mr. Delius showed any aptitude whatever for opera-writing.

*The Musical Standard*, 26 February 1908

All that *The Musical Times* could find to say about it was:

… as all who are acquainted with Mr Delius's other compositions would be led to expect, [it] is full of graces and refinements, and characteristic originality. But it is too little dramatic and the rhythmic interest is slight. The work, admirably performed as it was, did not greatly attract.

April, 1910

*The Times* critic wrote at length, in a not very readable style:

Mr Frederick Delius, who in this work comes before the English public for the first time as an opera composer, is no unknown name to those who frequent concerts. His healthy desire for originality of form and expression marks him out as one of the factors to be reckoned with; and if he has not as yet proved very conclusively that the new forms are more inspiring than the old, he has still shown that he has something to say on his own account.

The libretto of the opera is constructed (by the composer, we understand) on a story by Gottfried Keller; to its many shortcomings are no doubt due the many weaknesses in the impression made by the opera. It is always difficult, in the first place, to feel deeply interested in characters which require two interpreters each ... The audience, or some of them, may regret that the lovers were not more separated, for there is a strangely monotonous succession of duets between them, to the number of four or five, with hardly any intermission but a change of scene.

... For a subject of this kind it is beyond all things necessary that the composer should have at command a wealth of musical ideas wherewith to express the different aspects of love, whether in good fortune or bad. Some of the duets are sincere in expression, and the love-theme, which appears in a kind of anticipatory way in the prologue, is quite cleverly handled. The composer does not as yet know how to keep alive the interest of the scene during the course of the theme's development, and there are a good many unnecessary waits while nothing is happening on the stage. The orchestral texture of the work is a great deal more interesting than in anything the composer has yet given us; he is content with a band of no excessive size, and there is a real dexterity of workmanship in his treatment of the accompaniment as well as of the voice parts.

There are several quite pleasing instrumental numbers – as, for instance, the solemn wedding music in the dream scene, the interludes between the two scenes into which both the first and second acts are divided. Mr Delius seems to have remarkably little sense of dramatic writing for the voice.

The piece is staged very elaborately and all the scenes are admirable. In spite of the absence of any striking moment in the action, the opera was favourably received and the composer was called at the end.

23 February 1910

Although he mentioned neither Beecham nor the orchestra, the critic was quite generous in his praise for the singers. But, despite his favourable comments on the opera's staging and reception, in 1910 opera production and stage management (as well as audience behaviour) were pretty poor compared with today's standards: there had to be an eight-minute pause for a scene change, during which, Beecham complained, the chatter of the audience and banging onstage completely drowned *The Walk to the Paradise Garden*.[139]

Delius had returned to England from France at the beginning of the month, staying for a week with Gardiner at his cottage in Ashampstead, near Reading, before moving to London for the rehearsals. Although all his English friends

[139] *AMC*, p. 88.

no doubt saw the opera, and were full of praise, he must in fact have been very disappointed in the critics' reaction.

After performances of 'orchestral selections' from the opera which Beecham conducted in 1915 and 1916, reviews were still mixed:

> The selection, although divorced from stage action, served very well to exhibit the composer's peculiar idiom and to convey the feeling that he has something interesting to say.
>
> *The Musical Times*, January 1915

> The programmes of the Hallé concerts continue to be notable for much fine music new to us. *The Fair Scene* and *The Walk to the Paradise Garden* ... were repeated and left those who heard it still in the mood to declare that Delius here strikes a more truly individual note than any composer living today.
>
> *Musical Opinion*, January 1916

> A very long item was an orchestral selection from [the opera] ... There is much to allure in this varied and expressive music, but surely for concert purposes an abbreviated form would make it even more attractive. As it is, it frequently deludes the listener into the belief that it is about to end.
>
> *The Musical Times*, December 1916

## LEBENSTANZ
## (LIFE'S DANCE – RONDE DE LA VIE)
(1901–12: *RT* VI/5; *CE* vol. 24a)

*A* VILLAGE *Romeo and Juliet* was followed by *Lebenstanz* – a revised version of *La Ronde se déroule*. Scored for large orchestra, the structure is essentially a rondo in which the dancing main theme, jauntily announced by horns and bassoons and then developed *tutti*, with strenuous passage-work for the strings and woodwind, is quarried for a series of dreamier interludes. The first of these is especially striking for its yearning violin and cello solos and soaring lines for violas and violins; Philip Heseltine called it '… an uncanny phrase … one of the most vital moments in all music, suggesting as it does one of those flashes of insight that leave one overawed and dazed.'[140] The opening treatment eventually returns, but after a forceful *presto* climax it collapses into a reflective, hushed coda. Jelka Delius quoted her husband as saying that he wanted to depict 'the Turbulence, the joy, great striving of youth – all to end at last in the inevitable death'.

The first performances of *Lebenstanz* were in 1904, first in Düsseldorf under Buths and then at Elberfeld under Haym, and, four years later, in 1908 by the London Symphony Orchestra conducted by E. F. Arbos in London's Royal Albert Hall:[141]

> The title 'Life's Dance,' written on the autograph score suggests … the true character of the piece, the aim of the composer evidently being to depict some of the vicissitudes common to earthly existence … [The] composition heard at the Albert Hall is strong and significant music that attests to exceptional talent. It is laid out for a very large orchestra, and the part-writing is most complex. The two principal subjects are a dance motive, and a love theme which exerts great influence. The episodical matter is rationally introduced, and although the dissonances are at times extreme, a masterful purpose is always felt. The work was remarkably well rendered under the skilful direction of Mr. Arbos.
>
> *The Musical Times*, February 1908

In 1912, a revised version (dedicated to Oscar Fried)[142] was published by Tischer & Jagenberg of Cologne, who paid the composer 4,000 marks for the full rights in it. Delius told Dr Gerhard Tischer that '[it is] my best orchestral work … the ending did not please me very much but at last I have found what

---

[140] Philip Heseltine, 'Some Notes on Delius and his Music', *The Musical Times* 56 (1915), 137–42, at p. 138.

[141] Designed by two officers in The Royal Engineers, the hall was opened by Queen Victoria in 1871 as part of a national memorial to her late husband, Prince Albert. It now has a capacity of 5,544.

[142] See below, Chapter 4.

I was looking for and it is now complete.' That version was first performed the same year by Fried with the Berlin Philharmonic, and heard in England for the first time when Balfour Gardiner[143] conducted it, on 25 February 1913, at the sixth of his celebrated series of concerts almost entirely devoted to English music – after which *The Musical Times* gave the work a nonchalant single sentence:

> By far the most striking feature of the concert was the fascinating 'Lebenstanz' by Delius.
>
> April 1913

What a long, hard way Delius had travelled as a composer between 1899 and 1912!

I N more practical terms, in the first half of 1901 he had travelled to Berlin and the Loire valley. The first excursion was, of course, continuing his efforts to get his music published and played more often (although without success), but he also heard Tchaikovsky's Symphony no. 6 and Verdi's *Requiem* and *Falstaff*, and met several good friends. The second trip was pure holiday – he bicycled around with another friend – no doubt doing a little wine-tasting on the way.[144] Even with his return to Grez, however, he did not achieve much in the way of composing, although he did start his next opera, a one-act 'thriller'. It was written for the Sonzogno Prize at the 1904 Italian Concorso Melodrammatico Internazionale – but, as Beecham later said, it never had the slightest chance of winning.[145] Delius had by now, of course, acquired a complete affinity with France, and Paris in particular, so it is no wonder that, with the wide variety of painters and writers who must have accompanied him to all manner of different cafes, entertainments and theatres, he decided to compose something essentially Parisian, but appreciably less staid than even the wilder parts of *Paris*. That something was *Margot la Rouge*.

---

[143] Balfour Gardiner: see below, Chapter 5.

[144] Delius was in fact a serious and knowledgeable wine-drinker, and had a splendid cellar in the garden at Grez (see below, Chapter 10).

[145] *TB*, p. 122.

## MARGOT LA ROUGE
### (1901–2: *RT* I/7; *CE* vol. 5)

T HE libretto was almost certainly by one of the Molard circle in Paris, Berthe Gaston-Danville, who used the pen-name of Rosenval.[146] As has already become apparent, Delius rarely told anyone about the music he was writing, but with *Margot* for once he did. In a letter to Jelka in the spring of 1902 he said:

> I am hard at work on "Margot la Rouge", and have already sketched two scenes. I wonder what you will think of the libretto. I may make something good of it after all.

Then, on 3 June 1902, 'I am nearly at the end of my opera and shall have done in three or four days.' Later the same month he wrote that 'My opera (Margot) was quite finished on the 6th June.' It was not, however, performed for another eighty years: a BBC studio broadcast on 21 February 1982, conducted by Norman Del Mar;[147] and then, on 8 June 1983, Eric Fenby conducted it in St Louis, Missouri. It was finally done in England the following year, when Clive Timms conducted three performances as part of the Camden Festival on 28, 30 and 31 March.[148]

There is only one act, with eight separate scenes covering three distinct phases of the action: scenes 1 to 4 set up the atmosphere of the Parisian café and its drinking clientèle, and either introduce directly, or refer to, the three protagonists: Margot, Thibault and the Artist (although the latter is never specifically named and is seemingly intended as a 'type'); scenes 5 and 6 focus on the recognition by Margot and Thibault that they once shared a pure form of love for each other, and on their hopes that this can be renewed and fulfilled; scenes 7 and 8 concern the double murders of Thibault by the Artist, and of the Artist by Margot, ending with her arrest.

The opera opens with a brief orchestral prelude of great beauty containing two striking themes:

Ex. 3.30

---

[146] *Paris Years*, pp. 59, 80–1.

[147] Norman del Mar, CBE (1919–94): English horn player who became a conductor at the age of twenty-eight. He specialised in English music and that of Richard Strauss (about which he wrote the principal English textbook). There is an excellent obituary online at http://www.independent.co.uk/news/people/obituary-norman-del-mar-1392549.html [accessed 3 April 2014]; for a review of his *Margot* performance, see David Eccott, '*Margot la Rouge*: World Première Broadcast', *DSJ* 75 (1982), 22–4.

[148] Reviewed in *DSJ* 83 (1984).

Ex. 3.31

Three decades later this ravishing prelude would be recycled as the opening to *Idyll*, based on a Walt Whitman text (see below, Chapter 8). Its function here in the opera is simultaneously to suggest the lovers' repressed sexuality in their past meeting, and to prefigure the unbridled, if unfulfilled, passion of their reunion – as will be revealed. An important motif which Delius puts to work almost obsessively throughout the opera is introduced by the cor anglais right at the start of the scene:

Ex. 3.32

The general texture is slightly Wagnerian – somewhat in the style of *Das Rheingold*. The opening dialogue between the drinkers in the café and later between the soldiers in Scene 4 is mainly in this vein. Rather more interesting is a liltingly expressive passage in which the devious Lili Béguin, whose spiteful intrigues against Margot will set in motion the tragic outcome of the story, lays bare her desire for the Artist.

In a piece of rather obvious symbolism, Delius's librettist works in a gathering storm in Scene 2. Just as things seem to be bogged down in an atmosphere of unrelenting gloom, a contrast is offered by the appearance of a jovial character called La Poigne in Scene 3. Having picked a pocket or two, he facetiously offers to treat the company to a large bowl of salad. Subsequent banter between him and the drinkers at the bar is punctuated by the appearance of Margot. She utters one word, 'Non!', on a low D sharp and then remains a silent, brooding presence for a further two hundred bars or so. Her former lover, Thibault, expresses himself far less laconically in Scene 4 as, in a series of eloquent solos, he begins to piece together his memories of the golden-haired seventeen-year-old he loved and lost as a young man.

Margot's unnatural silence finally ends as Scene 5 begins, ushering in some glorious music for the two lovers, material that would also offer such rich pickings when recycled thirty years later as part of *Idyll*.

Lili makes a brief appearance from her hiding place where she has been spying on the couple. This is the composer at his most lyrically inspired, more than enough to make us forget the contrived situation as Thibault rediscovers the girl known to him formerly as Marguérite. The music really takes off and soars, ignited by a striking passage at bar 634 with a warm texture of two solo violas and divided cellos (voice parts are not shown):

Ex. 3.33

This builds sequentially in more and more urgent repetitions, and is perhaps the closest Delius ever got to suggesting the erotic textures of *Tristan*. The voices join in a true duet; both have different texts making intelligibility impossible, but it scarcely matters at this point. The music reaches an ecstatic climax, but the rest of the opera is unfortunately bathetic. The musical depiction of the double murders in Scene 7 is commonplace, with Delius trying his hand at *verismo* but able to speak its language only falteringly, as if with a foreign accent. Scene 8, the arrest of Margot, lasts barely more than a minute.

There is no question that, musically, the richest parts of this forty-minute drama are the orchestral prelude and the central scenes of love music. The commonly held view that the melodramatic or *verismo* demands of the plot stimulated only weak and atypical musical invention from Delius is not without foundation. *Margot* is a terribly uneven work. It unquestionably has some glorious music, notably in Scenes 5 and 6, which rise to heights of inspiration fully worthy of the composer of *A Village Romeo and Juliet*. In places, however, there is much pedestrian and uninspired material, making those outlying portions of the score a letdown.

The Saint Louis performances were quite widely reported in local papers, almost all of which, as might have been expected, commented on the disparity between the music and the action on the stage: 'Delius's orchestra sings away dreamily, as if divorced from the happenings on stage'; 'The disparity between Delius's subtly evanescent score and the bloody *verismo* subject is at times awkwardly apparent'; 'But Delius's vocal writing is much less interesting than his orchestra score, and the plot … is little more than a dramatic scenario – there's no development of character, no place for the story to go except a violent ending.' On the other hand, the English critic Andrew Porter, writing in *The New Yorker*, was far more sympathetic: having described the six Delius operas generally as 'strange, beautiful works in which an aristocratic disdain for the operatic conventions yields, at times, to disconcertingly clumsy attempts to observe them', and *A Village Romeo and Juliet* specifically as 'a masterpiece: tender, poignant, ecstatic, breathtakingly beautiful, and like no other work in the repertory', he went on to say of *Margot*:

> As verismo plots go, it's not a bad one, but the dramaturgy is ineffective: more than half the forty-minute opera is taken up with desultory conversation among the clientele, and nothing much of interest happens until Margot and Thibault start reminiscing … The opera was performed

behind a gauze semi-cylinder, played upon by slide projections of Paris facades, streets, and bridges, with the singers in pools of light behind. This cinematic mode of presentation can be effective, but often it seems to me more decorative than theatrical: it dissipates dramatic tensions by pulling the eye away from the living actors. The slender work might well seem stronger if concentrated in the single, realistic set of the composer's prescription – one whose seaminess would throw into contrast the lovers' dreams. On the whole – if not always – operas are most successfully produced in the way their creators intended, and the dreamy, 'drifting' aspects of Delius's music need no visual underlining.

JULIUS Delius died on 4 October 1901. His daughter Clare wrote that 'He passed away as he had lived – dictatorial, generous to a fault, incredibly stubborn ... he pursued the way of life he had marked out for himself with such Prussian exactness until six or seven weeks of his death.'[149] Delius went back to Bradford for the funeral, reporting to Jelka afterwards:

> We buried the old man on Monday and indeed he died just in time to save the whole family from ruin ... My brother is a soft headed mope & broke down at the grave altho I know he has been waiting 18 years for this & really did not care a straw. I was surprised to see him kneel & do a bit of praying when the Parson drawled out his prayers.

Delius & Co. had been in financial difficulties for a very long while – the secretary had written to Delius some eight years earlier saying:

> It is the general opinion of employees that your father is not abreast of the times, and unless he ceases to manage, not a customer worth a straw will be left in six months time.

Nevertheless, Julius was quite a rich man. He had kept accurate records of all that he had spent on, or given to, his various children, and in his will he specified that what each had received should be taken into account in dividing up his estate, then worth around £50,000. Delius had certainly been the principal beneficiary of his lifetime generosity (in particular the original purchase of Solana Grove, and its subsequent handing-over to Delius), with the result that he only received £539.[150] In view of Julius's many years of unrelenting opposition to Delius's pursuit of a musical career (despite having paid him a modest allowance, both when he was in Leipzig and in Paris), it is perhaps understandable that Delius does not seem to have mourned deeply for his father. Indeed, judging by the quality of the music that he wrote from here on, it is hard to avoid the conclusion that Julius's death was in fact a tremendous psychological release.

[149] *MMB*, p. 140.

[150] *AJ*, p. 50.

# The Great Noontide[1] and Beecham

*Appalachia – Beecham – Sea Drift – A Mass of Life*

I T seems appropriate now to take stock of what had happened in the rest of the musical world during the time covered by the previous chapters, and of where Delius stood at the end of it.

Although he had been composing seriously for fourteen years, only a few of his works had been heard in public: *On the Mountains, Over the Hills,* the *Légende,* the incidental music to *Folkeraadet, Mitternachtslied Zarathustras, La Ronde se déroule* and *Paris,* with excerpts from *Koanga* – all just once each (except for *On the Mountains,* which had been played twice) and all, except for *Paris,* at the 1899 St James's Hall concert. Despite the apparent success of that venture, between then and 1907, when the Piano Concerto was given its second performance, nothing else is known to have been performed anywhere in the United Kingdom. Delius had not yet broken through the barrier of acceptance.

Since the time of Johann Sebastian Bach, music had played a much greater part in everyday German life than it did in England – every town of any size, particularly in the Rhineland and Thuringia, had its director of music, an opera house, an orchestra and choirs – and there was therefore a continual movement of conductors, performers and, consequently, musical news between them. It was accordingly not in the least unusual that Buths moved from Elberfeld to Düsseldorf; or that Cassirer went from Lübeck to Posen, then to Saarbrücken, to Elberfeld, and finally to Berlin. Over a period of years many more German concert-goers got to hear much more new and unfamiliar music – even that of Delius – than was the case in England. By 1902, German audiences had heard, and seemed to have no great difficulty with the extraordinary complexities and new sounds of, the first four of Mahler's symphonies, all Strauss's tone poems except for the *Sinfonia domestica* and *Alpensinfonie,* the first two of Scriabin's symphonies and his early piano music, as well as Rachmaninoff's Symphony no. 1 and Piano Concerto no. 2 – while Schoenberg had started his huge and strange *Gurrelieder.* Admittedly (apart from Schoenberg) those composers had all had a proper musical education, but nevertheless their music was worlds away from what was concurrently being played in England.

However, one only has to compare two of the three works considered in this chapter, *Appalachia* and *Sea Drift,* on the one hand with any of those Austrian, German or Russian works, and on the other with Parry's *Invocation to Music* (1895), Coleridge-Taylor's *The Song of Hiawatha* (1900), Elgar's

---

[1] The phrase 'the great noontide' is taken from Friederich Nietzsche, *Thus Spake Zarathustra.*

*Coronation Ode* (1902) or Stanford's *Songs of the Sea* (1904), to appreciate the extent to which, even by this stage in his career, Delius's music was radically different from virtually everything that was being performed and written by his contemporaries in any of these countries. Apart from the new works of Parry, Stanford and Elgar (which were, of course, still written in the Germanic tradition) and the standard German classics, in 1901 and 1902 the concert-goers in Queen's Hall, the Philharmonic Hall in Liverpool, Manchester's Free Trade Hall, or at one of the big choral festivals (such as Three Choirs, Leeds and Birmingham) only rarely heard any new music more demanding than, for example, the cantata *Emmaus* by Elgar's friend, the organist of Gloucester Cathedral, Herbert Brewer (1865–1928); the dramatic oratorio *The Legend of St Christopher* by the American Horatio Parker (1863–1919); *The Phantasy of Life and Love* by Frederic Cowen (1857–1935); the overture *Di Ballo* by Arthur Sullivan (1842–1901); and the *London Day by Day* suite by Alexander Mackenzie (1847–1935). The task of winning those audiences over to 'more difficult' music was therefore going to be enormous. It is fair to comment that few, if any, of the new German works heard at Elberfeld, Essen, Düsseldorf or Munich in the same concerts at which Delius's music was premièred would have conceivably ever been played in England (and probably never have). Given, however, that English audiences were nowhere near as advanced in their listening as those in Germany, Delius's early, undemanding, orchestral pieces ought to have been well received, had he been able to get them played – but it was not to be.

His problem was very simple: a complete lack of interest on the part of the publishers and concert promoters whom he approached. After the first flush of success in getting some songs published in the early and mid-1890s, all his efforts proved useless – in 1896 he wrote to Jutta Bell:

> My money matters are as bad as ever, nay! even worse. I cannot sell a song; it seems ridiculous when one comes to think of it but I cannot make a fiver.[2]

He also lacked a 'highly gifted compatriot with the insight, the money or the influence to do for Delius what Beecham did in the following decades'.[3]

One other possibility is that, although he was born here, people would not necessarily have considered Delius as being English – both his parents were, of course, German, and he had lived as long in America and France as he had in England. On the other hand, he would not have readily admitted his German genealogy, and in terms of general 'feel', his music rarely reflects either that or the German countryside, let alone German history or culture. Indeed, he told Fenby many years later that he had a deep dislike of 'the music of the Immortals'.[4] For whatever reason, however, Delius now took to calling himself

[2] Letter 67.

[3] Arthur Hutchings, *Delius* (Macmillan & Co., 1948), pp. 30 and 32. For Beecham's first meeting with Delius, see below, Chapter 5.

[4] *Fenby 1*, p. 195.

Frederick, rather than Fritz. Bearing in mind that his music was still only being performed in Germany, not in England, that perhaps seems a little surprising – but as France now appeared destined to become his permanent 'home', he may well have wanted to distance, if not dissociate, himself from his family's origins. He is now, of course, rightly considered to be a 'cosmopolitan' composer.

The period between 1900, when Delius began *A Village Romeo and Juliet*, and 1905, at the end of which he completed *A Mass of Life*, was 'six magnificent years of passionate and creative activity when the composer was at the very height of his powers'.[5] Of the three works covered in this chapter, *Appalachia* was the one in which his maturity as a composer and his unique style first completely flowered, *Sea Drift* is arguably the finest that he ever wrote, and *A Mass of Life* certainly has a very similar claim.[6] With *Sea Drift* and the *Mass*, it is, of course, a comparison of opposites, in terms of size, styles of music and subject matter – the one about the transience of life, the other a paean to the joy of it – and whereas *Sea Drift* has only three characters, the *Mass* embraces the whole world.

Early in 1902, Delius spent a couple of months in Berlin – still trying to persuade conductors and concert promoters to include his works in their programmes. He and Jelka then went there together in October, to hear Busoni conduct *Paris*, and then on to Elberfeld for *Mitternachtslied Zarathustras* under Hans Haym. Jelka's mother died in June, and she had to deal with difficulties over the estate – but it was a relatively peaceful period for Delius, and much of it was spent at Grez, working on his next composition.

---

[5] Ibid., p. 119.

[6] Many discerning Delians would bracket *A Mass of Life* and *An Arabesque* together (*An Arabesque* is discussed below, Chapter 6).

## APPALACHIA
### (1902: *RT* II/2; *CE* vol. 9a)

T HOUGH the two pieces are totally different, *Appalachia* derives from the
nine-minute long, brash and lively *American Rhapsody* of 1896, which
Delius now expanded into a much larger work for eight-part chorus and
orchestra, with a short baritone solo to be sung by a member of the chorus.
His experiences in Florida – the sounds and sights of the forests, the negroes
and the mighty St Johns River – had impressed themselves so deeply into his
consciousness that some six years later, and despite the completely different
atmosphere of Grez, he had no difficulty in vividly evoking them in by far the
largest work he had yet written.

*Appalachia: Variations on an Old Slave Song with Final Chorus* is the full
description on the front of the score and, as befits this panoramic view of the
New World, Delius sets himself up with an extremely large orchestra: three
flutes, all of which double on piccolos; three oboes; a cor anglais; and four
clarinets – a pair in B flat, plus a bass clarinet and an E flat clarinet. The latter
can reach a perfect fourth higher than the B flat instrument and has a shriller
sound. It was pre-eminently used in military bands to brighten and strengthen
the top octave, and Delius does the same – in fact this is the only time he
included it in a score. He also requires three bassoons, a double bassoon, six
horns, three trumpets, three trombones, a tuba, timpani, percussion (triangle,
side drum, bass drum, cymbals and gong – all used very sparingly indeed), two
harps, and a 16–16–12–12–10 string section.[7]

The composer noted on the title page of the original manuscript score:

> Appalachia is the old Indian name for North America. The composition
> mirrors the moods of tropical nature in the great swamps bordering on
> the Mississippi River, which is so intimately associated with the life of
> the old Negro slave population. Longing melancholy, an intense love of
> Nature, child-like humour and an innate delight in dancing and singing
> are still the most characteristic qualities of this race.[8]

The ground plan of *Appalachia* is relatively straightforward: the theme
and main body of variations – fourteen of them – are framed by a substantial
introduction and by what might be termed a choral epilogue (Delius's 'final
chorus'). Although sets of double bar-lines provide some visual clue throughout
the score as to the way the music is punctuated in terms of structure, the
variations are not numbered individually. In fact, once they are under way, they
more often than not flow into each other so that the ear is not necessarily aware

---

[7] I.e. sixteen each of first and second violins, twelve each of violas and cellos, and ten
double basses. Wagner required the same for *Der Ring des Nibelungen*, but only
eight double basses.

[8] *RT Catalogue*, p. 59.

of the joins. Delius surely meant this work to be heard more as a rhapsodic entity than as a series of separate compartments. Table 4.1 shows the general structure of the work. The fourteen variations make up three-quarters of the music in terms of duration. There is the definite feeling of a midway point in the score after Variation 6; Variations 7 and 8 are a musical point of repose before Delius takes up his journey again – and it is significant that he begins to recapitulate some of his earlier material from that point on.

Table 4.1 *Appalachia* structure

| Section | From | To | Key-centre | Total bars |
|---|---|---|---|---|
| Introduction | Bar 1 | B+11 | E♭ | 55 |
| | B+12 | E+7 | B/C♭ | 23 |
| | F+1 | G+7 | C | 21 |
| Theme | G+7 | G+15 | C | 8 |
| Variations | | | | |
| Var. 1 | G+15 | H+8 | Fm | 8 |
| Var. 2 | H+8 | I+1 | F | 8 |
| Var. 3 | I+1 | J+1 | F | 20 |
| Var. 4 | J+1 | L+13 | Dm/F | 59 |
| | M+1 | M+12 | Dm/Am | 12 |
| | M+12 | N+10 | Dm/F | 26 |
| Var. 5 | O+1 | O+21 | Cm/F | 21 |
| Var. 6 | O+21 | Q+31 | F/C | 52 |
| Var. 7 | R+1 | R+14 | F | 14 |
| Var. 8 | R+15 | T+5 | Cm/C | 46 |
| Var. 9 | U+1 | U+42 | Fm/F | 42 |
| Var. 10 | V+1 | X+12 | Fm/Bm/F | 37 |
| Var. 11 | Y+1 | AA+8 | C | 64 |
| Var. 12 | BB+1 | CC+1 | Am/C | 19 |
| Var. 13 | CC+1 | CC+15 | C | 14 |
| Var. 14 | CC+16 | CC+50 | Am/A♭ | 35 |
| Epilogue | DD+1 | DD+9 | A♭ minor | 8 |
| | DD+9 | DD+20 | A♭ | 12 |
| | DD+20 | FF+28 | F | 50 |

As an introduction, the first ninety-nine bars are an exquisite example
of mood-painting, setting the scene in a three-part structure that begins
affirmatively in the key of E flat (Ex. 4.1) with a series of horn calls that ring
out three times: 3rd and 4th horns in octave unison at bars 1–5 and 13–17;
and the 3rd alone at bars 25–8. If one imagines Delius depicting the great
swamps bordering the Mississippi, then the distant echoes that occur seem to
come from the opposite bank of the river (1st horn: bars 5–8, 17–20, 29–32).
The overall mood (highly reminiscent of a similar texture at the start of the
opening movement of the *Florida* suite) is hushed and expectant, with faint
quiverings from tremulous, muted strings, feather-light woodwind chords,
and upward-floating harp arpeggios pointed and imitated by piccolo, clarinet
and oboe, and with just the faintest tremor of a pedal B flat from the timpani
below:

Ex. 4.1

A flattened seventh (D flat) has crept into the underlying E flat harmonies,
increasing the sense of nervous uncertainty; then suddenly (A+12) the mood
is broken by a vigorous, upward-thrusting figure on divided violas and cellos,
doubled by clarinets and bassoons: it is the familiar Delian fingerprint, the
rhythmic figure of a triplet followed by a longer note value, usually leaning on
the second beat of the bar, and often appended (as in *A Village Romeo and
Juliet*) by a little arching phrase ending in a falling perfect fifth. Delius probably
absorbed it from *Tristan*, but he made it very much his own. Ex. 4.2 is a variant
of it taken up by the 1st clarinet (A+22), followed by the 1st oboe, and then
passed on to other solo woodwind instruments, the little phrase weaving in and
out of a rustling accompaniment (Ex. 4.2). This first section of the introduction
comes to a close with the initial five notes of the horn call restated low down
by double basses, 3rd bassoon and double bassoon, and coming to rest on an
unexpected harp chord of G major. Suddenly there is a complete change of
mood – a masterly example of Delius's orchestration skills, worth showing in
full score (Ex. 4.3).

Here is the perfect example of Delius's reference to the natives' 'innate
delight in dancing and singing', as that essential instrument of 'the old Negro
slave population', the banjo, is brilliantly captured with the most economical
but telling of means: *pizzicato* violas and 2nd violins, doubled by bassoons
and the cor anglais in the bright, metallic key of B major, enhanced by the
tangy plucking of both harps. It is as if a shaft of sunlight has suddenly pieced
the primeval gloom of the misty swamp, and the whole orchestra starts
swaying to the beat: violins cascading, flutes and oboes trilling and flurrying,

Ex. 4.2

lower woodwind dancing away in 12/8 rhythms – so that within fifteen bars the texture has thickened, leading to a double *forte* climax (D+5) that is underpinned by a new pentatonic idea in E major (i.e. an idea based on five different pitches in an octave, see Ex. 4.4). This idea is broad and virile, and very American in flavour in its feel of wide-open spaces. It is introduced at D+1 by the bass clarinet, 1st and 2nd bassoons, 3rd, 4th, 5th and 6th horns, and the cellos. Soon it is taken up by *tutti* brass and horns, reinforced higher up by strings in Delius's ripest *Florida* vein. It will also be recalled by the choir in the final pages of the work (Ex. 4.4).

The music peaks and then swiftly backs away, a double bar-line is drawn, all the sharps in the key signature are cancelled. The third section of the introduction (F+1) is marked by the brilliant stroke of foreshadowing the appearance of the main theme which will not actually appear in full until twenty-one bars later (G+6). For now, Delius quotes just the first part of it three times in swift succession (see the figure marked *x* in Ex. 4.5): in the minor on the 1st oboe, E flat clarinet and 2nd trumpet; then in the major on the cor anglais, B flat clarinets, bass clarinet, 1st horn and violas; then on 1st and 3rd horns in unison. Delius also sneaks in three advance references to the end part of his theme (marked *y* in Ex. 4.5), firstly on the 1st and 2nd oboes (F+7 to F+8), then on the cor anglais (F+11 to F+13), then on a solo 1st horn (F+13 to F+14) – an ingeniously subtle way of planting the gist of the theme in the listener's musical subconscious.

The textures thin out and the music, with some characteristically Delian chromatic jostling, settles down onto a rich string chord of C major with the added sixth of the scale (A natural). After this evocative, tripartite introduction to the 'moods of tropical Nature' and its indigenous peoples (a lot has been

Ex. 4.3

Ex. 4.4

summed up, musically, in just under a hundred bars) 'the old Slave Song' itself makes its first appearance:[9]

Ex. 4.5

It was a stroke of genius to assign the unveiling of the theme to that most melancholy and poignant of instruments, the cor anglais, and – not only that – to have it accompanied by bass clarinet and three bassoons, giving a richly dark-hued and oily timbre to the passage. Note how simply constructed the tune is, though it is obviously not by Delius himself: it is an ideally suitable case for treatment. The tune is mostly built on a C major triad in second inversion: the first six of its eight bars only use the notes C, E, and a G at two different octaves. The 'tag' phrase at the end (i.e. the last two bars) really only takes in an additional D and A as passing notes; overall, therefore, this eight-bar phrase is constructed entirely from just five notes of the scale.

It is also pentatonic (playable, transposed, on just the black keys of the piano), a feature it shares with the first eight bars of Jerome Kern's immortal melody evoking the Mississippi, *Ol' Man River* – a song Delius would come to admire, though it was not written until 1927. Delius's slave song also bears a marked resemblance to the main theme of the quartet in Act 3 of Verdi's *Rigoletto* (to the words 'bella figlia dell'Amore' – literally, 'beautiful daughter of Love'), though whether there is meant to be any significance to this is a question that is probably best left unanswered!

After the theme, the variations proper begin, with a more angular harmonisation of the theme in F minor, the 1st horn taking over the melody from the cor anglais, and with some occasionally caustic string writing as accompaniment. Then minor yields to major as the pace increases a little to a

---

[9] According to Fenby, Delius first heard this sung by a worker in a tobacco factory when he was working his passage home from Jacksonville in 1886: 'Eric Fenby in Interview with Fred Calland', *DSJ* 106 (1991), 11–21, at p. 16.

steady *moderato*, and the E flat clarinet, with the 1st bassoon doubling at the octave below, gives another straightforward account of the theme, this time in F major and cushioned by flowing strings, with a chromatic bite in the last three bars.

These first two variations dovetail, as does the third, a vigorous *più vivo* which takes the *x* figure of Ex. 4.5 and reworks it as a partially dotted triplet rhythm: this can be heard on the 1st and 3rd horns and in the 1st trumpet right at the start of the variation; then, six bars later, on the 2nd and 3rd oboes, cor anglais and E flat clarinet; finally, all the upper woodwind get in on the act. The timpani also reinforce this idea. In addition, another motif appears in counterpoint to it: this follows the outline of Ex. 4.2 and is introduced by the 1st violins. It is subsequently multicopied by cellos, bass clarinet, flutes, horns and brass, etc. Downward-flowing quaver passages, together with trills in strings and woodwind, supplement the texture of the first thirteen bars of this third variation – in fact, there is a lot going on, recalling Fenby's judicious comment that *Appalachia* is 'the answer to those who regard Delius as a gifted amateur lacking technique enough to write vital music ... [and it] proves that Delius, in his own way ... can play the technicians at their own game.'[10] There is indeed no surer way of exposing compositional inadequacies than in a lengthy orchestral work in variation form; Delius passes the test with flying colours.

Seven bars before letter J, the busy nature of this section is quelled, as the music pulls up slightly for a brief chorale-like and *molto cantabile* statement of the theme by the strings and clarinets; then come three cadential punctuation marks over a timpani roll from, respectively, the upper woodwind, the brass, and, finally, the bassoons and horns. This culminates in a double bar-line and a different time signature (6/8), ushering in the fourth variation. This is the most substantial of the entire set in terms of number of bars (ninety-six) and duration (around four-and-a-half minutes).

It is in a three-part structure, A–B–A, and is started off by the cello section dancing to a D minor idea (Ex. 4.6), blithe but at the same time dignified, and clearly inspired by the earlier dotted-rhythm treatment of the *x* figure in Ex. 4.5. The second half of the tune (marked *x* in Ex. 4.6), a reply to the cellos from the 1st and 2nd violins, obviously pleased Delius as he refers back to it on several occasions later on, notably in the choral epilogue. An English pastoral mood seems to be in the air, such as Edward German was then writing, or Peter Warlock[11] would write, in mock-Tudor style. Then, after the full string section has answered its cellist colleagues, Delius elaborates the treatment for another fifty bars or so, with woodwind scales as decoration, and the horns and trumpets taking up the dotted rhythmic impetus. The 3rd oboe, cor anglais and the violas initiate a chain-sequence of quotations from the first part of the slave song (K+2 to K+5), deliberately emphasising the original duple metre

[10] *Lloyd*, p. 170.
[11] See below, Chapter 6.

Ex. 4.6

against the prevailing groups of three quavers in 6/8. That trend is eventually passed down, via horn and trumpet, to the trombone section and the tuba, which extend the quotation in full. At letter L+1 the textures overflow with exuberant *bonhomie* – and even Richard Strauss at his best could not be more effective in his orchestration than Delius is here. Suddenly the plug is pulled: the swirlings of harps, wind and strings gurgle away, and the opening of the theme sounds again in lower strings and bassoons, as the texture thins and mutes are applied in preparation for an extraordinary interlude marked 'Lento' – a mere twelve bars in length, but a highly significant part of the score.

These bars (they follow M+1) are scored solely for muted strings in shades of *piano* with just a few notes from the bassoons at the end, and they are not ostensibly connected with the main theme, melodically or harmonically. They are in Delius's most intimate manner, the harmonies unique to his sound world. Eric Fenby called them 'his moment of revelation',[12] seeing them as a significant spiritual and visionary development in Delius's work, and a signpost to the great *idée fixe* of his maturity: the transitory nature of mortal life in contrast to the perpetual renewal of Nature. 'At last he knew what was in him to do', says Fenby, and adds that henceforth entire works were to be shot through with the same poetic vision that imbues these twelve brief bars and which, in his view, elevates them from the level of mere 'tunefulness' and gives them a transcendent significance. If one concurs with this, then *Appalachia* can be seen as a tremendous advance on previous works such as the *Florida* suite and *Paris*. This passage from the fourth variation certainly haunted Fenby when he visited Florida in 1966, prompting him to say later that 'whatever Delius may have meant by it in the context of the work, to the end of my days it will conjure up the mysterious peace of Solano Grove, the spiritual birthplace of his most personal art.'[13] These are difficult matters to evaluate subjectively, but it is fairly obvious what Fenby was getting at. In the context of *Appalachia*, the eighth and fourteenth variations are further evidence of this emerging spiritual

---

[12] *Lloyd*, p. 173.

[13] Eric Fenby, 'Revisiting Solano Grove: Delius in Florida', *Composer* 21 (Autumn 1966), quoted in *Lloyd*, p. 175.

quality in Delius's music, which makes the work a major turning point in his output.

Returning to the fourth variation, after the *lento* interlude the cellos recapitulate their initial idea (M+7) and the strings take it up as before, but this time they develop it slightly differently. A brief coda, characterised by semiquavers and the discreet assistance of the woodwind, brings this variation to a close.

There is a flavour of Elgar and Strauss in the fifth variation, which is led off again by the cellos in an upward-moving *con moto* idea, which does not so much break new ground as recall elements of the previous two variations, notably a dotted-rhythm treatment of figure *x* from Ex. 4.5. But here it is expounded much more forcefully in a complex *tutti* with militaristic overtones; a percussionist is finally called into action on the triangle (O+15) as horsey rhythms canter along to a background of upwardly rushing woodwind scales.

Variation 6 lifts the tempo a further notch (P+1) with a *giocoso* solo from the E flat clarinet, who plays a delightful melodic variant on the main theme, doubled by the first and second desks of the cellos. It is another imaginative piece of orchestration: the more nasal quality of this particular variety of clarinet, reinforced by the cellos playing high up in their register – Delius takes them up to a B flat above the stave in the treble clef – gives a most vivid shrill effect, akin to a bugle. Lower strings accompany lightly, keeping pace with a running triplet figuration in the 1st and 2nd bassoons, the whole texture aerated by great upward sweeps of the two harps. After a fuller orchestration of the clarinet's ideas, there is another beautifully conceived passage at Q+1, marked 'più tranquillo': there are scale-like triplets and arpeggios from athletic strings and clarinets who work off their energy behind a trumpet solo that follows the melodic development of the slave song heard earlier from the E flat clarinet and cellos. The harp writing is exhilarating: could Delius have been influenced by Richard Strauss's seventh variation in *Don Quixote* (1897), where the blindfolded knight 'flies off' on his wooden horse? Strauss uses a wind-machine as well as harps, but the effect is comparable.

Delius's equally vivid music rises to a magnificent climax, built up from the momentum of rushing triplet figurations given to most of the orchestra. The 1st and 3rd trombones make an important entry at Q+17, with the theme (Ex. 4.7) complemented by a counter-subject that was foreshadowed a few bars earlier by the bass clarinet doubled by the cor anglais (Q+13), and is now pitted against the brass (in augmentation) in the violins, flutes and oboes (Q+18). Delius was notorious for dismissing what he called 'Protestant counterpoint', but he certainly knew how to write it himself when the occasion arose.

The music reaches an incandescent triple *forte* (Q+24) and then contracts, dying down in tempo and dynamic. At this point, Delius has a trick up his sleeve: the tenors and basses of his chorus enter *pianissimo* in the final three bars, gently singing 'La, la, la ...'. What an effect that must have had on the 1904 audience – and it can still take anyone new to the work completely by surprise. At the slight risk of overdoing the effect, Delius repeats the gesture at the end of

Ex. 4.7

variations 8, 9 and 10 – but he carefully instructs the singers to remain sitting for all of these brief interjections, and only to stand for their final 'chorus' at letter BB.

The following two variations, which dovetail, contain some of the most memorably poetic pages in the whole score, and are in fact at the midway point: taking timings from Beecham's 1952 recording with the Royal Philharmonic Orchestra, which has an overall duration of about thirty-seven minutes, the introduction, 'slave song' theme and Variations 1 to 6 take around sixteen minutes, which is matched more or less exactly by the duration of Variations 9 to 14 plus the choral epilogue. That leaves Variations 7 and 8 as a five-minute central point of repose, where Delius draws breath before starting to recall material from the introduction as a form of recapitulation in the second half of the work.

Variation 7 begins with a solo from the 1st horn, 'Lento e molto tranquillo', accompanied *espressivo* by chromatically moving strings at a very slow crotchet pulse of around fifty-four beats to the minute. This is a beautiful melodic variation of the main theme, with other members of the woodwind family adding little wisps of figuration around it, including a hint of the counter-subject mentioned above (Ex. 4.7), heard here in the cor anglais (R+4 to R+5). The overall mood is not unlike that of *Summer Night on the River* – a starlit night into the bargain – as this variation drifts on into the next one, marked *misterioso*. The strings, much divided, are spaced out in ethereal chords to provide a halo of sound for the icy triplet figurations of the 1st harp, and for pairs of falling thirds in the woodwind (notably flutes and clarinets). It is a telling piece of orchestration with a glittery feel.

Snatches of the upward triplet figuration first heard in the introduction recur (see Ex. 4.2): here, initially, they come from pairs of clarinets and divided violas (R+21); shortly afterwards from bassoons and bass clarinet, amongst others. The shuddering *tremolandi* in the lower strings just before letter S also recall a similar passage from the opening pages (A+15). This is part of the musical recapitulation referred to earlier, and it is also revealed in the reappearance (S+9 to 12) of the opening horn theme from the introduction (Ex. 4.1), and a reminiscence of the harp arpeggios from that same section (twelve bars before A). The 1st horn is not only given the statement but also the echo seven bars later (S+19 to 22). By now the strings are muted, with the violins reaching right up to the heavens, triple *piano*. There is a further reminder of the 1st horn call, this time muted (S+29 to S+32), ushering in the most magical entry of all – that of the male voices of the chorus: the 1st basses singing as quietly as they dare, answered by the 2nd basses and the 1st tenors. Bows are hardly touching the strings at this point; the upper woodwind play two unresolved little figurations, introducing the uncertainty of an F sharp into the basic C major chording (a reminiscence of a similar passage at the end of the fourth variation, three bars before letter O). The listener is suspended in time and space in a quintessentially Delian way.

But not for long: the spell soon breaks, to begin the return journey, with a waltz-like variation initiated (as were Variations 4 and 5) by the cellos. The time signature is actually 6/8 rather than 3/4 but this *andante con grazia* music still sounds like a slow waltz – and there is even a concert master present in the form of a solo violinist adding a counter-subject to the cello tune. The harps and main body of violins then follow his lead, as they accompany the main theme when it recurs on the 1st horn, doubled by the cellos at U+9. Since Delius is now seeking ways to recall some of his earlier material, it is not surprising, given the dance-like affinities between this ninth variation and the fourth, that he quotes part of the principal melodic idea of the latter in the 2nd and 3rd flutes, E flat clarinet and 2nd violins. A comparison of U+12 to U+14 with J+5 to J+7 will make this clear. Further snatches of the slave song theme recur (in the E flat clarinet and 1st violins, U+17 *et seq.*) as the waltz becomes more complex and builds to a *tutti* climax, pulling up the tempo and then returning to it, but with the tension taken out, 'a tempo, ma tranquillo'. A sequential rocking figuration in the 1st violins and woodwind moves steadily downwards in pitch and dynamic, momentarily interrupted by a snatch of the main theme from the 1st trumpet, robustly doubled by the bass clarinet and 1st horn (U+30 to U+33).

At this point, the tenors and basses add their third, and longest, interpolation so far: they have ten bars of 'La la la', not dissimilar to passages in the third movement of Part 2 of *A Mass of Life*. As before, this *vocalise* effect rounds off the variation beautifully, as the voices echo each other and die away over a hushed bed of strings, with touches of horn and bassoon.

After a moment of silence, variation 10 continues the mood of tranquillity as the woodwind meander downwards in frosty chromaticism and then play wisps of figuration over sustained – and more warmly harmonised – string chords. But soon there is a chill in the air again, emphasised by the appearance of the main theme in an unexpected B minor, a potent combination of bass clarinet, 1st bassoon and 1st trumpet. The orchestration here (V+8 to V+14), with its open spacing, its perfect fifths in lower strings and horns, and its starkly outlined woodwind, is a foretaste of the *North Country Sketches* of a dozen years later.

Then we turn the corner into F major (W+1) with, once again, the 1st horn, doubled by the cellos, playing the original slave song in full, and as it was first presented to us in the home key of C major – another example of Delius recapitulating his material in this second half of the work. And – dare one say it – this most unacademic of composers actually introduces a nice little hint of fugal counterpoint by dovetailing the last two bars of the theme with a further entry of it (a fourth higher, in F) by 1st flute, 1st oboe, E flat clarinet and 1st violins (reinforcing the horns at this point by giving them some doubling from the 3rd oboe, cor anglais and 1st trumpet). It in fact works as a strict canon, either at a one-bar or two-bar interval, though Delius resists the temptation.

After the build-up of texture in the bars before letter X, there is a dying fall to this tenth variation: *pianissimo* major and minor thirds from the two harps over sustained string chords recall similar passages in Variation 8, while the bass clarinet breathes a soft reminiscence of the slave song, and the men's voices enter for the fourth time but now far on the horizon, a fleeting and distant echo in just five haunting bars.

Military music would seem an uncongenial field for Delius, and yet he offers a very creditable pastiche of fife and drum in the eleventh variation. 'Allegro alla marcia' is the unequivocal direction, and the percussionists (who have been neglected since making a first appearance in Variation 5 to play the triangle for one bar or so) at last have some work to do, in fielding side drum, bass drum and cymbals (albeit just a single, off-the-beat, crash for the last). Delius writes a swaggering march based on the fanfare-like possibilities of the first half of the theme, with dotted rhythms for added colour. The 1st trumpet, 1st flute and piccolo, in three-octave unison, give the lead whilst the strong, two-in-a-bar, nature of this music (actually a compound-duple 6/8) is emphasised by the rest of the orchestra. The march asserts itself in a *tutti* passage of great brilliance (Y+22 *et seq.*) with the dotted rhythms pounded out, and aided by another reference to a melodic idea from Variation 4 (marked *x* in Ex. 4.6) in the upper woodwind (Z+1). There is a perfect evocation of a military wind-band nine bars after Z, at which point all three flautists have taken up their piccolos to join the cor anglais, E flat clarinet, B flat clarinets, all six horns, timpani and side drum, anchored by a *tremolo* G natural, triple *forte*, from the double basses – a marvellous effect. Again, this is reminiscent of Strauss's orchestral *militaria* in *Ein Heldenleben* and *Don Quixote*: Delius can certainly hold a candle to him. There is a thrilling climax with lots of rushing semiquavers, reined in with an *allargando*, after which the music collapses in on itself. A brief triadic passage for the brass heralds sudden gloom as F minor and A minor are juxtaposed, and we are invited to witness the natural appendage of a battle scene in the form of a funeral march.

This makes up the twelfth variation, in which Delius even finds within himself a touch of Elgarian pomp and circumstance. It is an impressive moment, with the whole orchestra eventually contributing to the arch-like design which has a span ranging from relatively diatonic *mezzopiano* harmonies for strings and woodwind to searing *fortissimo* chromaticism scored for full brass, timpani and bass drum. The music then thins in texture and dynamic as two surreptitious little fanfare motifs in the key of C are heard from the 1st trumpet, ushering in, for the first time, the full four-part chorus (sopranos, altos, tenors and basses) and the thirteenth variation – a beautifully harmonised, unaccompanied version of the slave song stated in full, and beginning with these words:

> After night has gone comes the day;
> The dark shadows will fade away;
> T'ords the morning lift a voice:
> Let the scented woods rejoice;
> And echoes swell across the mighty stream.

The actual words are of no consequence – Fenby considered them 'doggerel'. What matters is the poignant sound of the close harmony singing. The choir becomes effectively a double chorus in eight parts for this fourteen bar passage: Ex. 4.8 quotes just the last six bars which themselves are an extension of the basic eight bars of the main tune, and illustrate so well the harmonic complexity of the vocal writing. It is utterly Delian. (The German translation of the text, which is in both the full and vocal scores, is an apt reminder of the composer's high standing in Germany at that time).

Although Delius has at last released his full chorus into the open for this *a cappella* moment, he does not give them more to do until the fourteenth (and final) variation – at the very end of its thirty-five bars. By now, however, the listener should be used to the voices coming and going unexpectedly, and in any case the orchestra still has some potent magic of its own to weave. There is no evidence that Delius's powers of invention have begun to flag as he nears the end of his musical journey: on the contrary, this 'Misterioso lento' passage contains some of the most spell-binding pages in the entire score. The key-centre is initially A minor, with muted strings, the three flutes and the three oboes oscillating between open-spaced chords (Ex. 4.9) while the E flat clarinet, the cor anglais and a solo viola provide an *ostinato* inner voice. Muted horns, bassoons and harps add a bass part to the chords and the result is a textbook example of Delius's marvellous ear for orchestral colour.

A solo violin, doubled by the 1st flute, adds a haunting voice to this ghostly landscape which is given the additional sheen of four soft gong strokes; it offers a painfully chromatic variant of the opening to the main theme (CC+25 *et seq.*). As the textures thicken, so too does the harmonic writing, which veers now towards A flat; a solo viola picks out the inner-voice part (Ex. 4.9), which is also taken up by other instruments, including the solo violin. The strings and woodwind stretch themselves out in full semibreve chords as the chorus enters with two sustained added-sixth chords in A flat, quadruple *piano*, their text no longer 'La' but a more expressive, sighing 'Ah!' Words cannot convey the effect of this exquisite variation; it is surely one of those moments which Fenby would claim as evidence that Delius knew what was in him to do. Fenby also mentions[14] being struck by the strange colours of the trees growing in the swamps near Jacksonville: a dull, milk-chocolate hue juxtaposed with the

[14] Ibid.

Ex. 4.8

Ex. 4.9

grey of the moss enveloping them; seeing them for the first time made him understand some of the musical tone-colours in *Appalachia*, and he may well have been thinking of this particular passage.

The final three or four minutes of *Appalachia* are in the nature of a choral epilogue, introduced at DD+1 by a brief, eight-bar passage in A flat minor, scored for woodwind only, and offering a variant harmonisation of the main theme. (Robert Threlfall, in his editorial notes on page 68 of *CE* vol. 9a, mentions that Delius intended to make this woodwind passage optional, and that consequently, in an early lithographed Universal Edition of the full score, eight bars of empty staves were retained with no explanation. The current version of the score retains the passage – and quite rightly, as it seems musically necessary.) A baritone soloist, instructed to sing from his place amongst the chorus, suddenly breaks in, *forte* and in A flat major, with a new tune to words that express the fate of those who must be separated:

> O, honey, I am going down the river in the morning ... Aye! Honey, I'll be gone when next the whippoorwill's a-calling,[15] and don't you be too lonesome, love, and don't you fret and cry.

Delius must have remembered how the leader of a 'singing bunch' in the tobacco factories, or stemmeries, started off a song which the other workers would take up, in close harmony, as they shredded the tobacco leaves – and that is exactly what happens here, with the jubilant 'Heigh-ho' of the male voices breaking in immediately after the soloist, followed by the women. However, the sadness of separation is not the dominant mood ('don't you fret and cry'), for the music veers into the brightness of F major as though lit with a sudden shaft of sunlight. There's the promise, for those who remain faithful, of being reunited – either here on earth or, symbolically, in the afterlife.

At this point, the words 'For the dawn will soon be breaking, the radiant morn is nigh' are set to the music of the pentatonic idea from the end of the second section of the introduction (Ex. 4.4). Interestingly, it also has close

---

[15] A medium-sized nocturnal bird with a distinctive call, found in Central and North America.

affinities with the similarly shaped rise and fall of the last six notes of the main theme. The music gradually increases in tempo, with the textures anticipating equally jubilant passages in *A Mass of Life*, emphasised by the chorus's abandoning words for some more La la la-ing (sopranos at EE+14, full choir at EE+18) in a musical repeat of the little dancing phrase from the fourth variation that was noted earlier (*x* from Ex. 4.6). The main slave song is not forgotten by Delius, though, and it rears up *molto marcato* and *fortissimo* in the bass clarinet, bassoons, 5th and 6th horns, 3rd trombone, tuba and double basses, permeating the exuberant texture until it is taken up by the full orchestra and by the chorus, who match their text to its final phrase.

The music now begins to slacken in intensity as the voices, seemingly lost for words in their excitement, resort to a simple 'Ah!' in a downward chordal passage, while the initial horn call of the whole work (Ex. 4.1) returns *fortissimo* on four horns (FF+7 to FF+10). The triplet figuration from the introduction (Ex. 4.2) emerges again, principally in the upper woodwind, and dominates the final bars once the voices have fallen silent. It is heard on full strings underpinned by horns, and is then echoed by the woodwind. That gives the strings a moment to fix their mutes, and they have the final word in the simple, but utterly beautiful, cadence which ends this great work.

$A$PPALACHIA is the first of Delius's works that can be said to be utterly 'Delian', wrote the celebrated critic Neville Cardus:[16]

> Only the highest order of inspiration can work as simply as this. It is strong music, tender music, majestic music and music aching with the Delius nostalgia ... From the point of view of fine musical craftsmanship and fine musical thinking; from the point of view of intensely imaginative expression, *Appalachia* is a masterpiece over which is suffused a beauty so slender that it catches us suddenly and inexplicably by the throat, yet with all its ache of sensibility, the music goes through masculine and even rough weather before it dies away into the mists which concealed the secret places of the heart of the most poetic composer born in England.[17]

The première of *Paris* having (it would seem) gone so well from Delius's point of view, he had no further qualms about Hans Haym's abilities – indeed, Haym told him that 'Appalachia has grown very dear to me ... I find the whole

---

[16] (Sir) John Frederick Neville Cardus, CBE (1888–1975): an English (Mancunian) writer and critic, largely on music and cricket, who was for many years on the staff of *The Manchester Guardian*. Unlike most of his contemporaries, his style was romantic and subjective.

[17] Neville Cardus, *Ten Composers* (London: Jonathan Cape 1945), pp. 145–6. Interestingly, writing in *The Manchester Guardian* in December 1929, he suggested that Constant Lambert's *The Rio Grande* owed something to *Appalachia* (and *The Song of the High Hills*): quoted in Andrew Motion, *The Lamberts: George, Constant and Kit* (London: The Hogarth Press, 1987), p. 175.

thing superb and as rich as an entire life'.[18] So, notwithstanding the fact that the work was dedicated to Julius Buths, three years later, on 15 October 1904, Haym, with his local orchestra and choir, gave the first performance in the Stadthalle at Elberfeld.

On the day of the concert, a local paper printed an 'introduction' to the work written by Haym:

> Frederick Delius is still almost completely unknown today, even amongst musicians. It can, however, be only a question of time before his name will often be mentioned, and that its resonance will be registered, as only a few names in the history of music achieve. I regard Delius as one of the most original and gifted of living composers, one who firmly believes in forging new ways, which the majority at first hesitate to follow.
>
> *Taglischer Anzeiger für Berg und Mark*, 15 October 1904

The reports of the concert, although certainly not effusive, were not entirely damning:

> Next came the Symphony of F. Delius,[19] which had been heard already several times in Elberfeld.[20] This Symphony depicts moods in Florida and is called 'Appalachia', the old Indian name for N. America. Right from the beginning the artistry had an erotic character. It did not, however, show itself in an obtrusive way; the Negro singing was only discreetly discernible. Various really melodious parts were prominent. There were others, however, which were quite the reverse, and much seemed to derive from Richard Strauss, especially in counterpoint and orchestration. A simple motif, built from the intervals of a broken chord, that also plays a role in 'Rigoletto', runs through the composition, but does not, however, appear to prevent the work holding together. The a cappella choir was most effective, and had music to sing which made an immediate appeal, but the modern direction of some other parts refused to appeal in the same way. Mr Delius has undoubtedly talent; one could wish that he soon turns in the direction of clarity – on to the tracks of elucidation: he could then be very content with his success. Thanks to the outstanding work of Dr. Hans Haym, it was an interesting evening.
>
> *Elberfelder Zeitung*, 17 October 1904

---

[18] Letter 171.

[19] Delius often referred to his bigger works as symphonies, but 'Symphony' is not part of the title of the work, and curiously it was not used in the poster for the concert. However, in the programme for Buths's 1905 performance in Düsseldorf (see below), the title was given as *Appalachia (Dixieland) (Eindrücke aus dem Süden [Impression from the South]): Introduktion, Thema mit Variationen und Finale. Symphonische Dichtung [Symphonic Poem] für grosses Orchester, Baritone-Solo und Chor.*

[20] The work had not, of course, been performed anywhere before.

Many of those attending the performance of 'Appalachia', a Symphony with Choir, by Frederick Delius, will reflect on the work with a few doubts and uncomfortable feelings. Symphony with Choir? Did not someone else write such a one, that one immediately thinks of, when hearing this description? Beethoven and his Ninth! But with this one, Delius does not wish to tread in his footsteps. In Beethoven, a powerful build-up of sound and architecture from which bursts the hymn; in Delius, a row of erotic mood pictures, scenes from Florida and the Negro life, which have an outward connection in the constantly recurring motto-theme which is well known from the song: 'Einen goldnen Wanderstab' ['A golden walking stick']. The work is not at all too extravagant; the works of Richard Strauss have seen to it that the 'modern music' of his disciples is not too foreign-sounding to the ears. At various melodic places here and there, where ... the bizarre dominates, one could enjoy Mr. Delius' talent. Unfortunately, one often heard the loud verdict: 'Boring!' As in the Wagner [*Parsifal* excerpts] and Brahms [*Alto Rhapsody*], the Choir was a powerful element in the performance – and the relatively brief farewell song of a Negro to his sweetheart stood in stark contrast to the elaborate musical construction. Dr. Hans Haym ... devoted as much love and care to the new Symphony of Mr. Delius as to the works of the Masters Brahms and Wagner ... and provided an interesting evening.

*Taglicher Anzeiger für Berg und Mark*, 18 Oct 1904[21]

The next hearing of *Appalachia* was in Düsseldorf on 15 June 1905 under Buths. Oskar Fried (1871–1941) conducted its third performance some eight months later, in Berlin on 5 February 1906. Originally a horn-player, Fried studied composition in Munich with Humperdinck.[22] Following the success in Berlin in 1904 of his choral work *Das trunkene Lied*, setting words from Nietzsche's *Also sprach Zarathustra*, as Delius would later in *A Mass of Life*, Fried turned to conducting. He worked in Berlin from 1904. In the years from 1923, he made many appearances with the Berlin Philharmonic Orchestra, when Wilhelm Furtwängler was its principal conductor, particularly in the symphonies of his friend Gustav Mahler. In 1934, he was forced to leave Germany; he lived for the rest of his life in the Soviet Union. Fried first met Delius in 1905 – it seems almost certain that it was either Buths or Haym (or possibly both) who introduced them – and that summer Fried and his wife spent a while at Grez.[23]

---

[21] There is another criticism of the concert in Martin Lee-Browne, 'Four Conductors', *DSJ* 141 (2007), 52–66, at p. 53.

[22] Englebert Humperdinck (1854–1921): German composer who became a friend of Wagner and helped with the première of *Parsifal*.

[23] For a major article on Fried, see Lewis Foreman, 'Oskar Fried: Delius and the Late Romantic School', *DSJ* 86 (1985), 4–22.

Fried became really excited about the work, although perhaps a little apprehensive: 'Appalachia is damned difficult!' he said to Delius in a letter of 4 January 1906, and he complained in no uncertain terms about the poor condition of the full score and parts (still, of course, only in manuscript), from which he and his orchestra would be expected to play it:

> Come to Berlin at *once!* The orchestral parts of Apalachia [*sic*] really are in an incredible state! I have not enough time to put them in order, and we have certainly not got enough rehearsals to put up a good performance with the music as it is. No signatures! No dynamic markings – or very deficient ones! Whether flute or piccolo is not clear! With the two bassoons one never knows whether tenor or bass clef! The material must be put right before the first orchestral rehearsal, otherwise I cannot perform it. You must realise that we have no time here in Berlin for reading-rehearsals! The material must be clear and distinct, otherwise the musicians will certainly approach this new and difficult work with reluctance.
>
> So please set out as soon as you receive my letter and help me to put the orchestral music in order, otherwise the performance will come to nothing.
>
> Telegraph me as to when and whether you are coming. Great haste is essential.[24]

Delius duly went to Berlin for the performance[25] – with Busoni, who was 'so overcome with emotion that, when he came into the artist's room to congratulate the composer, he burst into tears'.[26]

Delius went to London in early April 1907. On the 15th he had dinner with Gardiner and 'they played Appalachia thru (a few musicians were there) all were tremendously taken with it. This really is my field.'[27] 'They' were undoubtedly some of the Frankfurt Gang and their friends[28] – but from what music did they play? It could have been from the full score published the previous year (see below), but the first edition of the vocal score was not produced (by the Leipzig firm of C. G. Röder & Co.) until 1907, although exactly when is unknown. There is no evidence of anyone having made a piano duet or two-piano arrangement, so it is nice to think that perhaps Delius came to the party bearing the very first copy of the vocal score. Otherwise, 'they' seems to indicate that two people, somewhat remarkably, sight-read from the 1906 full score as a duet. An interesting little conundrum!

---

[24] Letter 187.

[25] Two reviews of the concert can be found in *DSJ* 141 (2007), 60–2.

[26] *PW*, p. 70.

[27] Letter 211.

[28] See below, Chapter 5.

In April 1907, Delius lent scores to the critic Robin Legge and to Percy Grainger;[29] the following month, he gave Grainger one to take to show Grieg, who was 'keenly interested'; two months later, Wood lent a copy to Arthur Fagge, the conductor of the London Choral Society.

The English première of *Appalachia* was given by Fritz Cassirer, who had fallen completely under its spell. He came to tour in England in the autumn of 1907, and had originally intended to do both *Sea Drift* and *Appalachia*, using the Leeds Festival Chorus and the London Symphony Orchestra. However, the expense of bringing the former down to London and hiring the latter proved to be far too much: 'The concert would cost 7000M *without* a choir, without a baritone. Horrendous!'[30] He therefore set about finding an alternative. Someone told him that the young conductor Thomas Beecham had recently enlarged his New Symphony Orchestra, and – famously, for it was the beginning of the Delius–Beecham relationship – after their concert on 14 October 1907 Cassirer and Delius, full of admiration for the orchestra's playing, went to the artists' room, and asked Beecham if they could hire them.[31] Beecham was intrigued,[32] and negotiations were satisfactorily concluded a day or two later. In the event, *Sea Drift* had to be dropped from the programme, but on 22 November Cassirer conducted *Appalachia* with the orchestra and the Sunday League Choir in Queen's Hall.[33] Delius was, of course, there, as were Havergal Brian,[34] Cyril Scott,[35] Granville Bantock,[36] Wood, Grainger and Beecham (who had attended some rehearsals as well, and whose first experience of hearing any of Delius's music this was). At last a Delius work was extremely well received:

> the performance had a reception so unrestrainedly enthusiastic that the composer was surprised and amused. He was called for by name to appear on the platform, and it can safely be said that this work, not one of his supreme masterpieces, was the first wholly to capture English listeners and critics. A novelty it obviously was, as contemporary reviews

---

[29] No doubt copyist's copy.

[30] Letter 227.

[31] *RT Supplement*, p. 26, says it was before the concert, but that does not tie-up with Beecham's report of the discussion in *AMC*; perhaps Cassirer and Delius went to a rehearsal.

[32] There is a full description of the historic meeting and its consequences in Beecham's autobiography, *AMC*, pp. 63–4.

[33] Then London's premier concert hall, in Upper Regent Street. Built in 1893, close to where the BBC's Broadcasting House now stands, it was the long-time home of the Promenade Concerts until it was destroyed in an air-raid in 1941.

[34] Havergal Brian (1876–1972): English composer, especially of long symphonies.

[35] Cyril (Meir) Scott, on whom see below, Chapter 5.

[36] (Sir) Granville (Ransome) Bantock (1868–1946): English conductor and composer who was later (with Delius and Elgar) involved in the formation of The Musical League (see below, Chapter 5).

show, but the epithet is usually applied to *jeux d'esprit*, and the novelty was made highly palatable by the honeyed English sweetness of the writing.[37]

The eminent musicologist and author Percy M. Young seems to have thought that the audience reaction was rather different, but was right as regards the novelty of the work:

> the English were again reminded of the limits set on their musical appreciation by the academic and otherwise restrictive conventions that prevailed. *Appalachia*, not without praise for its effective atmospherics, was a bewildering experience.[38]

The finest critique of all was written by Ernest Newman[39] in the *Birmingham Post*:

> If Mr Frederick Delius would only have the cynical wisdom to die while he is still young, as Schubert and Hugo Wolf did, he would be recognised by Englishmen as a composer of the first rank. As he prefers to keep on living, he must be content to attain fame more slowly among his sluggish fellow-countrymen. Few of them, indeed, have in all probability heard his name until the last week or two, and even those, it is safe to say, have no idea of the greatness of the man. In spite of his foreign-looking name, Mr Delius is an Englishman, having been born in Bradford, Yorkshire in 1863 [*sic*] … In 1897 [*sic*] he gave a concert of his own compositions in London, which only had a mediocre success. London can go into hysterics (as it has done in the last fortnight, over a new prima donna singing faded and intellectually destitute stuff like 'Traviata' and 'Lucia di Lammermoor'), but open its ears very slowly to a new composer of genius … In Germany he is already enough of a celebrity for a biography of him to be published;[40] it is only in his native country that he is unknown. If our Festival Committees realised the significance of this new voice in English music, a festival without Mr Delius would be as unthinkable as one without Elgar.

---

[37] Hutchings, *Delius*, p. 36.

[38] *Young*, p. 537.

[39] Ernest Newman (1868–1959): the premier British music critic in the first half of the twentieth century, working for *The Birmingham Post* from 1906 until 1919, and then *The Sunday Times* from 1920 until his death. He was introduced to Delius late in 1907 by Granville Bantock, and had a deep understanding of, and admiration for, Delius's music – although, for some reason or other, Delius did not (or, at least, did not always) admire his reviews (see Letter 455). Rather than adopting the subjective approach of other critics, such as Neville Cardus, Newman wrote with an objectivity that was reflected in his books on Richard Wagner, Hugo Wolf, Richard Strauss and others.

[40] Max Chop, *Frederick Delius*, 3 vols (Leipzig: C. F. Kahnt, 1906–9).

'Appalachia' on Friday night made a great impression on a large section of the audience, the composer being enthusiastically recalled three or four times. The critics, too, were friendly next day, though it is asking too much of poor human nature to rave over the brains of a man of genius as they did over the larynx of Tetrazzini. 'Appalachia', it should be said, is the old native Indian name for America ... The object of the composer has been to paint the melancholy of the vast forests that lie about the Mississippi, and the corresponding melancholy, flecked now and again with humour or gaiety of the negroes. The theme itself is a beautiful one; its opening notes, by the way, bear a superficial resemblance to the tenor solo with which the great quartet in 'Rigoletto' begins ... The theme itself would be judged by most musicians as *a priori* ill-fitted to provide material for variations; of the four phrase-groups into which it falls, the first three are composed of precisely the same notes, so that apparently there is not much material to pass through the metamorphoses of variation form. One can understand, then, the objection of two of the ablest London critics – that the melody is not big enough to support the weight of the variations and that the theme is always in evidence – though the objections seem to me to rest on a misunderstanding of the work. Mr Delius's aim has not been to write a set of variations for their own sake, each independent of the others – pure exercise in musical inventiveness, like the 'Enigma' variations of Elgar and the 'St Anthony' variations of Brahms. He could easily have done this had he wished to, for the sheer musicianship of the work is of the most masterly kind. What he wanted to do, however, was to keep always before us, so to speak, the negro and the Mississippi forests, only exhibiting them to us in the variety of their moods. So far, then, from the persistent reminders of the main theme being a defect, they are of the essence of the work. One only needs to remember – what my London friends seem to have forgotten – that the theme never recurs twice with the same atmosphere enfolding it; the psychological and pictorial change of the music are even more important than the thematic changes. And no one seems to have known the work well enough to be able to recognise the many technical excellences of the writing.

One gift that Mr Delius has that only the big men have – is that of casting a long work in one mould, of weaving the tissue of it in one continuous fabric. Perhaps the best example he has given us of this quality is 'Sea Drift', which is one of the most remarkable works of our time;[41] here, in spite of all the changeful moods of the music, the total

---

[41] The first English performance of *Sea Drift* would not take place for another year, in October 1908, and it therefore seems that Newman might have gone to the première in Germany in 1906 or the second performance in Basle in 1907 – which would have been very unusual for a critic in those days.

impression is one of extraordinary unity – the secret lying mostly in the nature of the harmonic writing.[42] There is a similar unity in 'Appalachia', also partly harmonic in its essence, such as the curious addition of the sixth to many of the common chords throughout the work – an effect ultimately traceable to the melodic line of the last phrase of the main theme – and the use in the final bars of a scale with a whole-tone instead of a half-tone fourth, that had already been forced on our attention as early as the second variation. And anyone who will take the trouble to study the score will see just how full the work is of rich invention of just the type that the variation form demands – how easily all kinds of rhythmic and harmonic changes are rung upon the theme, and how naturally one variation follows upon another, instead of shutting itself up in its own frame in the usual way. To me, at any rate, the dominant impression given by the work, over and above all its beauties of detail, is its oneness, its air of pressing on steadily and unbrokenly from the first bar to the last. Of its orchestration there is no need to speak; everyone agrees that it is very beautiful, marvellously sure, and decidedly original. The only objection to the work I would permit myself, after a long study of it, is that one or two of the harmonic complexities in which Mr Delius indulges hardly justify themselves, though one's opinion on this point may possibly change in time. There can be no question that in Mr Delius we have a composer of unquestionable ability, with a style and outlook entirely of his own, and a technique of the utmost freedom and finish.

The orchestral part of the work was excellently rendered by the New Symphony Orchestra – 120 strong – under Mr Fritz Cassirer. The new orchestra has been founded by Mr Thomas Beecham. It is mostly composed of younger men who, with hardly one exception, are English. The material of it is excellent, the wind being equal, perhaps superior, to that of any other orchestra in England. With a little more experience, the band will be quite the equal of the two other leading London Orchestras. Mr Beecham is to be heartily thanked for having done such a service to the cause of music in England, in bringing the main body of the band down[43] to Birmingham on the 27th for the first concert of the City Choral Society. Mr Fritz Cassirer, who conducted, is a young Berliner who made his first appearance in England on this occasion. He is a brilliant conductor, with a temperament of his own and a perfect knowledge of the most complex scores.

The chorus employed in Mr Delius's work was that of the Sunday

---

[42] The full score of *Sea Drift* had been published in 1906.

[43] Its was usual in those days to go 'up' to London (as the principal city in the country) and 'down' to anywhere else: perhaps this was a sign of a 'proprietorial' attitude to Birmingham on Newman's part!

League. They sang very badly and with next to no understanding of their music. Their work was the only blot on the performance.

*The Birmingham Post*, 23 November 1907

Grainger wrote to Nina Grieg in his usual, inimitable, style:

... last Friday I had a jolly evening. Mother & I went and heard F. Delius's 'Appalachia' performed at the Hall. I do so wish you could have heard it. I dont say it's a perfect work *at all*, or even a work of pure genius; but it did strike me as poetic, & individual & genuine, & *most corageously* [*sic*] *experimental*. The new things he tried for seemed to me really plucky & of vital interest & not the usual dull commonplace (& usually perfectly 'safe') wheezes of so much so called 'modern' stuff. Then such a lot of it was piano & tender-colored, & that is such a relief & refreshingness.[44]

Far more important, however, was Beecham's immediate excitement and deep sense of identity with the music – which was now to flower into possibly the most celebrated relationship between a composer and a conductor ever to have existed. He wrote a quite masterly overview of the work that would encourage almost any music-lover to listen to it.[45]

I T is now appropriate to say something about Beecham. He was born in St Helens, Lancashire, on 29 April 1879, the great-grandson of a shepherd. His grandfather, also Thomas Beecham (1820–1907), became a self-taught veterinary herbalist, and progressed to making pills for people. The venture prospered, and the eventual product, Beecham's Pills, sold for over 150 years. The pills were both a laxative and a cure-all, mainly made of aloe, ginger and soap – 'worth a guinea a box', as the advertisement ran, but costing only nine pence at the time. Beecham's father, Joseph Beecham (1848–1916), took over the highly successful business in 1895, and was created a baronet in 1912.[46] Thomas was educated at Rossall School in Lancashire and Wadham College Oxford (where he only survived for a year) – and from a very early age he showed astonishing musical abilities. He spent some time in 1897 or 1898 at the Liverpool College of Music, where he was taught composition and harmony by Frederic Austin,[47] and his first conducting experience, when he was twenty, was

---

[44] Letter 240, endnote.

[45] *AMC*, p. 64

[46] Officially styled as 'of Ewanville in the Parish of Huyton in the County Palatine of Lancaster'. On his death, Thomas succeeded to the baronetcy.

[47] Frederic (William) Austin (1872–1952): one of Delius's very great friends. A celebrated English baritone who virtually started his singing career under Hans Richter, and was one of the principal baritones with the Beecham Opera Company between 1912 and 1920. He was an interesting composer, and the arranger of the music for Nigel Playfair's celebrated 1920–3 production of John Gay's *The Beggar's Opera* at The Lyric Theatre, Hammersmith. He was Artistic Director of The

with a largely amateur orchestra he had formed in St Helens. The second could not have been more different. His father had engaged the Hallé Orchestra from Manchester to play at a celebration of his re-election as the Mayor of St Helens, hoping that the celebrated Hans Richter would conduct; the maestro, however, declined, and Thomas persuaded his father to let him do so instead. The programme included Beethoven's Symphony no. 5, the overture to *Tannhäuser*, and Berlioz's *Rákóczi March* – and (because the orchestra obviously knew them well) there was only one rehearsal. A local paper reported that Beecham had a tendency to exaggerate *sforzandi* 'perhaps due to enthusiasm', but that generally 'his work was very clever indeed. It was more than merely a correct interpretation of the music; he put life and energy into his conducting.'[48]

Beecham then travelled widely, hearing all the music he possibly could, and in 1902 he got his first job, as an assistant conductor with the imposingly named The Imperial Grand Opera Company – 'a travelling operatic soup kitchen',[49] giving popular operas and operettas in the London suburbs. His first London concert was with the Queen's Hall Orchestra in the Bechstein (now Wigmore) Hall on 5 June 1905,[50] but for the second, in 1906, he used the newly formed New Symphony Orchestra, whose regular conductor he became a year later. In 1909, however, he fell out with them, and set up the Beecham Symphony Orchestra. Then, in 1910, he formed The Beecham Opera Company, whose opening productions at Covent Garden included the first performances in England of Richard Strauss's *Elektra*[51] and Delius's *A Village Romeo and Juliet*. From then on, until 1939, he reigned supreme over the English musical scene, spending quite astonishing amounts of his time and money in the opera houses, where the repertoire for his annual (sometimes biannual, and even triannual) seasons was nothing short of astonishing – German, French, Italian, Russian, and very occasionally English – raising orchestral standards, and giving brilliant performances night after night.[52] In all, he conducted

British National Opera Company in the 1920s, and later a professor of singing at The Royal Academy of Music. In 1935, he and Beecham were appointed the first Music Advisers to The Delius Trust. He was for many years a director of the Royal Philharmonic Society, and was appointed one of its Honorary Members in 1951. He was Martin Lee-Browne's grandfather.

[48] *St Helens Newspaper & Advertiser*, 9 December 1899; quoted in *Lucas*, p. 15.

[49] Neville Cardus, *Sir Thomas Beecham* (London: Collins, 1961), p. 89 – a phrase actually written of another contemporary opera company, but equally appropriate to this one.

[50] In which Austin sang a Mozart concert aria and the first performance of Cyril Scott's *The Ballad of Fair Helen of Kirkconnel*.

[51] These were the first performances of the work in English, and Austin sang Orestes in the last two performances of nine – without any prior musical or stage rehearsal!

[52] As with orchestral music, Beecham almost invariably conducted opera from memory – including the first performance of *Elektra* in England mentioned above. There is a story (possibly apocryphal) that one evening he appeared in the pit, leaned over to the leader and whispered 'It is *Carmen* tonight, isn't it, Mr ...?' The

over ninety different operas, giving the first performances in this country of more than a few of them. He worked continuously with all the major English orchestras, and his enormous repertoire included Haydn, Mozart, Schubert, Berlioz, Wagner, Tchaikovsky, Richard Strauss, Sibelius, most of the later French composers, and Russian composers. He championed a large number of contemporary English composers too (again, often giving first performances). Between 1908 and 1920 he conducted Delius's music more than seventy times, and by the end of his life the total exceeded a thousand; he also gave two festivals exclusively devoted to Delius, and edited most of the choral and orchestral music. He formed The London Philharmonic Orchestra in 1932, and The Royal Philharmonic Orchestra in 1946.

'Sensibility' is probably the word that best captures Beecham's extraordinary qualities as a conductor: an acute sensibility to the character, shape, rhythms and orchestral colour of a truly vast variety of music. His performances were always elegant and vital, with wondrous *pianissimos* and sonorous *fortissimos*, weaving magic spells over his players and singers, and consequently over his audiences. Without his efforts (and to a much lesser extent those of Haym, Cassirer and Wood) Delius's music could very well have remained in almost complete obscurity in this country for ever.

T HE second English performance of *Appalachia* was given at the Victoria Hall at Hanley, in the Potteries, on 2 April 1908, by the Hallé Orchestra and the celebrated North Staffordshire District Choral Society (which was based in Hanley), conducted by Delius himself – the first of the only three appearances he ever made on the rostrum in public concerts.[53] His skills were, to put it kindly, abysmal,[54] and Beecham subsequently commented wickedly on his ability to beat five in a 4/4 bar.[55] That all was not well on the platform was noticed by many people, *The Manchester Courier* putting it very politely:

> in music abounding in daring harmonic innovations and complex rhythmic devices, where absolute confidence in the playing is essential, it was not surprising to detect last night signs of hesitancy, an element which seemed to be accentuated by some lack of absolute understanding between the players and the conductor.

leader replied, 'Oh, no, Sir Thomas – it's *Tannhäuser*'– at which Beecham turned not a hair, and proceeded to conduct a characteristically brilliant performance.

[53] The others were the première of *In a Summer Garden* in Queen's Hall on 11 December, 1908, and the première of *A Dance Rhapsody* [no. 1] at the Three Choirs Festival in Hereford on 8 September 1909. He did, however, also conduct at a few rehearsals.

[54] See Stephen Lloyd, 'Delius as Conductor', in *MA&L*, pp. 15–35; see also under *In a Summer Garden*, below, Chapter 5.

[55] *AMC, p.* 79. Beecham also said, in a television interview on 22 November 1959, 'I have never come across such an abysmal ineptitude in the way of conducting as revealed by poor old Frederick': quoted in Lloyd, 'Delius as Conductor'.

The same critic, obviously 'knowing his Delius', nevertheless went on:

> In nothing else of Delius's with which we are yet acquainted is the many-sided nature of his pronounced personality so strikingly revealed as in *Appalachia*, which is a combination of brilliant craftsmanship, erudition and poesy but rarely met with in the choicest works of genius.[56]

Meanwhile, the often vitriolic J. H. G. Baughan (the editor, or 'conductor' as he styled himself) of *The Musical Standard*[57] thought that the theme was 'of meagre quality', and that:

> [If the work were] just half its present length there might be the probability of tolerating it. As it is, interest soon begins to flag and is eventually dried up by the monotonously dull atmosphere without any occasional glow of brightness to afford relief, and the excess of dissonance must have put both the players and singers in a maze of entanglements difficult to get out of, whilst the choral epilogue was the most thankless piece of vocal writing I have yet heard in any work.
>
> 18 April 1908

A FEW weeks before Fried's Berlin performance, Delius had had the most exciting change of fortune – indeed, another of the turning points in his career: following a recommendation by Casssirer, the Berlin publishers, Harmonie Verlag, wrote to him on 1 January:

> We take the liberty of bringing our publishing house to your notice and of asking you to consider our publishing and distributing your works. In commending our services to you, we shall be pleased to give you any further information.[58]

Even though they were a completely unknown firm, he must have leapt at the proposal, for negotiations were quickly completed, and the contract for the publication of *Appalachia* was signed on 20 February. Apart from the semi-private production of vocal scores of *Margot la Rouge* in 1905 and *A Village Romeo and Juliet* in 1906, it was the first of any of his major works to appear in print – which meant, of course, that a substantial number of musicians could get to know it. Between then and June 1907, further contracts were signed with Harmonie, for *Sea Drift*, *A Village Romeo and Juliet*, *A Mass of Life* and the Piano Concerto.

Oscar Wilde wrote his play *Salome* in 1891, and it had its first performance at the Théâtre de l'Œuvre in Paris in February 1896. Although the theatre is in the ninth *arrondissement*, some way across the river from 33 rue Ducouëdic where

---

[56] Reginald Nettel, *Music in the Five Towns, 1840–1914* (London: Oxford University Press, 1944), p. 99.

[57] In which post he followed his brother E. A. Baughan.

[58] *M&C*, Letter 5.

Delius was then living, given that he was frequently in the company of writers and artists, it is highly probable that he went to see it. In 1903 he approached the solicitors acting for Wilde's executors with a view to securing the rights to produce a libretto from the text of the play.[59] However, perhaps because they took a long time to reply (and perhaps luckily for posterity), he began to have second thoughts. When he learned from Haym that Richard Strauss was planning to use the play as the subject for another opera himself, he abandoned the project – notwithstanding that Haym wrote to him saying 'What a pity that Strauss took the material away from you! Couldn't you do it nonetheless, and especially now?'[60]

Beecham suggested[61] that another reason for Delius's decision was that he was becoming increasingly interested in the writings of the most important American poet of the time, Walt Whitman, and of the great German philosopher-poet Friedrich Nietzsche. During the next three years, he set some of the former in *Sea Drift*, and some of the latter in *A Mass of Life*. The breadth of Delius's conceptions, the assurance of his composition, the sensitive setting of the words, and the sense they can give the listener of having travelled a miraculous journey, could only have been the product of a happy and contented mind.

Until now, though, Delius had almost certainly not had that. Even after he and Jelka had become 'inseparable', he undoubtedly continued to indulge in indiscriminate flirtations and affairs, and he had written to her at the beginning of 1901: 'I am not affectionate – and regret it also, but I cannot alter myself.'[62] As Beecham, who was deeply fond of them both, also suggested, it would not therefore

> be surprising if during the intervening years some of her blind devotion to Frederick had abated, to be replaced by a cooler estimate of him as a man and potential lover. But she could not have failed to note and be moved by the trying and seemingly endless material difficulties against which he had been fighting ever since he had landed himself with the wretched Florida encumbrance, while her profound belief in his artistic future never faltered for a moment. I have little doubt that there came a critical moment when Frederick, tired of amatory excursions and commercial alarums, and longing for the sort of peace in which he could work out the new and glowing inspirations which were crowding his brain, turned to the one individual who, like a rock in a troubled sea, bore herself in any emergency with unruffled dignity, and never failed to irradiate sympathy and understanding.[63]

[59] Letter 148.
[60] Ibid., n. 1.
[61] *TB*, p. 122.
[62] *Letters 1*, p. 182, n. 1.
[63] *TB*, p. 123.

So on 23 September 1903, some seven and a half years after they had first met, Delius and Jelka were married, in the Mairie at Grez. On 28 September he wrote to Grieg:

> It really was a pleasure to me to receive your kind letter & to hear something in more detail about you again – On the 25th I married my friend Jelka Rosen here in Grez.[64] (Civilement of course) have [*sic*] got even further away from God and Jesus. We lived together for 6 years, but we found it really more practical to legalise our relationship – One gets everything cheaper & one receives free & without further ado a certificate of honesty and good manners.[65]

As a wedding present, Jelka's mother generously gave up her share in the house at Grez, and, no doubt to Jelka's great relief, that resulted in Delius giving up his flat in Paris – the 'City of pleasures / Of gay music and dancing / Of painted and beautiful women'.[66] Even so, that did not mean entirely giving up his close association with a number of his Parisian friends (possibly including one or two not very proper ladies) – for example, he and Edvard Munch remained close, and even in 1934, shortly before Delius's death, they were still writing to each other[67] – but nevertheless Ida Gerhardi had written to her sister on 21 August, 'I hope that Delius will remain as peaceful and calm as he is now.'

In that comfortable state of mind – with *Appalachia* finished, but his American experiences and the attractions of vocal music still dominating his thoughts – he began a setting of part of a long poem by Walt Whitman.[68]

---

[64] Their marriage certificate in fact gives the date as 23 September. Thereafter, Jelka sometimes used 'Jelka-Rosen' as her christian name.

[65] Letter 156.

[66] From the lines written on the original score (see above, Chapter 3).

[67] Letter 598.

[68] Walt Whitman (1819–92). For an extremely interesting article, see Professor R. K. R. Thornton's 'Whitman: Leaves of Grass and Sea Drift', *DSJ* 139 (2006), 20–29.

## SEA DRIFT
### (1903–4: *RT* II/3; *CE* vol. 9b)

W HITMAN was one of a group of now celebrated American writers born at the beginning of the nineteenth century – including Ralph Waldo Emerson, John Greenleaf Whittier, Edgar Allen Poe and Henry David Thoreau. He was brought up on the Atlantic shoreline of Long Island, on the Maine coast north-east of New York, and his roots remained there. His masterpiece, *Leaves of Grass*, was first published (as a slim volume) in 1855, and he spent the rest of his life enlarging and reworking it: the final edition, containing 383 poems grouped in fourteen sections, came out in 1892. 'Sea Drift' is Whitman's title for one of those groups – eleven poems about the sea or the seashore – and Delius used that same title for his setting of 101 of the total 183 lines from the first poem in the group, *Out of the Cradle Endlessly Rocking*.

Whitman has been called the father of American free verse, nearly always writing in lines of different lengths with little or no discernable metrical pattern:

> Flood tide below me! I watch you face to face;
> Clouds of the west! sun there half an hour high! I
>     see you also face to face.
>
> Crowds of men and women attired in the usual cos-
>     tumes! how curious you are to me!
> On the ferry-boats, the hundreds and hundreds that
>     cross, returning home, are more curious to me
>     than you suppose;
> And you that shall cross from shore to shore years
>     hence, are more to me, and more in my med-
>     itations, than you might suppose.
>
> From Crossing Brooklyn Ferry

Not surprisingly Delius – who only very rarely nodded his head to any of the standard musical forms or techniques, such as counterpoint or sonata form – developed a strong affinity with Whitman's experimental and unconventional forms; moreover their philosophies of life overlapped to a large degree.

It is almost certain that Jelka suggested to Delius that he should take the text for his new work from *Leaves of Grass* – she was very well read, and used to write out what she thought were appropriate pieces of poetry, 'put [them] on his desk, leave them there and hope for the best'.[69] It could well be, however, that during the last eighteen months or so of his time in America, Delius had already become familiar with Whitman's enormous work, and very possibly some of the poems in it, and that before he left he had already had the first inspiration which would lead him to portray the Long Island shore in music

---

[69] Fenby, 'Jelka Delius', p. 10.

of moving simplicity and power. Although Delius only stayed at Bradford Grammar School until he was sixteen, he almost certainly developed a basic interest in poetry there (although probably not at Isleworth) – and in due course he became very well read in the poetry of several European countries. It is known, for example, that Thomas Ward gave him a copy of Byron's poems.[70] After he left Solana Grove in 1885, Delius spent a year or so teaching at 'big houses' in Danville, Virginia – a town that, notwithstanding its setting in a very sparsely populated part of America, was far from being a cultural desert. Although most of his life there was taken up with music, it seems certain that, as an Englishman with good looks, an engaging personality and an obviously enquiring mind, he was entertained in some of those houses, meeting people with wide interests, including literature, and that he learnt something of Whitman's poetry in general, and *Leaves of Grass* in particular. What cannot be in doubt is that Whitman captured Delius's imagination – in the same way as he later did Ivor Gurney's:

> Walt Whitman is my latest rediscovery, and he has taken me like a flood. One of the greatest of teachers. And as a poet, he among others has this enormous virtue – that when he has nothing to say, you may divine it a mile off. A marked copy may be read in half an hour; but oh, what gorgeous stuff it is![71]

Whitman's poetry played a prominent part in the English Musical Renaissance. Vaughan Williams was introduced to it in 1892 by the philosopher Bertrand Russell, and his teacher, Stanford, had already set part of Whitman's *President Lincoln's Burial Hymn* in 1884.[72] The results were Vaughan Williams's settings of Whitman's words in *Towards the Unknown Region*, *A Sea Symphony* (his astonishing first symphony, the words of the first three movements of which are taken from other parts of Whitman's *Sea Drift*), and *Dona nobis pacem*. In *The Works of Ralph Vaughan Williams*, Michael Kennedy wrote:

> Composers found [Whitman's] untrammelling metre an outlet for musical settings which would seem to be at one with the words, despite the oddity of some of the similes ... The reason for Whitman's appeal to Vaughan Williams is fairly obvious, apart from the sheer technical challenge to his musical powers. In Vaughan Williams' nature there was a strong vein of mysticism ... He was a romantic; he was also an agnostic, a questioner ... Whitman presented a love of nature plus a combination of plain statement with mystical yearnings.[73]

---

[70] William Randel, 'Delius in America', in *Companion*, pp. 147–66, at p. 154.

[71] Letter from Ivor Gurney to his friend Ethel Voynich, September 1915: *Ivor Gurney, Collected Letters*, ed. R. K. R. Thornton (Manchester: Carcanet, 1991), pp. 41–2.

[72] The *Elegiac Ode*.

[73] Michael Kennedy, *The Works of Ralph Vaughan Williams* (London: Oxford University Press, 1964), p. 82.

All that could equally well apply to Delius.

Was there something else that inspired Delius to write *Sea Drift*? He left Danville for New York in June 1886, on his way home to Bradford, and on the way he spent either 'a short while' or 'ten days' on Long Island with a friend. According to Beecham[74] it was for a short while and the friend was from Jacksonville – if that were in fact the case, the friend might perhaps have been Ward. However, Heseltine said the friend was from the college at Isleworth, although that seems a little unlikely, and that Delius was on Long Island for ten days.[75] Whoever the friend was, this visit could well have been the genesis of *Sea Drift*. Whether or not Delius already knew the poem, the place clearly caught his imagination, and either then or later the reality of the seashore and the emotion of Whitman's words combined to make him realise that he could reflect them in music. It certainly seems possible that he came away with a feeling of identifying deeply with both Whitman's poetry and the place.

There is, however, no evidence of any specific motivation or spur behind the composition of *Sea Drift*. In a letter to Jelka, from London on 18 December 1898, Delius had prophetically said: 'I have my Walt Whitman and Nietzsche here so that I am not quite alone' – but the dates when it was begun and finished have not been established with any accuracy. Delius's sister Clare said it was written in 1903,[76] but Lionel Carley suggests that it was probably started that year and finished in 1904.[77] Almost the only other mention of it is in a letter of 28 February 1905 to Delius from Max Schillings: 'I would gladly propose that we put Sea Drift on the programme' – that is, on the programme for the 1905 annual Tonkünstlerfest (Composer's Festival) of the Deutsche Musikverein (General German Music Association), which that year was to be held at Graz in Austria.[78]

*Out of the Cradle Endlessly Rocking* is the poignant recollection of a boyhood summer spent on the sea-shore of Long Island observing two birds, migrants from warmer climes, nesting by the sand. The boy is spell-bound, especially by the singing of the he-bird, and, 'cautiously peering, absorbing, translating', he silently watches the devoted pair every day. Then, unexpectedly, the female disappears, never to return, and her bewildered partner is left alone, distressed and grieving. Thus the boy experiences his first heartbreaking awareness of the meaning of loss and, by implication, the transience of life – a theme that Delius so often sang, but perhaps never more poignantly than in *Sea Drift*. In his 'Additions, Annotations and Comments' in Heseltine's biography of Delius, Hubert Foss wrote:

---

[74] *TB*, p. 31.

[75] *PW*, p. 45.

[76] *MMB*, p. 140.

[77] *Letters 1*, pp. 210 and 235.

[78] Letter 179.

It is impossible without quoting the whole poem to give an adequate impression of the wide range of its emotion, and of the way in which the passion of the words and music rises and falls with a perfection of poise and cadence that seems to echo the very sound of the sea itself, uniting the story and its setting in a single vision that grips the imagination with an almost uncanny tenacity. In this music we seem, to hear the very quintessence of all the sorrow and unrest that man can feel because of love. It is the veritable drama of love and death, an image of the mystery of separation. The soul, distracted by doubt, rises in impassioned protest against the unheeding stars; but confronted at every turn by darkness and silence, it sinks down into a sort of numbness of endurance, and, when all that it has loved and hoped for seems to have fallen away, it rises again to re-create the past, to clothe it in a vesture of imperishable reality. The unity and formal perfection of this work embody the realization that all was fore-ordained, the future implicit in the past. Fate is accepted from the beginning: only for a moment does rebellion stir; and in the tragic annihilation of all that life has seemed to offer is found in the end a deeper truth and a more lasting beauty. [79]

In an article written in 1929 by Constant Lambert under the title 'The Art of Frederick Delius', the distinguished conductor and composer took the view that *Sea Drift* is one of the handful of works for chorus and orchestra in which Delius found his 'free-est emotional expression and, strangely enough, his most satisfactory formal expression'. [80] That notion of informal freedom of musical thought finding its most effective outlet through some sort of formal discipline is not really the paradox it might at first seem. It can be seen from a different perspective in Delius's comment to Fenby about the nature of a good work always shaping itself to the laws of its own inner being:

> For instance, take *Sea-drift* [sic], which, I think is one of my best works. The shape of it was taken out of my hands, so to speak, as I worked and was bred easily and effortlessly of the nature and sequence of my particular musical ideas, and the nature and sequence of the particular poetical ideas of Whitman that appealed to me. [81]

We may also infer from this that *Sea Drift* was a true inspiration, one of those relatively rare acts of creation when the pen or brush seems to move over the paper of its own accord, almost involuntarily. Other musicians and artists have noted the phenomenon. But *Sea Drift*, for all its apparent spontaneity, is certainly not just a piece of automatic or improvisatory writing. There is

---

[79] *PW*, p. 100.

[80] Constant Lambert, 'The Art of Frederick Delius', *Apollo*, November 1929; reprinted in *Companion*, pp. 75–7.

[81] *Fenby 1*, pp. 35–6.

abundant evidence of the craftsman at work, consciously moulding his material and shaping it. Even the most casual examination of some of the details in its construction will bear that out. It also reveals, as so often with Delius, the futility of trying to package the music neatly into any predetermined form – *Sea Drift* does not work like that. Though it falls readily into sections or paragraphs, it also evolves according to its dramatic nature, its inner laws, as Delius himself implied.

Delius employs a huge orchestra: triple woodwind plus cor anglais, bass clarinet and double bassoon; six horns; and a full brass section of three trumpets, three trombones and tuba (although they are used with great restraint). Timpani, a bass drum, two harps and strings complete the extensive palette of orchestral colours. The mixed chorus is kept in four parts for most of the work, the one major exception being the unaccompanied section at Fig. 19+1, where Delius indulges in some *divisi* writing to enrich the vocal texture by up to eight parts. Finally, there is a solo baritone, who must have a strong upper range: he is summoned up to a top F sharp above the stave on a couple of occasions – most notably on the word 'love'.

*Sea Drift* opens with forty-five bars of orchestral introduction, a miniature tone poem setting the Maytime scene by the sea-shore on Long Island (or 'Paumanok', the old Indian name that Whitman uses). Delius nearly always writes magical openings and this, with the sunlit sea gently lapping the briars in which the two sea-birds have built their nest, is no exception. Could the evocative beginning of Bax's *The Garden of Fand* (1913) have been influenced by a knowledge of these masterful opening pages?

Ex. 4.10

The divided upper string chords sustaining the harmony (marked *x* in Ex. 4.10) suggest the stillness of the scene, wrapped in the hazy heat of the day; the descending melodic lines (*y* in Ex. 4.10) are given to the woodwind, passing in a chain from flute to oboe to clarinet, like an evocation of waves calmly unfurling on the shore; meanwhile the two harps, cellos and double basses give an essential impetus to the texture (*z* in Ex. 4.10), suggesting the gently rocking ocean. It is, as Fenby commented, 'music of unexampled accuracy, suggestion and poignance'. And it is that last quality which Delius portrays so vividly. The key signature of four sharps indicates either E major or its relative minor, C sharp, and in fact the music oscillates between these two key-centres, lending it a sense of ambiguity as well as a strong premonition of something bittersweet to come.

This opening material is most important and Delius will draw on it again at key moments later on in the score, binding the whole work together. He also returns full circle to it at the very end, a symbolic gesture that extends Whitman's poetic theme of transience and loss from the specific to the universal, a situation that will recur again and again in other places and in other ages.

The choir enters at Fig. 2+1 and sets the scene in words, the orchestral texture continuing much as before. A familiar Delian rhythmic trademark, the triplet motif, makes its appearance at Fig. 3+1 in the 1st oboe, followed by the cor anglais and 2nd clarinet; then the 3rd clarinet, 1st bassoon, and 3rd and 4th horns. This little figure (Ex. 4.11) soon permeates the whole of the rest of the orchestra:

Ex. 4.11

The baritone soloist makes an undramatic entrance at Fig. 4+4, emerging from the choral texture with the comment 'And every day the he-bird to and fro, near at hand ...'. The chorus almost at once makes way for him as he continues his narrative.

At this point a word is necessary about the treatment of the voices, both soloist and chorus, because it is relatively original for a work of this sort. For example, Delius often responds to Whitman's rather allusive poetic style by overlapping or layering the text, and Ex. 4.12 shows this (it is part of the choral passage just before the soloist enters). The layering effect is a natural result of the staggered entries by the various choral voices, but it does overlap separate words in the text. For example, on the first beat of the fourth bar of Ex. 4.12 we have simultaneously the syllables *bri-* (from 'briars'), *sea-* and *-shore* (both from 'seashore'), and *two*. Likewise, a few bars later, we hear the *gue-* of 'guests', *two*, the *fea-* from 'feathered', and the *-ba-* of 'Alabama', again all sung simultaneously on the first beat. Moreover, it is not only a question of the same line of text being overlapped or unaligned: there are also examples of totally different phrases laid over each other – as when the baritone soloist at Fig. 4+4 is singing 'And every day the he-bird ...', whilst the chorus is telling us about 'four light-green eggs spotted with brown'. This technique must not be taken as gaucheness or amateurishness on the part of the composer – it was obviously a conscious artistic decision and he used it at several points in the score. On paper it looks as if the text will be jumbled or obscured, but it does not sound like that in practice. Surely what Delius was trying to get across was a sense of fluidity and improvisation, with different voices interrupting and talking over each other, as people tend to do in everyday speech. That is relatively unusual

Ex. 4.12

in secular choral works of this period: Coleridge-Taylor in his *Hiawatha* trilogy (1898–1900) hardly ever overlaps choral text; on the other hand, Elgar, in *The Dream of Gerontius* (1900), and Stanford, in his *Elegiac Ode* (1884 – also a Whitman setting), both do.

The various roles that chorus and soloist play in the story are also a very fine example of Delius matching the spirit of the poem to his musical treatment. After the choir's initial scene-setting, the baritone has the narrative of the early part of the poem, but later he and the chorus separately become the voice of the he-bird. This is a reflection of the whole process of what the narrator calls, at the outset, 'absorbing, translating'. In other words, there are not necessarily any fixed points of view for chorus and soloist: like the treatment of the text itself, there is a symbolic overlap throughout as we hear the story from different vocal perspectives – variously those of the poet-speaker, the boy, the he-bird, and the sea. Indeed, it is up to the reader of the poem to decide who is speaking, as Whitman does not make it immediately obvious – but the task is not too difficult.

Another voice – an orchestral one, in the shape of a solo violin – is used imaginatively and poignantly by Delius at selective points in the score. The first is at Fig. 4+1, where the violin emerges from the surrounding texture, and then comes into its own *forte* for a half-dozen bars just before Fig. 5+1, while the rest of the orchestra is marked right down in dynamic. A further example occurs at Fig. 6+16, again adding to what Beecham once referred to as the 'tender pathos' of this magical score.

At Fig. 5 itself the music subsides into a texture of pure string chords, pointed slightly with touches of solo woodwind and bass drum – the relative simplicity here matching the baritone's description of himself as 'a curious boy'. How strikingly Delius colours that word 'curious' with a *sforzando* discord; then, after the phrase 'cautiously peering, absorbing, translating', responding accordingly with a few bars that have a slightly hesitant feel to them, with the 1st flute and 1st violins uttering quivering trills over the most delicate of accompaniments. Small things, but very telling in their effect.

Then suddenly, at Fig. 6+1, comes the great *coup de théâtre* that Constant Lambert so admired: the chorus takes on the roles of the two migratory birds, raising an ecstatic shout of 'Shine! Shine! Shine! Pour down your warmth, great sun!' Musically, Delius refers us back to the very opening, the chords in the first two bars of Fig. 6 being the same as those in the opening four bars of the score, whilst the shape of the vocal lines reflects the initial falling phrases of the woodwind. The scene floods with light, as if the sun had burst out from behind a cloud, the warmth of its rays echoed in a now unambiguous affirmation of E major. The mood is rapturous and is given the fullest texture so far. Although at this point Delius finally unleashes all six of his horns, never more than five are heard simultaneously; likewise he keeps his maximum orchestral forces in reserve, with the brass section still being held back: only the 1st trumpet plays here, and then just for five bars. The brass will have their moments later, but not yet.

At Fig. 7+1, the pulse expands into a consistent six beats in a bar rather than four: one of those swinging, ecstatic and dance-like passages that Delius was so fond of; here it reflects the fervour of the mating birds, 'Singing all time, minding no time'. But the composer does not linger; a few bars later he puts the brakes on, reining the music right in as he swiftly lightens the texture, and brings the dynamic down to *pianissimo*. Delius the dramatist is in full command of his powers as a new chapter in the music begins at Fig. 8+1; the key signature changes for the first time in the piece, the tonal centre of E major / C sharp minor being shed for the chilling suggestion of F minor as the baritone spells out the tragic news that the she-bird has not returned to the nest, and 'never appeared again'. The baritone solo here is in a style that is typical of the work, an example of what Beecham called the *arioso recitativo* – a type of recitative that is part way between a sparer, more traditional style of declamation and a warmer, more lyrical one with a fuller sense of melodic line. For Beecham, as he wrote in an article on *Sea Drift* for *The Daily Telegraph* in 1953, Delius was an expert in this technique.

The passage at Fig. 9+1 is masterfully done, as the baritone recounts how the he-bird sits waiting in vain all summer long for his mate to return. The key signature of four sharps is reinstated and Delius returns to his opening material, but in skeletal form: the shimmering sound of the violins is absent and instead the familiar chords are softly outlined in woodwind and horns above the rocking motion of the cellos, double basses and harps to evoke the restless 'flitting from briar to briar' of the forlorn 'solitary guest from Alabama'. There is his own cry of incomprehension on the 1st violins and cor anglais four bars before Fig. 9 (Ex. 4.13a), and then again in augmented form at Fig. 10+1 (Ex. 4.13b), this time with a rising interval of a fifth rather than a fourth; this little motif also returns briefly on the 1st flute at Fig. 12+15, where the baritone describes the 'lone singer, wonderful, causing tears'; there is also an affinity, in shape at least, with a motif that occurs in the music of The Dark Fiddler in *A Village Romeo and Juliet* (Ex. 4.13c) – a conscious or unconscious self-quotation.

A choral interjection along the lines of 'Shine! Shine! Shine!' begins at Fig. 11+1, but here treated quite differently, to a new F major melody which drives fluently along in 6/4 in one of the fullest textures of the work so far (at Fig. 11+13 all six horns are at last momentarily heard, though there is still no other brass in evidence). The memorable passage in Ex. 4.14 is a plea by the he-bird to the sea-winds to blow his mate back to him.

Ex. 4.13

(a)

(b)

(c)

Ex. 4.14

This mood is only sustained for some two dozen bars before there is another transformation in sound at Fig. 12+1. So far the score has been bathed in the clear sunlight of a late spring day; now Delius ushers in the ominous, shadowy atmosphere of night-time which will be the backdrop to events until just before the end. How wonderfully the composer evokes the glistening stars of the night sky in scoring that prefigures similar passages in both *The Song of the High Hills* and *North Country Sketches*. It is very simply done but so effective: the harps provide the image of glittering starlight set against a lightly touched-in background of muted string figurations and little dabs of *pianissimo* woodwind – a master orchestrator at work. The 3rd trombone and tuba make their first appearance at Fig. 12+25, but, far more significantly, the solo violin is used again (Ex. 4.15), doubled an octave below by the 1st clarinet and then the 1st oboe, to give voice to the despairing call of the he-bird to his lost mate:

Ex. 4.15

This evocative nocturne is the prelude to a major new section beginning at Fig. 13+1, 'A tempo, molto tranquillo', gradually increasing in pace as the metre changes from four beats in a bar to six, and then to nine, sweeping onwards to reach a great climax at Fig. 17+1.

Delius begins by reverting to the tonal centre of a warm E major as the poet-speaker, from a retrospective standpoint, now reveals his own identification with the plight of the sea-birds: 'He poured forth the meanings which I of all men know' – and the boy looks back to his boyhood, to the furtive excitement of his nocturnal visits to the beach as a 'curious observer' in warm lyrical phrases that are cushioned by sustained strings and horns, with the solo violin weaving triplet figurations above. A reference to 'avoiding the moonbeams' is another instance of Delius's skill in instrumentation, a wonderful effect as the harps take over the undulating triplets of the solo violin and transform them into something more glittery. Then, after a brief pull-up, the texture fills out and we plunge into a new metre – 9/4 – at the same time replacing the four sharps of the key signature with a single flat.

Delius more than matches the growing ecstasy of the poetry, with its images of the 'breakers tirelessly tossing' and the wind 'wafting' the hair of the 'curious boy' (an illustrative harp *glissando* at Fig. 14+2) whilst the chorus has the last of its triple invocations ('Soothe! Soothe! Soothe!'), this time a call to the waves 'embracing and lapping, every one close'. The 2nd violins begin a rushing chain of quavers at Fig. 14+5 that is handed on to the 1st violins and then to the woodwind. The trombones and tuba at last make their first significant contribution to the score, beginning at Fig. 14+9: as noted earlier, Delius has held them in reserve until now, showing remarkable restraint, given that this is almost the mid-point of the score. The impetus of the music becomes irresistible, well-captured in a striking phrase (Ex. 4.16) that emerges in the sopranos and is typical of the invigorating momentum of this whole section:

Ex. 4.16

Meanwhile, as the baritone sings of how 'madly the sea pushes upon the land, with love', Delius increases the tempo a notch further. The vividly erotic imagery of the poetry becomes insistent in the music: swirling woodwind figurations, splashes of *glissandi* from the harps, the strings throbbing vigorously with eighteen quavers to the bar, the chorus interjecting such phrases as 'With love!' and 'High and clear', whilst the melodic lines of horns and voices reflect the swell of the sea in contours that are sometimes smooth and sometimes strenuously angular:

Ex. 4.17

Delius is enormously skilled at building his music gradually to a climax and then suddenly deflating it – and here is a perfect example: the music boils over at Fig. 17+1 in the loudest moment so far – 'You must know who is here, is here, you must know who I am, my love, my love' – and then, in just two bars, descends from triple *forte* to *mezzopiano*, followed by a double bar at Fig.18+1, reining in the speed a little and marking the return of four sharps in the key signature. The groundswell of the bass line still heaves a little before all the previous orchestral turbulence is banished, and then comes one of the most magical passages, not only in *Sea Drift*, but in the whole of Delius's music.

It is significant that at this precise moment Delius chooses to focus his musical expression on the sound of unaccompanied voices, both choral and solo. From Fig. 19+1, his expansive orchestra sits silent for twenty-six bars, with only the 3rd bassoon and double bassoon coming in, *piano* and almost imperceptibly, to underpin the cadence at the very end of this *a capella* section, three bars before Fig. 20+1, and then being joined on the final chord by the quiet flick of a *pizzicato* from cellos and double basses. The 'tender pathos' identified by Beecham as one of the major characteristics of the score is at its most memorable in the choral harmonies that begin (unambiguously this time) in C sharp minor, but resolve eventually onto a ripe chord of E major. Delius in fact includes a scored accompaniment for this passage, using just clarinets and bassoons, but he asks in a footnote that the woodwind should only play 'in case of necessity' – i.e. if the chorus cannot hold its pitch. He is not renowned for always being so practical. It is interesting that in Variation 13 of *Appalachia*, written only a year earlier, there is no such fail-safe provision for the chorus, even though they are given fifteen bars of moderately chromatic *a cappella* harmony to cope with. Delius may have thought that the *Sea Drift* passage would be harder to sing in tune; certainly it is a case of better safe than sorry, although having any sort of accompaniment, however discreet, will spoil the effect. It is a masterstroke on his part to focus on the unaccompanied chorus and soloist, which is why this passage should be always one of the highlights in any performance of *Sea Drift*.

What also catches at the throat is the juxtaposition of the choral text, with its pathetic hopes that 'Perhaps the one I want so much, will rise with some of you', set against the contradictory assertion of the baritone soloist 'Shake out ... solitary here, the night's carols! Carols of lonesome love! Death's carols!' Delius's overlapping technique is here at its boldest but most effective. This is the moment when hope is for the first time undermined, and this unaccompanied section, all over in less than a minute, provides an important emotional focal point for the listener. *Sea Drift* does not, incidentally, stand alone in Delius's works in stilling the orchestra and letting the voices come centre stage at a key moment: there are parallels in *Appalachia* and *The Song of the High Hills.*

The soloist will not yet give in to total despair – that moment is still to come – and he clings to the infectious hope of the chorus in the yearning music that follows the re-entry of the orchestra at Fig. 20+1: 'Somewhere I believe I heard my mate responding to me'. Shortly afterwards comes a motif in 1st flute and cor anglais (Fig. 21+8) that is soon taken up by other instruments and begins to dominate, just as it will do again in the final pages of the score. Ex. 4.18 shows it in its most developed form as it appears at Fig. 22+1 in the 1st violins:

Ex. 4.18

The chorus, now in the guise of the beloved, warns the he-bird that his hopes are futile: 'Do not be decoy'd elsewhere, that is the whistle of the wind, it is not my voice ...'. A dragging, melancholy downward fall of a semitone characterises this section, most poignantly and bitterly expressed – 'O darkness, O in vain' – at the *largamente* ten bars after Fig. 22:

Ex. 4.19

This terrible cry ushers in one of the two instances in the score when the full orchestra, brass included, is deployed triple *forte* (only at Fig. 17+1 is there a comparable display of strength). There is a dramatic cut-off and, over the barely perceptible rumble of timpani and double basses, the baritone finally gives way to utter despair in the line, marked *ad libitum*, 'O I am very sick and sorrowful'; the string and low woodwind harmonies which underscore the word 'sorrowful' are of unbearable poignancy. There is a fine example of Delius's attention to detail one bar before Fig. 23, where he writes a little downward-falling motif, in dotted rhythm, played consecutively by 3rd flute, 1st oboe and then 1st flute. Its significance is only apparent when the same phrase is repeated eleven bars later as a setting for the word 'uselessly' in the soloist's phrase, 'I singing uselessly all the night'. A little psychological detail that may go unnoticed, but it is there, all the same. The chorus softly echoes the word 'night' and the music seems about to sink into oblivion. But Delius has one more potent effect up his sleeve: at Fig. 24+1 the warmth of E major returns quite unexpectedly as the soloist sings eloquently of past happiness that can never be recaptured, with Ex. 4.18 quoted in turn by 1st and 3rd horns, 1st flute and strings. It is the quintessential Delian expression of transience and loss, here redeemed only by the glowing quality of the orchestral accompaniment as the soloist sings movingly of his past happy life 'In the air, in the woods, over fields'. This is not so much an affirmation of that other great Delian theme, renewal in Nature, as an acceptance that if physical love is over, then at least transfigured, spiritual love remains in the memory. *Sea Drift* does not end in despair but in a dignified resignation that is beautifully – indeed, perfectly – expressed in the final two pages of the score. The strings, with just a sparing use of horns and selective woodwind, have the last say as the baritone falls silent, musing on the words 'We two together, no more, no more!', with the chorus scarcely daring to breathe an echo of this. Delius brings back figure *z* from Ex. 4.10, the rocking harp figure from the very opening of the work, underscored by the faintest tremor of the bass drum. And so we come full circle, musically, back to where we started, a symbol of the eternal nature of Whitman's and Delius's theme. The harmonies of the opening are quoted once more in the final bars, interwoven with a low B natural on a muted horn, marked *morendo* – dying away. The ambiguities of major and minor are finally laid to rest as the C sharp of the penultimate string chord resolves onto a B natural and the music fades into nothing.

It is an unforgettable ending to one of the most perfect works that Delius ever wrote, perfect in the sense that there is nothing that needs to be taken away and nothing that needs to be added. And the composer himself knew it. Just a few days before he died Delius said to Fenby: 'Yes, I think if I had anything worth saying, my boy, I said it in *Sea Drift*.'[82]

FOR whatever reason, Schillings did not include the work in the programme for Graz, and the first performance took place the following year, on 24 May 1906, when the Tonkünstlerfest was held in Essen. Delius had instructed the Berlin firm of Harmonie to publish the full score and C. G. Röder the vocal score, but getting these to the performers in time must have been something of

[82] *Lloyd*, p. 176.

a nightmare, for on 8 May Harmonie wrote to Delius saying that they had just learned that:

> Speiss of Brunswick, the Court Opera singer, who was to have taken the baritone part, is not now going to do so, presumably owing to other engagements, and in 2 days we shall be told who is taking his place at Essen, we shall then immediately send this gentleman a copy of the vocal score. Herr Witte,[83] the orchestra conductor in Essen, received a fully corrected proof, together with a good full score of 'Sea Drift' in the middle of last week, which is in good time.[84]

Witte therefore had less than three weeks for the rehearsals, and Josef Loritz, the replacement soloist, something in the order of a fortnight in which to learn his extremely difficult part. As if that were not enough to worry Delius, Witte had written to him the previous month: 'I should like ... to ask whether you will permit me to "touch up" the choral parts a little in the interests of more comfortable singing and a better rendering of the German text.' Not unnaturally, Delius was furious, but Haym persuaded him simply to refuse the request.[85]

The concert was inordinately long by today's standards: in addition to *Sea Drift*, there was a symphonic poem by Rudolf Siegel, a fantasy for violin and orchestra by Otto Neitzel, another symphonic poem by Richard Mors, a symphony by Hermann Bishoff, an orchestral song by Walter Braunfels and a *Festgesang* by Humperdinck. Delius was there, and in the event he must surely have been pleased, for:

> the large Auditorium was completely sold out, reflecting the importance of the event ... Almost all the composers and musicians of whom the German people had reason to be proud had appeared; as well from Essen itself, as from outlying places, all who came brought with them a serious interest in and understanding of music; in any case such an attentive and, at least in very large part, such a knowledgeable public has never filled our beautiful Municipal Garden Hall since its foundation, as on this evening.
>
> *Essener Volks-Zeitung*, 26 May 1906

Interestingly, in a letter of 19 March 1906[86] Schillings wrote:

> None of the scores is especially difficult (like Strauss) or needs special musical forces. Delius is harmonically strange, technically not difficult; Siegel and Mors modern 'Normalstyle' (a bit thick);

---

[83] Georg Witte (1843–1929): a Dutchman who had by then been the Director of Music at Essen for some twenty-four years.

[84] Letter 193.

[85] *TB*, p. 135.

[86] To an unidentified recipient.

> Bischoff makes the greatest demands: he asks for the complexity of
> 'Eulenspiegel'.

but few players or singers today would agree with the view that *Sea Drift* is not
technically difficult.

*The Musical Times* was critical of the Festival as a whole – which it described
as 'The Annual Festival of Cacophony – for that it is more and more tending
to become' – but whoever wrote up this concert achieved an extremely good
grasp of *Sea Drift* in that one evening (and possibly at a previous rehearsal),
and definitely approved of it:

> ... But whether the greater part, or even a small fraction of the novelties,
> proved really enjoyable to any but the most advanced of the young
> 'Heaven-stormers' amongst musicians, critics and amateurs, may be
> doubted. Mr Delius's Sea Drift was generally acknowledged to be, with
> one exception,[87] the most important work of the Festival. It is a striking
> piece of musical impressionism, marvellously coloured, and, in spite
> of many extravagances, harmonically fascinating. There is no thematic
> material to speak of; chords and modulations, sound experiments and
> mood picturing alone produce an astonishing effect, and express the
> composer's poetic idea in such a convincing manner that the listener feels
> persuaded, almost against his inclination, that he has heard a masterpiece
> of a very individual and novel kind.
>
> July 1906

Two local papers were kind, although not totally convinced:

> The work earned exceptional applause, which, coming from such a
> distinguished and varied audience, was indeed doubly valuable ... The
> text is of great poetical beauty, and its meaning is enhanced and deepened
> by the music ... the whole made an extraordinary impression ... The first
> item after the interval was doubtless the most worthwhile work of the
> whole evening: the Symphony in E major, by Hermann Bischoff.
>
> *Essener Volks-Zeitung*, 26 May 1906

> If we were to dispense with the solo and choir, there would remain in
> the unique orchestral score so much left that is captivating, fascinating
> and moving, so that the listener could derive the purest joy from it. What
> interpretation, painting and illumination in this part of the work! Truly,
> the audience correctly felt, as it applauded so enthusiastically, celebrating
> this composer, that he is worthy to stand in importance alongside
> Hermann Bischoff.
>
> *Rheinish-Westfälischer Anzeiger*, 26 May 1906

---

[87] Presumably Mahler's Symphony no. 6, which was also premièred there.

The critic in Germany's foremost musical periodical, *Die Musik*, really disliked the work, but nevertheless thought that it should be repeated:

> ... a work of depressing cheerlessness such as I have scarcely heard before. One constantly has the feeling that the composer has composed with disregard for natural harmony; certain regularly recurring discordant progressions (seconds, sevenths, etc.) do not make for comfortable listening, which the sharply rhapsodic text by no means justifies. What is the good of all the ingenuity that is turned to such a piece if its effect is so miserable? Nonetheless, I am convinced that a whole string of conductors, true to their own principles, will not let slip this sea serpent next winter, and that a 'well brought up' public will give the appropriate palpable expressions to its satisfaction that even such a piece has an end.
>
> *Die Musik* 5(3), Bd 19 (1905/6), 50

Meanwhile, another musical journal was very intrigued:

> As chance would have it, it was a rebel in his art-form who, apart from Mahler, gave most food for thought at this festival: Frederic [*sic*] Delius. Mahler strives for extreme clarity in his themes and instrumentation. He loves the diatonic scale and clear rhythms, and all that is precisely defined. Delius, on the other hand, in his Sea Drift (Im Meerestreiben) has given us a work which is quite different. We can almost say that it consists only of chords and sounds, and that it seeks to restore music to its original elements ... liberation from fixed clear forms; very free harmony and mood-painting ... It is a rejection of all that has come down to us – the object being to penetrate the heart of poetry, and at the same time create something new
>
> *Neue Zeitschrift für Musik* 73, Jahrgang 24, 13 June 1906

Among the audience was the young conductor Carl Schuricht, who wrote to Delius later in the year:

> Dear Maestro ... How much inspiration, pure delight and joy 'Sea-drift' [*sic*] awakened in me and left imprinted on me, I will not describe to you in more detail, but just tell you that the mere knowledge of your physical existence has given me a source of inner warmth and joy in activity that enriches me in all my artistic undertakings ... I should be very grateful if you could send me, on loan, chiefly for detailed study, a copy of the score of your 'Sea-drift'.[88]

---

[88] Letter 199. Carl Schuricht (1880–1967) became a strong champion of Delius's music, and he conducted *Sea Drift* at Wiesbaden on 7 November 1910 and at least three times subsequently (including a recording issued on CD by Archiphon (ARC-3-0) in 1999 – the only one ever to use the German text). He also conducted *A Mass of Life*. There is an extract from another letter from Schuricht to Delius in *Pictures*, p. 54.

Cassirer, too, was tremendously taken by the work:

> To my surprise Herr Max Chop,[89] to whom I played through the whole
> of your opera 'R & J', brought me your songs and Seadrift [sic] in piano
> score. I had no idea that the things were already out. I have now got to
> know Sea-drift [sic] today! – What am I to write? I could have almost
> howled with delight. I will say no more. I am quite beside myself and
> wanted just to let you know briefly. Does Zarathustra have nothing but
> this sort of stuff too? I hope that I shall soon come into possession of
> the score. You are now glorious in your maturity. Sitting comfortably
> and plucking the fruits from the tree! Round and ripe and sweet, it says
> everything that one simply forgets the artist ... I got Herr Chop utterly
> intoxicated![90]

while Hermann Suter[91] of Basel also wanted to do it:

> For this winter it seems to me that it would be wiser for me if at a time
> when I am making some major demands on my choir (Berlioz Requiem,
> Bach B minor Mass) I could also make some lesser demands on them. In
> this way my whole Society, which as such has not yet sung anything of
> yours, might become acquainted with your style and won over for you by
> means of a smaller work. I have 'Seadrift' [sic] in mind, which enchants
> me more each time I play it. I feel that if I can get Messchaert for the
> baritone solo the work will be interpreted ideally. Who, by the way, sang
> it in Essen?[92]

In the event it was he who conducted the second performance, given in Basel's
Musiksaal by the Basel Gesangverein on 2 March 1907.[93] Delius was naturally
there, and he also attended the final rehearsal the previous day, which

> ended in the following little dramatic incident: After 'Sea Drift', the
> audience applauded enthusiastically, as did Mr Suter, the conductor,
> who repeatedly called for the composer. There was then hissing as well
> as applause. The conductor, Mr Suter, was incensed and called out that
> that was bad manners and that he would not tolerate any hissing. A voice
> from the audience cried out, 'We are allowed to express our disapproval
> too!' On Saturday (at the concert itself), there was only applause,

---

[89] Max Chop (1862–1929): a German composer, music critic and writer, whose
*Frederick Delius* (1904) was the first scholarly book on the composer.

[90] Letter 200.

[91] See p. 95 above. At Leipzig Conservatorium, he had been a pupil of Carl Reinecke,
an influential and versatile, but very conservative musician. That probably accounts
for his apparent predilection for Classical composers, and the difficulty he thought
his choir would have with *Sea Drift*.

[92] Letter 197.

[93] The programme was nearly as heavy as in Essen.

and the composer was obliged to mount the podium to thank the audience.

*Basler Nachrichten*, 5 March 1907

Two other reviewers of the concert said:

'Sea Drift' by Delius begins with the following text, which we wish to bring to our readers' attention because it shows what we are sometimes offered in the name of 'poetry' – bad taste and nonsense: [There followed the first nine lines of the poem]. Haven't composers got ears to hear such linguistic absurdities? The use of verbs is apparently something too vulgar, too common for the translator of the English poem, Jelka Rosen.

This incredibly obscure poem blows up a minor incident (which is just about good enough for a little story, told in the nursery) into an event of high tragedy, and it does so in as tasteless a manner as possible. It is a poem that, in our opinion, is not particularly suitable for setting to music, and we find it hard to understand how one can set such large forces in motion for material of this kind.

Delius's music gave us absolutely no pleasure whatsoever, and, if we are honest, then we must admit that seldom have we been so dreadfully bored. It did not appear to contain a single comprehensible motif and the constant formless seething of the music has an unspeakably monotonous effect. After a few minutes listening to this work, we were so tired that it was only by making a great effort and summoning up all our energy that we were able to follow the course of the music. We consider it completely impossible for anyone who is not perfectly acquainted with the piano arrangement or the score to follow the endless harmonic labyrinths, which are totally contrary to all that we have understood up to now under the heading of musical euphony. The whole thing made a very wishy-washy impression on us.

*National Zeitung (Basel)*, 6 March 1907

The beginning is so unclear that, until I learnt otherwise, I mistook the town of Paumanok for the hero of the poem, a love-sick male bird … A strongly elegiac mood is evoked by the text and the resonance of this mood is re-enforced by the composer's use of quite daring devices. Rarely have so many excruciating dissonances been strung together; but one senses an artistic will and sensitivity behind it all, and for this reason, one cannot reject this music out of hand. Our ears have got used to so many things over the years, and perhaps the Delian[94] processions of ninths and sevenths will, one day, be familiar fare.

*Schweizerische Musikzeitung und Sängerblatt*, 9 March 1907

Unfortunately, it is not known what Delius thought of either the Essen or the Basel performances.

---

[94] It is interesting that this expression was in use as early as 1907.

In January 1907 Delius had sent scores of *Appalachia* and *Sea Drift* to Henry Wood, presumably at his request, and his acknowledgement of them must have been very exciting for Delius: 'The latter work I am pushing very strongly with the Sheffield Festival Committee, and I hope that it will be included in our scheme.'[95] The Committee indeed agreed to Wood doing *Sea Drift* at the 1908 Festival. The young Frederic Austin had sung for him at Promenade Concerts and elsewhere since 1903 – many years later Wood wrote in his autobiography: 'I purposely asked for Frederic Austin to sing the solo part [in *Sea Drift*] because I knew of no one else who could be trusted to sing it *con amore*.'[96] Things did not, however, go all that smoothly on the non-musical front. The Festival Committee had for long been determined that 'their' performance should be the first English one, and in November 1907 they sent a letter to Delius expressing their considerable disappointment at learning that there was apparently to be a performance in London the following February – eight months before their Festival: 'When we undertook to perform this work at our next Festival, it was on distinct understanding that it was to be the first performance in England.'[97] Delius reported this to Granville Bantock:

> Dear Friend ... The reply from Sheffield was almost rude. They said in 4 lines that the Committee refused my offer & it would either play it or take it off the programme. It really seems preposterous (there never having been any question of 1st performance) they should now take up this attitude. Just fancy to require the first performance of a work 2 years before the Festival without any remuneration. Wood is of course behind it all. I feel quite sure he could have arranged it if he had wanted to. It really is taking my bread and butter away from me; for, all I get from the editor is a percentage on the music sold and performances. They seem to be able to pay him (Wood) a big fee! However, I don't care whether they play it or not.[98]

But in the event the proposed London performance did not take place, and Wood did conduct it at Sheffield. Then in June 1908 Beecham – who, only some six months after they first met, was rapidly becoming the composer's strongest supporter of all – wrote to say that he simply loved *Sea Drift*, now knew it very well, and gave him the marvellous news that at the end of the year he would be bringing the North Staffordshire District Choral Society ('the Hanley Choir') up to London to give it with the New Symphony Orchestra, seventy-five strong.[99]

---

[95] Letter 204.

[96] Sir Henry Wood, *My Life of Music* (London: Gollanz, 1938), p. 213.

[97] Letter 249, n. 3.

[98] Letter 249.

[99] Letter 284.

After the dinner party at Balfour Gardiner's house (mentioned above in connection with *Appalachia*), Delius wrote to Jelka, 'There is a splendid Baritone here a Mr Austin, very musical and I hope he will sing Sea-drift [*sic*] at Sheffield & later the "Messe"'.[100] Austin and Delius quickly became good friends: in October, Delius received an intriguing letter from him:

> I was delighted to get your letter. Please forgive my scandalous treatment of it, but until now I've been working against time to get a Rhapsody of mine finished – which Wood is playing on the 16th. I'm so glad you're here for a long visit & look forward to meeting you again very much. Apparently there's to be an opportunity on Saturday, as I've just had a letter from Gardiner talking of a party for the Middlesex.[101] We're both free & will come with pleasure. We have a friend staying with us whom we must bring along if you don't mind. A lady – but who will be quite game. Where shall we all meet? If we are going to be a large party on Sat? [*sic*] it would be well to get seats beforehand – box seats are the ones we generally affect. Perhaps, as you are in town comparatively, [*sic*] you wouldn't mind getting 3 for us? Last time we went we had great difficulty.[102]

and then:

> 'Sea Drift' is going well; I have rehearsed it three times already with Wood, and there are the choral & orchestral rehearsals still in front of me – so you may count on our thoroughness and enthusiasm. When do you come to London? I should very much like to go through it with you before the final rehearsals if possible.[103]

It is difficult today to appreciate the difficulty the choruses who took part in these early performances must have faced in learning and singing this new music – particularly bearing in mind that very probably more than half their members were using Tonic Sol-fa scores.[104]

[100] Letter 213. Delius would in fact have already heard Austin, as he sang the aria *Komm, süsses Kreutz* (*Come, Blessed Cross*) from Bach's *St Matthew Passion* in the Queen's Hall concert on 22 October 1907, when Szántó gave the first performance of the final version of Delius's Piano Concerto.

[101] A well-known music hall in Drury Lane. One of the oldest in the country, its origins went back to the seventeenth century, and Nell Gwynn was said to have been associated with it. Originally known as The Mogul, it was rebuilt in 1911 by the great theatre architect Frank Matcham. One can imagine Delius, with his deep love of 'la vie parisienne', thoroughly enjoying himself there.

[102] 21 September 1907 (coll. Martin Lee-Browne).

[103] Ibid.

[104] Tonic Sol-fa was a system of musical notation invented in 1853 by the Reverend John Curwen (1816–80). The notes of any scale are named 'Do', 're', 'me', etc., and those 'symbols' are printed below the notes they represent. In 1889, it was being used in 21,643 elementary schools: *Musical Opinion*, March 1908, p. 423. John

'Experienced in flights of Handelian semiquavers, the dramatic choruses of *Elijah*',[105] and even in the long contrapuntal lines of Bach, grasping music such as Ex. 4.12 (even though there are four quite independent lines) would not have been too difficult, but passages where there are up to eight lines (as at 'O rising stars'), or where almost every note is prefixed by an accidental (such as 'Those are the shadows of leaves'), must have taxed them sorely.

The performance was given in the third concert of the Festival, on 7 October 1908 in Sheffield's Albert Hall, with the Queen's Hall Orchestra and the 300-strong Festival Chorus. In addition to *Sea Drift*, the programme included York Bowen's Overture in G minor, Walford Davies's *Everyman* (in which Austin also sang the part of Everyman), the Bach E major Violin Concerto (with Kreisler – who played the famous unaccompanied *Chaconne* as an encore), and finally Strauss's *Till Eulenspiegel*. The programme note, by J. A. Rodgers, the chief critic of the *Sheffield Daily Telegraph*, gave a beautiful description:

> There is no formal structure to the work. The composer dispenses with representative themes; nothing is developed; only in one or two instances does a motive or harmonic expression recur; in fact the work is without organised plan. It is an impression in music of the pictures and emotions conjured up by the text. Yet, if devoid of formal design, it is far from being incoherent. The changing words of the text are mirrored and intensified in the music. Though phrases and harmonic patterns arise and disappear without orderly design or sequence, like the changing hues and cloud patterns on a summer sea – the entire work resolves itself into a composite whole, to linger in the memory as does the fixed impression of some exquisite Nature-scene – formless yet enchanting.

Despite an apparent breakdown in the middle (see *The Staffordshire Sentinel* report below), everyone on the platform seems to have been reasonably well rehearsed. The next day, Delius wrote to Jelka:

> Dearest. Just a word to say that the performance went off very well – It was a huge success – altho' I dont believe anyone really understood it – Austin sang wonderfully – The Chorus was wonderfull [*sic*] – Woods Orchestra knew it perfectly, but he did not always take the right Tempi – Sometimes too slow and then too fast[106] – However, it went quite well – I will keep some notices for you – Newman's and some others are awfully good – I have only read one at present – but Austin read some more …[107]

---

Curwen also founded the music publishers J. Curwen & Sons (later The Curwen Press).

[105] Geoffrey Attwell, '*Sea Drift*: Triumph – or Tragedy?', *DSJ* 108 (1992), 9–14.

[106] Wood was not generally regarded as a good Delius conductor. For instance, on 14 February 1914, Philip Heseltine wrote to his girlfriend Olivia Smith that 'Henry Wood did the Delius "Dance Rhapsody" disgracefully badly … "Enery J" has no idea whatsoever where Delius is concerned': *PW Letters*, Letter 382.

[107] Letter 293.

He talked to one of the local newspapers as well:

'The Sheffield Choir was wonderful', Mr. Frederick Delius, the famous Anglo-German composer, could hardly express with sufficient warmth his appreciation of the singers who last night gave his delightful setting of 'Sea Drift' so magnificent a rendering. 'The Sheffield choir is wonderful', his voice vibrating with enthusiasm. A representative of the Sheffield Independent had asked him for his impression of the way in which his work was given, and he most readily told the journalist of his enthusiasm for the singers. 'The rendering of my work', the composer said with obvious sincerity, 'was excellent – excellent – excellent.' 'You were perfectly satisfied?' 'Satisfied? Delighted! What can I say of so fine a performance except that it was really excellent? Mr. Austin was splendid. The only pity is that you have such a small hall here. The Chorus might well sing in a larger hall; but for what they did I am most grateful!'

*The Sheffield Daily Independent*, 8 October 1908

The reviews of all the first four performances in England well illustrate the fact that the music critics of provincial papers were generally quite as sensitive and well informed as many of those working on London papers or writing for musical periodicals, and often more so. Perhaps the London critics became jaded, but in those days, of course, 'local' papers were much more serious, and the standard of writing in them was far higher than it is in their counterparts today. Their almost daily reviews of concerts (and many other events) in London invariably appeared in the following day's paper, and they were by some of the most celebrated critics – Samuel Langford and later Neville Cardus at the *Manchester Guardian*, Ernest Newman with the *Birmingham Daily Post*, and (albeit at a later period) Ernest Bradbury for the *Yorkshire Evening Post*.

One of the fullest and most perspicacious criticisms was the one by Newman to which Delius had referred – the report of the whole concert was an almost complete broadsheet column in a very small font size. He may well have owned a score (published in 1906), but nevertheless, at one hearing (like Rodgers) he had acquired an astonishing understanding of the music:

For those who have been watching the progress of English music over the last few years, tonight's concert, with the first performance in this country of Mr Frederick Delius's 'Sea Drift' was the most interesting part of the Festival. Mr. Delius is a composer of pronounced individuality who so far has made little effort to become known in his own country, but who is highly honoured in Germany. 'Sea Drift' ... is based on a fine poem by Walt Whitman, in which there is, for that poet, a rather unusually deep vibration of purely lyrical feeling ... [Mr Delius's] idiom is entirely his own, which can be said of very few living composers, and, whether we like it or not, there is no denying that here is a new, quite independent personality to be reckoned with. I cannot always follow him in the

working out of his harmonic texture, and some of the vocal writing ...
seems more appropriate to instruments than to voices, but in the case
of a style so novel as that of Mr. Delius it is wise to suspend judgement
on these points for a while. The writing for the solo voice is amazingly
poignant in expression, and the general atmosphere of Whitman's
scene – the lonely beach with the sad, grey outlook, the hollow surge and
boom of the sea, the sting of salt in the air, and the mournful brooding
of the stricken bird – all this is painted with most singular power in
the orchestra. Most admirable of all, perhaps, is the singular unity of
the composition. Mr Rodgers, in his admirable programme note ...
points out that there is apparently no formal structure to it, and no use
of representative themes. That is precisely where Mr Delius shows his
originality and his modernity ... As music grows more subtle in feeling
we want a more subtle system of structure, a system that shall dispense
with the older external scaffolding and build more from the inside. That
is what Mr. Delius does in 'Sea Drift'. The work has a quite remarkable
unity. There is any amount of variety of expression in it, but, like a fine
painting, it all seems bathed in the one atmosphere which is no small
achievement in a work lasting an hour and a half [*sic*]. Anyone can score
well these days, but Mr Delius is one of the few composers with an
orchestral colour scheme all of his own ... To this, no doubt, is due the
satisfactory feeling or organic unity the work gives us. The melody, the
harmony and orchestration are indivisible ... One can hardly overpraise
the masterly singing of the baritone solo by Mr Frederic Austin.

*The Birmingham Daily Post*, 8 October 1908

*Musical Opinion's* local correspondent had obviously thought quite seriously
about it too:

It is quite a short composition on the most modern lines: but it is marked
by an absolute sincerity of purpose and a rare feeling of beauty for musical
atmosphere. Judged from an architectural standpoint, it is somewhat
lacking; but as a musical transcription of an emotional fragment of
beautiful poetry, it is almost unique. My own impression is that it will
be recognised as one of the most successful and beautiful works of the
transitional period through which we are passing.

November 1908

while his opposite number on *The Musical Standard* was also well pleased:

Compared with his other compositions, the harmonic basis of 'Sea
Drift' is more rational and the ear is not punished with crude bunches
of dissonance. The writing for chorus and solo baritone is entirely free
and independent of the orchestration, and is one continuous series of
changing hues, a state of moody reflectiveness with a feeling for Nature;
the roll of the 'husky-noised' sea ... the chorus responded to every nuance
of light and shade quite as loyally as the orchestra, and the effect upon

the listener was a tribute to Mr Wood's careful conducting, and, withal, a triumph for a composer of character and originality. Mr Frederic Austin was the exponent of the solo, and was an inevitable partner in what was the most brilliant success of the week.

*October 1908*

*The Times* of 8 October thought that 'the composer has written music of such haunting loveliness', and another critic felt that the work should be given a fair chance:

Many of the audience shook their heads at this work and failed to catch its idiom, perhaps because it was performed somewhat perfunctorily. The idiom of the work is strange and subtle. Many of the designed effects did not come off, mainly because the instrumental and choral tone demanded a far finer adjustment than what was attempted ... Mr Delius's music may be difficult to follow, if only because of its comparative formlessness. As I have said above, many felt untouched, but others discerned a consistency of treatment in the music and an atmosphere born of the poem. It may be hoped that the work may be heard again soon under ideal conditions of choral and orchestral balance.

*The Musical Times*, November 1908

Delius and Beecham must, however, have been greatly amused by one report which said, 'Mr Delius seems to have exhausted the whole gamut of aquatic emotion.'[108]

Beecham had heard the North Staffordshire District Choral Society earlier in the year, and he was hugely impressed by their ability to learn new music, their tone, their tuning and great sensitivity:

'Why did you go to the Potteries[109] for your choir, Mr Beecham?'

'Because I couldn't get a good enough choir in London!'[110]

In his biography of Delius, Beecham wrote similarly:

This choir ... was at that time in my view the most completely equipped for the interpretation of this particular kind of music. Under its excellent choirmaster, James Whewell, it had a bright ringing tone, undeviating pitch and a sensibility that marked it apart from most other large choral bodies of the day.[111]

This, then, was the choir Beecham used for the two performances he had promised Delius back in the summer. The first was in the Victoria Hall at Hanley on 3 December 1908:

---

[108] *TB*, p. 155.

[109] The area of Staffordshire in and around Stoke-on-Trent, where the country's primary china and earthenware industries were concentrated.

[110] Charles Reid, *Thomas Beecham* (London: Gollanz, 1961), p. 59.

[111] *TB*, p. 154.

Mr. Whewell's singers, on whom perhaps the brunt of the performance lay, sang as if inspired, and with the aid of the magnificent orchestra carried themselves through flawlessly.[112]

The second was in Queen's Hall on 22 February 1909. They also gave the piece in Manchester the day after the Hanley concert, when, as Beecham amusingly describes in *A Mingled Chime*,[113] there were about 400 members of the orchestra and chorus on the platform, performing for an audience of 300 in a hall capable of holding 2,600. One local paper observed:

> Manchester has invented a new way of showing that enthusiasm for music which it is so confident that it possesses. The method of proof consists in staying away from one of the most interesting concerts of the season. So Mr. Beecham, the New Symphony Orchestra and the North Staffordshire Choral Society went through the programme for the benefit of as fine a collection of empty chairs and benches as anyone could pray to be delivered from seeing.
>
> [Manchester] *Daily Despatch*, 5 December 1908

Austin was the soloist in all three of Beecham's performances, and the New Symphony Orchestra played for the first two (notwithstanding that Beecham did not now have much time for them, because they were unwilling to give him total control over their concerts); for the London concert, however, Beecham used the Beecham Symphony Orchestra – the first of the three 'bands' which he formed and owned over the years – then making only its second public appearance. In very high spirits after that performance, and clearly thrilled with his 'band', he sent some reviews to Delius, saying that *Sea Drift* had gone 'stunningly'.[114]

The orchestra was indeed hugely praised by all the critics, but one commentator was unimpressed by Beecham himself:

> Mr Beecham is a fine conductor, but his violent and often-times unnecessary gestures detract greatly from the merits of his conducting.
>
> *The Staffordshire Sentinel*, 5 December 1908

*The Times* was almost less enthusiastic after the Queen's Hall performance than it had been about the Hanley one:

> Much of the setting of Walt Whitman's beautiful rhapsody on the bird mourning for his dead mate is of the usual atmospheric vagueness, and it is not until the last few pages of the vocal score that the music contrives to express anything particular. When it does, it becomes really emotional, so that at the end the hearer forgets the tedium of the opening ... The choir deserve the utmost credit for finding their notes so accurately

---

[112] *The Staffordshire Sentinel*, 4 December 1908.

[113] *AMC*, p. 81.

[114] Letter 309.

in music that is singularly ill-fitted for the voice. In particular, the disposition of the chords in a passage in seven-part [*sic*] harmony is so ineffective that they might just as well be in four parts. The composer was called at the close of the work.

23 February 1909

Mr Baughan, meanwhile, worked himself up into yet another veritable frenzy:

We are afraid that Mr. Beecham will scarcely succeed in making Delius' 'Sea Drift' a delight to listen to. The composer would seem to be on the wrong path. We listened attentively to the music last Monday, and there seemed no excuse for its dullness and labouredness. Indeed, we venture to say that the spirit of the music is not the real spirit of Walt Whitman's poem. We were very sorry for the vocal soloist Mr. Frederic Austin: he had abominably monotonous, barbarous and totally ineffective stuff to tackle. He was extremely enthusiastic, but not once did he – nor could anyone – touch us in the remotest manner ... What we strongly object to, apart from the laboured character of the music, is the ugly and meaningless dissonance of 'Sea Drift'. We are scarcely convinced that it is the work of a master-musician of the first rank. Let Mr Delius study (say) the Prelude to 'Tristan and Isolde' and endeavour to understand how clumsy, seriously lacking in contrast and often downright bad is his own music from a harmonic standpoint. He will also see the value of melody. There is melody *and* melody, but 'music' without melody is not music at all.

*The Musical Times*, 1 January 1909

The majority of the critics, however, approved of the work:

The orchestral scoring is brilliantly illustrative of the anguished fantasy of the irregular verses of the poet, and the choral writing, although extremely exacting, is often impressive and even fascinating. The treatment, of course, is essentially modern, but there is no question of an allegation of a formless cacophony being hurled at the [audience] ...

*The Musical Times*, 1 March 1909

'Sea Drift' is an astonishing work. For all its new scheme of harmony, so rich as to be almost congested, it is an extraordinarily simple work – as simple as the beautiful, direct English of Walt Whitman's poem. Surely descriptive sound can go no farther than this. The swell and reach of the breakers rolling onto the beach, tearing and nagging at the sand below; the sense of infinite space, and the loneliness of the bird hovering on outstretched wings, looking for its mate; the poignant grief when the bird realises that he is singing uselessly in the night, and that he and his mate will be 'together no more' – these aspects of nature, and of the emotions in animate and inanimate nature are transferred into sounds by Mr. Delius with a poignant fidelity that is almost bitter in its truth.

*The Manchester Courier*, 5 December 1908

Many years later, the writer Hubert Foss described it very simply:

> Delius ... is the subjective mood-painter, the anthropomorphic dreamer about the brown birds; impressionistic in style, subtle and accomplished in technical expression, nostalgic, musing on memories, touched emotionally more by what is not there than what is. He broods in an exquisite musical rhapsody.

Curiously, five of the first six performances of *Sea Drift* were beset with problems: the short rehearsal period at Essen; the apparent breakdown at Sheffield mentioned in the next quotation; the famous disappearance of the full score before the Hanley concert (which Beecham proceeded to conduct from memory – *The Musical Times* of 1 January 1909 saying, in blissful ignorance, 'Mr Thomas Beecham showed his enthusiasm for the music of Delius by conducting from memory a performance of "Sea Drift"'); the tiny audience in Manchester; and, finally, an extraordinary crisis at Queen's Hall reported by *The Staffordshire Sentinel*:

> The run to Euston was good, the train pulling up at one of the principal platforms on scheduled time. The party went Westward by means of the tube railway. Tea was awaiting them, and after tea a rehearsal was called for. It transpired, however, the Suffragettes were in possession of the Queen's Hall, and would not be dispossessed long past the time for the band and the choir to meet. As a consequence, the band and the choir did not get together until the concert, though Mr Beecham had a quarter of an hour with the orchestra. Considering the character of the music, it was a dangerous thing to do, but thanks to the enthusiasm and efficiency of the choristers, the adaptability and executive perfection of the instrumentalists, and the clear, definite and inspiring control of Mr Beecham, nothing approaching a hiatus occurred. What a triumph this was for all concerned, and will be better appreciated, perhaps, if it be mentioned here that in the original performance of 'Sea Drift' at Sheffield, notwithstanding the splendour of the forces employed, and the time expended in rehearsal, an actual breakdown occurred, so difficult and unconventional is the work.[115]

Continuing his devoted championing of Delius's music at Elberfeld – the 'Elberfeld Tradition' – Haym conducted *Sea Drift* there early in 1911, with the distinguished Wagnerian bass, Felix von Kraus, as the soloist.

*Sea Drift* was only the fourth of Delius's works to be recorded – by Beecham on 11 November 1928 in the Portman Rooms, London, with Dennis Noble, the Manchester Beecham Opera Chorus and the London Symphony Orchestra.

---

[115] Perhaps surprisingly, neither the suffragettes nor the breakdown at Sheffield appear to have been mentioned elsewhere. If the latter was true, Delius might be expected to have said something about it in his to letter to Jelka quoted above.

D ELIUS was an atheist – he passionately believed that God did not exist. In his childhood, religious education in schools was not compulsory, but his parents were regular worshippers at Bradford's German Church, and when he was seven he was prepared for confirmation: unfortunately, however, his youthful high spiritedness got the better of him, and he chose to laugh at the most serious point in the service. Eric Fenby believed that:

> Already as a youth, when he had left Bradford on his first visit to Florida, Delius was at heart a pagan. A young mind, such as his, that had been nurtured chiefly on detective stories and penny dreadfuls, was not likely to forget that incident he had witnessed in Bradford when Bradlaugh[116] had stood, with his watch in his hand, calling on his Creator to strike him dead within two minutes if He existed! Delius had never forgotten that two minutes. It had made a lasting impression on him.[117]

Many years later, when Fenby had come to live at Grez, they were discussing Haydn's *The Creation*, and Fenby said: 'There is one enchanting passage, Delius ... it goes "And God created great whales and every ..." "God?" interrupted Delius. "God? I don't know Him."'[118]

Friedrich Nietzsche's wide-ranging ideas on truth, morality and religion, philology, aesthetics, history, nihilism, power, and the meaning of existence have exerted an enormous effect on Western philosophy and intellectual history. He challenged the very foundations of Christianity and traditional morality, reaching the conclusion that 'God is dead'. Much of his work was concerned with what he called 'master morality' and 'slave morality': the former measuring actions in terms of 'good' or 'bad' *consequences*, and the latter actions in terms of 'good' or 'bad' *intentions*. He believed in life, creativity, health, and the realities of the world in which people actually lived, rather than those in a world beyond.

How Delius first learned of Nietzsche and his writings in 1889 is mentioned in the section about *Mitternachtslied Zarathustras* in Chapter 3. Although they never met, Delius found in him a true kindred spirit, and he and Whitman together became the strongest of all the literary influences on Delius. As he said in a letter to Heseltine some years later:

> I consider Nietzsche the only free thinker of modern times & for me the most sympathetic one – He is at the same time such a poet. He feels Nature. I believe, myself, in no doctrine whatever & in nothing but in Nature & the great forces of Nature ...[119]

---

[116] Charles Bradlaugh, MP (1833–91), was a radical and free thinker in the tradition of Voltaire and Thomas Paine, famous for his championship of individual liberties.

[117] *Fenby 1*, p. 171. Between pages 164 and 183 of the book there is a fascinating description of Delius's attitude to religion.

[118] *Fenby 1*, p. 178.

[119] Letter 366, n. 1.

The eminent Delius scholar Christopher Palmer wrote:

> Through Nietzsche's *Also sprach Zarathustra* Delius experienced his
> true spiritual awakening, just as later Bax was to come to terms with his
> inner self for the first time through a reading of Yeats's *The Wanderings
> of Usheen* ... it may be useful here to recall briefly what Nietzsche taught
> Delius. He taught him that every man stands at an open door, that no man
> with an imaginative cast of mind need face a life twisted by drudgery; that
> man's pride as a man need not be measured by his capacity to shoulder
> work and responsibilities which he detests, which bore him, which are
> too small for what he could be; that such a man's strength should not
> be gauged by the values of the mystique of suffering. He instilled in him
> (or strengthened, for it was there already) an unutterable loathing of the
> society into which such a man is born: the stultifying mediocrity, the
> philistinism, the smug, directionless self-display of a bourgeoisie whose
> viciousness so often masquerades under the hypercritical leer of virtue.
> Delius had Olympian standards of refinement and discrimination, in
> music as in life, and those who proved themselves incapable of living up
> to them were ruthlessly cast aside. He was not cruel but he was hard; and
> we should remember that, in a way, his personality held a touch of the
> schizophrenic. What was the impulse which prompted the hard-headed,
> pragmatic, intolerant [Delius] to a continuous outpouring of unfettered
> rhapsody on the evanescence of life and love, inextricably intertwined
> with profound obeisance before the mystery and beauty of nature? Few
> artists can have segregated the conflicting elements of their personalities
> into such mutually exclusive compartments.[120]

It was inevitable that Delius should set more of Nietzsche's words to music
than just in *Mitternachtslied Zarathustras*, and quite early in 1904 he began
what would turn out to be, together with *Sea Drift*, his most deeply felt work
for voices and orchestra, and certainly the most epic of them all in its scale and
intellectual conception.

---

[120] *Palmer*, p. 96.

## A MASS OF LIFE
## (EINE MESSE DES LEBENS)
### (1904–5: *RT* II/4; *CE* vol. 10)

[*A Mass of Life*] may be regarded as being essentially an ecstatic dithyramb in praise of life here on earth, as opposed to that of a possible future state: a hymn of joyful acceptance and gratitude for all that it has to give, rather than of renunciation in the hope of achieving salvation: a paean in honour of Man and the human virtues of beauty, strength, nobility, plenitude and power (i.e. 'master morality'), rather than of God and the saintly virtues of humility, weakness, poverty and resignation (i.e. 'slave morality'), which are the articles of conventional Christianity and morality.[121]

*A Mass of Life* ... is a choral celebration of the Will of Man to say 'Yea' to life in certain joy of the 'Eternal resurrection' – Nietzsche's perennial theme – in face of the Christian slaying of self to gain the promise of Life Eternal.[122]

As is almost always the case, Delius's published correspondence says nothing at all about the 'gestation process' for *A Mass of Life*. Fritz Cassirer, however, gave him much help with the words – the title page of the score generously says 'zusammengestellt von [in collaboration with] Fritz Cassirer' and, undoubtedly as a direct result of that, the work is dedicated to him: 'Meinem Freunde Fritz Cassirer gewidmet'.

This time Delius was determined to have the full score and parts published and printed before the première. He approached Harmonie and the contract with them was signed in April 1907. The words were to be printed in German and English, and Delius had originally wanted the writer and critic Alfred Kalisch to undertake the translation. However, Harmonie made another suggestion:

We regard the fee which Herr Kalisch wants for translating as extremely high and advise looking for another translator. We have a very good English translator available, in the person of Mr John Bernhoff, and think that he would certainly not ask the fee of Mk800 which Herr Kalisch wants.[123]

In a letter to Delius a month later Henry Wood wrote:

---

[121] Fenby, programme note for the 1929 Delius Festival for 1 November.

[122] Fenby, programme note for a Royal Philharmonic Society concert on 5 December 1984.

[123] *M&C*, Letter 7.

I believe that John Bernhoff is a very clever man, and hope that he will make a great success of the translation of your work into English. I need not say I have looked through your score several times with the keenest interest ...[124]

In the event Delius went along with them. With the printing about to begin, however, he must have been somewhat taken aback to receive this:

> 5.7.7
> Blankenesse bei Hamburg
> 22 Parkstrasse
>
> Dear Sir,
>
> I have noted from the newspaper enclosed that you intend to bring out a choral work under the title 'Lebensmesse'. Presumably you do not know that I have published a choral poem under the same title, and that this title was invented by me personally; the word 'Lebensmesse' did not exist in the German language before. My poem has also been set to music several times; admittedly none of these compositions has yet been performed, but negotiations are in progress.[125] So it is as much in your interest as in mine that you should choose another title for your work. I am very sorry that I must ask this of you; but you will realize that I cannot waive my copyright. Moreover you will easily find in Nietzsche himself a title which fits your Zarathustra choral work as well, or even better. In any case I hope that, as an artist whom I highly esteem, you will sympathize with the embarrassing position I am forced to take up, and not take my request amiss.
>
> Yours very sincerely
> Richard Dehmel.
>
> N. B. I should like a reply as soon as possible.

Richard Dehmel (1863–1920) was a controversial Dutch poet, and very sympathetic towards Nietzsche's philosophies. If Delius did reply – which, in the circumstances seems unlikely – his letter has, sadly, not been published.

The vocal score, with the piano arrangement by Otto Singer (1863–1936, a choral conductor who worked in Leipzig and Berlin), was published at the same time as the full score and parts, and (in the same letter) Harmonie reported:

> He wrote to us that it would appreciably diminish the amount of work he had to do if he received two scores to make the arrangements from. He would then not have to copy the choruses but could just stick them together and set the piano part underneath. We envisage the production for the Mass as follows: We will have the English translation made from the original score and entered on it and we will then have the

---

[124] Letter 218.

[125] *Eine Lebensmesse* was written *c.* 1904, and first performed in Arnhem in 1911.

hand-written reproduction printed, from which Herr Otto Singer can make the piano arrangement.[126]

*A Mass of Life* is divided into two unequal parts, of five and six numbered movements respectively, Part 2 being roughly twice the duration of Part 1. An unnumbered, purely orchestral introduction (On the Mountains) precedes the first movement of Part 2.

The work is written for soprano, contralto, tenor and baritone soloists; a mixed double chorus; and the biggest orchestra Delius ever used: 3 flutes (1st doubling piccolo); 3 oboes; the rare bass oboe;[127] cor anglais; 3 clarinets; bass clarinet; 3 bassoons; double bassoon; 6 horns; 4 trumpets; 3 tenor trombones; bass tuba; timpani; bass and side drums; percussion (cymbals, triangle, castanets, glockenspiel, tam-tam and tubular bells); 2 harps; and no fewer than 68 strings, including 12 double basses. The indication in the original 1907 score 'Basshoboe [*sic*] auch Englisch Horn' would imply that the bass oboe and the cor anglais can be doubled by the same player: in fact they cannot be, as they play simultaneously in the second and fourth movements of Part 2.

Throughout the work Delius treats the soloists and double chorus as completely independent from the orchestra in the sense that their musical lines are virtually never doubled by other instruments. Indeed, he appears to think of the voices as separate instruments in their own right. The vocal writing in places can seem awkward to articulate and to pitch, and there are many instances of Delius placing huge demands on vocal technique, particularly for choral singers. But these characteristically angular vocal lines, dictated by Delius's acute harmonic sense, are very much a feature of his vocal writing and there are many similar examples in the operas and in the other big choral works.

When it comes to setting words, Delius often follows a precedent he set in *Sea Drift* and overlaps text between different voices singing at the same time. A typical example of this in *A Mass of Life* is at Fig. 28, where three of the soloists sing three different texts simultaneously; and at Fig. 39, where for some dozen bars or so the contralto soloist offers a completely different message from that of the choral basses. But this is presumably the effect Delius wanted.

It is perhaps surprising that there are relatively few cross-references to thematic material between the separate movements; notable exceptions are the bell theme (Ex. 4.24) and Zarathustra's theme (Ex. 4.28). That means that there is relatively little unifying material to bind this vast score together and therefore individual movements often stand alone thematically. Had Wagner or Richard Strauss written it there would no doubt be hundreds of separate *leitmotifs* representing the abstract concepts of Nietzsche's text. But that was not Delius's way.

---

[126] *M&C*, Letter 7.

[127] Delius would later use it in *Songs of Sunset, Fennimore and Gerda, An Arabesque,* the *Requiem* and *Eventyr.*

Part 1

*Movement I*

This is a purely choral and orchestral movement with two main sections.

A ('Animato, con fervore'): the music begins abruptly as if *in media res*, indicative of some introductory pages which were subsequently eliminated.[128] The opening bars have a great onward sweep, relentlessly driven by a powerful motor of repeated triplets in the woodwind and upper strings (it puts one in mind of Schubert's *Erlkönig* – not that Delius would have welcomed the analogy). The implied key is F major but the harmonic centre is immediately ambiguous as the sopranos and tenors flatten the seventh of the scale to an E flat and the music veers off into a rapid sequence of A flat–F minor–D minor, etc.:

Ex. 4.20

The key of F is not conclusively re-established until twenty-seven bars later (Fig. 1+13). The vocal writing is strenuous (sopranos going up to top B flats, later even to a top C natural). One of Delius's favourite rhythmic motifs is heard in woodwind, trumpets etc. (Fig. 1+15), the 'monogram' with which he signs so many of his works:

Ex. 4.21

[128] Robert Threlfall, *Frederick Delius: Complete Works: Editorial Report* (London: Delius Trust, 1990), p. 74.

A bridge passage ('Più tranquillo') forms a second subsection (Fig. 2+1); a third subsection ('Maestoso con grandezza') unveils a memorable D major theme in flutes, horns, harps and unison strings (Fig. 3):

Ex. 4.22

Maestoso con grandezza

Perversely, given its singable quality, it is not given to the voices but forcefully repeated in the key of A flat by the brass (Fig. 4+5). Two bars of trumpet fanfares (Fig. 6+1) then lead to:

A2: this is a telescoped repeat of section A, about one-third shorter; initially (Fig. 6+3) it has an identical text and musical setting, but it diverges (Fig. 7+13) to omit the *più tranquillo* subsection and goes direct to the 'Maestoso' theme (Fig. 8+1), now soaring out in F major. The music broadens with a *sostenuto* marking (Fig. 9+6), the 1st sopranos proclaiming 'Siege!' ('Triumph!') on a top C, and the music pulls itself up for the final bars in an exhilarating, blazing coda.

*Movement II: 'Recitative: Animoso con alcuna licenza'*

The most succinct movement of the entire *Mass* and a counterweight to the fourth movement of this Part. Here the vocal setting is for the baritone soloist alone, the first four bars being accompanied in classical recitative style. But Delius soon goes his own way, writing from the fifth bar onwards in his favoured 6/4 metre as the invitation to laughter and dance is extended. The dance itself begins most obviously at Fig. 11+1, where there is some fine orchestral word-painting for 'Diese Krone des Lachenden' ('this crown of laughter') in the woodwind, horns, trumpets, harps and triangle. Other examples are at Fig. 12+3: 'Dem Winde tut mir gleich' ('the wind is akin to me') with harp *glissandi*; Fig. 12+5: 'nach seiner eignen Pfeife will er tanzen' ('he'll dance to his own whistling') evoked in trills for flute and clarinet; and Fig. 13+1: 'unter seinen Fusstopfen' ('his feet stamping') underlined firstly by the rhythms of the violins and then by triangle and castanets.

*Movement III*

This movement, the most extended of Part 1, introduces the three remaining soloists. It falls into five main sections:

A ('Andante tranquillo con dolcezza'): the most lyrical music so far is ushered in by a quietly pulsing, muted 1st horn above a bed of arching cello figurations and a pedal open-fifth on the tonic (B major), joined in the second bar by the altos of Choir 1 singing a tune to the syllable 'Ah!':

Ex. 4.23

The tenor soloist enters in the fifth bar, followed by the soprano soloist (Fig. 16+1) as the key-centre moves up a notch to C; then the contralto soloist puts in an appearance with choral sopranos joining the altos (Fig. 17+1). The texture builds, permeated by the rhythm of a swaying quaver-crotchet-quaver rhythm.

B ('Poco più mosso ma moderato'): a new key signature (F major) (Fig. 19+1) and time signature (4/4) introduce this section, characterised by vocal solos, a duet (Fig. 20+9) and finally a trio (Fig. 21+9), accompanied throughout by 'La, la, la'-ing in the sopranos and altos of Choir 1. The orchestral texture gradually fills out as the solo voices become more impassioned, marked *più animato* and with a shift into 3/4 (Fig. 22+8), changing gear metrically in preparation for the next section.

C ('Con moto'): the chorus proclaims this to be a 'Tanz über Stock und Stein' ('a dance up hill and down dale') and we get a foretaste of the *Dance Rhapsodies* to come. Delius weaves a texture that looks and sounds suspiciously like counterpoint, a rare excursion for him into such territory. If hardly fugal, there are certainly plenty of imitative entries for the voices. Both choirs are involved, singing a mixture of text and *vocalise*, with the soloists (less the baritone) often singing three different texts at once (e.g. Fig. 28+1), another example of Delius's overlapping technique mentioned above. The orchestration swings along with a dominance of arpeggio figuration in strings and wind and the whole section reaches a climax (Fig. 32 *et seq.*). In a typically Delian way, it then deflates over the space of just a few bars (Fig. 33+6) as the tempo broadens (*slargando*) and the 'La, la, la's are briefly repeated by distant altos.

D ('Andante tranquillo'): this is in the nature of a bridge passage, consisting of a brief solo for the baritone (Fig. 35+1) expressing his delight in what he has just heard and thereby encouraging a fragmentary repeat of the melodic *vocalise* of Fig. 19, this time shared between the altos and tenors of Choir 1.

E ('Quieto, molto tranquillo – più lento'): this is the emotional heart of the movement: first there is an imposing statement by the contralto soloist (Fig. 38+1) in the unexpected key of E flat as she upbraids Zarathustra for his lack of faith to her ('O Zarathustra … du bist mir nicht treu genug!'), prophesying that when he wakes at midnight and hears 'eine alte Brummglocke' ('the ancient, booming bell') he will remember her words. The bell itself tolls low down in the 2nd horn (Fig. 39+5) (*mezzo piano marcato*), and then with the addition of both harps (Fig. 39+10): it is a little melodic fragment built on rising perfect fifths that will later assume much importance:

Ex. 4.24

Whilst the contralto is still only half-way through intoning her warning, the basses of Choir 1 enter *sotto voce* and *pppp* with the important *Mitternachtslied* (*Midnight Song*). First drafted sometime in the 1890s for baritone and piano, this was (as Jelka said) 'music of deep import, beyond anything he had done before'; that first version can be seen in the appendix to *CE* vol. 18b, where it is called *Noch ein Mal*. In 1896 Delius arranged it for baritone solo, male chorus and orchestra as *Mitternachtslied Zarathustras* (see above, Chapter 3), and he used it twice in *A Mass of Life*: here at Fig. 39+1, and then later in the sixth movement of Part 2 (Fig. 127+1) (Ex. 4.30). There are some minor variants in this first appearance from the original version for voice and piano: the time signature is 4/4 rather than 4/2; there are some alterations in notes (Fig. 39+2: the final crotchet is F sharp rather than D sharp) and in rhythm (Fig. 40+7: a sequence of four crotchets rather than two sets of dotted minims plus crotchet). We should also note that here in Part 1 the orchestral accompaniment is utterly different from that of the repeat in Part 2, where it is only more or less faithful to the original. The soprano soloist adds her observations (Fig. 40+9) in a coda of exquisite beauty scored for hushed strings with wisps of flute, oboe and horn.

*Movement IV: 'Agitato ma moderato'*

A counterpart to the second movement, this is another declamatory baritone solo, again with the feel of a recitative, only this time with additional commentary from both choirs. The mood is dark and desperate, matching Zarathustra's troubled spirit, though a change of key to F major (Fig. 46+1), just after the words 'Die Stunde naht' ('The hour draws near'), seems to clear the air and bridges the movement to the one that follows.

The bell motif from the third movement (Ex. 4.24) recurs in the 3rd bassoon and 1st horn (Fig. 42+5) at the mention of the 'Mitternachtsherz' ('Midnight Heart'), and, later, on the 3rd trombone, tuba, cellos and double basses (Fig. 45+2); it is heard again two bars further on, played by the 3rd bassoon, double bassoon, 2nd and 4th horns, cellos and double basses; and it also reappears, *pizzicato*, in cellos and double basses (Fig. 45+10).

There is an additional motif that needs to be identified (since it will recur in Part 2) when the soloist sings 'Spinne, was spinnst du um mich?' ('Spider, what are you spinning around me?') (Fig. 43+7):

Ex. 4.25

It is a suitably convoluted idea, woven first by the 1st bassoon and then at Fig. 44+1 by the 1st oboe and bass oboe, etc. Delius will quote it later, in the fifth movement of Part 2 (Fig. 113+1).

*Movement V*

This is the climactic moment of Part 1, and in mood it harks back to the more intimate passages of *Sea Drift* whilst foreshadowing the nocturnal magic of such pieces as *Summer Night on the River*. Overall the choral writing is the most lyrical so far, whilst the orchestration is suitably dark-hued and greyer in feel. There are four separate sections, encompassing two emotional peaks at Figs 49+9 and 53+10:

A ('Andante molto tranquillo'): the basses of both choirs evoke the coming of night; the harmonic language remains chromatic but is anchored on pedal notes, i.e. the F natural in bars 1 to 12. The orchestration of the opening is most striking, Delius at his most typically imaginative as he combines horns, clarinets and bass oboe: just a handful of instruments but exactly the right ones. The baritone soloist enters (Fig. 47+11) with long-spun, lyrical lines.

B ('Poco a poco più agitato'): this brief section, a transition really, begins at Fig. 49+1 and is propelled by repeated quaver movement in the cellos, commenting on the baritone's feelings of unfulfilment and interspersing choral 'ah!'s; this reaches a succinct climax (Fig. 49+13 *et seq.*).

C ('Meno mosso, più tranquillo'): the orchestral textures are suddenly quite spare here (Fig. 50+7), reflecting Zarathustra's sense of loss and loneliness, and are rooted once more on pedal notes (Fig. 51+1).

D ('Meno mosso, più tranquillo'): the opening text of the movement returns (Fig. 51+12), 'Nacht ist es', and Delius repeats the material of his opening A section, if not note-for-note then in overall mood. Quite unexpectedly, growing from next to nothing, the music swells in just a few bars to a heart-rending climax (Fig. 53+9 *et seq.*) as Zarathustra cries out 'nun erst erwachen alle Lieder der Liebenden' ('now awaken all lovers' songs'). A leading motif is heard *fortissimo* in the bass oboe, bassoons, horns and violas (Fig. 53+11):

Ex. 4.26

This will be recalled at the climax of the fifth movement of Part 2; but for now, the texture rapidly deflates and 'dies away to the end' (*calando al fine*) to the sound of the bass clarinet, a pair of horns, some soft punctuation from harp and timpani, and lower strings fading out *pppp*.

### Part 2

*Introduction: 'Andante – On the Mountains'*

This is an early example of Delius making an excursion to his beloved 'High Hills' and is one of his most exquisite journeys: horn calls echo across the peaks, high above misty valleys evoked by slow-moving chromatic harmony in muted violins and violas, while the lower strings remain with their feet on the ground, anchoring everything on plain C and F naturals. Delius specified three horns for this section, two of them providing echo effects which, following a suggestion in the most recent edition of the score, can be enhanced by placing the players off-stage. A magical transition occurs right at the end (Fig. 57+18), when the 1st flute unexpectedly enters and plays just four notes, *pppp*, while the harmony shifts to pure A major: it is as if a shaft of sunlight has suddenly pierced the mists (Ex. 4.27).

Ex. 4.27

*Movement I*

The musical equivalent of the opening pæan of Part 1: another vigorous outburst by the double choir – 'Herauf! nun Herauf!' ('Arise! Now arise') – but joined this time by the soprano, contralto and tenor soloists. Again, there are three main subsections with the first and last mirroring each other:

A ('Con elevazione e vigore'): as before, Delius hardly establishes a key-centre before he moves off it: A major swiftly gives place to C major and to a harmonic sequence that does not really re-establish the home key until some twenty bars later (Fig. 59+1).

B ('Meno mosso, più tranquillo'): the soloists are heard as a trio (Fig. 60+1), observing that spring has given place to the height of summer (harps add a shimmer of heat haze to the texture). The tranquillity is short-lived as the textures build again (Fig. 62+1) and the choral affirmations become more homophonic and declamatory. Ex. 4.21 breaks out again (Fig. 63+1) on the 1st and 2nd trumpets, and trombones. There is a sudden hush (Fig. 64+1) as the three soloists breathe the phrase 'Nachbarn der Sonne!' ('Neighbours of the sun') and then *tempo primo* bursts out again.

A2: this is an exact recapitulation of section A, with the same text and orchestration until six bars before the end (Fig. 66+9) when it diverges into the brief coda.

*Movement II: 'Andante'*

As in the opening of Part 1, Delius follows an extrovert movement highlighting the role of the chorus with an introverted one for the solo baritone. In 6/4, with austere orchestration and harmony, it has the feel of much later works, such as *An Arabesque* or *North Country Sketches*; it is similarly infused practically throughout by downward-falling quaver figurations (Fig. 67+3 *et seq.*). Delius rests all the brass whilst retaining four of the horns. There are two particularly intense moments from the soloist: his 'deine Rede wurde reif' ('your speech ripened') (Fig. 68+4); and 'Ihr höheren Menschen, riecht ihr's nicht?' ('You higher-born ones, do you not scent it?') (Fig. 69+5).

*Movement III*

This is the most substantial movement of the entire work and falls into five distinct parts.

A ('Lento'): in this purely instrumental section, which begins with woodwind and hushed, muted strings *divisi* evoking a mysterious, amorphous texture reminiscent of Sibelius, Delius anticipates Zarathustra's mental anguish – 'Wohl bin ich ein Wald und eine Nacht dunkler Bäume' ('I am indeed a forest and a night of dark trees'). The tempo picks up (Fig. 72+1) ('Con moto moderato') with some plaintive writing for the cor anglais over *tremolando* violas and nervously meandering chromatic figurations in the woodwind (Fig. 72+9 *et seq.*). Meanwhile, a significant theme, associated with Zarathustra, is presented for the first time (Fig. 72+6) on the cor anglais, 3rd bassoon, double bassoon, cellos and double basses and from this point on it is repeatedly woven into the texture:

Ex. 4.28

B: Abruptly (Fig.75+1), the women's voices of both choirs break in on Zarathustra's rêverie in a pastoral 6/8, vocalising 'La, la, la's which continue for some forty-four bars, the tempo becoming more lilting at Fig. 76+1 ('Molto moderato, con grazia') as Delius switches between 9/8 and 12/8 metres. For the most part, the voices are lightly accompanied by dancing wind and strings, and there is some effective writing for the harps. Delius's notion of what the human voice can do – at least, choral human voices – is ambitious, to say the least. This section of the *Mass* is particularly difficult to perform. A single bar of notation for the choral sopranos (Fig. 76+9) will suffice to show what his demands can be; if one did not know, it might be thought Delius was writing here for a pair of clarinets:

Ex. 4.29

Neither are the mocking 'ha, ha, ha's (Fig. 77+7) all that easy to bring off. As mentioned earlier, there is no hiding for the performers, because Delius refuses to double the voice parts in the orchestra, as kinder composers might have done.

C ('Moderato'): the voices die away as the baritone takes centre stage again (Fig. 81+1) for an extended monologue. Ex. 4.28 is heard in the cellos and double basses with a variant of it later (Fig. 82+5) doubled by the 3rd bassoon and double bassoon. Dancing rhythms return at Fig. 83+1 ('Più leggiero'); the text is at its most sibylline, and the best course is to grasp at its meaning from Delius's music. The bell motif (Ex. 4.24) is quoted (Fig. 84+1) in the 1st and 3rd horns, and the 1st harp, a bar before the sopranos of Choir 1 make the only choral intrusion in this section, with some mocking laughter. The text at this point refers to Zarathustra's previous penchant for sleep, and we remember how the contralto had prophesied that the midnight bell would eventually waken him. A rhythmic variant of Ex. 4.28 protrudes sternly on the 3rd bassoon, double bassoon, cellos and double basses (Fig. 86+8), as this section draws to a close.

D ('Con anima'): the women's voices return in pages reminiscent of section B, but with much thicker and more complex orchestral textures; indeed, the dance becomes almost bacchanalian and reaches a frenzy at Fig. 92+1 (*tutta forza*). It then rapidly calms down as *tremolandi* in the 1st harp, 2nd violins and violas (Fig. 93+5) usher in the final section.

E ('Lento molto'): this is a beautiful coda to the movement, centred in B major until the D major of the final pages. The women are heard in the distance (Fig. 96+1) as night falls, the tempo slackens and the music dies away with just a last wisp of the *vocalise* lingering in the air.

*Movement IV*

The text symbolically evokes the noontide of life, with Zarathustra, as prophesied, content to doze in the torrid heat of day, refusing to relinquish his daydreams. There are some astonishing contrasts of mood and texture in this fairly extended movement – which has five shortish subsections:

A ('Lento molto'): an exquisite orchestral introduction with a pastoral mood tellingly evoked by a short modal trio for the 1st oboe, cor anglais and bass oboe (bar 1 to Fig. 98+15), the reed instruments stealing in softly one by one in imitation, over muted lower strings and soft timpani rolls. Both choirs also enter quietly (Fig. 99+1), followed by a short passage for the tenor soloist quoting some of Nietzsche's most evocative lines to a delicate accompaniment. We seem suspended in time: this is indeed 'the secret hour of solemn silence when no shepherd sounds his flute'.

B: the mood is momentarily broken as Zarathustra stirs: 'Was geschah mir? ...' ('What befell me? ...') (Fig. 102+1). He talks eloquently in his sleep of his heart-broken rapture; the choirs repeat the 'zerbrich!' of his following 'O zerbrich, zerbrich Hertz' ('O now break, now break heart') like an echo (Fig. 103+2).

C: even the contralto soloist seems reluctant to intrude (Fig. 104+1), though the bell motif is sounded very quietly as a warning (Fig. 104+13) by the 1st horn and 1st harp.

D: now the soprano soloist has her say (Fig. 105+1), and is then joined by the tenor soloist as the music suddenly explodes with passion in a fully scored *tutti* passage (Fig. 106+1) which finishes with the double choir comparing Zarathustra to a god. A solemn chord intoned by the brass is followed by a pause, and the opening mood is re-established (Fig. 107+1).

E: in the final section, the contralto attempts to waken Zarathustra (Fig. 108+1) above a bed of weaving, highly chromatic strings; but he will have none of it and prefers to remain basking in his drowsy happiness. The choral voices whisper this desire like an incantatory refrain: 'O Glück!' ('O bliss!'), and the movement comes peacefully to a close, winding down in the strings with delicate touches by the 1st flute.

*Movement V: 'Allegro ma non troppo, con gravità'*

A passionate, brief outpouring of Zarathustra's resigned realisation that he is prophesying to deaf ears and that his message will never be widely understood. This baritone solo with chorus is in one, onward-sweeping section. There are two quotations of previous material, Ex. 4.25 from the fourth movement of Part 1 in the cellos and double basses (Fig. 113+1) at the chorus's words 'Nun kam Abend und Mitternacht' ('Now came evening and midnight'); and Ex. 4.26 from the fifth movement of Part 1, forcefully recalled (Fig. 115+5) by the bassoons and full brass to the words 'Lust ist tiefer noch als Herzeleid!' ('Joy is deeper still than heartfelt grief!'). An F sharp timpani roll then links us directly to the final movement.

*Movement VI*

The climax of the whole work unfolds in four sections:

A ('Largo con solennità'): Delius incorporates into this movement the *Mitternachtslied* he had written in 1898 – following the original orchestral manuscript note for note, but making a few changes to the chorus parts (see section C, below). With the timpani still playing softly, the cellos and double basses take up Zarathustra's theme (Ex. 4.28), which is then repeated by the cor anglais, bass clarinet and 1st horn (Fig. 116+2) with an *ostinato* harp arpeggio added during the previous bar. The baritone soloist enters at Fig. 117+1 with his warning that the hour has arrived when the midnight bell will toll. The music modulates from B major into B flat (Fig. 118+1), and Delius writes a very fine passage indeed, Wagnerian in its majesty, that includes reiterations of Zarathustra's theme (Fig. 118+2) in the bass clarinet and then, a few bars later, again by the bass clarinet, but this time reinforced by the bassoons, double bassoon, 3rd trombone and tuba (Fig. 118+10), and with three *glissandi* from the 1st harp (Fig. 118+9 *et seq.*) and the bell theme (Ex. 4.24) (Fig. 119+1) as additional orchestral colour to herald this solemn moment.

B ('Poco più mosso'): the tam-tam imparts its own aura of mystery (Fig. 120+2) before Ex. 4.24 underpins the texture in the form of a harp *ostinato*, reinforced by the 1st and 3rd horns (Fig. 120+13); bell-imitations permeate this section. Zarathustra's theme makes further important entries in the bass clarinet (Fig. 121+11) and then in cellos and double basses; the baritone himself grows more impassioned, with triplets and arpeggios infusing clarinets and divided strings as he calls his followers to attention. We are now ready to hear the great Midnight Song itself (Fig. 127+1).

C ('Lento molto'): Zarathustra utters his solemn and somewhat cryptic message to Mankind: 'O man, mark well! / What tolls the solemn Midnight Bell? / I lay asleep till haunting dreams broke slumber's spell / The world is deep and deeper far than day can tell / Deep is her woe / Joy deeper still than grief of heart / Woe says "Begone!" / But Joy would have Eternity / Ne'er ending, everlasting day!' Divided strings in the rich key of B major form the essence of the accompaniment (Ex 4.30). Delius makes only one change from the 1898 version by adding choral interjections for tenors and basses. (Fig. 127+4 *et seq.*). The song is then taken up by full chorus (Fig. 129+1) this time with the male voices singing the baritone part whilst sopranos and altos provide the interjections.

D ('Più animato'): The final ode to joy and to eternity, 'Alle Lust will aller Dinge Ewigkeit!' ('All joy craves eternity for all things!') (Fig. 132+1) involves not only the chorus but, significantly, the four soloists singing for the first time as a concerted quartet. Delius gradually unleashes all his orchestral forces to reach a monumental climax 'Maestoso con tutta forza' (Fig. 137+9) on the word 'Ewigkeit!' ('eternity!') with the bell theme clearly tolling in glockenspiel and timpani above the thick texture; but the final sounds are, characteristically, not triple *forte* but triple *piano*: Delius releases the tension (Fig. 138+1) for the final eight bars as the chorus softly intones 'Ewigkeit!' again, and the orchestration dims to a magical whisper of just lower woodwind, horns and strings, bringing this extraordinary work to a deeply moving close.

Ex. 4.30

EVEN before the first performance, Delius's conductor-friends showed considerable interest in the *Mass*: Fritz Cassirer wanted a copy,[129] and Max Schillings told Delius 'Your Mass score has just arrived, now I will see that it is secured for the Festival.'[130] The Festival in question was the 1908 Tonkünstlerfest of the Allgemeine Deutsche Musikverein in Munich, and Schillings was almost as good as his word. Unfortunately, however, it would be conducted by the unknown and only recently appointed director of the choral society there, the Münchner Hofkapelle, Ludwig Hess,[131] and on 1 April 1908 Schillings had to write to Delius telling him that:

[129] Letter 227.

[130] Letter 234.

[131] Ludwig Hess (1877–1944): he was originally an opera singer, but in 1907 he turned his hand to conducting and the Munich post was his first. He succeeded the

I am afraid that it is impossible to perform the *whole* of your work. Ludwig Hess and his choir cannot master it *all*; for that, *months* of rehearsal would be necessary, and you know yourself how enormous the difficulties are for a choir which is not composed of professional musicians. Hess suggests Part 2. Please get in touch with Ludw. Hess München, Kaulbachstr. 93 & arrange details with him (assuming that you agree to a performance of parts of your work). The question of soloists is extremely important. Whom do you suggest for the baritone part? He must be *a first-class* artist. The question of the material is also important. Provisionally Hess has borrowed the choral material at his own risk. But as you know, the A. D. M. V. [Musikverein] cannot acquire the material for the works it performs as it has no use for it. So some agreement with your publishers would have to be reached through your intercession. Please write to Hess about that too. – I hope you agree to our plan, so that we shall have the pleasure of bringing your work to the public, to begin with in parts. I look forward to it very much.[132]

Within a week, Delius wrote to Hess – who replied:

A thousand apologies for not answering your very friendly lines of 7th April until today, and then only dictating via typewriter. I have been so unbelievably overburdened by my threefold work that there is simply no other way.

Your 'Messe des Lebens' is one of those works where I have the feeling that there is such power and vitality in it that for the artist who renders it, putting all his power and love into it must make it an intensely rewarding experience for him. Rest assured that the preparatory work will be pursued with as much conscientiousness as pleasure on the part of all concerned.

With reference to the choice of soloists, I was unfortunately not able to wait for the wishes expressed in your letter, as the Festival is so close at hand and the Theatre management in particular had to know as soon as possible. However, I have chosen for each of the four solo parts the person I considered to be most suitable, taking into account poetic, musical, vocal and intellectual qualities, to be precise, for the most important part the baritone Rudolph Gmür, whom I consider to be the most highly gifted interpreter of parts of real character, for the contralto part, Else Schünemann or the very talented young Olga von Welden, for the soprano Fräulein van Lammen or Frau Grumbacher de Jong. I hope you agree; I chose according to the best of my conscience.

Now for two other important matters.

Firstly, please send me as soon as possible a fair copy of your score, as your manuscript is illegible from a certain distance.

distinguished Wagner conductor Felix Mottl (1856–1911).
[132] Letter 267.

Secondly, I can only perform the Tanzlied if you agree to its being performed by the two lady soloists and ten of the best female voices from my choir, in other words as a threefold quartet; because on 4th May we have a performance of Liszt's Missa Solemnis and Bruckner's 150th Psalm, and four weeks later your work has to be christened in fitting style! That is a physical impossibility, even for a Choral Society that has been in existence for 100 years. Please let me have your view on this; I can imagine the effect would be very pleasing. Finally another minor artistic scruple: I fear that the *frequent* repetition of the words La La spoils the sonorities of the Mädchentanz; could you possibly agree to a cut there? Please write to me soon.[133]

Delius's response must have been realistic, because in the event only Part II was heard complete (even so, with some cuts), preceded by just the second movement of Part I (the first baritone solo). The *Mass* was part of a huge afternoon concert – which Delius naturally attended – with four other works by eminent contemporary German composers (now long forgotten), including a second choral piece and two symphonic poems.

One of *Die Musik*'s critics, Dr Eduard Wahl, was pretty upset by the whole concept of the work, and was not overwhelmed by the performance either, but the music itself pleased him a little more:

Nietzsche's words contain, on the one hand, so much music of their own that setting them to music seems unnecessary, even disturbing. Secondly, they reveal – and conceal – so much deep thought that to add to that music is a monstrous profanity. Nietzsche's very well-known standpoint on contemporary music would certainly have turned him away in disgust from Delius's conception of his work. If, however, out of a sense of goodwill, one disregards all that, one can state that Delius has much to say that extends beyond the usual, the obvious, the mundane. He purposely avoids a rigid framework, his sounds are only to paint moods and create atmosphere (a certain relationship with the French School, not least with Debussy, is noticeable here), and he succeeds in this, supported by clever, indeed very often perfect, instrumentation, even if perhaps his capability for variety of expression seems much restricted. Next to complete misconceptions like the baritone solo 'Erhebt eure Herzen' – for the unsatisfactory effect of which, the baritone Rudolf Gmür was not entirely without blame ... – the combined efforts of the Choir, Orchestra and Soloists (the ladies Mientje van Lammen, Olga von Welden; and the gentlemen Benno Haberl and Rudolf Gmür) earned much praise. There were passages of the most noble kind as in: 'Die Sonne ist lange schon hinunter' [Part 2/III] or in the 'Mittagsphantasie' [Part 2/IV] in which the silent quivering of the warm air is so well expressed in the deep

---

[133] Letter 268.

woodwind. The noise at the end with the bells, however, is tasteless and deafening.

*Die Musik* 7(3), Bd 27 (1907–8)

Granville Bantock – with whom Delius had by now become the firmest of friends – had very much hoped to go over to Munich, but was unable to do so on account of a last-minute obligation to the Lord Mayor of Birmingham (in his capacity of Professor of Music at Birmingham University) to conduct 15,000 children and fourteen bands in Victoria Square. After the performance Delius wrote to him:

> My 'Mass' made an enormous impression – In fact much more than I ever expected – the Chorus was superb & the Tanzlied went splendidly … It is going to be performed in several towns in Germany next season …[134]

and Balfour Gardiner (to whom Delius had sent an inscribed copy of the newly published vocal score at the beginning of the year) wrote:

> First of all, hearty congratulations on the success of your Messe des Lebens. I hope that you yourself were pleased with it, & have returned full of desire to work.[135]

The first English, and full, performance was naturally to be given by Beecham, but he absolutely refused to use Bernhoff's translation:

> Fully convinced of this gentleman's fitness for the task, [Harmonie] were now endeavouring to foist it on me. This I naturally opposed, and engaged the best man I knew in London to provide me with something that could be both sung and understood. This was William Wallace, one of the most versatile figures of the day …[136]

Beecham approached Wallace, who said in one of his letters to Delius:

> Every German firm should have an Englishman as adviser as to translations. German or semi-German composers … are not the best judges of what a good text is, and though Bernhoff may have letters from many thanking him for his work, they fail to see that the English will be criticized by Englishmen and not by Germans. Take the first line of Bernhoff. This will be sung 'O thou my wi – ill'. Page 8: the word 'cleped' is obsolete, and probably not one in 100 of your audience will know what it means. Page 14: who will understand what is meant by 'prepared to mine ego', etc? Page 56: last line of text 'Wilt thou my hound' etc.,

---

[134] Letter 276.

[135] Letter 279.

[136] *TB*, p. 161. William Wallace (1860–1940) was a Scottish composer and writer, whose first career was as an opthalmic surgeon. He wrote powerful music – mainly orchestral and for voices and orchestra – and became the Dean of the music faculty at London University.

is not grammar. 'That is a dance' is foolish; *now for a dance* is English. 'Pitiless Columbine'!!! Page 113: 'Rages' has two syllables, not one. Page 131: 'ululating, inebriating' is simply putting a weapon in the hands of your critics. Page 180: what singer will have the assurance to get up and declare 'I'm a temulent dulcet lyre (liar)'? On Page 184 it is the turn of the poetess to be 'temulent'! Page 202: that word 'awfuller' gives the text away. You cannot afford to have your critical taste in English shown up with this sort of thing. Every musician who has seen B's text has said that it will damn the work if it is printed in the programme. I understand that 'Harmonie' says, 'We have no objection to a performance with the new text, on the supposition that it will be sent to us for disposal with all rights'. I made the new text for the sake of yourself and Beecham, and I will not allow it to be used for any other performance. If 'Harmonie' thinks that it is to their advantage to cancel Bernhoffs, they will have to pay for their mistakes like other people.[137]

Delius certainly liked the new words, and told Beecham: 'Wallace's new translation is ripping and reads like an English poem.'[138]

The translation was not, however, the only problem, for Delius wrote to Harmonie:

I have received the two copies of the 2nd part of the Mass and thank you very much for them. I have just heard from England that my Mass cannot be rehearsed there without choral parts in the English 'Tonic Sol-fa' as is customary in England. You will remember that you also had this done for Sea Drift and I beg you to apply to the same person at once and have it effected immediately, as the performance planned for London will be impossible otherwise. So it is of the greatest importance that it should be done at once. I have already had a telegram about it.[139]

In a letter on 28 January 1909, Beecham recommended that Delius should use the English publishers J. Curwen & Sons – whose founder had invented Tonic-sol-fa[140] – to produce a version.[141] Although there does not seem to be any actual evidence that they did so, the first English performance can only have been given with the chorus using a Tonic-sol-fa edition, and it was eventually published (by Universal) in 1932.

The concert was on 7 June 1909, in the Queen's Hall, with the Beecham Orchestra (as it was called then), the Hanley choir,[142] Cicely Gleeson-White,

---

[137] Ibid., pp. 161–2.

[138] *M&C*, Letter 46. Beecham and Wallace were, though, legally unable to have it printed, and it is not known ever to have been (*M&C*, Letter 46, n. 62).

[139] Ibid., Letter 33.

[140] See n. 104 above.

[141] Letter 305.

[142] In October 1909 this had 266 members: see Richard Walter, *A History of The North Staffordshire District Choral Society* (Hanley: Wood, Mitchell & Co., 1909).

M. G. Grainger-Kerr (who always seems to have concealed her Christian names), the tenor Webster Millar and the American baritone Charles Clark.[143] Even though most of Delius's music divided opinion at first hearing in those days (as it does today), it rarely produced such a passionate, almost vitriolic, piece of invective as that written by Mr Baughan in *The Musical Standard* (it is an enormous piece, of which the following is but a few extracts):

> Utterly impossible is it to declare that Mr. Frederick Delius' 'A Mass of Life' is a success, or even a half-success ... It was only a strict sense of duty that caused the writer to occupy his seat until the final bar had been dealt with: long before, he would have given anything, so to speak, to get out of Queen's Hall into the open air. When he did leave his seat, he had a feeling similar to that produced by having eaten something extremely indigestible ... But [the reception by the audience] was really misplaced enthusiasm: the whole of it laboured and self-conscious music of the kind presented could not possibly produce *sincere* enthusiasm. The labouredness of the music of Delius' 'A Mass of Life', a marked feature of its wearisome character, is just the same wearisomeness we have experienced in listening his other compositions performed in London, including 'Sea-Drift.' If Delius were a man of great talent – we are convinced he is nothing of the kind – it would be possible for him to write really impressively or inspired while the act of composition is governed by the method he imposes upon it ... Our point is the method of his music is a bad example to the budding composer, and not a success in itself ... The work opened with some hideous and badly felt writing, reaching no real climax, for chorus and, and later on there was another outburst of the same unreasonable and absurd character. Occasionally there are pages in the score of beauty of a quiet character; but we were never convinced that that beauty was really creative ... Of the vocal principals, Mr. Charles W. Clark greatly distinguished himself: it was wonderful what he made of a totally inexpressive series of notes – a series of notes no composer has any right to call upon a singer to deliver. And the other singers struggled with the ineffective writing assigned to them, and did their best. The chorus, whose doings we have already referred to, made a veritable triumph for itself in spite of the ungrateful and ineffective stuff it had to tackle ... We may say we read the very excellent English text with much enjoyment the night before the performance of the 'Mass,' and cannot say the Delius music enhanced that pleasure in the slightest degree ... Personally we have not the slightest wish to attend another performance of Delius' 'Mass': the contemplation of the act, even, is too terrible ... Mr. Thomas

---

[143] According to the review in *The Times* (see below) there was a second baritone, Mr Stanley Adams, who presumably sang in just the final quartet, the only place in the score that Zarathustra's part is not marked 'baritone solo'.

Beecham showed wonderful insight in his interpretations of the score.

*The Musical Standard*, 12 June, 1909

There was a more thoughtful judgement from an (as always) un-credited reviewer[144] in *The Times*:

Mr. Frederick Delius's setting for solo voices, chorus, and orchestra of words chosen from Nietzsche's Also sprach Zarathustra raises again the difficult question as to what is suitable literary material for musical treatment. Mr. Fritz Cassirer, to whom the work is dedicated, has put together a libretto on the same principle as that adopted by the compilers of Biblical oratorios ... On the dramatic side we have the person of Zarathustra more or less closely identified with a baritone solo voice, and the chorus used dramatically to represent the 'higher-born mortals' and the group of dancing girls in the forest. Elsewhere the words are treated impersonally and the voices are used according to principles of musical contrast alone ...

The words contain passages of great descriptive beauty, which give splendid opportunities to a musician with that power of using colour which Mr. Delius possesses so conspicuously. Such words as these: 'Night reigneth; now louder murmur the leaping crystalline fountains, and like them my soul is a fountain leaping upwards.' from the nocturne which ends the first part, and others in the 'Invocation to his Lyre' and the 'Noontide' movements seem made for lyrical expression. In spite of them, however, the philosophic thesis remains the main purpose of the work, and neither the descriptive imagery, the dramatic moments, nor the purely lyrical ones are sufficiently constant to make a scheme which demands music from first to last. There is necessarily a great portion of the work where the philosophy is less poetically clothed, and where consequently the vocal music becomes mere declamation and the elaborate orchestral texture seems inappropriate. Such passages give the work a certain ponderousness, which could only be avoided by concentrating the didactic second part into a smaller space.

The general characteristics of Mr. Delius's music are now fairly familiar from 'Appalachia' and 'Sea-drift,' [sic] as well as works for orchestra alone. Most of them appear again in the *Mass of Life*, from the masterly orchestration to the arresting and angular harmonic progressions. But the largeness of the scheme requires a larger musical plan than any of the former works, and its subject calls for a depth of thought, the lack of which could not be made up for by any amount of technical facility and orchestral effectiveness. Mr. Delius has responded to these demands in a remarkable way, and the sincerity of expression is the first quality

---

[144] Presumably not, however, their senior critic J. A. Fuller Maitland, as he had a well-known dislike of Delius's (and other English composers') music.

which is felt. We have shown that the work is divided into clearly defined movements, and the unity of design in each one is kept by the use of a few representative themes. The most conspicuous of these is the simple bell theme of four notes, which appears early and gradually becomes more insistent till it dominates the whole of the last scene. The only sign of weakness is in the composer's choral writing. In the big first chorus he gives the singers very few phrases which are interesting to sing in themselves. He seems bent on making the words felt by hurling (as it were) great blocks of harmony at the hearers; and though the chorus which opens the second part is more distinctive, its phrases are more instrumental than vocal and the most characteristic theme sounds much more effective on the trombones than it does when shouted out by the basses. The dancing chorus (women's voices, sung without words) is disappointing, and gives the impression that the composer had not calculated the effect accurately. The orchestration is often too heavy for the voices, the rhythm becomes monotonous.

But against these and other crude places, some of which are hard to bear, must be set passages of such conspicuous beauty as the beginning of the 'Song of Life', where the altos of the chorus sing a lovely refrain to the tenor solo, the melody set to the words 'O Man, mark well,' which recurs in the finale, and the theme on the horns in the nocturne. The orchestral introduction to the second part suggesting the hour before dawn, the undulating quavers which accompany the 'Invitation to his Lyre', the ending 'Now the aged midday sleeps' (Part II, No. 4), and the whole building up of the finale upon the bell theme are things which could not fail to make their right impression.

The performance ... was a careful and in many respects a good one. The *ensemble*, however, is so difficult and the composer treats his voices so ruthlessly, writing passages for the sopranos which lie round G and A and not infrequently go up to C, that it was scarcely wonderful that some queer screams were heard, and the intonation was not very perfect. With more refined playing, too, it is probable that the orchestration would not overweight the voices to the same extent as it did at this first performance. Still, since it was a first performance, great perfection of detail was scarcely to be expected ... There was a fairly large and appreciative audience, and Mr. Delius was called to the platform and heartily applauded.

*The Times*, 8 June 1909

Even having prior access to a full score, that is an amazing piece of writing to have produced between the end of the concert and when the presses started to roll! Although, of course, the critics of the other papers came away with many different impressions of the work, by and large they were favourable.

The first full performance in Germany came almost exactly six months later – on 11 December 1909 in the Stadhalle at Elberfeld, when the faithful

Hans Haym conducted the Elberfelder Gesangverein, with Emma Tester, Meta Diestel, Matthäus Römer and Charles Clark, again, as the soloists. This time, it was reported more widely, and the reviews were very full. The *General Anzeiger für Elberfeld–Barmen* for 14 December said:

> That was a thought-provoking Saturday evening, indeed a Red Letter Day in the annals of the Elberfeld Concert Society and particularly for their conductor, Dr. Hans Haym, who deserved much praise. The performance of this 'Mass', this paean, this praising of Life, was the first complete German performance, as at the Music Festival in Munich two years ago only excerpts were performed. It really is a work of art and without doubt one of the chief events of the season. Frederick Delius is a man with an individual feeling; a striver and an achiever, who has something new and personal to say, and with lofty ideals. With this work, Delius has discovered new territory. That the 'Mass' represents one of the most important works of the last twenty years, is unquestionable ... [he] has used all the colours of his palette to illustrate the mood of the text in his own musical language. The instrumentation moves from noble simplicity to the highest refinement. With him, colouristic and impressionistic effects are used only as a means to an end; he does not apply them for their own sake, but does so with such artistic sensitivity that his unprejudiced ear creates a magic which is found in all his music. On the other hand, it seemed that, for all its dark depths and sparkling heights of poetic output, in an effort to avoid well-worn paths, the soloists' parts are somewhat lacking in inspiration. However, it might be that on hearing the work again, this impression would change ... [The reviewer then mentioned a number of highlights] ... The performance was absolutely outstanding. Conductor, orchestra and choir covered themselves in glory. Everything was there: peace, a sure touch, power, beauty. Everything was clearly well-prepared and rehearsed, and the soloists also did very well ... The composer, who appeared at the finish to the accompaniment of lively applause, will probably be just as contented with the performance as we were. The significant success of the work is well-earned by him and all concerned in its production.

while the distinguished *Neue Zeitschrift für Musik* for 23 December was equally enthusiastic:

> The composer ... wanted to sing a song of high praise – a sacred song, a hymn – to earthly life. This idea had its roots in, and took its shape from, Delius's absorption in Nietzsche's 'Zarathustra'. The poem already glows through and through with music, and Fritz Cassirer sensitively chose the most beautiful songs and texts, although without putting them in a logical sequence. As in Bach's Magnificat, Zarathustra speaks sometimes through one or more soloists, at other times through the choir. The continuous thread through the work, and all its individual

sections, is this firmly-held basic precept: glorification of earthly life with all its highs and lows. Delius avoids monotony through contrasts and intensification ... but he follows paths that have been little trodden by others. The highly interesting full score reveals no 'Leitmotivs' (continuously recurring themes), but contrapuntal handling of voices, flexible themes and a strong shape, and the sound colours are kaleidoscopic – perfectly painting the mystical mood of Nietzsche's poem. The descriptions of Nature are the most successful, perhaps explained by the fact that the composer developed an intimate acquaintance with woodlands, fields and meadows when he was running a farm in Florida.

The best of the mood-pictures are 'Heisser Mittag schlaft auf den Fluren' [Hot midday sleeps on the meadows]; the dance-song, a baritone solo with accompanying women's chorus (Dance and laughter are the symbols of human freedom); and the 'Mittags' [Midday]. Although Delius's harmony is better than his melody, even so he often reveals an elegant, melodic creative power, for example in the Midnight Song for baritone and bass choir voices. There, Zarathustra's dying thoughts are softly expressed in elegiac music. In the powerful closing dancing sequences, there are strong accents, a marvellous sense of celebration in the 'Das trunkne Lied' [The Drinking Song] ... the double choruses at the beginning of the First Part ('O du mein Wille, du Wende aller Not') [Oh, thou my Will, dispeller of care] and in the Second Part ('Herauf nun, du grosser Mittag') [Arise, now, glorious noon-tide] have a thrilling power and energy.

A performance presents great problems for all the participants. Only very musical, note-confident singers and a highly-trained orchestra may risk approaching this giant work under the secure direction of an experienced conductor ... all performed extremely well.

*Die Musik* was even more impressed:

a work that can be regarded as one of the most important additions to the contemporary musical scene ... One can say what one wishes about the choice of text, but one must admit that the Zarathustra poem has a great swing to it, and the chosen extracts set by the composer offer an excellent basis for a series of musical mood pictures. And that Delius is a master of mood-painting, he has already shown in his symphonic poems 'Paris' and 'Appalachia'; also in his opera 'Coanga' [*sic*], which has already been performed in this theatre. He uses quite unique orchestral colours from his palette, and quite wonderful sounds faithfully reflect those of Nature voices. With a 'modern' composer like Delius, there are complicated harmonic structures, disharmonies and, yes, quite strange sounds, but they are partly occasioned by the text. Among the most magnificent numbers and happiest melodic inspirations, we can cite the grand 'Mitternachtslied' [Midnight Song] in the First Part, the 'Abend' and 'Mittags' scenes in the Second Part and the splendid celebration ending.

Dr. Haym has [been a true pioneer] on Delius's behalf, and brought great enthusiasm to his newest work. He has not only taken the trouble, in both a talk and a printed Introduction,[145] to try to give an understanding of Delius's music, but also expended great energy in the preparation for the performance of this difficult work – to which the Choir, the considerably augmented Municipal Orchestra and the soloists all made splendid contributions.[146]

Few, if any, of Delius's earlier works had been really enthusiastically received at their early English performances – but that was certainly not the case in Germany with the *Mass*. Indeed, bearing in mind the difficulty of the music, the huge forces needed and the cost, it is a mark of the tremendous impact the work made that over the next six years it received six performances there. It was done twice in Vienna on 18 and 19 February 1911 (for the Workers' Symphony Concerts); Haym gave his second, and, it seems, wonderful performance (which Delius attended) as part of a festival in Elberfeld between 20 and 22 October 1911 to celebrate the centenaries of the Choral and Concert Societies there;[147] it was done in Munich again on 20 January 1913 (conducted by Eberhardt Schwickerath); and in Wiesbaden and Frankfurt in 1914. The next performances, however, were not until 1925, when it was done in Coblenz, in Wiesbaden again (a marvellous performance conducted by Schuricht), and Berlin, as well as in Prague. After the Vienna concerts, the Hungarian composers Béla Bartók (1881–1945) and Zoltán Kodály (1882–1967) jointly wrote very enthusiastically (albeit briefly) to Delius[148] – and Bartók was so struck by the two *tanzlieder* that he subsequently wrote an essay about Delius's use of a wordless chorus.[149] Interestingly, because the vocal scores were bulky and heavy, in the autumn of 1911 Delius (perhaps a little over-optimistically) ordered 1,000 copies of the choir parts – which only have one line of music (for example, just the tenors' line, with 'cues' for the other voices) – but he was upset when he learned how much Harmonie wanted to charge for them.[150]

At a performance by Beecham on 10 March 1913, there was a problem with Charles Clark, the Zarathustra, who was brought in at the last moment: because he could not sing in German, he and the chorus used the English text and the other three soloists the German one! It is curious that Clark's linguistic limitations had not apparently prevented him taking part in Haym's

---

[145] Of which Balfour Gardiner made an English translation for Paul von Klenau's London performance in 1925 (see below).

[146] *Die Musik* 9(2) Bd 34 (1909–10).

[147] That performance was in fact the last of Delius's music given by Haym.

[148] Letter 353.

[149] *Letters 2*, p. 69.

[150] *M&C*, Letter 64.

1909 performances – and that there was no mention in any of the reports seen by the present writers that 'mixed languages' were used. Furthermore, the chorus – again the Hanley choir – was not thought to have sung as well as it did in 1909.[151] Neither Beecham nor Delius can therefore have been particularly pleased with the outcome, but Jelka reported to Ida Gerhardi that:

> Fred said that, apart from the singers, in this performance the orchestra was for the first time just as he had conceived it, & Munich & Elberfeld so bad that he had had doubts about the quality of the music.[152]

Finally, mention must be made of a memorable Royal Philharmonic Society concert in Queen's Hall on 2 April 1925, given by Miriam Licette, Astra Desmond, Walter Widdop and Roy Henderson,[153] the Queen's Hall Orchestra and the Philharmonic Choir,[154] conducted by the Danish conductor and composer Paul von Klenau – another great champion of Delius's music:[155]

> Above all, [Paul von Klenau], is clearly an exceptional choral conductor, for the Philharmonic Choir has never sung so well. ... All [the soloists] were good, but undoubtedly the best was Mr Henderson, who took the part of Zarathustra. He sang not only musically, but with rare artistic intelligence. He has a fine voice and uses it well. ... He should go far. ... There was a very large audience.
>
> *The Star*, 3 April 1925

The combination of Nietzsche and Delius was too much for a number of worthy souls, who fled from the Philharmonic Concert on Thursday, after this section or that, with an air of being anxious to go while the going was good. Those of us who remained to the end had one of the richest experiences of our lives. We may say what we like about Delius's artistic faults and his technical weaknesses – his monotony of mood, his mannerisms of harmony, his sometimes haphazard writing; the fact

---

[151] *WS&SS*, p. 19.

[152] Ibid.

[153] Roy Galbraith Henderson, CBE (1899–2000), was one of the finest English baritones of the twentieth century, equally celebrated in opera, on the concert platform and in recital. This was first of many marvellous performances of the part of Zarathustra; he was called in at the very last moment, and sang from memory.

[154] The precursor of the present-day London Philharmonic Choir. Martin Lee-Browne's mother was a member of it, and sang in both this performance and the first performance of *The Song of the High Hills*. See also below, Chapter 5.

[155] Paul August von Klenau (1883–1946) studied in Copenhagen, Berlin, Munich and Suttgart (where he was a pupil of Max von Schillings), and he became an extremely experienced conductor, working in both opera houses and concert halls. He also composed (mainly in the styles of Bruckner and Strauss), his major works being seven symphonies and seven operas, and he became a close friend of Alban Berg and Arnold Schoenberg. He wrote an interesting article, 'The Approach to Delius', for *The Music Teacher*, January 1927, 19–21, reprinted in *Companion*, pp. 31–6.

remains that here is some of the very finest music of the last twenty-five years, music that often leaves us drunk with beauty. Mr. Paul Klenau is evidently a Delius enthusiast. He conducted the work with the most sensitive feeling for its peculiar quality, and drew some fine playing from the orchestra and some good singing from The Philharmonic Choir. Of the soloists, Mr. Roy Henderson, a young man whose name I had not heard before, was head and shoulders, figuratively speaking, above his fellows. His voice is a baritone of good quality and range, the high G coming quite easily to him. His diction is first-rate, and that he is a born musician was shown not only by his exquisite phrasing but by his having committed the whole of the difficult baritone part to memory. No oddity in the harmonies or the colours around him could confuse for a moment either his ear or his larynx. He sang the music precisely as it should be sung, with philosophic fervour but without false dramatisation. His colleagues were all too much the slaves of their books to get anything like his freedom into their singing, though Miss Licette did some very beautiful things. Mr. Widdop sounded strained, and as regards interpretation took too operatic a view of the music. Miss Astra Desmond took too oratorioish and British cantataish a view of hers ... her singing [of the supremely beautiful section 'O Zarathustra'] was quite spoiled for some of us by the emotional over-emphasis she put into every phrase ... it might have brought the house down in 'He shall feed His flock' ... but it was not in the key of Nietzsche, and still less in the key of Delius, who has expressly marked the movement *quieto, molto tranquillo*.

> Ernest Newman in *The Sunday Times*, 5 April 1925

The performance will be remembered, for, if I read the signs aright, it marked a considerable step forward towards recognition of the great worth of this rare and choice music ...

> *The Telegraph*, 3 April 1925

Here, if anywhere is a philosophy not so much set to music as transformed and transfigured into music. But for its presentation the work wants performers who are at once musicians and philosophers. The other evening, we had the right man in charge.

> Ernest Newman in *The Glasgow Herald*, 9 April 1925

On Thursday, an event! ... The Royal Philharmonic Society (to whom, almost alone, this season we look for programmes of new or rarely heard music) is on Thursday ... to perform the Delius 'Mass of Life' ... 'A Mass of Life', from its first triumphal choral invocation of the will of man to the stupendous closing hymn to Eternity wherein the heart would break for very excess of joy, is an epic of initiation, of the bringing to birth of God in Man.

> Percy Scholes in *The Observer*, 29 March 1925

Many, although not all, of the critics found the text difficult, to say the least, and Dyneley Hussey in *The Saturday Review* took a particularly blunt view:

> But a far more patent obstacle to the appreciation of the 'Mass' is its text. Apart from the slump in Supermen and all the other paraphernalia of the Nietzschean philosophy, it is difficult to get past the jargon of these excerpts from 'Also sprach Zarathustra', which are almost wholly unintelligible by themselves, away from the poem as a whole. How can a plain, blunt Englishman not laugh at the idea of his toes listening, and see beyond the verbal nonsense into the mystical sense which lies behind?[156]

Although Delius's music had been performed relatively widely in America since 1909 – when Max Fiedler and the Boston Symphony Orchestra gave *Brigg Fair, In a Summer Garden* and *Paris* – it was not until 12 January 1938 that the *Mass* was heard there (in a cut version), and the first performance of the whole work was conducted by Eugene Goossens in Cincinnati, eight years later, on 8 May 1946.[157]

D URING 1904, Delius had travelled extensively, sometimes to drum up interest and hear performances and sometimes on holiday. Early in the year, he spent around three months in Germany (including Düsseldorf and Elberfeld, the latter for the first performance of *Koanga* by Cassirer); June saw him and Jelka in Düsseldorf for *Appalachia* conducted by Buths; in the late summer he went to Brittany for a two-month holiday, with Cassirer joining him for a while, and in October he was back in Elberfeld for another two concerts. For most of 1905, however, he stayed at home in Grez working, with both Cassirer and Oskar Fried coming to stay. There must have been a lot of talk in the house about Jelka's painting and the Salon des Indépendants in Paris, where both she and Edvard Munch were exhibiting.[158] Munch had remained a staunch friend, and Delius was to give him help with his entries for the following year's exhibition.

The three years from 1905 to 1907 were without question the *anni mirabili* of Delius's life. At the age of forty-three, with these three masterpieces – *Appalachia, Sea Drift* and *A Mass of Life* – he really 'arrived' on the European musical scene. His music began to be heard in England, and he had met not only the man who was to become his greatest friend and benefactor, Balfour Gardiner, but also the one who was to be his strongest musical advocate for over fifty years, Thomas Beecham.

[156] *The Saturday Review*, 11 April 1925.

[157] Don Gillespie and Robert Beckhard, 'On Hearing the First Delius in America: Critical Reaction to Frederick Delius's Music in the United States, 1909–1920', in *MA&L*, pp. 57–98.

[158] Letters 176, 177 and 180.

# Acceptance and Friends

*Songs of Sunset* – *Cynara* – the Frankfurt Gang – *Brigg Fair* – the Musical League – *Three Part Songs* – *In a Summer Garden* – *A Dance Rhapsody* [no. 1] – *Fennimore and Gerda*

D ELIUS continued to be an inveterate traveller – sometimes with Jelka accompanying him – happily now more often than not attending rehearsals for, and performances of, his music. In the January and February of 1906 he was in Berlin helping Oscar Fried with *Appalachia*; in May it was Essen for the première of *Sea Drift*; and in the high summer he was in Norway for the tenth time, spending over two months at Aasgaardstrand,[1] where he did a lot of walking. From September until the end of the year, however, he was at home, revising the Piano Concerto and making a start on *Songs of Sunset*.

Delius had had seventeen songs published in London and Paris between 1890 and 1896, but otherwise all his attempts to interest publishers in his music failed completely. Between 1896 and 1905 nothing else was published, despite his having to his credit forty-five completed works (or movements of suites, etc., and including two operas), another twenty-five or so songs, and a few piano pieces. All performances were therefore given from copyists' manuscripts, or possibly, early on, from the original autograph full scores and orchestral parts in Delius's own hand. The use of copyists' parts of a number of Delius's works continued not only up to the end of his life, but even after it – for example *Paris* was not published until 1909; *Cynara* was written in 1907, first performed in 1929, but not printed and published until 1931; while, even more remarkably, the *Drei symphonische Dichtungen* of 1889–90, premièred in 1946, only appeared in print in 1951.[2]

Finding a sympathetic publisher simply proved extremely difficult – although certainly not for the lack of trying on Delius's part. He approached the Danish firm of William Hansen and, in Germany, Aibl Verlag, Forberg, Kahnt, Kistner, Lauterbach & Kuhn and Siegel – all to no effect. However, in 1906, he did eventually establish a relationship with Harmonie, who agreed to publish *Appalachia* and *Sea Drift* (see above, Chapter 4). In 1906 and 1907 Harmonie went on to publish *Five Songs*,[3] *A Village Romeo and Juliet*, *A Mass*

---

[1] A fishing village (but now a flourishing town) towards the southern end of the Oslo fjord, where Edvard Munch had a cottage.

[2] Even today in 2014, performances are still being given using lithographed copies of manuscript parts – although that might be due to high hire charges for proper printed material.

[3] *RT Catalogue*, p. 113.

*of Life* and the Piano Concerto. They were granted the publishing (but not performance) rights throughout the world, and Delius should have received 50% of the profits, but the arrangements were vague and proved unsatisfactory, to say the least. Contrary to what might be expected, Delius was in fact a hard-headed businessman who would tolerate neither inefficiency nor a lax attitude to money, and unfortunately almost all the publishers he used over the years suffered from both. Within a year, therefore, exasperation with Harmonie led to his going elsewhere – which was the start of a series of unhappy arrangements, because he proved unable to stay with virtually any of those with whom he tried to work. In 1907, he approached the 198-year-old Leipzig firm of Breitkopf & Härtel without success, and so in 1909 he came to an agreement with F. E. C. Leuckart of Leipzig; between then and 1915, they published *Paris, Songs of Sunset, Brigg Fair, In a Summer Garden, A Dance Rhapsody*, and *The Song of the High Hills*. In 1910, he entered into another contract – this time with the Cologne firm of Tischer & Jagenberg, established only three years earlier; they re-engraved all the previously published songs, and subsequently published *Life's Dance, On Hearing the First Cuckoo in Spring* and *Summer Night on the River*. Next, in 1913, he went to Universal-Edition of Vienna, but the relationship was not a particularly happy one, and the last work they published was the incidental music to *Hassan* in 1923. Regular problems were Delius's thorough dissatisfaction with both the poor quality of their proof copies of the scores and parts (albeit not the final ones), and their obfuscations about copyrights and accounting for royalties – in many cases downright awful – so Delius was writing letters of complaint, often in very strong terms,[4] almost continuously for some thirty years. Early on, the situation with Harmonie was much the same. Then, towards the end of the Great War, he turned to Augener again, and they published several larger works – the Violin Concerto and Double Concerto, *A Song before Sunrise*, the second *Dance Rhapsody* and *Eventyr* – and finally, during the Delius's last years, Boosey & Hawkes produced *Songs of Farewell, Song of Summer, Cynara, Idyll*, and a few smaller pieces.

In addition to those six firms, between 1906 and his death in 1934, Delius used another eight different publishers,[5] almost exclusively for small works and songs. The constant changes cannot have done him any favours, for, by the time one firm had published a few pieces and decided that he was a talent worth promoting, he had taken against them and gone off to another. Consequently, he never had the many benefits of a long-term arrangement – such as the happy ones between Elgar and Novello & Co., or Benjamin Britten's

---

[4] Early on he invariably started his letters 'Dear (or 'My dear') Herr Direktor', and finished by sending his and Jelka's (sometimes warmest) regards. Later, however, as matters got increasingly difficult, the correspondence became formal – 'Dear Sir' from Delius, 'Maestro Delius' from them, and both concluding 'Respectfully yours'.

[5] Including Forsyth Bros, Winthrop Rogers, Hawkes & Son, Oxford University Press, and Curwen.

with Boosey & Hawkes. Interested readers will enjoy the letters between Delius and his publishers (mainly Harmonie, Tischer & Jagenberg and Universal) in Robert Montgomery's and Robert Threlfall's excellent book on the subject.[6]

On the performance side, matters were improving. By the end of 1909 *La Ronde se déroule* had been played once, *On the Mountains* twice, *Over the Hills, Lebenstanz, Brigg Fair* and *A Mass of Life* three times each, *Appalachia* six times, and *Paris* and *Sea Drift* both an amazing seven times – almost all by first-class conductors, orchestras and choirs. At last Delius's future seemed bright, and Beecham would describe his next work as 'truly Delian'.[7]

D ELIUS'S friend Granville Bantock was one of the most important figures in English music in the first half of the century. He was born in 1868, and his path to becoming a musician was not dissimilar from Delius's. His father, a gynaecologist, decided that he should go into the Indian Civil Service, but poor health intervened, and Bantock then enrolled at the City and Guilds Institute in South Kensington; luckily, his inclination to go to music libraries rather than attend engineering lectures came to the notice of the principal, who managed to persuade Dr Bantock to let his son set out on a musical career. He went to The Royal Academy of Music (where he gained a scholarship), heard Wagner at Bayreuth, and was soon composing large-scale works; he began conducting in 1894,[8] and a year later he was appointed musical director of The New Brighton Tower Pleasure Gardens, near Liverpool. There, he turned the seaside military band into a full symphony orchestra, and played much English music, with (*inter alia*) Frederick Cowen, Elgar, Parry and Stanford coming to conduct their own works. Then, for thirty-four years from 1900, he was the extremely successful principal of the Birmingham and Midland Institute School of Music, and in 1908 he followed Elgar as the Peyton Professor of Music at Birmingham University. He was knighted in 1930, and died in 1946.

Delius seems to have been introduced to Bantock in the late summer of 1907, by Henry Wood's wife, Olga, a singer, who asked Delius if he had anything for soprano and orchestra that she could perform at one of Bantock's concerts.[9] Delius clearly had not, but on 19 September he wrote to Bantock saying:

I have just finished a cyclus of songs by Ernest Dowson, for Soprano, Baritone, small chorus and Orchestra. Would it be possible to have this

[6] Robert Montgomery and Robert Threlfall, *Music and Copyright: The Case of Delius and his Publishers* (Aldershot: Ashgate 2007).

[7] *TB*, p. 167.

[8] With the George Edwardes Gaiety Company, in Sidney Jones's *A Gaiety Girl,* on an international tour.

[9] He did, however, orchestrate songs 3 and 7 of the *Seven Norwegian Songs* for her, and she sang them twice during March 1908 in Liverpool and Birmingham: see *RT Catalogue*, p. 99.

done? Mr Austin would, I am sure, sing the Baritone part splendidly. The chorus is not difficult.[10]

That is the first written mention of the 'truly Delian' piece.

## SONGS OF SUNSET
(1906–8: *RT* II/5; *CE* vol. 11a)

ERNEST Christopher Dowson (1867–1900) was a *fin-de-siècle* poet, novelist and story-writer, one of the group centred around the artist and author Aubrey Beardsley and others generally associated with the Aesthetic and Decadent Movements of the 1880s and 1890s – and in particular with *The Yellow Book*. Generally regarded as the quintessential expression of the *fin-de-siècle* spirit, and as decadent and shocking by many people, *The Yellow Book* was a cloth-bound quarterly magazine containing criticism, drawings, essays, poetry and short stories, with contributions by many of the well-known artists and writers of the time – although, contrary to common belief, Oscar Wilde never had anything published in it, despite his being a friend of Beardsley and Dowson. Dowson's verse, much of which had Latin titles, was greatly influenced by that of Paul Verlaine, and reflects the conventional world-weariness of the 1890s, with an emphasis on lost love and a deep sense of the sadness of things. His life was a disaster, and he unsuccessfully tried to lighten his sorrows with alcohol and women, demanding, as time went on, 'madder music and stronger wine'.

Fenby says that Balfour Gardiner gave Delius a book of Dowson's poems,[11] while Heseltine believed that it was Jelka who discovered them.[12] In either event Delius decided to write this cycle, hoping to get it published in 1908, quite possibly for Bantock's concert. It is interesting that, notwithstanding her German upbringing, Jelka clearly had a serious interest in contemporary English verse. However, difficulties arose with Dowson's publisher, John Lane, over the copyright, and the music writer and critic Rosa Newmarch came to Delius's aid:

> When I last saw Mr Lane, I think that I made him see that it is unusual and practically impossible to get *a royalty on song words*. But he says he frequently gets 5 guineas for the rights to a single lyric and he could not ask the Dowsons to take a guinea a song. Of course, the value of these things depends, I imagine, on the demand and there had been rather a run upon the Dowson songs.[13]

Although that problem was obviously resolved, there must have been others,

[10] Letter 226.
[11] *Fenby 2*, p. 58.
[12] *PW*, p. 172.
[13] Letter 270.

for in the same year Beecham twice wrote to Delius asking for a vocal score.[14] In the event, *Songs of Sunset* was published by Leuckart, in both full and vocal score, in 1911.

The work was dedicated to Haym's Elberfeld Choral Society, but they did not sing it until 1914, three years after the first performance – perhaps because Haym did not think that it would become popular: in a letter to Ida Gerhardi in 1913, he said, 'this is not a work for a wide public, but rather for a smallish band of musical isolates who are born decadents and life's melancholics at the same time.'[15]

Bearing in mind the emphasis on large-scale concert works for voices and orchestra that characterised Delius's output between 1902 and 1905 – *Appalachia, Sea Drift* and *A Mass of Life* – one might expect his powers of invention to show signs of exhaustion when it came to yet another piece in the same vein. But *Songs of Sunset* marks a high point of inspiration. He would, of course, have been utterly fired up by Ernest Dowson's text which fulfils just about every criterion for the composer in terms of his personal world-view: all his philosophical *raisons d'être* are here, ranging from the poignancy of Man's transient existence on Earth compared with Nature's eternal renewal, to the austere belief that we come from nothing and return to nothing. The overall mood is consistently elegiac, equalled only by the *Requiem* and the *Songs of Farewell*, and it is not surprising to learn that Delius's first inclination for a title, according to the original manuscript, was *Songs of Twilight and Sadness*. Ernest Dowson provided the composer with exactly the stimulus he needed, and he did so in poetry that is far clearer and easier to grasp than the opaque mysticism of Nietzsche; no wonder Eric Fenby tells us that the composer's own copy of Dowson's poems was 'well-thumbed'.

The instrumentation is typically lavish for this period in Delius's career, and includes a family trio of oboe, cor anglais and bass oboe, whilst the three bassoons are reinforced by a sarrusophone (the double bassoon being the practical substitute for that nowadays). On the other hand, the choral writing is less ambitious than in *A Mass of Life* and only rarely do the voices divide. Moreover, they are generally duplicated by instrumental lines, a feature that is more characteristic of this score than of any other by Delius. There are two soloists, a baritone and a soprano (though mezzos have frequently claimed the part and it suits them well, as the vocal line does not lie consistently high). Delius sets a group of eight poems by Dowson, not separated into movements as such, but into self-contained sections divided by a double bar, as if to emphasise the work's structural and emotional unity. There is considerable variety between the settings in terms of vocal textures, and so we find a mixture of purely choral sections (the first and the third); those using a single soloist (soprano in the fourth, baritone in the fifth and seventh); a duet for the two soloists (the second); and all the forces combined (the sixth and eighth).

---

[14] Letters 282 and 288.

[15] Andrew Burn, note for Chandos CD CHAN 9214.

*A Song of the Setting Sun* contrasts images of sunset, barren fields on a winter day, and a faded flower to express a deep sense of loss and impermanence. The music, marked 'Quietly', begins with startling lack of introduction as we are plunged unexpectedly into a full choral texture on the second crotchet of the opening bar; it is rooted in a G natural pedal point, in the key of C, from 3rd bassoon, double bassoon and double basses (it is interesting to compare this with the opening of *A Village Romeo and Juliet*, which uses the same technique). The choral writing is serpentine and chromatic, tortuous to pitch, although Delius gives the singers some assistance by keeping most of the lines doubled in the strings. By this stage in his career he had learnt from experience to be more practical in the demands he made of choirs. The word-setting, unlike parts of *Sea Drift*, keeps the syllables 'in sync' to allow maximum clarity for the verse. The overall feeling of mortality is reflected symbolically in cascades of falling chromatic lines, with the strings providing the main bed of sound, and woodwind and horns sparingly used to colour and point up the texture (an utterly characteristic, Delian way of orchestrating). The three separate verses of Dowson's poem are not set to identical music, far from it, so there are striking responses to certain poetic phrases: the cold 'cynic moon' rising to a glittering E major harmony (Fig. 1-1) lit by woodwind and harp; the twinge of a muted 1st horn (Fig. 1+8) to suggest the bitter north wind; and the image of golden corn reflected in the rustling quavers of the woodwind (Fig. 3+1). The musical arch of the last of the three verses ('A song of a faded flower'), with its brief climax at the words 'fair and fresh for an hour' (Fig. 4-2), dies away to *pppp* to mirror the words 'faded it lies in the dust and low'. All these sensitive reactions to the poetry are typical, not just of this opening section, but of the work as a whole and they bear eloquent testimony to Delius's having just as fine an ear for words as for music.

Right at the end of this section (Fig. 4+6) there is a four-note phrase marked *mezzo piano* for the 1st flute and the cor anglais, and this will recur as a *leitmotif* throughout the work, in a variety of guises:

Ex. 5.1

Indeed, it surfaces immediately at the start of the next poem, *Cease smiling, dear!*, on divided 1st violins (Fig. 5-1) and is then consistently woven into the orchestral texture, initially on the 1st clarinet, then successively (in variants) on the oboe, 1st and 2nd violins, various woodwind instruments, horns, and so on (the cor anglais and 1st horn later take up the idea at Fig. 7-2, and there is a further rhythmic version in flutes, clarinets and oboes at Fig. 7+5.)

This second song is the true love duet of the work. Initially the soloists echo each other's thoughts, their words overlapping as they express Dowson's melancholic observations on the change and decay of old age ('taste no more the wild and passionate love sorrows of today'). Then, from Fig. 7+4 onwards, they declaim more forcefully as the mood becomes both ecstatic and erotic ('O red pomegranate of thy perfect mouth!'), a frank celebration of physical lovemaking. This develops, yet more pointedly, into a passage in octave unison (Fig. 9+5), culminating in an impressive climax with the line 'we shall lie, red mouth to mouth entwined' (Fig. 11-5), with soaring strings in three-octave unison (Fig. 11+1), a technique of scoring that Puccini used so effectively at moments of passion. This is the first orchestral *tutti* of the work: trumpets, trombones and bass tuba have only previously been heard briefly and quietly around Fig. 9; in fact the brass instruments are generally used very sparingly in this score, with only a handful of entries in all. A characteristically swift deflation, so typical of Delius, ushers in a memorable if melancholy close to the song at the words 'Here in thy garden' (Fig. 11+3), with the soloists steeped in gloomy thoughts of 'time and chance and change / and bitter life and death, and broken vows / that sadden and estrange', the accompanying texture consisting of just strings and horns with touches of woodwind (Ex. 5.1 on the cor anglais at Fig. 12-2, and again at Fig. 12+5). A yearningly expressive 1st horn solo (Fig. 12+3) brings this beautiful song to an end, *pppp*, on a chord of A flat with an added sixth of the scale (F natural) hanging like a question mark.

The chorus returns for the third song, *Pale Amber Sunlight*, which has a wonderfully hushed opening with woodwind descending chromatically over a sustained perfect fifth sounded in the depths (an F natural from cellos and double basses capped by a C natural from the 4th horn.) A quiet entry by the chorus sets the scene: trees reddening in the October sunset and swaying slightly in the breeze (flutes). A change of time signature from six beats in a bar to four (Fig. 15+1) marks the observation that 'misty Autumn' is the season of 'sweet twilight' that 'eludes a little time's deceit'. It is only a lull before the darkness of winter, itself a symbol of Death, and Delius matches these melancholy thoughts with two sequential phrases for the chorus: 'The twilight of the year is sweet ...' (Fig. 15+4) and, even more memorably, 'Our love, a twilight of the heart ...' (Fig. 16-1) (Ex. 5.2).

To accompany phrases such as 'dreamful Autumn', and, 'a little while then let us dream', Delius rivals that other dreamer of dreams, Elgar. A solo violin (Fig. 18-1) weaves a drowsy line in triplets above the voices as they twice whisper the single word 'dream' before dying away to nothing.

*Exceeding Sorrow Consumeth my Sad Heart!* is the only song set for just the soprano soloist, and Delius gives her grief-stricken utterances a chamber music accompaniment, the strings providing the underlay plus a mere handful of woodwind and horns to enrich the texture. A sense of imminent parting and loss imbues the text, which begs for the cessation of all activity ('cast thy viol away') and of all speech ('Be no word spoken'); any thoughts of the future are banished as a state of emotional paralysis takes hold ('only lay in silent sorrow thine head my way!'). Delius reflects this mood in a trance-like chromaticism, with descending figurations soured by accented passing notes. There are only

Ex. 5.2

two brief instances of *mezzo forte* or *forte* markings; otherwise the music is all shadings of *piano* to suit the mood of calm desolation. The music's resignation, however, is rooted in the major, not in the minor, key. For Delius, the idea of a life ended by total oblivion may be regrettable but it is not disastrous; a willingness to accept the inevitability of Fate transcends sorrow and lends it a poignant beauty of its own. Accordingly, Delius's musical setting deliberately shuns tragedy by tempering bitterness with the sweetest of harmonies. This is a most important concept to grasp, as it permeates Delius's mature works: nowhere is it exemplified more strongly than in the choice of a major key to close this song. The final thirteen bars are worth quoting in full; how beautifully the cor anglais is echoed by a solo cello (Ex. 5.3).

Next comes a song for the male soloist. *By the Sad Waters of Separation* is marked 'With quiet movement', and it opens with descending figurations from the woodwind somewhat reminiscent of the musical waves that lap the seashore at the start of *Sea Drift*. The poetry here hints at separation from a loved one who has 'gone beyond' and crossed the 'waste, gray sea' into the 'ultimate night' (i.e. Death.) The lone lover is fast losing all memories and recollections ('Hardly can I remember your face'), and for him even music holds no consolation (an echo of the shape of Ex. 5.1 in the 1st clarinet and the cor anglais at Fig. 29-5). A flowing cor anglais theme initiates a section marked 'Slower' (Fig. 29+8), which is passed to the oboe and then briefly to a solo violin above muted and divided strings, as the singer dimly hears 'the sigh of mine ancient adoration'. To temper the mood of grief, Delius begins a more forthright section at Fig. 32-4, returning to *tempo primo* for the words, 'If you be dead no proclamation sprang to me ...' The soloist becomes passionate as chordal brass adds severity to the texture in a fine passage, the first really loud music of the song, which begins, psalm-like, with the words 'No man knoweth

Ex. 5.3

our desolation'. Then the soloist sinks back into mourning at the mention of 'ultimate night' (Ex. 5.4).

Ex. 5.1 recurs in the cor anglais (Fig. 35+2), echoed by the bass oboe in augmented note values, and the music ends, like the previous song, not in the minor but in a resigned, though questioning, F major.

The composer rightly senses that by this stage some contrast in mood and tempo is needed, since the last fifteen minutes or so have been predominantly slow and inward looking. So he now gives us a joyful C major paean to the delights of springtime, *See how the Trees and the Osiers Lithe*, which brings all the vocal forces together for the first time. The chorus wax lyrical about the woods, the meadows and the birds (the fullest orchestral texture we have had for

Ex. 5.4

No man know - eth our de - so - la - tion; me - mo-ry
pales___ of the old de - light;___ while the sad___
wa - ters of se - pa - ra - tion bear us on to the
ul - ti-mate night.___

a while, with trilling flutes and upper strings, embellished with flickering harp
chords), but then the baritone soloist dampens their enthusiasm in a slower
passage (Fig. 37+3) warning them that 'the spring of the Soul / cometh no more
for you or for me.' The chorus tries, tentatively at first, to re-establish the joy
of the opening with a section in praise of Nature's flora and fauna (Fig. 38+2),
but is checked again, this time by the soprano soloist who warns, Cassandra-
like, that the 'flowers of the Soul, / for you and me, bloom never again.' A solo
violin joins her and as she falls silent the chorus mournfully repeats her gloomy
prediction, barely rising above *pianissimo* before Ex. 5.1 creeps in on oboe and
cor anglais (Fig. 41+6) and the song ends in a desolate A minor.

The penultimate song, one of the most beautiful in the cycle, is a baritone
solo: *I Was Not Sorrowful, I Could Not Weep*. It is permeated by the sound of
rain falling 'wearily upon the window pane', evoked initially by string *pizzicati*
and later (Fig. 43-2) by splashes of harp and woodwind. The flowing 6/4 of the
opening, reflecting a 'white and strange' river, gives way to a central section
in 4/4 expressing utter weariness of soul and body. The physical image of the
loved one has become blurred in the singer's mind so that only vague but
disturbing memories remain to him. Here the music returns to a triple pulse,
3/2 this time, with an expressive, arching cor anglais melody (Fig. 46-2) – how
beautifully Delius writes for this instrument, clearly a favourite of his – and the
same little motif is echoed by the 1st violins. The harmonies of the final nine
bars are exquisite (Ex. 5.5).

They lead without a break into the final song, using some of Dowson's most
famous lines: 'They are not long, the weeping and the laughter'. The soprano
and baritone spin their own independent melodic line in octave unison above
the chorus, pitting themselves against the fullest scoring so far. Delius has
been very sparing in his *tutti* passages up to now, but here he floods the score
with rich textures, most notably when the singers reach the lines 'They are
not long, the days of wine and roses'. This sumptuous passage (Fig. 48+4 *et*

Ex. 5.5

seq.) is marked 'Somewhat more animated' and it positively glows, but only for a relatively short spell. At the words '[our path] closes within a dream', the textures thin out drastically to just strings, bassoons and horns, and Delius writes a masterly *coda* (Ex. 5.6). Violas and a pair of horns rock gently to and fro above sustained fifths and fourths in B flat from cellos and double basses, with wisps of melody from the violins. The soloists have fallen silent but the chorus remains, twice uttering the word 'dream', *pppp*, as the 1st clarinet magically whispers Ex. 5.1 and the strings fade into the distance. Even for a composer who wrote so many poignant and beautiful final pages to his works, these are in a class of their own.

Ex. 5.6

IN the event, it was Beecham, not Bantock, who gave the first performance – at Queen's Hall on 16 June 1911, as part of an all-Delius concert with Julia Culp, Thorpe Bates,[16] the Edward Mason Choir[17] and the Beecham Symphony Orchestra. Delius and Jelka were naturally in the audience, as well as Bantock, Gardiner and the seventeen-year-old Eton schoolboy Philip Heseltine, whose subsequent friendship with Delius is dealt with in the next chapter. For once, the critics were generous:

[16] Julia Culp (1880–1970 – 'the Dutch nightingale') was an internationally celebrated, 'connoisseur's' mezzo; she made nearly 100 records. Thorpe Bates (1883–1958) was probably better known as an operetta and light-music singer, with many Promenade Concert appearances to his name. He seems never to have sung for Beecham again.

[17] Edward Mason (1879–1915) spent seventeen years on the Music Staff at Eton College. He was the principal cellist of The New Symphony Orchestra, then became an assistant to Beecham, and founded his celebrated Edward Mason Choir in 1908. He was killed on the Western Front (see also below, Chapter 6).

frankly they must be heard again. A first hearing seems to show that the songs are not all upon the same lofty level as that beginning 'Exceeding Sorrow', but we are glad to have made the acquaintance of a work that is of immense sincerity and truth ... Mr Beecham fully earned the applause that greeted him not only for his enterprise, but also for the wholly admirable manner in which he had carried it to a highly successful issue.

*The Daily News*, 17 June 1911

The Delius Concert given at Queen's Hall served both to introduce a new work by that composer, and to remind us of the existence of Mr. Beecham and his Symphony Orchestra. The new work was a cycle of 'Songs of Sunset' to poems by Ernest Dowson, expressing the mutually reasoned despair of two lovers on the eve of a separation. The best feature of the music was the intensity and dignity of its pathos. It perhaps falls short of Mr Delius's best work in inventiveness, but his characteristic harmonies and coloration are employed with abundance, and proportionate effect ... Mr Beecham conducted with all the ability and individuality of method with which he made us so familiar last year.

*The Musical Times*, July 1911

*The Times*, however, despite never having seemed to be much in sympathy with Delius's music,[18] not only had the most perspicacious comments on *Songs of Sunset*, but was also well disposed to the other works in the programme:

Mr. Beecham signalled his public return to musical life last night in the Queen's Hall by giving a concert with his orchestra and the Edward Mason Choir devoted to the works of Mr. Frederick Delius. The combination of these two musicians is eminently suitable, for Mr. Beecham, by his production last year of *The Village Romeo and Juliet,* and earlier still by putting the orchestral works into the programmes of his symphony concerts, has done more than any one else to introduce to London audiences a composer who had until then made less of a mark over here than he had done abroad. The programme last night contained three works which have already been performed and one new one. In this new work Mr. Delius has found inspiration, like Mr. Bantock, in the poetry of Edward [*sic*] Dowson, eight of whose lyrics he has strung together and set continuously for orchestra and chorus, with soprano and baritone solos ... Mr Delius, while treating all the poems lyrically, has nevertheless

[18] Its senior critic between 1889 and 1911 was J. A. Fuller Maitland. He was well known for his snobbish attitude to some composers: his support for the English Musical Renaissance was driven by the fact that Stanford and Parry came from well-to-do families and had been to the best universities, while he disdained Elgar and Delius because they did not. He edited the second (1904–10) edition of *Grove's Dictionary of Music and Musicians,* from which Delius's name was completely omitted – as it was from his nevertheless entertaining and interesting autobiography, *A Doorkeeper of Music* (London: John Murray, 1929).

avoided monotony in his setting. He has succeeded in doing this partly by making reflective and personal lyrics alternate. The personal note is never prominent, but at two places it is insisted on, once where the soprano solo sings the lyric beginning 'Exceeding sorrow consumeth my sad heart' (the third stanza of which reads almost like a version of Sully Prudhomme's 'L'Agonie') and once again where the two soloists break into the song called 'In Spring' with the refrain 'But the spring of the soul cometh no more for you or for me.' The baritone solo might have been expected to express a strongly personal note at the entry of the words 'I was not sorrowful,' but here the composer makes the solo singer do what the chorus has to do throughout the work, that is to say he makes the voice take part instrumentally in giving emotional expression to the words. The episode is not personal or dramatic (if it had been it would have destroyed the balance of the whole work), and the voice moving in and out chromatically with the rest of the instruments gives a poignancy to the words which could have been gained neither by the orchestra alone nor by the still too impersonal chorus. It also occurs at one of the most original passages of a work which shows that the composer is gaining strength and individuality in his expression and is also advancing at any rate towards one solution of the interesting problem of the relation of the voice to the orchestra. Another and even more instrumental way of using the voice for purposes mainly of colour is to be seen in 'Appalachia', which came first in the programme and which remains one of the most vital and most individual of the composer's works.

After the interval, the symphonic poem 'Paris' was played, which shows the composer's sense of beauty and poetry as well as anything he has written. It is quite free from French influences, being in fact the work of a sensitive 'resident alien', and is about as different from Charpentier's way of representing Paris as Whistler's is from Meyron's.[19] The 'Dance Rhapsody' (written, like 'Appalachia,' in the form of variations) made a pleasantly gay and buoyant *finale* to the concert, and the large audience warmly applauded the composer who came on to the platform to bow his acknowledgments. From his point of view, however, the programme might well have been inverted and given in the exactly contrary order, for it would then have started with the least original of the four works and made a gradual crescendo to his strongest.

17 June, 1911

[19] James Abbott McNeil Whistler (1834–1903): celebrated American painter who started his career in Paris. Charles Meryon (1821–68): French artist famous for his etchings of Paris, almost like architectural drawings, and in a style completely different from Whistler's.

## CYNARA
### (1907–29: *RT* III/5; *CE* vol. 15b)

T HIS next work is a setting of more of Dowson's poetry, and it is very likely that Jelka discovered the poem for Delius. Its provenance is Horace's *Odes* IV, 1, verse 1, where the poet pleads with Venus to stop tormenting him with love, as he is growing old and claims he is not the man he used to be when the gracious Cynara ruled his heart. Dowson's poem originally appeared in 1849 in *The Second Book of The Rhymers' Club*[20] (an anthology of contemporary verse), and then in Dowson's *Verses* two years later. The writer A. K. Holland thought that:

> With Jacobsen's *Arabesk* and the Verlaine songs, [Cynara] forms a chapter in Delius's work which touches more closely than any other on the sentiment of the closing years of the nineteenth century. For us of the present day, it is difficult to recapture that sentiment, which is apt to seem a little hollow and artificial, but yet haunts us with a sense of bygone beauty.[21]

Delius prefaces Dowson's first verse with a ravishing orchestral introduction of twenty-three bars in which the spirit of Cynara herself is unmistakably present in the sinuous line of a solo violin, weaving its way above divided and muted strings, coloured by harp and by dense, low-lying chords on clarinets, bassoons and horns who add their distinctive, dark hue to the texture. (Interestingly, a slightly larger woodwind section is required for *Cynara* than for *Songs of Sunset*, the additions being a piccolo, 2nd oboe, bass clarinet and 3rd trumpet; on the other hand, no bass oboe is needed.)

A double bar and a change of key-centre (E major to E flat) mark the entry of the baritone: 'Last night, ah, yesternight, betwixt her lips and mine / there fell thy Shadow, Cynara!' Delius quotes Ex. 5.1 from *Songs of Sunset* six times: on the 1st clarinet, *espressivo*, at bar 28; again on the 1st clarinet at bar 30, doubled by the oboe; on a solo cello (bar 32); on the 1st flute and 1st clarinet (bar 45); on 1st and 2nd clarinets (bar 49); and on the 1st and 2nd oboes (bar 53). Meanwhile, the music broods and grieves in sympathy with the poet's haunted soul, which is unable to dispel the overbearing presence of Cynara.

A change of metre to 3/2 (bar 56) introduces the second verse, describing a desperate night of debauchery with a 'bought red mouth'. Pulsating horns and strings (the solo violin returns as well) emphasise not so much physical gratification as mental torment from the inability to shake off memories of the

---

[20] The Rhymers' Club was a group of London-based poets, founded in 1890 by W. B. Yeats and Ernest Rhys. Originally a dining club that met at Ye Olde Cheshire Cheese in Fleet Street and the Café Royal, it produced anthologies of poetry in 1892 and 1894.

[21] A. K. Holland, *The Songs of Frederick Delius*, The Musical Pilgrim (London: Oxford University Press, 1951), p. 21.

past. The poignant line, 'I have been faithful to thee, Cynara! in my fashion' recurs as a tag to each of the four verses, although Delius does not fall into the obvious musical solution of setting it in the same way: each appearance is different.

As more extravagant emotions are stirred in the third verse ('I have forgot much, Cynara! gone with the wind ... Dancing, dancing to put thy pale, lost lilies out of mind'), a faster 3/4 metre takes off (bar 101), continuously quickening its pulse. Dance rhythms naturally predominate, but there is a sense of desperation about them, marked by crudely scurrying woodwind, *pizzicato* strings and blaring brass, whilst the percussion adds its own forced gaiety.

The third verse spills over musically into the fourth at bar 139 ('I cried for madder music and for stronger wine'), a demand which is swiftly reined in as despair follows with the realisation that the 'feast is finished and the lamps expire'. Ex. 5.1 returns on the 3rd and 1st horns (bars 162–5), and is widely quoted (1st violins and cellos at bar 169 etc.). The trombone chord on the final word 'Cynara!' is a spine-tingling moment as we are led back into a nine-bar *coda* that mirrors the opening with its haunting violin solo and, like *Sea Drift*, achieves a degree of resignation, *pppp*, on a juxtaposition of E major and C sharp minor, in this case from divided strings, bassoons and horns.

Heseltine says that this setting of Dowson's 'most perfect poem ... was to have formed the climax [of *Songs of Sunset*], but that it was wisely left out, as tending to disturb the proportions and interrupt the mood-sequence.'[22] For whatever reason, Delius stopped work at the words 'feast is finished ...', put his draft away and forgot about it. It may have been the right artistic decision not to include it in the *Songs*, but twenty years later the completion of this fine and moving work became the first achievement in the miraculous collaboration between Delius and Eric Fenby in the early 1930s (on which see below, Chapter 8). In 1968, Fenby related how it came about:

> In the spring of 1929, Sir Thomas Beecham wrote to Delius asking if he had an unpublished work for voice and orchestra to include as a novelty in the programmes of the festival of Delius's music which he was proposing to give in the autumn of that year. I was instructed accordingly to look through the piles of faded pencil sketches (all in full score) that had accumulated from a lifetime's work. Along with the sketches *of Songs of Sunset* was one I could not place. On playing it over to Delius, he recognised it immediately as a setting for baritone and orchestra of Dowson's best-known poem *Cynara* which he had abandoned, indeed quite forgotten, after judging its inclusion inappropriate in the scheme of *Songs of Sunset* for which it was intended initially. It was quite complete in every detail up to the words 'Then falls thy shadow, Cynara', at which there was a blank. Delius decided to fill it, and, after some painful and frustrating hours of work, managed to complete the remaining bars

---

[22] *PW*, p. 112, n. 1; see also below.

by dictation. I shall never forget my thrill when I took down the telling chord on the trombones on the final word 'Cynara'.

The success of this dictation was as crucial to Delius as to me. If it failed to sound well in performance he would give up trying to compose altogether. When at last I sat beside him somewhat apprehensively in Queen's Hall at the orchestral rehearsal, I had no idea that before leaving Grez-sur-Loing for England he had told his wife, Jelka, to sew three fivers into the lining of his jacket 'for Eric, if it comes off well.' I got my fivers and Sir Thomas his novelty.[23]

Beecham conducted the piece in Queen's Hall on 18 October 1929, as part of his big Delius Festival,[24] with John Goss and the British Broadcasting Orchestra:

The most marked characteristic which seems to reflect his inmost musical temperament is a kind of nostalgic emotion. *Cynara*, written in 1907 but only recently completed and now heard for the first time, deals in something stronger than home-sickness, but the kind of reaction portrayed in Ernest Dowson's poem is just that tinge of regret that lies at the heart of almost all Delius's contemplative music. *Eventyr*, or 'Once upon a Time', on the other hand, is an orchestral distillation of the essence of Northern fairy-tales. It is hardly programme music; indeed it is doubtful whether one ought to speak of programme music in talking of Delius's works, in spite of their significant titles, for he generalizes where another would particularize. This accounts for a certain diffuseness in works like *Eventyr*. It also accounts for the absence of word-painting in vocal works and his not too felicitous setting of words. In *Cynara*, as in *Arabesk*, also performed for the first time last night, the words are slowed down, cut up, made to halt by reason of the orchestra's need to enlarge its own text.

*The Times*, 19 October 1929

The critics in both *Musical Opinion* and *The Musical Times* were somewhat non-committal:

[It is] a work of highly coloured orchestral weaving, expressive of the excesses of passion and its subsequent reproaches.

*Musical Opinion*, November 1929

There was much in these works [*Arabesk*, *Eventyr* and *Cynara*] ... that is not characteristic of the composer as we have learned to know him.

*The Musical Times*, 1 November 1929

but after Beecham had conducted the piece subsequently, one critic gave his view on Dowson's poetry in no uncertain terms:

[23] *Lloyd*, pp. 195–6.
[24] See below, Chapter 8.

This work will hardly do except for infatuated Delians. Not but that the music is rich in beauty; but the faint moans of Ernest Dowson's poems come all too near being ridiculous.

*The Musical Times*, February 1934

In 1932, when this work and the 1925 *A Late Lark* were first published, the same paper had an article about them both, which took an even more haughty view of the text.[25]

A T the end of the nineteenth century, there were only five degree-awarding music colleges in England,[26] and it was common for young English composers to go and study in Germany: Arthur Sullivan and Ethel Smyth were at Leipzig, Cowen and Stanford went to both Berlin and Leipzig, while Mackenzie was at Sondershausen. Dr Hoch's Conservatorium in Frankfurt was founded in 1878 (thirty-five years after the one at Leipzig), and it became famous in English musical history as the *alma mater* of five young composers – always known as the 'Frankfurt Gang'[27] – four of whom were to become Delius's greatest friends. Cyril Scott[28] (the one who did not) was there as a pianist in 1891–3, and again as a composer in 1895–8; Norman O'Neill[29] attended between 1893 and 1897; Henry Balfour Gardiner from 1894 until 1896, and then for another two years from 1900; Roger Quilter[30] from 1896 to 1901; while Percy Grainger[31] spent six years there from 1895 until 1901. Notwithstanding that they did not completely 'overlap', they all kept in touch and lasting friendships grew between them. In 1902 Grainger had settled in England, and he instituted a

[25] An extract from it appears below, Chapter 8, in the section about *A Late Lark*.

[26] The Royal Academy of Music (1822), Trinity College of Music (1872), The Guildhall School of Music (1880), The Royal College of Music (1882 – absorbing the 1873 National Training School of Music), and The Royal College of Organists (1864).

[27] See generally, Colin Scott-Sutherland, *Arnold Bax* (London: J. M. Dent, 1973), pp. 37–8; Stephen Lloyd, *H. Balfour Gardiner* (Cambridge: Cambridge University Press, 1984), *passim*; Martin Lee-Browne, *Nothing so Charming as Musick! The Life and Times of Frederic Austin* (London: Thames Publishing, 1999), pp. 18–19.

[28] Cyril (Mier) Scott (1879–1970): one of life's rebels, he wrote a vast amount of music in all genres, much of it then considered very *avant garde* – and it was probably for that reason that he did not remain in the 'Delius circle'.

[29] Norman (Houston) O'Neill (1875–1934): musically the 'lightest' of the five, he spent much of his career composing incidental theatre music – that for Maurice Maeterlinck's 1899 *The Blue Bird* becoming extremely popular.

[30] Roger (Cuthbert) Quilter (1877–1953): the son of a stockbroker (whose firm still exists in London), most of his output consisted of superbly lyrical songs (still a staple of recital programmes) and some theatre music that was very successful in its time.

[31] Percy (Aldridge) Grainger (1882–1961): born in Australia, a larger-than-life character who 'suffered from a surfeit of talent'. He became an international concert pianist, folksong collector, quirky composer and experimenter with musical machines – and a good friend of Delius. From 1915 onwards he lived in the USA.

series of regular 'get-togethers' of the Gang at his London house, and of *soirées* at other much grander ones, to perform and comment on each other's new, or sometimes only partly finished, songs and chamber music, and generally to put the musical world to rights. After a while, they moved to Gardiner's house, 7 Pembroke Villas in Kensington, and the numbers quickly increased. Charles Kennedy Scott[32] wrote fondly about those meetings:

> Everyone loved Balfour as a dear friend, who not only helped us all with unsurpassed largesse, but steered music into channels that literally inaugurated a new era of artistic freedom. If anyone deserved the title of a Maecenas it was Balfour. He generally lived in the country at that time, at Ashhampstead in Berkshire, but had a small house in London, just off Edwardes Square, Kensington, opposite to that of his friends Norman and Adine O'Neill. Here we would meet: Gustav Holst,[33] Delius, Percy Grainger, Frederic Austin, Roger Quilter, Benjamin Dale,[34] Cyril Scott, Norman O'Neill, Arnold Bax,[35] and occasionally others – though it was strange that Vaughan Williams was never of the number. I doubt whether before or since there has been such musical fervour in our midst, or such a banding together, in comradeship, of alert musical intelligence ... Many were the delightful evenings spent [there] when, with Balfour as a perfect host ...[36]

Sometimes the actor and amateur painter Ernest Thesiger (1879–1961), the tenor Gervase Elwes,[37] and the composer William Hurlstone (1876–1906) came

---

[32] Charles Kennedy Scott (1876–1965): an exceptional musician, and the finest choir-trainer of his time. He founded the brilliant Oriana Choir in 1904, and its successor The Philharmonic Choir in 1919. Arthur Hutchings wrote that 'He made musicians see the folly of supposing that Delius was unsympathetic in writing for choral forces': *Delius* (London: Macmillan, 1948), p. 98; see also below, Chapter 6, under *The Song of the High Hills*.

[33] Gustav Theodore [von] Holst (1874–1934): English composer and teacher. There is no evidence that he and Delius ever met.

[34] Benjamin James Dale (1885–1943): English composer and academic. In 1921 he would make a brilliant transcription of Delius's *Eventyr* for two pianos. In Germany in 1914, seeing Wagner operas, he was (with a number of other English musicians visiting or living there) interned at Ruhleben, near Berlin, for the remainder of the Great War.

[35] (Sir) Arnold (Edward Trevor) Bax, KCVO (1883–1953), Master of the King's Music (1942–52): a prolific English composer in all forms except opera, but particularly of symphonies and 'symphonic poems'. He was a celebrated sight-reader for whom no full score held any terrors, and he and Austin occasionally used to improvise piano duets at those gatherings.

[36] Scott-Sutherland, *Arnold Bax*, p. 38.

[37] Gervase (Henry Carey-)Elwes, DL (1866–1921): he did not begin his professional career until his late thirties, but then rapidly became the finest tenor of his generation. He specialised in oratorio, *lieder* and English art-songs, and he was the dedicatee of Vaughan Williams's *On Wenlock Edge*. He was accidentally killed by a

to meetings – and it seems very likely that other members of the arts world did so too.

Delius came to London on 7 April 1907 – taking rooms which Cyril Scott had found for him at 88 Oakley Street in Chelsea[38] – and he certainly had a busy time. He lunched with Henry Wood on the 12th, when they talked about the Piano Concerto and probably *Sea Drift*; on the 15th he had lunch with the conductor Percy Pitt,[39] and dinner with Gardiner; there he met some members of the Frankfurt Gang, and (as mentioned above, in Chapter 4) 'they played Appalachia thro'. Then, on or shortly after the 17th, Delius went with Cassirer and Hans Gregor, the director of the Komische Oper of Berlin (for whom he still seemed to have time, the problems over the first performances of *A Village Romeo and Juliet* notwithstanding), to see the company in Offenbach's *Tales from Hoffman* at the Adelphi Theatre.[40] On the 25th, the tenor John Coates,[41] a friend from Bradford Grammar School days, invited him to

> the annual dinner of our old Bfd Grammar School boys [*sic*] You are sure to know all of them – I shall sing a few songs afterwards – that is all – so you will have nothing to do but to sit and smoke & think of old times.[42]

The evening of the 25th was spent at Grainger's house, where Delius must have received a very warm welcome; and on the 27th he returned to Paris.

As a consequence of the dinner party on 15 April, Henry Balfour Gardiner unquestionably became Delius's greatest and most trusted friend, making the first of many visits to Grez later in the year.[43] He was born in 1877; as well as composing, he conducted, and in 1912–13 he promoted, entirely at his own expense, a famous series of concerts of music by his English contemporaries. It included *A Dance Rhapsody*, *Lebenstanz* and the Piano Concerto. Gardiner was, indeed, a major musical philanthropist – giving substantial financial

---

train in America, and subsequently his friends set up The Musicians Benevolent Fund in his memory.

[38] Letter 207. Curiously, there is no evidence as to how they had presumably already come to know each other.

[39] Percy Pitt (1870–1932): he spent a substantial part of his career at Covent Garden, working with Richter and Beecham, and then for the British National Opera Company. In 1926 he became the first General Music Director of the BBC.

[40] The performances were not well received: see *TB*, p. 143.

[41] John Coates (1869–1941): a well-known and highly respected English tenor (in fact originally a baritone) with a huge concert and operatic repertoire. He was famous for his Gerontius in Elgar's oratorio, and Beecham thought he was one of the most special musicians of the time.

[42] Letter 215. The dinner, which Delius attended, was held the following evening in The New Gaiety Theatre on the corner of Aldwych and The Strand: see Lewis and Susan Foreman, *London: A Musical Gazetteer* (London: Yale University Press, 2005), p. 230.

[43] Letter 220.

support to (among others) the Deliuses and Holst; to The Oriana Madrigal Society and the Philharmonic Choir; and to The Royal Philharmonic Society. Delius appointed him as one of his executors, but Gardiner did not in fact act, because of his dissatisfaction with the way in which Delius's wishes came to be carried out (as to which, see below, Chapter 10). Shortly before the start of World War II, this remarkable man gave up music entirely and retired to his estate in Dorset to grow trees, dying in 1950.[44]

On that same evening in April 1907, Delius almost certainly also met both O'Neill and Grainger, and they too became among his strongest friends. When Grainger was at Frankfurt, his composition teacher, Karl Klimsch,[45] somewhat improbably introduced him to the world of English and Scottish folksong. Grainger came to England in 1901, and spent the next ten years partly on worldwide concert tours and partly collecting English folksongs. Having heard a lecture 'On Collecting English Song' given to The (now Royal) Musical Association by the pioneering historian of the subject, Lucy Broadwood, he joined the Folk Dance Society in 1905 and, with the aid of a wax-cylinder phonograph, did an immense amount of fieldwork recording songs in many counties. His most celebrated 'find', in the same year, was *Brigg Fair*, which he heard at the Competitive Festival held in the Lincolnshire market town of Brigg, sung by Joseph Taylor, a seventy-two year old bailiff from nearby Saxby-All-Saints;[46] the following year, Grainger set *Brigg Fair* for unaccompanied solo tenor and mixed chorus – one of the most haunting pieces ever written by anyone.[47]

Delius and Grainger quickly discovered that they shared musical tastes and ideas, and at some stage Grainger showed Delius his *Brigg Fair* arrangement. Delius was so taken by it that he decided to write his own version (which he dedicated to Grainger), and it has been interestingly suggested[48] that he was intrigued by the song because the idea of its poem is curiously similar to the story of *A Village Romeo and Juliet* – a young man taking his sweetheart to the fair, and his deep devotion to her.

---

[44] He was the brother of the arborealist reviver Rolf Gardiner, and the uncle of the conductor Sir John Eliot Gardiner. Stephen Lloyd's *H. Balfour Gardiner* is an excellent biography.

[45] Karl Klimsch (1841?–1909/10?): see John Bird, *Percy Grainger* (Oxford: Oxford University Press, 1999), pp. 37–8.

[46] Ibid., p. 117.

[47] Joseph Taylor can he heard singing the song on the Hallé Orchestra's CD HLL 7503.

[48] John K. White, (unpublished) letter to Martin Lee-Browne as *DSJ* Editor, 31 May 2005.

## BRIGG FAIR
### (AN ENGLISH RHAPSODY)
#### (1907: *RT* VI/16; *CE* vol. 24b)

*B*RIGG *Fair* has to be ranked as one of Delius's out-and-out masterpieces. Although it lasts for little over a quarter of an hour, it is definitely not in the category of a miniature. Its lavish scoring necessitates fourteen separate woodwind players, six horns, and normal brass. A full complement of strings is essential not only for the purposes of balance but because Delius consistently divides them into ten parts. A publisher with a keen eye on the practicalities of performance might prefer to have in the catalogue an alternative, reduced scoring for a smaller orchestra; but that would be utterly inappropriate in this instance as the music rises to heights of grandiloquence that demand a sumptuous sound – surprisingly so, given the work's humble, folk-music origins.

The original manuscript full score is currently missing, and the published version is based on an edition by Beecham that incorporates a significant number of textual additions in terms of phrasing and, most notably, dynamics. For example, Delius had originally put no markings whatsoever in the last four pages apart from an overall *fortissimo* in all parts. But that was not good enough for Beecham when he came to perform (and later) edit the score – not that Delius himself ever had any quarrel with those amendments, such was his trust in the conductor's judgment.

*Brigg Fair* is certainly rhapsodic; it is also, in all but name, a set of variations. The poignant nature of the original tune, together with Grainger's chromatic voicing of his accompaniment to it, fascinated Delius and (according to Grainger) led to the somewhat confusing comment, 'but our harmonies are identical'. What he meant, in fact, was that their *use* of harmony and sense of harmonic *style* were identical.

Grainger's vocal transcription sets off to the fair immediately, but Delius has a more leisurely start to his journey, concerned to paint the scene as suggested in the opening verses: a fine, early morning in August, a lark singing in the meadows and a young man on his way to meet his sweetheart. This introduction, marked 'Slow – Pastoral', is frugally scored for divided, muted strings (their hushed entry in the third bar is an especially magical touch); arabesque-like solos for two flutes and clarinet suggest birdsong; harp arpeggios glisten like dew on the grass; and two sustained chords *pianissimo* from a quartet of horns add an aura of magic. These minimal ingredients provide the quintessence of the mature Delian sound-world – and all in just nineteen bars.

The folktune melody itself is now heard for the first time ('Simply – With easy movement'), quietly sung by the 1st oboe (Fig. 2+1) and accompanied by bassoons, clarinets and *pizzicato* strings. Grainger's arrangement, incidentally, is never plagiarised by Delius, who finds his own, constantly inventive, harmonisations:

Ex. 5.7

**With easy movement**

The modal nature of the melody lends it the characteristic of starting out as if in D minor but in fact turning back into G minor. It is short, only sixteen bars, and – following the dictum that having stated a folksong tune, all you can then do is to repeat it[49] – Delius does just that, giving it initially to the 1st flute (Fig. 3+7) and including an interesting variant (Fig. 4+6) in which the leading note of the melody is altered to F sharp (as opposed to remaining an F natural) so as to avoid a clash with a G flat with the lower violas (Delius makes a similar adjustment for harmonic reasons in variation 5, i.e. Fig. 27+7). The tune is then passed to the 1st violins (Fig. 5+4); and lastly to flutes and clarinets (Fig. 7+1), each time with varied harmonic treatment.

After this group of four statements of the basic tune, Delius begins a new paragraph (Fig. 9+1) which, though it is not marked with a double bar, can conveniently be thought of as inaugurating the first of a set of six variations. It consists of a group of three repetitions of the tune, the first of them quite a free variant, merely outlining the melodic and rhythmic patterns of bars 1 and 2 of Ex. 5.7; the central repetition quotes the tune on the 1st and 3rd horns (Fig. 11+5 *et seq.*); the last repetition allocates it to the 1st trumpet. Dancing semiquavers in strings, woodwind and harp weave in and out of the melody and lend a stylistic unity to the repetitions of this first variation. The music peaks *fortissimo* (Fig. 14+3), though not yet with the involvement of full brass; but it is only for a moment, as the texture, pace and dynamics swiftly contract to reach a double bar and a fresh variation (Fig. 15+1.)

This turns out to be an unforgettable inspiration, introduced by the same 'lark song' on the 1st flute as in the very opening bars of the work; then, muted 1st violins ('singing') give voice to a new melodic idea in which the first three notes of the folksong are evened out into a triplet followed by a descending

---

[49] Constant Lambert, *Music Ho!* (London: Faber & Faber, 1934), p. 146.

phrase, exquisitely harmonised and ending with a minor/major twist; around it, clarinets murmur like drowsy bees. Time seems to stand still:

Ex. 5.8

This beautiful thought is shared out (Fig. 17+6 *et seq.*) among the cor anglais, 1st clarinet and upper violas; then it is heard again as a solo for the 1st horn (Fig. 18+4) – sheer magic. The vision fades on a low-voiced F major chord (with an added sixth of the scale) from divided strings, whilst little snatches of birdsong (flutes and 1st clarinet) complete the spell. This is one of the most exquisite passages, not just in *Brigg Fair* but in all Delius.

After a double bar, a brief third variation reprises the folksong again on the 1st clarinet (Fig. 19+7) above chromatically shifting woodwind and horns, joined, in a repeat, by all three flutes. Delius effectively punctuates his thoughts with a little *ostinato* figure from the timpani, harp and *pizzicato* double basses (Figs 20+8 and 21+9). A more involved fourth variation follows (Fig. 22+1) in which the basic pulse quickens; the tune is heard in the woodwind in augmentation (i.e. longer note values) above dancing passage-work in the strings, ornamented with mordents or shakes, a good example of Delius being perfectly able to write good counterpoint when he wished:

Ex. 5.9

This leads to a climax marked by the very first appearance (and by now we are easily halfway through the work) of trombones and tuba (Fig. 22+7 *et seq.*) as well as the 3rd trumpet (Fig. 24+4). This is a typical example of how Delius liked to hold some of his orchestral forces well in reserve; it is a very effective touch, even though the players who have had to wait (with all those empty bars to count and with cold instruments to coax into life) might well curse him for it. The dancing mood briefly returns, and then the first true *tutti* in the work is reached (Fig. 25+1), with the entire orchestra deployed (apart from the percussionists). However, the loud dynamic is only briefly sustained, since the music soon subsides to a double bar and a complete change of metre and mood.

Marked 'Slow – With solemnity' this fifth variation (Fig. 26+1) irons out the rhythm of the folksong melody into a flatter 4/4 metre, which is played initially on the 1st trumpet and 1st trombone (in octave unison) with a tolling bell on the second half of the bar and strings playing offbeat quaver chords throughout:

Ex. 5.10

This striking treatment is then repeated a semitone higher in an expanded scoring for violins in octaves, augmented by the cor anglais, three clarinets and three horns, whilst the offbeat chords are marked by the lower strings *pizzicato*, joined by woodwind and brass and by occasional pulses from the bass drum. It is as if a funeral procession had emerged from the morning mists to pass briefly across the horizon, vanishing into shimmering strings and distant horn calls (Fig. 28+2). The ensuing bridge passage of some fifteen bars also serves as a sort of recapitulation, with flutes and clarinets evoking the birdsong of the introductory pages, this time with expanded wisps of melody from the cor anglais (Fig. 28+6) and bass clarinet (Fig. 29+3), the latter lending a particularly haunting sound to the texture.

This sense of coming full circle is reinforced at the double bar by the sixth variation, which returns to the folksong's original 3/8 metre and recalls the mood of the second variation with its dancing semiquavers. Now marked 'Gaily', the music begins to tread a rustic measure with splashes of timpani and triangle, harp and *pizzicato* cellos. The whole orchestra soon begins to sway to this irresistible rhythm of the dance, and the texture fills out (Fig. 35+1 *et seq.*). The tempo quickens but then expands *maestoso* into a broad metre of 3/2 (Fig. 38+7) for an unexpectedly overwhelming climax, in which trombones and bass tuba are given their moment of glory, twice rearing up *fff* to cut through the rest of the orchestra, who are engaged in augmented snatches of the folksong itself, underpinned with tolling bells. It is a glorious and uninhibited deluge of sound, but it is also very firmly controlled: as so often, Delius avoids overplaying his hand. Suddenly, the texture contracts and the 1st oboe returns (Fig. 40+7) for one final, heart-rending appearance of the folksong melody in its purest form, cushioned by strings. A few faint timpani beats are heard in the distance, like half-recalled souvenirs of the dance; wisps of 1st flute add a questioning G natural to the harmony before the music finally resolves, in the penultimate bar, onto a simple string chord of B flat major that dies away into silence.

*Brigg Fair* is one of the most satisfying and characteristic works of Delius's maturity, its form convincingly structured, its ideas fertile and memorable, its sense of direction and flow impeccable and its orchestration of the utmost imagination and sensitivity. If only one of his works could be quoted to give the lie to that tiresome cliché that Delius meandered and could not organise his music, then this is it. It certainly stands as a high-water mark of the level of artistry he had reached by 1907, and as a testimony to his development over the preceding decade. He had by now unquestionably found his own true voice.

D ELIUS and Bantock had become close friends. Within six months of their meeting, a letter from Delius ended 'With love to your wife and self from us both',[50] and another, from Bantock (in connection with The Musical League – see below), began in Yorkshire dialect:

---

[50] Letter 260.

My dear old pal,

Ow can thee axe me what I'es got agin ole country? Asn't tha gotten sacked at Liverpool? And you've been poomping and poomping at 'em pretty long and trying to bring a little fresh air into the musical atmosphere, and the question is, is it worth 'poomping' and spending our energy and strength on a musically apathetic race?[51]

Delius's lifelong relationship with Beecham had only just begun, so it was natural that Delius should ask Bantock to conduct the first performance of *Brigg Fair* – which he duly did, with the Liverpool Orchestral Society on 18 January 1908. *The Musical Standard* (doubtless in the person of Mr Baughan again) did not beat about the bush:

Delius … takes himself very seriously – so much so that, notwithstanding a great amount of technical cleverness and lavish use of every possible adjunct, even to a set of chimes, a full *batterie* of drums and an unusually large brass choir, I was heartily glad when the last bar sounded. I am sorry to say it, but the whole thing appeared to me – and I was not alone in the opinion – a case of 'much ado about nothing.' When I remember that the redoubtable J. F. R.[52] used to assume the *role* of John the Baptist so persistently in regard to Fritz Delius it is rather disappointing to find one's expectations (this is the second occasion) doomed to disappointment. I think that rather too much has been made of Mr. Delius' so-called English nationality, that it must not be forgotten that, although born in Bradford, his parents were not only German, but he received his musical education in Leipzig and has spent most of his life in America, Germany and France, so that those who are anxious to claim him as a 'British composer' ought to remember this.

1 February 1908

but *The Musical Times* gave Delius possibly the most favourable brief review that he had yet had:

This fine work is a slow movement in pastoral style, based upon a Lincolnshire folk song descriptive of a country swain journeying to meet his sweetheart at the fair. The music is of tranquil beauty, the central idea being surrounded by moving polyphony richly coloured. Before the close it reaches a climax of real grandeur, and all through betokens the mind and hand of a master.

1 February 1908

---

[51] Letter 312.

[52] J. F. Runciman (1866–1916): English music critic.

A month later, Landon Ronald[53] conducted *Brigg Fair* in Birmingham Town Hall with the Hallé Orchestra, and Beecham gave the first London performance, in Queen's Hall on 31 March:

> The novelties were a tone poem, 'Love among the Ruins' (by W. H. Bell) and an English rhapsody 'Brigg Fair' (by Frederick Delius). Each, in my humble estimation, seemed to suffer from undue length; especially 'Brigg Fair,' which I rather enjoyed for a time and of which I then grew weary.
>
> *Musical Opinion*, May 1908

> The general tone of the music is pastoral and meditative, and the harmonic treatment is very modern. A climax, in which bells took part, was somewhat trying to the ears, but at least the passage served as a foil to the beautiful quieter sections. It is reasonable to hope that many other opportunities will be afforded of hearing so important a work.
>
> *The Musical Times*, May 1908

In 1910, *Brigg Fair* was done in New York (under Walter Damrosch), in Zurich (by Volkmar Andreae), in Berlin (by no less a figure than Artur Nikisch) and Coblenz,[54] and Beecham gave two performances in London, followed by one in Liverpool in 1911. There was even one in Oxford in May 1912, which Heseltine attended:

> I wonder whether you were afflicted by a violent fit of the shudders last night at about 9 o'clock – because at that hour 'Brigg Fair' was being positively *murdered* … by one Dr H. P. Allen, directing an amateur orchestra, augmented by wind players from the London Symphony Orchestra. I am perfectly furious about the performance: *three in a bar*, just like at Coblenz, only *slower*, if anything!! … Can nothing be done to prevent further travesties of 'Brigg Fair' being perpetrated? I believe Dr Allen conducts over the country, and he might do it again. Awful thought!'[55]

A VERY un-Delius-like activity in 1908 was his acting as an adjudicator for the 29th Norwich Triennial Music Festival's Cantata Prize competition. The invitation came from Wood, the musical director of the festival, and having originally written to Delius in January 1907 (when Elgar and Bantock were mentioned as his co-adjudicators) he evidently forgot that he had done so, because he repeated the request on 20 April (when Elgar's name was not

---

[53] (Sir) Landon Ronald (1873–1938): he worked mainly with the London Symphony, New Symphony, and Royal Albert Hall Orchestras, and for twenty-eight years was the principal of The Guildhall School of Music.

[54] *PW Letters*, Letter 223.

[55] *PW Letters*, Letter 242. Dr Allen was then the organist at New College, Oxford. Heseltine (then aged eighteen) had been to the Coblenz performance.

mentioned!).[56] The libretto of the cantata was also the subject of a preliminary competition; ten or fifteen entries were expected, but in the event many more were received. Thirty-two settings of the winning poem, *Cleopatra* by Gerald Cumberland (1879–1926), many lasting half an hour or so, were considered, and Delius told Bantock that he had found the task hard work:

> My time has been entirely taken up with these prize Scores. Gracious! What a work. This will do me for ever, I believe, as adjudicator. One has the great desire to do no one injustice & feels oneself obliged to wade carefully and conscientiously thro miles and miles of dreary waste. The worst are those that try to be complicated like Strauss, without any of his mastery. There are one or two that are not so bad & where one feels talent and atmosphere, but these are badly scored – strange to say – My choice will no doubt fix on one of these.[57]

The reply was unsympathetic, as Bantock wrote back, 'I am amused when I think of you struggling with the rank vegetation of the Prize Cantatas.'[58]

The competition took place during the early months of 1908. Delius's co-adjudicators turned out to be Samuel Coleridge-Taylor[59] and the composer and critic Ernest Walker[60] – who, so *The Times* of 31 October said, were 'known to be in full sympathy with the most modern phase of literature and music'. The twenty-three-year-old Worcestershire composer Julius Harrison[61] won the first prize, and his work was played at the same year's festival, while the second prize went to Havergal Brian[62] for his forty-minute or so choral work *The Vision of Cleopatra*, which was performed for the first and only time at the 1909 Southport Festival by Landon Ronald.

---

[56] Letters 204 and 212.

[57] Letter 249.

[58] Letter 251.

[59] Samuel Coleridge-Taylor (1875–1912): born in London, the son of a West African doctor and an Englishwoman, he had a precocious musical talent. At the Royal College of Music, he was a pupil of Stanford, and wrote a considerable amount of music in all forms, including a symphony. His cantata *Hiawatha's Wedding Feast* (the première of which was conducted by Stanford while Coleridge-Taylor was still a student at the College) and its two sequels remained immensely popular among choral societies until the 1960s.

[60] Author of *A History of Music in England* (London: Oxford University Press, 1907).

[61] Julius Harrison (1885–1963): English conductor and composer. He assisted Arthur Nikisch and Felix Weingartner with Wagner operas, was a regular conductor for the Beecham Opera Company and provincial orchestras, and served on the staff of The Royal College of Music. He wrote a large amount of attractive music in nearly all forms. There is a review of the piece in *The Musical Standard* for 7 November 1908, p. 295.

[62] Havergal Brian (1876–1972): English composer who produced a vast quantity of music, including thirty-two symphonies, which has never found popular favour.

Delius's introduction to the Frankfurt Gang led to his involvement with The Musical League, the purpose of which was to promote the music of the younger generation of European composers. The idea was originally mooted in the first half of 1907, and many English musicians were connected with the League for varying periods over the next six years. In May 1907, Robin Legge told Delius[63] that Henry Wood had sketched a 'great scheme', but some two months later Wood wrote to Delius:

> I fear Mr Legge's 'scheme' has fizzled out altogether, as I have heard nothing more about it. I quite agree with you that it is high time something was done in London for a proper series of orchestral concerts which will not depend on door money, and which will be entirely subscribed for before the doors open, but so far I have failed utterly to bring this about.[64]

It could well, however, have been Delius who was the catalyst in furthering the idea. In October 1907, back in England again and staying with Gardiner at 7 Pembroke Villas, he had written to Bantock:

> I am getting up a great musical scheme, which I shall tell you all about when I meet you, and on Tuesday morning I am invited to lunch in order to meet Elgar, whom I shall also ask to join me.[65]

A year and a half later he said in a letter to Ethel Smyth '... it was with this hope that I started the Musical League ...', and Norman O'Neill once called him 'the inventor'.[66] The fact that three people – Legge, Wood and Delius – were all putting forward the same ideas for the similar reasons at much the same time must have been very exciting, but translating them into practice turned out, not surprisingly, to be a very difficult and time-consuming task. Ernest Newman was also involved at an early stage, asking William McNaught, the editor of *The Musical Times*, on 12 December 1907 to join the committee, and, with Mr Baughan of *The Musical Standard*,[67] to draft the constitution.[68]

Throughout 1907 and 1908, Delius was heavily involved in correspondence (much of it with Bantock) about the mechanics of actually getting the League to work:

---

[63] Letter 216.

[64] Letter 218.

[65] Letter 231.

[66] Letter 307, and n. 1.

[67] Perhaps a surprising member of the committee, given his obvious dislike of Delius's music – but perhaps Delius was in fact not appreciably affected by his frequent published criticisms.

[68] *The Musical League Papers*, The British Library, Additional Manuscripts 49600–49603.

I am anxious to speak with you about the Scheme. We have already decided that no music critic will be on the Committee – The few names you mention – if on the Committee – would cause the thing to fail entirely. Why! These old Johnnies who have had sufficient opportunity to shew what they can do & have done nothing – then I should prefer Elgar, you & myself to sign a letter & you may be sure that we shall have a good following. The others may join the Society & the more the merrier but not *lead* it, we know where they will all lead it to.[69]

In another letter he wrote '... in case you want to approach Percy Pitt, I would do so with pleasure ...'.[70] Then in yet another letter:

Don't you think we ought to have Beecham on the Committee? – This is an afterthought – There are now such a lot on that one more or less does not matter – Besides anyhow we shall have to have a working Committee – It was our original intention to get him to sign the memorial & he might be rather offended if he is not now asked.[71]

When Beecham did join the Committee he, too, was characteristically somewhat scathing about some of the 'possibles' for membership, and made an unkind remark aimed at Balfour Gardiner (with whom he never got on, and who for some reason was never invited to join).[72]

The League was publicly 'floated' in a letter to *The Times* on 23 March 1908, signed by, among others, Elgar (as the President), Delius (as the Vice-President), Mackenzie, Wood, Bantock, McNaught, Pitt and O'Neill:

We ask you to give publicity to the fact that we, the undersigned, have formed a new musical society, to be known as The Musical League. The objects of the league may be summarized as follows:–

(a) To hold an annual festival of the utmost attainable perfection in a town where conditions are favourable.

(b) To devote the programmes of these festivals to new or unfamiliar compositions, English and foreign.

(c) To make use, so far as possible, of the existing musical organisations of each district, and of the services of local musicians.

(d) To establish a means by which composers, executive musicians, and amateurs may exchange ideas.

---

[69] Letter 238.

[70] Letter 257.

[71] Letter 260 – and Delius wrote again some six weeks later asking, 'Have you any special reason for not putting Beecham on the Committee?'

[72] Letter 246.

Delius chaired the first Committee meeting – held in Birmingham on 10 April 1908, by which time there were seventy-nine members. Elgar was the chairman for the second, when the membership stood at 115, and there was £100 (equivalent to something over £10,000 in 2014) in the bank. Well-known musicians were constantly being invited to join the Committee, and by the end of 1908 it numbered around fifteen – although attendance at meetings was very variable, and gradually got smaller and smaller. The third one, in October, was again chaired by Elgar, with Delius and eight other members present, and it was resolved 'that a Festival consisting of at least one Orchestral and one Choral Concert be held in Liverpool towards the end of April 1909'. Delius and Beecham offered guarantees of £100 each, and just after Christmas 1908, Delius wrote to Bantock saying that he had succeeded in persuading Mahler, Debussy, Vincent d'Indy and Schillings to come and conduct one of their works at the festival – in Mahler's case his Symphony no. 2, no less![73] Foreign composers were, of course, firmly within the scope of the League's objectives, but as things turned out by the time it was wound up hardly anything but British music had been played. Although Delius may have been the instigator of the League, he began sending apologies for being unable to attend meetings – as did Elgar – showing, we may assume, a waning of enthusiasm. Once the time for actually organising the Festival drew nearer, they probably found they simply did not have the time to help with the hard work, and that October 1908 meeting was in fact the last Delius attended.

Sometimes things almost seemed to be going backwards, and Delius became increasingly disillusioned with England and the majority of its musicians – except, of course, Beecham, Bantock, his Frankfurt Gang friends, one or two others and some players. After a very depressing letter to Bantock,[74] the latter tried to cheer him up, mimicking Delius's use of Yorkshire dialect:

Dear Lad!

What hast tha gotten agin the ole countree? What's use o' crying aboot th' English Ears, if tha wa'nt do summat to help syringe 'em? What's use o' protesting? Lad, tha must keep on poomping and poomping at 'em, wi'out givin' o'em rest. The poor ignorant fools know dinna kenna no well better. Of course they'll suck Mendelssohn's soothing syrup, as long as they have hold o' the bottle. What we have to do is to get the bottle awa' from 'em, and ye canna weel do it, by pitching yer tent over the hills and far away, any more than I can by caravaning to Mecca, & visiting the Ka'abah. If ye can't drive the donkey or yer pigs to market the proper way, then you

---

[73] Letter 300. Only four months before the Festival, however, Mahler declined to come, saying that he would need at least four or five rehearsals for anything of his: see Letter 320. One wonders how and when Delius got to know Mahler sufficiently well to feel able to approach him in the first place, or whether he simply wrote 'out of the blue'.

[74] Letter 311.

must let 'em think they driving you, and once you get them to follow, why, lad, you can pull their noses all the time …

> Yer affeckshunet fayther
> Sambo[75]

But it was no use, and, although their correspondence continued spasmodically, Delius could not be persuaded to continue as an active member. In fact, for reasons which it has not proved possible to discover, the once stimulating relationship between Delius and Bantock, which generated letters like the one quoted, seems to have cooled: one letter from Delius to Bantock in October 1910 starts 'Dear Bantock' and ends 'Yours ever, Frederick Delius', and in 1913 Delius wrote to Ernest Newman, 'I wrote more than a year ago to Bantock … but got no answer.'

The first Festival eventually took place in Liverpool on 24 and 25 September 1909, with a chamber concert, an orchestral concert and a choral and orchestral concert. The orchestra was a scratch one – Vasco V. Akeroyd's Symphony Orchestra from Liverpool ('including a few first-rate professional players from the Hallé and the Liverpool Philharmonic'); Harry Evans, a noted choir-trainer, conducted the two big concerts, and The Liverpool Welsh Choral Union took part in the third. A large number of young British composers were represented in the programmes, including John McEwen[76] and Frank Bridge,[77] Ethel Smyth,[78] Vaughan Williams, Gardiner, Grainger (presumably regarded as an honorary Englishman), Scott, Austin, Bax and Delius – four of whose 'Seven Danish Songs' were sung by Edith Evans, the wife of Harry Evans.[79] (The songes were 'Wine Roses', 'In the Garden of the Seraglio', 'Through Long, Long Years' and 'Let Springtime Come, Then'.) Interestingly, it had been agreed early on that nothing by those involved in the organisation of the League would be played at any of the concerts,[80] and the only non-English music was Debussy's

---

[75] Letter 312.

[76] (Sir) John Blackwood McEwan (1868–1948), who wrote a large amount of attractive and interesting music.

[77] Frank Bridge (1879–1941): he studied under Stanford at the Royal College of Music, initially became a viola player, and then made a name for himself as an unflamboyant conductor. He wrote a large number of fine orchestral works, much chamber music and some sixty songs, and is celebrated as having been the teacher of Benjamin Britten (1913–76).

[78] (Dame) Ethel Mary Smyth (1858–1944) was one of music's more unusual characters, and a leader of the suffragette movement before the Great War.

[79] There is an effusive review of the Festival, well over 2,000 words long, in *The Musical Standard* of 2 October 1909.

[80] By the date of the concert, Delius was no longer a member of the committee. A letter to *The Musical Standard* (8 April 1908) commented, 'If [given the distinguished members of the Committee, that stipulation] is to hold good, whose compositions can be performed? … Holbrooke and Cyril Scott?'

*Nocturnes* (already ten years old), Rimsky-Korsakov's *Antar* and Bach's cantata *Praise Jehova*, which ended the Festival.

As mentioned below, Delius had intended to go to the Festival, but illness prevented him, so Adine O'Neill sent him a long and amusing letter commenting on the music and the performances.[81] He promptly replied with an equally amusing letter, which was, however, 'typical of the sarcastic attitude adopted by Delius towards England and the English at that time'.[82] Eighteen months later he wrote to Bantock:

> The musical [*sic*] League I suppose is dead, & will live on only in the salary of the undersecretary McNaught's son – No! I am afraid artistic undertakings are impossible in England – the country is not yet artistically civilised – There is something hopeless about English people in a musical and artistic way and, to be frank, I have entirely lost my interest and prefer to live abroad and make flying visits.[83]

This gives the impression that Delius was no longer involved at all, but it is not known whether he had already resigned, or was, indeed, still a member at the end.

Eventually, there were two more concerts in Birmingham in December 1912 and January 1913, but the League was virtually dead, and it was finally wound up in April 1913. Nevertheless, even at that stage there were some who still took a very up-beat view of the future, completely at odds with Delius's:

> No doubt the works performed had not quite the best of chances, but it was clearly the death-knell of the misery school – for, from what I know of the scores, no doubt remains in my mind that the development of European music lies in England.
>
> *The New Age*, 30 January 1913

With Bax, Arthur Bliss, Benjamin Britten, John Ireland, Alan Rawsthorne, Edmund Rubbra and Michael Tippett nearly all at the start of their careers, with the benefit of hindsight we can see there was actually no need for pessimism. It was not, however, the lack of up-and-coming composers that was the problem. The League's objects were impeccable, but its downfall was undoubtedly due to 'its conflicting personalities, too many men with too little time to spare and with vacillating conviction in the enterprise, especially when matters were not running smoothly'.[84]

---

[81] Letter 324.

[82] *Hudson*, p. 43.

[83] Letter 356.

[84] Stephen Lloyd, 'The Rumble of a Distant Drum', *DSJ* 80 (1983), 5–28, at p. 20.

T HE last significant event for Delius in 1907 was the death, on 4 September, of one of the most important figures in his life, Edvard Grieg – 'darling, sweet little Grieg', as Grainger called him.[85] He had been a friend and mentor since Delius's Leipzig days, and his influence was still just felt in parts of *A Village Romeo and Juliet*. He was to have come to England the following month – to conduct his Piano Concerto in Leeds, with Grainger as the soloist – when the Deliuses and the Griegs might well have met again. They had not in fact seen each other for many years, and their correspondence had dwindled, so it would in all likelihood have been a joyous reunion, for after Grieg's death Grainger told Delius that 'he was always talking of you, affectionately and admiringly, & told me lots of jolly anecdotes of your trips together in the High Hills.'[86]

Meanwhile, Delius had not yet given up his love of the high life of Paris – about which he doubtless had many somewhat different 'jolly anecdotes'. He had written to Bantock in December 1907:

> I do hope that you will manage to come over here for the *bal des quat'z arts* in April. Julian's ball is in February perhaps you might come for that also. It is nothing to get over here for a week if you can get off from the Institute. But the 4z arts is of course *the* one to go to.[87]

Bantock was unable to get there, for, as Delius reported afterwards:

> What a pity you could not come for the Bal – it was grandiose Gracious! What a sight it all was, and what lovely women were there – I dare not put down on paper what all took place – but I will tell you when we meet … Excuse this scrawl – I am rather rocky after the 4'z arts.[88]

1908 was a much busier year of travel for the Deliuses than 1907 – as always, sometimes he went away alone, and sometimes with Jelka. It was also a productive year, with, by the end of it, two good partsongs, *In a Summer Garden* and *A Dance Rhapsody*, all finished, and a start made on *Fennimore and Gerda*. There were four trips across the Channel: to conduct *Appalachia* and *In a Summer Garden*, and then to hear performances of *Paris*, *Lebenstanz* and the English première of *Sea Drift*. Next came Munich (for *A Mass of Life*) and Stuttgart (also for *Appalachia*). Finally, following the completion of *In a Summer Garden*, in July and August Delius went walking in Norway – with Beecham as an unlikely companion. They got on very well together, although Beecham's and Delius's descriptions of the former's fitness differ somewhat![89]

---

[85] Letter 224.
[86] Ibid.
[87] Letter 247.
[88] Letter 274.
[89] *AMC* p. 78; Letter 290.

However, his now quite prolific output and a good number of performances notwithstanding, Delius's music was still not appreciated by the critics:

Mr. Frederick Delius, in spite of his foreign name, is an Englishman. I confess that I do not understand his music. One of our foremost composers told me that in Delius we had a musician as significant, as rare and as epoch-making as Richard Strauss; and our foremost critic has said that the elements of greatness in his music are unmistakable. This is as it may be. I have heard his 'Brigg Fair' in rehearsal and in performance; but at no point could I enter its complex web of harmony and discover the beauty which I was told was there. His 'Appalachia' is founded on a theme worthy of Beethoven; but the harmonic structure of the variations is often grotesque and ineffective. 'Sea Drift' has imagination, but it is amorphous and extravagant. Throughout all the work of Delius with which I am acquainted one is met by great and gross lumps of discord, like malignant tumours in a human body. Why they are there it is hard to say. Nevertheless, I must confess that I have not yet finally made up my mind about this composer. I am told that, if I study him further and deeper, I shall be rewarded with some idea of his greatness: and I can believe that this may be so. In any case, he has a recognised and a high position on the continent and he is probably the only English composer who has had a whole book in a foreign language devoted to him in his own lifetime.

*Musical Opinion*, June 1908

## THREE PARTSONGS
### (1907–8: *RT* IV/2, IV/3 and IV/4; *CE* vol. 17)
### *On Craig Ddu; Wanderer's Song; Midsummer Song*

T HE first of these three partsongs for mixed voices had in fact been finished at the very end of 1907, and the other two were completed in January and April 1908.[90] In just a dozen lines, *On Craig Ddu* (pronounced 'Craig Thē'), an 'impression of nature' by Arthur Symons,[91] describes the sensory perceptions of the poet as he lies in the bracken, gazing up at the 'pallidly blue' sky, on the Welsh mountain-top of Craig Ddu, overlooking Caernarfon Bay. Sparingly, like a painter adding brush strokes to a canvas, Symons suggests the sounds of wind and water, of oxen lowing, sheep bleating and a farm dog barking down in the distant valley. Delius sensitively matches this poetic landscape with sure and fluent touches of harmony and a rich texture in which the male voices are divided throughout (usually in four but sometimes in five parts); the female voices are also divided but mostly only towards the end. 'Slow and softly' is the overall marking, and the dynamics are indeed relatively restrained. There is some striking word-painting from bar 14 onwards, evoking the rustling wind, which Delius shapes with a melisma of triplets for the sopranos on the word 'blew'. A reference to the sound of running water invading the silence inspires a harmonic sequence of great beauty (bars 23 to 28):

Ex. 5.11

The ending is deeply moving, with its somewhat unexpected close in the minor as the 2nd sopranos resolve the harmonic suspension by moving slowly down from A natural to G natural:

Ex. 5.12

---

[90] Letters 247 and 257; *M&C* Letter 22.

[91] Arthur (William) Symons (1865–1945): poet, critic, and translator, and another member of The Rhymers' Club. He was largely responsible for the successor to *The Yellow Book*, entitled *The Symbolist Movement in Literature* and published in 1899.

The words of *Wanderer's Song* are also by Symons. The first and third stanzas, depicting world-weariness ('I have had enough of women and enough of love ...', and, 'I have had enough of wisdom and enough of mirth ...'), are separated by contrasting lines that offer escape in the form of a call to the open road. This is matched musically by Delius in an A–B–A structure. The second A section essentially mirrors the first, but adds an extension and reworking of the last four bars to make a seven-bar coda. The scoring is for men's voices only, with tenors and basses divided throughout to give a four-part texture. The A sections both move from a moderate four-in-a-bar to a quicker six-in-a-bar, reflecting the poet's determination to forge a new way of life. This masculine decisiveness is contrasted at the start of the B section by a more reflective mood underlined by characteristically descending chromatic harmonies.

Delius fashions a striking coda out of the poetic references to Death as a 'sleep too deep to wake' when he inserts pungent and unexpected chords based on dominant sevenths on A natural, into an F minor tonality:

Ex. 5.13

*Midsummer Song* is a much more light-hearted affair – a call to make merry in the woods and enjoy 'youth, love and bliss', since night (i.e. again, Death) is not far away. The text of this hedonistic invitation is presumably by Delius himself, and the musical setting is far less complex than that of the previous two songs. The mixed voices are divided throughout into an eight-part texture, and the swinging rhythms of the 6/8 time signature soon lead into a central section consisting only of 'La-la-la's. This is a trait borrowed from the madrigal and to which Delius was oddly attracted – examples of it in *Appalachia* and *A Mass of Life* have already been noted. Here, it seems forced and not a little banal. Rooted in a fresh C major, the harmonies are correspondingly straightforward and mostly diatonic, though Delius throws in just enough chromaticism to keep the singers on their toes. It is a deceptive piece – not nearly as easy to sing as it looks on the page. There are some awkward intervals to negotiate, making it a good test for a choral competition – which indeed was its original function.

Delius sent a copy of the recently finished *On Craig Ddu* to Bantock at the end of 1907, saying:

> If you think it is any good I can have it published. The other one I attempted [*Wanderer's Song*] does not yet please me, so I must live with it a bit longer. I find I can never do anything in a hurry, but will try to do some of these things when the mood takes me.

*On Craig Ddu* was premièred at the 1910 Blackpool Music Festival, and (as another illustration of how Delius's music was becoming known) it was done again only two years later by The Barrow Madrigal Society, from the Lakes, who went all the way to London and included it in a concert in the Aeolian Hall on 7 March 1912[92] It has proved impossible to discover where and when the first public performance of *Wanderer's Song* was given, but that of *Midsummer Song* was in a concert by the Whitley Bay and District Choral Society conducted by W. G. Whittaker[93] in December 1910. Heseltine went to a concert of the Eton and Windsor Madrigal Society on 9 December 1912, and reported to Delius:

> I heard the 'Midsummer Song' in Windsor last Monday, and was only too thankful that you were not present, as the performance would have made you *writhe*! It was even worse than I had expected. Parratt[94] is a hopelessly bad conductor at the best of times, and well known to be out of sympathy with any modern music: he beat something which looked more like four in a bar than two in a bar, though what he actually meant to beat was not clear! The choir was sadly deficient in numbers, and, being accustomed chiefly to Palestrina and antique madrigals, obviously failed to grasp the music. I believe they call Stanford and Parry 'modern'! However, a striking testimony to the outstanding value of your part-song, as music, was afforded by the fact that, presented as it was under such adverse conditions, it was more appreciated by the audience than any other number on the programme! It was the only song that earned an encore, though the encore was not given. Applause, however, continued loudly until Parratt turned to make a speech, and said: 'The only people who will sing that again will be the audience' – a remark, apparently intended to be humorous![95]

When the *Three Part Songs* were sung at the 1929 Festival, however, they received an excellent performance:

> The unaccompanied partsongs … afford an opportunity for producing some of Delius's most lovely and characteristic effects by good chording. Half the character of his harmony is obtained by the spacing of his chords, and Mr. Fulton was able to obtain a kind of iridescence by careful shading of the different parts. The beauty of the two wordless choruses 'To be sung of a summer night on the water' lies in this kind of part-singing, and

---

[92] *PW Letters*, vol. 1, p. 239.

[93] William Gilles Whittaker (1876–1946): a much-respected academic musician (being an acknowledged expert on J. S. Bach's cantatas), composer and choral conductor.

[94] Sir Walter Parratt, who was the organist of St George's, Windsor for forty-two years until his death in 1924.

[95] It also soon 'became very popular with the London Glee Club', whose conductor was the celebrated Arthur Fagge: see *PW Letters*, Letter 274. The Edward Mason Choir also performed it.

the effect was heightened last night by their being sung off stage. Another happy instance was the ending of 'On Craig Ddu.' The imitation of bugles in 'The Splendour Falls' was perhaps a more doubtful matter.

*The Times*, 24 October 1929

A T the very end of 1907, Delius wrote to *Musical Opinion*[96] about the difficulties of trying to make a living as a composer:

Since I have been in London [says Mr. Delius, the composer of 'Appalachia'] many of your promising composers have complained to me that they rarely get a second hearing of their works. They should be exceedingly thankful that they get *a first!* In Germany the competition is much worse than it is in England. The principal society for the encouragement of music – the Tonkünstlerversammlung, with headquarters in Berlin – received, last year no fewer than two hundred and eighty symphonies, from which number *only six* had to be selected for public performance. Just think of the years spent in composing these works; and then the great disappointment save to the mere half dozen. No earnest musician should think of becoming what I may call a professional composer unless he has private means. A man who knows that his three meals a day are assured can devote himself to real individualistic composition and can wait for whatever good fortune may be in store for him. He could of course make a livelihood by writing shop ballads, many of which (while popular in England) would not be listened to in Germany. No; there is not much money to be made out of music until you are at the top!

The principal sources of income for composers at that time were sales of printed music, hire fees and performing rights (which were either Grand Rights for stage works, or Small Performing Rights for non-stage performances), and by the time of Delius's death he was still only receiving very modest fees for broadcasts, and even smaller ones for mechanical rights [i.e. recordings – of which twenty-nine had by then been made]. Even in 1927 he received only £89 from the Performing Rights Society (PRS), equivalent to £4,580 in 2014, and three years later £241 (or £12,880 in 2014). He also, of course, received fees from his publishers, albeit extremely small ones. As a comparison, in 1934 the average teacher earned £480 (£28,900) and the average solicitor £1,238 (£74,500) – while in 1922 rank and file orchestral players earned around £1 (£41.20) for a concert and probably a single rehearsal. Interestingly, at the end of their lives, Delius and Elgar were receiving very much the same in royalties from the PRS.[97]

Ever since Delius and Jelka began their life together at Grez, their garden had been a very special place indeed, both for them and their friends (and it

---

[96] December 1907.
[97] All those figures are taken from *M&C*, pp. 19–20.

has continued to be so for those who have lived in the house, and the hundreds of people who have visited it). Jelka had, of course, painted there, *en plein air*, even before she and her mother bought the property together, and it must have been the garden which was the main reason for their decision to do so. Only a few months after Delius died, Philip Oyler, an English agriculturist and author, wrote a long article in *The Music Student* about the garden which has become a classic – and in view of the garden's significance in the Deliuses' lives it is appropriate to quote quite extensively from it:

> ... its setting is an inspiration for all who are affected by the sight of beautiful things ... We have been standing in deep shade on the north side of the house and as we go out on to the other side, our eyes are dazzled by a rich sunlight falling on the courtyard. When they grow accustomed to this, they are amazed at a mass of flowers, so vividly intense, that one wonders what they are. We approach to satisfy our curiosity and find that they are roses of all sorts and annuals covering the ground completely between them ... a riot of colour throughout six months of the year, for the annuals, regularly watered, seem to delight in the hot sun and bloom as one never sees them in England: petunias, salpiglossis, cosmos, phlox, nicotiana, marigolds in the most astounding luxuriance, with here and there a madonna lily growing amongst them and looking down upon them as a sort of benediction.
>
> When we have satisfied our eyes with this feast of colour, and look around us, we find that the house has wings at each end that project southwards, thus forming the courtyard, and that where the wings end, old stone walls continue, and indeed lead right down to the river Loing below, giving perfect seclusion. Moving out of the courtyard, where climbing roses spread in profusion on all sides, we notice in the east, and barely a hundred yards distant, the towering ruins of a Norman castle round which the jackdaws are ever circling and in which they find ideal nesting places. On the west, and even nearer stands the old church with its noble twelfth-century tower, beautiful in its stern simplicity. On either side, too, one sees the roofs of old houses, barns and sheds of many shapes and sizes, but all covered with mellowed brown tiles that seem to have deep purple shades in them, a most pleasing combination with the grey stone walls, and entirely satisfying to the eye ...
>
> Beyond this the path forks, and both parts descend with pleasant windings till at length they reunite at the landing place by the river. Whichever one takes makes no difference. They are equally beautiful with fruit trees of various kinds growing on either side in luscious grass, with here and there a large clump of peonies. But it is really impossible to keep to either path. Between them in a little natural valley is a pool of enchantment, furnished by a never-failing spring of clear water. On its northern bank a weeping-ash – a Chinese variety – stands like a dignified guardian; at its southern end bamboos grow in luxurious profusion to

fifteen feet high and more, while yellow iris fringe its sides, and, if one approaches quietly, a pair of water hens will be seen at home. The hand of man has had very little to do with this lovely spot, and perhaps that is why it promotes a delight which one does not feel in beholding an artificial lily pond, no matter how rich in aquatic flowers.

Certainly it is not easy to pass on, yet when we do it is only to arrive at another beautiful place, a roughly circular lawn between the pool and the river. Here again there is an extraordinary natural charm. A beech with polished boles and of great height keeps guardian, this time at the northern end, apple trees are along the sides, and forming the border between it and the river, rise gigantic plane trees with the sun shining on their flaked boles – simple indeed all of it, but majestic in effect, a sight one could never forget.

And so to the river Loing, a wide, silent current with magnificent trees overhanging it on the village side, and pleasant meadows opposite ... an interesting row of silver-stemmed poplars on the opposite bank [which Delius] planted in 1910 ...[98]

and Eric Fenby wrote:

the white courtyard would blaze with myriad flowers, and Nature rim his little world by the great trees at the water's edge. Indoors, apart from works by his friends Gauguin and Munch, all the paintings on the walls revealed colourful studies of the garden in summer mood from the brush of his talented wife, Jelka. But the garden itself was her masterpiece, and the musical imagery it worked in her husband's mind was dedicated fittingly to her.[99]

In such surroundings, the theme of Delius's next work was perhaps inevitable.

---

[98] Philip Oyler, 'Frederick Delius in his Garden', *The Music Student* 14 (July 1934), 121–3; reprinted in *Companion*, pp. 49–54.

[99] *Lloyd*, p. 153.

## IN A SUMMER GARDEN
(1908: *RT* VI/17; *CE* vol. 25a)

H E originally considered eight possible titles, all of which are written on an early draft score: *Summer Night, Rhapsody, Summer Sounds, Summer Rhapsody, A Song of Summer, A Summer Eve, A Summer Song, Summer, On A Summer's Eve* and *In a Summer Garden.* Still not happy, however, he headed page 1 of the original manuscript score *Summernight – Slowly with simplicity,*[100] and it seems clear that for a long time *A Summer Rhapsody* was the title he favoured most strongly. When he finally opted for *In a Summer Garden* is not known – but that title was used in the programme for the première, and it was never changed again. Likewise, he had many second thoughts about the music itself, and he made numerous amendments to the first pencilled manuscript before writing out the 'clean copy' used by the copyists for producing the orchestral material for that performance.[101]

This exquisite work was dedicated to Jelka, and Delius placed these lines by Dante Gabriel Rossetti[102] at the head of the score:

> All are my blooms; and all sweet blooms of love to thee I gave,
> While Spring and Summer sang.
>
> Spring 1908 – Rossetti.[103]

For many admirers of Delius's music, *In A Summer Garden* holds a special place in his output. A concise but unforgettable synthesis of his style, it represents the best of him – all contained in under fifteen minutes of music. He made further extensive revisions after the first performance, and the analysis below follows those second thoughts, as published by Leuckart in 1911. Delius liked to let the titles of his works speak for themselves, so it was must unusual that when the score was reissued by Universal in 1921, he included a brief description setting the scene (which had originally been included in a programme note for a performance in Germany in 1913):

> Roses, lilies and a thousand sweet-scented flowers. Bright butterflies flitting from petal to petal, and gold-brown bees murmuring in the warm, quivering summer air. Beneath the shade of the old tree flows a quiet river with water-lilies. In a boat, almost hidden, two people. A thrush sings faintly in the distance.[104]

---

[100] *RT Supplement*, p. 173; *Pictures*, p. 64.

[101] *RT Supplement*, p. 173.

[102] Dante Gabriel Rossetti (1828–82): painter, illustrator and poet, who in 1848 founded the Pre-Raphaelite Brotherhood with William Holman Hunt and John Everett Millais.

[103] From Rossetti's *The House of Life*, part 1: *Youth and Change*, sonnet LIX, lines 9–10.

[104] Translated from the original German: 'Rosen, Lilien und tausend duftende Blumen. Bunte Schmetterlinge flattern von Kelch zu Kelch und goldbraune Bienen summen

In this case, the task of pinpointing Delius's artistry in words is even more frustrating than usual, but at least an idea of the structure of the work can be communicated: it is a tour of the garden in three sections, with the river playing a central part. Though Delius employs a sizeable orchestra, his instrumentation is refined and more akin to chamber music, with the use of *tutti* passages deliberately restricted. A wind quintet of flute, clarinet and three bassoons establishes a cool G minor tonality in a chordal phrase echoed immediately by muted strings, above which two significant but fragmentary melodic ideas are heard. The first is voiced by the 1st oboe:

Ex. 5.14

This is complemented by a more lyrically expansive theme, given to the 1st flute:

Ex. 5.15

Ex. 5.14 is scattered amongst the woodwind instruments and grows organically (Fig. 3+4) into a more lyrical form with which Delius makes great play, developing it extensively throughout the opening section:

Ex. 5.16

in der warmen zitternden Sommerluft. Unter schattigen alten Bäumen ein stiller Fluss mit weissen Wasserrosen. Im Kahn, fast verborgen, zwei Menschen. Eine Drossel singt – ein Unkenton in der Ferne.'

The first *tutti* breaks out (Fig. 5+1) with a jauntier motif (a development of Ex. 5.15) which is like a sudden burst of sunlight. Now, after the greyness of G minor, the temperature warms up considerably as the garden blossoms musically and our ears become more and more attuned to the sounds of nature, including trills on strings which suggest the buzzing of insects (Fig. 6+4). Descending chords on woodwind and harp (Fig. 7+7) are a colourful touch and the string writing becomes more vivacious (Fig. 10+3 *et seq.*). Then the pace slackens – 'more reposeful' is how Delius marks it – and there is a change of metre to 6/4, halving the previous *tempo*. Undulating quavers in the upper woodwind, which tell us we have reached the riverbank, decorate a wisp of a theme for the violas, 'singing', as Delius directed, above sustained and muted strings, and with a counter-melody added for the 1st horn:

Ex. 5.17

In a masterly touch, Delius gives this idea two further treatments: he repeats it a minor third higher, reinforcing the violas with the 1st horn as the former move out of their richest register, and also adding rhythmic harp chords; then putting the violas right up in the treble clef, a minor sixth higher, with the 1st trumpet *dolcissimo* adding an edge to the sound – a wonderful example of Delius's subtle skills in orchestration. The music dreams on as the overall texture fills out and the strings, now richly divided, soar aloft with the 1st violins being given Ex. 5.17 to sing. Then the orchestration suddenly collapses in on itself as we seem to turn away from the river and head back across the garden. The initial 3/4 pulse returns ('Mysteriously' is Delius's instruction to the conductor and players) and Ex. 5.15 is recalled, inciting the orchestra to a sudden outburst of passion spread over several pages, the music exultant and in full flood as Delius lets the players off the leash *fff* (Fig. 16+6). There is an equally memorable passage marked 'Softer and more quietly' (Fig. 16+8) as the music, still in a richly scored texture, reaches a double bar and a *sostenuto* followed by a sudden hush, coloured by upward scales on the harp (Fig. 17+6) and by dense string writing which culminates in three lush string chords, a pause marked over each. We must now retrace our steps.

Lyndon Jenkins[105] has given a striking insight into this third and final section of the work by pointing out that Delius does not offer a recapitulation pure and simple of the opening section, so much as a new vision of it:

It is as if we have chosen the alternative path for our return journey: the same garden is seen from slightly different angles; we see similar sights

---

[105] A former chairman of The Delius Society, and author of *WS&SS*.

to before but the effect is different even as some phrases familiar from earlier on are recalled.[106]

Exactly so: Exs 5.15 and 5.16 are revisited but in strikingly new ways and always treated instrumentally with the greatest invention and imagination. Finally, the music seems to withdraw and disappear into the distance, the last pages given over to murmuring, muted strings with arabesques on two flutes – the barest of means but utterly magical as the music comes to rest *pppp* on an almost inaudible chord of G major, the sixth of the scale added as a harmonic by just half of the 1st violins. Then the vision fades – but it has been an ecstatic experience.

*I*N *a Summer Garden* was finished in June 1908, and, notwithstanding the experience of *Appalachia*, Delius unwisely offered or agreed to conduct the first performance himself at a concert of the Philharmonic Society in Queen's Hall on 11 December 1908 – although who first suggested it is a mystery. On 17 July, the secretary of the Society, Francesco Berger, wrote 'We ... are happy to agree to your conducting the first performance of your "A Summer Rhapsody"', but Delius told Theodore Szántó in a letter of 21 September that the Society had invited him, and offered what he thought was a very ungenerous fee of £25. He reported this to Bantock: 'so in spite of your severe criticism on [*sic*] my conducting, I shall try again!'. Bantock replied, 'Better £25 than nothing – Eh? Don't beat 4 however in a 6/8 measure.' Nevertheless, Delius confessed to Jelka that in the rehearsal he *had* beaten 'once or twice 3 in a 4 bar – absentmindedness!', but hoped he would do better in the performance; we must accept his report to her afterwards that:

> I was quite cool when I found myself on the conducting stand & made no mistake ... I don't believe many people understood the piece but they received it very favourably and called me three times.[107]

That last sentence indicates that on balance the audience liked the work. But, as was so often the case, the critics took a different view. *The Musical Standard*, forthright as always, not only delivered a stern rebuke, but was also clearly unimpressed by the music:

> He would have been well advised to have entrusted it to other and more experienced hands, for his conducting lacked any ray of animation and his beat was uncertain and difficult to follow. The opening slow movement certainly created an 'atmosphere' of considerable musical interest, but it struck me that this remarkably modern impressionistic music comes dangerously near acting as a soporific. There are plenty of special effects and tubular bells and a glockenspiel are effectively introduced. But clever

---

[106] Lyndon Jenkins, '*In a Summer Garden*', *DSJ* 140 (2006), 29–34, at p. 33.
[107] Letter 298, and n. 1.

instrumentation is by no means all, and the whole of the work seems to be carefully planned and painfully laboured: and the scanty thematic (and to me uninteresting) material did not justify its length.

19 December 1908

*The Musical Times* made a sly dig at Delius's conducting by comparing it with that of Landon Ronald (who was in charge of the remainder of the concert), and was generally not much more enthusiastic than the *Musical Standard*:

The work cannot be said to have made a distinct impression. A certain vague, musing dreaminess characterises most of the music, but there are sections that have undoubted beauty. The moods portrayed seem at a first hearing of the work to be too persistently melancholy. Perhaps the general effect suffered from a somewhat hesitant and flabby performance … Brahms's second Symphony was also performed, and here again Mr. [Landon] Ronald distinguished himself by his fine reading of the music.

19 January 1908

*The Times* critic took a haughty attitude:

a work in which the modern 'atmospheric' effects have been thoroughly studied and reproduced. But as there is no organic idea in the piece, no thematic germ of any consequence, it is a little like a play in which there should be nothing but scenery and lime-light, or still more like the effect of an unimaginative country organist who is obliged to extemporise until the clergyman is ready to begin with the service. The poverty of material would possibly be unnoticed if it had not been necessary to augment the orchestra for the realisation of the composer's desire for effects of orchestral colouring: but the list of extra instruments at the end of the description of the work in the programme leads ordinary hearers to wonder what is the object of employing so many players to say so very little. The work, played under the composer's direction, was received with favour if without much enthusiasm. Brahms' Second Symphony came like a breath of sweet country air in the second part of the concert after the exotics of the first part.

12 December 1908

Following the publication of the score in 1911, *In a Summer Garden* was played a gratifyingly large number of times in America and Germany. Among early performances, the conductor of the New York Philharmonic Society, Josef Stránský, gave it in Dresden in 1911, and again in New York on 25 and 26 January 1912; it was then done in Boston some three months later by Max Fiedler; in 1913 in Germany at the Jena Tonkünstlerfest in June, and in Berlin in November. The American critics – like their English colleagues – were greatly divided in their opinions.[108] The British Isles, though, had to wait for a performance until 18 December 1913, given in Edinburgh by the Scottish Orchestra (formerly the Glasgow Orchestral Union) under its Polish conductor Emil Młynarski, and the piece was not heard in London until 27 March 1914, when the Queen's Hall Orchestra played it under Geoffrey Toye. By that time *The Musical Standard* had changed its mind:

> Mr Toye also conducted a revised version of Delius's 'In a Summer Garden', which is an orchestral poem full of shimmering suggestion, dreaming and dainty effects: it creates just the impression its title would suggest.
>
> 1 April 1914

Beecham, who had a very high opinion of the piece,[109] conducted it for the first time some three months later, on 8 July, in an all-Delius concert at the Royal Academy of Music. *The Times* reported:

> No one who heard this programme could deny the extraordinary beauty of Delius's orchestral sound, or that that beauty is achieved in a great variety of ways. ... there is the way of the dreaming pieces of spring and summer, in which tiny details of phrase supplied by different instruments make up a very varied scheme of colour by very simple means. There is the way of 'Brigg Fair' ... which he also pursues in the 'Dance Rhapsody' ... There is the way of the dreaming pieces of spring and summer [i.e. *In a Summer Garden*], in which tiny details of phrase supplied by individual instruments make up a very varied scheme of colour by very simple means ... And yet one feels that, taken in bulk, it is weak music; its beauty is so largely a matter of colour, so little carried on by a sustained line of rhythmic energy.
>
> 9 July 1914

However, *The Musical Times* for November 1915, reporting on a performance in Manchester by the Hallé, also under Beecham, said that it was 'morally certain of an early repetition'.

I N 1909 Delius managed to spend from January to May at Grez working on *Fennimore and Gerda* – but after that his and Jelka's travels continued apace. He visited England in June, to be present at Beecham's rehearsals for, and then the first performance of, *A Mass of Life*; in July he went on a walking holiday in Austria with Norman O'Neill, doing up to 20 miles a day; then he and Jelka travelled to Hamburg, and the country estate of Palsgaard, on the Baltic coast of Jutland, which belonged to some new friends Einar and Elisabeth Schou.

---

[108] See Don Gillespie and Robert Beckhard, 'On Hearing the First Delius in America: Critical Reaction to Frederick Delius's Music in the United States, 1909–1920', in *MA&L*, pp. 57–98.

[109] *TB*, p. 167.

Einar Schou managed the world's then biggest margarine factory at Southall (at that time still virtually detached from London), and Elisabeth, a very musical amateur singer, used to go regularly to concerts. Towards the end of 1908, she was at a recital of Cyril Scott's chamber music and songs at which Frederic Austin sang, and she and Austin met at a supper party afterwards. They got on famously, and the two families became good friends – to the extent that the Austins holidayed at Palsgaard several times. In the summer of 1909, the Austins took the Deliuses with them, and they made the following entries in the visitors' book:

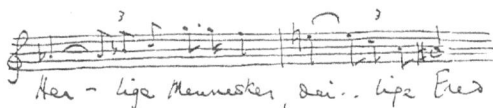

In September, Delius was back in England, to conduct the first *Dance Rhapsody* at the Hereford Three Choirs Festival. While there, he became ill, and although he managed to conduct the *Dance Rhapsody* he was unable to go on to the Musical League's Festival in Liverpool, and went straight back to Grez. After less than a couple of months there, however, he was off again – this time to Elberfeld, for Haym's performance of *A Mass of Life*; the year finished with a visit to Berlin to discuss the problems of his Harmonie contract with his German lawyers. The main causes of his concern were Harmonie's accounting calculations and their seemingly capricious and unhelpful attitude to the fees and prices they were charging for the hire and sale of full scores and parts (the copyright in which, as was the usual practice, they bought from the all their composers – usually for what are now regarded as extremely small sums). There were also, however, problems over corrections to proof copies, Harmonie's inability to deal promptly or accurately with Delius's requests for copies for his own use, and his relations with their London agents, Breitkopf & Härtel.[110]

Robert Montgomery and Robert Threlfall have pointed out[111] that there was not in fact 'much in it' for publishers who took on unknown composers: the copyright was virtually worthless, and they were reliant on hire fees which they often had to share with the client – but if works did not receive reasonably regular performances, the hire fees would be minimal too. Naturally, perhaps, publishers' contracts were therefore somewhat vague on the details, and in Delius's case neither party came out satisfied.

One marvels at the way that Delius pressed on regardless, despite the difficulties with Harmonie and the fact that it was very rarely indeed that any of his first performances had a really enthusiastic reception from the critics. Until 1909, apart from what had been played at the St James's Hall concert and the Piano Concerto, every single one of the first performances of Delius's works (and indeed a good many subsequent ones) had been given in Germany – but thereafter the tide did begin to turn. His music gradually fell out of favour with German audiences or conductors (or both), probably in the face of the rising interest in the Second Viennese School – but happily Wood, Bantock, and particularly Beecham, were beginning to serve him very well over here. In 1908, there were sixteen performances of his music over here, as against a handful in Europe. In addition to two concerts in which Beecham programmed *Paris* for the sixth and seventh times, he gave performances of *Brigg Fair, Over the Hills and Far Away, Appalachia*, and *Sea Drift* (twice); then, in 1909, *Sea Drift* again, and his first première – the complete *A Mass of Life*. As Lionel Carley put it:

> It is now clear that within little more than a year Delius had made a mighty mark on the English musical scene, a fact that did not escape the notice of one of his German critics, who laconically noted that the composer 'from now on wants to be an Englishman and wishes therefore to be acknowledged as such by us'.[112]

That critic was, of course wrong, however, because Delius certainly never wanted to be considered an 'English composer', and in fact probably never cared what people might class him as.

D ELIUS must have been extremely pleased when, on 17 April 1909, he was invited by the organist of Hereford Cathedral, G. R. Sinclair,[113] to direct a 'short orchestral work of yours' at the Three Choirs Festival there that year. Happily, he had already written it.

---

[110] *M&C*, pp. 55–83.

[111] *M&C*, p. 45.

[112] *Letters 1*, p. 329.

[113] George Robertson Sinclair (1863–1917). He was a great friend of Elgar.

## A DANCE RHAPSODY (NO. 1)
### (1909: *RT* VI/18; *CE* vol. 25b)

APART from continuing with *Fennimore and Gerda*, all that Delius managed to write during 1909 and 1910 was one work – his first *Dance Rhapsody* (not referred to as 'no. 1' until after the completion of the second in 1916). There is, as usual, no information about what inspired it or when Delius began or finished it, apart from letters to Bantock of 17 February and 24 April 1909 in which he referred to it as recently finished.

Delius never wrote a full-length ballet, but dance rhythms often infuse his music and his two *Dance Rhapsodies* give an encouraging indication of what he might have accomplished for the stage, had he tried his hand at something more substantial. Interestingly, the two-dozen bars of introduction to this first *Dance Rhapsody* have a strong affinity with the incidental music written fifteen years later for *Hassan*, foreshadowing the latter's sinuous texture and 'oriental' melodic intervals. The opening, sketching the two main themes on which Delius builds a chain of continuous variations, is just as remarkable for its scoring: divided cellos, initially centred on a chord of C sharp minor, accompany a duet for cor anglais and bass oboe which together produce a deliciously reedy sound, as if they have strayed from a North-African *souk* or middle-eastern bazaar:

Ex. 5.18

The duet continues with the 1st clarinet replacing the cor anglais; it will shortly evolve into a jaunty, dotted theme for the oboe:

Ex. 5.19

The similarly dotted rhythm played by the 2nd horn (Fig. 2-4) blossoms into a motif heard on the 1st flute:

Ex. 5.20

Ex. 5.19 has an 'oompah' accompaniment for plucked cellos and double basses doubled by the 3rd bassoon and sarrusophone (double bassoon), whilst Ex. 5.20 is given similar impetus by the 1st harp, double basses and three horns. Both ideas have a modal flavour: that is to say, that while ostensibly written in A major, the fourth of the scale is sharpened by a semitone from D natural to D sharp. The whole of the first section of the work (up to Fig. 7+1), plays with these two ideas in continuous variation form so that there are no clear-cut sections as there are in *Brigg Fair*.

Incidentally, at Fig. 6-1, with reference to the string section, we find the indication *Kleines Orchester*: this is meant to indicate a reduction in the number of players and was apparently a practical suggestion made to the composer by the dedicatee, Hermann Suter. It helps the balance of the strings against the wind in more delicately scored passages. Likewise, Delius writes *Grosses Orchester* when he wants the full complement restored.

After a double bar, a *vivo* section, almost twice as quick, introduces a wilder and more abandoned episode. With its swirling woodwind writing and chromatic harmonies, one feels that Delius has been eavesdropping on that wily story-teller Scheherazade and has picked up a few tips from Rimsky-Korsakov, certainly in the outline of Ex. 5.21:

Ex. 5.21

Exs 5.19 and 5.20 are also reintroduced in counterpoint (Fig. 12-4 *et seq.*) and the tempo begins to relax a little as we reach the end of this central section with a double bar (Fig. 15+1). A third and final section then offers another perspective on the opening material, not an exact recapitulation but a reworking of the material in different arrangements and instrumentations – Delius never likes to repeat himself. In a sudden burst of high spirits, the music achieves lift-off (Fig. 17+2) and reaches its climax *fortissimo* at Fig. 18+1, before beginning to unwind gradually (Fig. 21+1 onwards). We are nearing the end of the dance, but not before a truly beautiful passage (Fig. 23+1) marked 'molto adagio' which acts as a coda. It is scored for divided strings alone, playing *pianissimo* with their mutes on and accompanying an unmuted solo violin, far up on the fingerboard. The underlying harmonies are consistently chromatic in Delius's most characteristic vein and the overall effect is of a touchingly bittersweet

lyricism. The cor anglais reappears briefly (Fig. 24+7) ushering in a final set of solos for horns, the 1st clarinet, bass clarinet and then, more extensively, the bass oboe, now quite low in its register and singing its reedy lament above a hushed string chord of A major.

Some will wish that Delius had ended the piece at this exquisite point of repose, which, musically, would have brought us full circle. It is debatable whether the 'Molto vivace e fortissimo' ending of fourteen additional bars, scored blaringly for the full orchestra (including triangle), adds anything at all artistically. Granted, it finishes the piece with a bang and doubtless stimulates applause in the concert hall, but it tends to come across as gratuitous and somewhat crass.

E VERYONE was amazed that Delius had agreed to the request to conduct the first performance, on 8 September 1909 at what was known as the 'Secular Concert' in Hereford's Shire Hall, with the usual 'pick-up' orchestra, largely composed of individual players from the London Symphony Orchestra. Afterwards, Hubert Parry, well on the way to becoming the Grand Old Man of English music, was appalled: 'Delius was so excited about the performance of his work that he had to remain in his room all day and live upon gruel. He conducts very badly – stiff, amateurish.'[114] Although not able to be there, Beecham later wrote a highly amusing (and celebrated) account of what seems to have been a near catastrophe, including the tragi-comic ineptitude on the part of the amateur lady bass oboe player.[115]

*The Times* of 9 September 1909 said 'Mr Delius's "Dance Rhapsody" [was] heard for the first time [and requires] more comment than it is possible to give at this late hour of writing.' However, the following appeared the next day – and without any doubt Delius and the orchestra must have wished that it had not, even though the mention of the hapless player was pretty matter-of-fact:

> Of Mr Delius's 'Dance Rhapsody' one cannot speak so whole-heartedly. He has done so many better things that it seemed a pity to produce this in a place where his work is very little known. In the hands of an experienced conductor the contrasted *tempi*, too rich orchestral colouring, and the fantastic harmonic variations which decorate the theme would no doubt produce a vivid effect. But the performance last night under the composer's direction only served to impress the mind with the second-rate and second-hand character of the tunes. The duet

[114] Delius was in fact unwell, and probably stayed in his room for that reason! Although he and Parry never met, neither had a good word for the other. Writing to Bantock (Letter 319), Delius said that being at Hereford would 'afford me an opportunity of hearing "Job" by our mutual friend H. P. How a man rolling in wealth, the lord of many acres and living off the fat of the land can write anything about Job beats me entirely.' It was actually the first performance of the work, with Frederic Austin singing the name part.

[115] *AMC*, pp. 79–80. He mistakenly thought that the concert had been in the cathedral.

between the cornet and hecklephone [*sic*] (a kind of bass oboe) was robbed of its misty atmospheric effect by the fact that the player who had learned the hecklephone specially for the occasion, had to struggle to produce the notes in any way possible. Then the prosaic dance tune and the still more commonplace pendant to it were emphasized without one gleam of humour or rhythmic lightness in the phrasing; and only in the last section, just before the end, when the tune is played very slowly by a solo violin, was there any compensating beauty of tone. It really is unkind to allow a composer to dissect his score in public.

*The Times*, 10 September 1909

One reviewer was kind enough not to refer to the problems on the platform:

The second novelty, Mr. Delius's 'Dance rhapsody,' is as much in the style of the present day as Mr. Bantock's suite [also played in the concert] is in that of three hundred years ago. Its grace and charm expressed in modern idiom is great. Much effect is secured from the fresh colour derived from the use of the heckelphone, a bass oboe, and the harmonic scheme is new and striking.

*The Musical Times*, 1 October 1909

The next performances were two years later, in 1911, in Berlin, and in Beecham's Queen's Hall concert on 16 June, when *Songs of Sunset* was given its première. Henry Wood conducted the work in 1914, again at the Queen's Hall, when *Musical Opinion* described it as 'Delius's clever but over-elaborate Dance Rhapsody'.[116]

H EALTHWISE, 1909 had not been a good year for Delius, nor indeed for Jelka. He had influenza, a chest infection and stomach trouble – none of them perhaps helped by worries about his relationship with Harmonie – and by 1910 his general condition was worse, for he was beginning to suffer from a nervous disorder. In May he went alone to Zurich for a performance of *Brigg Fair* (which Bartók, Haym and Carl Schuricht also attended), and then took the opportunity of seeing a specialist; as a result, he went for a month to a sanatorium at Mammern on Lake Constance. It was a miserable time for both him and Jelka,[117] and, although he felt much better by the end of his stay there, on the way home in July the problems recurred. By November he was still weak and without energy, so he spent about two months at a clinic near Dresden, where the syphilis that he had caught in his younger days was diagnosed as having reached the tertiary stage.[118] One comfort, though, was the renewal of his friendship with Ida Gerhardi, who became extremely concerned about his

---

[116] 14 February 1914.

[117] *Letters 2*, p. 37.

[118] See *DSJ* 98 (1988), pp. 3–8; 106 (1991), p. 21; 132 (2000), p. 17; and 143 (2008), pp. 68–71.

health, and it was probably she who had finally persuaded him to seek advice in Germany.[119]

The last work of the period covered by this chapter is Delius's sixth and – as it turned out – final opera.

## FENNIMORE AND GERDA
### (1909–11: *RT* I/8; *CE* vol. 6)

A s a result of his trips to Norway for Delius & Co. and later, Delius acquired a deep interest in Norwegian plays and poetry, and came to know some of its most important writers of the time personally. His last song to Norwegian words had, however, been written in 1890 or 1891, and from then on (although he also set a number of French texts) Danish poets became the most powerful 'national' influence on his work. But, as John Bergsagel observes:

> One cannot help wonder how he came into contact with Danish literature – and in what language he learned to know it. It has often been claimed that Delius, who was so enthusiastic about Norway, quickly mastered the Norwegian language, but it is striking that nearly all his extensive correspondence with Scandinavian friends was carried out in German, exceptionally in English, but never in Norwegian or Danish ... The question then must be whether the composer was able to receive inspiration from the works of the Scandinavian authors he so admired in their original languages, or if it was through the many translations that spread the reputation of modern Scandinavian literature throughout the length and breadth of Europe, especially in Germany, from the 1870s that he got to know them?[120]

Delius decided to base *Fennimore and Gerda* on a novel by Jens Peter Jacobsen,[121] *Niels Lyhne*, using his own German libretto. Many years later, in 1929, he wrote an interesting letter to Ernest Newman:

> You know how difficult it is to translate to music. This is the reason why, in composing 'Fennimore & Gerda' and the 'Arabesk' – to avoid a language like Danish, which has no public – I composed to german words. German is so very similar to Danish that much of the original wording of J. P. Jacobsen would be retained.[122]

Some authorities date this opera to 1908–10, but the manuscript full score has 1909–10, and Delius wrote to Bantock in April 1911 saying 'I am putting

---

[119] Letters 329 and 333.

[120] John Bergsagel, 'An English Composer and Danish Poets in 1899', *DSJ* 142 (2007), 44–54, at pp. 46–7.

[121] See above, Chapter 3.

[122] Letter 533.

finishing touches to Niels Lyhne.'[123] It was published in 1919 by Universal, initially only in vocal score, with just Delius's German text. A second vocal score followed in 1925, using only Philip Heseltine's English translation (he having sent Universal a copy of the original vocal score with his words pasted over the German). Finally, a full score, with both sets of words, was produced in 1926.

*Fennimore and Gerda* is a ground-breaking and complex work, enriched with a hauntingly beautiful score that deserves to be better known. Yet, in the opinion of many, it has a crucial flaw in its construction which hinders it from being universally accepted as a masterpiece. Despite a promising reception in Germany, where the première was given in Frankfurt in 1919, it has never – like all Delius's other operas – entered the general repertoire. Delius had already favoured Jacobsen's poetry in six of the *Seven Danish Songs* of 1897, and he would return to it in 1911, in more extended form, for the text of *An Arabesque*. Jacobsen was a kindred spirit, initially a scientist whose study and translations of Darwin led to an uncompromising atheism, hence Delius's affinity for his writings.

Delius's specific choice of title, *Fennimore and Gerda*, shifts the emphasis from the hero himself onto the two women he loves, though the opera is also subtitled *Two episodes from the Life of Niels Lyhne, in eleven pictures, after the novel by J. P. Jacobsen*. It is important to grasp from the outset that this opera is essentially a psychological drama rather than a drama of action. So much so, that only a few sentences are required to summarise the plot of what is basically a love triangle featuring 'ordinary', middle-class Danish characters. Two young friends, a writer (Niels) and a painter (Erik), are in love with the same woman (Fennimore). To the despair of Niels, she chooses to marry Erik, but their relationship turns sour and they become locked in an unhappy union. Eventually, Fennimore realises that it was Niels to whom she was really attracted to all along. The two declare their love, but shortly afterwards, when Erik meets his death in an accident, Fennimore's guilt so overwhelms her that she violently renounces Niels and will have nothing more to do with him. A few years later Niels returns to his childhood home and falls in love with the teenage Gerda, who accepts his proposal of marriage. Delius chooses to end the story on this optimistic note rather than continuing the plot of the novel, which goes on to depict the death of Gerda and her baby son, followed shortly afterwards by that of Niels himself, who enlists in the army and is mortally wounded in battle.

The happy ending disappointed Heseltine, and confounded Beecham – who, perversely, only ever performed the final, Gerda, section. It cannot be denied that while the two episodes are undoubtedly contrasted, they are also unbalanced since the Gerda sequence accounts for less than a quarter of the total running time. It does, however, include two outstandingly beautiful orchestral interludes (prefacing the tenth and eleventh 'pictures', as Delius

---

[123] Letter 356.

called them) which were married up by Eric Fenby to form a continuous five-minute sequence known as the *Intermezzo from Fennimore and Gerda*. But it is not only a question of relative durations. The events concerning Fennimore are mainly expressed in intense and searingly powerful music that comes from another emotional world to that of Gerda, whose depiction is two-dimensional, trite and even falls into bathos. Many have questioned why Delius did not close the opera at the end of the ninth picture, with Erik's death and Fennimore's brutal rejection of Niels. He seems to have considered doing so, but is on record as saying that such a 'gloomy and unresolved ending' would have been too downbeat, going on to argue that 'the Gerda episode is necessary after all to round off the opera [and] the work has undoubtedly gained from this conclusion.'[124] The problem is, though, that we learn nothing about Niels's life after the crucial split with Fennimore, only (in the short, tenth picture) that he has given up writing and professes to be 'healed'. A few months later (picture eleven), he gets engaged to Gerda and the opera ends unconvincingly (and too loudly) with a forthright C major chord. Heseltine aptly summed up the case for the prosecution when he noted that:

> It is the disproportion and psychological falsity of this last section that jar. It is like a sugar-plum designed to take away the taste of the preceding tragedy, and one resents this, for the tragedy is convincingly complete in itself …

The structure of the opera is of considerable interest in the way it reflects Delius's desire for 'short, strong emotional impressions given in a series of terse scenes'. The effect is cinematic, with the eleven pictures (*Bilder* in German) not necessarily following on sequentially: three years elapse between the first two pictures and the central sequence (the former depicting Fennimore's acceptance of Erik, and Niels's despair at losing her; the latter, which begins with the third picture and ends with the ninth, describing episodes in the disastrous marriage of Fennimore and Erik). Then a further three years elapse before the final two pictures showing how Niels woos and wins Gerda. This selective presentation of a storyline was not new in opera – indeed, Puccini's librettists used a similar technique in the plots of *Manon Lescaut* and *La Bohème*, where a considerable period elapses between some of the acts.

*Fennimore and Gerda*, which at eighty minutes or so is relatively concentrated, is intended to be given without an interval. Several of the pictures flow on, one to another, even when the setting is not the same (i.e. the first to the second, an interior to an exterior scene); on the other hand, Delius also asks for significant pauses between certain pictures, specifying the exact timings for them: five minutes after the second picture; three minutes after the sixth and seventh; four minutes after the ninth. Many of the pictures begin with startling abruptness: it is as if we have opened a door and walked into a room where a scene is already half-way through. The very opening of the opera is an

---

[124] Letter 375.

example of this: there are just four bars of very quiet orchestral introduction before Niels's opening line, 'How peaceful, how still! I wish I could always sit beside you and watch you.' Quite what has occasioned this remark and why it makes Fennimore smile, is not explained. The beginning of the fourth picture, a conversation between Niels and Erik sitting over their cigars and drinks, and which also begins *in media res*, is another case in point.

A good proportion of the dialogue in *Fennimore and Gerda* is allusive and understated, offering in this respect a parallel with the language of Debussy's *Pelléas et Mélisande* of 1902. This was a deliberate artistic choice by Delius, who wrote to Universal:

> whatever is purposely not expressed in words ... is made complete by the music. The text is simply there as the basis and situation for the music and must in consequence absolutely not give the impression of being something complete in itself.

The fourth picture offers a good illustration of this at the point where Erik asks Niels whether he has thought about death at all: 'Oh, yes', replies Niels and Erik retorts, 'By death, I mean not sickness and dying.' What exactly he does mean is never expressed in words but it is implied in the music, which stops short on a brief pause, suggesting Delius's own belief that there is nothing beyond the grave. Similarly at the end of the fifth picture, when Fennimore offers friendship to Niels after admitting the problems in her marriage, she and Niels fall silent and it is the orchestra that reveals their unspoken thoughts (Fig. 60 *et seq.*). There are other instances of this kind of implied subtext.

In fact we also learn very little about these characters or their backgrounds. Fennimore herself is an unpredictable, enigmatic figure; Niels, we do know, wants to be a writer, but is making painfully slow work on a novel (why?); Erik is a painter but his attempts to translate his visions onto canvas (in the fifth picture) are frustrating him, and leading him more and more into drink and despair. Although it may seem disproportionate to focus so much on the structure and form of Delius's libretto, it is important if only because it was relatively novel and original for its time; contemporary audiences would have been quite puzzled and disorientated by it.

*Fennimore and Gerda* also breaks new ground in Delius's musical language: vocal lines are more angular, harmonies more astringent and orchestral textures more complex. The music rarely remains in one key-centre for long, but is constantly shifting this way and that in chromatic twists of considerable subtlety. Resolved and unresolved dissonances, suspensions, enharmonic shifts – all these techniques are used as a matter of course, rather than occasionally. Some may find this excessive and, in the end, conducive to aural saturation, but there is no denying the sheer craftsmanship and virtuosity involved in spinning such complex harmonic textures.

As in Delius's other operas, there is no extended use of *leitmotifs* or recurring themes attached to specific characters, and it could be argued that the vocal lines are less memorable than in, say, *A Village Romeo and Juliet*. For all its abundant lyricism, the overall impression is of a strongly unified atmosphere within which there are highly effective individual moments.

Another distinguishing feature of this score is its great sense of rhythmic freedom engendered by the conversational style of the text: this is reflected in constantly changing time signatures to accommodate natural speech rhythms. The libretto is the least high-flown of all Delius's operas and includes such commonplace exchanges between Erik and Niels (at the end of the third picture) as: "'Have a cigar, old man!" – "Many thanks!"' This would have seemed even more startling when the opera was new than it does today, and recalls the exchange in Puccini's *Madama Butterfly* (1904) where Pinkerton famously offers his guest Sharpless 'Milk punch or Whisky?'

Ex. 5.22

Make your-self at home.   My dear old friend!

Have a cig - ar, old man!   Ma-ny thanks!

In contrast to such down-to-earth dialogue, there are many passages of intensely expressed emotion, such as Fennimore and Erik's declarations of love (Ex. 5.23). Note here the passionate underlay of the orchestra, with the accented dissonances in the chords on the first beat of bars five and six (i.e. B flat clashing with A natural, G sharp with G natural), adding significantly to the emotional tension. High-voltage musical electricity is also generated by Fennimore and Niels's passionate exchanges at the close of the seventh picture, sparked by a turbulent orchestra (Ex. 5.24).

Similarly powerful discharges occur elsewhere in the score: Erik's revelation to Niels in the fourth picture that he fears the loss of his talents: 'The soul of a man can be bruised and broken, and no one knows how deep down in a man his soul extends' (Figs 44+4 to 45+1); Fennimore's despair when she hears of Erik's accidental death (eighth picture, Fig. 92 *et seq.*); and Fennimore's heartless rejection of Niels, induced by her inordinate feelings of guilt, which, together with his bewildered reaction, are masterfully pointed up in the orchestral texture through a marked use of harmonic dissonance (Ex. 5.25).

In contrast to these emotional highlights, there are many haunting moments of repose that linger in the ear. Right at the start, in the opening picture, there is a passage where Erik mentions the weather ('There'll soon be a downpour' – Fig. 6+7) and the orchestral texture marvellously suggests the pattering of the rain in diatonic, off-beat *pizzicato* chords for the strings. The song that Fennimore sings at Erik's suggestion shortly afterwards is a lovely inspiration, scored for harp and strings, stylistically a throwback to one of Delius's Danish song settings from the 1890s. Of a different kind, but no less telling, is the moment where Erik's corpse is brought into the house at the end of the ninth

Ex. 5.23

picture by 'four dark figures' (Fig. 104+11) and Delius comes up with an eerie funeral march in which divided string chords are punctuated by timpani beats.

Where the pictures follow without a break, the transitional passages for the orchestra are often musical highlights, as might be expected with Delius. For example, the interlude linking the first and second pictures is astonishingly beautiful in the way it subtly leads us from the house down into the garden bordering a fjord, where the waters of the sea, according to the libretto, sparkle with phosphorescence. A wordless tenor voice floats across the scene, recalling the similar effect of the boatmen at the close of *A Village Romeo and Juliet* and foreshadowing the lapping rhythms and textures of *Summer Night on the River*. It is an unforgettable passage and the scoring (rocking woodwind and horns, subtle use of harp and succulent harmonies for divided strings) should be quoted in every textbook on orchestration.

Ex. 5.24

(They sink down upon the mossy ground in a passionate embrace.)

Ex. 5.25

Niels
You don't know what you're say - ing
Fennimore (freeing herself violently from him.)
(He lays his hand lightly on her shoulder.)
Leave me a -
Come in now and calm your - self.
cresc
- lone! Can't you see how much I hate you?
cresc

The two most memorable passages of the Gerda section are likewise not vocal but instrumental, and they have already been referred to above; it should be stressed that the first of them is even more poignant when heard in the context of the opera itself, since it follows on from the shattering ending to the previous (ninth) picture. A simple diatonic melody on the flute is accompanied by the most beautifully varied harmonisations, including two that did not find their way into the concert version and are worth quoting (Exx. 5.26, 5.27).

Ex. 5.26

Ex. 5.27

Since it remains something of an elusive work, *Fennimore and Gerda* demands detailed study to do it justice; it needs to be sympathetically and patiently explored before it will yield up its riches – it is an ideal 'gramophone opera'. Delius's bold conception led him, not untypically, to make his own rules for this extraordinary inspiration and the score demands to be accepted on its own terms or not at all. The rewards that lie in store are plentiful indeed: page after page of arresting invention, both vocal and instrumental. But it is not a genial work: the prevailing mood of intense melancholy and unrelieved gloom are quintessentially Nordic, reminiscent of the bleak mood of an Ingmar Bergman film. As Eric Fenby pointed out, this 'laconic Danish opera' – and 'laconic' is the *mot juste* for it – inexorably reveals what made its creator tick, and it stands in close relationship to those equally uncompromising works *An Arabesque*, *Requiem* and *North Country Sketches*.

As might have been expected, the first staging of the opera was in Germany, and Delius had to wait eight years for it. The possibility of one performance in Cologne in 1914 came to nothing, but on 21 October 1919 an unknown staff conductor at the Opera House in Frankfurt, Gustav Brecher, led a cast of what were probably in-house singers who appear to have performed very well.[125] The Deliuses went to Frankfurt the previous month so that Delius could attend many of the nine orchestral rehearsals, and he was thrilled with the result, particularly as he was called on to the stage many times at the end. He wrote afterwards to Heseltine:

> The performance at Frankfort was very good – Singers excellent and the regisseur the best I ever knew … No expense was spared – I am satisfied with the new work & it is certainly a step in the right direction – perhaps the only direction that 'Singspiel' has any future – There are no tedious moments – The drama plays wonderfully well and is clear to the public – Almost every word is heard – Brecher was not as good as I had thought – but gradually got into the spirit of the whole …[126]

Furthermore, a major German journal said that:

> Fennimore and Gerda … had a successful première at the Frankfurt Opera House. This intellectually and technically secure work made a strong impression because its style is far from traditional, and its warmth and intimacy were extraordinary.
>
> *Neue Zeitschrift für Musik* 44/5 (6 November 1919), p. 294

It was another ten years (almost to the day) before a note of the work was heard again, and even then it was only the *Gerda* section, the two final pictures. Beecham gave them at Queen's Hall on 24 October 1929 as part of his Delius Festival, with Pauline Maunder and John Goss as Gerda and Niels:

> The concert last night contained two short scenes from the opera *Fennimore and Gerda*, which has never been performed in England. Like the excerpt from *A Village Romeo and Juliet*, heard at the first concert of the festival, it rouses the desire to hear the work given complete on the stage. The orchestra provides a frame for these 'pictures', as Delius prefers to call his scenes; the text is not so much set to music as declaimed without emphasis against the orchestral tissue in which the whole essence of the situation is depicted. It is the method employed in *Sea Drift* – Wagnerism carried further – and although difficult to justify by ordinary canons, does achieve a wonderful unity of its own when it is used successfully, as it is here.
>
> *The Times*, 25 October, 1929

Although the opera was dedicated to Beecham, and he included Fenby's *Intermezzo* in concerts and recorded it, no doubt to Delius's huge disappointment he never conducted any part of the work again. He in fact

---

[125] Paul Hindemith was a viola player in the orchestra.

[126] Letter 449.

disliked it from the start – describing the three main characters as miserable people and complaining that in was in effect a 'non-opera'.[127]

There was then a further long wait before the next performance, given on the BBC Third Programme on 27 March 1962:

> The work, completed in 1910, has always lain under something like a cloud. Those who knew it admitted that it was completely individual in form and manner, but were inclined to dismiss it as excessively restrained and conversational ... although [Fenby] saved from it the beautiful intermezzo which is in reality a conflagration of two orchestral interludes.
>
> This broadcast showed the extravagance of such denunciations. True there is an over-generous measure of discontented, neurotic Fennimore to a ha'porth of sweet, girlish Gerda – these are the two lovers of the Onegin-like protagonist. But the unbalanced construction does suggest the idea that the deepest, most hectic love may be for a tiresome woman, and that it is at least equalled in value by a gentler love that brings more happiness.
>
> True that Heseltine's English translation is deplorably flat in diction; one can hardly sit unmoved when Erik declaims 'Sit down and have a cigar, my friend' to a vocal line that would not sound out of place in *Sea Drift*. But in this matter-of-fact level at which the story moves forward, and in the brevity of each scene (reminiscent of many more recent operas), is the individual and decidedly intriguing flavour of the whole. Anyone who has warmed to the melodic diction of *Sea Drift* or *A Village Romeo and Juliet* must find himself at home to the vocal lines of *Fennimore and Gerda* – or so we would think had Beecham not written as he did. Mr. John Cameron certainly found plentiful warmth in the part of the protagonist (though his voice is rather dry); and Miss Sybil Michelow made a strong and impressive character of Fennimore. Mr. Stanford Robinson conducted with a real feeling for the flexibility and sensuous values of the music.
>
> *The Times*, 28 March 1962

Finally, a few months short of fifty years after the première, the opera was staged for the first time in England, on 23 May 1968 at The Old Town Hall, Fulham Broadway, in West London:

> It is all too easy to say what is wrong with Delius's opera *Fennimore and Gerda*, an undramatic idiom, flat characterization, a want of variety in texture, harmony, and pace, a theatrically inconvenient length (one and a half hours). It is easier still to be deceived by all this into overlooking its merits, which are great and real.

---

[127] *TB*, pp. 164–5. Given his comments there, it is perhaps not surprising that he never performed it in its entirety. It was quite possibly the only work of Delius's that he did not appeciate.

Last night's English stage première by Hammersmith Municipal Opera under Joseph Vandernoot ... gave it less than a fair chance: the orchestral playing was imprecise and weak in rhythm (faults to which Delius's fragile language is particularly susceptible), the longish intervals dissipated much of the emotional force, and the principal soprano was variably accurate.

The opera is oddly constructed ... the last two scenes ... emerge as an epilogue designed to end the opera cheerfully; they are worth having mainly for the nature-music of their preludes.

[The critic felt that what was lacking] in the first half of the opera, despite many patches of poetic and evocative music (notably a gorgeous song over the water, with murmuring accompaniments) was a chance for the music to unfold and expand. 'Long dialogues and wearisome narrations must go', Delius once said, 'and will be replaced by short strong emotional impressions ... in terse scenes'. In spite of himself, the seventh to ninth pictures do expand: forest music. Then a glorious passionate love duet, a scene for Fennimore which is tantamount to an aria expressing love with a hectic cabaletta expressing guilt, and finally the lovers' parting. The musician, happily, overruled the theorist. It is a superb, intense scene.

*The Times*, 24 May 1968

Since then there have been a welcome number of productions in England,[128] Germany and the USA.

D URING the five years covered in this chapter, notwithstanding that Delius's health caused him and those closest to him considerable concern, and that he would have been aware that his syphilis was incurable, he had achieved a great deal. First and foremost, he had settled down contentedly with Jelka at Grez, where the calm of their house and garden provided an ideal environment for work. He had composed two more masterpieces, *Brigg Fair* and *In a Summer Garden* – the first (for anyone who cares to explore it in detail) a technical *tour-de-force* that was also marvellously approachable, and the second one of the most evocative pieces of nature music ever written – as well as another substantial choral work, *Songs of Sunset*. While the critics were continually disparaging his music, it was being played increasingly often, to a

---

[128] The one by English National Opera in late 1990 was notable for the inspired conducting of Sir Charles Mackerras (and Lionel Friend in some performances), for the singing of Sally Burgess as Gerda, and the quite 'pretentious and incomprehensible' production, which even enraged the musical press: see Roger Buckley, *'Fennimore and Gerda'*, *DSJ* 107 (1991), 15–19. Amends were made in May 2012, when Ardente Opera under Julian Back gave an excellent concert performance in London at St John's Church, Waterloo.

very high standard, both in England and abroad.[129] Delius had also probably learned the lesson that the conducting of his music was best left to others, and his involvement with the Musical League must have convinced him that he was not a committee man. Finally, he had made a host of new friends on the English musical scene – his happy relationship with some of whom would prove to be lifelong.

[129] In 1910, *Paris* was played in Wiesbaden, while *Sea Drift* was not only given there by Haym, but was also conducted by Schuricht in Elberfeld; Beecham included the Piano Concerto in the programme for a London concert in 1910 and gave it again in Birmingham in 1911, as well as providing a further performance of *Appalachia*, the première of *Songs of Sunset,* and conducting the *Dance Rhapsody* in both Berlin and Manchester.

# Inspiration Unabated

Philip Heseltine – *An Arabesque* –
*The Song of the High Hills* – *Two Pieces for Small Orchestra* –
*Two Songs for Children* – *North Country Sketches* –
*Requiem* – Violin Sonata no. 1

A<small>FTER</small> a bad start to the beginning of 1911, by the spring Delius was beginning to recover:

> The cure in Dresden only made Fred worse – awfully thin and haggard and he only picked up in Wiesbaden and everybody thinks he looks very well now. He is working again and we take nice walks.[1]

He and Jelka left the clinic in Dresden in January, went to Wiesbaden (where they heard Schuricht conduct *Sea Drift*), and were back in Grez by the first week in March. Delius was able to receive visitors again, and Beecham came twice. In March he brought with him his new friend (and lover), the American-born London society hostess, Lady Cunard, who had apparently come to like Delius's music, and at the beginning of June Beecham drove over to Grez in his car, and took Delius back to London, with Jelka following by train. They stayed at 9 Hans Place, near Harrods, the home of the wealthy art-collector Frank Stoop[2] and his wife, whom they had come to know quite well. Delius met Bantock on the 16 March and, with Jelka, they went to the first of Beecham's all-Delius concerts, which included the première of *Songs of Sunset*, with *Appalachia*, *Paris* and the first *Dance Rhapsody*. During the interval, Delius first met Philip Heseltine, the seventeen-year-old schoolboy who was to play a large part in his life for almost the next twenty years.

Philip Arnold Heseltine was born, somewhat incongruously, in The Savoy Hotel on Piccadilly (or 'on the Embankment', as he later put it)[3] on 30 October 1894. The men in his family had been successful stockbrokers and solicitors, and his father was also a solicitor. However, he died when the boy was only three, and two years later his mother – a very domineering woman, with

---

[1] Jelka Delius to Adine O'Neill, Letter 355.

[2] In 1933, he gave his important collection of modern paintings (by, among others, Cézanne, Picasso and Matisse) to The Tate Gallery. Ida Gerhardi was also a friend of the Stoops. See also *PW Letters*, vol. 1, p. 216.

[3] Barry Smith, *Peter Warlock: The Life of Philip Heseltine* (Oxford: Oxford University Press, 1994), p. 2.

whom he developed an almost Oedipal relationship[4] – remarried and moved to a large, old house in the middle of Wales. Heseltine went to Eton, where he was taught music by two remarkable men, Edward Mason[5] and Colin Taylor, the second of whom remained a confidant and friend for life. They introduced him to Delius's music in 1910,[6] and he quickly acquired a deep love and, indeed, an obsession for it.

Taylor took Heseltine to that concert, and the yong man was completely overwhelmed. The following day he wrote a 330-word letter to Delius, eulogising over the music and Beecham's conducting, and cheekily asking the composer if he would 'be so kind as to do me the honour of a visit in Mr Beecham's motor car'.[7] By then, he was already an assiduous writer of vital, amusing and extremely long letters – several are between 3,000 and 4,000 words, with one to Delius approaching 6,000.[8] Almost more often than not they ran to around 750 or 1,000 words.

By far the largest number were to his mother, Edith Buckley-Jones (as she became on her remarriage), followed by Delius, Colin Taylor and Cecil Gray;[9] then there were his girlfriend Olivia Smith, other short-lived loves and, from 1916, his wife 'Puma'. As he increasingly became an important and well-known figure in English artistic life, he corresponded regularly with such figures as the critic Ernest Newman, the composers Benjamin Burrows and Bernard van Dieren, the violinist André Mangeot, and the writers Bruce Blunt and Robert Nichols. The letters cover innumerable subjects – for example, Christianity and religion; Verdi's *Falstaff*; the psychologist Havelock Ellis's book *Studies in the Psychology of Sex*; the times of the trains from Grez to Paris; the poetry of Shelley; the nine issues of the controversial magazine about contemporary music, *The Sackbut*, which Heseltine edited between 1920 and 1921; and directions on how to get to Land's End. Even while still at school, he acquired a wide knowledge of the latest goings-on in the English musical world – the personalities and the gossip about them, the newest works, the most recent opera productions – and the letters to Delius, in particular, are crammed with vivid reports of his concert- and opera-going.

Through their correspondence and occasional meetings, Delius, thirty-seven years his senior, rapidly became Heseltine's mentor and a father figure, while for his part Heseltine proved himself of the utmost help in correcting proofs, translating and improving texts, making vocal scores and transcribing

---

[4] See, for example, *PW Letters*, Letter 184, written after she had sent him a bunch of violets for his birthday.

[5] See above, Chapter 5. There is a photograph of both of them in Smith, *Peter Warlock*.

[6] *PW Letters*, Letter 178.

[7] *FD&PW*, Letters 1 and 2.

[8] Ibid., Letter 62.

[9] Cecil Gray (1895–1951): a Scottish composer, music critic and Heseltine's most Bohemian companion.

orchestral ones,[10] and giving advice to the composer. It has to be said, however, that the relationship of father and son, guru and disciple, did not commend itself to some, including Beecham.

As a composer, Heseltine was a miniaturist, with a great sense of style. His reputation as a composer stands on his 150 or so songs, some of which bear comparison with the best written by his contemporaries. All his music, except for possibly a few of his early songs, was published under the pseudonym Peter Warlock.[11] He also edited neglected Elizabethan and Jacobean music, and had a finely developed literary taste – although a wicked, and sometimes offensive, sense of humour made him some enemies.[12]

Sadly, his life disintegrated, both psychologically and physically. He became an alcoholic; he grew almost to dislike Delius's music, and while Delius and Jelka retained their affection for him, his once fierce love of them dwindled, and although until the late 1920s their friendship had known almost no bounds, thereafter hardly any letters passed between them. Tragically, he died from gas poisoning at his flat in Chelsea – probably committing suicide – on 17 December 1930.

A FTER Delius's bad experiences in Dresden, it was probably not until the end of the summer of 1911 that he felt like writing again; by the autumn, however, he had finished *An Arabesque*. In *RT Catalogue*, this comes after *The Song of the High Hills*, but subsequent research has shown that they were composed in the reverse order, 'Autumn 1911' being on both the manuscript and the printed scores of *An Arabesque*. It seems quite probable that it was partly rewritten in 1915, when the Deliuses were staying in a house outside Watford that Beecham rented for them.[13]

---

[10] *Brigg Fair* (1911 – with which Delius was very pleased: see Letter 361), *Lebenstanz* (1912), *In a Summer Garden* (1912–13), both *Dance Rhapsodies* and *North Country Sketches* (1921), *A Song before Sunrise* (1922) and *On Hearing the First Cuckoo in Spring* and *Summer Night on the River* (1931).

[11] He adopted the pseudonym towards the end of 1915 to disguise his identity from the editor of *The Music Student*, to which he was contributing, but used it very rarely for signing letters to anyone, be they friends or not. Given his maverick character, it is not surprising that he chose that name, with its many connotations, and that he later became interested in 'black magic'.

[12] Smith, *Peter Warlock*, pp. 270–1.

[13] *RT Supplement*, p. 40; Letter 404.

## AN ARABESQUE
## (EINE ARABESKE)
(1911: *RT* II/7; *CE* vol. 12a)

*A*N *Arabesque* is still very much underrated and hardly ever performed. It sets a complex text by J. P. Jacobsen for solo baritone, mixed chorus and orchestra, and lasts some twelve or thirteen minutes. Fenby thought it 'superb' and amongst the very best of Delius. Beecham also loved this work: he made a pioneering recording of it with Einar Nørby (singing in Danish) in 1955, and had a very high opinion of it.[14] He also claimed that it must always be performed in Danish, as any attempt to render it in translation makes a nonsense of its elusive meaning, despite the fact that Delius originally set it in a German translation by Jelka; the English version also given in the full score was added later by Philip Heseltine.

Getting to grips with the poem is not easy, clothed as it is in dense imagery and symbolism. It is not so much a narrative, as a portrait of an unnamed female figure. She is an ambivalent creature, seductive but treacherous. Though compared to 'jasmin's sweet-scented snow', she also has the 'red blood of poppies [circling] in her veins'. A *femme fatale* with 'sighing in her laughter' and 'gladness in her pain', she seemingly drinks allegiance to her lovers, but her pledge is drained from 'the dazzling chalice of a poisoned lily' and those who desire her are doomed.

The work is freely rhapsodic and there is seemingly very little in the way of recapitulated musical material. As in *Fennimore and Gerda*, there is an overall austerity about the score, particularly in its harmonic language, that marks a significant evolution in Delius's style. This may make it a difficult work to assimilate at first; however, repeated listening reveals a consistently high level of musical invention, with many extraordinarily imaginative passages.[15]

In the opening pages, the strings brood chromatically in groups of flowing quavers, crowned by arabesque figurations in the woodwind, suggesting the rustling of the 'gloomy forests' mentioned in the first line of the text (Ex. 6.1). The enigmatic question, 'Knowest thou Pan?' (i.e. as the god of woods and fields, flocks and herds) receives the answer: 'Yes, I have known him, but [...] only as the god of Love' (i.e. implying pagan lust, with Pan as half-man, half-goat). The 1st flute, coloured by celesta and harp, adds a shrill imitation of the pan-pipes (Fig. 2+5) and continues to spin a virtuoso line as the music swirls us away, out of the forest, and into a 'sunbathed meadow' where a flowering herb grows, the deceptively alluring symbol of the beloved. The chorus adds its voice to the texture (Fig. 4+3) in a chromatic descent (none too easy to pitch,

---

[14] *TB*, p. 168.

[15] There is a much longer description of the work than there is space for here in *Palmer*, pp. 71–8.

Ex. 6.1

With slow and flowing movement
2nd vln + vcl 8va basso
pp cresc
strs
fl
cl
mf
1st vlns + 8va
ob
c.a.
fls
ob

and typical of the vocal challenges of the score as a whole). The voices serve a triple function: sometimes wordless, as in this first entry; sometimes echoing the soloist's observations as a means of emphasis; and sometimes carrying the weight of the text itself. All in all, the composer treats them with the utmost flexibility.

Despite first impressions to the contrary, the score does in fact have musical motifs binding it together, though they are fragmentary rather than expansive: the most important of them is the 1st violin melody in the third and fourth bar of Ex. 6.1, which recurs later (Fig. 5+7) when it is shared by the 2nd violins. The shape of the line, if not its exact intervals, is also explored by the chorus (Fig. 6+5) when describing the woman's 'death cold hands'; it subsequently appears on 1st and 2nd violins (Fig. 9-3), and, as a slower variant, on 1st violins alone (Fig. 11-3); its final transformation, in the upper strings (Fig. 13+3), is a synthesis of these various versions, and this time the celesta (doubled by harp) adds a full harmonization:

Ex. 6.2

Delius could be very sparing in the way he deployed a large orchestra, but in this score he keeps most of his players busy throughout, in textures which are vividly conceived and executed. On the other hand, he is also capable of substantial restraint, achieving miracles of instrumentation from remarkably slender means. In this respect, the final pages are exemplary: Love has drunk from a poisoned chalice, and, as the baritone and chorus whisper despairingly that 'All is past' (Fig. 15-3), the scene shifts to a barren, bleak landscape in the grip of winter. The dominant image is of a lonely thorn bush, its leaves scattered by 'black winds', gradually shedding its glowing, blood-red berries onto the snow-whitened ground. Upper strings sustain icy chords (Fig. 16+2), whilst violas and cellos, *pizzicato*, evoke the berries themselves, as they drop relentlessly to the ground (Ex. 6.3). The 3rd bassoon, double bassoon, 1st and 2nd horns, 1st trumpet, and double basses playing open fifths, are masterfully blended into the scoring as the baritone and chorus, 'like a sigh', repeatedly breathe the opening interrogation, 'Knowest thou Pan?' (Fig. 17+5), a phrase now imbued with the utmost poignancy. It is one of the most spellbinding and unforgettable codas that Delius ever wrote.

IT was originally intended that the first hearing of the work should be in Vienna, and Delius set off, on his own, on 20 November 1913. However, the performance never materialised – probably because Universal Edition (which

Ex. 6.3

had now supplanted Harmonie and Tischer & Jagenberg as his publishers) were unable to produce the full score and parts, although they had printed a vocal score. Instead, Delius went with Hans Gregor to see an opera by Goldmark. Three years later, in three separate letters to Grainger, he listed the work as being unperformed, and then, on 16 January 1919, he again said that it had still not yet been done.[16] When a performance did eventually materialise, it could hardly have been in a more unusual place or given by a less likely combination of musicians: 'thanks to the enterprise of Mr Cyril Jenkins',[17] at Newport in Monmouthshire, on 28 May 1920, Arthur E. Sims conducted the Welsh Musical Festival Choral Society and the London Symphony Orchestra, with Percy Heming[18] as the soloist. Very surprisingly, neither that nor the next

---

[16] *RT Catalogue*, p. 68.

[17] *TB*, p. 188. Cyril Jenkins (1889–1978) was a Welsh composer and a musical administrator. He studied with Stanford and for a short while with Ravel, and his music includes works for brass-band competitive festivals.

[18] Percy (Alfred) Heming (1883–1956): a well-known singer of the time, with a beautiful voice and very musical, he was a member of the Beecham Opera Company (with whom he sang the Dark Fiddler in the first performances of *A Village Romeo and Juliet*), and then of the British National Opera Company (of which Frederic Austin was the Artistic Director). Later he became heavily involved in the management of opera.

performance (on 18 October 1929 at Beecham's 1929 Delius Festival, when the soloist was John Goss with the London Select Choir and 'the BBC orchestra') seem to have been reported other than as to matters of fact, without any attempt to consider the music.[19]

Hard on the heels of *An Arabesque* came the next piece, *The Song of the High Hills*.

## THE SONG OF THE HIGH HILLS
### (1911–12: *RT* II/6; *CE* vol. 11b)

I have tried to express the joy and exhilaration one feels in the Mountains & also the loneliness & melancholy of the high Solitudes & the grandeur of the far wide distance. The human voices represent man in Nature: an episode, which becomes fainter & then disappears altogether.

T HAT is the description of the work that Delius uncharacteristically asked Norman O'Neill (who was now the treasurer of The Philharmonic Society)[20] to include in the programme note for the first performance in February 1920.[21] It is one of the very few explanations of his music that Delius ever gave, and it matches a quotation from the poem *The Open Air* by the 'nature mystic' Richard Jefferies[22] that Frank Bridge put at the head of the score of the first of his orchestral *Two Poems (after Richard Jefferies)*:

Those thoughts and feelings which are not sharply defined, but have a haze of distance and beauty about them, are always the dearest.

There can be no doubt that *The Song of the High Hills* was inspired by Delius's beloved Norwegian mountains, and presumably ideas had been going round in his head since his first visit in 1881:

The effect of [their] scenic wonders ... [had been] little short of cataclysmic on a youth who had felt intuitively, in the vastness and remoteness of the West Riding moors, that he might 'do something unusual' with his life ... Men like Delius who love hills find in them something more than a medium whereby they may express themselves in terms of physical force; for hills have the power not only to draw out the best from within a man, but to interpret his inmost thoughts in terms of an even greater awareness, an awareness that height somehow brings exhilaration, enhances life, quickens it to a finer rhythm. It is the unchanging quality in

---

[19] It is, however, frequently mentioned in *DSJ* 142 (2007).

[20] It became The Royal Philharmonic Society during its hundredth season in 1912.

[21] *Hudson*, p. 69.

[22] John Richard Jefferies (1848–87): essayist and novelist whose work was largely based on nature and rural life. His best-known books are the autobiographical *The Story of my Heart*, and *Bevis: The Story of a Boy*.

mountains which makes them so valuable to man: they are steadfast, they are perfectly in tune with the universal rhythms and harmonies of nature, they bring man into touch with those forces which mean happiness, and they are a medium whereby beauty can be expressed in its freshest, purest, freest form. In the high hills, Delius found the beauty he craved above all else.[23]

In a letter to Bantock on 10 June, Delius said, 'I am at work on a new work for Chorus and Orchestra', and to Heseltine a fortnight or so later, 'I am working hard on a new Choral and Orchestral work, and am already far advanced.'[24] There are two extant sets of sketches for this piece, one in the DTA and the other (twenty-four pages of early annotations) at The Grainger Museum in Melbourne; part of the former is headed *Symphonie*,[25] and various drafts had the titles *Poem of the Mountains*, *Song of the Mountains* and *The Song of the Mountains*.

There is no evidence as to what actually decided Delius to begin work on *The Song of the High Hills*, but many years later Percy Grainger claimed that:

> for all his 17 [*sic*] mountaineering trips to Norway it did not occur to him to write a work about the hills until he had heard my two *Hill Songs*, the first written 1901–1902, the second 1901–1907.[26]

Given the fact that the two composers were great friends, that is a curious remark – but even if Grainger did feel somewhat slighted, that did not prevent him from having a long involvement with the work: he prepared the chorus for a Delius birthday performance at Frankfurt in 1923; the same year he made an arrangement for two pianos; and on 28 April 1924 he conducted the American première.

Whenever Delius could not make progress on a particular work, he would put it aside and only start on it again when interest or inspiration returned, which was sometimes not for a very long time. Many years later, however, Fenby recollected what Delius had told him about the difficulties he had with *The Song of the High Hills*:

> 'Passages eluded me; one in particular, the eight-part chorus that wouldn't come right!' He remarked, too, that this was the only occasion on which he had not been able to bring himself to put a work aside.[27]

His absorption in the piece was, it seems, virtually complete from start to finish.

Towards the end of 1913, Delius asked Balfour Gardiner to correct the proofs (from his latest publisher, Leuckart), but Gardiner did not want to do it,

---

[23] *Palmer*, p. 40.

[24] *Letters* 2, p. 89.

[25] As was an early version of *Appalachia* – see above, Chapter 4.

[26] *PW*, p. 172.

[27] *Fenby* 2, p. 66.

and – no doubt with little difficulty – persuaded Heseltine to take over the task. Heseltine wrote to Olivia Smith that 'on Monday Balfour Gardiner came to tea with me and brought the proof sheets of a new orchestral and choral work of Delius, "The Song of the High Hills".'[28] Heseltine must then have worked fast, for exactly a month later he sent this to Delius:

Dear Mr Delius

I am returning the proof sheets of 'The Song of the High Hills' by this post, with many apologies for having kept them so long. It is very remiss of me not to have sent them back long-ago, and I sincerely hope you have not been inconvenienced by their non-arrival. Gardiner brought them at Oxford ...

Yours affectionately[29]

Those loose proof sheets were bound together at some stage, and, complete with Heseltine's corrections, they are also now in the DTA.[30]

In Beecham's autobiography of Delius, there is a characteristically affectionate description of the work, particularly remarking on the first entry of the chorus.

*The Song of the High Hills* describes a musical journey in three main sections, each of them subdivided, forming an arch-like structure whose central keystone is an extended outpouring of essentially slow-moving music. This constitutes the longest section of the work, the heart of the matter, and which, as the score unequivocally states, is a view of 'The wide far distance – The great solitude': a rare instance of Delius adding a verbal description to his music. The approach to that vista, and the retreat from it at a swifter pace, form the itinerary of the first and third sections. The schematic summary in Table 6.1 makes the plan clear.

The journey begins with one of Delius's most arresting openings: the sighing of the 1st violins, underpinned by the 2nd violins and pairs of clarinets and horns, is countered with upward flurries from the violas, pointed by cor anglais and bassoons (Ex. 6.4).

This sense of yearning is developed and extended in chains of rising and falling quavers in both woodwind and strings and, after a *tutti* outburst (Fig. 3+7), this undertow continues its relentless way (Fig. 4+1), 'Very quietly but not dragging', as the 1st flute and the 1st clarinet introduce a soaring melodic idea which steers us from the chilliness of G minor towards the warmer climate of E major (Ex. 6.5).

---

[28] *Gardiner*, p. 106.

[29] *PW Letters*, Letter 351.

[30] They were found in 1989 among the music of Frederic Austin's conductor son Richard – to whom they were probably given by Gardiner.

Table 6.1 *The Song of the High Hills* structure

| Section | | Description | From (Fig.) |
|---------|---|-------------|-------------|
| I | A | Exposition (i) | Opening |
| | B | (Interlude) | 8 + 7 |
| | C | Exposition (ii) | 15 + 3 |
| II | A | 'The Wide Far Distance – The Great Solitude' | 17 + 7 |
| | B | | 23 + 4 |
| | C | Combination of IIA & IIB | 27 + 7 |
| | D | Recapitulation of IIA | 30 + 1 |
| III | A | Recapitulation of section I with IB omitted | 35 + 1 |
| | B | Coda: Recapitulation of IIB | 49 + 1 |

Ex. 6.4

The woodwind hold all the interest at first, but then the roles are reversed (Fig. 5-1) with the 1st violins singing the tune while the flutes, soon joined by the clarinets, string out chains of quavers. Delius expands Ex. 6.5 with considerable ebb and flow, all six horns having a decisive say in the texture as it starts to build. Then a new idea (Fig. 7-1), rooted in the key of C and marked 'With vigour, singing', breaks out in flutes, oboes, cor anglais, clarinets and 1st trumpet, with the second half of Ex. 6.5 providing a counter-melody in bassoons and lower strings, joined shortly afterwards by trombones (Ex. 6.6).

The music reaches an exhilarating climax, marked by insistently repeated triplets high up in flutes and clarinets (Fig. 8-3) (Ex. 6.7).

The music soon collapses in on itself (Delius seldom prolongs his moments of ecstasy), quietening down from *fff* to *ppp* in fewer than a dozen bars. A solo from the third horn is echoed by the first horn, and they intertwine above a sustaining bed of strings in B major, marking the start of a magical interlude (Ex. 6.8).

Ex. 6.5

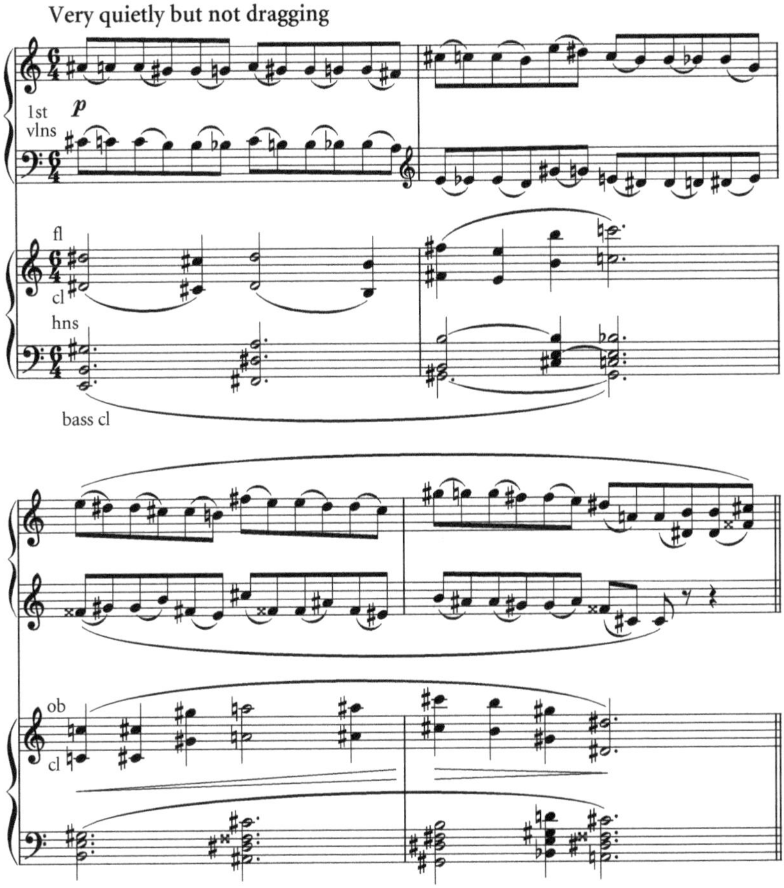


Ex. 6.6

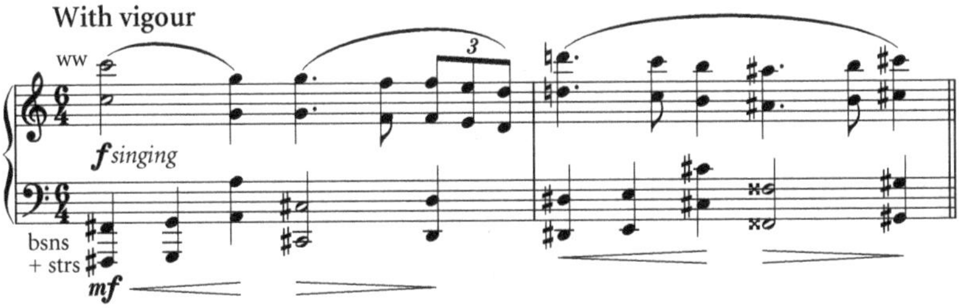


Ex. 6.7

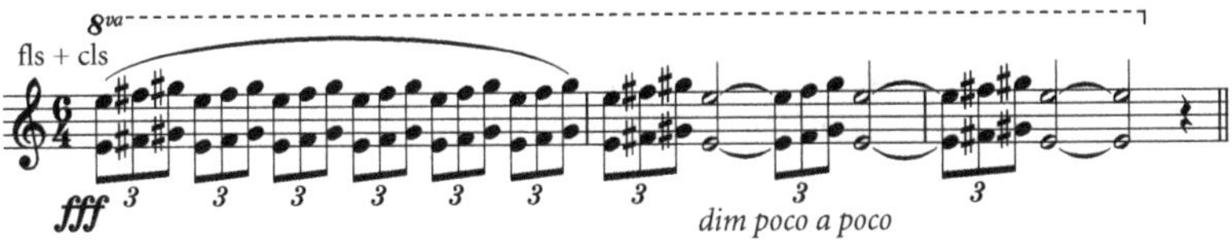

Ex. 6.8

The horns call to each other as if across a valley, whilst flutes and clarinets decorate the duet with the rhythm of the triplet figure in Ex. 6.7, additionally coloured (Fig. 10+1) by the celesta pointing up the chords of the divided strings, whilst the two harps sketch in a series of feathery, upward arpeggios. We might almost be back with Zarathustra on the mountains at the beginning of Part 2 of *A Mass of Life*.

The music unexpectedly flows into C major (Fig. 11+1), the strings still *molti divisi*. It is like a sudden splash of cold water from a mountain stream after the richness of the harmonic language employed up until now. A modal flavour infuses the writing, unexpectedly reminiscent of the language of Vaughan Williams, as the horn section continues to call out across the landscape. The interlude draws to a close as the texture begins to build again and the biggest *crescendo* of the work so far reaches its peak (Fig. 16-1) in an exhilarating passage marked 'With exultation' (Ex. 6.9).

Typically, the descent from this transcendental moment is swift: a mere half-dozen bars is all it takes, before we reach the end of the first of the score's three main sections. We seem to have climbed up through misty valleys and are now way up on the heights, vouchsafed our first undisturbed view of that 'Wide far distance – The great solitude'.

The central section begins (Fig. 17+7) with violins, violas and cellos each divided into multiple parts; the only other sounds are those of a remote horn and a wordless chorus, the tenors emerging first from the texture – one of the most magical moments in all Delius's music. Delius requests them to 'sound as if in the far distance', and in an ideal performance we should hardly even realise that they have begun to sing. Muted violins hint at a new melody which is elaborated a few bars later (Fig. 18+5) by the woodwind, 'Slowly and solemnly', in a beautiful, chorale-like harmonisation (Ex. 6.10).

Ex. 6.9

With exultation

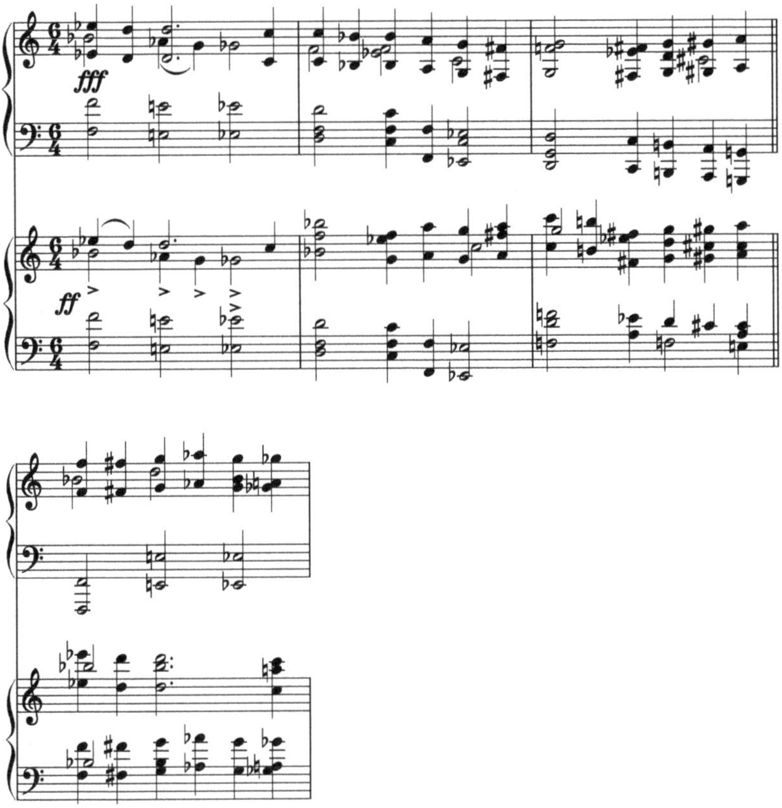


Ex. 6.10

Slowly and solemnly

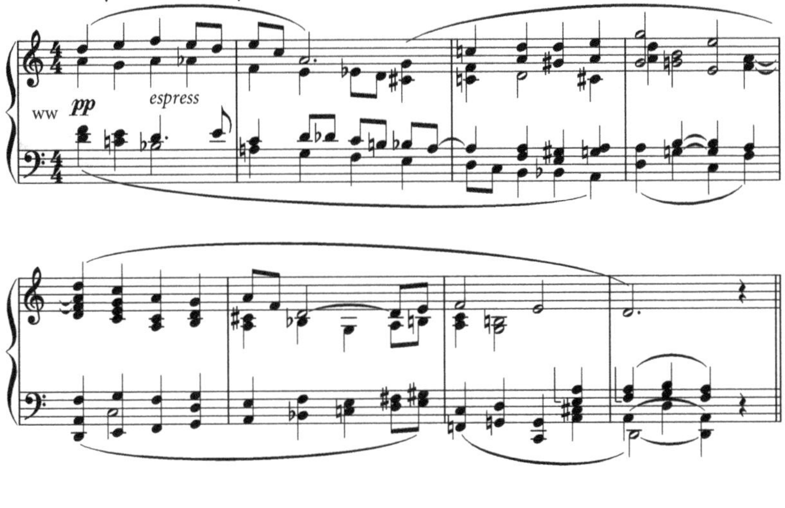

An equally eloquent idea, full of yearning, is offered by the strings (Fig. 20+1):

Ex. 6.11

This central episode can be subdivided into four sections. In the first, the strings provide a complementary answer of their own to Ex. 6.10. This is followed by a passage of exquisite stillness in which Delius's orchestration achieves miracles of imagination as undulating chords in divided strings are pointed up by celesta whilst the 1st harp touches in a series of upward semiquaver scales, the timpani rumbling in the background and a group of distant tenors sketching in a somewhat modal melody (Fig. 21+4).

A truly extraordinary passage follows, whose stark textures are a further consolidation of the novel musical language of *An Arabesque*. The violins, divided into four parts and placed high in their register (Fig. 23+4), give out a continuous stream of rustling semiquavers for some thirty consecutive bars, with not a single change in dynamic after an initial *pianissimo*. Against this eerie backdrop, Delius calls on the 1st oboe to give voice to a rather melancholy, plangent tune that hovers between D minor and A minor, and whose triplet rhythms work against the grain of the groups of quadruplets in the strings:

Ex. 6.12

A cor anglais joins the oboe, at first in imitation, and then in octave unison. Meanwhile the lower strings, aided by horns and bassoons, sustain a slow-moving chromaticism that gradually melts the frostiness, and edges us closer to warmer harmonies. Some of the voices join the texture (Fig. 26+5), but only *pppp* and marked 'As a sigh' – again, we hardly realise they are present. The music slows down and dies away, resolving into a more comforting F major with timpani purring gently in the background.

It may seem as if Delius is now ready to move on – but not yet, since the tempo picks up again (Fig. 28-4) for a short, third section, a mere two dozen bars, still very quiet. This ingeniously juxtaposes material from the first two sections. The melodic lines of the oboe and cor anglais return, but this time Delius adds a tenor soloist in counterpoint, gently outlining the melody of Ex. 6.10. The cellos and double basses sink deeper and deeper, and come to rest on a final octave E natural, providing the root of an E minor chord filled in by violas, horns and timpani, the 1st violins adding a major ninth. The music seems to be holding its breath.

The passage that follows (Fig. 30+1), forming the fourth and final part of this central keystone of the musical arch, is one of Delius's greatest inspirations. We hear the chorus, unaccompanied, in a complex elaboration of Ex. 6.10. They divide into an eight-part, double choir with the addition of two solo lines from a soprano and a tenor, who weave the previously heard modal motif of Fig. 21+4 into the texture. Strings join (Fig. 32-1) and soon the whole orchestra follows their lead, fusing into an ecstatic outpouring of melody harmonised as only Delius can. The summit is reached (Fig. 33+1) and the panoramic vista is held for barely a dozen bars, but as the music slackens in intensity, the opening idea of the whole work breaks in (Fig. 35+1) and we begin a recapitulation and a descent from high ground.

What follows is a skilfully condensed version of the opening material with the interlude omitted entirely: this is effected by means of a surreptitious cut, discarding the material previously heard between Fig. 7+1 and Fig. 15+3. The rest is pruned to three-quarters of its original length. Although there are no significantly new ideas, Delius often departs from his original orchestration in new arrangements as he reworks his material: for instance, Ex. 6.4 is given a fuller instrumentation (Fig. 35+1) incorporating more of the woodwind, as well as some of the voices, who are brought into the texture as if they were orchestral instruments. As a general rule, the harmonic colourings are darker and harsher in the course of this recapitulation.

The triplet rhythms of Ex. 6.7 return (Fig. 45+4), as does the very opening material (Fig. 46+5). This final statement has an acerbic quality to it, as if leaving a bitter taste in the mouth at having had to return to ground level from the heights. The cor anglais steals in (Fig. 49+1) with a recollection of Ex. 6.12, this time with *divisi* strings providing a halo of slowly undulating, sustained chords, very different from the icy rustlings of Fig. 23+4. The 1st horn briefly echoes the cor anglais as the harmony settles, with the music, as the score says, 'dying away to the end'.

Final impressions haunt the memory: the three timpanists very quietly play a tonic triad in G sharp minor, also rooted below in cellos and double basses. But the tonality is ambiguous, since the upper strings have the notes of a major seventh chord in B major. We are suspended between major and minor, symbolic of the disparity between the vision of the great solitude from the summit and the prosaic return to ground level; between the glimpse of eternity, now only a memory, and the realisation of Man's transience.

T HAT triple timpani chord caused a particular problem to Balfour Gardiner when he was correcting some reprint proofs of various works – as Grainger recalled:

> Gardiner kept asking about a kettle-drum passage ... in which the kettle-drummer, with only 4 drums, was required to play 5 different notes and with no time to tune between them. Gardiner insisted that the passage, as printed, could not be played. But all he got out of Delius was: 'I don't know how he plays them; I only know he *does* play them.' Gardiner was disconsolate: 'The trouble is that the drummer does *not* play the 5th note, but Fred never notices it.'
>
> (There was in fact some justifiable confusion on Gardiner's part for, while the published score in fact specifies two drummers, even so Jelka Delius could write to Grainger on 4 April 1924 that 'Fred wants me to tell you – the score of S. of H. H. only *two* drummers are marked – But that is a mistake, there ought to be 3 ...').[31]

Notwithstanding that Leuckart's proofs had been corrected by Heseltine in early January 1914, the work was not actually published until 1915 – perhaps for reasons connected with the War. It was then a further five years before the first performance – in Queen's Hall on 26 February 1920, with The Philharmonic Choir (making its first public appearance) and The New Symphony Orchestra, under Albert Coates.[32] The choir had been formed by Kennedy Scott from his brilliant Oriana Madrigal Society,[33] and it would become London's major choir, pre-eminent in Delius's choral music. Delius and Jelka were thrilled by their performance after this concert, as they would be again after the first performance of the *Requiem* in 1922; in a letter to O'Neill, Delius referred to them as 'the lovely Kennedy Scott chorus'.[34]

---

[31] *Gardiner*, p. 135.

[32] Albert Coates (1882–1953): Notwithstanding that Lady Elgar called him 'that brutal, selfish, ill-mannered bounder', a highly regarded conductor, as a young man he gained vast experience in German and Russian opera houses and at Covent Garden. He also composed seven operas, and orchestral works. His fee for this concert and its rehearsals would have been around £100.

[33] See below, Chapter 7, under *To be Sung of a Summer Night on the Water.*

[34] Letter 473.

Two days later, *The Daily Telegraph's* review, headed 'An Amazing Concert', was as joyous in its praise as any paper had ever been in the past, or would ever be in future, for any work by Delius:

Many and many a long day is gone since the ancient Royal Philharmonic Society of London, now in its 108th season, offered a concert like that of Thursday last, which overfilled Queen's Hall. As the fortunate ticket-holders walked up Regent-street to the hall they were met by a melancholy procession of unlucky wights for whom no room could be found. And why the crowd? Was it because of Mr Kennedy-Scott's new Philharmonic Choir, now trying its paces for the first time? Was it because of the new Delius work? Was it the 'Immortal Ninth' that attracted, or the promise of Coates conducting? It really does not matter. The point is that Queen's Hall was sold out for a concert that was one of the most amazing affairs of its kind in many years.

To the new work first. Delius entitles it 'The Song of the High Hills.' In it, he states, he has tried to express the joy and exhilaration 'one feels in the mountains and also the loneliness and melancholy of the high solitudes and the grandeur of the wide, far distances. The human voices represent 'Man in Nature'. The Russians have a term which, to some extent, conveys something of the same meaning – 'prostor'. It is a feeling rather than a descriptive term, a feeling, a sentiment, for the awful beauty of more or less illimitable space, and it seems to us to be this sentiment that the ever-meditative Delius has set himself to reduce to terms of musical sound.

As in 'Appalachia,' as in 'Brigg Fair,' as in 'Paris,' so here, plainly, it is not the material, but the mental aspect of a meditative man that is set before us. In 'Appalachia' it is not North America that Delius 'describes' through the medium of his basic negro melody; similarly, in the case of 'Brigg Fair' and 'Paris, it is not the concrete fair nor the streets, &c, of Paris that Delius records. So with 'The Song of the High Hills' – there is the same essentially characteristic meditativeness, an almost brooding, longing, introspective mental atmosphere. And how beautiful it is in its kaleidoscopic (mental) colour! Even Delius, with all his amazingly developed orchestral colour-sense, has set nothing of a greater loveliness. At the close he and Coates, who conducted superbly, were called time and time again to bow their acknowledgement for what was a complete triumph for both, no less than orchestra and chorus!!

*The Daily Telegraph*, 28 February 1920

Mr. Delius was the hero, too, of the Philharmonic Concert … the new Philharmonic Choir, organized by Mr. Charles Kennedy Scott, sang for the first time his ' Song of the High Hills,' which is a record of the composer's impressions of Norwegian mountain solitudes on a balmy summer night. For a brief moment the voice of Man intrudes, but grows fainter and fainter. A part of the work is in Delius's usual vein, but in the choral numbers he displays an amount of vigour unusual with him, and there is an unaccompanied section culminating in a massive climax which will probably be judged in future to be the strongest music he has ever composed. An interesting point about the work is that the chorus sings no words, but only varying vowel sounds. In the ninth Symphony of Beethoven, and Bach's Motet, 'Sing ye to the Lord,' the new choir showed that it has the makings of a body of voices that may in the not too far future venture to compare with a really high-class North Country choir, although it has yet a long way to go.

*The Musical Times*, 1 April 1920

Queen's Hall was crowded last night for the concert of The Royal Philharmonic Society, at which the new Philharmonic choir made its *début*. Mr. Kennedy Scott, who has trained the choir, conducted its first performance, Bach's eight-part motet without accompaniment, 'Sing to the Lord.' Mr. Albert Coates conducted the rest of the programme, which began with the prelude to *Parsifal*, included a new work for orchestra and choir by Delius, 'The Song of the High Hills,' and ended with Beethoven's Choral Symphony.

Such a rich scheme should attract a large audience if anything will, and the first concert in which the new choir took part will be an important landmark in the venerable Society's career. In the Bach motet, the choir showed itself fully worthy of the position it is to occupy. The singing was extraordinarily alert and full of rhythmic energy, each part clearly distinguished, and almost every word easily audible … In interpretation, the first principles which Mr. Kennedy Scott has instilled with such success require supplementing by greater elasticity and more expressive *sostenuto* … The ship has to 'find itself' after it is successfully launched.

Mr. Delius's new work is for orchestra with the addition of chorus. There are no words: for some time the voices only enter into the texture at intervals, like extra instruments, but there is a noble choral climax in which voices come well into the foreground. The prolonged singing without words always seems rather an unnatural business, and the effect of the thing struck us as a laborious attempt to maintain a mood of exaltation. As in certain other works of Delius, one is enchanted by the atmosphere and the rare colouring at the outset; later one longs for a change of mood, which does not come. But, after all, that is a matter of personal preference. Some never weary of the snow-clad peaks; others soon long for trees and the flowers of the valley. There is also such a thing as mountain sickness. Nevertheless, there is fine music in every part of the work, which was received with acclamation, the composer coming on to the platform repeatedly to acknowledge the applause.

*The Times*, 27 February 1920

Several months after the concert, Delius wrote to C. W. Orr, a new friend whom he had first met in 1915:[35]

> The Song of the High Hills also went off well – especially the chorus – Coates evidently did not know quite what to do with my music – It was unfamiliar to him & I am afraid that he had not occupied himself sufficiently with the score. However, no doubt, he will give a better rendering of it on 2 June when it is due to be repeated.[36]

And in 1922, Delius said to Grainger that he thought of *Song of the High Hills* as among his best works, and also as 'one of my works in which I have expressed myself most completely'.[37] That, too, was the opinion of *The Monthly Musical Record* after a performance by Kennedy Scott in 1929:

> Delius's *Song of the High Hills* is to be placed among his very finest works. The hasty, impatient listener might call this music bare and empty. It certainly makes no deliberately picturesque points. But as the landscape it depicts broadens out – a landscape singularly solitary and serene – we become aware of a beauty that attains to grandeur. The wordless chorus comes in with an effect of poetry hard to define-Perhaps it is that from the outlook on the mountain's height all the warring activities of man mingle harmoniously in nature's inscrutable scheme. The fourth piece in the programme was Balfour Gardiner's always welcome *News from Whydah*.
>
> July 1929

[35] Charles Wilfred Leslie Orr (1893–1976): inspired by reading Ernest Newman's book on Hugo Wolf's *lieder*, he became a significant, if relatively little-known, writer of lyrical songs. He was known to most people as C. W. Orr, and spent the last thirty-six years of his life at Painswick in Gloucestershire. An intensely keen admirer of Delius's music, Orr first met him by following him to a restaurant after a recital that included the Violin Sonata no. 1; through Delius he met Heseltine, who in turn introduced him to a number of other composers and helped him in dealing with publishers.

[36] Letter 454.

[37] Letter 475.

## TWO PIECES FOR SMALL ORCHESTRA
### (1911–12: *RT* VI/19; *CE* vol. 27a)
*Summer Night on the River;*
*On Hearing the First Cuckoo in Spring*
*(Introducing a Norwegian Folksong)*

As with *In a Summer Garden*, the peace and quiet of Grez must have been largely responsible for these two short pieces that reflect the surrounding village landscape – the second without doubt Delius's best-known work. The idea seems to have come from Percy Grainger:

> Around 1910 he had complained to me that his orchestral works were neglected in England. I wrote him saying that England was studded with fine amateur orchestras that would rejoice to do Delius works, but lacked the 3rd clarinet, 3rd bassoon, and 5th and 6th horns that his scores so often called for. 'Write some short pieces for small orchestra,' I urged, 'and English orchestras will devour them.' His next letter told that he had taken my advice, had already finished a short piece for small orchestra (based on a Norwegian melody).[38]

Dedicated to Balfour Gardiner, they were in fact written in reverse order, and a year apart – but it is convenient to deal with them together. *Summer Night on the River* dates from 1911, and *On Hearing the First Cuckoo in Spring* was written the following year. Tischer & Jagenberg, who published them together in one volume in 1914 as *Two Pieces for Small Orchestra*, appear to have lost the original autograph full score (as they may have also done with those of *The Song of the High Hills* and *A Dance Rhapsody*). Interestingly, at about the time he wrote *Summer Night on the River*, Delius acquired a pianola roll of Debussy's *L'Après-midi d'un faune*.[39]

There has been much speculation as to where Delius heard the cuckoo in question, but the most logical answer must be in the garden at Grez – for in a letter to Heseltine from there (admittedly in 1916) he recorded, with obvious pleasure, 'I heard the cuckoo for the first time the day before yesterday ...'.

Eric Fenby memorably captured the essence of *Summer Night on the River*, one of Delius's short masterpieces, when he wrote that 'one can almost see the gnats and dragonflies darting over the waterlilies, and the faint white mist hovering over willow-tressed banks and overhanging trees.'[40] Delius's aural imagination is at its most acute – which makes it all the more miraculous that the orchestral palette he works from is relatively small: just pairs of flutes, clarinets, bassoons and horns, a single oboe, and strings.

---

[38] *PW*, p. 172.

[39] *Palmer*, p. 141.

[40] *Lloyd*, p. 152.

A floating boat is evoked in the first eight bars by the woodwind and horns gently bobbing to and fro in a 12/8 rhythm, underpinned by muted double basses:

Ex. 6.13

When the rest of muted strings enter (Fig. 1+1), tracing angular, chromatic lines pointed by flute and clarinet, their silvery tone is like moonlight glittering on the water. A brief scurry from the woodwind gives way to undulating clarinets and flutes, and *pizzicato* 1st violins. Trills from 2nd violins and violas suggest the hum of insects. An important melodic idea emerges on a solo cello (Fig. 3+1), and this arching theme will dominate the rest of the work:

Ex. 6.14

Whenever it appears, this tune is sung to a light but very chromatic accompaniment whose figurations Delius varies most imaginatively. A subsequent, slightly varied statement of it, transposed up a minor sixth (Fig. 4+1), adds a solo violin in duet with the cellist. It also recurs (Fig. 5+1) in yet another guise, doubled in 1st flute, oboe, solo violin and solo viola, and leads to the loudest and fullest texture so far (Fig. 6-3) with all the strings gradually removing their mutes.

The current ceases to flow quite so fast as Delius steers into a backwater for a magical passage marked 'Very quietly' (Fig. 6+4) in which echoing horn calls are reminiscent of the off-stage horns at the beginning of the sixth scene of *A Village Romeo and Juliet*.

Ex. 6.14 returns (Fig. 7-1), doubled at the octave on solo violin and solo viola, and marked, 'becoming softer and softer as if dying away in the distance'. The pulse slackens still further, as a final fragment of the haunting theme is heard (Fig. 8-3). The boat rejoins the main river (Fig. 8+1), but it slowly drifts away downstream into the distance, 1st violins whispering trills with little off-beat pulsations from woodwind and *pizzicato* 2nd violins, a wonderful effect. These peter out and darkness swallows up the scene, the lower strings coming to rest on an A major chord, *pppp*, Delius yet again adding the questioning, sixth note of the scale.

O N *Hearing the First Cuckoo in Spring* is a flawlessly conceived and constructed work, and one of the most exquisite examples of Delius's mature artistry. It is masterfully orchestrated for divided strings plus a single flute and oboe, and pairs of clarinets, bassoons and horns. The manner in which the scene is set in the first three bars is unforgettable:

Ex. 6.15

Then, after a brief pause, a swaying rhythm ('With easy flowing movement') pulses gently to and fro in the strings, shaping the rise and fall of a sweetly inflected, pentatonic melody, and foreshadowing in mood and outline the folksong we have been promised by the work's subtitle. This is introduced some fifteen bars further on by the flute (Fig. 3-1) and then by the oboe, and it is the same melody that Grieg arranged for solo piano, and which he published in 1896 as the fourteenth of his *Nineteen Norwegian Folksongs*, op. 66: *I Ola-dalom, I Ola-kjønn* ('In Ola Valley, in Ola Lake'). Grieg had a beautiful way of colouring this haunting tune:

Ex. 6.16

Delius has his own equally idiosyncratic methods of harmonising the folktune in each of his varied statements of it; he knows how to add just the right amount of piquancy to counter the sweetness of the original (Fig. 8-4):

Ex. 6.17

The clarinet impersonates the cuckoo of the title on two occasions (Fig. 5+7 and Fig. 8+5), with characteristic descending intervals of a third. Ornithologists may point out the calls are not the same, in that the first set uses the interval of a minor third, and the second that of a major third. Perhaps we are hearing different cuckoos? Or is it just that Nature is capable of infinite variety? More importantly, this enchanting miniature goes beyond merely heralding the beginning of spring: its bittersweet harmonies cause a melancholy shadow to fall over it, suggesting that Delius wants us to bear in mind that the springtime of life itself will not last long. However, since he himself is quite resigned to this, he cannot consider it a tragedy and ends by unexpectedly diverting the harmonic flow onto a dominant seventh on B natural, marked by a pause (Fig. 11+8), before letting it die away gently on a simple G major chord.

A RTHUR Nikisch conducted the first performance of both pieces, on 23 October 1913 in Leipzig. Delius was naturally there, and on the day of the concert (the rehearsal for which was sold out) he wrote to Jelka:

This morning Wed. was the Hauptprobe – ausverkauft [final rehearsal – sold out]. Nikisch played the 1st piece (Spring) much too slow – but very expressively the 2nd He played most beautifully – perfect – I asked him to play the 1st one faster at the Concert so I hope it will go off alright – Orchestra splendid ...[41]

On the following day he reported that 'The first he took rather too slow – The public seemed to like it best – although I like the 2nd best.'[42]

The first English performance, three months later, at a Royal Philharmonic Society concert in Queen's Hall on 20 January 1914, was given by the Dutch conductor Willem Mengelberg:[43]

Two charming pieces for small orchestra by Delius were played for the first time. The first, 'On hearing the First Cuckoo in Spring,' is a fantasy on a Norwegian folk-melody, and the second, 'Summer Night on the River,' is an imaginative study in quiet tones based on a barcarole rhythm. Only strings, woodwind (flutes, oboes, clarinets and bassoons), and horns are used, but the composer shows his mastery of orchestral effect in the delicately varied combinations of tone which he achieves from them. The 'Cuckoo' piece errs a little, perhaps, in prolonging its existence just a few bars longer than the rhythm warrants. One misses a direct point of contrast, and the repetitions of the cuckoo's notes on the clarinet become a trifle monotonous, but, after all, that is true to life. The 'Summer Night,' with its greater variety of detail, its sinuous interweaving of themes, and its interesting harmonic scheme, is more engrossing if less obviously attractive. Both were excellently played.

*The Times*, 21 January 1914

It is long since we have heard an important new work from the pen of Frederick Delius, and it cannot be said that the spell is yet broken. Neither of these tone-poems, in spite of their great charm, could be described as important. They are small, both in design and character, but within their range they are completely successful. Their delicate tone-painting and subtle, shifting orchestral and harmonic colours reveal the hand of a master at every point.

*The Musical Times*, February 1914

Beecham included both pieces in a mammoth all-Delius concert by the Beecham Symphony Orchestra in The Duke's Hall at The Royal Academy of Music on 8 July (which unfortunately attracted a somewhat small audience):

---

[41] Letter 384.

[42] Ibid., n. 2.

[43] Willem Mengelberg (1871–1951) was the eminent conductor of the Concertgebouw Orchestra of Amsterdam from 1895 until 1945.

Mr Thomas Beecham in his enthusiastic generosity was in all probability responsible for the Delius concert at the Duke's Hall. We know his sympathies are much with this young representative of the newer school, and, on the whole, the composer's reputation withstood this unfair drain upon it. Very few composers are of sufficiently diversified character to maintain interest without clash or contrast with works in other mood or of other times, and certainly if this had been [a public concert] the world of music would have been the gainer on this occasion if a flavour of laughter had lifted us into another world. Mr. Delius is splendid as a musician, but depressed as a thinker. This is no kind of use. Much splendid musicianship is ebbing to waste in sadness and tragedy – the easiest things in the world! Even when Mr. Delius hears 'The first cuckoo in spring' he does not seem to jump joyously. But if we ask him nicely, he will change all this.

*The Musical Standard*, 18 July 1914

The rest of the programme was *Brigg Fair*, *The Walk to the Paradise Garden* and the final scene from *A Village Romeo and Juliet* (with Frank Mullings and Agnes Nicholls, who also sang three songs),[44] *In a Summer Garden* and the *Dance Rhapsody*. Afterwards, Delius told Jelka, 'I never heard Beecham play my things so beautifully.'[45]

COMPOSITION did not occupy a great deal of Delius's time in 1912 – all he managed was the finishing of *The Song of the High Hills*, the writing of *On Hearing the First Cuckoo in Spring*, and making some revisions to *Lebenstanz*. There was, though, more travel: Berlin in early March, to hear Fried conduct *Paris* – 'excellently', Delius told Heseltine; then Munich and, in April, Venice. It seems likely that it was in Venice that he met an extremely interesting and like-minded American sculptor and painter, Henry Clews, Jr., and his wife Marie.[46] they became extremely good friends, and remained so for the rest of Delius's and Jelka's lives. The visit to Munich was thoroughly frustrating; Delius

---

[44] Agnes Nicholls (1876–1959): a mainly dramatic soprano who was equally happy in the concert hall and the opera house c. 1910–25. She was the wife of the conductor (Sir) Hamilton Harty (1879–1941). Frank Mullings (1881–1953) was a heroic tenor, notably in Wagner roles, and they were both members of the Beecham Opera Company and the British National Opera Company.

[45] Letter 398, n. 1.

[46] Henry Clews, Jr (1876–1937): he made a mask of Delius in 1916 (see *Letters* 2, plate 17c). For many years, he and his wife had a huge home, Château de La Napoule, a medieval fortress on the shore of the Mediterranean, half way between St. Tropez and the Italian border, which they spent many years restoring (see *Letters* 2, plate 40b). According to Marie, his and Delius's conversations were 'scintillating' – yet although they also had violent quarrels, they then happily made them up. See the note on Marie's unpublished memoirs in *Letters* 2, pp. 205–6, and Jelka's letter to her on pp. 453–4. See also *TB*, pp. 169 and 182–3.

went there (with Jelka) to have a showdown with Alexander Jadassohn, the head of Harmonie, over their accounting procedures – which, to say the least, Delius found opaque. When they got to Munich, however, notwithstanding their appointment, Jadassohn was in Berlin; Delius was not prepared to drop his complaints, so there was nothing for it but to return to Grez from Venice via Munich again. For the second time Jadassohn failed to keep the appointment. This was particularly vexing for Delius, whose Berlin accountant had gone with him, and led directly to Delius severing his connection with the firm. He took legal advice, but the wheels of justice turned very slowly, and his claim never got to court before the start of the Great War. In the second half of the year, in September there was a visit to the Birmingham Festival for *Sea Drift*, and then down to London, via Gardiner's cottage at Ashampstead in Berkshire for a few days, to hear the Piano Concerto and *Dance Rhapsody*; then it was back to Berlin to hear Fried conduct his music for the second time in the year – *Lebenstanz* in its revised form; and finally home to Grez in October. The stay with Gardiner might have proved fatal: Gardiner drove them to look at Oxford, and on the way back the steering broke, and, but for the fact that they were going slowly through a village, the resulting accident could have deprived English music of two important, albeit very different, personalities.[47]

English audiences were increasingly getting to know and appreciate Delius's music. He would have been amused by a comment in *The Musical Times* for May 1912, under the heading 'Music in Manchester':

> The past season has witnessed the laying of the Delius-bogey; this fearsome ultra-modernist has been represented by the 'Brigg Fair' and 'Appalachia' Variations, in addition to the [Dance] 'Rhapsody', and the Manchester public has vigorously applauded, evidently finding him much to its taste.

and pleased by a review of *Sea Drift* at the 1912 Birmingham Festival:

> This is a striking instance of how quickly an unfamiliar type of music may be assimilated, for when it was heard at Sheffield a few years ago many people found it almost unintelligible, yet now its beauties seem perfectly clear ... A great deal of its beauty lies in the balance of harmony and the contrasts of colour between the voices and the orchestra. It is rather weak in rhythmic design, and that is why it needs close knowledge to make it successful.
>
> *The Times*, 4 October 1912

[47] *Gardiner*, p. 101.

A year later, on 18 December 1913 the Polish conductor Emil Młynarski gave *In a Summer Garden* in Edinburgh; as *The Musical Standard* observed, 'The ultra-modern British school, in which Delius is frequently classed, has been given a fair hearing at these concerts this year.'[48]

Although Delius obviously wanted as many performances of his music as possible, there was one he refused to allow; in May 1912, his sister Clare, an amateur singer, received this:

> You would do me the greatest favor by *not* giving a recital of my songs in London ... do not try to 'battre monnaie' by being my sister & singing my old songs ... Dont be hurt at what I say – I have always liked you better than the others – Please let me continue to do so & do not do something which I should never forgive you for ...[49]

He was also getting less tolerant of other composers' music. He wrote to Jelka from the Birmingham Festival:

> Today I tried to hear the Mathew Passion but could not stand more than 40 minutes of it – I see now definitely that I have done for ever with this old music. It says nothing whatever to me – Beautiful bits – Endless recitations and Chorale My goodness! How slow![50]

The Deliuses never seemed to tire of travel. January 1913 saw them in Munich again for *A Mass of Life*, and in March they came back to England to hear Beecham give its second English performance at Covent Garden. Beecham and Lady Cunard also plunged them, probably somewhat reluctantly at first, into the social whirl of the good and great in London. Very probably with a view to strengthening her relationship with Beecham, Lady Cunard succeeded in parading Delius in many of the great houses – to the extent that he and Jelka even had lunch with the Prime Minister, Herbert Asquith, at 10 Downing Street.[51] Lady Cunard had become amazingly good at persuading people to attend Beecham's concerts and opera performances, for:

> There appeared to be no limit to the number of boxes she could fill. Her will-power was sufficient, her passion for music fervent enough, to make opera almost compulsory for those who wished to be fashionable. She had grasped the fact that in the London of the time, in order to ensure the success of an art-luxury such as Grand Opera, it was absolutely necessary to be able to rely upon a regular attendance by numskulls, nitwits and

---

[48] *The Musical Standard*, 10 January 1914.

[49] Letter 367.

[50] Letter 371.

[51] There is an interesting pen-picture of Delius at one of her at one of her lunch parties in (Sir) Osbert Sitwell's *Great Morning: An Autobiography* (London: Macmillan & Co. and The Book Society, 1948), pp. 252–3. For an amusing reminiscence of another such party, see Eugene Goossens, *Overture and Beginners* (London: Methuen & Co., 1951), pp. 126–7.

morons addicted to the mode, even if they did not care in the least for music.[52]

In May Delius went to Paris to see Serge Diaghilev's[53] legendary Ballets Russes in Stravinsky's *The Firebird*, and six days later he went to the notorious first night of *Le Sacre du printemps*; he did not have a ticket, and therefore wrote to Stravinsky that he would call for him on the way to the theatre, so that they could go in together.[54] He also met both Diaghilev and his principal dancer Vaslav Nijinsky.[55] Having returned home via Cologne and the annual Tonkünstlerfest in Jena, Delius was back in Paris in the middle of June to hear Beecham give a 'pitiful performance' of *Appalachia*: 'the Orchestra was 2nd rate & the Chorus awful & Beecham seemed to be entirely out of his water', wrote Delius to Heseltine.[56] The problem was almost certainly that the French orchestra had probably never played a note of Delius before. Only a few weeks later Delius set off for Norway, leaving Jelka to work on the décor sketches for the planned October première of *Fennimore and Gerda* in Cologne (which was in fact postponed, and not given until 1919); she later joined him, and they stayed until early September – but before the end of the year he had been to both Leipzig (to hear Nikisch give the *Two Pieces for Small Orchestra* their first hearing) and Vienna (where he hoped *An Arabesque* would be played, though in the event it was not). At last, however, in early December he was back at his desk in Grez again.

At some stage in the year, Delius must have been persuaded to write a piece for the American school music Progressive Music Series, and the result (which probably gave him a little amusement) was the *Two Songs for Children* (1913: *RT* V/29; *CE* vol. 17). The first, 'Little Birdie', a setting of part of Tennyson's poem *Sea Dreams* (1860), is for unison voices and piano. The two verses of the text (both beginning 'What does little birdie say, / in her nest at peep of day'), are set to the same music. In the context of the poem, they are a lullaby sung to a three-year-old, and whilst they would undoubtedly strike the modern child as too twee and sentimental, they would surely not have seemed so cloying at the time. In fact the music is charming and Delius is careful to make the vocal line relatively simple, without involving awkward intervals. On the other hand, there is no suggestion that he is writing down for his youthful singers, since their part is accompanied by fairly chromatic harmonies, using chords

---

[52] Sitwell, *Great Morning*, p. 251. *Plus ça change!*

[53] Serge Diaghilev (1872–1929): Russian impresario. He formed the Ballets Russes in St Petersburg in 1909, completely revolutionising the traditional art form and attracting the finest contemporary performers, choreographers, designers, producers and composers. The company was disbanded on his death in 1929.

[54] Letter 379. How Delius first met Stravinsky is a mystery.

[55] Nijinsky was possibly the finest male dancer ever. Diaghilev and Nijinsky had been lovers, but Nijinsky married in 1913.

[56] *FD&PW*, Letter 56.

and modulations that are instantly recognisable as being very much in the composer's mature style.

The companion piece, 'The Streamlet's Slumber Song' (which in the event was only published in 1924), is a rather more ambitious affair and benefits from a text that is less childish, in all senses. The words are by May Morgan, her two verses evoking the sights and sounds of summer at its height ('Bees are droning lazy tunes through the sultry noons'); musically, we are in the world of *In a Summer Garden* or *Summer Night on the River*, with highly chromatic chordal writing for the piano in a flowing, languorous, 3/2 metre. The voice parts are divided throughout, and are slightly more challenging than in the first song, though not unreasonably so. The mood is relaxed and nostalgic with an elegiac flavour matching a reference in the verse to the season's end when 'bee and brook will sing no more, summer will be o'er'. The final bars are beautifully written, with the voices gradually fading away in delicate, sustained phrases; this much-neglected song is really something of a little gem.

H IS travels notwithstanding, Delius found time during the year to start a third major orchestral work: at the end of a letter to Heseltine he said, 'I could not come to England as I was hard at work on something new.'[57]

---

[57] Letter 380.

## NORTH COUNTRY SKETCHES

(1913–14: *RT* VI/20; *CE* vol. 26)

*Autumn: The Wind Soughs in the Trees – Winter Landscape –*
*Dance – The March of Spring: Woodlands, Meadows and*
*Silent Moors*

ALTHOUGH little or nothing is known of Albert Coates's relationship with Delius at this time, *North Country Sketches* is dedicated to him. They do not seem to have met until 1919, six months before Coates conducted the première of *The Song of the High Hills* – as a result of which, and another performance, Delius had a high regard for his musicianship – but this work was finished six years before that. A mystery!

Delius gave no indication that the *North Country Sketches* describe any particular places, except that the title of the fourth movement includes the words 'Silent Moors'. Christopher Palmer wrote: 'After Grieg's death ... Delius found himself turning more and more to the Northlands for inspiration: ... [including] the orchestral suite *North Country Sketches*'.[58] However, there can really be no doubt that Delius was thinking of Yorkshire. There could hardly have been a sharper contrast between Delius's distaste for his home town, Bradford, with all its grimy industrial legacy, and his appreciation of the nearby hills and moors, which he loved so much.[59] Although she did not mention the work in her book, Clare Delius did talk of two walks over the moors when Delius would have been a teenager – one with a friend, and the other with his brother Max (a long one over Rumbold's Moor, between Bradford and Ilkley) – as well as his riding on Rumbold's Moor, and long walks which she had with him.[60] Most importantly, though, Fenby wrote that *North Country Sketches* was 'the one instrumental work in which he recalls expressly his impressions of the Yorkshire countryside he had known as a boy,' and 'It was England, though, not Scandinavia, that impelled his major orchestral impressions of the northern scene he had known as a boy when riding his pony on the Yorkshire moors.'[61]

*North Country Sketches* is a vivid testimony to Delius's love for the countryside, although there is nothing nostalgically sentimental or cosy in the music. Indeed, an austerity and bleakness characterise this four-movement suite, and they are given full expression in astringent harmonies and stark textures. The warmer months of summer are entirely absent, and we are presented instead with the harsh and chilly climes of autumn, winter and spring. Even the *Dance* has a bracing, severe quality to it.

The poetic word *sough* in the subtitle of *Autumn* means 'sighing' or

---

[58] *Palmer*, p. 44.

[59] *PW*, pp. 143 and 175.

[60] *MMB*, pp. 38 and 50; the last is confirmed by Heseltine.

[61] Bradford Delius Centenary Festival programme (1962), and sleevenote for HMV ASD3139 (1972), both in *Lloyd*, pp. 157–8.

'murmuring', and the whole movement is relatively restrained in terms of dynamics and instrumentation (brass, percussion and harps, for example, are entirely absent.) The emphasis is on the strings, who are frequently divided into as many as twelve parts, and who play for most of the time with their mutes on, giving a silvery, ghostly quality to the sound. The imaginative opening, marked 'Slow, with even flowing movement', perhaps implies a moonlit scene:

Ex. 6.18

Slow, with even flowing movement        1st hn (muted)

muted strs

*ppp*

2nd hn (muted)    strs

A general characteristic of this work is the great emphasis it puts on textures and timbres: in that respect, it is one of Delius's most impressionistic scores. Certainly, in the opening two movements, only undeveloped wisps and fragments of melodic ideas emerge; the following are all from the opening pages:

Ex. 6.19

hns 1.2

*p dolce*

ob

*mp espress.*

vlas

One striking example of the overall predominance of texture over melodic interest is a melancholy passage (Fig. 2+8 *et seq.*) that consists of chains of descending chromatic scales in divided strings, anchored on slow-moving pedal notes in cellos and double basses. There are occasional flutterings on woodwind instruments (Fig. 4+4 *et seq.*), but generally the landscape, unlike that of, say, *Brigg Fair*, is bereft of birdsong. Flowing, semiquaver movement, expressive of the soughing of the wind, is heard in the flutes, before passing to the strings (Fig. 7-2). It eventually reaches full strength (Fig. 10-3) (but still only marked *forte*) in one of several passages in the score that are reminiscent of the style of Debussy. Then the wind drops almost entirely, with a change of mood marked 'Slower and more deliberate' (Fig. 11+1). The texture suddenly becomes more chordal and static, the harmonies more opaque, as if mist has enveloped the moors:

Ex. 6.20

Now there is only the faintest soughing of clarinets and horns, and just one brief arabesque from the cor anglais (Fig. 14-2). In the final six bars, the strings fall away across the stave above a pedal G natural in cellos and double basses, finally coming to rest on a chord of C, voiced with chilly fourths and fifths, the only warmth being provided by the violas gently adding an E natural.

After this vivid opening movement, Delius follows it with an equally memorable *Winter Landscape*. A bleak and monotonous *ostinato* figuration on oboes and cor anglais, tinged with what Fenby called 'icy fingerings from the harps', is surrounded by a halo of string harmonics (not shown in Ex. 6.21), beneath which a wispy, melodic fragment emerges on the cellos:

Ex. 6.21

The textures of the entire movement are formed from these basic elements in varied arrangements. The cellos' melodic fragment is passed to the violas; to the 1st horn (Fig. 15+1); to the clarinets and violas (Fig. 15+6); to the violins (Fig. 16+1); to the cor anglais (Fig. 16+ 6); and so on. The violin version is a more forceful affair:

Ex. 6.22

The final bars recall the texture of the very opening, though this time with a solo cello, reinforced by the 1st bassoon, playing the melody of Ex. 6.21. The 'icy fingerings' cease abruptly as the strings fade away on a widely spaced chord, grounded on an open fifth (D to A) juxtaposed with the dissonance of a diminished fifth (B to F) from 2nd violins and violas – a thoroughly eerie conclusion.

After two predominantly slow movements, both of them brooding and mysterious, Delius provides plenty of contrast in the remaining pair, a *Dance* and a *March*. The former has no explicitly seasonal connotations; its function is to provide a link between the depths of winter and the onset of spring and it is very much in the manner of one of Delius's *Dance Rhapsodies*. 'Mazurka tempo', characterised by a strong accent on the second beat of the bar, introduces a jaunty theme with dotted rhythms, given initially to the 1st flute:

Ex. 6.23

This is taken up by the 1st oboe (Fig. 20-2) and then, much more boldly and in a slightly quicker tempo, by the 1st violins (Fig. 21-2). The brass, hitherto absent from the score, now put in an appearance (Fig. 22+5 and Fig. 25+1), the latter entry marking a slower and more deliberate section in 4/4 which introduces a new idea on the strings, with strong family resemblances to Ex. 6.23:

Ex. 6.24

This is characterised by the so-called 'Scotch snap', which inverts the normal order of dotted notes so that the shorter of them comes first, rather than last. It is a rhythmic trait that Delius was fond of, using it, for example, in the second subject of the second movement in his Violin Sonata no. 3. Oboes play a variant (Fig. 26-2), which is repeated by the 1st flute and the 1st clarinet in octave unison. The tempo fluctuates, as does the time signature (between three and four beats to the bar), and the orchestra passes the various dance themes around, with yet one more variant (Fig. 29+3) introduced by the 1st violins, violas and oboes:

Ex. 6.25

Now the texture fills out considerably, involving some vigorous and strenuous passage-work for the strings (Fig. 31+1). A few bars for solo violin (Fig. 32+1) introduce the final section of the dance, which really takes off in some imaginative scoring that includes chordal figurations darting upwards in strings and harps (Fig. 33+2), and sinuous chromatic lines for the woodwind and brass. The strings insist on a variant of Ex. 6.23 in octave unison, while the brass provide rhythmic thrust by playing mainly on the second beat of the bar as the music soars and reaches a *fff* climax (Fig. 39-4). Then, so typical of Delius, the texture deflates and contracts in just a few bars, as the dancers seem suddenly exhausted and the music dies down with a few final quotations of Ex. 6.23 by the woodwind, before the strings sign off with two F sharp minor chords, *pizzicato*.

Eric Fenby considered the final sketch, *The March of Spring* 'the most difficult movement to bring off successfully in all [Delius's] orchestral music'.[62] The challenge in performance lies in the lack of thematic development in what is an overtly rhapsodic movement, as Delius flits from idea to idea, taking up a melodic fragment, playing around with it for a while, but then moving impetuously on to something else. However, there is a more substantial (and recurring) melodic idea in the form of upward arpeggios, heard in the opening bars from a solo cello:

Ex. 6.26

This idea is imitated and extended by a solo viola (Fig. 41-4), the music dancing along, as the score instructs, 'With a light, lively and throbbing

---

[62] *Lloyd*, p. 157.

movement, never dragging'. Downward chromatic flourishes on the strings (Fig. 42-4), followed by off-beat trills, are reminiscent of Debussy's *La Mer*:

Ex. 6.27

In the slower passage which follows, Delius makes great play of a triplet motif, introduced by the 1st oboe (Fig. 43+3):

Ex. 6.28

This is taken up by the strings against murmuring woodwind figurations, pitting groups of four semiquavers against three. Another little fragment which takes the composer's fancy, incorporating intervals of falling sevenths, is introduced by the 1st flute, 1st oboe and 1st clarinet (Fig. 46-4), and shortly afterwards accompanies a return of Ex. 6.26 (Fig. 46+2), which itself is repeated (in longer note values) by the 1st oboe (Fig. 47+3). This, along with other previously heard material, gives us some sense of a recapitulation. The restless pulse ebbs and flows as the time signature fluctuates between three and four beats to the bar, leading to a swift and unexpected climax (Fig. 51+1) with tricky passage-work for the strings that settles into a unison repeat of Ex. 6.26 (Fig. 51+5), and is then passed on to the clarinets (Fig. 52+1). A bridge passage, with descending chromatic chords on harps and woodwind, leads abruptly into the final *March of Spring* (Fig. 53+4). This treads a deliberate measure, fully scored and sounding more Scottish than English in its jaunty, dotted rhythms:

Ex. 6.29

**Very rhythmically, marchlike and sustained**

The tempo relaxes as the texture thins, with a clutch of solos for the woodwind based on Ex. 6.29, culminating in the 1st clarinet repeating, like an *ostinato*, a falling minor third above a murmuring 3rd bassoon. The strings come to rest on a soft and widely spaced chord of F major with, as so often in Delius's final chords, the addition of the sixth of the scale.

T HE première was given by Beecham – the first Delius première he conducted – on 10 May 1915, in Queen's Hall. It was part of a series of five concerts with the London Symphony Orchestra, and immediately preceded three entitled 'A Festival of British Music', which included *Sea Drift*[63] and the Piano Concerto. The critic of *The Musical Times* seemed blissfully unaware of the Yorkshire inspiration:

> The first two [movements] are very realistic in an appropriately bleak manner, the third contains suggestions of a dance of Highland origin, and the fourth depicts the gradual awakening of nature – apparently over the Border, judging from the 'snap' in the rhythm of the march section. The sketches were well received.
>
> 1 June 1915

but *The Times* (for once) gave the work a fine review:

> The 'Four North Country Sketches' by Delius, which were played for the first time, provided yet another and a very remarkable interest in the programme. Three of them are wonderfully beautiful impressions in tone colour of aspects of nature. 'Autumn, The Wind soughs in the Trees' and a 'Winter Landscape,' both for small orchestra, strike one at once by their delicacy and the extra-ordinary power which Delius has of preserving a unity of tone colour without falling into musical monotony. The third piece is simply called 'Dance' and some of its treatment recalls the 'Dance Rhapsody,' but its themes are stronger and its rhythm more closely knit. The last, 'The March of Spring,' is larger in design, but less strikingly beautiful at a first hearing than its two companion landscapes; but both its opening and its ending with the cuckoo's note have delightful suggestions which make one want to know it better.
>
> 11 May 1915

---

[63] The solo part of *Sea Drift* was sung by the celebrated baritone Herbert Heyner (who would soon be commissioned into the Artists' Rifles).

## REQUIEM
### (1913–16: *RT* II/8; *CE* vol. 12b)

APART from three songs, the only other work that Delius started in 1913 was the *Requiem* – the second to which, surprisingly in the light of his views on religion, he gave a 'Christian' title. Probably the first reference to it is in a letter to Ernest Newman in October:

> A question! If you had to characterise the 4 principal religions in music – which religious melodies used in the several religious ceremonies would you choose? In other words – what themes do you consider would characterise the best the Christian – Mahomedan – Jewish & Boodhist religions? If you can help me out I should be very grateful.[64]

A few months later, Delius wrote to Heseltine simply saying 'I am working at my requiem' – which suggests that Heseltine already knew of the project – and he used exactly the same words again in July 1914.[65] It must however, have taken him much longer to complete than he had expected, for Beecham recalled him still working on it during 1915, and in another letter to Heseltine in January 1916 he said, 'I am hard at work on the end of my "Requiem"'[66] – so the finishing touches were probably made quite shortly after that.

The words are taken partly from the Book of Ecclesiastes and partly from the writings of Friedrich Nietzsche. There was originally some doubt as to who actually put them together, and, as no attribution is given in either the finished manuscript or the printed copies, it was believed that Delius had produced the text himself; later research, however, has shown that its 'author' was his friend Heinrich Simon.[67] Delius must, however, surely have had considerable input, for he was mischievous enough to play the Devil and cite Scripture for his own purposes.

Delius only twice gave his own written descriptions of what his music was 'about': once in the programme notes for the first performances of *The Song of the High Hills*, and once for this work.[68] Here, he provided an 'Explanation' which shows him to be well versed in philosophy – mainly Nietzschean, of course, but not entirely:

---

[64] Letter 383. In that letter, Delius reveals an interest in Beecham's recent performances of Strauss's *Elektra* – in two of which Frederic Austin had sung the part of Orestes.

[65] *FD&PW*, Letter 61, and *Letters*, Letter 399.

[66] Letter 416.

[67] Heinrich Viktor Simon (1880–1941): German polymath – political economist, writer, translator, art historian, musicologist and musician: see Lionel Carley, 'Delius's *Song of the Earth*', *Fanfare from the Royal Philharmonic Society* 3 (Spring 1994), 3–4; reprinted in *The Delian*, October 1997, 5–6.

[68] He did, however, put quotations on the preliminary pages of the manuscripts of *Paris* and *In a Summer Garden*.

It is not a religious work. Its underlying belief is that of a pantheism that insists on the Reality of Life. It preaches that human life is like a day in the existence of the world, subject to the great laws of All-Being. The weakling is weighed down thereby and revels in magic pictures of a cheerful existence hereafter. The storm of reality destroys the golden dream-palaces, and the inexorable cry resounds, 'You are the creature of the day and must perish.' The world tries to soothe the fear of death; 'the highways of the world give birth to gods and idols.' The proud spirit casts off the yoke of superstition, for it knows that death puts an end to all life, and therefore fulfilment can be sought and found only in life itself. No judgment as to doing and not doing good and evil can be found in any ordinance from without, but only in the conscience of man himself. Often a man is judged worthless to the world and its laws, who should be exalted by praise for his human goodness, and the love of which he freely gives. Thus independence and self-reliance are the marks of a man who is great and free. He will look forward to his death with high courage in his soul, in proud solitude, in harmony with nature and the ever-recurrent, sonorous rhythm of birth and death.[69]

That last sentence ties in with the dedication of the work 'To the memory of all young Artists fallen in the War' – which was presumably added after 1918. Despite the composer's attempt to clarify his approach, however, the work must have puzzled many in the audience at the first performance, some of whom might well have lost relatives or friends in the conflict.

The text of the first of the five, linked movements, treads ideologically familiar ground for Delius: 'Our days here are as one day, for all our days are rounded in a sleep.' Man is mortal and must die; there is no such thing as an afterlife, and those who believe in it merely deceive themselves. The music is marked *Solemnly* (*Feierlich*) and Delius begins his sermon in severe mood, with bare fourths and fifths from the strings in the opening two bars followed by chromatic harmony given a sense of direction by a finely conceived bass line. Delius's musical language had by now toughened and grown more astringent and sinewy, a development in style that had begun with *An Arabesque* and *North Country Sketches* (Ex. 6.30).

The chorus is divided for much of the work into two choirs, and the second of these enters before its counterpart (Fig. 1+7); both work independently in this movement to give a rich, eight-part texture – their lines, as is usual in Delius's later choral works, being shadowed instrumentally. The way in which this opening is notated – in 3/2, with the minim as the main pulse – lends it a weighty tread, with a symbolically hymn-like look to the score, soon dispelled when a vicious *pizzicato* from the strings (Fig. 3+8) leads to a bad-tempered outburst in recitative style by the baritone soloist, denouncing the self-deception and falsehood of those who deny man's ultimate extinction.

---

[69] *MMB*, p. 195.

Ex. 6.30

His words are echoed more lyrically by both choirs (Fig. 5+7), shrouded by murmuring woodwind and strings. The baritone then launches out into another provocative denunciation of 'weaklings ... [who] drugged themselves with dreams and golden visions', a passage that is typical of the score in its vivid and imaginative orchestration: in this case a high-pitched solo violin spins a mendacious web as it builds 'a house of lies to live in'.

Delius now returns (Fig. 8+3) to the solemnity of the opening material (Ex. 6.30) as the baritone issues fresh warnings of 'a storm with mighty winds', and this duly erupts *ffff*, octave unison A flats from the six horns clashing with woodwind D naturals (creating an augmented fourth, the so-called 'Devil's interval') and grinding against open fifths, G–D, in the strings, the voices adding F naturals to the mixture.

A forceful and didactic pronouncement, resounding to 'trumpet tones' (Delius reinforces three of them with three horns), pronounces sentence on mankind: 'thou art mortal and needs must thou die.' It is admittedly an overly dramatic gesture and one that is ammunition for those who have no time for bombast. This rude blast is echoed softly by the two choirs (Fig. 10+2) as pulsing timpani lead into a recapitulation of the opening text and music, this time with a varied harmonisation.

A *maestoso* bridge passage (Fig. 13+1), graphically scored to include full brass, treads purposefully towards a double bar and a *coup de théâtre* as the second movement bursts in without a break. To the accompaniment of drumming quavers in timpani, cellos and double basses, marked 'With vigour and fervour', the women of the chorus reiterate shrill cries of 'Hallelujah' in counterpoint to male-voice shouts (labelled 'The Crowd') of 'La il Allah'. Reinforced with a beefy, deliberately crude orchestration of full brass and lower woodwind, it is a passage unique in Delius (a fact which some might consider to be a mercy.)

This multicultural Tower of Babel fades away as the baritone returns in a slower tempo (Fig. 16+7), musing ('Very deliberately' is the marking) on those who are able to see through 'Gods and idols' and effectively distance themselves:

Ex. 6.31

'for fame and its glories seem but idle nothings'. An even slower section, accompanied by strings and lower woodwind (with cor anglais, bass oboe and contra bassoon to the fore) finds the soloist pondering the inescapable finality of death, his words echoed gloomily by the two choirs.

But Delius has finally spent his rage and delivered his uncompromising sermon. From here onwards, he is ready to return to a more familiar idiom of wistful resignation, composed to some of the most beautiful and imaginative music he ever conceived. Indeed, real warmth at last enters the orchestration (Fig. 19+7) with cellos and double basses marked *cantabile*, as the baritone urges us to rejoice in the primary functions of life: good food, wine, love-making and rewarding work. Sensuousness radiates through rich chords in the upper strings, softening the stoicism urged by the text. The ending of

Ex. 6.32

this movement is a fine piece of writing, the basses of the first choir intoning ('without expression') the conclusion that 'at the touch of Death [those who are living] lose knowledge of all things', whilst the music dies away, resolving at the very last moment on to a hushed chord of B flat from strings and cor anglais, with the 2nd violins adding the sixth of the scale.

The third movement is a poignant love song, in which the baritone soloist evokes memories of cherishing his beloved 'like a flower … whose fair buds were folded lightly and she open'd her heart at the call of Love.' The images recall Dowson and Delius's settings of *Songs of Sunset*, so much so that this movement could be an *addendum* to that same work. Up to this point the baritone's vocal lines have been angular and frankly unmemorable, but they now blossom forth into some truly lyrical writing, mirrored by beautiful orchestral textures (Ex. 6.31).

The chorus makes a brief contribution of just six bars, though it is very effective in context (from here on it is treated as a single unit rather than a true double choir). The baritone continues to delve nostalgically into his past, and, in the final bars, *più tranquillo*, he is accompanied by a filigree of woodwind, including Delius's favoured cor anglais and bass oboe. The ending of this movement is as magical as anything Delius ever wrote, including two bell-like chords for the celesta (Fig. 27+9), repeated a few bars later as the woodwinds tiptoe quietly from the scene, leaving the strings to resolve onto a hushed chord of F major with the timpani adding a soft pulse. All passion is spent.

The patient soprano soloist has had to wait nearly twenty minutes to sing, but she now begins energetically in praise of the 'man who can love life, yet without base fear can die. He has attained the heights and won the crown of life.' As in the previous movements, Delius uses the chorus to echo the soloist's sentiments. There is a most striking passage for the strings (Fig. 31-2) as the 1st violins gradually ascend toward the top of their range to mirror a description of the soul ascending to the mountain top, a beautiful piece of orchestration with its horn calls and sonorous C major chord for low-placed trombones (Ex. 6.32).

The final pages of this movement are equally outstanding, as Delius embellishes textual references to the sun going down and to night arriving, symbolic of the onset of the dreamless sleep of Death (Fig. 35+2). Descending string chords are ornamented with slowly falling arpeggios in solo oboe, flute and cor anglais before the music apparently comes to rest; but then Delius smudges the sound as double basses continue to shift down on open fifths, with a single, distant horn note and the 1st bassoon playing an enigmatic downward arpeggio to render the harmony opaque (Ex. 6.33).

Ex. 6.33

Ex. 6.35

The composer saves the best till last: the fifth movement resonates with the joy of Life. It is a real *tour de force*, a masterpiece of orchestration in which Delius offers some of his most original and startling effects. It is his claim to Modernism if ever there was one, though it has few parallels elsewhere in his work, with the possible exception of *North County Sketches* and *An Arabesque*.

The text has shed its dogmatism and instead imparts a familiar Delian message, that of Nature eternally renewing itself (symbolised by the coming of spring) in contrast to Man's doomed existence. The first ten bars, glittering with pentatonic, F sharp figurations in upper strings, flutes and celesta, aptly depict snow, described by the baritone as lingering on the mountains. Then the soprano soloist points out budding trees and hedges, golden willows and red

almond blossom, as bass clarinet, 3rd bassoon, harp and double basses weave a
strange pattern, startlingly atonal for Delius:

Ex. 6.34

References in the text to birdsong are vividly illustrated in the orchestra
(Fig. 38-2), with trilling strings, stuttering woodwind and pentatonic harp
clusters underpinned by bass clarinet, double bassoon and double basses – an
extraordinary effect. In an ever-swelling texture, the chorus makes a thrilling
entry with repeated cries of 'springtime, springtime'. The horns, held in reserve
up to now, make their own effect, swaying to and fro above string arpeggios as
the tempo is halved (Fig. 39+2) and lyrical passages for the baritone and chorus
depict woods, forests and brooklets 'full of silence'. The ripening corn, soon to
be cut down, is a symbol of death, but we are reassured that 'everything on earth'
(i.e. in Nature) 'will return again'. Here Delius once more rises to the height of
his powers with a choral entry (Fig. 41+6) of great poignancy (Ex. 6.35).

A final section in praise of the seasons is equally inspired, as the soloists join
their voices for the first time, the choir echoing them antiphonally and rising
to ecstatic heights (and a top B natural for the 1st sopranos.) The final cries of
'Springtime' are thrilling (Fig. 43+8 *et seq.*), with celesta and harp chords added
to the mixture. Then, as the voices break off, the final pages are given over to
the orchestra alone (Fig. 45+1 *et seq.*).

Searing *fortissimo* chords scored for woodwind, brass and strings, are
interspersed with gentle *piano* chords for horns, tuba and strings, leading to
the coda (Fig. 46+2), *molto tranquillo*, introduced by the 1st oboe with a dotted,
swaying theme passed on to the 1st and 2nd flutes. Bells toll, pitched in thirds
and imitated by harp, 1st clarinet and by the 5th horn. (Delius optimistically
envisaged the remainder of the horns, plus the trumpets, playing off-stage as
if in the distance, but this is quite impractical as he only gives them six bars
to leave the platform.) The pealing bells cease, the dotted theme on flute and
clarinet becomes fragmented, and horns, celesta and harp leave the scene as
well, as the strings and a handful of woodwinds fade away on a D major chord
with an added sixth.

In many pages of this challenging work, Delius's artistry is arguably
unsurpassed. It is undeniable that the first movement and part of the second –
where the composer is firmly astride his hobby-horse – are weak parts of the
score. Craftsmanship is never absent here, but musical invention for the most
part lags behind. One can respect his entrenched opinions, whilst noting that
he himself is hardly inspired musically by his dogmatism as a soap-box orator.
For vintage Delius, one must look instead to the closing pages of the second
movement and to what comes after, which still comprise over half the work's
total duration and in which his artistry shines out.

I N his *Frederick Delius*, Beecham let fly at the *Requiem* in a long paragraph that begins with a typically blunt and derisive comment, but ends in almost a spirit of pity and regret, as if he would have preferred that Delius had never written it.[70] On the other hand, in editing the work for the Complete Edition, Beecham spent considerable time balancing the dynamics – leading Robert Threlfall to comment that, 'had it been [Beecham's] most cherished score, he could hardly have worked with more care and affection.' Delius himself is on record as asserting, 'I do not think I have done better than this', whereas for Philip Heseltine the *Requiem* remained 'the weakest of all Delius's mature works'. Eric Fenby, given his strong religious faith, dismissed it out-of-hand initially ('the most depressing choral work I know'),[71] but changed his mind later after hearing it performed, lauding the final section in particular and even going as far as to claim that '(it might) well be rated by future generations as second only to the *Arabesque* as one of his most characteristic and commendable masterpieces.'[72]

For some Delians the *Requiem* will always remain a problematic, if not repellent, work. But we must be clear what their hostility stems from, and at least try to separate out any textual evaluation from a purely musical one – there is, after all, much in Nietzsche to take moral exception to, and that should not colour our musical judgement of *A Mass of Life*. The title 'Requiem', with its Christian connotations, was certainly meant to be deliberately provocative and chosen ironically, although, strictly speaking, this particular branch of religion is not singled out. For Delius, all religions that preached the immortality of the soul were equally to be condemned.

Six years passed before the work was heard in public, and the performance, in Queen's Hall on 23 March 1922, was the second Delius première given by Albert Coates and The Philharmonic Choir; the soloists were the almost-unknown Amy Evans and Norman Williams. The reviews were particularly thoughtful, but came to the much the same conclusions:

> The text which set out to do [what Delius had said in his 'Explanation'] ...
> was by an anonymous German, and a translation by Mr. Philip Heseltine
> was sung. [It is] clumsy and inchoate as only German prose-poetry can
> be, and unfortunately could only add to the restlessness of those whom
> the title 'Requiem' had struck as inappropriate. Some of the bitterness
> over this title was excessive, for Mr. Delius has numerous precedents in
> the use of the word in a non-liturgical sense. We think of Burns: 'While
> all around the woodland rings, / And every bird thy requiem sings.' ...
> Mr. Delius's music lasted for just half an hour. It was a very little while
> when we had to be persuaded of so much. Now and then there was a
> patch of good Delius, and we all know how fascinating that can be,

[70] *TB*, p. 172.

[71] *Fenby 1*, p. 102.

[72] Ibid., p. 245

seeing the composer's ultimate mastery in the shifting play of chromatic harmonies, charming as day-dreams. But there was nothing in this music, not any striking invention or consecutive argument, to claim the attention. The text bitten off was altogether more than it could, in fact, chew.

*The Musical Times*, 1 May 1922

The chief point of interest lay in the first performance of Delius's since much-discussed Requiem for soli, chorus and orchestra. The composer has set his own words, which he claims have no religious significance, but although they express a noble stoicism they do not seem to have raised his inspiration to a pitch that the magnitude of the subject calls for. Mr. Delius gains much of his effect by a use of subtle and beautiful harmonies; but a Requiem imbued with the doctrine of pessimism calls as much for nobility of melodic outline as does that based on more conventional ideas. The second section especially contained some beautiful music, and the whole work was admirably sung ...

*Musical Opinion*, May 1922

*The Times* of 24 March said:

Delius's 'Requiem,' we were told, 'is not a religious work,' but it shares the disadvantage of a great deal of 'religious' music in that it is more concerned with preaching a dogma than with purely artistic expression. Its words are little more than a dry rationalistic tract, and are about as amenable to musical treatment as the Church Catechism would be. One is reminded of the Continental musician who said, 'Ah, yes, I know your British festivals. It is Hallelujah, Amen, for four days.' Only Delius's creed is the negation of 'Hallelujah, Amen.' There is, indeed, one choral passage where Hallelujahs are mingled with 'Allah il Allah,' but that is introduced apparently to suggest the equal futility of all the religious war-cries of the world. But the Delius standpoint is, as a whole, more arid than that of the most conventional 'religious' music, because a negation can generate no common impulse and arouse no enthusiasm. He seems to become conscious of the defect as the work proceeds, and to fight hard in the finale to quicken the pulses with the thought that 'Everything on earth will return again – springtime, summer, autumn, and winter, and then comes spring again!' but no one seemed to find it exactly exhilarating. Delius is not happy in setting words for voices: the vocal outlines, whether solo or choral, are stiff and ungracious, and neither Miss Amy Evans (soprano) nor Mr. Norman Williams (baritone) could disguise the fact that what they have to sing is so much obvious prose clumsily declaimed. Practically all the characteristic beauty of tone, the shifting harmonies, and the iridescent colours, lie in the orchestral commentary. The solemn awakening and the final movement of the awakening spring give suggestions in contrasting moods of the finest qualities of Delius's previous works. Some of the choral passages give the opportunity to the choir to show the beauty of their tone in combination, the cry 'Thou art our brother,' for example, which was one of the few moments in the work which made any human appeal. Mr Kennedy Scott must be congratulated on the training of the choir, and Mr Coates on achieving a remarkable first performance of a complicated score.

T HE Deliuses would now come to be badly affected by the Great War. During the first eight months of 1914 all was fine. In January, Delius told Heseltine that he was working hard[73] – it was on the *Requiem* and finishing *North Country Sketches* – although clearly he would never again attempt anything on the scale of *Appalachia, Sea Drift* or *A Mass of Life.* The following month, he went to Wiesbaden, and to Frankfurt for very fine performances of *A Mass of Life.* Then, for three weeks in June and July, Delius again enjoyed the glittering London 'season' – staying with Beecham at 'The Cottage' in Hobart Place, near Victoria, and with the O'Neills at 4 Pembroke Villas in Kensington. He wrote to Jelka several times telling her what he was up to;[74] 'Un vrai Gotha',[75] was her comment. Despite the frivolity and doubtless many expressions of dubious *bonhomie,* the visit, like the previous one, was a tremendous boost for him. As Lionel Carley has written: 'It would be almost impossible to exaggerate the promise that London alone – and the highly influential friends it was providing – now held for Delius and his music.'[76] He was still an notably handsome man, a brilliant talker, tall and distinguished, and people must have been attracted to him at dinners and parties – notwithstanding that he was 'shy and diffident in social life, and the acidity and irony of his conversation when he did speak was often repellent to lion-hunters'.[77]

In August, however, everything changed. From the late 1800s, Germany, hitherto the cultural centre of Europe, had determined to become the supreme military power as well, but was surrounded by the three military empires of Austro-Hungary, Russia and France. The last two were the real concerns, but Germany did not have the resources to fight on both fronts. Because it was thought that, if attacked, Russia would take longer to mobilise its army than France, the decision was made to annihilate France first. The German army invaded Belgium on 4 August and rapidly advanced towards Paris, with a view to encircling the French army. In the event, they did not reach it, but there was much military activity, with Fontainebleau full of British soldiers, and the Deliuses felt that they had to move away. On 30 August – three-and-a-half

---

[73] *Letters 2,* p. 116.

[74] Letters 395–8. They make particularly good reading.

[75] The *Almanach de Gotha:* a directory of the royal and noble houses, and the aristocracy, of Europe. First published in 1764, it still appears occasionally.

[76] *Letters 2,* pp. 117–18.

[77] Ibid., p. 205.

weeks after war had been declared – Percy Grainger wrote urging them to leave for England, and then go on to America, and in part they followed his advice. Delius wrote that:

> [having] buried the silver and about 1,000 bottles of our best wine, we took all the valuable paintings [apparently including *Nevermore*[78]] down – took them off their chassis & rolled them up to take with us.[79]

On 4 September they set off by train from their local station at Bourron-Marlotte down to Nantes, on the Loire, from where they hoped they get a boat to England. The journey must have been extremely distressing, for they travelled in great discomfort in a luggage van and then a horse-box, reaching Orléans in the middle of the night, the rest of which they spent on a bench outside the station. There was a refugee problem in the city, but the following day they managed to get a room in the Grand Hôtel d'Orléans – where (in true Delian style):

> we stayed a week and had a most interesting time & very good food & coffee and wine – at our table there were several officers, so we got the news before the rest of the town.'[80]

Following the Battle of the Marne (the allied victory that ended the German advance on Paris), they decided that they could safely return home, but after that experience Delius must have felt that the War would engulf him and all he stood for. As his sister wrote:

> The War [had come] to Fred, as to most artists, as a profound shock. While appreciating the spirit of self-sacrifice that it engendered, he refused to regard it otherwise than as a form of madness which had swept over the civilised world, destroying everything that was beautiful.[81]

Three felicitous chances, however, were to return the Deliuses lives to something approaching normality, and set him composing again. Firstly, in mid-November, at Beecham's invitation, they set off for London – partly to escape the war, and partly to hear the first performance of *North Country Sketches* (although in the event it was postponed at less than three weeks' notice). They initially stayed with Beecham at Hobart Place. Then, early in December 1914, Beecham took Delius to hear him conduct a Hallé Orchestra concert in Manchester, in which the main work was Brahms's Double Concerto,

---

[78] *AJ*, p. 73.

[79] Letter from Frederick Delius to Norman O'Neill, 15 September 1914; reproduced in Lewis Foreman, 'Watford sur Gade: Delius in Watford during the First World War', *DSJ* 130 (2001), 8–18, at pp. 9–10.

[80] Ibid.

[81] *MMB*, p. 190.

played by two remarkable sisters who were to become celebrated in the history of early-twentieth-century English music: May and Beatrice Harrison.[82]

In the 1890s, Colonel John Harrison, an officer in the Indian Army, and his wife, Annie, had four daughters – May and Beatrice, Monica and Margaret, who respectively became a violinist, a cellist, a singer and a pianist. Monica was the least musical of them, but the other three (Margaret before she was five) went to The Royal College of Music, and then to the Leipzig Conservatorium. May was thirteen when she first played in public, and Beatrice fifteen – both with Henry Wood in Queen's Hall. They never looked back, and were soon two of the most important players in the country's concert and recital halls – incidentally doing a great deal for the cause of women musicians. Beatrice became famous for her interpretation of the Elgar Cello Concerto,[83] and also for the broadcast on the BBC World Service of her playing to a nightingale in the garden of her Surrey home.[84]

Meeting the sisters after the concert, to their great delight (as Beatrice subsequently recollected), Delius told them that 'our performance was superb, so much so that he was inspired to write a double concerto and dedicate it to my sister and me.'[85] He kept his word, and began work a few months later.

Lastly, whether by chance or deliberately, Beecham had taken a lease of a delightful property with a mill-wheel, Grove Mill House, just to the north of Watford – and as it had become clear that the Deliuses were reluctant to return to France, he had little difficulty in persuading them to accept his generous offer that they should live there rent-free.[86] The future was beginning to look much less bleak.

---

[82] May Harrison (1890–1958); Beatrice Harrison (1892–1965).

[83] It was sometimes rumoured that she played it using only one string.

[84] A private recording of May playing the Violin Concerto with the Bournemouth Municipal Orchestra under Richard Austin was made from a BBC broadcast in 1937, and the same year she also made a private recording of the Violin Sonata no. 3 with (so it is believed) Arnold Bax.

[85] Katrina Fountain, 'In a Surrey Garden: The Story of the Harrison Sisters', *DSJ* 87 (1985), 3–12, at p. 7.

[86] *TB*, p. 172.

## VIOLIN SONATA NO. 1
### (1914: *RT* VIII/6; *CE* vol. 31b)

H AVING composed nothing for the violin since the sonata in B major and the *Légende* in 1892, during this traumatic year Delius somehow managed to create this new Violin Sonata using some sketches he had made back in 1905. Exactly when and where he did so seems impossible to discover. He could have started it, but is unlikely to have finished it, before he went to London for the 'season', but he certainly would not have had the peace and quiet he needed between August and October. The likelihood, therefore, is that he began the sonata in Grez in the spring and finished it at Watford during the very last days of the year. There is no extant final manuscript, but the first printed copy, published by Forsyth Bros of Manchester in 1917, is dated 1914; interestingly, this copy was edited and revised for publication by the first performers, the violinist Arthur Catterall and the pianist R. J. Forbes.[87] In July 1917, Delius told Jelka that he was planning 'to send it with a "dedication" to May Harrison', but as none appears on the printed score, perhaps he was just too late to get it included.

Tasmin Little, who has extensive experience of playing all the violin sonatas, comments that this is 'the deepest and most complicated … it is also the most elusive, musically'.[88] Part of the problem would seem to lie in the discrepancy between the traditional expectation of what a sonata should be and Delius's idiosyncratic conception of it. Generally (and this holds true for all three of the mature sonatas, as well as for the Cello Sonata) he is not interested in following a conventional construction involving two contrasting ideas in different keys, which are then developed, before being recalled in the same key – the essence of textbook sonata form. It is no use trying artificially to force Delius's sonatas into this pattern. As we shall see, he may have as many as four, rather than two, main themes on the go, and any potential interplay between their different keys is the least of his concerns. Eric Fenby also made a most important point when he noted that 'Delius tends to announce a theme and develop it instantly on stating it, merging statement and expansion into one.'[89] This explains why it is futile to look for any separate development sections in these sonatas, because the music is continually evolving. Indeed, this is a fundamental concept to grasp in approaching Delius's music in general.

---

[87] Arthur Catterall (1883–1943): a celebrated English violinist who led the Hallé Orchestra for eighteen years, and in 1929 became the founding leader of the BBC Symphony Orchestra; he also conducted, and directed the third concert of the 1929 Delius Festival. Robert T. Forbes was a well-known accompanist before World War II, and between 1929 and 1953 he was the principal of the Royal Manchester College of Music (which became the Royal Northern College of Music in 1972).

[88] CD booklet, Conifer 75605 51315–2.

[89] *Lloyd*, p. 198.

This first Violin Sonata is written in one continuous movement which falls into three main sections: pages 1–8 ('With easy movement but not quick'); pages 8–11 ('molto moderato'); pages 12–21 ('With vigour and animation').[90] A genial idea in 6/4 opens the work, relaxed in mood, with a slightly modal feeling about it:

Ex. 6.36

Delius has barely begun to expand this (1/8–11) before a fresh thought occurs to him; initiated by the piano (1/12), it is taken up in triplets by the violin:

Ex. 6.37

The piano writing here is characteristic of Delius's way with the instrument: the pianist has to cope with the swift juxtaposition of widely spaced, highly chromatic chords, often involving filled-in tenths in the left hand. These are awkward to play without having a large stretch, and need the utmost care in execution if they are not to sound clumsy. Most importantly, a way has to be found of bringing out the melodic shape and line of these chord sequences, which are sometimes hidden in internal parts. Given that such obvious pointers

---

[90] As there are no bar numbers, rehearsal letters or figures in the printed score, references are to page numbers and bars in the piano part in *CE* vol. 31b – e.g. 6/3.

as phrase markings are often entirely absent from the page, the performer is left without much help, though the composer would doubtless have expected him or her to have an instinctive understanding.

Another new idea (1/17) comes after a double bar and a change of metre:

Ex. 6.38

This third theme, in 4/4, receives considerable exposure, propelled by quaver triplets and semiquaver passage-work in the piano part, before it yields to yet another new idea, which reverts to 6/4 and is again set off by a double bar (3/1):

Ex. 6.39

This idea, with its counter-melody in the piano, is repeated just once by the violin, an octave higher, before it is swept aside by Ex. 6.38. This is a typical example of the way that Delius abruptly dismisses material, turning aside almost wilfully to take up something else. It can make his intentions hard to follow, certainly on a first hearing. There is a surprisingly minimalist element to his chamber music in which the presentation of ideas and their connecting material are pared down to essentials. (This suggests an interesting analogy with Debussy's late sonatas for violin and cello.)

The violin's impatient and forceful manner with Ex. 6.38 yields to a downward flourish from the piano (3/12) before Ex. 6.39 returns, this time with melody and counter-melody swapped around between the instruments. The music grows in intensity, helped by a fluid piano part with sweeping arpeggios in the left hand (like the chordal writing, somewhat awkward to execute.) The violin launches passionately into two bars of cadenza-like triplets leading unexpectedly to yet another change of direction, marked 'Quicker' and with the character of a dance (5/1). Dotted rhythms in the violin are set against quaver triplets in the piano; but this is really no more than a bridge passage leading to four bars of *tranquillo* music which hint at the melodic shape of the opening and a return home.

Indeed, once a double bar is passed, there is a textbook recapitulation of Ex. 6.36 (6/1) in the original key. Ex. 6.37 also returns (6/13), as does Ex. 6.38, presented with some exquisite new harmonisations. As that comes to rest (Ex. 6.39, incidentally, is not recalled) there is a double bar (8/12) and a marking of 'molto moderato' – the start of what is effectively the sonata's slow movement. This is dominated by a lushly harmonised melodic fragment which Delius plays with over and over again, as if fascinated by its shape and possibilities:

Ex. 6.40

There is one notable variant of it which is based on the contour of the downward semiquavers, and which receives such extensive treatment (9/1 – 10/12) that it becomes a separate theme in its own right:

Ex. 6.41

The descending crotchets are imitated by the piano (9/6 *et seq.*) in a set of harmonic sequences interspersed with occasional intrusions by Ex. 6.40, which then returns definitively (10/13) to dominate the beautifully dreamy close to this section in which both instruments seem spellbound. The music pauses on a simple G major chord.

The awakening is abrupt, as an aggressive theme in B minor thrusts its way centre-stage, marked 'With vigour and animation' (12/1):

Ex. 6.42

This soon takes on the character of a march, with vigorous, off-beat piano chords (12/12 *et seq.*). There are two secondary themes in this section, the first introduced by the piano, 'Più tranquillo ed espressivo' (13/1), its dotted rhythms clearly in sympathy with Ex. 6.42:

Ex. 6.43

The other secondary theme is warmer and more lyrical:

Ex. 6.44

Note how it dovetails ingeniously into the second half of Ex. 6.42. After further restless treatment, the music becomes softer and slower, before launching unexpectedly into a dark and extended interlude of some twenty-nine bars, marked 'Slow and mysteriously'. The piano plays a menacing role, spinning rows of chromatically inflected quavers in 12/8 time, as it reaches down into the depths of the instrument. The whole section has a highly sinister feel, perhaps reflecting fears of the War and the destruction it would bring.

After building to a *fortissimo* climax (17/2) the music sinks back in seeming despair, but the violin is determined to break the mould and, with an upward flourish, brings back Ex. 6.42 (18/19) and its companion themes. This eventually leads to a substantial coda (page 21) with forceful and vigorous writing for both players. The end is a complete surprise: the final chords are decisively, and unexpectedly, in B major. It is as if, despite the forebodings of these last pages of the score, some sort of private but unspecified battle of the soul or mind has in fact been won.

R ELATIVELY few new chamber works receive three performances within about six months of being finished, but the Violin Sonata did: by Catterall and Forbes in Manchester on 24 February 1915, and then on 29 and 30 April in London. The second performance was at The Music Club:

> Mr. Delius was the guest of the evening on April 29, when the chief feature of an enjoyable programme of his works (carried out by Madame Emily Thornfield and Messrs. D'Oisly, Catterall, Forbes, and Bax[91]) was the first London performance of his Sonata for violin and pianoforte. This consists of three movements – the first and second without break – of which the third is perhaps the most effective at first hearing. The work throughout, however, is full of the elusive charm and interesting harmonic colour that we now expect from the composer, and will no doubt be

---

[91] Bax and May Harrison recorded the Sonata in 1929 – one of the few recordings of Delius's music made before his death.

frequently heard. It was beautifully played by Mr. A. H. Catterall and Mr. R. T. Forbes.

*The Musical Times*, 1 June 1914

The third performance was also mentioned there, albeit very briefly.

The Music Club was part of Lady Cunard's various socio-musical circles, described by Arnold Bax as:

> a dressy concert-cum-supper affair presided over by Alfred Kalisch, critic of The Star, and a pious thurifer before the altar of Richard Strauss ... The Club members were mostly elderly, and notable for wealth, paunchiness, and stertorous breathing. Bulging pinkish bosoms straining at expensive décolletages, redundant dewlaps, and mountainous backs were generously displayed by the ladies, whilst among the men ruddy double chins, overflowing their collars at the back of the neck, and boiled eyes were rife. The assemblage indeed was ever inclined to bring to mind Beardsley's famous drawing – 'The Wagnerites'.[92]

While we can smile at it now, the Club did provide a hearing for a great deal of interesting, mainly new, music played by extremely good musicians, often in the presence of the composers.[93]

One would not have thought that the Sonata presented any interpretative difficulties to sensitive musicians, but Eric Fenby remembered an occasion when 'a certain violinist and his colleague'

> came to Grez to treat the composer to their conception of his Sonata for Violin and Piano No. 1. Their stay was almost as brief as their rendering, for, in the silence of the turn of the page between the slow movement and the energetic last movement, a voice from the corner was heard to say, 'Good afternoon. Take me away, please, and, Jelka, make the lady and gentleman some tea!'[94]

---

[92] Arnold Bax, *Farewell, my Youth, and other Writings*, ed. Lewis Foreman (Aldershot: Scolar Press, 1992), p. 49.

[93] For example, on 14 January the previous year, Schoenberg had been the guest; the string sextet version of *Verklärte Nacht* was played and Frederic Austin sang five of his songs.

[94] *Fenby 1*, p. 187.

# Winding Down

---

*Air and Dance* – Double Concerto – Cello Sonata –
*A Dance Rhapsody* no. 2 – String Quartet ('Late Swallows') –
Violin Concerto – *Eventyr* – *To be Sung of a Summer Night
on the Water* – *A Song before Sunrise* –
*Poem of Life and Love*

---

O N top of all their other problems, Delius and Jelka's 'close and multi-layered friendship'[1] with Ida Gerhardi now came under considerable strain. It dated back to Jelka's and Ida's time at the Académie Colarossi, and remained very strong until about 1902, when, for unknown reasons, Delius began to turn his back against Ida, and the friendship seriously cooled and possibly even came close to extinction. The problem, of course, was that Ida and Jelka had always been rivals for Delius's affections, and Ida – who had very recently finished her second portrait of him – must have been devastated when he married Jelka in the autumn of 1903. There was a reconciliation in 1909, perhaps brought about by Ida's learning of Delius's increasing health problems, and all three of them attended a number of concerts of his music together. In 1912, however, Ida caught pneumonia and pleurisy, and gave up her studio in Paris, and the following year she went back to her family home in the Westphalian town of Lüdenscheid – where she remained, a permanent invalid, until her death in 1927. As a result, she was cut off from the Deliuses, and this time, once the War had started, it was probably her very strong pro-German inclinations that seriously risked bringing the relationship to an end for a second time: she wrote to another friend, 'the Deliuses are so *very* English that, since understanding is impossible, I have broken off from them; they were particularly malicious in Copenhagen.'[2] Nevertheless the underlying bond proved sufficiently strong for such manifest and seemingly entrenched attitudes not in fact to endanger the friendship',[3] with Jelka telling Grainger in 1925 of her disappointment that Ida could not come to help her cope with Delius's ill-health.[4]

Reasonably happily ensconced in Grove Mill House – although he complained about the cold – it was not long before Delius began writing again.

---

[1] Annegret Rittmann, '"Our Prophetic Little Lady Friend": The Artist Ida Gehardi', in *MA&L*, pp. 168–83, at p. 180 – a most interesting chapter.

[2] Ibid.

[3] Ibid.

[4] Letter 499.

## AIR AND DANCE
### (1915: *RT* VI/21; *CE* vol. 27b)

T HIS is Delius's only work for string orchestra – attractive and relatively brief. The *Air*, with its stepwise melodic line and predominantly dotted rhythms, introduced by a solo violin, has the flavour of a Celtic folksong. The rest of the strings punctuate the melody with offbeat chords, whose harmonies never reach for the obvious, but which colour the melody in fresh and unexpected ways. The tune is eventually given, in octaves, to divided 1st violins (B+6); then to a solo viola (D+6), joined, four bars further on, by the rest of the section; and, finally, to the 1st violins again, this time in unison (E+6).

The *Dance* follows without a break but in a somewhat quicker tempo (G+2). Its dotted rhythms are modelled on those of the *Air*, but the note values are halved, and it has a more modal feel. Delius continues to show great ingenuity in finding novel and, at times, poignant harmonies, especially towards the end, where there is a change of texture as the strings relinquish their busy streams of crotchets and are quietly poised on minims and semibreves as the initial *Air* is recalled by a solo cello:

Ex. 7.1

The conclusion is brisk with a straightforward *pizzicato* cadence and a forthright, bowed chord of E minor.

ADY Cunard was still figuring in Delius's life, and she persuaded him
and Beecham that *Air and Dance* should first be heard in her house.
Beecham duly conducted it there, presumably with a 'pick-up band' and no
doubt to decorous applause, in 1915, although exactly when no one seems to
know.[5] Then, before Delius and Jelka returned to Grez when the War was over,
Delius was invited to visit The National Institute for the Blind, which had just
published a piano version of *On Hearing the First Cuckoo in Spring* in Braille.
As a result, the Institute became the unlikely dedicatee of *Air and Dance*,
fourteen years after it was written, and just before its first public performance.
That was given by Beecham in the Aeolian Hall on 16 October 1929 as part of
the second concert of that year's Delius Festival,[6] after which *The Times* gave
the piece a generous, albeit short, mention:

> But songs, piano pieces, and little works like the new Air and Dance for
> strings, come from the same composer [as works for larger orchestra],
> and being his made a unique and precious contribution to the small class
> of exquisite miniatures.
>
> 17 October 1929

In reviewing the published copy in June 1931 *The Musical Times* said:

> Its full worth can be made evident only by players of ability and
> experience, but I cannot imagine a better introduction for accomplished
> amateurs to Delius's style. It would also be difficult to discover a work
> better suited to the study of tone-values.

VER since his Leipzig days, Delius had had no time for the classics – as
already mentioned, he once said to Fenby 'You needn't ask me to listen to
the music of the Immortals! I can't abide 'em! I finished with them long ago!'[7] In
this period, however, Delius renewed his interest in writing concertos, of which
there are three major examples, as well as two other works with relatively
abstract, non-descriptive titles. Delius, of course, had no intention of meekly
following either the eighteenth- and nineteenth-century precedents or, as
we shall see, the musical forms that such works had traditionally employed:
characteristically, he would chart his own course.

[5] Robert Threlfall, 'Frederick Delius: *Air and Dance*', *DSJ* 109 (1992), 8–9.

[6] The programmes for the Festival are listed in full below, Appendix 3.

[7] *Fenby 2*, p. 195.

## DOUBLE CONCERTO FOR VIOLIN AND CELLO
### (1915: *RT* VII/5; *CE* vol. 30)

I N December 1914 Beecham went to conduct the Hallé in Manchester, and Delius went with him. Although the programme included two excerpts from *A Village Romeo and Juliet*, what really attracted Delius's attention was a magnificent performance of the Brahms Double Concerto by the Harrison sisters (mentioned above, Chapter 6). After the concert, they were introduced to Delius by the huge, bearded and untidy Samuel Langford, the doyen of the music critics of the time, who worked for the *Manchester Guardian*[8] and wrote that 'Their unanimity in attack, phrasing, rhythmic treatment and every other grace of style was next to marvellous'. Although what Delius felt about the music is not recorded, his imagination was immediately fired, and, throwing off his composing lethargy, he offered to write a concerto for them. He began work on it only a few months later.

Before Brahms completed his Double Concerto in 1887, there were hardly any other examples of the genre. Apart from Vivaldi, who wrote six double concertos for violin and cello (with string accompaniment), there were only isolated examples by a handful of seventeenth- and eighteenth-century composers, including such figures as J. C. Bach, Reicha and Stamitz. Delius was therefore breaking relatively new ground, and his concerto ranks as one of his masterpieces in terms of beauty of sound and melodic invention.

True to his word, Delius began work on the Double Concerto in April 1915. In one continuous movement, it is structured in three sections of equal duration. The only marking given at the head of the score is one that affects the dynamic ('Quietly'), and there is no overall indication of tempo: Delius clearly expects his interpreters to have an intuitive feeling for what works best. A grave, stately and somewhat classically inflected idea in C minor is announced by the 2nd violins and violas, an octave apart, above an open fifth on the cellos, and austerely reinforced by octave G naturals from the horns; 1st clarinet and 1st bassoon then give their reply:

Ex. 7.2

[8] Samuel Langford (1862–1927): one of the most remarkable music critics, he followed Ernest Newman on the paper and was succeeded by Neville Cardus, who later wrote of him, 'Langford was a great man, and a writer on music without parallel': Neville Cardus, *Autobiography* (London: Hamish Hamilton, 1947), p. 212.

This introductory motif (for it is little more that that) will make just one further appearance, and even then only towards the very end of the work (Fig. 45+1). It does, though, exert considerable influence on later ideas, notably through its emphatic use of the interval of a perfect fourth. Generally speaking, the material of this concerto is interrelated: the themes have a family likeness about them, and a sense of affinity. There is also a yearning quality about the melodic material which unifies it.

The two soloists enter forcefully in the ninth bar with just a suggestion of Ex. 7.2 (rather than a direct quotation); a short, cadenza-like flourish from the violin leads to a slight gathering of breath, before an important theme is heard:

Ex. 7.3

Any composer who sets out to write a double concerto must consider the respective roles of the two soloists. Here we have an obvious case of them working in tandem: the violin tends to have the main melodic interest, with the accompaniment in the cello, though the roles are often swapped (e.g. Fig. 5+1 where the cello takes centre stage and the violin steps into the background). But it was not always so: in earlier drafts, before suggested revisions by the Harrisons, Delius favoured giving the violin and cello a shared melodic line, often placing them an octave apart.[9] This invited problems of intonation and balance, and Delius was right to follow the advice of his performers and, for the most part, avoid such a texture. Not only is the modification more practical, but it is also far more interesting to the ear not always to have the players in unison. But, at those moments where the two players do actually share a melodic line (e.g. between Figs. 22 and 24), the effect can be utterly arresting – and all the more so for being sparingly employed.

For a while, the soloists reiterate Ex. 7.3 in a sequence of different keys; then they embark on a broader passage, to a swaying rhythm, marked 'Rather quicker', in the key of B minor (Fig. 4+1). The accompaniment, with its offbeat quavers from woodwind and *pizzicato* lower strings, gives a sudden and exhilarating impetus to the music:

---

[9] See Robert Threlfall, *Frederick Delius, The Complete Works: Editorial Report* (London: The Delius Trust, 1990), p. 196.

Ex. 7.4

The initial melodic shape of Ex. 7.4 (a rising minor third followed by a falling semitone) is identical to that of Ex. 7.2, whilst the intervals of fourths and fifths which characterise Ex. 7.3 also find their place in Ex. 7.4; this is one example of what was referred to above as a family likeness in the concerto's material.

Ex. 7.4 sounds as if it is ripe for development, but with Delius nothing can be assumed, and in fact he goes on to return to Ex. 7.3, this time in E minor (Fig. 5+1) with the soloists exchanging roles as they weave contrapuntally around each other, the cello sometimes soaring above its partner. The music begins to relax a little – up to now there has been a surfeit of nervous urgency – and a series of quietly insistent, repeated C naturals from the timpani mark the end of a paragraph (Fig. 8-4). But, again, Delius goes his own unexpected way, as the pulse quickens once more (Fig. 8+1) and the strings introduce a brisk, chordal march in the unexpected key of A flat/G sharp. (Ex. 7.2 is suggested by the dominating fourths and fifths, Ex. 7.3 by the descending figurations at the close of the theme):

Ex. 7.5

At first, the soloists decorate this new idea with chromatic passage-work (Fig. 9+1), but it is not long before they take up the melody itself (Fig. 10+1). The oboe and the violinist sketch in a glancing reference to Ex. 7.3 (Fig. 11+1), before both soloists in turn have the fragment of what appears to be a new motif:

Ex. 7.6

In fact, this has evolved from Ex. 7.3 by decorating it with passing notes, and as if to emphasise this, Delius immediately appends Ex. 7.3 itself, first in the solo cello (Fig. 11+6) and then in the solo violin (Fig. 12-1). Trumpets and trombones make a delayed first appearance in the score (Fig. 12+1) – up to this point Delius has favoured the horns. The orchestral texture fills out as Ex. 7.6 is repeated *espressivo* by the soloists, high in their registers (Fig. 12+5), with triplet figurations in woodwind, harp and lower strings, in similar style to the accompaniment of Ex. 7.4 (another indication of unity through cross-reference). Vigorous passage-work for the violinist leads to a *cantabile* variant of Ex. 7.3 (Fig. 14+3), echoed two bars later by the cellist and, three bars further on, by the 1st trumpet. The orchestra takes up the shape of Ex. 7.3 in sequences of marching crotchets (Fig. 15+2 *et seq.*) and this leads to the first real *tutti* of the whole work. As so often, Delius prefers to use the full orchestra sparingly.

Just as characteristic is his manner of descending swiftly from a climax soon after reaching it, and in the space of just four bars, marked *smorzando* (dying away), the tension is released over a pedal F sharp from the double basses, underlined by timpani rolls (Fig. 17+1). A double bar, and the instruction 'Slowly and quieter', indicate the central section of the concerto, introduced by solos from the 1st horn and the cor anglais, pre-empting a new motif that is now given definitive form, *espressivo*, by the cello soloist (Fig. 18+1):

Ex. 7.7

With its beautiful, arching shape, this is a striking invention, and the violinist cannot resist trying it out too, immediately joining the cellist in an elaboration (Fig. 18+5 *et seq.*), to an accompaniment of imaginative harmonisation in the strings and horns, with added arabesques from the woodwind – quintessential Delius. One development of the theme (Fig. 19+7) is worth noting for its characteristic triplet figure, which is deliciously echoed by flutes, oboe and cor anglais:

Ex. 7.8

The violin soloist goes on to quote Ex. 7.7 in full, before this exquisite passage, perfectly orchestrated, is interrupted by the 1st flute and the oboe reminding us of the opening theme (Ex. 7.2) (Fig. 21+1), with pulsing timpani in the background, and the solo cello adding a counterpoint of triplet arpeggios.

At this point (Fig. 21+5) Delius introduces the last significant new theme of the concerto:

Ex. 7.9

This idea will be singled out for recall in the coda; meanwhile, the two soloists give exquisite voice to it, the cello high in its register. This is one passage which Delius was determined to present in (mostly) octave unison, and he was quite right, as the radiant effect this gives is simply stunning. The pulse slows (Fig. 24+2) as the soloists return to musing on Ex. 7.7, as if lost to the world.

However, the spell must be broken, for it is time to move on towards a recapitulation. Delius does so in a passage which serves as a cadenza for the soloists. At first, the violinist plays semiquaver arpeggios, whilst the cellist descends chromatically (Fig. 26+1); then both instruments create a four-part harmonic texture, by means of double-stopping, with chords which see-saw up and down, whilst the 1st flute hints at the shape of Ex. 7.2. The soloists soar aloft in semiquavers, to land on a sustained diminished chord, which is punctuated by a harp arpeggio, before they begin their descent with eerie harmonics, accompanied by harp chords and a meandering, chromatic flute line.

The solo violinist outlines the shape of Ex. 7.2 (Fig. 29-2), which is imitated by the oboe and 1st flute, and then, impetuously, by the whole orchestra, leading to an *accelerando* and the marking 'Tempo I' (Fig. 30+1), as the solo cellist boldly reiterates Ex. 7.3.

The recapitulation of previously heard themes more or less follows the scheme of the opening section, though Delius, who hates to repeat himself, varies his presentation of the material, particularly in terms of orchestration. It is worth noting how his boundless invention leads him, for example, to recall Ex. 7.4 (Fig. 33+1) with the soloists' roles reversed in terms of melody and accompaniment (cf. Fig. 4+1); when Ex. 7.5 returns (Fig. 36+1), it is again given to the strings, but this time they play *pizzicato* with reinforcement from 4th horn and full brass (cf. Fig. 8+1), and this is followed by two completely new variations of the idea, both involving the soloists (Figs 37+1 and 38+3); later, Ex. 7.6 is recalled, but now combined contrapuntally with Ex. 7.3 (Fig. 40-1 *et seq.*).

A lively bridge passage (Fig. 41+1) marks the transition to the coda, with the 1st and 2nd horns playing what sounds like a fanfare (Fig. 42-2), echoed by the clarinets among busy figuration from the soloists. This flourish is echoed distantly by the 1st horn, and then a double bar marks the start of the coda itself, one of the most glorious and exalted passages in all Delius – though the codas of the cello and violin concertos rival it for sheer beauty. The soloists enter quietly and expressively (Fig. 43+1) with Ex. 7.9, an octave apart in C major. They then repeat the theme, more and more ecstatically, before embarking on frenzied arpeggios as they hand the melody over to the 1st and 3rd trombones (Fig. 44+ 4); two bars later, the theme is taken up by the full string section, spaced three octaves apart, with supporting horns, brass and harp – an overwhelmingly thrilling effect.

Then comes an unexpected return to the gravity of the very opening bars of the concerto (Fig. 45+1): this time the soloists have a descending scale to add as a counterpoint to the melancholy of the theme itself. But the concerto is destined to end not in despair but in tranquillity: Ex. 7.9 returns for the final time, given to the soloists in octave unison (Fig. 46+1), with the 1st clarinet, followed by the 1st flute and the oboe, adding the little dotted rhythm of Ex. 7.2 in counterpoint. Once again Delius seems inclined to linger, but finally the soloists soar aloft to end affirmatively in C major, backed by strings and by rhythmic flickers from the 1st bassoon, the 1st flute having the last say in Delius's favoured imprint of a rising quaver triplet. The music then fades away to nothing.

As the work progressed, Delius frequently consulted the Harrison sisters on many aspects of the solo parts, often going down to their house in Kensington; by the end of June 1915, the concerto – 'For May and Beatrice Harrison' – was finished. Just under four years later, on 21 February 1920, they gave its first performance at Queen's Hall, with Wood conducting:

No completer contrast [to Granville Bantock's *The Sea Reivers*] can be imagined than Mr. Delius's Double Concerto for violin and violoncello, produced at the same concert, which seems to have been conceived and executed in the closely guarded aloofness of a conservatory in the South. It is a very delicately and carefully wrought composition in the composer's typically meditative and languorous mood ... and its performance by Miss May and Miss Beatrice Harrison leaves no room for adverse criticism.

*The Musical Times*, 1 April 1920

The work seems chiefly important as an addition to the repertory of the two sisters, whose performance of Brahms' Double Concerto is now famous. The general mood bears a resemblance to the recently heard Violin Concerto of Delius. The melodic ideas are intimately dovetailed into one another, and stress is laid on the palpitating sentiment of the central slow movement. Delius is most attractive in the world of dreams ... The beauty of the instrumental colour with which the ideas are clothed, and the opportunities it gives for an intimate *ensemble* between the soloists and the orchestra, are things which should give the concerto a definite place among the very few of its class which exist.

*The Times*, 23 February 1920

After Bantock, Delius. After the nationalist, the idealist. With that superb detachment from labels and influences which is most characteristic of Delius, he gives us a 'New Concerto' called thus, tout court – for violin, violoncello and orchestra. He adopts and adapts the classical concerto form, the old three convention movements being there in substance, though not cut-and-dried. Double concertos are not made every day, and one can safely say that no work, of quality like this has been heard in England for generations. (To find a parallel one would have to refer back to the seventeenth and eighteenth centuries). It is not one form that is especially interesting, nor the ensemble chosen – nor any wild challenge to his contemporaries, that Delius may have made in this work that arrested the audience on Saturday. It is simply that within the limit of an octave divine melodies could still be written, that harmony no less divine could be found for those melodies – and more than that that – that harmony and melody were one and interchangeable. It is to be hoped that the work will be repeated soon, and often. As an essay in colour it is unusually interesting to the student of orchestration, Delius arriving at his effects by baffling simplicity; the mere crossing of registers between solo fiddle and 'cello had, in the 'slow' movements and in parts of the first, a new significance.

*The Daily Telegraph*, 23 February 1920
(probably Robin Legge)

THE concerto finished, the Deliuses decided that they had had enough of England, and in any event Delius's health had taken a turn for the worse. As he wrote to Heseltine:

> I understand your state of mind entirely as I felt somewhat similarly before leaving England – a certain depression had absolutely taken possession of me – I luckily could forget as long as I was working; But Watford is like an unpleasant dream to me now.[10]

Before they left, however, Beecham made them yet another generous gesture. Even at this early stage in the War, Delius's royalties on the Continent were drying up, and (his publishers being German) little of his music was available in England. He and Jelka were therefore in difficult financial straits, and so Beecham bought seven works – the new Violin Sonata (for £300), the *Légende* (£150), *North Country Sketches* (£250) and three songs (£250). The total of £900 was payable over three years, and, having published them at his own expense, he would then reassign the copyright to Delius.

Although inspiration was now starting to flow again, *Air and Dance* and the Double Concerto were – perhaps unsurprisingly given the circumstances in which Delius and Jelka had found themselves – all he had managed to produce in the last twelve months. He started, however, to feel well again, and there were increasing numbers of performances, both in England and in New York, with Grainger (who had gone to live there permanently in 1914) persuading several well-known conductors to include Delius in their programmes – as he did himself.

All this time, too, Heseltine had continued to work away on Delius's behalf with total dedication: in January he was editing the *Légende* and writing a programme note for *Paris*; the March issue of *The Musical Times* had six pages on Delius, five of which were an article by Heseltine ('Some Notes on Delius and his Music'); and at the end of the year, he was correcting proofs of the first Violin Sonata. He was still continually writing to Delius on subjects as diverse as those mentioned above in Chapter 6: a project to publish only books that 'are found living and clear in truth'; the trials of being a music critic in London; conscientious objection to compulsory military service; how to produce *A Village Romeo and Juliet* and other operas; and living with D. H. Lawrence in Cornwall.[11] It is clear from Delius's replies that he still greatly appreciated Heseltine's friendship, undoubtedly because they had so much in common: 'Both were from well-to-do backgrounds; both suffered parental disapproval of the musical profession; both were strongly anti-establishment and rebels by nature, and both were largely self-taught, developing their own unique musical language.'[12]

---

[10] *FD&PW*, Letter 132.

[11] Ibid., Letters 141, 144, 146 and 152.

[12] Ibid., p. xv.

Being back in Grez was obviously doing Delius a lot of good, for very early in 1916 he was at work on his next piece – the Cello Sonata.

## CELLO SONATA
### (1916: *RT* VIII/7; *CE* vol. 31c)

D ELIUS had clearly been very taken by Beatrice Harrison and her playing, as this piece was also written for, and dedicated to, her. It is one of Delius's finest achievements in the field of chamber music, brimming over with memorable invention; nevertheless, its interpreters must prepare it carefully if its overall shape and structure are to be made clear in performance. As Eric Fenby said:

> No work by Delius has been more misread through failure to grasp the sense of flow in the subtle inflexions of the cello lines which he found he could not convey on paper, but left to the soloist's intuition. The pianist's role upholds the flow and underlines its musical sense in a rich poetry of chordal textures characteristic of Delius's art.
>
> Wigmore Hall programme note, 19 November 1980

And again:

> There is a touch of rapture already in the cellist's opening phrase of this remarkable duo if played with rubato as Delius intended it. In fact I contend that this free interpretation of flow is essential to a definitive performance of his music, being mindful of its basic tempo.
>
> New York recital programme, 14 November 1991

The Cello Sonata is an admirably concise work in one continuous movement, in three, clearly defined sections. The first of them, marked 'Allegro, ma non troppo', begins as if in mid-phrase, with both instruments entering simultaneously, *mezzopiano*, the cello floating a lyrical, free-ranging line which in fact proves not to be the dominant idea – that is assigned instead to the piano (Ex. 7.10). The cello has to bide its time until bar 18, before being allotted the piano theme. However, shortly afterwards, it makes two significant contributions of its own, the first of them at the end of bar 25 (Ex. 7.11).

The second idea, introduced by the cello at bar 30, evolves immediately from Ex. 7.10; more forceful and angular, it is treated sequentially (Ex. 7.12). Though the phrases come in two-bar groups, the shape of the musical line is expansive and broad, and it needs to be given a strong sense of direction, despite the fact that Delius has indicated no overall phrase marks, only slurs between notes. But, as Fenby also remarked, this is a typical, and deliberate, omission – though it is arguable that Delius might have given his interpreters just a little more guidance.

These ideas, or at any rate variations of them, inform the whole of this opening *Allegro* – Ex. 7.11, for example, is explored by the piano in a solo

Ex. 7.10

Ex. 7.11

Ex. 7.12

passage in bars 46–52. Broadly speaking, Delius demonstrates the technique he uses so extensively in his first Violin Sonata, and, indeed, in most of his major orchestral works: evolving and developing his melodic ideas almost immediately after he first states them, so that a separate development section becomes virtually redundant. Delius's piano writing is also idiosyncratic, for it contains bar after bar of complex, highly chromatic and widely spaced chords, which change on every beat. The effect is often one of great sonority, but it is as if he is writing for a string orchestra rather than for just ten fingers. In the case of this particular sonata, the two players are put relentlessly to work, seldom being allowed to draw breath; the cellist, for example, is silent in only thirteen out of the total of 264 bars.

After two pages of highly charged and passionate music (bars 82–113), the tension slackens and there is a change of texture and dynamic, characterised by a series of gentle piano triplets (bar 127 *et seq.*) which accompany a quiet cello line, marked 'dreamily'. The indication 'Lento molto tranquillo' appears to herald the start of the central section, but in fact this is just a transition; the slow movement really begins eight bars further on at a change in time signature (to 6/4), where the cello is given a theme marked 'with much expression':

Ex. 7.13

The cello sings its heart out, not only in repetitions of the above but in wistful recollections of ideas from the opening *Allegro* – notably Ex. 7.11, whose melodic line is most beautifully varied and extended in a return to a 4/4 metre (bar 141 *et seq.*):

Ex. 7.14

This whole section is one of the great Delian reveries, and the composer is clearly reluctant to break the spell: 'rather slower and more dreamily', he insists at bar 162. The cello sinks drowsily down onto a *pianissimo* F sharp trill, but then begins to shake off its torpor in hesitant recollections of Ex. 7.10. The piano follows its lead, helping to propel the music towards 'Tempo 1' at bar 177.

The concluding section re-examines the material of the opening, compressing its duration in the process by one-third. Delius normally fights shy of offering a mirror impression when he returns to earlier material, but in this case he does not. Apart from two bars at the start, which are placed an octave higher for the cello, the recapitulation, as far as bar 221, is an exact repeat of the exposition up to bar 45. After that, bars 221–44 are a transposed version of bars 45–68, with some variants, before the music heads into a coda at bar 244, which breaks off as the cello reaches up to a searing G natural and falls back to a C sharp (bar 253). Both players then launch into a final 'Maestoso' statement of Ex. 7.10, which exuberantly sweeps all before it, to end on an emphatic D major tonality in the piano and a high D in the treble clef for the cello; the arpeggio chord which Delius notated in the following bar is arguably an unnecessary gesture, and is often omitted.

T HE first performance did not take place until 1918, when Beatrice Harrison and Hamilton Harty[13] played it at the Wigmore Hall on 31 October; then, in 1929, the Sonata became one of the very first of Delius's works to be recorded. In the August issue of *Gramophone* its founder, Compton Mackenzie, candidly admitted that:

> The Delius 'cello sonata, played by Miss Beatrice Harrison and Mr. Harold Craxton, is rather beyond my capacity for enjoyment at present. It wanders about over four sides of two discs with what, to the average man, will sound like a good deal of dull repetition. The recording is splendid, and I hope I shall grow to like it. I don't seem able to extract a sonata from it as yet, and if it isn't a sonata, why call it one? Poets do not write poems in eight lines and call them sonnets. Nobody wants to deny a composer the liberty of experiment, but why should he put new wine in old bottles? However, I expect that this is a perfectly good sonata all the time and that my own stupidity is to blame for not recognising it as such.

Beecham was also gently critical. He had no quarrel with the form of the work, and felt that the cello part was well written – but he thought that it was not the most characteristic Delius, insufficiently spontaneous and warm, and the

---

[13] (Sir Herbert) Hamilton Harty (1879–1941): born in Ireland, he became 'the prince of accompanists', and then a celebrated conductor of the Hallé Orchestra. He was particularly noted for his championship of the music of Berlioz. Throughout his life, he also composed orchestral, chamber and vocal music, much of it Irish-inspired. He was married to the singer Agnes Nicholls.

fact that the cellist plays virtually without pause prevented him from strongly recommending it.[14]

## A DANCE RHAPSODY NO. 2
### (1916: *RT* VI/22; *CE* vol. 26)

ELIUS continued to compose at an incredible speed, for the manuscript of this work is similarly dated 'Spring 1916'. There are no clues as to why he wrote it, and it has to be said that it is very rarely played – perhaps because, despite being just nine minutes long, it is a difficult work to programme. That is a pity, for it repays getting to know, and, as Fenby said, 'it is one of the composer's most under-appreciated achievements.'[15]

This second *Dance Rhapsody* is more concise and tautly constructed than its predecessor. It has a tripartite structure, with the opening section featuring two main ideas; the first is in the tempo of a mazurka, with a characteristic stress on the second beat, as well as an attractive, stylish elegance:

Ex. 7.15

The other main idea, scored for woodwind, brass, celesta and harp, is, by contrast, more forthright, and bursts onto the scene (bar 14) in a quicker tempo:

---

[14] *TB*, p. 181.
[15] Sleevenote for Unicorn-Kanchana UKCD 2071.

Ex. 7.16

Quicker

The opening section, some 150 bars in duration, features these two ideas in a series of continuously varied treatments. The scoring is enhanced by percussion (notably triangle and cymbals), and by celesta and harp; Delius also displays his artistry in shaping engaging solos for the woodwind, and in finding ingenious new harmonisations for Ex. 7.15, of which the following (bars 91–7) is a striking example:

Ex. 7.17

Very gracefully - slower

After a brief return to the opening material in its original form (bar 134 *et seq.*), Delius begins a new paragraph (bar 147) in a more wistful, restrained style:

Ex. 7.18

Tranquillo

This in fact marks the start of the central section of the piece. Ex. 7.18 is treated sequentially: the oboe theme is passed, a minor third higher, to the piccolo and flute (bar 151), then back to the oboe (bar 155), then on to the 1st violins (bar 160), who are joined, an octave lower, by the 2nds (bar 164) – and so on. Gradually, the orchestral texture builds to reach a *forte* climax (bar 176); as it relaxes again, two gentle flights of arpeggios from the harp are answered by *pianissimo* woodwind and brass chords, pre-empting the return of Ex. 7.16, which erupts on celesta, harp and strings (bar 190) with flourishes from triangle and cymbals. Ex. 7.15 now returns (bar 197), but not as an exact repeat: this time, a variant of the original tune, with a feel of C major about it, is given to the 1st oboe, with the accompaniment appearing on *pizzicato* strings, sustained by two bassoons, and the four horns providing the lilting, second beat of the mazurka:

Ex. 7.19

Tranquillo

This third section complements the first, though it is only a third of its length. A quickening of pace from bar 211 onwards, in combination with a thicker instrumental texture, leads to an impressive *fff* climax at bar 234, the brass prominent in a descending stream of chromatic chords, the harmony changing with every quaver.

So far, this dance has been a relatively jovial affair; but now the skies cloud over and darken, and an ominous shadow falls over the scene (Ex. 7.20). The triplet figurations in woodwind and horns are unsettling and lead up to a *sforzando* discord; the muted brass and horn triplet, tinged with oboe, is distinctly sinister, especially when Delius adds to it a roll on a military drum (its first appearance in the score). It is a macabre touch, but, given the date of the score, leads to the obvious conclusion: just as the pre-1914 world has disintegrated, so what began as a light-hearted mazurka, has turned into a Dance of Death. A desolate cor anglais adds its voice (bar 256) to an F minor harmony, spiked with *sforzandi* from bassoons and horns, as the two flutes, in

Ex. 7.20

fourths and fifths, wander up the stave in bewilderment. Further drum rolls underpin distant chords on muted brass and horns. The dancers stand frozen in grief as the music falters and loses its way: it never really recovers, and an attempt at re-establishing an F major tonality in the last five bars remains unconvincing.

As explained below, by the time of the first performance of this *Dance Rhapsody* in 1923 Delius's relationship with Beecham had cooled considerably, and Henry Wood[16] had become his main supporter. Five years earlier, Delius had offered him the work, and he and Jelka visited England from France to discuss it. To Wood's astonishment, as soon as they arrived, Delius 'proceeded to unbutton his waistcoat, shirt and top trouser buttons', and produced twenty-six sheets of manuscript music![17] Although the Armistice had recently been signed, he was obviously concerned at the possibility of having them taken from him by some 'brutal and licentious soldiery' or a customs official. Why the première was delayed is unknown, but Wood eventually conducted it in Queen's Hall in the last night of the Proms on 20 October 1923, in the unlikely first-half company of (apart from Grieg) Humperdinck, Puccini, Schubert, Sullivan, Parry and Weber.[18]

---

[16] Who had been knighted in 1911.

[17] Sir Henry Wood, *My Life of Music* (London: Gollanz, 1938), pp. 306–7.

[18] None of the regular reviewers appears to have thought the concert worth reporting.

## STRING QUARTET
### (1916–17: *RT* VIII/8; *CE* vol. 32)

DELIUS'S inspiration was still flowing fast and furious, for he wrote to C. W. Orr at the end of May (i.e. probably before the Cello Sonata was completed), telling him that he was 'just finishing a string quartet'. The autograph score is, like those of the Cello Sonata and the second *Dance Rhapsody*, dated 'Spring 1916' – so Delius was in fact composing three new works almost simultaneously. He gave the slow movement the title of 'Late Swallows' – he saw the birds around the house at Grez, and mentioned them in a letter to Heseltine: '& the swallows also have returned 3 or 4 days ago, so the weather has become warm and lovely.'[19]

The String Quartet originally had only three movements – the first, third and fourth, as we know them today. The following year, though, Delius substantially revised the slow movement, and added a *scherzo* based, as Fenby identified,[20] on the final bars of all that survives of the *scherzo* from the abandoned 1888 quartet mentioned in Chapter 2.

If Delius ever had any intention of following traditional sonata form in the opening movement, then his is an eccentric interpretation (as in the Double Concerto and Cello Sonata), and one which deviates from the textbooks in several significant ways. For example, it is shaped in two substantial paragraphs, each subdivided into three parts, and there is no separate development section as such. The key structure is also idiosyncratic: the opening theme, which begins on the 2nd violin but soon transfers to the 1st, looks as if it is going to be in C major or A minor, but this is not the case (Ex. 7.21). The presence of G major is soon undermined by passing hints of C, before the tonal centre shifts to D, somewhat obscured by chromaticism; then at Fig. 1+7, a complementary phrase appears – and now we find ourselves in F sharp minor (Ex. 7.22).

The descending figuration of the first four notes, with its rhythm of crotchet – two quavers – crotchet, is derived from the second, third and ninth bars of Ex. 7.21 (the figures marked *x*). Delius makes great play of this during the next twenty or so bars – a prime example of how he often spotlights a rhythmic fragment as a means of propelling the music forwards.

A new idea, initiating a second section, is stated quietly by the 1st violin at Fig. 4+6; in this case, despite its chromatic shape, there is no doubt about its tonality, which is an unequivocal C major (though in orthodox sonata form, given the opening feeling of G, the more likely choice would have been D major) (Ex. 7.23). For a while, Delius examines the possibilities of this theme, notably in conjunction with a figuration that has a fascinating, upward curl (Figs 5+9 and 7+2). Then a new departure is made, marking a third section: this begins (Fig. 7+10) by elaborating a phrase for the 1st violin which descends

---

[19] *FD&PW*, Letter 147. The whole quartet is often wrongly referred to as *Late Swallows*.
[20] *Lloyd*, p. 202.

Ex. 7.21

With animation

Ex. 7.22

Ex. 7.23

Rather quieter

in semitones and owes much to Ex. 7.23. It is given an airy, mostly *pizzicato* accompaniment, and further elaborated in an extended passage marked 'more and more animated' (Fig. 10+7 *et seq.*). (Meanwhile, there has been an unmistakable visit from Ravel in the four bars beginning at Fig. 9-3; Delius might well have known his String Quartet of 1903).

Eventually there is a forceful declaration by all four players (Ex. 7.24). The tension is then released and Delius slips unobtrusively into a note-for-note recapitulation of the opening material (Fig. 14+4), though this time around Ex. 7.21 is given over just to the 1st violin. The second section returns in G (Fig. 19+2) in an abridged version (though allowing time for Ravel to appear again), and then the original third section is recalled in full (Fig. 21+7). It is transposed (Ex. 7.24 is even more compelling a major third higher), and the movement is then rounded off with a brisk coda which ends, surprisingly, on a solemn chord of E minor.

Delius has attempted a bold scheme for this movement which, arguably, does not quite come off: the third section, the least inventive of the three,

Ex. 7.24

**Very deliberately**

rather outstays its welcome, especially when repeated in full; in general, the music lacks a sense of cohesion.

We are on much more straightforward ground with the second movement, which presents no structural complexities. Delius was astute to quarry material from his earlier 1888 quartet for the opening theme; marked 'Quick and lightly', it is worthy of a Mendelssohn *scherzo*, and bounces idiomatically off the strings:

Ex. 7.25

**Quick and lightly**

The 1st violin introduces a subsidiary motif, shaped by the main theme, though in major mode, rather than minor:

Ex. 7.26

This is treated imitatively (Fig. 3+5 *et seq.*) by the cello, the 1st violin and the 2nd violin; the music then pauses briefly over a dominant seventh on C, before setting off again with imitative entries of Ex. 7.25 in A minor, to end (like the previous movement) in an unexpected E minor.

The central section, or trio, introduces a lyrical melody that could well have been composed by Grieg, though perhaps Delius was recalling another of his own youthful compositions?

Ex. 7.27

Cantabile (rather slower)

This charming idea is given to the cello at Fig. 9+4 (accompanied by a version of Ex. 7.25 in the 1st violin). Snatches of the theme are then passed around the other players, before a full version emerges again on the 1st violin (Fig. 18+1) and the trio ends with a quiet but decisive chord of C major.

The opening section is then repeated note for note, apart from a minor change in the distribution of the parts around Fig. 25+6 where the viola, rather than the 1st violin, has the interest. After a minor extension to the final bars, the movement ends, once again, with a *pizzicato* E minor chord.

The third movement, 'Late Swallows', is marked 'Slow and wistfully', and has led an independent life out of context[21] – deservedly so, since it is a deeply affecting piece in its own right. Delius bases the opening and closing sections on a lyrical idea of outstanding beauty: a descending, melodic chain of fourths and fifths, balanced by a gently soaring line, imitating the darting swallows themselves (Ex. 7.28).

Delius's skill in investing Ex. 7.28 with variants and fresh harmonisations is never less than poetic. Even more touching is the central section, with its dreamlike, hypnotic atmosphere evoked through muted *ostinato* quavers (Ex. 7.29).

The pulse changes from a slow triple to duple (Fig. 4+6), as Delius introduces an expressive theme on the 1st violin which belongs to the world of his early American works, *Florida*, *Koanga* and *Appalachia* (Ex. 7.30). This haunting melody is repeated by the 2nd violin (Fig. 5+4) and by the viola (Fig. 6+3.) The music slows down and the vision fades to *pppp*. Six mysterious bars in a 3/2 metre (Fig. 8+1), with hymn-like chordal progressions, provide the link

---

[21] Often being played on its own, and in Eric Fenby's 1963 arrangement for string orchestra (retaining the title). He also similarly arranged the whole quartet as *Sonata for String Orchestra* in 1977.

Ex. 7.28

Ex. 7.29

Ex. 7.30

to a return of the opening material. Delius finds yet more ways of reworking Ex. 7.28 melodically and harmonically, before finally letting the music come to rest in a sixteen-bar coda (Fig. 10+6 *et seq.*), whose sequence of imaginative harmonic progressions finally resolves onto a hushed D major chord.

The fourth movement opens with a quick and vigorous introductory passage containing the seed of an idea (Fig. 1-1) that will germinate later. Its crushed (*acciaccatura*) notes, coupled with modal intervals, have all the earthy quality of folk-music:

Ex.7.31

Two main themes emerge once the music gets under way (Fig. 3-4); the first is introduced by the cello:

Ex. 7.32

**With bright and elastic movement**

The second, not dissimilar in shape or style, is given to the 1st violin (Fig. 5+5):

Ex. 7.33

**Broader**

These two ideas, interspersed with brief interludes, lend the movement the feeling of an exuberant *rondo*. Ex. 7.31 eventually comes into its own (Fig. 11-1) marked *pesante* ('heavily'), after which the music slows down to catch its breath, before setting off again, led by the viola (Fig. 13+2), with a return to Ex. 7.32. The material is developed much as before, and Ex. 7.31 is given the final word, ending the quartet in spirited fashion.

T HE original, three-movement, version had its première in London's Aeolian Hall in 1916, played by the London String Quartet:[22]

> The concert given on November 17 was distinguished because it introduced a new String Quartet by Delius. As might have been expected, this composition is a serious contribution to musical art – the most important, in fact, that has been heard in London during the present season. We will not affect to be able to plumb the depths of the music merely after one hearing. At most we can venture upon a statement of general impressions, and we can but hope that this splendid quartet party will find it possible to repeat the Quartet at an early date. Whatever the ultimate 'placing' of the new work may be, it is certain that it deserves the attention of all who value the highest art. Delius has accustomed us to expect originality and a peculiar idiom that is not readily analysable. But it must be said that in this Quartet the construction and harmonic features are comparatively easy to follow. The first movement is full of fine things in chord contrasts and warmth of expression, and we

---

[22] Of which Albert Sammons, to whom Delius dedicated the Violin Concerto, was the leader.

are conscious of the composer's firm grip of his material. The second movement has unquestioned charm. It is entitled 'Late Swallows,' and the direction of the composer is that it should be played 'with slow, waving movement'. The sad, pining mood which Delius so well realises in 'Sea-drift' is there. The movement seemed too long for the material. The third and last movement has great vitality and thematic interest, but on first hearing it did not leave a distinct impression. With this imperfect criticism we must leave the work at present, and simply hope to whet the curiosity of quartet lovers.

*The Musical Times*, 1 December 1916

Heseltine wrote:

> The performance of your String Quartet last Friday week would have confirmed your darkest doubts as to the musical understanding of English players. It is, of course, always difficult to speak of the rendering of a work with which one is not already familiar. But I think I probably understand your work well enough to be able at any time to perceive the real you peeping out from the adumbrations of unintelligent performers ... the first movement, headed 'with animation' was accorded a monotonous, spiritless, rhythmless performance, about as far removed from animation as any performance could be – while in the lovely 'Late Swallows' section, nothing was audible except the persistent four-note figure which is quite obviously a background. One heard snatches of beautiful melody for a second or two from the other instruments, and then everything was blurred again. The whole rendering resembled nothing so much as an unintelligent pianola-performance where, by reason of the mechanism, every note comes out with equal strength and only the top part is really heard! It was horrible to hear such beautiful music smothered ...[23]

to which Delius replied:

> I had to smile at your description of the string quartet performance – I have always had my doubts about S [Albert Sammons][24] as a musician – you were very keen on him in London at the time my Sonata was being played – What you say about the quartet is quite right – The figure which you noticed so persistently is marked – ppp sotto voce – The melody & harmony ought to be heard most. However all my works have been very difficult to *accoucher* ... Hard frost up to 22° Centigrade & Sun – not a cloud ...[25]

---

[23] *FD&PW*, Letter 156.

[24] See below.

[25] *FD&PW*, Letter 157. Heseltine really did dislike the London String Quartet, for in a letter to Delius some eighteen months later he said, 'I have neither heard nor seen any work of yours since the String Quartet was raped by that lecherous party of players in London': *FD&PW*, Letter 160.

It seems that the revised work was heard for the first time on 27 May 1917, in France. Delius told Heseltine that 'I have rewritten my string quartet & added a scherzo – heard it in Paris – there was a little too much double stopping – I think it is now good.'[26] Who played it and where, however, is unknown; very probably it was a group of Delius's French friends. The first time the revised version was heard in London was on 10 February 1919, again at the Aeolian Hall with the London String Quartet.

## VIOLIN CONCERTO
### (1916: *RT* VII/6; *CE* vol. 30)

IN a letter to Heseltine in October 1916, Delius said, 'I am writing a Violin Concerto now.'[27] As Jelka's letter to Marie Clews on 20 January the next year[28] contains the first reference to *Eventyr*, Delius had presumably finished the concerto before Christmas. That those two mentions of it to Heseltine seem to be Delius's only 'advance notice' of its appearance is typical – he liked to keep these things to himself. Although there is no evidence of what initially spurred him to write it, it must surely have been a combination of his own love of the instrument from the days of his lessons with Mr Bauerkeller and then Hans Sitt, and May Harrison's playing.

As in the Double Concerto, Delius prefers not to divide his thoughts into separate movements, but instead to set out his material in one, unbroken span of three sections, A–B–A, followed by a fourth, which is linked thematically to what has come before, and which serves as an extended coda. (The Cello Concerto, written only a few years later, also follows this scheme.)

Two decisive bars from the strings serve as the briefest of introductions:

Ex. 7.34

Then, in the third bar, the soloist plunges straight in (Ex. 7.35). Delius never liked to keep his soloist waiting, and this no-nonsense gesture gives the work an appealing sense of immediacy. In Ex. 7.34, the manner in which the stress is placed on the second beat of the bar is characteristic of several of the

---

[26] Ibid., Letter 159.

[27] *Letters*, Letter 422. He said it again ten days later: see *FD&PW*, Letter 153.

[28] *Letters 2*, p. 176.

Ex. 7.35

concerto's themes.[29] For example, the interval of a descending perfect fourth at the beginning of bar 2 of Ex. 7.34, emphasised on the second beat, finds a counterpart in the stressed E natural of the diminished fourth in bar 5 of Ex. 7.35. Moreover, the initial violin entry is in itself a fertile breeding ground for subsequent ideas; for example, the rhythmic pattern in the second bar of Ex. 7.35 (the figure marked *x*) recurs as an ingredient of much of the melodic material.

Two further ideas appear in quick succession and though, at this stage, they pass swiftly by, as fleeting melodic fragments, nevertheless they are important. Both are introduced by the soloist in a swaying 12/8 pulse:

Ex. 7.36

Ex. 7.37

Delius makes much play of these motifs, before Ex. 7.35 returns 'With vigour' (Fig. 3+1) in octave unison in flutes, oboe, cor anglais and clarinets, as well as being restated by the soloist. The soloist then goes on to introduce yet another new idea, one which folds over on itself chromatically:

Ex. 7.38

[29] Deryck Cooke traced the growth of the whole work from just these first two bars: see his 'Delius & Form: A Vindication', *The Musical Times* 103 (1962), 392–3 and 460–5; reprinted in *Companion*, pp. 249–62, at p. 249.

By now, Delius has offered us a generous – some might say bewildering – range of themes, most of them only a bar or two in length. But this is Delius's way: he prefers to juggle several ideas at once. Most of them are barely stated before they begin to evolve and change shape, and the bridge passage which follows at Fig. 5+2 ('rather quicker'), is a case in point: it derives from Ex. 7.38 and is evidence of just how organic this concerto is.

So far the orchestra has been kept in the background, strings and minimal woodwind supplying the harmonic context; there has been no real *tutti*. Now we have one (Fig. 8+1) as Ex. 7.35 bursts in, backed by full brass and followed by a virtuoso semiquaver flourish for the soloist. The tempo broadens, and the mood relaxes, as the soloist muses on Ex. 7.38. But then, Ex. 7.34 thrusts itself vigorously to the forefront, in octave unison in the woodwind (Fig. 10+1). It is immediately followed by a new, fanfare-like motif, 'Maestoso', from the brass:

Ex. 7.39

This idea is taken up by the violin, combined with some strenuous passage-work, including a series of mounting octave triplets, snatches of Ex. 7.36, and the figure marked *x* in Ex. 7.35. But the heat begins to go out of the music and the tempo slackens, as upward arpeggios from harp and woodwind, backed by the strings on a quiet F major chord with added sixth of the scale, bring the first part of the concerto to a close.

The central portion of the work, marked 'Slower' (Fig. 12+1), is an extended poetic rhapsody based on two new melodic ideas. The first, a warmly lyrical theme in 6/4, is introduced by the soloist to an accompaniment of muted strings, with a counter-melody on the 1st horn (Ex. 7.40).

The flurry of semiquavers in bars 3 and 4, like a vocal melisma, recalls a similar characteristic of figure *x* in Ex. 7.35 and of Ex. 7.37 (see also Ex. 7.41, below) – once again, evidence of significant thematic unity. Some beautiful interplay between the soloist and the orchestra follows; note especially the delicately swirling triplets on the 1st flute (Fig. 13+3) and the return of the 1st horn's counter-melody at Fig. 13+5. With a change of time signature to 4/4 (Fig. 14+1), the violin presents the second main theme of this slow section, which has the characteristic dotted rhythm of the 'Scotch snap' (of which there are notable examples elsewhere in Delius – e.g. the third movement of *North Country Sketches*, and the second movement of Violin Sonata no. 3) (Ex. 7.41).

Ex. 7.40

Ex. 7.41

The more lyrical second half of the theme is complemented with exquisite writing for the 2nd horn and the harp; its semiquaver melisma also links it to Exs 7.35 and 7.40. Extensive restatements of both main themes follow but, as usual with Delius, the harmonisations and accompaniments are never mere repetitions. Subdued, muted strings provide a background not only for the violin, but also for solos from woodwind, horns and harp, the sort of writing Delius excelled at. Sometimes he reverses the procedure, as at Fig. 19+1, where he gives Ex. 7.41 to the 1st violins, together with a glorious counter-melody for the soloist.

Shortly after this (Fig. 20+1), the violin begins a series of arpeggios and virtuoso double stopping (i.e. two or more notes sounded together), at first unaccompanied, but soon backed by the strings (now unmuted), who are directed to 'follow the soloist'. This passage, the nearest the concerto comes to having a cadenza, is relatively extended, lasting for some thirty bars. It even introduces a new idea which Delius recycled from the first version of his Piano Concerto:

Ex. 7.42

Elgar has a similar accompanied cadenza in the finale of his Violin Concerto, completed five years earlier, though it is impossible to say whether Delius was influenced by this or not (or, indeed, whether he had even heard the work.) Here, the cadenza culminates for the soloist in a pair of high-altitude trills, with the two flutes cooing like doves in chromatic thirds, before the spell is abruptly broken with the return of Ex. 7.35, *forte*, for strings, horns and brass.

The material of the opening section is recalled in the same order as before, though this time around it is compressed to two-thirds of its original length. Neither is this a mirror-image in terms of keys or orchestral accompaniment, and Delius feels free to vary both, as a comparison of the relevant pages in the score will clearly show. When everything has been reviewed, the soloist vigorously states Ex. 7.35 in double-stopped sixths, which are aggressively interrupted by the full orchestra with the 'Maestoso' chordal tag of Ex. 7.39, and then the violin twice takes flight in ascending broken octaves, the second matched by the orchestra, shaking its fist, so to speak, in two emphatic exclamation marks (Fig. 31+5). There is a dramatic pause, and a double bar-line. We might reasonably expect a brief coda now, to wrap up the work. But this is not the way Delius intends to proceed.

Instead, he begins what is effectively a new section, marked 'Allegretto' and with a time signature of 12/8. At first the violin dances along in semiquavers, decorating a melodic line in woodwind and *pizzicato* strings which is not directly related to anything that has come before. After eight bars, the time signature changes back to 4/4 and the soloist presents a distinctive new idea (Fig. 33+1) − a surprise, coming, as it does, so far on in the concerto. It is a yearning, heartfelt theme of great beauty, with clear affinities in the shape of its line (especially in the semiquaver melisma) to Ex. 7.40:

Ex. 7.43

Delius adds his fingerprint of an upward triplet tied to a longer note value (Fig. 33+6) before the 12/8 metre returns, this time providing a perfect frame for the oscillating intervals of Ex. 7.43. A more impassioned statement of the latter returns in 4/4 (Fig. 35+1), but it is the 12/8 metre that dominates for the next few pages, involving the soloist in some strenuous, and occasionally ornamented, semiquaver passage-work. This finally slows up and broadens into the true coda of the concerto (Fig. 41+1), which draws its main material from Ex. 7.35, with the soloist singing eloquently, cushioned by the strings, and decorated with touches of solo woodwind arabesques. The music gradually winds down, but seems reluctant to take its leave, until the solo violin finally ends its serenade with a flourish of semiquavers, finishing on a sustained high A natural, against a hushed string chord of F major (with an added sixth) and a delicate *pianissimo* triplet figuration from the 1st flute.

I N the light of what he had said to Heseltine about the String Quartet's première, it is curious that Delius not only dedicated the Violin Concerto to Albert Sammons,[30] but asked him to give the first performance – which he did at a Royal Philharmonic Society concert in Queen's Hall on 30 January 1919, with the young Adrian Boult[31] conducting Delius's music for the first time. Largely self-taught, Sammons was at the centre of English music from 1899 (when, aged thirteen, he became the leader of the Earls Court Exhibition Orchestra) until illness forced him to stop playing in 1950. First gaining great experience in the light music world, he was drawn away to 'serious' music in 1908 by Beecham, who was taking tea at the Waldorf Hotel when he heard Sammons leading Ernest Bucalossi's Orchestra in the last movement of the Mendelssohn Violin Concerto. Afterwards Beecham sent him a note saying 'Splendid, but tempo too fast.' Sammons returned it, having written on it, 'Thanks, I will play it again a little later on.' On the strength of that, he was soon invited to become the leader of the Beecham Symphony Orchestra; he held the post for five years and served Beecham brilliantly.[32] A consummate technician and superb artist, he had a fulfilling career: before joining Beecham he had been the leader of the Casino Orchestra of Dieppe under the young conductor Pierre Monteux,[33] who then, just before the Great War, appointed him as leader of the orchestra for Diaghilev's Ballets Russes. He played Elgar's Violin Concerto more than a hundred times, took part in the first performances of Elgar's String Quartet and Piano Quintet, and enjoyed a partnership with the pianist William Murdoch for twenty-five years.

In the event, Delius was cock-a-hoop – writing to Clews:

Since I came to England [in September 1918] I have had four first performances of works completed during the war ... The success has been ever increasing & was quite enormous when the Violin Concerto was given last Thursday – Everybody musical in London was present (a

---

[30] Albert Edward Sammons, CBE (1886–1957), on whom see further below.

[31] (Sir) Adrian Cedric Boult, CH (1889–1983): he became one of the most distinguished English conductors, supreme in English music (including much Delius, but particularly that of Elgar and Vaughan Williams). In 1930 he was appointed the BBC's Director of Music to form the BBC Symphony Orchestra, and in his later years he enjoyed a strong relationship with the London Philharmonic Orchestra.

[32] *AMC*, p. 82.

[33] Pierre Monteux (1875–1964): he would become a justly celebrated and loved French conductor in Europe and America.

very big audience) & it was really quite an event. Albert Sammons the violinist played it most beautifully – Even the criticisms are splendid[34] – Am I becoming popular!! beware! beware! However what is really nice is that we are hearing a lot of music & a lot of my own music & I am realising that the war was not a barren & lost epoch for me ...[35]

Jelka wrote to Grainger's wife, Ella, that 'There was an enormous audience and the piece was awfully well received.'[36]

The audience were indeed very appreciative – 'they all shouted for Fred, who was tremendously cheered.'[37] The March issue of *The Musical Standard* carried one of the most enthusiastic reviews of any Delius première:

The concerto (and its creator) had a most deservedly enthusiastic reception. A wealth of melodious themes supported by a harmonic structure of much freshness and beauty are the outstanding characteristics of this beautiful work. One never had the least sensation of straining after 'effects' in the orchestration either – the impression produced was that the conception of all three, melody, harmony and 'colour,' had been simultaneous throughout. The themes are clearly stated and developed with the accustomed skill and individuality of the composer. The concerto will assuredly be included in the repertoire of violinists who are artists as well as virtuosi. It is gracefully written for the solo instrument, and is, above all else, absolute music. As it died away ppp (the voice of the flute is the last 'still, small voice') I sighed involuntarily; just as one feels how mundane the world is upon awakening from a beautiful dream.

*Musical Opinion* was almost equally fulsome:

The concerto is in one movement, but the sections vary much in their moods, and the thematic material is extremely beautiful and characteristic of its composer. Mr. Sammons played the many beautiful singing passages with which the concerto abounds as only he can. The work created a deep impression, and we hope that it will be repeated at the first opportunity.

March 1919

In *The Musical Times*, however, the author and critic Alfred Kalisch wrote:

This work breaks fresh ground in several respects. It is in one movement, and the solo instrument is employed almost continuously. Of development there is little. The work is a long soliloquy by the soloist, against a delicately-beautiful harmonic background. The mood is perhaps too consistently reflective for a work of such length, and we felt, too, that

---

[34] By now, Delius knew what usually to expect from them!

[35] Letter 443.

[36] Letter 441, n. 1.

[37] Jelka Delius to Marie Clews, 4 February 1919: *Letters 2*, p. 215.

a little more rest for the soloist would have conduced to variety. He was sometimes kept busy without any proportionate result. For example, the section in which the orchestra plays a kind of dance measure was not helped by the somewhat fidgety figuration given to the solo instrument. But when all is said, there remains the impression of a work full of singular and often haunting beauty. Mr. Albert Sammons played it as if he loved it, and Mr. Adrian Boult and the orchestra provided the right delicate and flexible accompaniment. The composer received an ovation.

1 March 1919

This is quite typical of Kalish's reviews of Delius. Although he had written the programme note for the first performance of *The Song of the High Hills*, and might therefore have been expected to be sympathetic towards the music, he often seemed grumpy and only partly approving when he reviewed Delius performances. Even a year later he was still distinctly cool:

Mr. Sammons played Delius's Concerto. It does not improve on acquaintance: The lack of anything like a broad melodic phrase for the soloist makes itself almost painfully felt. The constant figuration for the violin ends by sounding almost fussy. The atmospheric beauty of the music is, however, undeniable, and the last pages appeal to the heart. One wonders whether Delius had heard the ending of 'Don Quixote' before he wrote it.

*The Musical Times*, 1 March 1920

JELKA summed up 1916 in a letter to Marie Clews: 'Fred's work is going so well'.[38] Indeed, with the Cello Sonata, the String Quartet, the second *Dance Rhapsody* and the Violin Concerto, it was one of the most prolific, and happiest, years of his life. The beginning of 1917 also found him hard at work, but in the middle of the year he had another bout of depression, as well as trouble with his legs and feet; luckily a 'cure' in Normandy set him right again, and one day at the end of July he walked 10 kilometres.[39] Before those troubles, however, he had finished yet another sizeable orchestral work, dedicated to Sir Henry Wood.

---

[38] *Letters 2*, p. 162.

[39] Ibid., p. 176.

## EVENTYR
## (ONCE UPON A TIME)
### (1917: *RT* VI/23; *CE* vol. 26)

I T was now thirty-six years since Delius had first been to Norway, and it was probably on his third visit, in 1887 – when he went for pure enjoyment, not to recover from the *ennui* of a business trip[40] – that he became deeply interested in the country's culture and literature. Since 1888, when he had taken the words of his melodrama *Paa Vidderne* from Ibsen's poem of the same name, the writers Peter Christen Asbjørnsen[41] and Jørgen Engebretsen Moe[42] had published many of the country's fairy tales and much of its folklore. Delius became completely fascinated by them, and a good many years later they provided the inspiration for this fifteen-minute orchestral 'Ballad for Orchestra', as he originally subtitled it. The Norwegian word 'eventyr' means 'fairy tale' or 'folk tale', but these tales are far from the cosy bedtime stories that the work's subtitle might imply:

> Asbjørnsen's "fairies" are the Underjordiske ... the supernatural humanoid creatures ranging from dwarves and brownies to trolls, witches and giants, whose influence on the peasants in whose lives they intervene is sometimes benign but more usually malevolent.[43]

Moreover, the Norwegian concept of 'fairy tale' or 'folk tale' is not simply something of the imagination, but the telling, centuries later, of things that – so strong is the influence of the genre – it was still believed had actually happened.

When *Eventyr* was performed in Beecham's 1929 Delius Festival, the programme book included this, written by Jelka (and which Delius said was 'quite perfect and expressed exactly what he had meant'):

> 'Eventyr' is not based on any particular story of Asbjørnsen; it is a resumé-impression of the book ... the old legends still quite alive with lonely peasants, hunters and mountaineers. These people have a naive belief in the 'Underjordiske' (the Underearthly ones), Trolls, Heinzelmännchen, hobgoblins; who either help the humans or, if provoked, become very revengeful. A boy alone in a forest would imagine he heard them trotting after him, and get very frightened. At a wedding or Xmas meal a little dish of cream porridge is put on the loft for these underearthly ones, or else they might be offended – they have been known to fetch girls away (even the bride of a wedding) in such cases and dance with them furiously till they fall down unconscious. A hunter's luck would depend on their good

---

[40] He went walking in the vast mountain plateau to the east of Bergen, the Hardangervidda.

[41]  Peter Christian Asbjørnsen (1812-1885): Writer and scholar.

[42]  Jørgen Engebretsen Moe (1811-8820): Bishop and poet

[43] Barrie Iliffe, '*Eventyr* and the Fairy Tales in Delius', in *MA&L*, pp. 273–89, at p. 276.

or bad will. In the queer noises at night in lonely huts and woods you would imagine you heard the hordes of these mysterious beings galloping along in the distance.

Though we will never know which specific folk legends were at the back of Delius's mind when he composed the work, it is so pictorial and vivid (probably the nearest thing he wrote to a Straussian, or even more aptly, a Sibelian tone poem) that it strongly suggests a dramatic narrative. But the most useful approach to the score is not to speculate on its hidden sources (after all, Delius could have told us, if he had wanted to), but instead to make sense of it in more general terms. One way of interpreting it, followed below, is to see it as a struggle between good and evil: between wilful malevolence and simple, homely virtue.

A sense of menace undoubtedly pervades the opening pages, which are marked 'Slow and mysteriously'. Cellos and double basses whisper a fragment of what sounds like a melancholy folksong; they are accompanied by brooding bassoons and horns, and answered by sombre woodwind and a single timpani stroke:

Ex. 7.44

Ex. 7.44 is repeated a fourth lower, this time provoking strange *pizzicato* triplets from the strings. But then, quite unexpectedly, this ominous introduction gives way (Fig. 1-15) to a passage evoking a far more wholesome atmosphere:

Ex. 7.45

As the strings continue on their untroubled, lyrical way, dancing semiquaver triplet figurations quietly insinuate themselves into the texture (on the 3rd bassoon at Fig. 1-3; then, two bars later, on the piccolo and cor anglais; and on the oboe and 1st bassoon.) The context, however, suggests that mischief-making, rather than innocent pleasure, is really what this motif signifies:

Ex. 7.46

Appended to Ex. 7.46, is an angular little motif, like a burst of mocking laughter; it rears its head in an aggressive *crescendo* in the piccolo and the 1st clarinet, echoed by lower strings and then, more fully scored, in other woodwind instruments, as if to say, 'watch out, all is not quite what it seems':

Ex. 7.47

This unsettling interruption is ignored by the strings (Fig. 2+3) as they embark on another lyrical idea, *molto tranquillo*:

Ex. 7.48

Meanwhile, Ex. 7.46 has been chattering away sarcastically in the background; now Ex. 7.47 breaks in rudely on cellos, basses and strident woodwind (Fig. 2+12 *et seq.*). The strings are forced to abandon their comforting thoughts, as a violent interlude erupts (Fig. 3-5 *et seq.*), suggesting panic-stricken flight from evil spirits and other unseen horrors. Scurrying passage-work, insistent groups of *marcato* quavers, and galloping, dotted rhythms in woodwind and brass, result in a huge climax (Fig. 4+1), marked *fff*, and with percussion well to the fore (eleven instruments are specified): the xylophone plays an important role, cutting through the texture with a brittle motif of four semiquavers

(Fig. 3-2, subsequently much repeated), which could be taken as the scornful laughter of malignant trolls or goblins.

The mayhem subsides with a variant of Ex. 7.47 (Fig. 4+5) in the bass clarinet, 3rd bassoon and cellos, beneath pulsing bassoons and horns. A return to previous tranquillity is promised by Ex. 7.48 in the strings (Fig. 5-15) but this is short-lived. Soon the dance rhythms of Ex. 7.46 are heard again in strings and woodwind, a sign of temptation, significantly marked 'pleading' in the cor anglais (Fig. 5-1). Then, after a sudden shriek (Fig. 5+5), comes a second, far more extensive outbreak of general mayhem, which continues, with only an occasional respite, until Fig. 13+5.

It is a three-pronged attack: the first onslaught is launched by stomping rhythms in harps and *pizzicato* double basses (Fig. 5+7) as Ex. 7.47 breaks out mockingly in the xylophone and is echoed by the strings and woodwind. Ex. 7.44 returns (Fig. 6+1), not diffidently, as before, but loudly and 'very broad' in bassoons, cellos and double basses, reinforced by trombones and tuba (Fig. 7-3). Chattering triplets in woodwind, horns and trumpets are transformed into the frenzied dancing rhythms of Ex. 7.46, sounding more than ever like a cruel parody. The full force of the orchestra is unleashed, Delius marking the score 'Furiously' (Fig. 8+1).

Though the music suddenly quietens down, the second episode of terror is about to begin, the pulse changing to three-in-a-bar (Fig. 8+7), as *ostinato* triplet figurations in strings and then woodwind suggest some sort of chase or pursuit. Here it is feasible to pinpoint a specific piece of folklore in Asbjørnsen, namely the tale of *The Widow's Son*, featuring a lad who is escaping on a magic horse from a band of malevolent trolls, when he hears his pursuers shouting out behind him; this is exactly what happens in *Eventyr*. As the music gallops on, there is a wild shout of 'Hei' by men's voices at Fig. 9+4 (according to the score, these must number twenty, and should be 'behind', 'outside', and 'invisible', though for practical purposes, musicians on the platform are given the role). After further frenzied pursuit, the cry is repeated (Fig. 11-5).

After the second shout, the music slows right down, though its mood is still stormy: the pounding rhythms heard earlier at Fig. 3+2 return (Fig. 11+5), together with an aggressive reiteration of Ex. 7.47 in the strings, *fortissimo*. After a brief respite, the musical fury is unleashed for the third time (Fig. 12-3) in much the same manner as before, though the climax (Fig. 13-1) is marked, even more shatteringly, *ffff*.

But then a new force, essentially a benign manifestation, appears to predominate in a passage marked 'Maestoso' (Fig. 13+5), characterised by downward streams of crotchet chords in celesta, harps and strings, and with lyrical lines of quavers in the woodwind, set against a background of tolling tubular bells. The brass enter assertively (Fig. 14+1), and shortly afterwards the music dies down again, disturbed only by eerie twitterings in woodwind, celesta and violins (Fig. 15+2). A bell motif resounds four times in D flat (Fig. 15+5), though Delius avoids using the real thing, preferring an imitation of greater resonance by lower woodwind, horns, cymbals, harps and lower strings.

There are some vaguely menacing background noises, including a muffled roll of a military drum (cf. the ending of the *Dance Rhapsody* no. 2), but suddenly the simple, homely warmth of Ex. 7.45 returns (Fig. 16+3). A single chuckle from the 3rd bassoon (quoting Ex. 7.46) cuts loudly and irreverently into the texture (Fig. 17+4), but is ignored, as Ex. 7.48 returns (Fig. 17+7), at first 'very quietly' but then triumphantly in a defiant *fortissimo* climax (Fig. 18+2). Though the final pages contain vaguely disturbing elements, including mysterious semiquaver flickerings, the forces of evil have effectively vanished and the work ends tranquilly with a solo cello plucking an upward F major arpeggio. The nightmares are over – at least until bed-time tomorrow ...

B EECHAM'S father, Sir Joseph, had died in October 1916, leaving a huge mountain of debts. He owed the Duke of Bedford £1.75 million for his extremely complicated, £2-million purchase of eighteen-and-a-half acres of Covent Garden (including The Royal Opera House), and over £79,000 to the Inland Revenue for underpayment of income tax. In addition, the first instalment of death duties on his estate was £190,000.[44] The War was having a serious effect on the fortunes of the pill business, and the result was that between 1916 and 1920 Beecham had to spend increasing amounts of time trying to right his financial position. His conducting engagements fell and fell, so that whereas in 1915 he conducted Delius's music on twenty-five occasions, in 1919 he did so on just three.[45] Furthermore, in 1919 Beecham still owed Delius £300, the last instalment of his payment for the works he had bought in 1915. It is not therefore surprising that the Deliuses became increasingly disenchanted with him, and that Henry Wood had become their new conductor of choice. *Eventyr* was therefore given its first performance under him, in Queen's Hall on 11 January 1919 – another occasion when a manuscript score and parts were used. After the concert the couple was over the moon,[46] Delius writing to Grainger a week later and saying that Wood 'gave a ripping good performance & took no end of trouble with it'.[47] Furthermore, for once, *The Musical Times* critic definitely enjoyed some Delius:

> The hall was crowded on January 11, many people being turned away. One would like to think that music was the main attraction, but it was evident that the majority had come to greet Madame Calve, and to revive memories of past operatic joys ... The musical interest of the concert was centred in the first performance of an Orchestral Ballad by Delius, 'Once upon a time,' based on Norwegian folk-lore, but with no definite programme. The Ballad is highly imaginative in a fantastic way, and is beautifully scored. Thanks to some thrilling climaxes, it may possibly

---

[44] *Lucas*, pp. 111–12 and 138.

[45] *WS&SS*, p. 25.

[46] Letter 441, n. 1.

[47] Letter 442.

achieve the popularity that the composer's works have so far escaped. Mr. Delius was present, and had a very cordial reception.

1 February 1919

Fourteen years later, after Beecham was well back 'in the Delian fold', another (unidentified) critic also enjoyed himself, writing after Beecham's performance on 22 November 1933 that 'Delius's "Eventyr" had never sounded so beautiful.'

## TO BE SUNG OF A SUMMER NIGHT ON THE WATER
(1917: *RT* IV/4; *CE* vol. 17)

T HE last time Delius had written any small scale *a cappella* choral music was some ten years earlier – the *Three Part Songs* (see above, Chapter 5). Now, however, a few months into 1917, he turned to the medium again and wrote two wordless 'pieces of vocal impressionism [which] are, in their own way, brilliant and without blemish'. [48] After the première of *The Song of the High Hills*, Delius and Jelka always held Kennedy Scott's choir-training abilities in high esteem, so these little gems were dedicated to 'Kennedy Scott and his Oriana Choir', [49] and first sung at their concert in the Aeolian Hall on 28 June, 1921; before he and Jelka left for a holiday in Norway, Delius went to a rehearsal, and he later wrote to Heseltine: '*you must hear them* – to realise what one can do with a good chorus'. [50]

In the first song, Delius divides his tenors and basses, so as to create a six-part texture; in the absence of a text, he instructs the performers to 'sing on vowel "uh" as in "love" with very loose mouth, almost closed in the *pianissimo*, but which should be gradually opened or shut according as more or less tone is wanted ...' The mood is subdued throughout, apart from a single rise and fall in dynamic about half way through; the musical material stems entirely from the opening four bars (Ex. 7.49).

The soprano line (together with a slightly varied version of the initial group of quavers) is passed from voice to voice, each entry coloured by a different harmonisation in Delius's most expressively chromatic manner. Ex. 7.50, occurring towards the end of the piece (bars 17–20), is a fine example of his ingenuity.

---

[48] Donald Mitchell, 'Delius: The Choral Music', *Tempo* 26 (December 1953), pp. 8–17.

[49] The choir was in fact the Oriana Madrigal Society. Formed by Scott in 1905, it immediately became London's foremost hand-picked chamber choir, singing (*inter alia*) a large quantity of contemporary partsongs. Although, as was well known to the orchestras he conducted, Beecham had absolutely no voice, he took part in its first concert, as a bass, and occasionally wrote its programme notes. The Society continued to give chamber concerts under its own name until 1922, but was enlarged into The Philharmonic Choir in October 1919 (see above, Chapter 6).

[50] *FD&PW*, Letter 263.

Ex. 7.49

Ex. 7.50

Delius makes a practice of dividing the melodic line between different voices; as Ex. 7.50 demonstrates, he gives the first bar to the 1st basses, then hands the tune on to the 1st and 2nd tenors, then to the contraltos and 2nd tenors, and finally back to the 1st and 2nd tenors. The ending of the song is magical, the voices 'dying away to the end' and coming to rest in B flat, with the sixth note of the scale high up in the 1st tenor part.

The companion piece to this exquisite inspiration is in complete contrast; marked 'Gaily but not quick', it is in the style of a folksong. Delius keeps his male voices divided, and adds a separate part for a solo tenor, who is given very specific instructions: 'The solo voice should sing to syllables as indicated, introducing delicate *staccati* at appropriate places (which are generally where the syllable "luh" is put).' Apart from 'luh', the other syllables are a mixture of 'lah', 'hah', 'ha', and 'ah'. As in the first song, Delius gives a fresh twist to the accompaniment at each repetition of the tune, sometimes in quite sharp and astringent harmony, as in this version (bars 8–9) with the tune in the minor (Ex. 7.51).

These two partsongs prove that Delius, so often responsive and sensitive to language, did not necessarily need a text to inspire him.

Ex. 7.51

THE War continued to be a worry. Everything, particularly coal and wood,[51] was in short supply, and there were regular air raids on Paris – only some forty miles away from Grez. The Deliuses therefore began thinking about moving again, and by the end of 1917 they had planned to go to London – possibly to Balfour Gardiner's house. They were, however, thwarted, as in January 1918 Delius's health suddenly became a cause for concern again – a nervous condition and eye trouble – and he spent a while at a sanatorium on the outskirts of Paris. Returning to Grez in March, and feeling much better, he began writing again, but quite soon the decision was made to go to Biarritz for at least several months, and on 5 June they were there. Happily, Delius's condition improved, inspiration returned again, and the result was two further orchestral works.

---

[51] Letter 428, n.

## A SONG BEFORE SUNRISE

### (1918: *RT* VI/24; *CE* vol. 27a)

G IVEN the difficulties that the Deliuses were having to face during this
period, it is a miracle that he produced this tuneful, six-minute work,
needing only a modest-sized orchestra. Dedicated to Philip Heseltine, it is one
of Delius's happiest inspirations.

'Freshly' is the unpretentious marking at the head of the score, and it is all
that a conductor really needs to know: this music speaks eloquently for itself in
evoking the dawn of a new day. The opening idea is given to the 1st violins in a
buoyant 6/8 tempo:

Ex. 7.52

This is richly harmonised in a continuous stream of chords by the rest of the
strings, divided into nine parts in all, whilst woodwind arabesques decorate the
melodic line:

Ex. 7.53

A few bars further on (A+3), the 1st violins introduce a new idea:

Ex. 7.54

Snatches of Ex. 7.53 are neatly combined with this, as the music heads towards
a glorious outburst of sunny C major (B+5), illuminating a new melody on the
2nd violins, violas and cellos, placed three octaves apart:

Ex. 7.55

The violins take up the tune (B+9), as do the cellos ('broadly') at C-5, after which the music enters a more thoughtful, central section, no longer propelled purely by a chordal underlay, but inspired instead by an airy semiquaver figuration, first given to the two flutes (C+1) and subsequently featured by each woodwind instrument in turn:

Ex. 7.56

A variation of this is given to the strings (E-1 *et seq.*), and yet another version given to flutes and bassoons, scored in perfect fourths and marked 'Slower' (E+8). Shortly afterwards, a series of falling minor thirds on flutes and bassoons once more (E+11) suggest distant bird calls before a return to 'Tempo 1' (F+1), with an exact repeat of the opening section. After thirty-four bars (I +1) it diverges into a coda: sweeping arpeggios lead to a final statement of Ex. 7.55 in the cellos; in the final bars, bird-like chirrups from the woodwind break off abruptly, as the vision fades.

Perhaps surprisingly given its very modest proportions, the work had to wait five years for a performance, but it was eventually given by Wood – his third Delian première – in a Promenade Concert in Queen's Hall on 19 September 1923, only a month before *Dance Rhapsody* no. 2. Two days later *The Times* merely said that it was played.

## POEM OF LIFE AND LOVE
### (1918: *RT* VI/25; *CE* supp. vol. 1)

I N July 1918 Delius told Heseltine 'I am just finishing my new work – 'The Poem of Life and Love',[52] and a fortnight later Jelka said to Marie Clews that 'Fred has been working quite splendidly and has quite finished his Symphony'.[53] It was not, of course, a symphony,[54] but a symphonic poem, and he had not actually finished it – at least not to his own satisfaction. He either tinkered on with it, or simply put it aside, and well over two years later, on 1 December 1920, he wrote to Hertzka, the managing director of Universal, saying that it was not ready yet. Over a number of visits to Grez in the following years, Balfour Gardiner arranged the manuscript as far as it went for two pianos – it was probably about three-quarters finished. Nevertheless, Delius seems to have thought about it from time to time, because on the very afternoon of Eric Fenby's arrival to act as Delius's amanuensis, on 10 October 1928 (as to which see below, Chapter 8), Delius asked him to look at the manuscript of the full score and show him how he would finish it – a real baptism of fire! Fenby worked for the rest of the day, but nothing was said the following morning – because then Delius wanted him to look at the piano part of the Cello Sonata, as the celebrated cellist Alexandre Barjansky[55] was coming to stay; that evening, they duly played it together, and Delius was delighted. About a week later, Gardiner arrived, and, 'We played the arrangement [of *Poem of Life and Love*] through several times, but Delius merely thanked us and made no comment.'[56] Some while later, Delius asked Fenby to give his honest opinion of the piece – which, full of trepidation but encouraged by Jelka, he duly did:

> I soon warmed to my difficult task, and found myself criticising the work fearlessly. My first unfavourable comment electrified him, but it was not long before he saw my view and agreed with my opinion.[57]

A little later, Delius asked him to 'select all the good material, develop it and make a piece out of it yourself'[58] – and those passages eventually became part of *A Song of Summer*. It therefore seems logical to combine the description of the *Poem of Life and Love* with that of *A Song of Summer* in the next chapter.

Edited for performance by Robert Threlfall, *Poem of Life and Love* was first heard in a BBC broadcast by the BBC in 1999, with Norman Del Mar

---

[52] *FD&PW*, Letter 164.

[53] Letter 434, n. 1.

[54] See Chapter 4, n. 19.

[55] Alexandre Barjansky (1883–1961): a Russian cellist who greatly impressed with his playing of Delius's works.

[56] *Fenby 1*, p. 28.

[57] Ibid., p. 35.

[58] *Lloyd*, p. 161.

conducting the BBC Symphony Orchestra, and it seems that its only public performance to date has been in Suffolk, by the Haverhill Sinfonia, conducted by Kevin Hill, on 17 March 2002. It was, however, recorded by David Lloyd-Jones and The Royal Scottish National Orchestra in September 2010.[59]

D ELIUS and Jelka had not long settled into a routine in Biarritz before they learned that the house in Grez had been requisitioned by the French Army – and when they returned in mid-August they found that the officers billeted there had caused very considerable damage, and stolen many of the contents. Delius wrote a letter to the Clewses[60] describing the worst acts of the vandalism, and the dreadful condition in which the place has been left. So it was back to England again – this time staying for September in Henry Wood's house in St John's Wood, and then taking a flat at 44 Belsize Park Gardens over the winter and into the middle of 1919. Delius became very saddened by life in England – oppressed by 'the *God of Dullness* and Indifference to all things artistic', the weather, the shallowness of the upper-class society in which they for the most part moved in a sort of love–hate relationship; even Diaghilev's Russian Ballet was 'very poor and uninteresting'.[61] Lady Cunard – whom Delius had asked to see if she could find a buyer for Gauguin's *Nevermore*[62] – soon caught up with them, on one occasion taking them shopping in Selfridges, where she introduced them to 'a head man there, a most important persons [*sic*] and so we obtained a pot of jam without standing in a line'. Perhaps the thing Delius enjoyed most of all during this nine-month period was going to a boxing match in the Albert Hall, when he 'saw Jimmy Wilde knocked out by Mike O'Dowd!!'[63]

[59] Dutton Epoch CDLX7264.

[60] Letter 435.

[61] Letter 439.

[62] Letter 436.

[63] Letter 440.

# Fenby and the Last Years

*Dance* for harpsichord – *Hassan* – Cello Concerto –
*Five Piano Pieces* – *Three Preludes* for piano – *The Splendour
Falls on Castle Walls* – Violin Sonata no. 2 – *A Late Lark* –
Eric Fenby – *A Song of Summer* – the 1929 Delius Festival –
Violin Sonata no. 3 – *Songs of Farewell* – *Caprice and Elegy* –
*Irmelin Prelude* – *Fantastic Dance* – *Prelude and Idyll*

EVER since the Deliuses had left their comfortable home for Orléans in
September 1914, they had suffered one disruption after another, but by now,
despite bouts of depression and ill health, Delius had miraculously recovered
the energy and inspiration he needed to go on writing. 1914 had seen the
completion of *North Country Sketches*; 1915, the Double Concerto; and in 1916,
the *Requiem*, the String Quartet, *A Dance Rhapsody* no. 2, the Violin Concerto
and the Cello Sonata. Then in 1917 he finished *Eventyr*, revised the quartet, and
wrote two of his three most beautiful partsongs – and in 1918, he produced *A
Song before Sunrise* and most of the *Poem of Life and Love*.

Now, however, following the end of the War, the next five years were an
almost continuous round of journeys (most of them doubtless extremely
exhausting) to concerts or operas in London and Germany, holidaying in
Norway and southern Europe, and to German sanatoria for 'cures', with very
little time spent at Grez. Depression, indeed, rather than physical ailments,
became an increasingly serious problem – brought on by a number of things.
The vandalism of the house at Grez had upset the Deliuses beyond measure;
for a considerable time they had been virtual refugees in England, separated
from most of their possessions; Beecham had more or less given up conducting
Delius's music – indeed, he was hardly giving any orchestral concerts at all,
and what time and energy he had to spare from trying to resolve his financial
problems was spent in the opera house – so the Deliuses saw little or nothing
of their great friend; and finally they were short of money, unable to recover
assets which they held in Germany. Post-war England was a grim place:
inflation had almost doubled, the value of the pound had plummeted by over
60 percent, and:

> Music does not seem to be very flourishing in London at present: the
> price of everything goes up and there is no increase of audiences, but
> rather the reverse, so that the loss on concerts is greater than ever.[1]

---

[1] Letter from Gardiner to Rose Grainger: *From Parry to Britten: British Music in
Letters, 1900–1945*, ed. Lewis Foreman (London: Batsford, 1987), Letter 95.

Finally, the lawyer on whom Delius was relying in his dispute with Universal, Franz Heinitz, had died.

All that meant that the only music Delius wrote in 1919 was the *Dance* for Harpsichord and some sketches for a setting of a Verlaine[2] poem. What, in other circumstances, might have been an exciting prospect was the possibility of his writing something for piano and orchestra for Grainger – but nothing came of the idea.[3]

## DANCE FOR HARPSICHORD
### (1919: *RT* IX/6; *CE* vol. 33)

SOME twenty-one years earlier, in November 1898, Delius had gone from Grez to London to try to find sponsorship for his 1899 concert in St James's Hall, and he had been given a letter of introduction to (among others) the celebrated harpsichordist Violet Gordon Woodhouse.[4] Whether she gave him any help is unknown, but in late 1918, when he and Jelka retreated from France to England a second time, they were going to her house regularly. Jelka described her to Marie Clews: 'She is not young, and not got up "young"; but just dressed and to her fingertips in harmony with her dainty, delicate old instruments and her whole person.'[5] Delius was persuaded or bewitched into writing this two-minute piece and dedicating it to her. In the same year, he met A. H. Fox Strangways,[6] the music critic of *The Times*, who founded the quarterly *Music & Letters* in 1919 (and edited it for seventeen years), and Heseltine persuaded Strangways to publish Delius's *Dance* in its very first issue (dated 1 January 1920) – which also included an article by Mrs. Woodhouse.

The work is undoubtedly a curiosity: the harpsichord favours uncluttered textures, underpinned by harmony that alters relatively infrequently, and it is

---

[2] Paul(-Marie) Verlaine (1844–96): French poet who was one of the models for the Decadent movement.

[3] Letter 450.

[4] Violet (Kate) Gordon Woodhouse (1872–1948): a somewhat fearsome character, she was a brilliant player (also of the clavichord and the piano), and did much to promote the keyboard music of Bach, Scarlatti and Mozart. For some twenty years she lived in an eccentric *ménage à cinq* with her husband and three other men, which was reduced by two in the 1920s.

[5] Letter 439.

[6] Arthur Henry Fox Strangways (1859–1948): he followed Fuller Maitland as the music editor of *The Times* from 1911 until 1925, when he moved to *The Observer*. Heseltine described him as having a 'jocular-schoolmaster-out-of-school-hours manner, with his interminable and pointless conundrums – whether the respective lengths of violin bows and cello bows affected the phrasing with regard to the sex of the performer.' At their first meeting, he asked Delius, very tactlessly, who published his music: see Letter 99.

therefore unsuited to Delius's style and keyboard technique, with its swiftly changing chromaticism and densely voiced chords demanding to be sustained. The instrument, let alone the ear of the listener, simply cannot cope and the result is inevitably a clumsy, unpleasant jumble of sound. However, when transferred to the piano, the *Dance* comes into its own and is revealed as an utterly charming and fascinating synthesis of Delius's later harmonic style, captured in just two pages of score.

The main melody, marked 'With graceful dance movement, rather quick', nods in the direction of early music: it has the flavour of a *gavotte*, in the way it stresses the second half of the bar and uses ornaments with discretion. But there the similarity ends: Delius's harmonies belong firmly to the twentieth century, especially in the way discordant intervals (such as augmented fourths, minor seconds and major sevenths) are placed within chords that occur on strong beats but which are swiftly resolved:

Ex. 8.1

[With graceful dance movement, rather quick]

Delius, typically, does not bother to mark phrase lengths, and so the performer needs to work out carefully the shape of the musical paragraphs, as well as any melodic lines hidden within them, and – most importantly – the cadential points to which the music is leading. Once all that is secure, this apparently unassuming, not to say unpromising, little piece yields many subtle delights.

THE Deliuses left Belsize Park in June 1919, and a fortnight later they were, perhaps unexpectedly, at Sennen Cove, near Land's End. They did not enjoy the place, so at the beginning of August they went to Norway – where Delius's health always seemed to improve – and in mid-September they met their old friend Edvard Munch in Christiania. From there they went on to Frankfurt for the later rehearsals for *Fennimore and Gerda*, and attended its very successful première – at the end of which Delius was called on to the stage many times.

By the third week of October they were back at Grez, but after only a month they left again for London – staying 'in a funny little Restaurant and Hotel in Soho, where rather amusing artists frequented and discreetly disappeared upstairs with veiled femmes du monde!'[7] They immediately found themselves back in the revived social scene with the rich and famous, and Delius sat for a strong, red crayon portrait by the artist William Nicholson.[8]

Apart from a visit to London for the premières of the Double Concerto and *The Song of the High Hills*, Beecham's revival of *A Village Romeo and Juliet*, and meetings about their financial problems, with a short stay in Paris in the autumn, the Deliuses spent most of 1920 in Grez. In the middle of the summer, Delius had a letter from a complete stranger, the impresario Basil Dean.[9] Dean and the stage designer George Harris had been walking past Covent Garden one evening, seen that *A Village Romeo and Juliet* was on, and gone in just as the 'glorious music' of *The Walk to the Paradise Garden* was beginning:

> Never had I heard such a fountain of sound. I was enthralled. I turned to George and said 'This is the man I want for "Hassan".'[10]

He was referring to his forthcoming production of *Hassan (or The Golden Journey to Samarkand)*, a play by James Elroy Flecker. Born in 1884, Flecker read Oriental Languages at Cambridge, and then joined the Levant Consular Service as an interpreter. His first post was in Constantinople, and it was there that reading some farcical Turkish plays gave him the idea of writing his own – about the trials and tribulations of Hassan of Baghdad, a portly, middle-aged confectioner, and his love for the 'young and voluptuous' Yasmin. Flecker spent three years revising and enlarging his play, and just managed to finish it before dying of tuberculosis in 1915 – 'unquestionably the greatest premature loss that English literature has suffered since the death of Keats'.[11] Edward Marsh,[12] a noted personality in the arts world, became very interested in the play, had helped Flecker to improve it, and then, through a friend, showed it to Dean.

---

[7] Letter from Jelka Delius to Marie Clews: *Letters 2*, p. 210.

[8] (Sir) William Newzam Prior Nicholson (1872–1949): a distinguished artist, painting landscapes, still life and portraits, and carving many woodcuts. Of Delian interest are his drawing of Ernest Dowson and his oil of W. E. Henley.

[9] Basil Herbert Dean, CBE (1888–1978): he also acted, produced plays, directed films, and formed the film company which eventually became Ealing Studios.

[10] Basil Dean, *Seven Ages: An Autobiography, 1888–1927* (London: Hutchinson 1970), p. 129; quoted in Dawn Redwood, 'Flecker, Dean and Delius: The History of *Hassan* (Part II)', *DSJ* 51 (1976), unpaginated.

[11] Alec Macdonald, 'James Elroy Flecker', *Fortnightly Review* 115 (February 1924), 274–84.

[12] (Sir) Edward Howard Marsh, CVO, GB, CMG (1872–1953): a very influential figure, he was private secretary to many government ministers, a patron of the arts, translator, and editor of several books of poetry.

Dean realised that the play would benefit hugely from having incidental music, and he tried to interest a number of composers in the project – including Ravel. For various reasons none of them proved to be available or suitable (even Ravel, who at the time was writing *L'Enfant et les sortilèges*, and anyway did not understand English well). Dean's walk down Bow Street therefore happened at just the right moment. In fact, Delius refused his first approach, but, nothing daunted, Dean went over to Grez with a copy of the play, and his reading of it so completely changed Delius's mind that he began work almost immediately.[13]

Grez was, however, becoming no place for Delius and Jelka during the winter, so in the middle of November 1920 they set off for Frankfurt, enjoying the cultural life there to the full until the following March. Back in London, they took an apartment in Swiss Cottage (complete with a piano lent to them by Broadwoods), heard *Appalachia* conducted by Albert Coates – of whom Delius had now formed a very high opinion, and become extremely fond[14] – and there *Hassan* was finished.

---

[13] Marion Scott, 'Mr Delius Discourses on his Music to *Hassan*', *Christian Science Monitor*, 27 October 1923; available through www.musicweb-international.com [accessed 19 March 2014].

[14] Very unusually indeed for those days, at the end of that performance they actually embraced on the platform: Letter 465.

## HASSAN

### (1920–3: *RT* I/9; *CE* vol. 8)

T HE play was initially given on 1 June 1923, in Darmstadt, with a German translation of the text, but it was not a success. The London première, though, was one of the most eagerly awaited events of the London stage in the years after the Great War – particularly as it had encountered years of frustrating delays before finally being given a sumptuous production by Dean at His Majesty's Theatre in September 1923. It ran for a total of 281 performances, and Delius, having granted the stage rights to Dean's production company, received £25 a week in royalties throughout the run.[15] Hailed as 'the greatest poetic play since *The Tempest*', the extensive text in five acts, calling for a huge number of actors and elaborate stage-effects, presented a daunting challenge, but Dean was determined not to skimp. He engaged a star cast, headed by Henry Ainley, Leon Quartermaine and Cathleen Nesbitt, commissioned magnificent sets and costumes, complex lighting, and choreography by Mikhail Fokine. On the first two nights, the conductor was Eugene Goossens,[16] but thereafter Percy E. Fletcher was in the pit.[17] For the London production, Dean devised a more elaborate staging than that used at Darmstadt, which needed more music, and this was duly extracted from 'a loudly protesting composer … the most enchanting items in a score that did more to bring Delius to the notice of his countrymen than all his previous work'.[18]

The following synopsis shows how Delius's incidental music fits into the play; titles in italics refer to the individual numbers as they are listed in the full score.

(*Prelude to Act 1*) The scene is laid in Baghdad where portly, middle-aged Hassan, a confectioner by trade, has fallen deeply in love with one of his veiled customers. His friend, Selim, identifies her as Yasmin, a beautiful young widow. (*Interlude between Scenes 1 and 2; Act 1 Scene 2*) Hassan goes off at nightfall to

---

[15] *M&C*, p. 379. According to one conversion table, that £25 was equivalent to £1,196 in 2014.

[16] (Sir) Eugene Aynsley Goossens (III) (1893–1962): English conductor of Belgian parentage, whose father and grandfather had the same main names and were both conductors. He began his career as a violinst in the Beecham Symphony Orchestra, but turned to conducing and spent twenty-four years in the USA and Australia. He was the brother of the oboist Léon Goossens and the harpists Marie and Sidonie Goossens – Sidonie was a member of the orchestra for the production. In 1916, Delius told Heseltine that Goossens' *Phantasy Quartet*, op. 12, was the finest work that ever came from an English pen: *FD&PW*, Letter 510.

[17] Percy Eastman Fletcher (1879–1932) was music director for several West End theatres, and the resident one at His Majesty's Theatre from 1915 – hence his conducting most of the run. He also composed both light and serious music.

[18] Dean, *Seven Ages*, p. 146.

serenade her (*Serenade*) but, to his disgust, finds that Selim has tricked him by gaining entrance himself to Yasmin's house and winning her affections. As dawn breaks (*Melos*), the Caliph of Baghdad arrives on the scene, together with his vizier, his executioner and his court poet, all of them in disguise and looking for adventure. They hear mysterious music coming from an adjoining house (*Chorus behind the scenes*) and manage to gain entry, with the exception of the poet Ishak, who is disillusioned with his despotic master and arranges for Hassan to take his place.

(*Prelude to Act 2*) The dwelling turns out to be the home of Rafi, self-styled King of the Beggars and enemy of authority; his ragged followers entertain their guests with song and dance (*Fanfare preceding the Ballet; Ballet: Dance of the Beggars; Chorus of Women; Divertissement; General Dance*)[19]. Rafi is set on avenging Pervaneh, the girl he was once betrothed to, and who was carried off against her will to the Harem. When the visitors reveal who they really are, Rafi holds them captive (*Chorus of Beggars and Dancing Girls*), but Hassan is able to save the day by smuggling a note out of the building (*Act 2 Scene 2*). This is eventually handed over to the Chief of Police, who rescues the Caliph, and arrests Rafi and his band. Hassan's resourcefulness is rewarded by a high position at court; Ishak, who has offended the Caliph by a request to leave his service, manages to save his skin by improvising a flattering poem (*Music accompanying Ishak's poem*), and promising to take the naïve Hassan under his wing.

(*Prelude to Act 3; Act 3 Scene 1*) Hassan is installed in splendour at the palace but is wary of the intrigues of the court; the Caliph advises him to keep a low profile. (*Act 3, Interlude between Scenes 1 and 2*) Hassan is cynically approached by the ambitious Yasmin, who is clearly on the make. Though he tries to resist her, he cannot help himself and gives in to her seductive ways. (*Act 3 Scene 3;*[20] *Fanfares in the great Hall of the Palace; Entry of the Caliph*) The Caliph now reveals his ruthless and cruel nature: Rafi's followers are shown no mercy and are hanged; sentence is also passed on the Beggar King himself, who faces a horrifyingly slow and painful death. Pervaneh is now brought in and pleads for mercy. The Caliph offers the lovers an appalling choice: he will spare Rafi's life on condition that the young people part for ever and that she remain in the Harem; alternatively, they will be allowed one whole day in which to make love, after which they will be put to death in merciless torment (*Fanfares*).

(*Prelude to Act 4*) Hassan and Ishak are searching for Rafi and Pervaneh, who are incarcerated somewhere in the vaults of the palace; they bribe the guards to let them spy on the prisoners. (*Act 4, Interlude between Scenes 1 and 2*) The two lovers agonise over their decision; in the end it is Pervaneh who argues

---

[19] Percy Grainger helped Delius with this movement when he visited the Deliuses in Norway in 1923 (see below) – his manuscript is headed 'Sketch for "Dance" from "Hassan" late July 1923, Lesjaskog': *RT Catalogue*, p. 54.

[20] This is incorrectly identified in the score as Act 3, Scene 2.

that it is worth spending a day of bliss together, even if it entails an appalling death.

(*Prelude to Act 5*) Hassan pleads with the Caliph to spare the lovers but loses his temper in the process and, as a punishment, will be forced to witness the execution. (*The song of the Muezzin at sunset*) The hour has come (*The Procession of Protracted Death*) and the gruesome instruments of torture are displayed, followed by Rafi and Pervaneh, in chains, dragging their coffins behind them. Their grisly deaths take place off-stage. Hassan is horrified and remains in a state of shock, but Ishak urges him not to despair: let them put the moral filth and cruelty of Baghdad behind them and join the great Caravan, shortly to leave for the cities of the north, and known by pilgrims as 'The Golden Journey to Samarkand'. Suddenly the waters of a nearby fountain begin to spurt blood and Hassan and Ishak flee in terror as the ghosts of Rafi and Pervaneh appear, condemned to haunt the spot for ever.

(*Prelude to the Last Scene; Closing Scene*) Just inside the city walls, the caravan assembles with its band of merchants and pilgrims, among them Hassan and Ishak: they intend to seek out a prophet who may be able to explain to them the reason for the existence of mankind. The men and their beasts of burden set off, the watchman closes the gate to Baghdad, and, as the procession winds its way across the desert, the voices of the travellers and the bells of their camels are finally lost in the distance.

Delius wrote a substantial amount of incidental music for *Hassan* which, performed out of context, would last for just over an hour. There are twenty-nine separate numbers, scored for a theatre orchestra of twenty-four players, fairly large by the standards of the day (the optimistic composer had originally asked for thirty). The level of inspiration is consistently high, with the exception of the ballet music in Act 2, whose forced orientalism borders on kitsch – though, admittedly, it serves its function well enough in the theatre. Elsewhere, Delius identified strongly with the exotic nature of Flecker's extraordinary story, illustrating its melancholy, its pathos and, at times, its sadistic cruelty, in some of the most ravishing pages he ever wrote. The play itself is so rarely performed that the sheer range of the music is not just unfamiliar, but surprising. Some of the numbers consist of no more than a dozen bars, to cover brief scene-changes; others, such as the magnificent final scene, are substantial compositions. Only the *Serenade*, in a variety of arrangements, has led an independent existence. The music cries out to be given a lease of life in one or more concert suites, although a sequence of four excerpts, arranged and scored for full orchestra by Eric Fenby in 1929, went some way towards remedying this.

Hassan's attempt to woo Yasmin with his lute in Act 1 is the occasion for the *Serenade*, whose lilting rhythms and haunting tune fully justify its popularity. Delius's original conception was for the wordless melody to be sung by an off-stage tenor, but the vocal line was subsequently reallocated to a solo violin; yet another version, consisting of exactly the same music, serves as the interlude between the first and second scenes of Act 3, where it is rescored for woodwind, strings and harp.

But this number is not, by any means, the only highlight of the score: an equally atmospheric passage serves as the interlude between scenes 1 and 2 of Act 1, and is notable for the extreme delicacy of the instrumentation, with its imaginative use of solo woodwind and harp, and melodic intervals that give just the right *frisson* of the Orient:

Ex. 8.2

Delius uses a mixed chorus with great imagination, notably in the unaccompanied, off-stage vocal music that precedes the final scene of Act 1. The harmonies are wonderfully inventive:

Ex. 8.3

The *Procession of Protracted Death*, with its inexorable, menacing bass-line on lower strings and timpani, its harsh, discordant intervals, and its deliberately violent scoring (shrieks of pain are suggested by woodwind and strings), could scarcely be better done. There are also some remarkable pages in the *Prelude to the Last Scene* with its atonal harmonies, and strange, fluttering, ghostly figurations in woodwind and strings which evoke the restless spirits of Pervaneh and Rafi at the site of their grisly execution. Those extraordinary pages – the nearest Delius ever came to sounding like Schoenberg – lead straight into the masterly final scene, operatic in scope, with its *ostinato* arpeggio figurations on cellos and harp, the relentless drumming of timpani, the tinkling of camel bells and the fervent cries of the travellers and pilgrims:

Ex. 8.4

The final pages, as the procession disappears into the distance, are deeply moving and are realised with startling economy of means. The sparing use of distant voices, timpani, *ostinato* harp and string *tremolandi* haunts the ear long after it has ceased to sound. One cannot help feeling that Flecker, had he lived to experience a production of *Hassan* embellished with music, would have agreed that no composer could have been more sympathetic to the mood of his play, or served him more magnificently, than Delius.

THE following week, the theatrical weekly *The Stage*[21] devoted the equivalent of a full A3 page in a modest-sized font to the production, and, probably with every justification, had no criticism at all of the show:

'Hassan' was received with justifiable enthusiasm by a large and representative audience (including the dead author's Greek widow and his parents) on Thursday, from the moment when, behind an illuminated tableau curtain Mr. Henry Ainley, as the Baghdad confectioner, recited, by way of prologue, some verses from Flecker's long-published poem ... [A number of the other senior members of the cast then spoke, and] Mr Ainley, too, was constrained to say a few words of thanks, and express the hope that he and his comrades would have to make the Golden Journey many times. Thus auspiciously, indeed triumphantly, was carried through the opening stage in an enterprise resounding to the credit of those upholding the banner of the best dramatic literature, ancient or modern, though coming in but tardy and grievously belated recognition of that unhappy victim of consumption, James Elroy Flecker. In the success also shared that Bradford man, Frederick Delius, whose music, composed for the production, followed the Eastern mode closely enough ... Mr Esmé Percy doubled the effective role of the impudent and cowardly 'false friend' Selim with that of the Master of the Caravan who has to control the crowd in one of the most impressive and best-grouped scenes one has ever seen, even on the vast and spacious stages of His Majesty's and Old Drury, for instance ... Delius's most appropriate, and generally sombre, although by no means untuneful music, less abstruse than some he used to write, was rendered ably (as far as the chattering audience let one hear) at the opening performance by a special orchestra conducted by Mr. Eugene Goosens.

Unfortunately, however, the behaviour of the audience spoilt the evening for many. The Deliuses were 'acutely depressed',[22] and Heseltine was so appalled that he devoted the first quarter of the long article that he wrote about the play for *The Daily Telegraph* to the problem:

---

[21] 27 September 1923.
[22] Redwood, 'Flecker, Dean and Delius'.

'We want to hear the orchestra.' Clearly the author of this famous phrase will have to ... devise some method of retaliation if those who go to the superb production at His Majesty's Theatre as much for the music as for the play are to be frustrated in their attempts to hear it (as the representative of The Daily Telegraph appears to have been on the first night) by the chatter of folk who are oblivious of the disrespect they are showing to one of the greatest living composers.

29 September 1923

The conductor Ernest Irving[23] was also heavily critical in a letter to the same paper on the same day:

> Surely when a musician of the calibre of Frederick Delius writes a score for the theatre he should be entitled to a hearing! There is always in an English audience a certain number of mentally-maimed people to whom music means nothing, but good manners should prevent them from robbing those fortunate in the possession of all their faculties ... In any other country but this, there would be silence as a matter of course, and if your critic proves to be right it is a mournful reflection for an Englishman that we must wait for a concert performance in Queen's Hall to hear music written by one of the most distinguished living musicians specially for the theatre. No wonder managers think any rubbish good enough for incidental music.

All the reviews seem to have concentrated on the story and the production, and scant tribute was paid to the music. This is typical:

> The music of Frederick Delius struck us as more Eastern than seductive; but that is, of course, a matter of taste. There could be no two opinions about the success of the whole production, which does full justice to Flecker's fine work. There was a brilliant house, immense at the curtain-fall.
>
> *The Times*, 21 September 1923

[23] (Kelville) Ernest Irving (1878–1953): he was the Musical Director of Ealing Studios between 1935 and 1953, composing and conducting numerous film scores. In 1951, the Royal Philharmonic Society elected him and Frederic Austin as Honorary Members (its highest accolade apart from the Gold Medal) for their services to English music.

A FTER *Hassan*, Delius's creative urge rose again, and on 6 April 1921 he told Heseltine that he was working on a 'Violincello-Concerto'[24] – which proved to be the last music that Delius was able to write with his own hand. Probably the previous year, the Harrison family had moved from Cornwall Gardens in Kensington to an old farmhouse, The Waffrons, at Thames Ditton in Surrey. Beatrice's sister Margaret claimed that:

> Delius actually planned the Cello Concerto while sitting in our garden ...
> He had a favourite rose, the Gloire de Dijon. We had a magnificent
> specimen all over the wall and he sat under it, and he said that it was
> always the Gloire that made him write the 'cello work'.[25]

Beatrice also claimed that 'some of his works were composed in our garden.'[26] The fact is that no-one knows the exact truth – but it makes a romantic story. There is no doubt, however, that Delius went down to Waffrons a good many times to discuss the progressing concerto with Beatrice, and by September he was correcting the proofs. Interestingly, it seems that Delius and Orr were getting on well together, as there are both a *Stichvorlage* (the copy of a manuscript used by the engraver) of the full score, and a separate solo part written out by Orr for the publishers, Universal Edition.[27] As Orr acknowledged many years later, however, his version of the former was not well done, and the errors were not corrected until the work's publication as part of the Collected Edition.

---

[24] Letter 464. He had in fact begun sketching it the previous year.

[25] 'Margaret Harrison Remembers', *DSJ* 87 (1985), 13–18, at p. 13.

[26] Lionel Carley, 'The Harrisons, the Cello Concerto and The Waffrons', *DSJ* 148 (2010).

[27] *RT Catalogue*, p. 170.

## CELLO CONCERTO
### (1921: *RT* VII/7; *CE* vol. 29b)

O N E of Delius's masterpieces, the Cello Concerto is one of the finest in the repertoire, and a worthy successor to the earlier string concertos – indeed, he himself rated it the best of the three on account of its melodic invention. It is original and innovative in its structure (some might say, even to the point of eccentricity). For one thing, the cellist carries a heavy weight of responsibility, centre-stage for 80 percent of the time and absent from only fifty-eight complete bars out of a total of 358. Traditionally, a concerto soloist is pitted against the orchestra in a form of musical discussion or argument, but that is not the case here: the two are united in blended textures, rather than being separated by conflict. Delius also disdains to provide any marked contrast between his various thematic ideas, but instead lends them a family resemblance, so that they tend to flow in and out of each other, with textbook rules about contrasting key-schemes largely ignored. Nor is there extensive rhythmic variety: within the slowish pace of the majority of the score, Delius indulges his fondness for trochaic and iambic patterns (respectively *long–short* and *short–long*). The general effect is of an unbroken idyll or reverie.

There is also a free spirit abroad in terms of form. The concerto is in one continuous movement, framed by an introduction and coda, and presents an A section of interlinked themes, then a B section introducing fresh ideas in a similar way, before returning to a considerably edited A section. Though there is nothing revolutionary in that, the real surprise comes after the return of the A section, when Delius launches into a C section containing brand new material in a mainly faster pulse, which, unlike an identical scheme in the Violin Concerto, never refers back to the point of departure. As Fenby commented, 'one can but guess, but not explain, the mystery of Delius's motive here.'[28]

After a brief fanfare, marked 'Slow', for woodwind, echoed by horns, the cello soloist enters boldly in the fifth bar with bowed chords in a strong E minor tonality, a striking gesture which appears to constitute a main subject, though in fact the idea never returns. (Delius's sweeping arpeggio chords were modified by the cellist Herbert Withers in 1935, one of a series of revisions that affect around seventy-six bars of the original solo part; these are printed as alternatives in the full score and mostly concern passage-work, offering modifications that make more idiomatic sense on the instrument. Phrasing has also been added, as Delius had marked virtually nothing.)

The soloist's forthright, blunt introduction suddenly reaches up to a soft D natural in bar 12 and melts onto a downward arabesque, coloured by warmer accompaniment for flute, bassoon, horns and harp, with *pizzicato* cellos and basses, and prefiguring the rhapsodic mood to come. The orchestra muses

---

[28] *Lloyd*, p. 168.

alone ('Not quick; quietly') for eight bars before a change in metre (from 4/4 to 12/8) marks off the preceding pages as no more than an introduction.

We now hear the first main theme:

Ex. 8.5

Ex. 8.5 is utterly characteristic of the long, unbroken solo lines in this concerto, which exploit the full range of the instrument, particularly its penetrating upper register: Delius thinks of his cellist as a tenor, rather than as a bass or baritone, and he regularly takes the part up into the treble clef. The passage-work is frequently angular and chromatic (i.e. bars 3 and 4 of Ex. 8.5), soaring and swooping in wide leaps (i.e. bar 7). Some melodic ideas are chromatic in outline (bar 5), whilst others are shaped by the pentatonic scale (i.e. bars 8 to 10).

The 1st violins introduce a fresh idea (bar 36) which will be further developed; but for the moment, it is embellished by a countersubject from the cellist:

Ex. 8.6

The soloist now takes up a development of the violin theme (bar 43) before plunging into virtuoso passage-work, which is interrupted by a return of Ex. 8.5 in octave unison on violins and violas, and which leads to the first *tutti* in the work, albeit a brief one. Ex. 8.6 evolves still further (bar 56), appearing in F sharp in the cello, and with an important appendage (bars

58–61) to which Delius ingeniously introduces Ex. 8.5 in counterpoint on the 1st violins:

Ex. 8.7

A melodic motif in the cello (bar 60) (the figure marked *x* in Ex. 8.7), is only fleetingly referred to at this point, but it will become a major theme in its own right later on – an example of real organic growth. Indeed, one of the reasons why this concerto works as an entity, rather than just being a succession of musical moments, is that its themes are all of a kind, however much they subsequently evolve.

Ex. 8.7 sets the mood for a gradual increase in intensity, and the orchestral texture thickens, notably in bars 70–6 with their undulating woodwind accompaniment. The music builds to a fine climax at bar 77 with soaring strings in octave unison, and a downward, chromatic line for the trumpets, underpinned by trombones and tuba: a striking instance of how Delius uses his brass sparingly, but effectively. A brief quotation on the oboe of the first two bars of Ex. 8.5 (bar 80), leads to a further development of Ex. 8.7, which now captures Delius's interest (between bars 82 and 88 there is a good example of how the semiquaver passage for the cellist, needlessly taxing, was effectively modified by Herbert Withers). As the soloist scurries up the stave and then falls silent (bar 88), a punctuation point is marked by the brass and upper strings in unison, who die away as a harp arpeggio brings this initial A section to a close.

The predominant 12/8 metre gives way to a more relaxed 6/4 (bar 93) and a new tempo marking of 'Slow', which ushers in a new group of themes. The first of these is a lilting melody, warmly scored for strings, with touches of 1st flute:

Ex. 8.8

For the moment, the orchestra jealously guards this beautiful inspiration whilst the soloist muses rhapsodically, in short passages of recitative (bar 97 *et seq.*) punctuated by the rhythm of Ex. 8.8 on muted horns and on bassoons (bars 103–5). A double bar marks the arrival of a fresh idea, preponderantly lyrical (bar 114), introduced, in the mellow key of D flat, by the soloist:

Ex. 8.9

The melody begins by quoting figure *x* from Ex. 8.7, its swaying rhythms bearing a family resemblance to Ex. 8.8; moreover, the shape of the tune, as it unexpectedly turns aside into F major (Ex. 8.9, bar 6), is influenced by the cello line of Ex. 8.6. All of which is yet further evidence of Delius's remarkably organic method of composition.

Ex. 8.8 is recalled (bar 123) on flutes, clarinets and harp, and is now entrusted to the soloist, who begins a triplet embellishment of it (bar 125), followed, in a quicker tempo (bar 128 *et seq.*), by variations on Ex. 8.9 which continue for several pages. After a strong entry by the brass (bars 154–7), the soloist continues to be preoccupied with florid passage-work based on Ex. 8.9, as the 1st violins and cellos voice a new counter-melody (bar 158) that spreads through the rest of the strings (bar 168) and, once again, displays a resemblance to Ex. 8.7:

Ex. 8.10

This fresh and captivating theme is quoted by the 1st horn (bar 172) and also as a solo by the 1st clarinet; then again, very quietly, by the 1st clarinet and 1st bassoon (bar 185) with Ex. 8.9 in counterpoint on the solo cello, now high in its register, in the bright key of D major.

The central section now draws to a close, marked by a short solo for the oboe (bar 195), a pentatonic motif, slightly ornamented and immediately imitated by the cellist (bar 197). The woodwind and horns softly sketch a reminiscence of Ex. 8.8 before the music comes to rest on a general pause.

A recapitulation of material from section A follows, though shorn by two-thirds (it lasts twenty-six bars rather than seventy). The soloist reminds us of Ex. 8.5 (bar 205), this time with slight variations in the layout of the woodwind accompaniment; Ex. 8.6 follows (bar 216), and now the cor anglais takes up the counter-subject, and the solo cello has the main theme, the latter then passing to the strings (bar 221). Delius avoids recalling its evolution as Ex. 8.7 altogether, and instead delves into material from the B section for a snatch of Ex. 8.10 (bar 223), fairly high up on the solo cello, accompanied by chugging horns, and by flute and clarinet arpeggios. Then the music slows right down, with an A natural trill from the cello and an upward arpeggio on the harp, sustained by woodwind and horns. The recall of the opening material has been brief and it might seem as if Delius is about to lead us into one of his glorious, sunset codas. Indeed he will, but not yet: first, he has a surprise in store. Changing the time signature to three crotchets in a bar, and marking the score 'With animation', he invents a new and most captivating theme:

Ex. 8.11

This is the first of two brand new themes in this final C section, which itself is given spacious proportions in the concerto's structure, 128 bars no less, equivalent to a third of the total duration. Therefore, it can hardly be thought of as an extended coda, but, rather, should be considered as a section in its own right.

Ex. 8.11 is developed in an outpouring of melody carried on the shoulders of the soloist, who is given no rest but presses on with vigorous passage-work (bar 250 et seq.), the strings providing the harmonic background, punctuated by downward quavers on the harp. The rest of the orchestra follows the drift as the tempo picks up even more, and spiky figurations for flute and cor anglais (bar 260) lend the music the character of a rustic dance, enhanced by fifths and fourths in harp and strings and pizzicato chords from the soloist (bar 260); this is the quickest music of the whole concerto. After a copious stream of semiquavers from the cellist, an uninhibited tutti with full brass erupts at bar 275, before the texture thins and the pace relaxes.

Delius still has one, final melodic idea up his sleeve, which he marks 'Rather slower, very quietly':

Ex. 8.12

Rather slower, very quietly

The accompaniment is inspired: clusters of syncopated woodwind chords, with the harp strumming gently in the background and the strings gradually entering to fill out the harmonies. The cello makes much of the theme's downward semiquavers, and these are echoed by the 1st violins (bar 305), and by the oboe and 1st flute (bars 306–8). The cellist also hints (bars 311 and 313) at a little triplet figuration from the introduction (bars 14 and 15). Ex. 8.11 returns on full strings (bar 318) with a counter-melody from the soloist, before the tempo slows down and the music slips seamlessly into the real coda (bar 342). Here, the cello adds a poignant commentary, in a melodic fragment that descends chromatically, as the 1st flute adds a final reminiscence of Ex. 8.11 (bar 347). The ending is beautifully conceived: downward arabesques, based on Ex. 8.12, are scored for cor anglais, followed by flute and oboe, then cor anglais again, all of this over sustained strings and a held G natural from the soloist, with gentle pulsations from the harp. The strings die away to nothing, and a soft and radiant G major chord, spread *pizzicato* by the soloist, ends the work.

D ELIUS always remained faithful to the soloists who had particularly pleased him in giving first performances of his music – Albert Sammons, and now both Alexandre Barjansky and Beatrice Harrison. Although he wrote the Cello Concerto for Beatrice,[29] he neatly avoided favouring one cellist over the other by not dedicating the work at all. It was Barjansky, however, who first played it – in Vienna on 31 January 1923.[30] A month later, on 1 March, he repeated it in Frankfurt (where the Deliuses were staying), in an all-Delius concert in honour of the composer's sixtieth birthday. It was conducted by Paul von Klenau,[31] who had become tremendously taken with Delius's music.

*The Musical Times* report from Vienna said:

The performance of the Delius Concerto, given in honour of the composer's sixtieth birthday, was its first performance anywhere. It is harmonically simple, yet never primitive, and its orchestration is of unquestionable exotic charm. A subdued mood prevails throughout,

---

[29] Katrina Fountain, 'In a Surrey Garden', p. 8.

[30] With the elderly Franz Schalk conducting. Although 'rather diffident of "modern music"', at the second rehearsal he declared it 'ein Meisterwerk': Letter 478, n. 3.

[31] See above, Chapter 4, n. 155. The concert also included *North Country Sketches* and *The Song of the High Hills*, for which Grainger prepared the chorus.

without ever becoming monotonous, and the middle section, with its Scots dance rhythms, adds a pleasing national colour to the work.

*May 1923*

Two weeks or so later, Jelka wrote to Beatrice Harrison:

> I send you today piano score of the Cello Concerto marked very carefully with Metronome marks. Please copy them into your copy and send me back this one ... The Cello Concerto is perfectly lovely and had an enormous success ... the Delius Concert has been a great success. It was perfectly lovely and the audience quite spellbound. von Klenau, a Dane, conducted awfully well ...

and she wrote to Adine O'Neill that:

> [The whole concert] was beautiful and very stimmungsvoll, although the Symphonic Orch here is 2d or even 3d rate. The Public was most enthusiastic right through to the end and made great ovations.[32]

Delius only had to wait another four months before Beatrice gave the first English performance – on 3 July in Queen's Hall, with Eugene Goossens and the Goossens Orchestra.[33] Whether or not Delius had realized it, she seemed intent on displaying the theatrical side of her personality:

> Miss Beatrice Harrison's charity concert at Queen's Hall on July 3 was attended by no more people than half filled the hall. As a charity concert, then, it was a failure, but as a musical concert it was a success. Miss Harrison has lately lost a number of her mannerisms, and so has improved her already good playing, but she is still too good an actress to be in the first rank of musicians. At this concert she gave the Elgar 'Cello Concerto and a new work in the same form by Delius (written for herself), with some authority from the composer and her own ideas. Miss Harrison is not perhaps the best 'cellist in England to-day; there is, however, no one else who could play one of these works so well, and give of the other so good a first reading.
>
> *The Musical Times*, August 1923

*The Times*, however, concentrated on the music:

> Miss Beatrice Harrison played two 'cello concertos at Queen's Hall last night, accompanied by the Goossens Orchestra. Of these, Elgar's in E minor was conducted by the composer, while the other, by Delius, was given its first performance in England under Mr. Eugene Goossens. Another new work, 'The Happy Forest,' for orchestra by Arnold Bax, was also played for the first time. These two works provided an interesting

---

[32] Letters 479 and 480.

[33] Which Goossens had used, 105 strong, when he gave the first English performance of *The Rite of Spring* a month earlier. It only survived for a few years.

contrast in their treatment of the same theme, if trees and woods in spring can ever be said to provide the same theme to different men at different times and in different places.

Delius's Concerto in the course of its single long movement never leaves its one prevailing peaceful mood, though once or twice within that mood the pulse quickens. For ordinary mortals the life of contemplation is difficult, and its rarefied air may soon become exhausting. It says a great deal for the beauty in which this work abounds that the hearer is held by its serenity more securely than by any adventitious excitements. 'The Happy Forest' is more physical, an affair of colour and movement; yet it is no ordinary spring idyll, but something fantastic. It might well have been called 'The Enchanted Forest', for it suggested an appropriate setting for a German fairy tale in which the trees are all alive and in which anything might happen.

Artists so competent as Miss Harrison and Mr. Goossens, by the perfect finish which they impart to their work, create in the listener a sense of security which is at once a condition and the consummation of contemplative music, such as last night, not only in Delius's Concerto but in Elgar's and Mr. Goossens's own 'By the Tarn'.

*The Times*, 4 August 1923

A COMPLETELY new venture took hold of the Deliuses' imagination during the summer of 1921. He was well enough for them to go to Norway, and they stayed at an hotel in the little village of Lesjaskog in the Oppland area of central Norway. While they were there, he realized that he could now fulfil his dream of spending part of his life in Norway – so they arranged to have a little wooden house built on the slopes above the village, and called it Høifagerli. Early in 1922, however, Delius's health deteriorated again, the symptoms of his syphilis now very evident, and he virtually stopped working. In February, Jelka took him for a cure in Wiesbaden – where his limbs were so weak that he was confined to a wheelchair, although he could just manage some proof-reading – and three months later they were in the Black Forest for the waters. Those courses did him some good, for by the middle of June he had the energy to travel back to Norway for their first holiday in the new property. There he continued to check proofs, and may possibly have started composing again. Balfour Gardiner came to stay in the last few days before they left for home at the beginning of September,[34] and on their way they met Grainger in Oslo.

By now, Delius had lost the use of both hands, and had to dictate all his music and letters to Jelka; he was losing his sight, and it looked as though his

---

[34] While he was there, Gardiner worked on his own last major work, *Philomela* for voices and orchestra. Curiously some of his sketches are dated 10 September, 1922, three days after the Deliuses had left – so he presumably stayed on in the chalet alone for a while.

career as a composer was all but finished. Between then and 1928, he only composed eight short piano pieces, a lovely partsong, a violin sonata and *A Late Lark* for tenor and orchestra.

There was, moreover, no question that – even with Jelka, as always, caring and concerned for him with total commitment – they could any longer spend the winters in the relatively remote Grez. In November 1922 they therefore set off for Frankfurt again, and stayed there until the following April.

Another cure at Bad Oeynhausen, north-east of Düsseldorf, worked well enough for Jelka to be able to tell Marie Clews in May 1923 that 'Our beloved Delius is progressing so well now', and by the end of June they were back at Høifagerli. There, Delius was initially able to work on *Hassan* and Grainger spent three weeks with them; indeed, he gave Delius a bit of assistance with one of the numbers (see above). However, Delius's energy waned again, and early in October they returned to Grez, having managed to get to London for the first, and a subsequent performance, of *Hassan*.

Although the dates are not clear, during 1922 Delius began those piano pieces, the partsong and what became the second Violin Sonata. The miniatures that make up the ***Five Piano Pieces*** (1922–3: *RT* IX/7; *CE* vol. 33) contain music of no great profundity, but this is nevertheless an attractive collection of five vividly contrasted movements: *Mazurka – Waltz – Waltz – Lullaby for a Modern Baby – Toccata*. On the whole, Delius is satisfied with a less complex texture than he demands elsewhere in his piano writing. Though the *Mazurka* idiomatically emphasises the second beat of the bar, it is a wistful, melancholic conception of this lilting dance, and its chromatic harmonies could certainly never be mistaken for Chopin. The first *Waltz* is straightforward: a single melodic line, gentle and lilting, is accompanied by a syncopated accompaniment. The second is more complex and is a reworking of a much earlier piece, dating from 1891;[35] this later version is expanded to almost twice the length. The *Lullaby for a Modern Baby* is a curiosity, in that it includes an additional melodic line (notated on a separate stave) which Delius suggests should be either hummed by the pianist or played by a muted violin. The basic, rocking accompaniment is varied with longer, chromatic lines (bars 6–13); the overall mood, as might be expected, soft and tender. By contrast, the final *Toccata* is the most virtuoso piece in the set; mostly in a two-part texture, its energetic semiquavers, set against longer melodic lines, bring the suite to a flamboyant conclusion.

[35] See above, Chapter 2, Ex. 2.7.

## THREE PRELUDES

(1922–3: *RT* IX/8; *CE* vol. 33)

T HE *Three Preludes* represent the finest of Delius's solo piano music, and
sustain a far higher level of invention than that of the *Five Piano Pieces*.
They are fluid, quixotic, fleeting apparitions (none lasts longer than two
minutes) whose beguiling harmonies are very much in the manner of Debussy
and are akin to the composer's vocal settings of Verlaine's *Avant que tu ne t'en
ailles* or *La Lune blanche*.

The first piece, marked 'Scherzando', has an enchanting lilt to it and its
harmonies are fashioned from the whole-tone scale:

Ex. 8.13

The sweep of the semiquaver arpeggios propels the music forward (even though
the notes do not lie all that well under the hands and some redistribution is
advisable). The piece builds to a fine, chordal climax, 'Maestoso, poco più lento',
before recapturing the mood of the opening to end (as indeed each *Prelude*
does) with a dying fall.

The second of the set, marked simply 'Quick', has right-hand figurations of
broken fourths decorating a sweeping melody that would sound even more
effective on the cello. The ending is memorable: accented discords in the left
hand (bar 26 *et seq.*), resolving onto the third beat, lead to an upward flourish
and, in the final bar, a clash between a tonality of D major and C sharp, that
melts, via an F sharp crotchet, onto a hushed resolution.

The third prelude is marked 'With lively undulating movement'; it makes
great play of the whole-tone scale (Debussy is not far away) and consists
of melodic fragments coloured with pungent harmonies, in a rippling
semiquaver accompaniment. The ending is another beautiful example of
how Delius lets the music float away into the distance. These three pieces,
though they may appear slight on the page, are subtle, and richly rewarding to
play.

Nothing is known about when and by whom these eight pieces were first played in public – although, with one of the last hand-written letters that Delius ever wrote,[36] he sent a copy of the *Three Preludes* to Percy Grainger. Whether or not he included them in a forthcoming recital is unknown, but they were recorded in 1929 for Columbia, by the Deliuses' friend Evlyn Howard-Jones,[37] and since then other recordings have been made reasonably frequently.[38]

B Y now, the very well-read Jelka was finding all the poetry for Delius to consider setting: she would leave a copy of something she thought might inspire him on his desk, and sometimes the ruse worked, sparking off his imagination. In 1923, he seems to have been taken by Tennyson's verse, and in a letter to his friend Henry Clews[39] he quoted some lines from Tennyson's long poem 'The Princess': 'Tears, idle tears, I know not what they mean ...'. He then went on:

> I have no Tennyson with me and I quote from memory ... so this may not be quite correct, but it is the emotional and artistic way of looking back on the past. We luckily forget all the unpleasantness, the vileness etc etc that was mixed up in it all and therefore perhaps we become unfair to the present and exaggerate.

In that same year, again with Jelka's help, he used some other lines from the same poem for **The Splendour Falls on Castle Walls** (1923: *RT* IV/6; *CE* vol. 17) – the last of his partsongs. This is altogether a most imaginative response to Tennyson's verses, notable for the way that the composer employs an additional semi-chorus of tenors and basses, who are called upon to illustrate the line 'Blow, bugle, answer echoes, dying, dying, dying ...' by humming wordlessly, in imitation of distant brass. The harmonic language is fluent and characteristically chromatic, though not excessively so, whilst Delius surreptitiously changes the metre to give his setting a real sense of flow. The ending is truly striking: three cadential phrases mark three repetitions of the word *dying*, but each time unresolved, so that F major is juxtaposed with C major and the song ends in mid-air.

The first performance was given by Delius's beloved Charles Kennedy Scott and the Oriana Madrigal Society in the Aeolian Hall on 17 June 1924 – but unfortunately it has not proved possible to find any reviews of the concert.

---

[36] John Bird, *Percy Grainger* (Oxford: Oxford University Press, 1999), p. 220. See also *Letters 2*, plate 41.

[37] Evlyn [*sic*] Howard-Jones (1877–1951): his wide sympathies (in particular with the music of Brahms) made him much sought after, for both concert and recital work. He was one of the founders of The Music Club (*q.v.*).

[38] Including a recent version by Paul Guinery on Stone Records: 5060192760130.

[39] Henry Clews, Jr (1876–1937). See Chapter 5, n. 46.

## VIOLIN SONATA NO. 2
### (1922–3: *RT* VIII/9; *CE* vol. 31b)

THIS sonata was finished a little later, and concision is the key-word to bear in mind. The shortest of the four sonatas, it is a lean, tautly conceived work in one continuous movement, without superfluous gestures. That is not to say that it is laconic and difficult to grasp; compared to the troubled and complex first Violin Sonata, it has an open-hearted, sunny disposition, all the more remarkable given the difficult circumstances of its creation. The opening (theme A) unfolds in a calm and radiant C major, its leisurely melodic line spanning sixteen bars. The other significant ideas of this 'Con moto' section follow in rapid succession and without musical punctuation marks: theme B is a brief, rather angular motif (page 22, bars 17–18; page 23, bar 1); and theme C is broader, like a slow, descending arpeggio (page 23, bars 5–11):[40]

Ex. 8.14

The outline of this has evolved from part of theme A (i.e. the violin's downward arpeggio in bars 3 and 4 of the opening) – a good example of the way in which Delius thinks organically. The piano vigorously takes up Ex. 8.14 with a great sweep, and goes on to fuel the fragment of a new idea, theme D (page 23, bar 19 *et seq.*), characterised by insistent quavers, answered by semiquaver flourishes from the violin. Theme C returns in the violin (page 24, bar 3), as does theme B (page 24, bar 7); then C again (page 24, bar 15); a snatch of D (page 24, bar 17); B once more, 'Poco più tranquillo' (page 24, bar 18), and finally a version of C in diminution – i.e. with the dotted rhythms halved (page 25, bar 7).

Listing the themes in this rather bald way, does not of course do justice to the manner in which Delius unfolds his musical narrative, so that the sequential melodic ideas flow in and out of one another and are developed in an organic way. Other composers might have considered this the function of a separate development section – but not Delius, who always prefers a process of continuous evolution. There is a notable example about two-thirds of the way through this opening section, where the piano introduces (page 25, bar 15) an idea which appears to be new but which in fact can be traced back to the insistent quavers of theme D, and to theme C, in diminution:

---

[40] References are to page numbers in the piano part of *CE* vol. 31b.

Ex. 8.15

The pace slackens as the music changes metre to 3/2, and eases itself into a central episode marked 'Lento' (page 27, bar 5). This section consists of two passages of dreamy, lyrical outpourings from the violin, framing a 'Vivace' (page 28, bar 7) based on theme C. It seems quixotic of the composer to break the mood by returning to a theme which he has already extensively explored, especially when the rhapsodic material is as beautiful as this (Ex. 8.16).

The central section comes to a full close with a hushed cadence in C major. Then the piano launches off, 'Molto Vivace' (page 30, bar 16), into a virile, heroic theme of considerable energy. Delius then recalls ideas from the opening section of the work: Ex. 8.15 returns (page 31, bar 25; page 33, bar 4); theme A, which, surprisingly, has not been quoted *verbatim* since its initial appearance, is now restated twice (page 32, bars 9 and 19). In other words, the third section of the sonata also serves as a recapitulation of the first, with the 'Molto vivace' theme introduced as a framing device for the earlier material. This means that it has the final say (page 33, bar 18) and ends the work in forthright and ebullient style, both instruments sweeping on towards an affirmative, *fortissimo* cadence in C major.

Ex. 8.16

T HE following reviews are included here as much to show the somewhat whimsical style adopted by some music periodicals at this period, as to record the reception of the Sonata. The first performance, on 7 October 1924 took place in unusual circumstances:

> 'The Music Society' is rather a little Society but a big name. Such a name seems to embrace much. The little Society, which meets at St. John's Institute (just beside Westminster Abbey), has a restricted embrace, but what it gets hold of is usually good.[41]
>
> The concerts are between tea-time and dinner. One sits in a deck-chair, and smokes. The hall is barn-like, and rather too resonant. At the first meeting of the winter there was a programme of modern English music – and everyone there (Mr. W. J. Turner, of course excepted – if he were there), seemed to like it. Indeed, such English chamber-music as we heard – Vaughan Williams's Phantasy Quintet, Bax's Oboe Quintet and a new Violin Sonata of Delius – might reasonably expect a welcome. But we live in days of strange music-lovers. One might say that many are in truth music-haters (I have just been reading Mr. Turner's book!), and only endure music in this life in hopes of a remittance of purgatory. And none of these three pieces would succeed in beguiling those others

---

[41] The Music Society was formed in 1920 by the then well-known violinist André Mangeot.

who can take to nothing between the extremely archaic and the purest of atonality. Mr. Albert Sammons and Mr. Howard-Jones played Delius's Violin Sonata, called like its predecessor, 'No. 2.' It is a brief work, to the point. The composer has deigned to come outside his wood. He tells you that there was all the time a real human being amidst all those thick silvan shadows. The violin sings with an eagerness that is almost naïf. There are mercifully few notes for the pianoforte. There is one movement, or rather three short linked movements, and no sonata arguments – just a lyrical expansion.

*The Musical Times*, November 1924

The second recital, a month later, suffered from a surfeit of Delius:

One-composer programmes are seldom entirely satisfactory, except Bach or Wagner, and the Delius chamber concert at Wigmore Hall on November 8th proved this rule most conclusively. Close on two hours of this entirely original idiom – displaying throughout the curious, vague, impersonal aloofness possessed by Delius more than any living composer, and which shines most in direct contrast with more energetic and vital creations – proved, en masse, disappointing. Each sonata or group cancelled out the effect of the preceding one, as the ear quickly tires of endless unvaried chordal progressions for the piano and the wide spreading phrases, with little rhythmic pulse to support them, for the stringed instruments.

The two violin sonatas were played in a perfectly straightforward manner, with no subtleties of tone colour, by Messrs. Albert Sammons and Howard-Jones. Miss Beatrice Harrison's share in the 'cello sonata was *troppo rubato e sempre portamento*. Of six songs, interpreted by John Goss, the 'Chanson d'Automne' (Verlaine) was by far the most convincing, but all were suffused with a pleasing gentle melancholy; and one or two in a contrasted group of songs should be heard more frequently than heretofore. Mr. Goss also hummed a plaintive tune in the new piano piece quaintly entitled 'Lullaby (for a modern baby),' one of a set of six still in manuscript. Other piano pieces, especially the preludes, provided flowing passage-work effects which might have been utilised to advantage in the concerted works, but as contributions to pianoforte literature they are of small importance. Let us have a certain amount of Delius by all means, but a whole concert, No.

*Musical Opinion*, December 1924

In 1929, the celebrated viola player Lionel Tertis arranged the Sonata for viola and piano, and then recorded it for Columbia with George Reeves as his accompanist. When Delius had listened to the records, Jelka wrote to Tertis for him:

I have only just heard my 2nd Violin Sonata played by you for the 'Columbia'. It is marvellously beautiful, and I am overjoyed. I cannot imagine it better played. You have got *so* inside the music, and I never thought that the viola could sound so lovely. What a great artist you are! ... Please also thank Mr Reeves for his excellent collaboration.[42]

1923 was a marvellous year for first performances: the Cello Concerto, *Song before Sunrise*, *Hassan* and the second *Dance Rhapsody*, and Delius and Jelka must have been thrilled by that. Furthermore, their financial troubles were finally resolved, for Balfour Gardiner made another of his immensely generous gestures: he bought the house in Grez from them for 70,000 FF, on the basis that they would be able to live there until they had both died. Despite his bluff manner and occasional blunt remarks about people, Gardiner had a warm heart, and always stood by his friends – luckily being financially able to help them if they fell on hard times. Earlier in the year, Gustav Holst had fallen off a rostrum while conducting, and the resulting injury to his head prevented him from working for two years: so Gardiner not only took over his composition and harmony classes at both Reading University and The Royal College for a while, but gave him £8 a week to cover his loss of earnings. So far as the Deliuses were concerned, Stephen Lloyd put it beautifully:

> Through the love of his own cottage and the seclusion it afforded him, Gardiner would have been sensitive to the anguish that a separation from Grez would have caused Delius. Both men were autocrats and while Gardiner had neither the disdainful bearing nor the hardness of character that Delius possessed, they had certain things in common: they shared a liking for the finer comforts of life in which both were connoisseurs. Purchasing the house at Grez was in itself an act of preservation – of the house and the style of life associated with it.[43]

The first two-and-a-half months of 1924 were spent at Rapallo on the north-western Italian coast, followed by five weeks with the Cleweses at their Chateau de La Napoule. Back at Grez, they had the usual stream of visitors, but Delius's health continued to go up and down and they made two visits to Cassel for yet another cure. It would be tedious to continue regularly mentioning Delius's deteriorating condition – so suffice it to say that from now on he would become progressively physically weaker and weaker, although his mind remained as active as ever, virtually up to the end of his life.

ALTHOUGH at some point in the year he had started making sketches for a setting of W. E. Henley's poem *A Late Lark*, for tenor solo and orchestra, nothing else was written during 1924, and he only appears to have began work on it properly the following year.

William Ernest Henley was a Victorian literary polymath of considerable stature, being a critic, editor, poet and publisher. Born in Gloucester in 1849,

---

[42] Letter 540.

[43] *Gardiner*, p. 157.

the son of a bookseller, he suffered from a bone disease which resulted in his spending a large amount of time in hospitals, and even losing a leg. As a result, much of his best poetry reflects that aspect of his life and meditates on death – for example, the sequence of twenty-eight free verse poems *In Hospital* in his *A Book of Verses*,[44] and the defiant 1875 poem, *Invictus* (ending with the celebrated lines 'I am the master of my soul / I am the captain of my fate'). In a completely different vein, however, is *I. M. [In Memoriam] Margaritae Sorori*,[45] the first line of which is 'A late lark twitters from the quiet skies'.

## A LATE LARK

### (1924–9: *RT* III/6; *CE* vol. 15b)

I N extended images of the sun setting at the close of day and the onset of night, Henley's poem embraces, with tranquil resignation, the end of life for one whose 'task [is] accomplish'd and the long day done'. The text, in its obvious connotations with the disintegration of Delius's health, stimulated a work of the utmost poignancy. The image of the lark, late in migrating to a more congenial climate and lingering on instead, is given musical life in the opening bars of the work, by the oboe in a snatch of birdsong, characterised by dotted rhythms, above a hushed string chord. A twittering and trilling solo violin adds its voice (Fig. 1-6), whilst a soft horn call (Fig. 1-2) heralds the setting sun, shedding its farewell warmth over the scene, in a mellow D major from clarinets, bassoons, 2nd horn and strings, to which the oboe, once again, makes a lyrical melodic contribution, soon joined by the solo violin and further horn calls (Ex. 8.17).

Delius finds many ways of subtly illustrating the text in the orchestra. Rising arpeggios in the cellos (Fig. 2+1) mark the words 'The smoke ascends in a rosy and golden haze'; the oboe motif (Ex. 8.17) reappears high up in the violins as a radiant splash of A major (Fig. 3+1) just after the line 'The spires shine, and are changed'; the undaunted lark sings its heart out again in the guise of the solo violin (Fig. 3+5), soaring up to high F sharp trills at the words 'The lark sings on'. The poet's assertion that 'the darkening air thrills with a sense of the triumphing night' is marked by Delius with shuddering *tremolandi* in lower strings (Fig. 4+3); the flute has its share of birdsong (Fig. 5-2), leading to an imaginative change of harmony at the phrase 'So be my passing!', in which a D major tonality unexpectedly shifts to C minor (Fig. 5+1), marking the moment when the sun disappears below the horizon and the deathly gloom of dusk infuses the landscape. The lark appears for the final time on the solo violin and the oboe (Fig. 5+7), followed by Ex. 8.17, warmly played in E flat by strings, in three-octave unison, and mirroring the resignation in the text: 'Let me be gathered to the quiet west'.

---

[44] William Ernest Henley, *A Book of Verses* (London: Alfred Nutt, 1888).

[45] A 'dedication' to his sister Margaret, added ten years after the poem was written.

Ex. 8.17

The final bars are indescribably poignant (Ex. 8.18). The final F major chord, resting as it does on an A natural, the third note of the scale, seems to hang mysteriously in the air, and adds yet another masterly stroke to what has to be considered one of the most perfectly conceived and executed creations in the whole of Delius's output.

THE fact that, by the end of 1925, Delius was forced to put the work aside, with only a handful of bars needing completion – the vocal line petered out at 'splendid and serene', and the orchestral accompaniment two bars earlier – reveals just how suddenly and seriously his health declined. The piece lay untouched until April 1929, when Heseltine was sent over by Beecham to discuss with the Deliuses what Beecham might include in his forthcoming Delius Festival. Heseltine unearthed the manuscript, and in the first two weeks of May, Fenby helped Delius to complete it[46] – in time for it to be given its first performance on the opening night of the festival, 12 October 1929. Heddle Nash was the soloist and Beecham conducted the Orchestra of The Columbia Graphophone Company:

---

[46] Letter from Jelka Delius to Philip Heseltine, 12 May 1929; quoted in *FD&PW*, footnote to Letter 927. There is a description of exactly what they did in David Tall, 'The Fenby Legacy', *DSJ* 61 (1978), 5–11, at p. 7.

The new work (dating from 1925), 'A Late Lark,' which Mr. Heddle Nash sang with clarity of diction and outward understanding, though without much inner sympathy for this mood (which may be readily understood and forgiven in any healthy young man), explicitly utters the same sentiment which is implicit in almost all that Delius writes. Again, the work is formally perfect – in the sense that it expresses perfectly what it sets out to express – but it reveals nothing new. Like Sea Drift [which came at the end of the programme], it is a kind of distillation of the spirit that animates the words.

*The Times*, 14 October, 1929

Ex. 8.18

When the piece was published in 1931, *The Musical Times* had interesting things to say about both it and *Cynara*:

Two big Delius songs are issued by Boosey & Hawkes, and are of outstanding interest. Both are published with pianoforte versions of the original orchestral accompaniment: in both cases, however, the music is so essentially orchestral in style, and depends so much upon timbre for its colour, that a pianoforte version, even if it be as well done as these are, is unsatisfactory. 'A Late Lark', W. E. Henley's poem set for tenor voice, is perhaps the more successful of the two in their present form. The music suffers less from arrangement: it has a beautiful freshness of sound; and a contrasting middle section makes the real unity of the song apparent. 'Cynara,' set for baritone, seems less satisfactory, perhaps because the orchestral part makes bigger demands. Apart from this, the poem pulls down the level of the music, in which some of Delius's more obvious tricks of style amount almost to mannerisms. Beauty, naturally, there is. But, to be frank, it is becoming more and more difficult to take seriously these naughty boys of the 'nineties, Dowson particularly. We are tired of their self-conscious humourless debaucheries. We are not interested in all that went on 'between the kisses and the wine': we, too, are desolate and sick of the old passion. The poetry is not good enough. One could do with it, perhaps, if the phrasing were perfect, like some of Baudelaire's: Dowson is simply too amateurish. Delius skilfully reflects the spirit of the poem: those who like Dowson will like Delius's 'Cynara': if one dislikes the poem it is obviously hard to judge the music fairly.

                                                                    1 October 1931

B Y the end of 1925, the Deliuses had had many welcome visitors. One particularly so was a representative of The Royal Philharmonic Society, who came to present the Society's Gold Medal, its highest honour – Delius joining the ranks of, *inter alia*, Hans von Bulow, Brahms, Pablo Casals, Henry Wood and Elgar. Almost all the others were devoted friends: at Easter, Gardiner and Kennedy Scott joined them in Cassel; in May Austin and the Barjanskys came, the Barjanskys returning in July; Heseltine and his friend E. J. Moeran followed; then Evlyn Howard-Jones, and finally Grainger and Gardiner again. It must have been reassuring to have all that support, particularly as Delius must have felt totally frustrated that the medical profession was doing little for him other than more or less keeping him going. The impossibility of travelling to London or elsewhere (particularly Germany) for some of the ever-increasing number of performances of his works[47] was partly compensated

---

[47] The introductions to each year's correspondence in *Letters 1* and *Letters 2* mention a very large number of them. Although in the briefest of terms, they nevertheless give a good overview (which it would be impossible to provide here) of the extent

by the acquisition of a wind-up gramophone, and especially from 1927 onwards the first recordings of his own music by the Columbia Graphophone Company.

There were two great surprises in 1926: Delius was invited by Oxford University to accept an Honorary DMus (but had to refuse as he would have had to go to Oxford in person to receive it), and, at the very beginning of the year, the 1926 New Year's Honours List announced his appointment as a Companion of Honour – the sole gift of the Sovereign for 'recognised services of national importance'.[48] It might be thought that Delius would have been contemptuous of the gesture, but Beecham was right when he judged both Delius's and the public reaction to be welcoming, and organised his 1929 Festival.[49]

Between 1926 and 1929, Delius wrote nothing that has survived, but happily there was still a constant stream of visitors: in addition to most of those already mentioned, who came again, they included Arnold Bax, Fritz Cassirer, Norman O'Neill and Orr – as well as a Dr Heermann from the clinic in Cassel, who spent a week trying some new medical treatments. In the autumn of 1926, Edvard Munch stayed, and thereafter he and Delius continued to exchange occasional letters.[50] The BBC celebrated Delius's sixty-ninth birthday in 1927 with a broadcast concert conducted by Geoffrey Toye,[51] and, as Jelka wrote, 'they addressed a little speech to Fred, which seemed so personal and extraordinary; he enjoyed it all.'[52]

By 1928, many years had passed since there had been a 'defining moment' in Delius's life, but now the last of them arrived. The story of how, at the end of 1928, the twenty-two year-old Eric Fenby became Delius's amanuensis, and enabled him to continue composing for another four years, is the subject of his book, *Delius as I Knew Him*.[53] No one interested in Delius should fail to read it, and it is inappropriate to paraphrase or quote extensively from it here. Suffice it, therefore, to relate the way in which the amazing relationship came into being.

Eric William Fenby was born in Scarborough in 1906. His family were all musical and he enjoyed a happy childhood – beginning to learn several

to which Delius's music was now being played. Some figures for Delius's royalty income can be found on *M&C*, p. 19.

[48] Beecham had in fact campaigned unsuccessfully two years earlier for Delius to be appointed a member of the (higher) Order of Merit: see *Evening Standard*, 14 June 1917; *Lucas*, p. 187.

[49] *TB*, pp. 199–200.

[50] Letters 524, 527, 528, 597 and 598.

[51] (Edward) Geoffrey Toye (1889–1924): a versatile English conductor and composer who had strong links with the D'Oyly Carte Opera Company and Sadlers Wells Ballet.

[52] Letter 509.

[53] Eric Fenby, *Delius as I Knew Him* (London: Faber & Faber, 1936; rev. edn 1981) (here *Fenby 1*).

instruments, having perfect pitch, and able to read a full score well before he reached his teens. Just into them, he became the organist at the local church; he largely taught himself composition, and by the time he reached nineteen he had conducted one of his pieces in the Spa Grand Hall. One, if not the first, of his hearings of Delius was a broadcast of Kennedy Scott's performance of *A Mass of Life* in Queen's Hall on 16 May 1928 – he switched the radio on during a boring game of chess[54] – and: 'When at last, after weeks of enquiries and disappointments, I was able to peruse the score ... I stood spellbound in the little music shop in the main street of my native town ...'.[55] He then read somewhere about Delius's pitiful condition, and so fired was he by the combination of the two that he wrote to Delius, saying how much he had enjoyed the work; Jelka replied on Delius's behalf, thanking Fenby for his sympathy and appreciation. 'During the next few weeks the conceit that I could help [Delius] became an obsession ... and in the end I could not sleep for it.'[56] He therefore summoned up his courage and wrote again, with an offer to help the stricken composer in any way he could for three or four years – an offer which was, of course, accepted.

Fenby arrived at Grez on 10 October 1928, and (as described above, in Chapter 7) on that very afternoon he was given his first task.[57] Over a number of visits to Grez, Balfour Gardiner had been transcribing the manuscript full score of *Poem of Life and Love*, dating from 1918, into short score so that it could be played on two pianos. But it was still unfinished, and Delius asked Fenby to complete it. Neither the next morning, however, nor subsequently, did Delius ask how he had got on – until, one evening, Delius suggested that he would like to dictate a 'simple little tune':

> Throwing his head back, he began to drawl in a loud monotone that was little more than the crudest extension of speech, and which, when there was anything of a ring about it, wavered round a tenor middle B. This is something like what I heard: 'Ter-te-ter – ter-te-ter – ter-te-te-ter' – and here he interjected 'Hold it!' and then went on – 'ter-te-te-ter – ter-ter-ter – te-ter – hold it! – ter-te-te-ter – ter-ter-te-te-ter – hold it! – ter-te-ter-ter-te-ter-ter-te-ter – hold it! – ter-te-ter-ter-te-ter-ter-te-ter'.[58]

That was the well-known beginning of Fenby's labour of love – and, astonishingly, the two of them gradually evolved a *modus operandi* which resulted in the making of an orchestral suite out of the *Hassan* music, the finishing of *Cynara* and *A Late Lark*, and the complete composition of seven new works. Fenby repeatedly lost heart, and several times returned to England

[54] *Lloyd*, p. 13.

[55] *Fenby 2*, p. 6.

[56] Ibid., pp. 8–9.

[57] See above, Chapter 7, under *Poem of Life and Love*.

[58] *Fenby 2*, p. 31.

for a break – but he had become too fond of the Deliuses, and too determined to see his task through to the end, for him ever to give up.

The full story of how the breakthrough came about can be found in the first thirty-seven pages of *Delius as I Knew Him* – and in the event it was achieved remarkably quickly. Ever since Delius had finished *Poem of Life and Love*, he must have known in his heart of hearts that was not a satisfactory piece, but he had not had the will to put it to rights. Although he had made no further mention of the transcription, some two or three weeks after Fenby's arrival Delius asked him to criticise it:

> [I was very] conscious of Delius's cautious probing, and I dreaded the inevitable question I fear he would put to me. Well, it came all too soon: what did I think of the piece? Now Delius was a very difficult man, despite a certain charm and dry humour; a very private man; awesome and given to silence. And had I known how much he resented criticism of his music, I should never have dared to say what I did of the invention of some of the weaker sections of the work, which I thought might have been written by a student, and very much in Delius's early manner too. And here was I, little more than a student myself. However, my opinion had already been approved in private by his wife Jelka, and I gave it when asked with more candour than tact, and Delius was taken aback. Eventually he conceded. 'Then select the good material and make a piece out of it yourself. Take your time. I'll hear it when you're ready.' And with this he was carried away. Eventually the next dreaded moment came, but not without praise for my written effort. Delius said he could work with me; now he would see what he could do. I tore up my manuscript in triumph. I had managed to rekindle his interest.[59]

It seems to have been nine or ten months before they actually started work on what would become *A Song of Summer* – perhaps in August 1929.

[59] *Lloyd*, p. 161.

## A SONG OF SUMMER
(1929: *RT* VI/26; *CE* vol. 27b)

## POEM OF LIFE AND LOVE
(1918: *RT* VI/25; *CE* supp. vol. 1)

I T is unlikely that Delius would have wished the score of *Poem of Life and Love* to be available in circulation, after its 'dismemberment' (to borrow Robert Threlfall's vivid term) and subsequent reworking as *A Song of Summer* – though it has, in fact, now been published, and even recorded. Some may have reservations about this, but it does at least present valuable evidence of how justified Fenby was in standing up to the composer (as Jelka urged him to do) and pointing out the unevenness of the writing. The surgery was so skilfully done – indeed, the amputations were unavoidable if the patient was to survive – that we should be grateful for any insight into how it was achieved. After all, the invalid recovered and was reincarnated as a piece of vintage Delius.[60]

*Poem of Life and Love* has been likened to a symphonic movement,[61] a lengthy one, lasting for around twenty minutes. *A Song of Summer*, on the other hand, is roughly half that length, so it is obvious that a great deal of material was discarded. The instrumental requirements of the two scores are virtually identical, the only differences being the removal of a redundant bass drum, and the reduction of two harp parts to one. Otherwise, the retained portions of the score were not significantly reorchestrated, though, as will be noted below, some modifications were made.

This is not the place for a detailed comparison, which could only properly be shown on a bar-by-bar basis, but the following description of *Poem of Life and Love* should at least give some indication of what was rejected in the process of recomposition. Broadly speaking, it is the slower, lyrical sections, i.e. the poetry of Love rather than Life, that have been retained. In its overall form, the piece consists of a sequence of alternately fast and slow sections, which gradually introduce new material, whilst at the same time referring back to previous ideas, albeit without much in the way of logical development or evolution. If this seems confusing in theory, then it is also sadly true in performance: one of the great weaknesses of the work is that no overall sense of departure and arrival, of a journey accomplished, is apparent.

An eighteen-bar introduction, marked 'Very Slow', was cut in its entirety, though the cello theme which runs through it does survive, in modified form, as Ex. 8.19 (see below). This motif is initially no more than an upward-curving arabesque, hesitantly sketched out beneath slow-moving, chromatic woodwind chords. But at bar 19, as the pulse changes from 3/2 to 4/4 ('With animated but moderate tempo'), it becomes more assertive – presumably it is the heroic

---

[60] Fenby gives a detailed account of working on this in *Fenby 1*, pp. 131 *et seq.*

[61] Jelka, for example, referred to it as a 'Symphony': see Letter 434, n. 1.

life-force implied by the work's title – though, frankly, the impression it gives is simply that of an undistinguished idea accompanied by chugging quavers, doggedly reiterated on lower wind: a sort of poor man's *Heldenleben*.[62] This prosaic passage lasts for just over fifty bars and, like the introduction, was completely – and rightly – discarded.

The texture suddenly subsides after bar 70, and a new idea emerges in the 1st flute, imitated by the 1st bassoon: these two bars, 72 and 73, correspond to bars 14 and 15 of *A Song of Summer* and in fact the next section is carried over intact, with some very minor, but effective, additions to the scoring (for example, in the later score, Delius introduces a slow-moving melody for the cellos in bar 16 *et seq.*, whereas he originally held them motionless on a sustained F sharp; and in bar 24 *et seq.* he introduces a counter-subject for the 1st horn, which is not to be found in the earlier score).

The two works diverge again after bar 112 of the *Poem*, as the main cello theme from the opening is recalled, along with some of the slower melodic material of the passage that originally followed it. This section, of nearly 100 bars (marked 'Comodo'), was cut in its entirety. So too were the following 40 bars (marked 'Very slow'), which included a new idea shared by the 1st oboe and the 1st horn: a downward arpeggio, complemented by a triplet, which sounds as if might have been suitable for inclusion in *A Song of Summer*; in fact, it finds no place there (perhaps Delius felt it was too reminiscent of earlier works). The animated music of the opening main section returns (bar 247), now with a rather slower and broader tempo marking; again, this was not destined for recycling. A final section (bar 297 *et seq.*) reintroduces material recalled mainly from the work's slower interludes, and some of this was transferred across to the final pages of *A Song of Summer*, notably a passage beginning (in the earlier work) at bar 321 and which corresponds to bar 116 *et seq.* of the later score.

So much for *Poem of Life and Love*, a work whose inspiration is too uneven, and whose construction too diffuse, ever to be convincing. As Fenby was quick to realise – and Delius too, to give him credit – it was the more lyrical pages, usually in a slower tempo, that stood out from the rest and were the ones that cried out to be salvaged.

We can now consider the transformation of those passages into *A Song of Summer*. Delius's own description of the opening bars survives as an authentic vision of what was in his mind:

> I want you to imagine that we are sitting on the cliffs in the heather, looking out over the sea. The sustained chords in the high strings suggest the clear sky and the stillness and calmness of the scene ...[63]

The atmosphere is captured in a masterly piece of orchestration: against an

---

[62] This is the passage played by Christopher Gable in Ken Russell's 1968 BBC television film, *A Song of Summer*, that the youthful Fenby had the temerity to criticise.

[63] *Lloyd*, p. 160

unemphatic pulse of seven crotchets to a bar, a motif on cellos and double basses unexpectedly emphasises the augmented fourth (G sharp) and the flattened seventh (C natural) of the D major tonality, its repetitions suggesting waves gently breaking on the shore below; the flute and oboe figurations, using intervals of the whole tone scale, and a rhythmic flick in the tail, imitate the cry of seagulls; the murmuring triplets on the horns (bar 6) giving an additional sense of the sea's gentle swell:

Ex. 8.19

Just after the 1st bassoon takes up the flute and oboe motif, the metre changes to 3/2 and the tempo quickens considerably (bar 16), propelled by softly pulsing D major chords from the harp, whilst half of the cello section gradually climbs up the stave and the oboe shapes an idea evolved from the initial bars of the upper 1st violin part of Ex. 8.19, the various motifs worked out in fairly elaborate counterpoint:

Ex. 8.20

Delius expands the oboe theme of Ex. 8.20 in the 1st violins (bar 24) and broadens it. Two other significant motifs emerge: the first is in the woodwind (bar 28) and derived from the first three notes of Ex. 8.20; the second has a modal flavour and is given to the 1st oboe (bar 39), borrowing its dotted rhythm from the earlier flute motif (Ex. 8.19, bar 5), a thumbprint in Delius's later works (e.g. *North Country Sketches* and Violin Sonata no. 3):

Ex. 8.21

From these somewhat fragmentary melodic ideas, Delius derives virtually all the musical material for the rest of the piece. The texture thickens from bar 60 onwards, building up to a full orchestral presence at bar 70, where the upper strings recall (in octaves) the opening cello and double bass motif from Ex. 8.19. The mood becomes impassioned, but not for long, the music swiftly dying down again by bar 80, at which point 1st flute, cor anglais, 1st and 2nd bassoons, 1st oboe and 1st clarinet recall Ex. 8.19, relaying the idea from one instrument to another.

Harp chords (bar 90) indicate the return of Ex. 8.20, now in a tonality of B flat. Delius then recapitulates his earlier material, so that bars 90 to 116 correspond to bars 16 to 39, although the texture and orchestration are quite different. After bar 116 the music strikes out in a different direction, as the dotted rhythm of Ex. 8.21 begins to dominate in the woodwind and is then passionately given out, in octaves, by the strings (bar 124) before dovetailing seamlessly with Ex. 8.19, played by the full woodwind section.

Timpani rolls underpin a gradual relaxation of the tension and link into a coda of exquisite beauty (bar 139), the strings quietly providing a bed of sustaining harmony, above which the woodwinds play fragments of Exs 8.19 and 8.21. The 1st violins add their own recollection *espressivo* of Ex. 8.21 (bar 147), whilst the harp spins gentle arpeggios and the last cry of a seagull in the distance is heard on the 1st flute, the strings dying away on a simple chord of pure D major.

ACCORDING to the BBC Proms Archive,[64] the Promenade Concert conducted by Wood in Queen's Hall on 17 September 1931 was a veritable 'Deliusfest'. In addition to the first hearing of *A Song of Summer*, the programme included the *Dance Rhapsody* no. 1, *Autumn*,[65] the *Seven Norwegian Songs*,[66] the Violin Concerto, the Piano Concerto, *Brigg Fair*, and something from *A Village Romeo and Juliet* (unspecified, but presumably *The Walk to the Paradise Garden*). Almost as an afterthought came Grieg's *Six Songs*, op. 48, one song each by Frederick Nicholls and Stanford, and an unspecified excerpt from *Lohengrin*:

---

[64] Available online at www.bbc.co.uk/proms/archive [accessed 19 March 2014].

[65] Listed in the BBC Proms Archive as a piece by Delius and arranged by Beecham. Was it the 'missing' fourth movement of the *Drei symphonische Dichtungen*? (On which see above, Chapter 2.)

[66] Said to have been arranged by Beecham, so presumably only nos 1, 3 and 4: see *RT Catalogue*, p. 99.

Mr Delius has become a popular composer. Last night he had the whole of the programme to himself, and he filled the hall … the new work, 'A Song of Summer' is true Delius, in which there is a tune, but not a tune that one would want to call a theme. It is a fairly short work, meditative, but not wistful, that will take its place beside his other orchestral pieces – 'miniature' is too small a term, 'rhapsody' too big.

*The Times*, 18 September 1931

T HE relationship between Heseltine and the Deliuses had cooled appreciably over the last few years, to the extent that Heseltine could write to his mentor Colin Taylor at the beginning of 1925:

Delius, I think, wears very badly. His utter lack of any sense of construction, coupled with the consistent thickness of Texture and unrelieved sweetness of harmony (even at moments where sweetness is the most inappropriate thing in the world) get on one's nerves, and make one long for the clean lines, harmonic purity and formal balance of the Elizabethans and of Mozart – or else for the stimulating harshness and dissonance of Bartok, and the Stravinsky of *Le Sacre du Printemps* …[67]

and he did not revisit Grez between 1925 and early 1929.

Heseltine's reinvolvement came when Beecham, still in the early stages of planning his long-wished-for Delius Festival in October and early November 1929, realised that Heseltine would be just the right person to help with the planning, organisation and writing of programme notes for the huge venture. Having sent him to Grez early in the year – when the unfinished manuscripts of both *A Late Lark* and *Cynara* were discovered – Beecham went over himself only a few weeks before the Festival began, to persuade the Deliuses to come to England for it. There were two concerts of chamber music in the Aeolian Hall, and four of orchestral and choral works in Queen's Hall – with the Orchestra of the Columbia Graphophone Company and The Royal Philharmonic Society's Orchestra each playing for one of the latter (resulting in some recordings and live broadcasts), and the augmented BBC Wireless Orchestra for the remaining two. Delius apparently had only one concern about the arrangements – that Roy Henderson was not asked to take part; the two baritones whom Beecham chose, however, acquitted themselves extremely well. Details of the programmes are given below, in Appendix 3.

Beecham's persuasion worked, and Delius, Jelka and, of course, Fenby stayed (at Beecham's expense) in The Langham Hotel, immediately opposite Queen's Hall, from 9 October until the first week of November. Delius's presence at all the concerts undoubtedly contributed to the capacity audiences that flocked to the two halls, and the Festival was an unimagined success. Indeed, no other composer born in England had ever been given a series of concerts including

---

[67] *PW Letters*, Letter 917.

a very substantial proportion of his whole output (except for his operas) in the space of some twelve days.[68] The concert reviews indicate that the musical public genuinely appreciated the opportunity of hearing a large proportion of his music. At the end of the first concert, Delius

> was given a very cordial reception by the audience. He bowed his head and raised his hand in acknowledgement of the continued cheers, and Sir Thomas Beecham, speaking on his behalf, assured the audience that the composer was overjoyed at his return to his native land, and that the enthusiasm of the audience had given him great happiness.
>
> *The Times*, 14 October 1929

Equally satisfying was the fact that the press were more fulsome than it had ever been before about Delius's music:

> It is true that the orchestra is the ideal medium for Delius's harmonic style, but several of the songs sung last night showed that words supply him with a stimulus for mood-painting in lyric form. Indeed, it is surprising that several, at least of the early ones, do not enjoy wide popularity.
>
> *The Times*, 17 October 1929

> The third concert ... was designed to show that the composer's genius is able to express itself in a variety of subjects and in different moods. He has with some reason been accused of a monotony of idiom; the programme last night gave a reasoned answer to the charge, in that it contained works which were more objective, less autobiographical than much of his music ... Delius is one of the composers who can bear the weight of a whole programme. The interest in his music deepens, and enthusiasm for it increases, as the festival proceeds ... The concert, therefore, apart from its intrinsic merit, which was very great indeed, shed new light on Delius's work as a whole.
>
> *The Times*, 19 October 1929

> There was never any doubt as to the interest roused by this series of concerts ... there was the unmistakable something in the air of an 'event'.
>
> *The Musical Times*, 1 November 1929

> The great enterprise reflects honour on its promoters, in particular Sir Thomas Beecham. Delius's music has not been neglected quite to the extent that some have suggested; nevertheless, to hear it in such quantities and so well executed is a revelation of beauty. Some who, though always attracted and charmed by Delius's music, had doubted

---

[68] The biggest previous festival was the four-concert 'Commemoration' of Handel held in Westminster Abbey in May and June 1784 (see information available through www.westminster-abbey.org [accessed 19 March 2014]). The only major omission from the Delius Festival was *The Song of the High Hills*, which had been given in London relatively recently.

whether it had variety enough to maintain interest in such exhaustive programmes found that the spell positively grew on them; at the end of two and a half hours they came away saying that Delius after all could be properly appreciated only in large draughts. The composer, as all the world has been told, was able to come from his hermitage in France, in spite of his sad infirmities; and surely the very crown of the enterprise was his delight in the admirable series of performances and the fact, asserted by his intimates, that the experience had to all appearances given the afflicted musician 'a new lease of life.'

*The Monthly Musical Record*, 1 November 1929

The extraordinary enthusiasm which attended the recent Delius Festival and drew over-crowded audiences at the Aeolian Hall and Queen's Hall on each occasion is less a matter for congratulation than for reflection. No amount of argument can offer a genuine solution to the sudden popularity of a composer who not long ago was supposed to have but a few faithful friends. It may be chagrin to those few to know that Delius is now worshipped by many others, for some ten thousand attended the festival. Many, no doubt, heard each concert. The miracle lies in the sumptuous and exquisitely sustained interpretation.

*Musical Opinion*, December 1929

One can almost hear in the words of the dreamer, Niels Lyhne, Delius's own profession: 'I want no wider world than this.' It is a lovely world, none the less, full of colour, rich and fading. Analogies with other arts are dangerous, but I feel there is some similarity in texture to the vibrant, glowing palette of Renoir, something, too, of his luscious sensuality in the erotic works. This is not, however, quite the whole of Delius's world. He has his variety, more, indeed, as this festival has shown, than most of us had realized ... this autumnal poetry is the most characteristic note in his music, and after hearing one of the works, in which it is sounded, one feels, indeed, that 'summer's loss seems little on days like these.'

*The Saturday Review*, 2 November 1929

It must have been expected from the outset that, even with considerable financial support from the three organisations whose orchestras had been used, the Festival (meaning Beecham) would lose money. Nevertheless, it had undoubtedly achieved its purpose of making many more people aware of the attractions of Delius's music, and the critics seemed at last to have come round to accepting that the music was infinitely better than they originally thought.

Helping Beecham with the Festival was the last thing that Philip Heseltine did for Delius before he died from coal-gas poisoning at his London flat on the night of 16/17 December 1930. He was one of life's mavericks:

I cannot think of Warlock as having lived only in our time. There was something princely, something of the Borgias, about him. He seemed to me to combine, as it were, Thomas Nashe and Aubrey Beardsley.

His outlook was Elizabethan, he was a child of our age. The combination was astonishing. Let us hope that his death, so deeply to be regretted as the cessation of one of our best talents, will have the result of turning the attention of people to what he has left behind, his music.

*Monthly Musical Record*, 1 January 1931 (Author unknown)

But Heseltine's colourful personality did not affect his close friendship with Delius, and his youthful enthusiasm had been hugely helpful and stimulating. The Deliuses' shock at his death was dreadful. *Cynara* had not by then been dedicated or published, so Delius wrote on the manuscript score 'Dedicated to the memory of Philip Heseltine'.

The Deliuses have perhaps always been seen as recluses in France, but, of course, until now they had travelled extensively, and their friends continued to give them marvellous moral support. The long list of visitors in 1929 and 1930 included Barjansky, Gardiner (in both years, the second time with a young composer from Cambridge, Patrick Hadley), Roger Quilter (with whom Delius had kept in touch on an occasional basis since they first met at one of the Frankfurt Gang gatherings in 1907, and of whom Delius was particularly fond),[69] the musicologist Edward Dent (then the Professor of Music at Cambridge), Heseltine (bringing the conductor Anthony Bernard – who in 1929 made the first recording of *Sea Drift*, with Roy Henderson), as well as E. J. Moeran and a young composer, William Wordsworth.[70] Grainger and his wife Ella (married in 1928), O'Neill, and Bantock's son Raymond also paid visits, and at some point, too, Florent Schmitt went to Grez.

In that amazing year, Delius's paralysis improved somewhat, and – spurred by Fenby's quick mind, musical knowledge and constructive suggestions, and urged on, of course, by Jelka – he managed to compose his final piece of chamber music, a substantial work for chorus and orchestra, and a new piece for Beatrice Harrison. The first of these, dedicated to Margaret Harrison (who gave Delius and Fenby technical advice), was the Violin Sonata no. 3.

---

[69] *Fenby 1*, p. 57.

[70] Barry Smith, *Peter Warlock: The Life of Philip Heseltine* (Oxford: Oxford University Press, 1994).

## VIOLIN SONATA NO. 3

(1930: *RT* VIII/10; *CE* vol. 31b)

$\mathbf{E}$ RIC Fenby noted that 'scanty sketches' (some of them predating the composition of the second Sonata) already existed: 'the opening bars of three separate movements barely decipherable in his own hand'.[71] Those fragments had been elaborated in 1924 – the first twenty bars of the first movement were clearly written out, mostly in pencil, and there were six bars of the second movement (notated by Jelka); the last movement was for the most part complete, with around two-thirds (eighty-six bars in all) in pencil draft.[72]

The first movement, filling a concise framework of just ninety-five bars, opens in a leisurely tempo ('Slow') and presents three, clearly identifiable themes, each of them introduced with relative brevity. At the start, a bar or so of rather melancholy piano semiquavers establish a vaguely G minor tonality and precede the entry of the violin, which introduces an upward, modal scale, that touches a B flat on the way, but which arrives, in the fourth bar, on an unexpected B natural. The melodic line then pursues a rhapsodic course, with an accompaniment consisting of chromatic chords, which Delius made so much his own in, for example, the Cello Sonata. The pace quickens (bar 12) as the violin states a rather jaunty idea, taken up two bars later by the piano. This would appear to be a significant new theme, but that is virtually all we ever hear of it. Triplet figurations in the piano lead instead to the true second theme, announced by the violin (bar 19). In contrast to its predecessor, this has a downward flow to it, marked by falling intervals of major and minor thirds. Delius works the idea for a dozen bars, then reins in the tempo again at a double bar, and changes the metre to 6/4: the piano now introduces the third theme (bar 31), a lilting melody, richly harmonised in D major, and introduced by the piano before the violin takes it up (Ex. 8.22).

The music soon reaches a cadence at a double bar and returns to the opening theme, this time restated a tone higher and with a subtly altered underlying tonality (a dominant seventh on D) (bar 43). The material is freely developed in two, expansive statements (bars 43 and 60); during the first of these (bar 54), Delius includes a melodic fragment that he will recall at the very end of the movement.

The second theme returns (bar 65) with a different accompaniment (semiquaver triplet arpeggios and chromatic chords, rather than triplet quavers). After eleven bars, it dovetails with the third theme (bar 76), now in E major; the violin line remains, essentially, as before, but Delius varies the accompaniment from its original chordal style, to flowing quaver triplets. This leads directly to an eleven-bar coda (bar 85). The 'false' second subject (from

---

[71] *Lloyd*, p. 201.

[72] There is a detailed list of sources in *RT Supplement*, pp. 154–7.

Ex. 8.22

bar 12) is barely sketched, in just three notes in the piano part (bar 88), before the violin sweeps upwards above rising chromatic chords on the piano, and an *allargando* ends the movement in an exultant E major.

The second movement opens 'Andante scherzando' in 12/8; its dancing rhythms strongly suggest the music of the Dark Fiddler in *A Village Romeo and Juliet* and offer a contrast to the more intense music we have heard so far. But it is not allowed to overstay its welcome: after barely thirty bars, there is a complete modification of pace, metre and key-centre (from D minor to G minor) as a soulful melody is announced as a piano solo (bar 29), soon taken up by the violin (Ex. 8.23). The dotted rhythms have all the feel of a Celtic folksong. This is the 'simple little tune' that Fenby was asked to take down and whose idiosyncratic harmonisation must have surprised and delighted him. The interlude lasts a mere nineteen bars and a crotchet upbeat, before the opening material returns, a perfect fifth lower (bar 49), though soon steered back to the original tonality of D minor (bar 59) to follow its initial statement.

Ex. 8.23

It diverges again (bar 71) into a brief coda, which ends with energetic passage-work for both players and a *fortissimo* chord of D major.

The final movement begins with a slow introduction of great beauty: its rather formal, recitative-like melodic lines for the violin are underpinned by the piano with static and, for once, relatively unchromatic chords. A characteristic triplet motif appears briefly in both instruments (bars 13–15) before the music subsides onto a sustained chord of G for the piano (with added sixth), seemingly lost in thought.

However, the spell is broken by a double bar, as the third movement proper, marked 'Con moto', sets off in some agitation (Ex. 8.24A). In the space of just over forty bars, a handful of significant ideas, some only fragmentary, come tumbling out, one after another:

Ex. 8.24

These ideas, all introduced initially by the violin, are not overtly related to each other, though one of them (Ex. 8.24B) is linked back to the little triplet motif of the introduction. After their initial appearance, they then occur in kaleidoscopic fashion; for example, in the space of just thirteen bars, we hear, either in full or in snatches, Ex. 8.24B (bars 69 and 72); Ex. 8.24E (bars 77–9); Ex. 8.24C (bar 79); Ex. 8.24D (bars 80–3); and Ex. 8.24A (bars 83–5). Towards the end of the movement, Ex. 8.24E stands out from the crowd in a forceful statement by the violin (bars 92–6), *con passione*, with double-stopping soaring above *fortissimo* piano chords. The music finally subsides into an eleven-bar coda, marked 'Tranquillo', which re-establishes the introverted mood of the introduction and turns aside, in inconsolable grief, to end with dark piano chords in a sombre D minor.

O NLY some seven months later, May Harrison and Arnold Bax played the Sonata in The Wigmore Hall, and (through the good offices of Adrian Boult) they broadcast it in the following week:[73]

> The work is slighter than the second Sonata, but, although the composer finds nothing very new to say, this very slightness gives it a wistful charm. The melodies of the three movements are simple and characteristic and the writing is devoid of any complexities, the melodic line being supported for the most part by progressions of chords. Arnold Bax's second Sonata, which came later in the programme, made the greatest possible contrast to Delius's work. It has many beautiful moments in it, but its very richness of texture and decoration produces in the end a feeling of monotony no less than the bareness and mutual similarity of Delius's movements. Both these works were admirably played.
>
> *The Times*, 8 November 1930

Delius must have loved this review:

---

[73] Letters 544 and 547.

Two Sonatinas by Siegfried W. Müller for violin and pianoforte, in C major and G minor, show a good deal of ingenuity, but the harmonization is too advanced at times to be pleasant. Polytonality must do better than this before it can be accepted. There are moments in these Sonatinas when one feels convinced that two tonalities are not better than one. The difference between these and Delius's Sonata for violin and pianoforte No. 3 is that between darkness and light – for in the one case the harmony system is entirely artificial, while in the other it is as natural as the melody of a Schubert and as effective a means of musical expression.

*The Musical Times*, 1 May 1931

No doubt encouraged by Delius's letter to him about the viola arrangement of the second Sonata, Tertis did the same for this one, which was published, like the second, in 1932. On 13 February 1933, Tertis travelled to Grez, and he and Fenby played it to Delius (with Tertis's arrangement of the Serenade from *Hassan*). Jelka wrote again, full of enthusiasm:

> The remembrance of your masterly and heavenly playing, so full of deepest understanding, is with us all the time, and I hope you will come again when it is not so cold. Delius would love that. It was unfortunate that he had had one of his bad days when you came, and he cannot bear such icy weather. Yet he loved and enjoyed your playing which, he says, is quite unique. Kindest regards from Fenby who, of course, loved accompanying you.[74]

No one would have imagined that, at this stage in his life, Delius had the physical strength, the will or the inspiration to write a 'companion' piece to match the *Songs of Sunset* of over twenty years earlier. However, a friend of Delius recommended a Scottish hypnotist, Alex Erskine, who might help to restore his sight, and during June he spent a fortnight at Grez, seeing Delius every day for an hour. Delius's sight did not, however, improve, but his general physical condition did – to the extent that he rapidly became able to use his arms and fingers, could walk a little and climb a few steps. It was miraculous, and one can imagine his and Jelka's relief at this marvellous (albeit temporary) change in his health.

Back in 1920, Delius had begun a five-movement work for chorus and orchestra,[75] completing virtually the whole of the first movement in full score, and, in short score, the orchestral introduction to the second movement, together with extensive sketches and drafts for setting the rest of the text.[76] On 15 May that year, he wrote to Universal, saying: 'I am now busy on a new choral work, which I might be able to give to you', and the following day he

---

[74] Letter 576.

[75] Jelka Delius to Ernest Newman, 28 October 1930: *RT Catalogue*, p. 71.

[76] *RT Supplement*, p. 216; *Fenby 1*, p. 147.

told Orr that he was working on one.[77] Having made a start on it, however, he had further health problems, and then he had received the commission for the *Hassan* music – so he put it aside, and the manuscript lay on a shelf for ten years. After Fenby had been with the Deliuses for almost exactly eighteen months, either Jelka brought it out it as something which Delius and he might like to look at, or Fenby found it himself. Either way, they started work, and luckily Fenby left a detailed description of how they put the piece together.[78]

The words, taken from Walt Whitman's *Leaves of Grass* (which had, of course, provided the words for *Sea Drift* back in 1904), were chosen by Jelka, as was possibly the title too.[79]

## SONGS OF FAREWELL
### (1920–30: *RT* II/8; *CE* vol. 13a)

A SUBSTANTIAL amount of work had been done by Delius on this before he was forced to abandon it:[80] the first movement was fully composed and orchestrated, whilst extensive sketches and drafts existed, albeit only in short score, for the remaining movements. What is particularly interesting is that, in several instances, the accompaniment was fully drafted, with the words of the text written in above, but few indications of the vocal parts – a fascinating insight into Delius's priorities. As we know from Fenby's detailed accounts,[81] the compositional process was usually influenced by harmony rather than melody.

*Songs of Farewell* is an example of Delius at his most concentrated: the work lasts barely twenty minutes, with no place for self-indulgence or needless expansion. In terms of structure, the five Whitman passages inspired settings of roughly equal duration, the exception being the fourth, which follows straight on from the third movement and which is shorter than its companions.

The individual vocal parts are often highly chromatic, to match constantly shifting harmonies which rarely settle in one key for long, though the five individual movements are rooted in tonal centres, respectively the major keys of D, C, C (ending in B flat), F and D – all bright-sounding, clean-cut tonalities in the harmonic spectrum, well suited to the open horizons of a seascape.

Compared to *A Mass of Life* or *Sea Drift*, where Delius often expects an almost instrumental virtuosity from his singers, here the choral lines are more practical and gratifying to sing, with fewer leaps and bounds, or awkward intervals (though when it comes to high-pitched notes, Delius still makes considerable demands on technique and stamina). Moreover, he supports the

---

[77] Letter 454.

[78] *Fenby 1*, p. 147.

[79] See above, Chapter 4.

[80] *RT Supplement*, pp. 216, 184.

[81] *Fenby 1*, pp. 147 *et seq.* and appendix.

voices by doubling most of their lines in the orchestra, reflecting evidence we have from the sketches that the accompaniment often came first in the composition process.

The layout of the opening of the work shows this clearly enough: the 2nd sopranos are mostly doubled by the violins; the 1st altos by the 1st horn and then by the 2nd violins; the 2nd tenors by the violas; and the 2nd basses by the 2nd horn and then by the cellos. Similarly, the next choral entry (bar 17) has its eight-part choral texture doubled by the (divided) string parts. Naturally, there are moments when the voices do stand alone (for example, between bars 111 and 121 near the start of the third movement) but, on the whole, this is not typical.

Another major departure from the earlier choral works concerns the treatment of the poetry itself. In *Sea Drift*, Delius often superimposes different lines of text, but that is virtually never the case in *Songs of Farewell*, apart from a passage at the start of the work (bar 7), where staggered entries by 1st sopranos, 2nd altos, 1st tenors and 1st basses lead to a degree of linguistic confusion, with the words/syllables *backward, as in, silent, -erings* (from 'wanderings'), and *tracings* all being sung simultaneously. But this sort of textual overlap is the exception and not the rule. The choral writing is typically homophonic rather than polyphonic (i.e. the different voice-parts move together as a rhythmic entity, rather than against each other, in counterpoint).

The opening song, *How Sweet the Silent Backward Tracings!*, is marked 'Quieto, molto tranquillo' and plunges straight into the text in the second half of the very first bar, after just a soft chord on 1st clarinet, 1st and 3rd horns and harp, emphasised by *pizzicato* cellos and basses: Delius has packed his bags and is anxious to be off. The opening pages, as far as bar 33, are a general invocation to the 'remembrance of things past', before specific poetic images of Nature are recalled (apple orchards, wheat fields, lilac bushes, and so on). Four bars into the score, the 1st oboe, imitated almost immediately by the 1st flute and then by two clarinets, display one of Delius's best known calling cards: an ascending quaver triplet leading to a longer-held note, linked to a phrase that falls away.

The absence of any introduction to set the mood has its compensation in two memorable interjections by the orchestra: in bars 12–17, as the voices softly breathe the word 'dreams', flutes cascade gently down over quietly pulsing horns and a bed of hushed strings; then in bars 27–32, muted 1st and 2nd horns touch in similar arabesques against a counter-melody (marked 'echo') for the 3rd horn: a magical passage which also occurs in the opening of the prelude to Act 3 of *Hassan*.

Another arresting piece of orchestration helps to colour the augmented chord at the word 'voyage' in bar 25: fluttering woodwind and harp arpeggios evoke expectant sails, billowing in the breeze.

Whitman's beautifully poignant images of Nature dominate the second part of this movement and Delius responds with some of the finest mixtures of his orchestral palette: the 'Più animato' rustling of orchard blossoms in strings and clarinets (bar 33 *et seq.*); the cool of the early morning, captured in an unexpected C major harmony, with an added sixth, at the word 'freshness' (bar 41); the golden, hazy sun of late afternoon, reflected in a burst of radiant A major, 'Largamente', for the chorus:

Ex. 8.25

The music peaks *fortissimo* (bar 50) and then deflates with Whitman's final image of purple and white lilac, which Delius conjures up with woodwind arpeggios, upward figurations for violins and violas, and a whole-tone scale on the harp. The movement then comes to rest on a D major chord, burnished by full but very quiet brass, the 2nd trumpet and the 1st trombone just smudging the harmony with the sixth of the scale.

The second song, *I Stand as on Some Mighty Eagle's Beak*, is a seascape whose wide horizon is evoked in a short orchestral introduction, 'Lento molto'. The cellos, *espressivo*, suggest the movement of the waters in a broad, arching theme, soon reinforced by bassoons and cushioned by slow-moving string chords; a counter-melody in bars 69–70 is introduced by the 1st and 3rd horns:

Ex. 8.26

This horn theme is of some importance: apparently Delius wanted it to 'run through the movement', and so it does: on the 1st oboe (bar 71); then repeated and extended by the 1st clarinet (bar 72); on violas and 1st and 2nd bassoons (bar 75); on 1st and 3rd horns again (bar 78); high up, in octaves, on divided 1st violins (bar 81), etc. (This theme also appears in the last six bars of the prelude to Act 5 of *Hassan*).

The chorus contemplates the limitless horizon and the wild, restless sea 'seeking the shores forever', the vocal lines now less chromatic. There are many subtle touches in the orchestration: the swell of the ocean waters is evoked in an *ostinato* figuration, swinging back and forth between C sharp and C natural on 1st bassoon and violas (bars 78–81) at the words 'nothing but sea and sky'; 'tossing waves' rise up in the 3rd bassoon, double bassoon, horns, trombones, tuba, cellos and double basses (bars 81–4); a splash of a *sforzando* D sharp on all three trumpets (bar 83) colours the word 'foam'; the 'wild unrest' of the sea (bar 85) is suggested by a chord for three horns 'stopped' by the hands of the players to give a metallic buzz to the notes; and the timpani play for the first time in the work (in bars 85 and 89), all the more effective for having been held in reserve.

The movement reaches a climax of spray and spume at bar 88 ('the snowy, curling caps, that inbound urge and urge of waves') with Ex. 8.26 thundering out 'marcato ma espressivo' on all four horns, as we navigate through choppy seas (lower strings) with a gale blowing (woodwind and upper strings). But, typically for Delius, all passion is soon spent and three bars later the calm of C major has been restored ('Più tranquillo') in the initial metre of eight crotchets to the bar and the serene return of the arching cello lines (bar 93), this time with E naturals flattened by a semitone. Ex. 8.26 returns softly on divided 1st violins (bar 96) and is echoed by clarinets and bassoons, 'molto espressivo', as the music comes to rest on a C major chord, with added sixth.

There is a short orchestral introduction in triple metre, 'Andante tranquillo', to the third song, *Passage to You! O Secret of the Earth and Sky!* Scored for divided strings, its harmonies are somewhat reminiscent of Vaughan Williams: octave G flats in cellos and double basses clash with a B flat major triad in violins and violas (bar 102). The harmony sidesteps into B major and then into C as the chorus enters (bar 111) ('Passage to you!') combined with a cello figuration with a wavy, watery flow, a variant of Ex. 8.26:

Ex. 8.27

The rhythm of the vocal parts is borrowed by the strings for a richly harmonised motif (bar 122):

Ex. 8.28

The brass adds its own colour to the text ('you strong mountains of my land!' – bars 126–31) and the music begins to sway and dance. A reference to 'rain and snow' is illustrated in the orchestra by pattering rhythmic figurations in the woodwind (bar 137 *et seq.*). When Whitman evokes the planets and the stars, Delius responds (bar 145 *et seq.*) with divided string *tremolandi*, sustained woodwind, and splashes of harp. The pace quickens, matching a mood of exultation in the voices ('The blood burns in my veins!'), but holds back for three bars of 'Allargando' at the culminating cry, 'Away O soul, hoist instantly the anchor!' (bar 157). The full brass have been kept in reserve but now Delius unleashes them for this brief climax, which has the sopranos soaring up to top C and the tenors to a top B and B flat. (The *ad lib.* cymbal clash on the second beat of bar 157 was added at the suggestion of Eric Fenby, one of several dynamic and instrumental shadings by him; another is the soft harp chord that punctuates the very first beat of the whole work.)

The churning rhythm of Ex. 8.27 in cellos and double basses returns (bar 160), this time a perfect fourth higher; by now the voices have given their all and fall silent, and the orchestra is left to conclude this fine movement with a coda dominated by Ex. 8.27 and sustaining chords above in the woodwind and upper strings. The music eventually comes to rest in B flat.

Delius directs that *Joy, Shipmate, Joy!* should follow directly on (*attacca*) from the previous song, and this maximises the effect of the chorus bursting in with its exultant cries of joy. The music has the flavour of a triumphal march or hymn. The broad *legato* texture of the opening is effectively punctured at bar 185 by two clipped chords from strings and brass, as the anchor is hoisted. The harmonies are characteristically chromatic, with imitative entries for the voices from bar 190 onwards. Delius echoes the phrase 'She leaps!' most effectively in the voices, working into the texture his favoured triplet motif as a fanfare for trumpets and trombones (bar 196–7). The march continues with forceful choral shouts of 'Joy! Joy!' backed by full orchestra. The timpani, brass and double basses beat out a tonic-dominant tattoo in the final three bars, as the music rears up 'Allargando al fine' with a *crescendo* to *fff* (another suggestion by Fenby).

The final song, *Now Finalè to the Shore*, begins diffidently, weaving its way in chromatic harmonies that fluctuate between five and six beats in a bar. But that mood changes abruptly with a 'Più animato' (bar 227) as the metre swings into three in a bar ('Embrace thy friends') and a rising sequence sweeps us on towards another big moment, the 'Largamente' valediction ('Depart upon thy endless cruise old Sailor') which Delius underlines with a massively affirmative *fff* G major chord (bar 237); it is like being drenched in pure, ice-cold water.

Delius now steers into the calmer seas of D major with which the work began, for a hypnotic coda, 'Lento di molto', featuring yet another rocking, rhythmic variant of Exs 8.26 and 8.27, repeated over some twenty-one bars:

Ex. 8.29

Two sets of descending chordal clusters in the upper strings, together with corresponding woodwind phrases (bars 252–3) recall both the ending of *Sea Drift* (at the point where Delius sets the words 'no more') and the final pages of *A Village Romeo and Juliet*, which depict the sinking barge. In this case, though, we remain on the shore, hearing the waves lapping as the departing ship disappears over the horizon. There is just a final sigh of 'Depart!' from the chorus, *ppp*, in the last bar, marking the disappearance of the lonely voyager sailing over the horizon.

T HERE was sadly no question of Delius being able to travel to London for the work's first hearing, on 21 March 1932, and it was not broadcast, but he would probably have been pleased. The celebrated sponsors of those days, Samuel and Elizabeth Courtauld, offered to include it in one of their series of 'Courtauld-Sargent' concerts, originally intended to have been conducted by Bruno Walter. Walter was a surprising choice, because some years earlier he had criticised *A Village Romeo and Juliet*, but (whether or not Delius had a hand in it) in the event he was unable to get to England, and the concert was conducted instead by a newcomer on the Delian scene, Dr Malcolm Sargent, with The Philharmonic Choir singing their third Delius première, and the London Symphony Orchestra playing their second.

The concert was widely reviewed, and *The Times*'s piece had a gentle, valedictory quality:

The whole circumstance of [the songs'] production, the fact that they have had to be dictated (and it is marvellous that so rich a score could have been so committed to paper), the knowledge that if not Delius's last composition, the songs are intended to be in some sort the epilogue of his artistic career, caused their first hearing to be received in a spirit of reverence. They are not so much new music, as an heroic determination to extend the life of that music which we know as Delius a little further, perhaps to carry its aspiration a stage higher.

The first two numbers dream over again of the beauties of earth and sea, which have inspired so many of Delius's nature pictures. 'Passage to you' strikes a personal note; in 'Joy, shipmate, joy' the composer rouses himself to a height of rhythmic urgency unusual with him at any time, but doubly striking now. 'Now, finale to the shore' is what such a finale must be. After the words 'Depart upon thy endless cruise, old sailor', the orchestra is left to sail out into the complete serenity of a *pianissimo* ending … the whole work was treated with the ardent sympathy it calls for, and if the audience at the end were a little uncertain as to whether they ought to applaud, the hesitancy was certainly not due to apathy.

22 March 1932

while *The Musical Times* took a thoughtful view:

Only a specialist in Delius could decide whether these five pieces reveal the muse of Delius as going forwards or backwards or as stationary. To a neutral appreciation they were just Delius, a luscious fancy revolving round itself in its own plane of loveliness, and most characteristic when it was least concerned with any activity or articulateness outside itself. These are elements that are inevitably looked for when words are set to music.

1 May 1932

At the end of the previous year, *The Musical Times* had had well over half a page discussing the recent publication of Fenby's vocal score:

I declare them the richest offerings that choirs have had since Elgar's, and the richest tribute to Whitman since Vaughan Williams's, and Delius's own *Sea Drift*. There is a passion and quietness, and just here and there a trace of that tang that we noticed in the new orchestral work broadcast at a Prom. lately – *Song of Summer*. At least two of the pieces can be described as 'gorgeous' – and how rarely can we afford that adjective nowadays! … To me the quality of Delius's harmony suits Whitman's simple-hearted exuberance astonishingly well. Some may say that it is over-rich for the poetry, but I cannot imagine anyone not feeling the thrill of so magnificently upstanding an outburst as 'Joy, shipmate, Joy!'

1 November 1931

And Beecham later noted that the music had a strength almost resembling the great choruses in *A Mass of Life*.

## CAPRICE AND ELEGY
### (1930: *RT* VII/8; *CE* vol. 29b)

D ELIUS clearly still felt very affectionate towards Beatrice Harrison, who went to see him early in 1930 and asked for a new piece. Fenby found a few sketches for something for cello and piano, he and Delius set to work, and this was the result. Fenby thought that 'these miniatures are gems; simple as only genius would dare to offer in old age.'[82] Indeed, the *Caprice* uses the barest of means to produce its effects: harp arpeggios cascading downwards; gentle triplets in the cellos, oscillating between notes forming a perfect fifth; understated rhythmic emphasis from a handful of woodwind, with just the occasional arabesque on the flute; whilst the soloist pursues a jaunty melodic line (bar 6) which emphasises the interval of a perfect fourth, and is characterised by dotted rhythms. The brief initial statement over four bars is then expanded to eleven, and the whole section is heard again as a written-out repeat (the only difference in the orchestration being some additional double-bass *pizzicati*). The piece ends with a five-bar coda (bars 44–8), dying away on a luminous C major chord, with a B natural added at the top, reminiscent of the opening of *On Hearing the First Cuckoo in Spring*.

The *Elegy* is an altogether more extended and complex piece, with two main melodic ideas: the first is an angular, chromatic phrase which, like the main theme of the *Caprice*, folds over on itself, in this case a diminished, rather than a perfect, fourth. Subsequent repetitions are accompanied by unexpected harmonic shifts (Ex. 8.30).

A second idea, in B minor, has the feel of a stately, funeral march (bar 17); it is interrupted by a brief reappearance of the first idea (bar 22), but sets off again (bar 30), more purposefully this time and in D minor, to a soft tread provided by gently descending chromatic string chords. The two horns break in *mf* with an inversion of the intervals of the opening motif (bar 35), but the march ignores this and continues on its implacable way, reverting to B minor. *En route*, the initial idea is quoted in counterpoint on the clarinet and the bassoon (bar 46), and then is taken up by the solo cello again in a memorable coda, with shifting, minor/major harmonies as the music dies away to nothing.

The physical strength which Delius must have summoned up is simply incredible – for Harrison (the dedicatee) played the *Caprice and Elegy* on tour in the USA later in the year. Although she recorded the work for HMV in November 1930 with an unnamed orchestra conducted by Fenby, it was not, however, until 23 April 1931 that she gave the work its first hearing in

---

[82] *Lloyd*, p. 169.

Ex. 8.30

England – in The Wigmore Hall, accompanied by an unidentified pianist, who might well have been Fenby, as he had made that orchestral arrangement in 1930.

Delius would probably have appreciated this review too:

> Two pieces for 'cello and pianoforte by Frederick Delius may not take precedence over other works by the same composer, but they will be a boon to players. Both 'Caprice' and 'Elegy' possess the distinction of originality in thought and expression. Both achieve much with simple means.
>
> *The Musical Times*, 1 May 1931

IN September and October 1930, the Deliuses heard broadcasts of Wood's all-Delius Prom, and Beecham's performance of *A Mass of Life* at the Leeds Festival, which must have cheered them a little. Almost immediately, Fenby went back to England for a six-week break, but when the time came for him to return he was unwell, and he was not in Grez again, in good health, until mid-October 1931. During that time he had nevertheless worked hard on Delius's behalf, getting Boosey & Hawkes, who were now Delius's preferred (and final) publishers, actually to print and distribute scores. Having Fenby back, of course, acted as an immediate tonic for Delius, and in the six weeks up to the end of the year they managed to write two more works together.

## IRMELIN PRELUDE
### (1931: *RT* VI/27; *CE* vol. 27b)

ALTHOUGH the early opera *Irmelin* is deeply flawed, some of its thematic material was too good to languish in obscurity; this refurbishment of some of the more striking ideas has therefore proved a welcome addition to the concert hall.

Four themes were salvaged from the opera: three from the prelude to Act 1, and a fourth from the prelude to Act 3. The new scoring is a substantial reduction of the original, with the following instruments omitted: 3rd flute, 2nd oboe, 3rd bassoon, 3rd and 4th horns, all the brass (trumpets, trombones and tuba), timpani and percussion.

The new work follows a sequence of themes from the original orchestral introduction to Act 1 of the opera, but makes substantial cuts between them, in order to eliminate unnecessary repetition; a theme from Act 3 follows. Table 8.1 shows how ingeniously this has been done (references are to bar numbers). From then on, the piece diverges from its operatic source, and is newly composed.

Table 8.1  Revision of *Irmelin* Introduction for *Irmelin Prelude*

| Bars | | |
|---|---|---|
| Original operatic version | Irmelin Prelude | Notes |
| 1–4 | 1–4 | Theme 1 (originally from Act 1) |
| 5–6 | cut | |
| 7–10 | 5–8 | Theme 1 (originally from Act 1) |
| 11–20 | cut | |
| 21–5 | 9–13 | Theme 2 (originally from Act 1) |
| 26–7 | 14–15 | Theme 1 (originally from Act 1, slightly modified) |
| 28–31 | cut | |
| 32–7 | 16–21 | Theme 3 (originally from Act 1) |
| – | 22–3 | New material for Theme 3 |
| 38 | cut | |
| 39–48 | 24–33 | Theme 4 (originally from Act 3) |

There is no evidence that this five-minute miniature was ever performed in a major concert hall before Beecham used it twice in curious circumstances. First, he included it as an interlude in Act 3 of *Koanga*, in ten performances at Covent Garden and on tour in the north of England between 23 September and 23 November 1935; then, when he gave *Florida* at Queen's Hall on 1 April 1937, he substituted the *Irmelin Prelude* for the 'proper' second movement. Perhaps hardly surprisingly, neither of those performances seems to have been noticed at the time, apart from one report on the 1937 concert which said, 'Listening to "Florida" today, one doubts whether Sir Thomas Beecham would think of playing it if it bore the name of any composer other than that of Delius'.[83] Nowadays, however, the piece makes reasonably regular appearances in concerts, particularly those of pro-am orchestras.

## FANTASTIC DANCE
(1931: *RT* VI/28; *CE* vol. 27b)

THIS exuberant piece, with its straightforward A–B–A structure, is out of the same mould as the two *Dance Rhapsodies*. It shows how Delius could, when he wanted, shape his music from rhythm and a strong sense of pulse, rather than from harmony. The main theme of the first section, just three bars long, is introduced by the 1st flute and is characterised by two little whole-tone scales, beginning after semiquaver rests, and complemented by a falling phrase in minor thirds. Woodwind (and later brass) provide a strong pulse on the second and fourth beats of the 6/8 bars. The violins soon take over, and the melody is given full orchestral treatment, ending with horns and brass sliding down a chromatic scale as the music flows into the central section, still in the same tempo but marked 'più tranquillo'. Fragments of melody are passed around woodwind and strings, the 1st clarinet setting the trend with an off-beat rhythm, and then handing over to the 1st oboe and the 1st flute, against a background of little chromatic string figurations. Later, the 1st violins lead off *espressivo* with what promises to be a more intense theme (bar 34), but basically this section retains a light touch: there is no big tune, as such. The opening section then returns (bar 57) and is slightly extended to form a rumbustious coda in which the original horn and brass slides are now coloured with a full orchestration that includes the late appearances of glockenspiel and off-beat cymbal clashes. The dance ends in high spirits with a harp *glissando*, and a loud *pizzicato* C major string chord.

Unfortunately, on its first appearance, this piece did not appear to fare any better at the hands of the critics than its immediate predecessor. Adrian Boult included it in the concert of the BBC's 1934 British Music Festival on 12 January: 'The interest in Delius's short dance was largely pathetic. Though a characteristic bit of invention and scoring, it would not have won much attention in the days of "Appalachia" and the Dance Rhapsodies.'[84]

ALTHOUGH, during Fenby's absence, old friends continued to come – Gardiner and Austin, the piano-duo of Ethel Bartlett and Rae Robertson (who made an arrangement of the *Fantastic Dance*) and O'Neill – not many other things went right at Grez during Fenby's absence. In particular, Jelka's

---

[83] *The Times*, 2 April 1937.

[84] *The Musical Times* 75, February 1934.

burden was wearing her out. She had domestic (although not always very helpful) help in the house, but the work of moving Delius about the house and garden, and being with him during the day, had for many years been the task of a series of young German men, whom they knew as *Bruders*. Some were good and some were bad, but generally their turnover was quite rapid, and having to deal with them was another cross that Jelka had to bear. At the beginning of 1932, the Deliuses were delighted when Ida Gerhardi's niece, Evelin, arrived to give almost whatever help was needed. Delius's spirits rose, and in July the Lord Mayor and Town Clerk of Bradford came to present him with the scroll confirming his recent appointment as an Honorary Freeman of the City. The following year brought one of Delius's most distinguished visitors – Sir Edward Elgar, who flew from London to Paris. They got on extremely well together, and they subsequently exchanged fifteen warm letters.

Furthermore, a new work was being thought and talked about. One of Heseltine's many friends was the poet Robert Nichols,[85] and it seems likely that Delius was introduced to him by Heseltine – through the post, as he was then living in California.[86] In a talk to The Delius Society in 1983, Fenby remembered that, soon after his return to Grez on 1 September 1932, when he was playing through everything of Delius's that had never been published, Nichols arrived and Delius asked him if he would write a completely new libretto for *Margot La Rouge*. He declined the offer, however, as he was literally about to leave to take up a new job in the Far East – but he was well aware that the opera contained some exceedingly fine music, and virtually on the spur of the moment, in not much more than a few hours, with Fenby's help, he drafted a quite different text, selected from several different sections of Whitman's *Leaves of Grass*.[87] Delius and Fenby set to work and, as an afterthought, added the opera's sixty-five bar prelude. The task was completed by the time Fenby left for home again on 1 November.

---

[85] Robert Malise Bowyer Nichols (1893–1944): one of sixteen 'Great War Poets' who are commemorated on a memorial stone in Westminster Abbey.

[86] From where, among other things, he wrote a long and enthusiastic letter to Jelka about the first American performance of *Songs of Farewell*.

[87] *Lloyd*, pp. 121–2.

## PRELUDE AND IDYLL
(1932: *RT* II/10; *CE* vol. 13b)

T HIS is a fascinating example of how to give musical material a new lease of life: hardly an unknown phenomenon, but carried out here in an astonishingly ingenious way. Roughly 40 percent of the score of *Margot la Rouge* was discarded, affecting the end of scene 2, all of scene 3, most of scene 4, and all of scenes 7 and 8.[88] Some of the short opening scene was retained, as well as the majority of scenes 5 and 6, which comprise the opera's love duet. What is noteworthy is that, apart from one instance, the music of the *Prelude and Idyll* follows the same order in which it appears in the opera; in other words, it does not jump around, taking material from scenes out of sequence. The exception is at the very end, where the final pages (Fig. 11 *et seq.*) were derived from a portion of scene 4, with the addition of a handful of newly composed bars.

Moreover, the orchestral accompaniment was virtually kept intact, with only minor adjustments (such as replacing short notes followed by rests, with sustained notation through a bar); on the other hand, the original vocal parts were jettisoned and completely new ones created for soprano and baritone soloists, in order to fit the new Whitman text. The orchestration was not significantly altered in any way, apart from minor adjustments to cover the cuts, especially where these dovetailed. Indeed, the instrumentation for the two works is identical, with two minor exceptions: the piccolo part (which required a separate player and was not doubled by one of the flutes), as well as an unnecessary percussion part, were both omitted.

A tiny amount of new composition was required, such as the six bars preceding Fig. 7 (in order to effect a convincing join) and the final nine bars, though in each case the additions were merely an extension of what had come before. Occasionally, a silent bar was added to accommodate the vocal line (e.g. Fig. 4+2); the original notation was halved to introduce a greater sense of flow (e.g. Fig. 7+20 *et seq.*); and transpositions into different keys were made (e.g. Fig. 4+5).

Though this is not the place to give a complete concordance between the two scores,[89] it is worth giving a sample, at least, of the technique involved, showing how cleverly the original material was recast (bar numbers refer to *Margot la Rouge*, and figures to the *Prelude and Idyll*).

After the *Prelude*, two silent bars for the orchestra were added to accommodate the first phrase of the new text; bars 66 to 80 were cut, the orchestra entering (Fig. 1-9) with bar 81 (in the following bar, the woodwind chord was sustained, rather than being cut off; similarly with the string crotchets, extended to minims, two bars later); bars 90–2 were cut, so that

---

[88] For an account of *Margot La Rouge* itself, see above, Chapter 3.

[89] These can be found in David Eccott's article '*Margot La Rouge* Part Two: The Music', *DSJ* 70 (1981), 8–17; and *Lowe*, p. 166.

bar 89 segues into bar 93; the second half of bar 103 was omitted, the string chord sustained and the 1st clarinet upbeat from bar 134 added, before cutting to bar 135; bars 148–53 were cut (but the final crotchet F retained); bars 156–7 were cut; the string quaver chord in bar 162 was sustained for an extra bar; a silent bar (Fig. 4+2) was added; bars 180–1 were transposed up a tone, and the subsequent passage from bar 182 transposed; after bar 193 (Fig. 4+15), the following 181 bars were cut, rejoining the original at bar 374. And so on.

Ex. 8.31 shows the way in which the new text was superimposed on the existing orchestral accompaniment, by directly comparing the original vocal parts for Margot and her lover, Thibault, in their duet from scene 6 of the opera (bars 683–93), with the soprano and baritone lines setting Whitman's text, as a replacement.

Ex. 8.31

Ex. 8.31 *continued*

It is interesting how the music of *Margot la Rouge*, not considered one of Delius's more inspired works, appears utterly transformed when matched to a text that is infinitely superior to the original libretto. Delius made his musical selection with discernment; the fact that he supervised the task himself makes it especially valuable as an indication of how he could, when necessary, act as his own judge and jury in evaluating his material. The newly fashioned vocal lines soar above the original accompaniment and not only enhance it, but reveal it to be some of the most outwardly romantic music he ever wrote. It is uncanny how this transformation fits the poignancy of the new text like a glove, ranging as it does from an outpouring of passion that is truly Wagnerian in scale, to a much more intimate, but no less lyrical intensity. Delius did not always wear his heart on his sleeve but here he finds no place for understatement. We may only surmise whether the composer intended *Idyll* as a final love letter to his wife, a musical valentine in gratitude for her long years of devotion and selflessness. At any rate, the work magnificently recaptures the mood of earlier, happier days – the Paris of 1901 before 'the iron entered his soul'. Whatever its motivation, *Idyll* was a magnificent way in which to end Delius's composing career.

W ITH Delius's health clearly becoming worse by the month, every effort was made to give the première as soon as possible. The manuscript had to be checked, the full score and parts printed and proof-read, and a suitable concert selected in the orchestral season which would begin in the autumn; in the event it took place at a Promenade Concert in Queen's Hall on 3 October 1933. Beecham's rift with the Deliuses had healed to the extent that he coached the soloists, Dora Labbette and Roy Henderson (who had now become the Delian baritone without equal), but Delius had promised the performance to Henry Wood. It was a quiet success:

> In the last week of the Queen's Hall Promenade season was introduced a new work by Delius – or rather a new redaction of an old one, portions of his opera 'Margot la Rouge' having been adapted to a new text selected from Walt Whitman. This 'Idyll' takes the form of a prelude, a baritone recitative and a duet for baritone and soprano. If less than a masterpiece, it echoes the magical strains of the composer's masterpieces. The gist of the piece is a tragic separation of lovers; the end, however, is not despair, as in 'Sea-drift', but consolation attained in death. It is a beautiful piece.
>
> *The Monthly Musical Record*, November 1933

> The music is typical Delius, good Delius yet not making any real addition to what we already have, except in so far as the form and length and layout of the Idyll make it an extremely useful example of the composer's work that will fit into an ordinary concert programme conveniently. The mood is one of retrospect such as Delius most characteristically depicts; the voice parts, sung last night with beautiful clarity and sympathy by Miss Dora Labbette and Mr Roy Henderson, are typical of his method of setting words; the poem provides the starting-point for the orchestral meditation, and then the actual lines are set almost, it would seem, but not quite independently, or made to float upon the surface of the heaving sea of orchestral sound. The music itself is, if anything, more compactly wrought thematically than is sometimes the case with Delius. It is in fact a good little work.
>
> *The Times*, 4 October 1933

T HUS, and fittingly, Delius's composing life came to an end. His music had not become universally popular, nor would it ever; but virtually all that he had written was beautiful, sometimes powerful, of integrity, consistent in style, and marvellously orchestrated – and it remains unique.

# CHAPTER 9

# The Songs

S INGERS have no reason to complain that Delius neglected them. His six operas represent a substantial commitment, and the numerous works for voices and orchestra described in previous chapters cater for all sorts of vocal combinations, ranging from the epic grandeur of *A Mass of Life*, to the simple intimacy of the unaccompanied partsongs. The sheer range of these scores bears witness to Delius's abiding love for the human voice, an affection that never left him and which spanned his entire creative career.

In addition, there are over sixty solo songs with piano accompaniment – a neglected part of Delius's output, since only a handful are ever performed with any regularity. This chapter does not attempt to deal with each and every one, for that would require a book in itself. The intention is simply to offer a brief but representative survey, covering settings in six languages and ranging from the earliest examples, dating from the mid-1880s, to the final offerings of 1919. If a particular song has not been singled out for discussion, that does not by any means imply that it is unworthy; merely that the selection below is, by necessity, limited, and that the choices, inevitably, are subjective.

One of the problems in dealing with the songs is that, over the years, they have appeared in print in different formats: some were issued singly, others in collections; some appeared during the composer's lifetime, others only posthumously. Moreover, they were originally issued by a variety of different publishing houses, many of them no longer in existence; the situation can be confusing, to say the least. To give one example: the collective title 'Seven Danish Songs' is now accepted as a convenient way of referring to the group of stylistically related songs which were composed during the 1890s and which were all subsequently orchestrated by Delius in 1897. He himself referred to them in his letters simply as 'The Danish Songs' and obviously thought of them as a group. Yet they were never published as a complete set during his lifetime, though five of them were performed at his self-promoted 1899 concert in London. A collection with the title *Five Songs from the Danish* (i.e. omitting two) was published in 1906 by Harmonie-Verlag of Berlin in versions for voice and piano, and was subsequently reprinted by Universal Edition and by Boosey & Hawkes. However, an identically titled collection, published posthumously by Galliard/Stainer & Bell in 1973 as part of a volume of *Ten Songs by Frederick Delius*, contained a different selection, never grouped in that way by the composer. At various times, other publishers, such as Oxford University Press, have issued volumes of disparate songs by Delius of which they happened to hold the copyright. To complicate the situation further, some songs fell out of print and became difficult to obtain, even in second-hand copies; others had never even reached the press, despite the vigorous efforts of the composer (and his indefatigable wife) to have them published, and were thus hidden away and, effectively, unknown.

Fortunately the situation has been completely transformed thanks to the scholarship and authoritative editing skills of Robert Threlfall, who prepared the Collected Edition for publication. All the songs (and other vocal works) with original orchestrations by Delius have now been made available in print, many of them for the first time, and have been conveniently gathered together in the Collected Edition, volumes 15a and 15b. The songs with original piano accompaniments are available in volumes 18a, 18b and 19, together with a supplementary volume containing four previously unpublished songs. We can now see *all* the trees, as well as the wood, and gain an overall perspective of Delius's entire vocal output.[1] Most importantly, the scores themselves are accessible in modern, authoritative editions; what more could singers need to encourage them to explore such a rewarding repertoire?

One further problem specifically concerns those songs based on Scandinavian poetry, whether Norwegian, Danish or Swedish. In many cases, Delius claimed that he composed his music to fit a poem's original language, though there is conflicting evidence for whether or not this was so, particularly in the case of Norwegian.[2] What is certain, however, is that Delius fully realised (as did Grieg before him) that the market for songs in Scandinavian languages would be tiny and that, outside Scandinavia itself, there would be little chance of selling them to professional singers, let alone amateurs. From a purely practical and commercial point of view, Delius therefore had to provide his publishers with versions in English and/or German translation; often he or his wife took on the task; but there were several instances where others were commissioned, with appalling results. Delius was particularly distressed by bad English translations of his Danish songs,[3] though more recent editions have been able to repair the worst horrors (for example, during the late 1960s, the tenor Peter Pears produced far more accurate and singable versions.) In the process of adapting the vocal line to fit a translation, Delius would have had to alter some of his rhythmic notation; furthermore, the original languages were not even offered as a printed alternative, but were omitted and have not necessarily survived. This is a pity, as singers nowadays would perhaps be more willing to tackle Scandinavian languages than were their predecessors.[4]

Any reader wishing to explore these intricate problems of publication and translation is strongly recommended to consult the prefaces by Robert Threlfall

---

[1] There is also a complete list of the songs in this book, in Appendix 1, Part 2, below.

[2] See *RT Catalogue*, p. 93.

[3] Ibid., pp. 98–9.

[4] Those curious to hear them sung in Norwegian and Danish should seek out the recordings conducted by Bo Holten, which are sung in versions using the original languages and, in some cases, with his own orchestrations.

to the relevant volumes of the Collected Edition, as well as his *Editorial Report*[5] and *RT Supplement*, where such matters are discussed in some detail and clearly explained.

Where there are discrepancies over the exact title of the songs, or where alternatives exist (e.g. 'In the Seraglio Garden' / 'In the Garden of the Seraglio'; 'Summer Nights' / 'On The Sea Shore'), then the one given in the Collected Edition has usually been followed below. The titles printed in bold refer to the songs that have been selected for discussion and, in each case, references have been given as to which volume they can be found in.

One of the most useful ways in which a young and inexperienced composer can learn his craft is not by writing a symphony, but by penning a song. The reasons are not hard to fathom: songs are one of the oldest and most natural forms of self-expression, and we learn them (or used to) in our cradles; words not only provide extra-musical inspiration, they also involve an element of personal choice; the technique of voice and piano, the commonest vocal medium, is a relatively uncomplicated one; there is a much greater likelihood of actually hearing the results performed than with an orchestral work. Most importantly, because songs are relatively brief affairs, they do not present problems of having to manipulate large-scale, formal designs – and this means that errors of judgement can be quickly identified and some useful lessons learnt. If a song is not a success, then it is not too distressing to tear it up and write another, much better, one.

So it is not surprising that songs were among the earliest works that Delius attempted when he was taking his first, hesitant steps in composition. We do not know how many he may have written and subsequently discarded, but three have come down to us dating from 1885–6, when he was in his early twenties: one is a setting of Heinrich Heine ('Der Fichtenbaum'), whilst the other two show a precocious fascination with Scandinavian poets: the Norwegian Bjørnstjerne Bjørnson (in 'Over the Mountains High'), and the Dane Hans Christian Andersen (in **'Zwei braune Augen'**) (*RT* V/3; *CE* vol. 18a). The latter is musically the most promising of the group and does justice to the poet's moving description of how he has been captivated by the brown eyes of his beloved, which seem to radiate 'wisdom and a child-like peace … in them, lay my home and my world'. Delius's music has a pleasing, folksong lilt, implying that he knew Grieg's earlier setting (1864–5) and was influenced by it, particularly in its use of harmony. Nevertheless, Delius kicks up his musical heels when he attempts a startling trick in the last phrase, which, though it does not quite come off, at least shows a streak of independence: after modulating into E major for some dozen bars, he unexpectedly twists back into the home key of G, as if to punctuate, or underline, the poet's assurance of eternal devotion.

---

[5] See Robert Threlfall, *Frederick Delius, The Complete Works: Editorial Report* (The Delius Trust, 1990).

Delius's growing knowledge of Scandinavian poetry during the late 1880s and early 1890s resulted in a dozen settings inspired by Norwegian writers, and these were eventually published by Augener: five of them in 1890, and the remainder in 1892. The later collection, indeed, is most impressive in the way it demonstrates how far Delius had progressed in such a relatively short time; there is no doubt that he had learnt to write effectively and imaginatively for the voice. **'Twilight Fancies'** (*RT* V/9; *CE* vols 15a and 19) is one of the best known of this group of Norwegian songs – and deservedly so. Bjørnstjerne Bjørnson's original poem *Princessen* (which Grieg set in 1871) describes an aloof princess who at first is irritated when her solitary meditations are disturbed by a young lad sounding his horn; she tells him to stop, then changes her mind, realising that his playing fires her imagination. But her indecision has effectively killed the moment and, as the sun goes down, she is left alone, asking herself what it is that she really longs for, and what she wants from life.

It is a haunting poem, rich in subtext, but, wisely, Delius does not try to over-interpret it musically, and is content to respect its ambiguities, treating it more like a folksong. The distant horn calls are imaginatively portrayed in the piano, using perfect fifths that oscillate ambiguously between tonic and dominant, whilst the harmonic underlay is mostly provided by simple piano chords that allow the narrative to come through. The overall mood is one of mysterious melancholy, conjured from the simplest of means, which give the song an impeccably judged sense of unity and poignancy. As he often did in these early songs, Delius uses essentially the same music for each of the poem's three verses, though here the setting does in fact diverge at the end of the third stanza, in a sequence of drooping phrases that point to the princess's sense of bewilderment at her own feelings, as the horn calls are filtered through her consciousness like a distant memory (Ex. 9.1).

Another fine setting, also from the second collection of Norwegian songs, is **'The Homeward Way'** (*RT* V/9; *CE* vol. 19). This is a far cry from the claustrophobic, not to say neurotic, atmosphere of 'Twilight Fancies'; here instead we find the sweet and simple expression of memories of Nature and its beautiful landscapes. Recollections of a childhood spent amongst mountains, valleys and streams serve later in life to comfort and heal the jaded soul of an adult, tired and worn out by the grind of an urban life; this is a homeward journey being made in the mind rather than in a literal sense. Again, the musical setting is not complex: the vocal range, for example, is just over an octave, and the same music is used for each of the two verses. The harmonisations admittedly owe much to Grieg (who set the text in 1880) but not slavishly so, and there is clearly a free-thinking musical mind at work. Delius's own voice and style emerge unmistakeably in the lyrical opening bars, as well as in the phrase setting the words 'They fill my wand'ring thoughts with joys untold / it stills the noisy sounds of tedious day.' The song successfully avoids superfluous gestures and artistic self-consciousness, with the result that it has a feeling of naturalness and sincerity that is genuinely touching.

Ex. 9.1

Two songs from 1895 with Danish origins are worth examination. The first, **'The Page Sat in the Lofty Tower'** (*RT* V/17; *CE* vol. 18a), is from J. P. Jacobsen in an English translation by the composer himself. A page is trying to write a love poem, but struggles to find the right words, including, specifically, a rhyme for 'roses'. In despair, he tightly grips his sword and puts his horn to his lips, communicating his thoughts in music which rings out across the mountainside to reach his loved one. The image of a horn-playing youth – and by extension, the Artist struggling to express his emotions – has obvious parallels with 'Twilight Fancies'. There is also the shared idiom of a folksong, with the vocal lines declaimed over open fifths in the bass of the piano part. Later on in the accompaniment (bars 11 and 12), Delius aptly suggests the 'vain searching' of the would-be poet by writing hesitant, bare octaves for the right hand, followed by a fuller texture of diminished harmonies and sweeping chords. The culminating horn call is boldly sounded by the piano (bar 21), and the song ends with an unexpected modulation to G major, as if the page is asking himself whether he will ever receive an answer. As with 'The Homeward Way', this song is economical in expression despite its overtly romantic language, and is guided by an innate taste and judgement; yet it also breathes an atmosphere of great warmth and passion.

**'Im Glück wir lachend gingen'** ('In Bliss We Walked') (*RT* V/20; *CE* supp. vols 18 and 19) dates from the same period, the mid-1890s, and was also inspired by Danish poetry – verses by Holger Drachmann. It remained unperformed for many years. Though it was at one time engraved, it was never published – much to Delius's annoyance, since he rated it highly and, as late as 1929, continued to pester Universal Edition to bring it out. The song finally appeared in print in a posthumous (1981) edition. The text speaks of old age with its nostalgic, and occasionally tearful, recollections of the lost joys of youth; rather than give way to despair, one should be gladdened by the process of recollection, and ask for nothing more – a philosophy that obviously appealed to the composer. The setting itself is not all that typical of Delius and sounds much more like a mainstream English song – Butterworth, perhaps, or early Vaughan Williams. It has a hymn-like tread and an austere key-centre of F minor: its two verses hardly modulate and are not overtly chromatic, though there are subtleties of harmonisation to be found in the piano accompaniment (especially in bars 15–23, and their later equivalent in bars 35–44). The song has an admirable dignity and poise, as well as a clarity of musical expression that matches the text. There is a striking moment in the third bar from the end, where the German translation asks, 'Was will man mehr?' ('What more can one wish for?') and Delius places a most unexpected harmony (in essence A flat minor over a G flat in the bass) before adeptly resolving it.

Given that Delius was resident in France for such a long period, it would be natural to assume that he would turn to French poets, and yet there are only seven examples of this: 'Chanson de Fortunio' (Alfred de Musset, 1889); 'Nuages' (Jean Richepin, 1893); and five settings of Paul Verlaine, including one dating from 1895, **'Il pleure dans mon cœur'** (*RT* V/16; *CE* vol. 19). The last shows that when Delius did use the language of his adopted homeland, it touched off something unexpectedly French in his musical style. With its transparent texture, unexpected harmonic twists, and lyrical, melodic lines weaving in and out of a flowing accompaniment, the obvious comparison is to the style of Fauré (Ex. 9.2).

The mood of intense, yet controlled, melancholy characteristic of many French songwriters, including Debussy, is also to be found in Delius's other Verlaine setting from the same year, **'Le Ciel est, par-dessus le toit, si bleu, si calme!'** (*RT* V/16; *CE* vol. 19). The verse, written whilst the poet was serving a prison term for manslaughter, describes him gazing out through his barred windows at the blue sky, and experiencing an overwhelming sense of loss at what he considers to be his wasted youth ('Dis, qu'as-tu fait, toi que voilà, de ta jeunesse?'). Delius responds musically with unfailing sensitively, but without

Ex. 9.2

over-playing his hand: there are the merest suggestions of a tolling bell and of birdsong. Towards the end, the accompaniment consists of bare piano chords, with the vocal line transformed into recitative, to point up the essential message of the text. These subtle touches, in which less is undoubtedly more, are the marks of a natural songwriter.

The majority of Delius's songs involve a piano accompaniment; however, the 'Seven Danish Songs' of 1897, based on texts by Drachmann and Jacobsen, though originally with piano parts, were subsequently orchestrated by the composer himself. Since they gain immeasurably from their skilful, instrumental colouring, it is those versions which are discussed here.

**'Silken Shoes'** (*RT* III/4; *CE* vols 15b and 18b) is an ecstatic love song, marked 'with elevation'. 'Silken shoes upon golden lasts! I've won a maiden fair ...', reads the text. Delius's vocal line darts impulsively over the stave, in wide-ranging, angular intervals. This rhapsodic outpouring of young love includes many inventive touches of orchestration: the soaring strings at references to 'sky' and 'snow' (bars 12–13); the warm, burnished sound of horns and bassoons at the words 'But my heaven is filled with earthly bliss' (bars 15–16); and the richly scored climax of the song (bars 17–18, 'flames flare out of the snow'). At the same time, Delius knows the value of restraint: the four horns are only used as a quartet for a mere three-and-a-half bars out of twenty-two – whilst the trumpet plays only nine notes in all. This refinement of technique is typical, in general, of the orchestration of these songs. Also noteworthy is the characteristic imprint of an upwardly rising triplet followed by two longer note-values (the 1st flute has this figuration in bar 1, for example, and the 1st oboe and 1st flute have it in the penultimate bar).

'Irmelin' (*RT* III/4; *CE* vols 15b and 18b) is in the style of a ballad, each stanza concluding with the phrase 'Irmelin, loveliest of all!', which Delius sets in three subtly different ways, thereby avoiding the obvious. The text is based on the legend that provided the composer with the plot of his first opera, *Irmelin*, and it concerns a beautiful heroine, much courted, but whose heart can only respond when the right man comes along. Irmelin's theme in the opera (Ex. 2.10) recurs frequently in the song's accompaniment, sometimes as a direct quote (e.g. on the 1st violins in bars 13–14), sometimes in slightly varied forms (e.g. on the 1st clarinet in bars 7–8; and on the 1st oboe in bars 9–10). As this motif is different in mood from the narrative parts of the rest of the song, it subtly emphasises the princess in her world apart.

'Summer Nights' (alternative title: 'On The Sea Shore') (*RT* III/4; *CE* vols 15a and 18a) was also set earlier, in 1891, to different music (a version known as 'Dreamy Nights'), but this later setting is an altogether more sophisticated affair. The title of the original Danish poem, *Lyse Nætter*, invokes the particular quality of twilight experienced in Scandinavia: the word *lyse* literally means 'light' or 'bright', whilst *nætter* means 'nights', so *lyse nætter* refers to the season when true darkness is replaced by a luminous twilight, neither night nor day. Delius's setting is a magical piece of writing, barely rising above *piano*, and economically scored for muted strings (divided into ten parts) and four horns, which are used so sparingly that the 2nd and 4th play only one note apiece, in the space of just one bar. The soloist is instructed to be as free from any sense of rhythmic constraint as possible, and indeed the beautifully contoured vocal line is very much in the nature of a recitative (Ex. 9.3).

'In the Seraglio Garden' (*RT* III/4; *CE* vols 15b and 18b) is a superb piece of oriental mood-painting. Marked 'slow and dreamily', it is delicately enhanced by the orchestration, which has discreet touches of glockenspiel and harp, as well as pentatonic flurries from flute and clarinet; again, Delius happily resists the temptation to overdo these effects. There are some striking harmonic progressions colouring the words 'the pine trees are swaying so silently in drowsy air' (bars 8–11); and, immediately following, 'silvery fountains are playing so dreamily' (Ex. 9.4).

Four years later, at the very opening of the third movement of Part One of *A Mass of Life*, Delius would include the pentatonic figuration which is played by the 1st violins in the fourth bar of the above example as an embellishment of the solo tenor line by wordless alto voices; it is hard to say whether this is a conscious or unconscious self-quotation.

'Wine Roses' (*RT* III/4; *CE* vols 15a and 18a) opens as a raucous drinking song, extolling the virtues of Burgundy (we hear the clinking of glasses on triangle and cymbals). But then, as the pulse slows, the text unexpectedly evokes 'A faded day, a time gone by', with chains of triplets rising poignantly

Ex. 9.3

in the woodwind (bars 11–13); the deep ruby-red of the wine recalls the colour of roses, symbols of love. Past love-affairs are like wild roses along the 'great highway', which are 'gone as a strain of music goes'. Here the music sighs with heartbreaking beauty and eventually fades away in despair.

'**Through long, long years**' (alternative title: 'Red Roses') (*RT* III/4; *CE* vols 15a and 18a) originally had four verses, but Delius set only the first, a melancholy expression of long atonement for a trifling pleasure – a situation all too familiar to the composer. Red roses are once again invoked as an image of love, from which 'sorrows grow and hot tears flow'. Musically, the setting is hushed and restrained and scored without brass.

'**Let Springtime Come, Then**' (*RT* III/4; *CE* vols 15a and 19) sets off optimistically with swaying rhythms from flutes, 1st violins, cellos, double basses and timpani, all of which suggest the annual burgeoning of nature. But there is no springtime in the poet's heart, as a dark, seven-bar interlude, *più lento* (bars 17–23), clearly indicates. A third section mirrors the first, but more succinctly, as the poet resigns himself to awaiting 'my own spring. When? When?'.

Though he grew up bilingual, Delius made relatively few settings in German: there are half a dozen isolated songs from the 1880s and early 1890s, including four with texts by Heine; in addition, there is a set of four, dating from the late 1890s but unpublished until 1924, which all have iconoclastic texts by Nietzsche. Stern and austere in mood, their rugged individualism sets them apart from the rest of Delius's vocal output, so that they seem to stand aloof, like pillars of

Ex. 9.4

granite. As in *A Mass of Life*, the singer declaims the Nietzschean philosophy in a suitably monumental way. The vocal line of **'Der Einsame'** (*RT* V/19; *CE* vol 18b), for example, is starkly set against a powerful chordal landscape (Ex. 9.5). Other settings – such as 'Der Wandrer und sein Schatten' – are more enigmatic; none lasts more than a few minutes and all are in a slow tempo; they benefit greatly by being performed as a set.

More typical is **'Autumn'** (*RT* V/21; *CE* vol. 18b), dating from 1900, one of the finest of the songs to flower from Danish roots (in this case a poem by Ludwig Holstein). It deals with a quintessentially Delian obsession: Man's transitory status on earth and his subsequent consignment to oblivion. There are three verses (a fourth in the original was not used) and the first two are

Ex. 9.5

set to identical music: a child asks its father about the destination of swans seen in the sky, and then clouds. The third verse, which has a more chordal accompaniment, is very finely conceived in terms of its harmony; there is a poignant outburst from the child, by now distraught, who asks about Man's own destination and is given the implacably bleak answer, 'No one knows whereto!'

From the same year, **'The Violet'** (*RT* V/21; *CE* vols 15b and 18b) is an even more striking song, inspired by the same poet; it has some highly individual harmonic progressions, particularly where it slips into D flat at the beginning of the third bar, followed by equally unexpected modulations that stray into E major (bar 9). The song is startlingly brief – just two short verses, each occupying seventeen bars of identical music – yet it encapsulates an entire world. The orchestration is sparing, with a single flute and oboe, pairs of clarinets and bassoons, and minimal use of four horns (the 2nd clarinet and 4th horn play one note in each verse, the 2nd bassoon just two.)

**'I Hear in the Night'** (*RT* V/23; *CE* supp. vol. 19) is a noteworthy setting dating from 1901, inspired by verses of Drachmann; Delius considered publishing it in 1910, though nothing came of this. The text has all the quality of a nightmare: a sleeper is awakened by a despairing cry from a dark and ominous forest, and calls out, 'Who's there?', only to be answered by the echo of his own voice. Unable to sleep, he lies awake, torturing himself with questions such as 'Who am I? Where am I bound?' The piano part, imitating the rustling forest, makes virtuoso demands, consisting of forty-four consecutive bars of very fast (and very quiet) semiquaver chords, alternating between left and right hands. The harmonic language is stark and somewhat uncharacteristic for Delius.

Another example of a song which Delius orchestrated himself dates from the following year, 1902: **'Summer Landscape'** (*RT* V/24; *CE* vols 15a and 19) is an exquisite description of Nature, and its instrumentation (including parts for cor anglais, timpani and harp) evokes fields seen through the twilight haze of summer, and dusky woodlands trembling in a faint breeze. Here, Delius works all his customary magic in arrangements of great delicacy; the string textures, in particular, unfold in a passage of memorable beauty to accompany the phrase 'on every leaf, sweet memories dwell'. The best is saved for last: the final dozen or so bars swell poignantly at the words, 'a poem is born in the dark'ning sea of trees', before the strings die away gradually to *pppp*. This is a minor masterpiece.

Delius turned infrequently to English poetry, at least for his solo songs – there are only eleven examples in his output – but in 1910 he made a memorable setting of a poem by William Ernest Henley, **'The Nightingale has a Lyre of Gold'** (*RT* V/25; *CE* vol. 19). The humble blackbird's song ('And he plays but a boxwood flute') is preferred to the sophisticated calls of nightingale and lark, because it once formed the musical backdrop to a lovers' meeting, when lips and hearts joined as one. The music begins in triple time, with a languorous piano introduction in the style of a *mazurka* whose characteristic stress on the second beat of the bar, sounds like an offcut from the second *Dance Rhapsody*. This leads to a quicker section in 4/4, with a triplet accompaniment that passionately drives the music forward, as memories of the spontaneous declaration of love come flooding out (Ex. 9.6).

The mood of the opening is then recalled, with the last word given to the pianist, whose concluding four-bar postlude, coloured by semiquaver triplets, is again reminiscent of the second *Dance Rhapsody*, but which hints that this particular love-affair has almost certainly faded and died. A whole sequence of conflicting emotions is thus captured in just three, concise pages.

Equally succinct is a setting from 1910 of lines by Verlaine: **'La Lune blanche'** (*RT* V/26; *CE* vol. 19) – a text that also attracted many French composers, including Fauré, Hahn and Debussy. Delius's setting reflects the complexity of the poetic form, in which single lines at the end of each of the three verses ('O bien-aimée', 'Rêvons, c'est l'heure', and 'C'est l'heure exquise') form a separate, coded dialogue between the lovers in the moonlit landscape: in the song they are marked off musically from the rest. The rocking accompaniment

Ex. 9.6

is hypnotic and adds an unforgettably dreamlike quality to this exquisite setting (Ex. 9.7).

Delius responded equally well to the romantic, Celtic-inspired poetry of Fiona Macleod (a *nom de plume* for the Scottish writer William Sharp) which fascinated several English composers, notably Rutland Boughton, who made it the basis for the libretto of his opera *The Immortal Hour*. Delius fell under the spell in 1913, and the result was one of his most haunting, if uncharacteristic, songs: **'I-Brasil'** (*RT* V/28; *CE* vol. 19). The title refers to a mythological Celtic island off the west coast of Ireland, and the text is imbued with a mysterious sense of how peace may be found there 'where the last stars touch the sea'. This poignant expression of an acceptance of ultimate extinction could hardly have

Ex. 9.7

failed to appeal to Delius, and indeed he responds to it with great tenderness and sensitivity (Ex. 9.8).

The folksong mood is sustained throughout, as is the presence in the piano part of dotted rhythms, suggestive of Celtic song and occuring in several other Delius works, such as the last of the violin sonatas. Indeed, bar 5 of Ex. 9.8 is identical to a passage in the middle section of the Violin Concerto (Ex. 7.41). Though the vocal line is relatively straightforward, the chromatic harmonies of the accompaniment have anything but a folksong simplicity; nevertheless they lend it a feeling of intense melancholy.

Elizabethan poets (Shakespeare, Jonson, Nashe and Herrick) provided inspiration for Delius during his enforced exile from France during the

Ex. 9.8

Slow
voice
pno
mp
There's
con Ped
cresc poco
sor-row on the wind, my grief, there's sor-row on the wind,
mf
p
Old and grey! Old and grey! I
hear it whis-per-ing, call - ing, where the last stars touch the sea,
3

Great War, and the results were published in 1919 as *Four Old English Lyrics*. The last of the set, Herrick's **'To Daffodils'** (*RT* V/30; *CE* vol. 18b) fitted the composer like a glove, with lines comparing the short life of the flowers to that of Man: 'We have as short a spring, as quick a growth to meet decay, as you, or anything.' Delius's setting, one of the finest of his later songs, begins in recitative style for the singer, whilst a triplet figure features consistently in the piano accompaniment. The vocal line acquires a lyrical intensity at the words 'We will go with you along', suffused with a warm E major tonality:

Ex. 9.9

A few lines further on, Delius colours the word 'decay' with an A flat minor chord over an F natural in the bass, and then initiates a more chordal tread in the accompaniment, leading to a climax which falls away into the tenderest of codas: two bars for the piano, again characterised by triplet figures, give a perfect expression of resignation and acceptance.

The same year in which that setting appeared, Delius embarked on his last song, which did not appear in its final form until 1932, when it was prepared for publication. Delius returned to Verlaine for inspiration, and **'Avant que tu ne t'en ailles'** (*RT* V/31; *CE* vol. 18b) adheres to the formal technique of 'La Lune blanche' in juxtaposing or weaving together two separate poems. Delius's musical setting does not attempt to unravel them, but aims at a fluidity in which the singer and the pianist work together as equal partners, almost more so than in any other Delius song. The ending is beautifully conceived: an ecstatic moment for the singer, a plea to make haste while the golden rays of the sun are still in the sky, then leaves the final word to the piano in a poignant coda suggestive of 'all passion spent'; Delius could hardly have chosen a more fitting way to say farewell to his music for the solo human voice, which had proved such a rewarding means of expression for him over so many years.

Ex. 9.10

# CHAPTER 10

# 1934 and After

FREDERICK Delius died at his home in Grez-sur-Loing on 10 June, 1934, in appalling agony, with Jelka beside him in a wheelchair.[1] Jelka herself had been very seriously ill for several months before Delius's death, having two major operations, and on 16 May she wrote to Fenby:

Dearest Eric

I am afraid I am very ill; I have gone on until I could not any more ... Please, Eric, be an angel and come here as quick as you can and stay with Fred and keep him company ... please, dear, do not fail us

Yours ever affly
Jelka Delius[2]

He was there within days. The contrast between the beautiful French countryside he had come to love and his friend's condition was dreadful, and as soon as he arrived, he went upstairs, 'took the delicate hand he offered me and kissed his brow, for he was weeping like a child'.[3] Over the next three weeks Delius's condition alternated between slight improvement and increasing deterioration, and it had not been helped by the news of the deaths of Elgar on 23 February, and Norman O'Neill ten days later. Local doctors and nurses performed temporary wonders, but there was no question but that Delius would soon follow them.

Many years before, Delius had told the Harrison sisters' mother that he wanted to be buried in a country churchyard in England,[4] but as a temporary measure he was laid to rest in the cemetery at Grez on 12 June.[5] In due course, St Peter's Church at Limpsfield in Surrey was chosen, and almost exactly a year later Fenby accompanied the coffin from France for the reburial on 26 May 1935. It was estimated that the occasion drew about 1,000 people to the church; Beecham gave an *oraison funèbre*, and conducted a section of the London Philharmonic Orchestra in *Summer Night on the River*, the serenade from *Hassan* and *On Hearing the First Cuckoo in Spring*. Tragically, Jelka came down with pneumonia on her way to England for the

---

[1] Letter from Jelka Delius to Marie Clews, *Letters 2*, p. 453. Fenby, however, said that he was beside Delius when he died, and that Jelka was in bed in the next room (*Fenby 1*, pp. 225–6). Such is the confusion in people's memories after the event.

[2] Letter 606.

[3] *Fenby 1*, p. 219.

[4] *WS&SS*, p. 72.

[5] The day before which a plaster death-mask and an impression of his right hand had been made.

service, was unable to attend, and died on 28 May 1935 in a Kensington nursing home.[6]

The Deliuses had made a joint will in 1918, for some unexplained reason based on the very unlikely expectation that they would die together. It simply set up a fund to cover annual awards of up to £200 to young English composers – with no provision for whichever one of them might be the survivor. Balfour Gardiner, Philip Heseltine and Percy Grainger were named as the executors. In November 1925, however, Delius, with his failing health, seems to have realised the possibility of his predeceasing Jelka, and he therefore made a new will, apparently containing nothing about the award scheme and simply leaving everything to her.

However, when in May 1934 Jelka was suddenly taken ill, Delius decided to revise his 1925 will, and he wrote to Balfour Gardiner on the nineteenth asking him for help, saying, 'You are the only one of my friends who I can entirely rely on.'[7] When Gardiner arrived on 7 June, Delius had become weaker still, and all that Gardiner was able to do was to take down in his pocket-book Delius's wishes for a codicil. Fenby would receive £1,000 and all Delius's 'printed manuscripts', and everything else was to go to Jelka for her lifetime; after her death, the estate and the future royalties would be used to fund a yearly concert of The Royal Philharmonic Society. Beecham would conduct it, and there would be one piece of Delius's in every concert, with the rest of the programmes made up of works by young British composers who merited public performance. Beecham was also to choose a committee to plan the programmes. Finally, Austin and Kennedy Scott were left the contents of the wine cellar, and Gardiner had already been told that he was to have the furniture.[8]

Delius died three days later, with the codicil neither legally prepared nor signed, so those bequests could never take effect. Thus, when Jelka died on 28 May 1935, she became entitled to the whole of Delius's estate under his 1925 will. She obviously wanted her inheritance to be used for the perpetuation of Delius's music, and must undoubtedly have known of the concert plan when she set about making a new will herself. Beecham, however, persuaded her to abandon it, and in its place set up what is now The Delius Trust. Its object was 'the advancement in England or elsewhere of the musical works of my late Husband Frederick Delius,' through recordings of his music, the creation of what was to become the Collected Edition under Beecham's editorship, and the financing of concerts that included Delius's works.

Gardiner was still one of Delius's executors – but he and Beecham had never got on together, and when Jelka told him that, in making her new will, the concert scheme had been dropped, Gardiner was extremely upset. Loyalty was

---

[6] See *Letters 2*, p. 456: David Howarth, 'The Funeral'.

[7] Letter 607.

[8] There is a copy of the notebook entries in 'Balfour Gardiner on Delius', *DSJ* 85 (1985), 10–17, at p. 15.

one of his strongest characteristics, and because he would no longer be able to carry out Delius's wishes, expressed to him at his great friend's deathbed, he honourably renounced his executorship. It has to be said, though, that the Trust has turned out to be an infinitely better way of remembering Delius and his music than his original idea would ever have been.

The first Trustees were an English solicitor, Philip Emmanuel, and Barclays Bank, with Beecham and Austin named as Musical Advisers. The Trustees were required 'to obtain and observe the advice and opinion of Sir Thomas Beecham'. Subsequently, in 1964, the Trustees successfully applied to the Charity Commissioners for a scheme for the future management of the Trust, which is still in force.

In 1946, Beecham organised a major festival of Delius's music in London, the programmes for which are set out in Appendix 3. This was how *Musical Opinion* reviewed the tribute:

Sir Thomas Beecham's Delius Festival, consisting of seven generous programmes, began on October 26th at the Albert Hall ... The undertaking brings back to mind Sir Thomas's similar festival of 1929, and although the conditions of 1946 are less propitious it should be said at once that the conductor's feeling for the music seemed to be more passionate and deeper than ever, and its expression of surpassing fineness. The Royal Philharmonic Orchestra gave in the course of this series the best performances by far of the autumn's multifarious music-making, and the festival stands out as the distinguished feature of the season ... Some of the music brought forward was secondary, and if hardly any of it was without some magical gleam one was aware that this depended on the conductor's personality and passionate exertion to a degree that does not promise well for the future of secondary Delius ... It is clear that if Delius's music is to survive Beecham the publication of a Beecham edition is necessary.

When there is no longer a Beecham to bring his burning sympathy to this music the vocal works are likely to be the first to fall into the background ... *Songs of Sunset* were beautifully sung by Nancy Evans and Redvers Llewellyn, but the composer's complaisance towards the feeble moans of his poet, Dowson, excited impatience. And yet it was one of the vocal works, *Sea Drift*, which stood out as a pure masterpiece. We have heard many routine performances of *Paris* that made it sound at least twice too long, but on this occasion, thanks to Sir Thomas's unflagging energy and unrivalled command of dynamics, the playing of the Royal Philharmonic Orchestra invested the music with a sense of urgency and direction that compelled attention throughout its considerable length.

The Festival came to a triumphant conclusion at the Albert Hall on 11 December when the BBCSO and BBC Choral Society ... gave the great *Mass of Life* ... the BBC Choral Society sang splendidly and made light of the work's formidable problems ... as for the orchestral playing, only

Sir Thomas could have evoked the spell-binding sound of, *inter alia*, the preludes to the sixth and seventh movements, or shown so firm a grasp of the massive structure. The Festival has served the valuable purpose of demonstrating the remarkable variety and richness of Delius's output … and in our view has also fully vindicated Sir Thomas's estimate of Delius as the greatest composer since Wagner.

T HE following quotations would seem to provide a fitting summary of Delius's priceless bequest to present and succeeding generations of music lovers:

> With the death of Delius there has died a world the corresponding loveliness to which it will be a long time before humanity can create for itself again. It may be that, as some think, we are now in the first hour before a new dawn in music. But that hour is grey and chilly: and those of us who have been drunk with the beauty and the glory of the sunset of civilisation as we knew it must find our consolation in the melting colours of the cloud-shapes of the music of this last great representative of that old dead world.[9]

> His music looks back on days intensely lived through; it knows the secret of the pathos of mortal things doomed to fade and vanish. At bottom Delius is pagan and epicurean. His music will never be familiar to a large crowd; and the few who have come to love it will try hard to keep it to themselves.[10]

> The most precious part of this man is the immortal part – his spirit as revealed in his work; and in whatever sphere that spirit is, I should like our greetings to pass beyond the confines of this earthly sphere, and let him know that we are here, not in a spirit of vain regret, but rather in a spirit of rejoicing that his work is with us and will remain with us for evermore.[11]

---

[9] Ernest Newman, 'Delius: The End of a Chapter in Music', *The Sunday Times*, 17 June 1934; reprinted in *Companion*, pp. 97–100, at p. 97.

[10] Neville Cardus, *Ten Composers*, (London: Jonathan Cape, 1945), pp. 145–6.

[11] Beecham at Delius's graveside: see *WS&SS*, p. 170.

# Delius's Works in Chronological Order

## PART 1 ORCHESTRAL, VOCAL AND CHAMBER WORKS

| Date | | RT | CE | First performance* | Instrumentation |
|------|---|----|----|--------------------|-----------------|
| CHAPTER 1 1862–1888 Youth | | | | | |
| 1885 | Zum Carnival Polka (Piano) | IX/1 | vol. 33 | n/k | |
| 1885 | Pensées Mélodieuses (Piano) | IX/2 | vol. 33 | n/k | |
| 1887 | Florida | VI/I | vol. 20 | 1888 – 1 Apr 1937 Leipzig – QH, Beecham | picc.2.2.[ca]†.2.[bscl].2 – 4.2.3.1 – timps, perc, harp – str |
| 1887 | Norwegischer Schlittenfahrt (Piano version) (aka Sleigh Ride) | IX/3 | – | 24 Dec 1887 Delius to Grieg & Sinding | |
| 1888 | Hiawatha | VI/2 | supp. vol. 6 | 23 May 2009 Dorchester, Oxon, Lloyd-Jones | 3.2.2.2 – 4.2.3.1 – timps, perc, harp – str |
| CHAPTER 2 1888–1892 The Young Composer | | | | | |
| 1888 | Zanoni | I/1 | – | n/pf | |
| 1888 | Rhapsodische Variationen | VI/3 | supp. vol. 4 | n/pf | picc. 2.2.2.3 – 4.2.2 cornets.3,1 – timps, perc – str |
| 1888 | Paa Vidderne (Melodrama) | III/1 | vol. 14 | 17 May 1983 Norway TV – Farncombe | male speaker – picc. 2.2.ca.2.2 – 4.2.3.1 – timps, perc – str |
| 1888 | Three Pieces for String Orchestra | VI/4 | – | n/pb | |

* Place and artists shown where known
† Instruments in [ ] used in certain movements only

n/k = not known
n/pb = not published
n/pf = no known performance

AH = Aeolian Hall, London
CH = Central Hall, London
QH = Queen's Hall, London
RFH = Royal Festival Hall, London
SJH = St James's Hall, London
SJSS = St John's, Smith Square, London
WH = Wigmore Hall, London

| Date | | RT | CE | First performance | Instrumentation |
|---|---|---|---|---|---|
| 1888 | String Quartet | VIII/1 | supp. vol. 32 | n/k | |
| 1889 | Romance for Violin & Piano | VIII/2 | vol. 31a | n/k | |
| 1889 | Idylle de printemps | VI/5 | vol. 21c | 11 Feb 1895 SJSS, London, Corp | 3.2.2.2 – 4.0.0.0 – timps, harp – str |
| 1889 | Petite Suite d'orchestre [no. 1] | VI/6 | supp. vol. 2 | n/k | |
| | Marche | VI/6(1) | | | picc.2.2.2.2 – 4.2.0.0 – timps, perc – str |
| | Berceuse | VI/6(2) | | | 1.1.1(2).1 – 1.0.0.0 – harp – str (no dbs) |
| | Scherzo | VI/6(3) | | | picc.2.2.2.2 – 4.2.0.0 – timps, perc – str |
| | Duo | VI/6(4) | | | 2.2.2.2 – str |
| | Tema con Variazione | VI/6(5) | | | picc.2.2.2.2 – 4.2.0.0 – timps, perc – str |
| 1889 | Sakuntala | III/2 | 15b | 19 Jun 1987 York, Partridge, Seymour | ten soloist – 3.2.ca.2.bscl. 2 – 4.0.0.0 – timps, 2 harps – str |
| 1889–90 | Suite de 3 morceaux caractéristiques | VI/6(a) | | | |
| | La Quadroone (Une Rhapsodie floridienne) | VI/6(a)(1) | vol. 21c | n/k | picc.2.2.ca.2.2 – 4.2.3.1 – timps, perc – str |
| | Scherzo | VI/6(a)(2) | vol. 21c | n/k | picc.3.2.ca.2.2 – 4.2.2.1 – timps, perc – str |
| | Marche caprice (extended version of VI/6(1)) | VI/6(a)(3) | vol. 21a | 21 Nov 1946 Central Hall, Beecham | picc.2.2.2.2 – 4.2 cornets.2.3.1 – timps, perc – str |
| 1889–90 | 3 symphonische Dichtungen | VI/7 | vol. 21b | | |
| | Sommer Abend (Summer Evening) | VI/7(1) | vol. 21a | 18 Nov 1946 Central Hall, Austin | 3.2.2.2 – 4.2.3.1 – timps – str |
| | Winter Nacht (Sleigh Ride) | VI/7(2) | vol. 21b | | picc.2.2.2.2 – 4.2.2 cornets.3.1 – timps, perc – str |
| | Frühlings Morgen (Spring Morning) | VI/7(3) | vol. 21b | | 3.2.2.2 – 4.2.3.1 – timps – str |

| Date | | RT | CE | First performance | Instrumentation |
|---|---|---|---|---|---|
| 1889–90 | Two piano pieces (Valse & Reverie – uncompleted) | IX/5 | vol. 33 | n/pf | |
| 1890 | Légendes (Sagen) (Pf & orch – uncompleted) | VII/2 | supp. vol. 4 | n/pf | solo piano – picc.2.2.2.2 – 4.2.3.1 – timps, perc – str |
| 1890 | Marche française (uncompleted) | VI/6(b) | – | n/pb | picc.2.2.2.4 – 4.2.2 cornets.3.1 – timps, perc – str |
| 1890 | À l'amore (or À l'aurore?) | VI/8 | – | n/pb | 3.2.ca.2.2 – 4.2.3.1 – harp – str |
| 1890 | Petite Suite d'orchestre [no. 2] | VI/9 | supp. vol. 2 | n/k | 2.2.2.2 – 2.1.0.0 – timps – str |
| | Allegro ma non troppo | VI/9(1) | | | |
| | Con moto | VI/9(2) | | | |
| | Allegretto | VI/9(3) | | | |
| 1890–1 | Suite for Violin & Orchestra | VII/1 | vol. 28 | 24 Mar 1984 SJSS, Holmes, Handley | solo violin – 3.2.2.2 – 4.2.3.1 – timps – str |
| | Pastorale | | | | |
| | Intermezzo | | | | |
| | Élégie | | | | |
| | Finale | | | | |
| 1890–2 | Irmelin | I/2 | vol. 1 | 4 May 1953 Oxford, Beecham | 8 soloists + chorus – picc.3.2.ca.2.bscl.3 – 4.2.2 cornets. 3.1 – timps, perc, harp – str |
| 1890–2 | On the Mountains (otherwise Paa Vidderne or Sur les cimes) | VI/10 | vol. 22 | 10 Oct 1891 Christiania, Holter | picc.2.2.2.bscl.2 – 4.2.2 cornets.3.1 – timps, perc – str |
| 1891 | Maud | III/3 | vol. 16 | n/k | ten soloist – 3.2.ca.2.[bscl].2 – 4.2.3.1 – timps, harp – str |
| | Birds in the High Hall-Garden | | | | |
| | I was Walking a Mile | | | | |
| | Go Not Happy Day | | | | |
| | Rivulet Crossing my Ground | | | | |
| | Come into the Garden, Maud | | | | |

| Date | | RT | CE | First performance | Instrumentation |
|---|---|---|---|---|---|
| 1892 | Violin Sonata (B major) | VIII/3 | vol. 31a | 12 Apr 1958 BBC, W & B Lehmann | |
| 1892 | Légende (Violin & piano version) | VII/3 | vol. 28 | n/k | |
| 1892–3 | String Quartet | VIII/4 | – | n/pb | |

CHAPTER 3 1893–1901 Coming to Maturity

| Date | | RT | CE | First performance | Instrumentation |
|---|---|---|---|---|---|
| 1893–7 | Over the Hills and Far Away | VI/11 | vol. 23a | 13 Nov 1897 Elberfeld, Haym | 3.2.2.3 – 4.2.3.1 – timps, perc – str |
| 1894–5 | The Magic Fountain | I/3 | vol. 2 | 30 Jul 1937 Golders Grn, del Mar | 5 soloists + chorus – picc.3.3.ca.3.bscl.3.sarrusaphone – 4.3.3.1 – timps, perc, 2 harps – str |
| 1895 | Légende (Violin & orchestra version) | VII/3 | vol. 28 | 30 May 1899 SJH, Dunn, Hertz | solo violin – 2.2.2.2 – 4.0.0.0 – timps – str |
| mid-1890s | Badinage (Piano) | IX/4 | vol. 33 | n/pf | |
| 1895–7 | Koanga | I/4 | vol. 3 | 30 May 1899 SJH, Black, Russell, Hertz / 30 Mar 1904 Elberfeld, Cassirer | 7 soloists + 9 bit-parts + ch – picc.2.2.ca.2.bscl.3.contra – 4.2.3.1 – timps, perc, 2 harps – str |
| 1896 | American Rhapsody (Appalachia) | VI/12 | vol. 22 | 10 Dec 1986 RFH, Downes | picc.2.2.2.3 – 4.2.2 cornets.3.1 – timps, perc, 2 harps – str |
| 1896 | Romance for Cello & Piano | VIII/5 | vol. 31c | 22 Jun 1976 Helsinki, Lloyd Webber | |
| 1897 | Folkeraadet (aka Norwegian Suite) | I/5 | vol. 7 | 18 Oct 1897 Christiania, Wige | 2.2.2.2 – 4.2.3.1 – timps, perc – str |

| Date | Work | RT | CE | First performance | Instrumentation |
|---|---|---|---|---|---|
| 1897 | Seven Danish Songs (also with piano accompaniment) | III/4 | | 30 Mar 1899 (Pt) SJH, Andray, Hertz<br>16 Mar 1901 (Pt) Paris, Andray, d'Indy | sop/mezzo soloist – max 2.2.2.2 – 4.0.0.0 – timps, perc, hp – str |
| | Silken shoes | | vol. 15b | | |
| | Irmelin (Rose) | | vol. 15b | | |
| | Summer Nights | | vol. 15a | | |
| | In the Seraglio Garden | | vol. 15b | | |
| | Wine Roses | | vol. 15a | | |
| | Red Roses | | vol. 15a | | |
| | Let Springtime come, then | | vol. 15a | | |
| 1897 | Piano Concerto (3 movt version) | VII/4 | supp. vol. 3 | 24 Oct 1904 Elberfeld, Buths, Haym | solo piano – 3.2.bscl.3 – 4.2.3.1 – timps – str |
| 1904–9 | (1 movt version) | | vol. 29a | 22 Oct 1907 QH, Szántó, Wood | solo piano – 3.2.ca.2.3 – 4.2.3.1 – timps, perc – str |
| 1898 | Mitternachtslied Zarathustras | II/1 | – | 30 May 1899 SJH, Powell, Hertz | bar soloist + t & b chorus – 3.3.ca.3.bscl.3.contra – 4.3.3.1 – timps, perc, 2 harps – str |
| 1899 | La Ronde se déroule (1st version of Lebenstanz) | VI/13 | n/a | 30 Oct 1899 SJH, Hertz | picc.3.3.bscl.3.contra – 4.3.3.1 – timps, perc, harp – str |
| 1899–1900 | Paris | VI/14 | vol. 23b | 14 Dec 1901 Elberfeld, Haym | picc.2.3.ca.3.bscl.3.contra – 6.3.3.1 – timps, perc, 2 harps – str |
| 1900–1 | A Village Romeo & Juliet | I/6 | vol. 4 | 21 Feb 1907 Berlin, Cassirer | 5 soloists + 18 bit-parts + chorus – picc.2.3.ca.3.bscl.3.contra – 6.3.3.1 – timps, perc, 2 harps – str (+ on-stage band: solo vln – 6 hns, 2 cornets, 2 trbns, perc – organ) |
| 1901–12 | Lebenstanz (Life's Dance) | VI/15 | vol. 24a | 21 Jan 1904 Düsseldorf, Buths | picc.3.3.ca.3.bscl.3.contra – 4.3.3.1 – timps, perc, 2 harps – str |
| 1901–2 | Margot La Rouge | I/7 | vol. 5 | 8 Jun 1983 St Louis, MO, Fenby | sop, ten & bar soloists + 14 bit-parts + chorus – picc.2.2.ca.2.2. – 4.2.3.1 – timps, perc, harp – str |

| *Date* | | *RT* | *CE* | *First performance* | *Instrumentation* |
|---|---|---|---|---|---|
| CHAPTER 4 1902–1905 The Great Noontide | | | | | |
| 1902 | Appalachia | II/2 | vol. 9a | 15 Oct 1904 Elberfeld, Haym | 8 pt chorus (incl. bar soloist) – 3.3.3.ca.2.Eb cl.bscl.3.contra – 6.3.3.1 – timps, perc, 2 harps – str |
| 1903–4 | Sea Drift | II/3 | vol. 9b | 24 May 1906 Essen, Loritz, Witte | bar soloist + 8 pt chorus – 3.3.ca.3.bscl.3.contra – 6.3.3.1 – timps, bd, 2 harps – str |
| 1904–5 | Eine Messe des Lebens (A Mass of Life) | II/4 | vol. 10 | 17 Jun 1909 (complete) QH, NStaffs CS, etc., Beecham | satb solos – satb × 2 – 3(alt picc).3(incl. ca). bsob.3.bscl.3.contra – 6.4.3.1 – timps, perc, 2 harps – str |
| CHAPTER 5 1906–1911 Acceptance and Friends | | | | | |
| 1906–8 | Songs of Sunset | II/5 | vol. 11a | 16 Jun 1911 QH, Culp, Bates, Mason Choir, Beecham | sop & bar soloists + satb chorus – 3.1.ca. bsob.3.3.sarrus (contra) – 4.2.3.1 – timps, perc, harp – str |
| 1907–29 | Cynara | III/5 | vol. 15b | 18 Oct 1929 QH, Goss, Beecham | bar soloist – 3.2.ca.3.bscl.3.contra – 4.3.3.1 – timps, perc, harp – str |
| 1907 | Brigg Fair | VI/16 | vol. 24b | 18 Jan 1908 Liverpool, Bantock | 3.2.ca.3.bscl.3.contra – 6.3.3.1 – timps, perc, harp(s) – str |
| 1908 | In a Summer Garden | VI/17 | vol. 25a | 11 Dec 1908 QH, Delius | 3.2.ca.2.bscl.3 – 4.2.3.1 – timps, perc, hp(s) – str |
| 1908 | A Dance Rhapsody [no. 1] | VI/18 | vol. 25b | 8 Sep 1909 Hereford, Delius | 3 (incl. picc).1.ca.bsob.3.bscl.3.sarrusaphone (contra) – 6.3.3.1 –timps, perc, 2 harps – str |
| 1908–10 | Fennimore and Gerda | I/8 | vol. 6 | 21 Oct 1919 Frankfurt, Brecher | 7 soloists + 8 bit-parts + chorus – 3 (incl. picc).2.ca. bsob.3.bscl.3.sarrusaphone (contra) – 4.3.3.1 – timps, perc, 2 harps – str |

| Date | | RT | CE | First performance | Instrumentation |
|---|---|---|---|---|---|
| CHAPTER 6 1911–1914 Inspiration Unabated | | | | | |
| 1911 | An Arabesque | II/7 | vol. 12a | 25 May 1920 Newport (Mon.), Hemming, Sims | bar soloist + satb chorus – 3.2.ca.bsob.3.bscl.3.sarrus (contra) – 4.3.3.1 – timps, perc, harp – str |
| 1911–12 | The Song of the High Hills | II/6 | vol. 11b | 26 Feb 1920 QH, Philharmonic Choir, Coates | satb chorus × 2 (incl. sop & ten soloists) – 3(incl. picc).2.ca.3.bscl.3.sarrus (contr) – 6.3.3.1 – timps (3 players), perc, 2 harps – str |
| 1912–13 | Two Pieces for Small Orchestra | VI/19 | vol. 27a | 23 Oct 1913 Leipzig, Nikisch | |
| | On Hearing the First Cuckoo in Spring | VI/19(1) | | | 1.1.2.2 – 2.0.0.0 – str |
| | Summer Night on the River | VI/19(2) | | | 2.1.2.2 – 2.0.0.0 – str |
| 1913–14 | North Country Sketches | VI/20 | vol. 26 | 10 May 1915 QH, Beecham | 2 [incl. picc].2.ca.2.2 – 4.[2.3.1] – [timps, perc,] 2 harps – str |
| 1913–16 | Requiem | II/8 | vol. 12b | 23 Mar 1922 QH, Philharm. Choir, Coates | sop & bar soloists + satb chorus × 2– 3(incl. picc).2.ca. bsob.3.bscl.3.sarrus (contra) – 6.3.3.1 – timps, perc, harp – str |
| 1914 | Violin Sonata [no. 1] | VIII/6 | vol. 31b | 29 Feb 1915 Manchester, Catterall & Forbes | |
| CHAPTER 7 1915–1918 Winding Down | | | | | |
| 1915 | Air and Dance | VI/21 | vol. 27b | 16 Oct 1929 AH, Beecham | strings |
| 1915 | Double Concerto | VII/5 | vol. 30 | 21 Feb 1920 QH, Harrison sisters, Wood | solo vln & cello – 2.1.ca.2.2 – 4.2.3.1 – timps, harp – str |

| Date | | RT | CE | First performance | Instrumentation |
|---|---|---|---|---|---|
| 1916 | Cello Sonata | VIII/7 | vol. 31c | 31 Oct 1918 WH, Harrison & Harty | 2(incl. picc).2.ca.2.2 – 4.2.3.1 – timps, perc, cel, harp – str |
| 1916 | A Dance Rhapsody no. 2 | VI/22 | vol. 26 | 20 Oct 1923 QH, Wood | |
| 1916–17 | String Quartet (Late Swallows) (original version) | VIII/8 | vol. 32 | 17 Nov 1916 AH, London String Quartet | |
| | (Revised, 4 movt, version) | | | 1 Feb 1919 AH, London String Quartet | |
| 1916 | Violin Concerto | VII/6 | vol. 30 | 30 Jan 1919 QH, Sammons, Boult | solo violin – 2.1.ca.2.2. – 4.2.3.1 – timps, harp – str |
| 1917 | Eventyr | VI/23 | vol. 26 | 11 Jan 1919 QH, Wood | picc. 2.2.ca.3.bscl.3.sarrus – 4.3.3.1 – timps, perc, cel, 2 harps, str, 20 men's voices (offstage) |
| 1918 | A Song before Sunrise | VI/24 | vol. 27a | 19 Sep 1923 QH, Wood | 2.1.2.2 – 2.0.0.0 – 1 timp – str |
| 1918 | Poem of Life & Love | VI/25 | supp. vol. 1 | 17 Mar 2002 Haverhill, Suffolk, Hav'll Sinfonia, Hill | 3.2.ca.3.bscl.3.sarrus – 4.3.3.1 – timps, bd, 2 harps – str |

CHAPTER 8 1919–1934 Fenby and the Last Years

| Date | | RT | CE | First performance | Instrumentation |
|---|---|---|---|---|---|
| 1919 | Dance for harpsichord | IX/6 | vol. 33 | 1919? Violet Gordon Woodhouse? | |
| 1920–3 | Hassan | I/9 | vol. 8 | 20 Sep 1923 HM's Theatre, London, Goossens | satb chorus (incl. ten & bar soloists) picc.1.ca.1.1 – 2.1.1.1 – timps, perc, harp – str |
| 1921 | Cello Concerto | VII/7 | vol. 29b | 31 Jan 1923 Vienna, Barjansky, Löwe | solo cello – 2.1.ca.2.2 – 4.2.3.1 – timps, harp – str |
| 1922–3 | Five Piano Pieces | IX/7 | vol. 33 | 1924? | |

| Date | | RT | CE | First performance | Instrumentation |
|---|---|---|---|---|---|
| 1922–3 | Three Preludes (Piano) | IX/8 | vol. 33 | 1924? | |
| 1923 | Violin Sonata no. 2 | VIII/9 | vol. 31b | 7 Oct 1924 Sammons & Howard-Jones | |
| 1925–9 | A Late Lark | III/6 | vol. 15b | 12 Oct 1929 QH, Nash, Beecham | ten soloist – 1.1.ca. 2.2 – 2.1.3.0 – str |
| 1929 | A Song of Summer | VI/26 | vol. 27b | 17 Sep 1931 QH, Wood | 3(incl. picc).2.ca.3.bscl.3.contra – 4.3.3.1 – timps, harp – str |
| 1930 | Violin Sonata no. 3 | VIII/10 | vol. 31b | 6 Nov 1930 WH, Harrison & Bax | |
| 1930 | Songs of Farewell | II/9 | vol. 13a | 21 Mar 1932 QH, Philharmonic Choir, Sargent | satb chorus × 2 – 2.2.ca.2.bscl.3.contra – 4.3.3.1 – timps, harp – str |
| 1930 | Caprice & Elegy | VII/8 | vol. 29b | 23 Apr 1931 WH, Harrison & piano | solo cello – 1.1.ca.1.1 – 2.0.0.0 – harp – str |
| 1931 | Irmelin Prelude | VI/27 | vol. 27b | 1 Apr 1937 QH, Beecham | 2.1.ca.2.bscl.2 – 2.0.0.0 – harp – str |
| 1931 | Fantastic Dance | VI/28 | vol. 27b | 12 Jan 1934 London, Boult | 2.2.2.2 – 4.2.3.1 – timps, perc, harp – str |
| 1932 | Prelude and Idyll | II/10 | vol. 13b | 3 Oct 1933 QH, Labette, Henderson, Wood | sop & bar soloists – 2.2.ca.2.2 – 4.2.3.1 – timps, harp – str |

## PART 2 SONGS

| Date | Title | RT | CE |
|------|-------|-----|-----|
| | PART SONGS (See Chapters 1, 5, 7 & 8) | | |
| 1885–7 | Six Part Songs | IV/1 | supp. vol. 17 |
| | Lorelei / (Heinrich Heine) / (not by Delius: probably an arrangement – not published in *CE*) | | |
| | O Sonnenschein (An den Sonnenschein) / O shining, golden Sun / (Robert Reinick ) | | |
| | Durch den Wald / Through the Woods / (von Schreck) (?) | | |
| | Ave Maria / (Emanuel Geibel) | | |
| | Sonnenscheinlied / Song of Sunshine / (Bjørnstjerne Bjørnson) | | |
| | Frühlingsanbruch / The Coming of Spring / (Carl Andersen) | | |
| 1891 | Her ute skal gildet staa / Here we shall feast / (Henrik Ibsen) / (in draft score only) | IV/1 (notes) | supp. vol. 17 |
| 1907–8 | Three Unaccompanied Part Songs | | vol. 17 |
| | On Craig Ddu (An Impression of Nature) / (Arthur Symons) | IV/2 | |
| | Wanderer's Song / (Arthur Symons) | IV/3 | |
| | Midsummer Song / (Words unattributed – probably by Delius) | IV/4 | |
| 1913 | Two Songs for Children | V/29 | vol. 17 |
| | Little Birdie / (Alfred Tennyson) / (voices in unison, with piano) | | |
| | The Streamlet's Slumber Song / (May Morgan) / (voices in two parts, with piano) | | |
| 1917 | To be sung of a summer night on the river / (wordless) | IV/5 | vol. 17 |
| 1923 | The Splendour falls on Castle Walls / (Alfred Tennyson) | IV/6 | vol. 17 |
| | SOLO SONGS (See Chapter 9) (Songs marked * were also orchestrated by Delius) | | |
| *c.* 1880 | When other lips shall speak / (Alfred Bunn?) / (not by Delius: probably an arrangement) | V/1 | n/pb |
| 1885 | Over the Mountains high / (Bjørnstjerne Bjørnson) | V/2 | vol. 18a |
| 1885 | Zwei braune Augen / (Hans Christian Andersen) | V/3 | vol. 18a |
| 1886 | Der Fichtenbaum / (Heinrich Heine) | V/4 | vol. 18a |

| Date | Title | RT | CE |
|------|-------|-----|-----|
| 1888 | Fünf Lieder (aus dem Norwegischen) / Five songs from the Norwegian: | V/5 | vol. 18a |
| | Der Schlaf / Slumber Song / (Bjørnstjerne Bjørnson) | | |
| | Sing, Sing / The Nightingale / (Theodor Kjerulf) | | |
| | Am schönsten Sommerabend war's / Summer Eve / (John Paulsen) | | |
| | Sehnsucht / Longing / (Theodor Kjerulf) | | |
| | Beim Sonnenuntergang / Sunset / (Andreas Munch) | | |
| 1888 | Hochgebirgsleben / (Henrik Ibsen) | V/6 | vol. 18a |
| 1888 | O Schneller mein Ross / (Emanuel Geibel) | V/7 | vol. 18a |
| 1889 | Chanson de Fortunio / (Alfred de Musset) | V/8 | vol. 18a |
| 1889 | Sakuntala / (Holger Drachmann) / * (see notes below) | III/2 | vol. 15b |
| 1889–90 | Sieben Lieder (aus dem Norwegischen) / Seven songs from the Norwegian: | V/9 | vol. 19 |
| | Wiegenlied / Cradle Song / (Henrik Ibsen) | | |
| | Auf der Reise zur Heimat (Heimkehr) / The Homeward Way / (Aasmund O. Vinje) | | |
| | Abendstimmung / Twilight Fancies / (Bjørnstjerne Bjørnson) / * | | |
| | Kleine Venevil / Young Venevil / (Bjørnstjerne Bjørnson) | | |
| | Spielleute (Spielmann) / The Minstrel / (Henrik Ibsen) | | |
| | Verborg'ne Liebe / Hidden Love / (Bjørnstjerne Bjørnson) | | |
| | Eine Vogelweise / The Birds' Story / (Henrik Ibsen) / * | | |
| 1890–1 | Skogen gir susende, langsom besked / Softly the Forest / (Bjørnstjerne Bjørnson) | V/10 | supp. vol. 18/19 |
| 1890 | Songs to words by Heine: | V/11 | vol. 18a |
| | Mit deinen blauen Augen | | |
| | Ein schöner Stern geht auf in meiner Nacht | | |
| | Hör' ich das Liedchen klingen | | |
| | [Aus deinen Augen fliessen meine Lieder] (now known not to be by Delius: words, von Schwerin; music, Franz Ries) | | |
| 1891 | Maud / Alfred Tennyson / * (see notes below) | III/3 | vol. 15b |
| 1891 | Three Songs, the words by Shelley: | V/12 | vol. 19 |
| | Indian Love Song | | |
| | Love's Philosophy | | |
| | To the Queen of my Heart | | |
| 1891 | Lyse Naetter / Dreamy Nights / (Holger Drachmann) | V/13 | vol. 18a |

| Date | Title | RT | CE |
|---|---|---|---|
| c. 1893 | Jeg havde en nyskaaren seljefløjte / I once had a newly cut willow pipe / (Vilhelm Krag) | V/14 | supp. vol. 18/19 |
| 1893 | Nuages / (Jean Richepin) | V/15 | vol. 18a |
| c. 1894–7 | Seven Danish Songs: | III/4 | vols. 18a/18b |
| | Silken Shoes / (Jens Peter Jacobsen) / * | | |
| | Irmelin / (Jens Peter Jacobsen) / * | | |
| | Summer Nights (On the Seashore) / (Holger Drachmann) / * | | |
| | In The Seraglio Garden / (Jens Peter Jacobsen) / * | | |
| | Wine Roses / (Jens Peter Jacobsen) / * | | |
| | Red Roses (Through long, long Years) / (Jens Peter Jacobsen) / * | | |
| | Let Springtime come, then / (Jens Peter Jacobsen) / * | | |
| 1895 | Deux Mélodies, poésies de Paul Verlaine: | V/16 | vol. 19 |
| | Il pleure dans mon cœur | | |
| | Le ciel est, par-dessus le toit | | |
| 1895? | Pagen højt paa taarnet sad / The Page sat in the lofty Tower / (Jens Peter Jacobsen) | V/17 | vol. 18a |
| c. 1898 | Traum Rosen / (Marie Heinitz) | V/18 | vol. 18a |
| 1898 | Vier Lieder nach Gedichten von Friedrich Nietzsche / Four Nietzsche songs: | V/19 | vol. 18b |
| | Nach neuen Meeren | | |
| | Der Wanderer | | |
| | Der Einsame | | |
| | Der Wanderer und sein Schatten | | |
| 1898? | Noch ein Mal / (Friedrich Nietzsche) | See below | vol. 18b |
| 1898 | Im Glück wir lachend gingen / In bliss we walked with laughter / (Holger Drachmann) | V/20 | supp. vol. 18/19 |
| 1900 | Two Songs from the Danish: | V/21 | vol. 18b |
| | The Violet / Das Veilchen / (Ludvig Holstein) / * | | |
| | Autumn / Herbst / (Ludvig Holstein) | | |
| 1901 | Schwarze Rosen / Black Roses / (Ernst Josephson) | V/22 | vol. 19 |
| 1901 | Jeg hører i natten / I hear in the night / (Holger Drachmann) | V/23 | supp. vol. 18/19 |
| 1902 | Summer Landscape / (Holger Drachmann) / * | V/24 | vol. 19 |
| 1906 | They are not long, the weeping & the laughter / (Ernest Dowson) | See below | vol. 18b |
| 1907 | Cynara / (Ernest Dowson) / completed 1929 / * (see notes below) | III/5 | vol. 15b |

| Date | Title | RT | CE |
|------|-------|-----|-----|
| 1910 | The Nightingale has a Lyre of Gold / (W. E. Henley) | V/25 | vol. 19 |
| 1910 | La Lune blanche / (Paul Verlaine) | V/26 | vol. 19 |
| 1911 | Chanson d'automne / (Paul Verlaine) | V.27 | vol. 19 |
| 1913 | I-Brasîl / (Fiona Macleod / William Sharp) | V/28 | vol. 19 |
| 1915–16 | Four Old English Lyrics: | V/30 | vol. 18b |
|  | It was a Lover and his Lass (William Shakespeare) |  |  |
|  | So white, so soft, so sweet is she (Ben Jonson) |  |  |
|  | Spring, the sweet Spring (Thomas Nashe) |  |  |
|  | To Daffodils (Robert Herrick) |  |  |
| 1919 | Avant que tu ne t'en ailles / (Paul Verlaine) | V/31 | vol. 18b |
| 1924 | A Late Lark / (W.E. Henley) / completed 1929 / * (see notes below) | III/6 | vol.15b |

NOTES

1. The titles above are as listed in the *RT Catalogue*; any English translations are as they appear in the contents of the published volumes. Alternative English titles are given in parentheses.

2. With the exception of *Noch ein Mal*, Delius notated the voice part of the above solo songs in the treble clef, including the *Four Nietzsche Songs*, although these can be performed by a baritone without transposition. The compass of each song is given in the *RT Catalogue*.

3. Detailed notes on all the songs are to be found in *RT Catalogue*.

4. *Noch ein Mal* is a setting of lines from *Also sprach Zarathustra*; see *RT Supplement*, p. 166.

5. 'They are not long, the weeping and the laughter' is an early version of the closing section of *Songs of Sunset*: see *RT Supplement*, pp. 166–7.

6. *Sakuntala, Maud, Cynara* and *A Late Lark* are included here (as well as in Appendix 1, Part 1) for the sake of completeness, though they were originally written with orchestral accompaniment; however, each has subsequently been published in vocal score with piano reductions by Philip Heseltine, Eric Fenby and Robert Threlfall. In the case of the *Seven Danish Songs*, orchestrated in 1897, these were later published with Delius's own, original piano accompaniments. The exact dates of composition are problematic; for further details see *RT Catalogue*, p. 78 and *RT Supplement*, p. 59.

7. *Paa Vidderne* (RT III/1) is a (spoken) melodrama and is not included here; see Appendix 1, Part 1 and Chapter 2.

# Delius's Diploma and Reports from the Leipzig Conservatorium

Mr Fritz Delius of Bradford (England), was born at the above mentioned place on 29 January 1862, he was accepted as a student at the Royal Conservatorium of Music in Leipzig on the 30 August 1886 (sub.no. 4486) and at Easter 1888 he was honourably discharged from the above mentioned place. In this period he undertook study in the Theory of Music; in Practical Piano, in Practical Violin, as well as in the History and Aesthetics of Music performance and, assisted by a strong capacity [for this work] he has made 'substantial and most respectable' progress. Mr Delius has a very advanced and excellent knowledge of the Theory of Music; in Practical Composition 'he is on the way through solid practice to a most valuable development'; he has 'some knowledge' in the History and Aesthetics of Music.

Mr Delius's moral demeanour at the Conservatorium has been 'exemplary'.

The unanimous conclusion above is based on the particular assessments by the relevant teachers at the Institute as well as on personal knowledge.

Directorial-diploma conferred on Mr Fritz Delius of Bradford and completed to-day in good faith.

Leipzig 17 January 1889.

Particular results have been awarded personally by the following undersigned teachers from the Institute. [Signatures follow.]

# Report 1
## (September 1886–March 1887)

*Theory of Music*

He was a hard-working and conscientious student for quite a while. He did not attend during the latter stages of the course. He worked thoroughly through the course in theory up to fugue. He was not here for Easter but before that he was hard-working and composed some nice things.

*Carl Reinecke*

*Violin*

He was a student of mine for a short time only and made a substantial effort to master the work set.

*Sitt*

*Ensemble Work*
He came occasionally.

*Carl Reinecke*

*Aesthetics and History of Music Lectures*
[No entry]

*Oscar Paul*

*Singing*
Did not attend.

*Klesse*

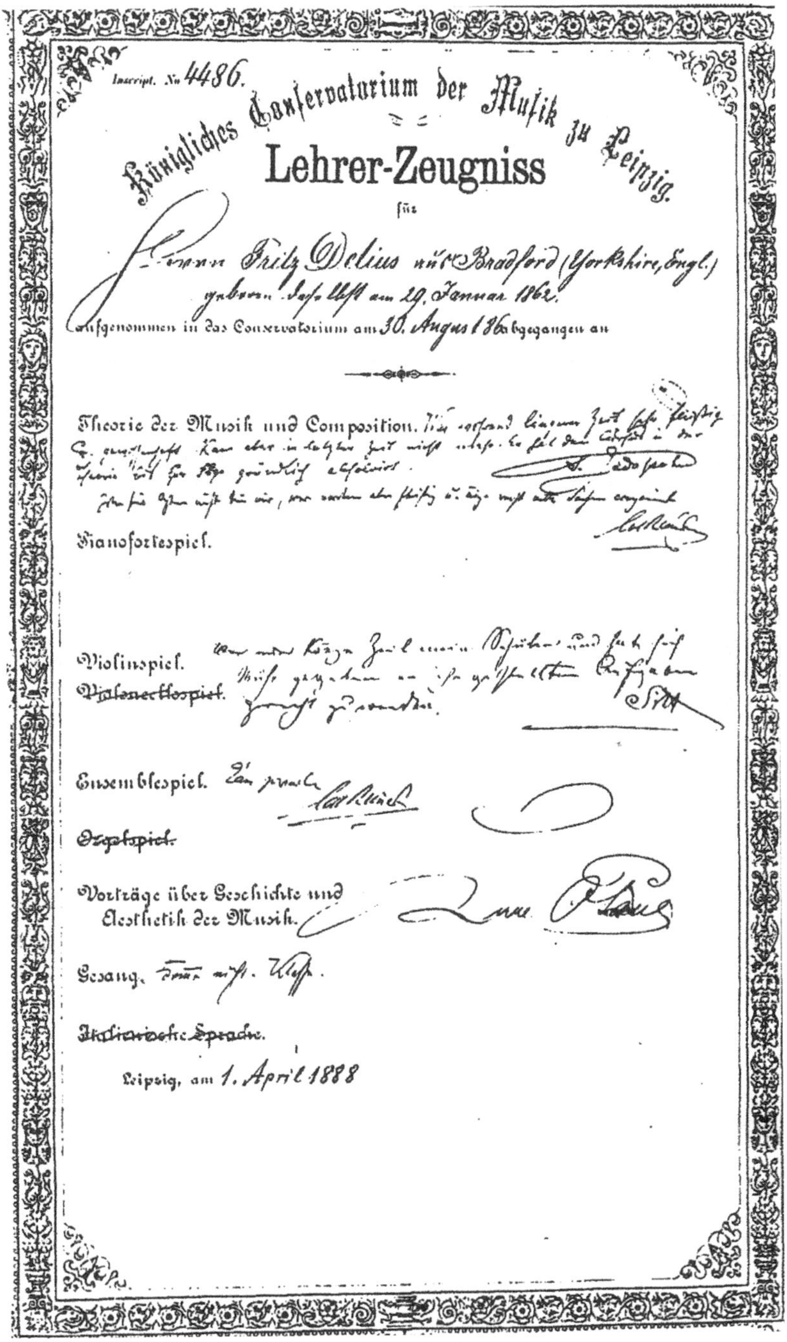

Inscript. No. 4486.

Königliches Conservatorium der Musik zu Leipzig.

Lehrer-Zeugniss

für

Herrn Fritz Delius aus Bradford (Yorkshire, Engl.)

geboren daselbst am 29. Januar 1862.

aufgenommen in das Conservatorium am 30. August 186 abgegangen am

Theorie der Musik und Composition.

Pianofortespiel.

Violinspiel.

~~Violoncellospiel.~~

Ensemblespiel.

~~Orgelspiel.~~

Vorträge über Geschichte und Aesthetik der Musik.

Gesang.

~~Italienische Sprache.~~

Leipzig, am 1. April 1888

Report: April 1887 – March 1885

# Report 2
## (April 1887–March 1888)

*Composition*
Herr Delius has attempted to play the piano for years, but he is not talented enough to achieve anything at all as a performer.

*Carl Reinecke*

*Theory of Music*
Very hard working; he has made a thorough study of counterpoint, including fugue.

*S. Jadassohn*

*Piano*
He is totally unknown to me!

*Paul Quasdorf*

Attended about 20 of my classes from Easter to September 1887 and then did not attend at all; was not without talent but achieved very little and was not a serious piano student; played Etudes from Op 807 by Czerny, Two part Inventions by Bach, C sharp minor Sonata and F minor Variations by Haydn, but not fluently.

*B. Zwintscher*

*Ensemble Work*
Came [but did nothing!]

*Carl Reinecke*

*Aesthetics and History of Music Lectures*
Came occasionally.

*O. Paul*

*Singing*
Did not attend.

*Klesse*

# Programmes for the 1929 and 1946 Delius Festivals

## The 1929 Festival

12 October    Queen's Hall

Orchestra of the Columbia Graphophone Company; conducted by Sir Thomas Beecham

*Brigg Fair*

*A Late Lark* (first performance: Heddle Nash)

*A Dance Rhapsody* no. 2

*Sea Drift* (Dennis Noble, London Select Choir)

*In a Summer Garden*

*A Village Romeo and Juliet* (excerpt: Pauline Maunder, Heddle Nash, London Select Choir)

16 October    Aeolian Hall

An unnamed small orchestra conducted by Sir Thomas Beecham

*A Song before Sunrise*

Seven songs (Olga Haley)

Cello Sonata (Beatrice Harrison and Evlyn Howard-Jones)

*Summer Night on the River*

*Air and Dance* (first performance)

Six songs (John Goss)

*Three Preludes*

*Dance* for harpsichord

*Five Piano Pieces* (*Mazurka and Waltz, Waltz, Lullaby, Toccata*)  } Evlyn Howard-Jones

Six songs (John Armstrong)

*On Hearing the First Cuckoo in Spring*

18 October    Queen's Hall

BBC Wireless Symphony Orchestra; conducted by Sir Thomas Beecham

*Eventyr*

*Cynara* (first performance: John Goss)

Piano Concerto (1906 version: Evlyn Howard-Jones)

*An Arabesque*

*Appalachia* (Royal College of Music Choral Class and BBC National Chorus)

23 October   Aeolian Hall

Dora Labbette, Heddle Nash, Arthur Catterall, Evelyn Howard-Jones, London Select Choir, Virtuoso String Quartet

Three unaccompanied partsongs:

  *The Splendour Falls*

  *On Craig Dhu*

  *Midsummer Song*

Four songs (Dora Labbette)

Violin Sonata no. 1

*Three Songs (The words by Shelley)* (Heddle Nash)

*To be Sung of a Summer Night on the Water*

Four songs (Dora Labette)

String Quartet

24 October   Queens' Hall

Royal Philharmonic Orchestra; conducted by Sir Thomas Beecham

*North Country Sketches*

*Songs of Sunset* (Olga Haley, John Goss and London Select Choir)

Violin Concerto (Albert Sammons)

*A Dance Rhapsody* no. 1

*Gerda* (the last two 'pictures' of *Fennimore and Gerda*) (Pauline Maunder, John Goss, London Select Choir)

1 November   Queens's Hall

BBC Wireless Orchestra, Miriam Licette, Astra Desmond, Tudor Davies, Roy Henderson and Philharmonic Choir; conducted by Sir Thomas Beecham

*A Mass of Life*

## The 1946 Festival

26 October   Royal Albert Hall

Royal Philharmonic Orchestra and Luton Choral Society; conducted by Sir Thomas Beecham

*Over the Hills and Far Away*

*Song of the High Hills* (Freda Hart and Leslie Jones)

Incidental music to *Hassan*

*Appalachia*

4 November    Royal Albert Hall

Royal Philharmonic Orchestra and BBC Choral Society; conducted by Sir Thomas Beecham

*Paris*

Piano Concerto (Betty Humby Beecham)

*Sea Drift* (Redvers Llewellyn)

*On Hearing the First Cuckoo in Spring*

8 November    Royal Albert Hall

Royal Philharmonic Orchestra; conducted by Sir Thomas Beecham and Richard Austin

*On the Mountains* (first performance)

*In a Summer Garden*

Violin Concerto (Jean Pougnet)

*Koanga*, Act 3 (Oda Slobodskaya, Leslie Jones, Roderick Jones, Trevor Anthony, Bruce Clark and Croydon Philharmonic Society, cond. Richard Austin)

15 November    Royal Albert Hall

Royal Philharmonic Orchestra and BBC Choral Society; conducted by Sir Thomas Beecham and Richard Austin

*Eventyr*

*Brigg Fair*

*Songs of Sunset* (Nancy Evans and Redvers Llewellyn)

*A Village Romeo and Juliet*, Scenes 5 and 6 (Freda Hart, Heddle Nash, Leslie Jones, Redvers Llewellyn *et al.*, cond. Richard Austin)

18 November    Central Hall, Westminster

Royal Philharmonic Orchestra and Croydon Philharmonic Society; conducted by Sir Thomas Beecham and Richard Austin

*A Dance Rhapsody* no. 2

*Idyll* (Elsie Suddaby and Roderick Jones, cond. Richard Austin)

*Songs of Farewell* (first four movements only)

*Three Small Tone Poems* (first performance, cond. Richard Austin)

Five songs (Elsie Suddaby)

*Summer Night on the River*

*A Song before Sunrise*

*Cynara* (Roderick Jones)

Double Concerto (Paul Beard and Anthony Pini, cond. Richard Austin)

21 November    Central Hall, Westminster,

> Royal Philharmonic Orchestra and Luton Choral Society; conducted by Sir Thomas Beecham, Richard Austin and Arthur Davies
>
> *North Country Sketches*
>
> Three unaccompanied partsongs (cond. Arthur Davies)
>
>> *The Splendour Falls*
>>
>> *On Craig Ddu*
>>
>> *Midsummer Song*
>
> *An Arabesque* (Gordon Clinton, cond. Richard Austin)
>
> Five songs (Marjorie Thomas)
>
> *Irmelin Prelude*
>
> *Marche Caprice* (first performance)
>
> Five songs (John Kentish)
>
> *La Calinda*
>
> *Folkeraadet*, Act 3 Prelude

11 December    Royal Albert Hall

> BBC Symphony Orchestra and BBC Choral Society, Lilian Styles-Allen, Muriel Brunskill, Francis Russell, Redvers Llewellyn; conducted by Sir Thomas Beecham
>
> *A Mass of Life*

# Selected Further Reading

Banfield, Stephen, *Sensibility and English Song: Critical Studies of the Early Twentieth Century* (Cambridge: Cambridge University Press, 1985)

Bartók, Béla, 'Delius's First Performance in Vienna', *Zeneközlöny* 14 (1911), 340–2

Bennett, Joseph, programme book for Delius Orchestral Concert, St James's Hall, 30 May 1899

Bergsagel, John, 'J. P. Jacobsen and Music', in *J. P. Jacobsens spor i ord, billeder og toner*, ed. F. J. Billeskov Jansen (Copenhagen: C. A. Reitzels Forlag, 1985), pp. 283–313

Cahill, Mary, *Delius in Danville* (Danville: Virginia Historical Society, 1986)

Carley, Lionel, 'Hans Heym: Delius's Prophet and Pioneer', *Music & Letters* 54 (1973), 1–24; rept. in *Companion*, pp. 187–217

—— 'Carl Larsson and Grez-sur-Loing in the 1880s', *DSJ* 45 (1974), 8–26

Clews, Marie, 'The Memories of Marie Clews', in *Letters* 2, pp. 205–6

Cooke, Deryck, 'Delius: A Centenary Evaluation', in *Vindications: Essays on Romantic Music* (London: Faber & Faber, 1982), pp. 116–22

—— 'Delius & Form: A Vindication', in *Vindications: Essays on Romantic Music* (London: Faber & Faber, 1982), pp. 123–42; rept. in *Companion*, pp. 249–62 [an analysis of the Violin Concerto]

Delius, Frederick, 'At the Cross-Roads', *The Sackbut* 1, no. 5 (September 1902); rept. in, *inter alia*, *Companion*, pp. 37–43

—— 'Musik in England im Kriege', *Musikblätter des Anbruch* 1, no. 1 (November 1919), 18–19; rept. as 'Music in England during the War', trans. L. Carley, *Delius Society Newsletter* 32 (Autumn 1971), 6

*The Delius Society Newsletter* 1–42 (July 1962–74)

Diamond, Harold (ed.), *The Delian*, 1990 [newsletter of The Delius Society, Philadelphia Branch]

Dowson, Ernest, *The Poetical Works of Ernest Christopher Dowson*, ed. D. Flower (London: Cassel & Co., 1934)

Elgar, Sir Edward, 'My Visit to Delius', *The Daily Telegraph*, 1 July 1933; rept. in *Companion*, pp. 93–7

Elkin, Robert, *The Annals of The Royal Philharmonic Society* (London: Rider & Co., n.d.)

Foreman, Lewis, 'Oskar Fried: Delius and the Late Romantic School', *DSJ* 86 (1985), 4–21

—— *From Parry to Britten: British Music in Letters, 1900–1945* (London: Batsford, 1987)

—— 'Watford sur Gade: Delius in Watford during the First World War', *DSJ* 130 (2001), 8–18

Gerhardi, Evelin, 'My Reminiscences of Frederick and Jelka Delius at Grez-sur-Loing', *DSJ* 52 (1976), 4–9

Grainger, Percy, *The Farthest North of Humanness: The Letters of Percy Grainger, 1901–1914*, ed. Kay Dreyfus (London: Macmillan, 1985)

Hadley, Patrick, 'Frederick Delius', in *Dictionary of National Biography 1931–1940*, ed. L. G. Wickham Legg (London: Oxford University Press, 1949), pp. 218–20

Harrison, Beatrice, *The Cello and the Nightingales: The Autobiography of Beatrice Harrison*, ed. Patrick Cleveland-Peck (London: John Murray, 1985)

Huismann, Mary Christison, *Frederick Delius: A Guide to Research* (London: Routledge, 2005)

Jacobsen, Jens Peter, *Niels Lyhne*, trans. Hanna Astrup Larsen (New York: Twayne Publishers Inc. and The American–Scandinavian Foundation, 1967)

Keller, Gottfried, *A Village Romeo and Juliet*, trans. Peter Tegel (London: Blackie, 1967)

Klenau, Paul, 'The Approach to Delius', *The Music Teacher*, January 1927; rept. in *Companion*, pp. 31–7

Krohg, Christian, 'Fritz Delius', *Verdens Gang*, 23 October 1897; trans. L. Carley, in *Lowe*, pp. 172–4

Lloyd, Stephen, 'Beecham: The Delius Repertoire', and other articles, in *Letters 2*, pp. 467–8

Nietzsche, Friedrich, *Thus Spake Zarathustra: A Book for Everyone and No One*, trans. R. J. Hollingdale (London: Penguin 1961)

Orr, C. W., 'Frederick Delius: Some Personal Recollections', *Musical Opinion*, August 1934; rept. in *Companion*, pp. 49–54

Oyler, Philip, 'Frederick Delius in his Garden', *Music Student* 14, no. 7 (July 1934), 121–3; rept. in *Companion*, pp. 55–64

Parker, Maurice, *Sir Thomas Beecham, Bart, CH, 1879–1961: A Calendar of his Concert and Theatrical Performances*, 2 vols (1985), with *Supplement* by Tony Benson (s.l.: s.p., 1998)

Pilkington, Michael, *Delius, Bridge & Somervell*, English Solo Song: Guides to the Repertoire 3 (London: Thames Publishing, 1993)

Redwood, Dawn, *Flecker and Delius: The Making of Hassan* (London: Thames Publishing, 1978)

Rossi, Jérôme, *Frederick Delius, ou Une Célébration de la vie* (Geneva: Editions Papillon, 2010)

Sadie, Stanley (ed.), *The New Grove Dictionary of Music and Musicians* (London: Grove, 1980)

Thornton, R. K. R., 'Whitman: Leaves of Grass and Sea Drift', *DSJ* 139 (2006), 20–9

White, John, 'A Mass of Life: Nietzsche's Invitation to the Dance of Life', *DSJ* 144 (2008), 12–19

Whitman, Walt, *Leaves of Grass*, ed. David McKay (Philadelphia, PA: David McKay, 1900)

# Index